Anonymus

Letter from the Secretary of the Treasury

Anonymus

Letter from the Secretary of the Treasury

ISBN/EAN: 9783742874900

Manufactured in Europe, USA, Canada, Australia, Japa

Cover: Foto ©Thomas Meinert / pixelio.de

Manufactured and distributed by brebook publishing software
(www.brebook.com)

Anonymus

Letter from the Secretary of the Treasury

LETTER

FROM THE

SECRETARY OF THE TREASURY,

TRANSMITTING

REPORT UPON THE MINERAL RESOURCES

OF THE

STATES AND TERRITORIES WEST OF THE
ROCKY MOUNTAINS.

WASHINGTON:
GOVERNMENT PRINTING OFFICE.
1867.

IN THE HOUSE OF REPRESENTATIVES,
January 23, 1867.

On motion of Mr. LAFLIN, chairman of the Committee on Printing,

Resolved, That there be printed for the use of the House five thousand extra copies of the report of J. Ross Browne on the mineral resources of the country.

Attest: EDWARD McPHERSON, *Clerk.*

LETTER

THE SECRETARY OF THE TREASURY,

TRANSMITTING

A report upon the mineral resources of the States and Territories west of the Rocky Mountains.

JANUARY 8, 1867.—Referred to the Committee on Mines and Mining and ordered to be printed.

TREASURY DEPARTMENT, *January* 8, 1867.

SIR: I have the honor to transmit a preliminary report upon the mineral resources of the States and Territories west of the Rocky mountains by Mr. J. Ross Browne, who was appointed special commissioner under a provision of the appropriation act of July 28, 1866, authorizing the collection by the Secretary of the Treasury of "reliable statistical information concerning the gold and silver mines of the western States and Territories."

An introductory communication from Mr. Browne is also enclosed, which will indicate the scope of the report, with some suggestions in regard to the future prosecution of the inquiry into the situation and prospects of gold and silver mining in the United States.

The commissioner has evidently availed himself of the best experience of the State of California, especially in the department of geological and mineralogical observation; and the present compilation of its results cannot fail to be a welcome contribution to the public information.

If Congress shall make the necessary appropriation for this object, it is the purpose of the Secretary to secure a similar body of scientific and statistical information in regard to the mining districts of New Mexico, Colorado, and Montana. A report upon the production of gold and silver in those Territories, and in the Vermillion and Alleghany districts of the United States, by Mr. James W. Taylor, will be forwarded from this department to the House of Representatives at an early day.

I am, very truly, your obedient servant,

H. McCULLOCH,
Secretary of the Treasury.

Hon. SCHUYLER COLFAX,
Speaker of the House of Representatives.

LETTER OF INSTRUCTIONS.

TREASURY DEPARTMENT, *August* 2, 1866.

SIR: In entering upon your duties as special commissioner to collect mining statistics in the States and Territories west of the Rocky mountains, it is important that you should clearly understand the objects designed to be accomplished by this department and by Congress.

The absence of reliable statistics in any department of the government on the subject of mines and mining in our new mineral regions, and the inconvenience resulting from it, induced Congress at its last session to appropriate the sum of ten thousand dollars for the collection of information of all kinds tending to show the extent and character of our mineral resources in the far west.

The special points of inquiry to which your attention will necessarily be directed are so varied, and embrace so large a scope of country, that it will scarcely be practicable for you to report upon them in full by the next session of Congress.

I entertain the hope, however, that you will be enabled by that time to collect sufficient data to furnish, in the form of a preliminary report, the basis of a plan of operations by which we can in future procure information of a more detailed and comprehensive character.

The success of your visit to the mineral regions, in carrying out the objects contemplated, must depend in a great measure upon the judicious exercise of your own judgment, and upon your long practical acquaintance with the country, your thorough experience of mining operations, and your knowledge of the best and most economical means of procuring reliable information.

The department will not, therefore, undertake to give you detailed instructions upon every point that may arise in the course of your investigations. It desires to impress upon you in general terms a few important considerations for your guidance, leaving the rest to your own judgment and sense of duty.

1. All statistics should be obtained from such sources as can be relied upon. Their value will depend upon their accuracy and authenticity. All statements not based upon actual data should be free from prejudice or exaggeration.

2. In your preliminary report, a brief historical review of the origin of gold and silver mining on the Pacific coast would be interesting in connection with a statement of the present condition of the country, as tending to show the progress of settlement and civilization.

3. The geological formation of the great mineral belts and the general characteristics of the placer diggings and quartz ledges should be given in a concise form.

4. The different systems of mining in operation since 1848, showing the machinery used, the various processes of reducing the ores, the percentage of waste, and the net profits.

5. The population engaged in mining, exclusively and in part; the capital and labor employed; the value of improvements; the number of mills and steam-engines in operation; the yield of the mines worked; the average of dividends and average of losses, in all the operations of mining.

6. The proportion of agricultural and mineral lands in each district; the quantity of wood land; facilities for obtaining fuel; number and extent of streams and water privileges.

7. Salt beds, deposits of soda and borax, and all other valuable mineral deposits.

8. The altitude, character of the climate, mode and cost of living; cost of all kinds of material; cost of labor, &c.

9. The population of the various mining towns; the number of banks and banking institutions in them; the modes of assaying, melting, and refining bullion; the charges upon the same for transportation and insurance

10. Facilities in the way of communication; postal and telegraphic lines; stage routes in operation; cost of travel; probable benefits likely to result from the construction of the Pacific railroad and its proposed branches.

11. The necessity for assay offices and public depositories; what financial facilities may tend to develop the country and enhance its products.

12. Copies of all local mining laws and customs now regulating the holding and working of claims.

13. The number of ledges opened and the number claimed; the character of the soil and its adaptation to the support of a large population.

Upon all these points it is very desirable that we should possess reliable information. Whatever tends to develop the vast resources of our new States and Territories must add to the wealth of the whole country.

I am extremely solicitous that the information collected should be ample and authentic.

Trusting that you may be enabled to make such a report as will be of great public utility, and at the same time promote the interests of the miners to whose industry and energy so much is due,

I am, very respectfully, your obedient servant,

H. McCULLOCH,
Secretary of the Treasury.

J. ROSS BROWNE, Esq ,
 Washington, D. C.

LETTER

FROM

J. ROSS BROWNE,

SPECIAL COMMISSIONER FOR THE COLLECTION OF MINING STATISTICS,

TO THE

SECRETARY OF THE TREASURY.

SAN FRANCISCO, CALIFORNIA,
November 24, 1866.

SIR : I had the honor to send you by last steamer a preliminary report on the mineral resources of the States and Territories west of the Rocky mountains.

Congress, at its last session, appropriated ten thousand dollars " to enable the Secretary of the Treasury to collect reliable statistical information concerning the gold and silver mines of the western States and Territories," &c. Under a letter of appointment, dated August 2, 1866, and in accordance with detailed instructions of same date, I entered upon the discharge of the duties assigned to me, immediately upon my arrival at San Francisco, September 3, ultimo.

The views of the department as to the impracticability of reporting in detail by the next session of Congress were fully realized when I came to consider the magnitude of the subject and the immense scope of country over which the inquiry extended.

You were pleased to express the hope, however, that I would be enabled to collect by the meeting of Congress " sufficient data to furnish, in the form of a preliminary report, the basis of a plan of operations " by which information of a more detailed and comprehensive character could be procured in future.

To obtain any geological or statistical data whatev , within the brief space of two months, precluded the possibility of a personal visit to the mineral regions prior to the transmission of my report. The experience of Mr. William Ashburner and Mr. A. Rémond, members of the State geological survey, satisfied me that it would be utterly impracticable to examine the mines of a single district, much less of all the States and Territories west of the Rocky mountains, within that time. Mr. Ashburner spent eight months in procuring data for a single table, showing the operations of the principal quartz mills in Mariposa, Tuolumne, Calaveras, Amador, Eldorado, Plumas, Sierra, and Nevada counties. Mr Rémond spent three months in visiting the principal mines and mills in that part of Mariposa and Tuolumne counties lying between the Merced and Stanislaus rivers, and three months more in preparing tables showing the results of his observations.

Under these circumstances, and in view of the fact that I had already visited nearly every mining district within the range of my instructions, and was familiar with the topography of the country and the general condition of the mining interest, I deemed it best to avail myself of such reliable sources of information as were immediately accessible. San Francisco being the central point of trade and commerce for the Pacific coast, afforded facilities in the way of statistical data and scientific aid which could not be obtained elsewhere. From this point nearly all the capital radiates, here the records of all mining enterprises are kept, and here centre the products of the mines.

The report to which your attention is respectfully invited embodies the results of many years of careful and laborious research. It is compiled from original data furnished by the most intelligent statisticians and experts known on this coast, as well as from notes made by myself during the past three years.

In many respects this report is imperfect. No reliable system has hitherto existed for the collection of mining statistics, such as the governments of Europe have long since deemed it expedient to establish. The existing system in the British colonies of Australia and North America, though not adapted to our mineral regions, or to the habits and customs of our people, is both thorough and comprehensive. Surveyors and registrars are appointed for each district, and all mining operations are carried on under their inspection. Monthly and quarterly reports are made by them, under the direction of a supervising officer, whose duty it is to collect and arrange all the data thus furnished for publication. These reports show the actual condition of every branch of mining industry from month to month and quarter to quarter, so that at the expiration of the year a complete history is given of the progress of development and the profits and losses of mining. A permanent system like this, established upon a somewhat different basis, is greatly needed in our country.

One of the difficulties already experienced in the collection of mining statistics on this coast is the disinclination of parties interested to expose the secrets of their business. Either the business is not remunerative and they desire to encourage further investments by false representations, or by withholding the truth; or, if unusually successful, they may consider it to their interest, in view of further purchases, arrangements, or contracts, to avoid giving publicity to the facts. I am inclined to believe, however, that the advantages of fair and truthful statements, in the encouragement of immigration, the reduction of the cost of labor, the promotion of confidence in mining enterprises, and the establishment of a more uniform system of laws, will soon become apparent. Indeed, the difficulty to which I refer is not so general, even now, as might be supposed. I have found mining companies, doing a steady and reliable business, nearly always disposed to furnish the desired information. The cases of refusal are exceptional, and there is usually a cause for it, well understood by persons familiar with mining enterprises.

Another difficulty, which, however, will not exist to so great an extent hereafter, has been the conflicting character of statements made by different parties. In many instances where the sources of information are equally reliable, but where conflicting influences prevail, it is almost impossible, after the lapse of any great length of time, to get at the exact truth. Even facts, seen from different stand-points, appear differently to the most conscientious persons. In cases of this kind, where the proofs on either side are not positive, I have preferred—sometimes at the expense of prolixity—to give the different statements, especially where there is a general concurrence of testimony as to the main facts. Thus, it will be seen that the amount of bullion produced on the Pacific coast is variously estimated by the best informed and most intelligent men. Mr. Ashburner's estimates are somewhat lower than those usually accepted by the public, but I believe they are well-considered. Gold and silver are so generally blended together under the head of "bullion," that none of the express companies or bankers have hitherto kept separate records of the products of each. It would be very difficult to obtain correct returns on this point, unless the numerous assay offices and the authorities at the branch mint could furnish details of the quantity obtained by parting, or by estimating the bullion passing through their establishments—the two metals are so universally alloyed with each other.

Mr. Swain, superintendent of the branch mint at San Francisco, a gentleman possessing both the means and the disposition to inform himself on this subject, estimates the product of gold and silver for Oregon, California, Nevada, and Washington Territory, as follows :

In 1861	$43, 391, 000
In 1862	49, 370, 000
In 1863	52, 500, 000
In 1864	63, 450, 000
In 1865	70, 000, 000

Well-informed parties estimate the product for 1866 as follows :

California	$25, 000, 000
Montana	18, 000, 000
Idaho	17, 000, 000
Colorado	17, 000, 000
Nevada	16, 000, 000
Oregon	8, 000, 000
Other sources	5, 000, 000
Total	106, 000, 000

Great differences of opinion, however, exist as to the accuracy of this estimate. To some it appears exaggerated, while others pronounce it far below the actual yield. The imperfect returns received for the last nine months would seem to warrant the conclusion that it is not an unreasonable estimate. For instance, the product of Oregon is assumed to be $8,000,000. Statistical tables, supposed to be worthy of credit, show a probable yield for that State of $20,000,000. In 1865 the generally accepted estimate for Oregon was $19,000,000, though that was probably above the actual product. There is good ground for believing that the result this year will be considerably above that of the last year. The same may be said of the Territories of Idaho and Montana.

In like manner, the capital in circulation in California, and necessary for the transaction of business within the limits of the State, is variously estimated at from $25,000,000 to $50,000,000. It is believed that $10,000,000 is annually shipped up to the mines to defray the current expenses of mining; but there is no record of the return of this amount in the form of a circulating medium.

Assuming the estimate of the product of bullion, as above given, to be approximately correct, it will be seen that the States and Territories on the Pacific slope produce annually upwards of $100,000,000 of the precious metals, a quantity more than four times as great as the total product of the world less than thirty years ago. The improved processes for the extraction of these metals from their ores, made within the past two years, and the constantly increasing area over which gold and silver mines are being developed, furnish strong guarantees that there will be no abatement in the product for years to come, provided government places no impediments in the way by impolitic legislation. The recent financial panic in Europe afforded an illustration of the importance of encouraging this branch of industry. Within sixty days during that panic there was exported from San Francisco the enormous sum of $12,000,000 in gold and silver, without which, it is well known, the commercial interests of the United States would have suffered in sympathy with those of our best customers in England. The shipments of specie from San Francisco to New York during the first eight months of 1866 amounted to $27,729,010.

There is a more striking form in which the importance of the gold and silver mines of the Pacific coast on the national welfare may be illustrated.

The product of these metals for the present year exceeds in amount all the gold and silver in the national treasury, and in all the banks in all the States.

The report of the Secretary of the Treasury shows that the bullion in that department on the 1st of August last was $61,000,000
The banks at New York, at same date, report having 5,000,000
The banks at Boston and Philadelphia report 600,000
The last quarterly report of all the national banks in the United States, outside of the above cities, reports. 1,600,000
State banks outside of those cities estimated at 1,500,000

Total 69,700,000

The approximate estimate already given of the gold and silver product of the Pacific States and Territories for 1866 shows a total of $106,000,000, or nearly double the combined bullion of the government and all the banks in the country.

For convenience of reference the report transmitted to you is divided into sections and clauses, of which the following is a brief summary:

Section 1 contains a historical sketch of the discovery of gold and silver in the territory of the United States west of the Rocky mountains; the excitement consequent upon the development of rich placer diggings in California; the crude means adopted in the early stages of gold mining on the Pacific coast; the introduction of improved processes, and the extraordinary results that followed in the sudden increase of commerce and the extension of the area of civilization. In this section a sketch is also given of the discovery of the Comstock lode and the development of the silver mining interest east of the Sierra Nevada mountains.

Section 2 refers chiefly to the geological features of California, and the prominent characteristics of the principal lodes in the great mineral belt. The present production of the gold mines is given from actual data derived from investigations made by Professor Ashburner, of the State geological survey, and a comparison is made between the products of California and Australia. Detailed descriptions are given of a few leading mines in Grass valley and Mariposa, showing the expenses and profits of gold mining as a permanent business.

Section 3 gives minute details and statistics of the gold and silver mining interests on the Pacific coast; the improved processes and results; the exports of treasure from San Francisco, with the amount received from the mines; cost of extracting the ore and reducing it; the average yield; the machinery in use; capital and labor employed, and cost of working.

Section 4 gives a historical and topographical sketch of Nevada; the prominent characteristics of the principal silver mines; the alkali lakes, salt-beds, wood and water privileges, and general products. Carefully prepared statistics are given in this section, showing the expenses of silver mining, the various processes of crushing and amalgamating the ores, the number of mills in actual operation, the profits and losses, with a general review of the condition of the mining interest. It also contains brief sketches of Utah, Idaho, Oregon, Washington Territory, Montana and Arizona, with such reliable data, showing the condition and prospects of the mines, as could be obtained.

Section 5 is devoted to the copper mines of the Pacific coast. In this paper a history of the discovery of every notable copper lode is given; the extent of the veins; the quality of the ore; the process of reduction; the costs of machinery and working; the yield, and the profits and losses. Special attention is called to the great national importance of this interest.

Section 6 contains a report on the quicksilver mines of California, with statistics of production.

Section 7 gives the history of the discovery of borax in California; the process of working the borax deposits; their extent and value; some account of the sulphur deposits; and reports on the tin mines of Temescal, and the coal and iron resources of the Pacific coast.

Section 8. Mining regions, population, altitude, &c.

Section 9. An annotated catalogue of the minerals found west of the Rocky mountains.

Section 10. Mining titles; the laws and customs of foreign governments; the crown right, and peculiar doctrines held under that right; the recent legislation of our own government; recommendations of the Secretary of the Treasury; passage of a law for the sale of mineral lands, and general approval of the policy adopted.

Section 11. Local customs; difficulties arising therefrom; the necessity of some uniform system; importance of congressional legislation for the systematic working of the mines, and the establishment of a permanent policy for the development of the great mineral resources of the country.

Section 12. A list of the most important works published in reference to the geology, mineralogy, and metallurgy of the Pacific coast.

Section 13. Population of the mining regions; agricultural resources; table of distances, &c.

From the above synopsis it will be seen that an earnest attempt, at least, has been made to meet the wishes of the department as expressed in the letter of instructions hereto appended. Want of time for a more systematic arrangement has been the only serious obstacle to more satisfactory results.

One of the most important subjects considered in the report is the discrepances existing between the local rules and customs upon which a material part of the late mineral land law is based and the statutes of the States and Territories. The policy of granting titles to the miners in fee-simple has met with such universal approval, and the time has been so short since the law went into operation, that I have serious doubts as to the expediency of an immediate change. Attention has been called to some of the difficulties arising from the loose interpretations given to local rules and customs, and in many cases the entire impracticability of determining what they are or ascertaining where they are to be found. Some provision requiring official records to be kept might, perhaps, have a beneficial effect. Reasons doubtless exist for the differences in the size of the claims in different districts. The rules which would apply to the Reese River district, where the ledges are extremely narrow and close to each other, would scarcely be applicable to districts in which the ledges are of great width and far apart. Still, without descending to details in a general law, some regard should be had to uniformity; and especially some fixed principle should be adopted as to the local laws which shall govern in all conflicting cases. The policy of giving every advantage to the practical miner over the mere speculator will at once be conceded. This, I think, can only be carried into effect by national legislation. A general law, based somewhat upon the principles incorporated in the mining law of Mexico, but more liberal in its provisions, will probably be required before long. The holding of claims without working; the seizure of mining property for debt; the abandonment of claims; the destruction of timber; the monopoly of salt-beds; these are subjects worthy of serious consideration.

In the preparation of a preliminary report I have been compelled to depend chiefly upon the labors of other and abler hands. To Mr. Hittell, author of a very excellent work on the resources of California, Professor Whitney, Mr. Ashburner, and Mr. Gabb, of the State geological survey, Professor Blake, author of various standard works on the geology and mineral resources of California, Baron Von Richthofen, the distinguished German savant, Mr. Degroot, an experienced statistician and topographer, Mr. Bennett, a mining expert, thoroughly familiar with the mineral regions, to Dr. Blachley, of Nevada, and others, I am indebted for nearly all that is really valuable in the report.

It is my intention to visit the various mineral districts of the Pacific slope during the coming spring and summer. Personal examination of the mines, increased experience, and sufficient time for the careful preparation of the material collected, will enable me, I trust, to present for your consideration, before the next meeting of Congress, a report better worthy of your approval than that just submitted. Reliable statistics and valuable information, showing the resources and products of our new States and Territories, cannot fail to result beneficially to the country and the government. Nothing can tend in a greater degree to encourage immigration and the investment of capital.

The question arises, how can the object be best accomplished in the future ? A statistical bureau for the Pacific coast has been recommended.

It is manifest to my mind that the work cannot be properly done by bureau organization. Information derived from interested parties by means of blanks and circulars, sent out over the mining regions. would be very imperfect and for the most part unreliable.

The plan that appears to me most feasible would be—

1st. To authorize the appointment in each State and Territory of an able and experienced geologist, familiar with all the operations of mining.

2d Annual reports to be made by each officer so appointed and assigned to duty, under official instructions, to the supervising commissioner at San Francisco.

3d. The commissioner to make a visit every year to each mining district, for the purpose of personal inspection of the mines, and conference with his assistants ; after which he would be prepared to make his annual report to the Secretary of the Treasury.

Proper measures, of course, would be taken to secure the official returns of assessors, surveyors, tax collectors, and other local State or territorial officers.

The expense would be comparatively trifling, inasmuch as the services of professional experts could be had without requiring their entire time. A small compensation to each would be an object of some importance.

An appropriation of $25,000 would probably be sufficient to inaugurate such a system, though a much larger amount could be advantageously expended.

In the hope that these suggestions, hastily made and informally stated, may at least furnish some ground for action, I have the honor to be, very respectfully, your obedient servant,

J. ROSS BROWNE,
Special Commissioner.

Hon. H. McCULLOCH,
    Secretary of the Treasury.

SECTION 1.

HISTORICAL SKETCH OF GOLD AND SILVER MINING ON THE PACIFIC SLOPE.

1.—FIRST MENTION OF GOLD.

The first mention of gold in California is made in Hakluyt's account of the voyage of Sir Francis Drake, who spent five weeks in June and July, 1579, in a bay near latitude 38°; whether Drake's bay or San Francisco bay is a matter of dispute. It certainly was one of the two, and of neither can we now say with truth, as Hakluyt said seriously, "There is no part of the earth here to be taken up wherein there is not a reasonable quantity of gold or silver." This statement, taken literally, is untrue, and it was probably made without any foundation, merely for the purpose of embellishing the story and magnifying the importance of Drake and of the country which he claimed to have added to the possessions of the English crown.

If any "reasonable quantity" of gold or silver had been obtained by the English adventurers, we should probably have had some account of their expeditions into the interior, of the manner and place in which the precious metals were obtained, and of the specimens which were brought home, but of these things there is no mention.

Neither gold nor silver exists "in reasonable quantity" near the ocean about latitude 38°, and the inference is that Drake's discovery of gold in California was a matter of fiction more than of fact.

2.—GOLD FOUND BEFORE 1848.

Some small deposits of placer gold were found by Mexicans near the Colorado river at various times from 1775 to 1828, and in the latter year a similar discovery was made at San Isidro, in what is now San Diego county, and in 1802 a mineral vein, supposed to contain silver, at Olizal, in the district of Monterey, attracted some attention, but no profitable mining was done at either of these places.

Forbes, who wrote the history of California in 1835, said "No minerals of particular importance have yet been found in Upper California, nor any ores of metals."

It was in 1838, sixty-nine years after the arrival of the Franciscan friars, and the establishment of the first mission, that the placers of San Francisquito, forty-five miles northwest from Los Angeles, was discovered. The deposit of gold was neither extensive nor rich, but it was worked steadily for twenty years. In 1841 the exploring expedition of Commodore Wilkes visited the coast, and its mineralogist, James D. Dana, made a trip overland from the Columbia river, by way of Willamette and Sacramento valleys to San Francisco bay, and in the following year he published a book on mineralogy, and mentioned in it that gold was found in the Sacramento valley, and that rocks similar to those of the auriferous formations were observed in southern Oregon. Dana did not regard his discovery as of any practical value, and if he said anything about it in California no one paid any attention to it. Nevertheless, many persons had an idea that the country was rich in minerals, and on the 4th of May, 1846, Thomas O. Larkin, then United States consul in Monterey, a gentleman usually careful to keep his statements within the limits of truth, said in an official letter to James Buchanan, then Secretary of State : "There is no doubt but that gold, silver, quicksilver, copper, lead, sulphur, and coal mines are to be found all over California, and it is equally doubtful whether, under their present owners, they will ever be worked."

The implication here is that if the country were only transferred to the American flag, these mines, of whose existence he knew nothing save by surmise, or by the assertion of incompetent persons, would soon be opened and worked. In sixty-six days after that letter was written, the stars and stripes were hoisted in Monterey, and now California is working mines of all the minerals mentioned by Larkin save lead, which also might be produced if it would pay, since there is no lack of its ores.

3.—MARSHALL'S DISCOVERY.

The discovery of the rich gold fields of the Sacramento basin is an American achievement, accomplished under the American dominion, by a native of the United States, and made of world-wide importance by American enterprise and industry, favored by the liberal policy of American law.

It was on the 19th day of January, 1848, ten days before the treaty of Guadalupe Hidalgo was signed, and three months before the ratified copies were exchanged, that James W. Marshall, while engaged in digging a race for a sawmill at Coloma, about thirty-five miles eastward from Sutter's Fort, found some pieces of yellow metal, which he and the half dozen men working with him at the mill supposed to be gold. He felt confident that he had made a discovery of great importance, but he knew nothing of either chemistry or gold mining, so he could not prove the nature of the metal or tell how to obtain it in paying quantities. Every morning he went down to the race to look for the bits of the metal; but the other men at the mill thought Marshall was very wild in his ideas, and they continued their labors in building the mill, and in sowing wheat. and planting vegetables. The swift current of the mill-race washed away a considerable body of earthy matter, leaving the coarse particles of gold behind. so Marshall's collection of specimens continued to accumulate, and his associates began to think there might be something in his gold mine after all. About the middle of February, a Mr. Bennett, one of the party employed at the mill, went to San Francisco for the purpose of learning whether this metal was precious, and there he was introduced to Isaac Humphrey, who had washed for gold in Georgia. The experienced miner saw at a glance that he had the true stuff before him, and after a few inquiries he was satisfied that the diggings must be rich. He made immediate preparation to go to the mill, and tried to persuade some of his friends to go with him, but they thought it would be only a waste of time and money, so he went with Bennett for his sole companion.

He arrived at Coloma on the 7th of March, and found the work at the mill going on as if no gold existed in the neighborhood. The next day he took a pan and spade and washed some of the dirt from the bottom of the mill race in places where Marshall had found his specimens, and in a few hours Humphrey declared that these mines were far richer than any in Georgia.

He now made a rocker and went to work washing gold industriously, and every day yielded him an ounce or two of metal. The men at the mill made rockers for themselves, and all were soon busy in search of the yellow metal.

Everything else was abandoned; the rumor of the discovery spread slowly. In the middle of March, Pearson B. Reading, the owner of a large ranch at the head of the Sacramento valley, happened to visit Sutter's Fort, and hearing of the mining at Coloma, he went thither to see it. He said that if similarity of formation could be taken as proof, there must be gold mines near his ranch, so after observing the method of washing, he posted off, and in a few weeks he was at work on the bars of Clear creek, nearly two hundred miles northwestward from Coloma. A few days after Reading had left, John Bidwell, now representative of the northern district of the State in the lower house of Congress, came to Coloma, and the result of his visit was that in less than a month he had a party of Indians from his ranch washing gold on the bars of Feather river, seventy-five miles northwestward from Coloma. Thus the mines were opened at far distant points.

4.—THE DISCOVERY OF GOLD IN PRINT.

The first printed notice of the discovery was given in the California newspaper published in San Francisco, on the 15th of March, as follows:

"In the newly made race-way of the saw-mill recently erected by Captain Sutter on the American Fork, gold has been found in considerable quantities. One person brought thirty dollars to New Helvetia, gathered there in a short time."

On the 29th of May the same paper, announcing that its publication would be suspended, says:

"The whole country, from San Francisco to Los-Angeles, and from the sea-shore to the base of the Sierra Nevada, resounds with the sordid cry of *gold! gold! gold!* while the field is left half planted, the house half built, and everything neglected but the manufacture of picks and shovels, and the means of transportation to the spot where one man obtained one hundred and twenty-eight dollars' worth of the real stuff in one day's washing; and the average for all concerned is twenty dollars per diem."

The towns and farms were deserted, or left to the care of women and children, while rancheros, wood-choppers, mechanics, vaqueros, and soldiers and sailors who had deserted or obtained leave of absence, devoted all their energies to washing the auriferous gravel of the Sacramento basin. Never satisfied, however much they might be making, they were continually looking for new placers which might yield them twice or thrice as much as they had made before. Thus the area of their labors gradually extended, and at the end of 1848 miners were at work in every large stream on the western slope of the Sierra Nevada, from the Feather to the Tuolumne river, a distance of one hundred and fifty miles, and also at Reading's diggings, in the northwestern corner of the Sacramento valley.

5.—EXCITEMENT ABROAD.

The first rumors of the gold discovery were received in the Atlantic States and in foreign countries with incredulity and ridicule; but soon the receipts of the precious metal in large quantities, and the enthusiastic letters of army officers and of men in good repute, changed the current of feeling, and an excitement almost unparalleled ensued. Oregon, the Hawaiian islands, and Sonora sent their thousands to share in the auriferous harvest of the first year; and in the following spring all the adventurous young Americans east of the Rocky mountains wanted to go to the new Eldorado, where, as they imagined, everybody was rich, and gold could be dug by the shovelful from the bed of every stream.

Before 1850 the population of California had risen from 15,000, as it was in 1847, to 100,000, and the average increase annually for five or six years was 50,000.

As the number of mines increased, so did the gold production and the extent and variety of the gold fields.

In 1849 the placers of Trinity and Mariposa were opened, and in the following years those of Klamath and Scott's valleys. During the last sixteen years no rich and extensive gold fields have been discovered, though many little placers have been found, and some very valuable deposits, previously unknown, have been brought to light in districts which had been worked previous to 1851.

6.—PAN WASHING.

In the first two years the miners depended mainly for their profits on the pan and the rocker. The placer miner's pan is made of sheet iron, or tinned iron, with a flat bottom about a foot in diameter, and sides six inches high, inclining outwards at an angle of thirty or forty degrees.

We frequently see and hear the phrase "golden sands," as if the gold were contained in loose sand ; but usually it is found in a tough clay, which envelops gravel and large boulders as well as sand. This clay must be thoroughly dissolved ; so the miner fills his pan with it, goes to the bank of the river, squats down there, puts his pan under water and shakes it horizontally, so as to get the mass thoroughly soaked ; then he picks out the larger stones with one hand and mashes up the largest and toughest lumps of clay, and again shakes his pan ; and when all the dirt appears to be dissolved so that the gold can be carried to the bottom by its weight, he tilts up the pan a little to let the thin mud and light sand run out ; and thus he works until he has washed out all except the metal which remains at the bottom.

7.—THE ROCKER.

The rocker, which was introduced into the California mines at their discovery, is made somewhat like a child's cradle. On the upper end is a riddle, made with a bottom of sheet-iron punched with holes. This riddle is filled with pay-dirt, and a man rocks the machine with one hand while with a dipper he pours water into the riddle with the other. With the help of the agitation, the liquid dissolves the clay and carries it down with the gold into the floor of the rocker, where the metal is caught by traverse riffles or cleets, while the mud, water, and sand run off at the lower end of the rocker, which is left open. The riddle can be taken off so that the larger stones can be conveniently thrown off.

In places where there was not water enough for washing, and where the gold was coarse, the miners sometimes scratched the metal from the crevices in the rocks with their knives ; but the pan and rocker were their main reliance for three or four years.

In many places the rich spots were soon exhausted, and there was a rapid decrease in the profits of the miners. It was necessary that they should devise new and more expeditious methods of working, so that they could wash more in a day, and thus derive as much profit as they had obtained by washing a little dirt.

8.—MINING DITCHES.

The chief want of the placer miner is an abundant and convenient supply of water, and the first noteworthy attempt to convey the needful element in an artificial channel was made at Coyote Hill, in Nevada county, in March, 1850.

This ditch was about two miles long, and, proving a decided success, was imitated in many other places, until, in the course of eight years, six thousand miles of mining canals had been made, supplying all the principal placer districts with water, and furnishing the means for obtaining the greater portion of the gold yield of the State. Many of the ditches were marvels of engineering skill.

The problem was to get the largest amount of water at the greatest altitude above the auriferous ground, and at the least immediate expense, as money was worth from three to ten per cent. per month interest. As the pay-dirt might be exhausted within a couple of years, and as the anticipated profits would in a short time be sufficient to pay for an entirely new ditch, durability was a point of minor importance. There was no imperial treasury to supply the funds for a durable aqueduct in every township, nor could the impatient miners wait a decennium for the completion of gigantic structures in stone and mortar. The high value of their time and the scarcity of their money made it necessary that the cheapest and most expeditious expedients for obtaining water should be adopted. Where the surface of the ground furnished the proper grade, a ditch was dug in the earth; and where it did not, flumes were built of wood and sustained in the air by frame-work that rose sometimes to a height of three hundred feet in crossing deep ravines, and extending for miles at an elevation of a hundred or two hundred feet.

All the devices known to mechanics for conveying water from hill-top to hill-top were adopted. Aqueducts of wood and pipes of iron were suspended upon cables of wire, or sustained on bridging of wood; and inverted siphons carried water up the sides of one hill by the heavier pressure from the higher side of another.

The ditches were usually the property of companies, of which there were at one time four hundred in the State, owning a total length of six thousand miles of canals and flumes.

The largest of these, called the Eureka, in Nevada county, has two hundred and five miles of ditches, constructed at a cost of $900,000; and their receipts at one time from the sale of water were $6,000 per day. Unfortunately these mining canals, though more numerous, more extensive, and bolder in design than the aqueducts of Rome, were less durable, and some of them have been abandoned and allowed to go to ruin, so that scarcely a trace of their existence remains, save in the heaps of gravel from which the clay and loam were washed in the search for gold.

As the placers in many districts were gradually exhausted, the demand for water and the profits of the ditch companies decreased; and the more expensive flumes, when blown down by severe storms, carried away by floods, or destroyed by the decay of the wood, were not repaired.

9.—MINERS' "RUSHES."

The year 1850 was marked by the first of a multitude of "rushes" or sudden migrations in search of imaginary rich diggings.

The miners, although generally men of rare intelligence as compared with the laborers in other countries, had vague ideas of the geological distribution of gold, and the marvellous amounts dug out by them, sometimes ascending to thousands of dollars per day to the laborer, excited their fancy so much that they could scarcely have formed a sound judgment if they had possessed the information necessary for its basis. Many believed that there must be some volcanic source from which the gold had been thrown up and scattered over the hills, and they thought that if they could only find that place, they would have nothing to do but to shovel up the precious metal and load their mules with it. More than once, long trains of pack animals were sent out in the confident expectation that they would get loads of gold within a few days.

No story was too extravagant to command credence. Men who had never earned more than a dollar a day before they came to California were dissatisfied when they were here clearing twenty dollars, and they were always ready to start off on some expedition in search of distant diggings reputed to be rich. Although the miners of to-day have better ideas of the auriferous deposits than they had sixteen years ago, and no longer expect to dig up the pure gold by the shovelful, they are now, as they have been since the discovery of the mines, always prepared for migration to any new field of excitement.

10.—GOLD LAKE AND GOLD BLUFF.

In the spring of 1850 a story was circulated that gold was lying in heaps on the bank of Gold lake, a small body of water eastward of where Downieville now is. Thousands of men left good claims to join this rush, but after weeks or months they returned much poorer than they started. The next year witnessed a rush to Gold Bluff, on the ocean shore about latitude 41°.

The sea beating against a high auriferous hill had left a wide beach containing much gold, which was mixed with sand that was very rich in spots, but was shifted about under the influence of a heavy surf. A gentleman of much intelligence, secretary of a mining company which claimed a portion of the beach, examined the place and seriously wrote to his associates that each one would receive at least $43,000,000 if the sand proved to be only one-tenth as rich as that which he had examined.

Several other similar statements were made in corroboration. The mining population were wonderfully excited by these reports, and preparations were made for a large migration to the golden beach; but more precise information was soon published, and most of the adventurers who had started were disenchanted before the vessels in which they were to sail could get to sea.

11.—THE "TOM."

The construction of hundreds of ditches within three or four years after the successful experiment at Coyote Hill gave a great impulse to placer mining, and had much influence to change its character. Before the water had been carried in artificial channels to the tops or high upon the sides of the hills, nearly all the miners spent their summers in washing the dirt in the bars of the rivers and their winters in working the beds of gullies, which were converted into brooks during the rainy season. In the gullies the supply of pay-dirt was usually small, and the claims were exhausted in the course of a few weeks.

On the bars the water was below the level of the pay-dirt, and had to be dipped or pumped up by hand.

These circumstances were favorable to the use of the rocker; but the ditch brought the water to places where the dirt was far more abundant and could be obtained with more facility, though it was poorer in quality, and, therefore, the washing of a larger quantity would be necessary to yield an equal profit.

New modes of working and new implements must be introduced to accomplish the greater amount of work, and the tom and the sluice came rapidly into use. The tom had been employed for years in the placers of Georgia, and some Georgians had their sluices in Nevada county in the latter part of 1849, and in February of the following year a party at Gold Run, in that county, finding that the bed of the ravine did not give them enough fall, made a long board trough on the hill-side leading down to their tom, and the pay-dirt from the claim was thrown up to a board platform, and from that thrown up to the head of the trough, and the water carried the dirt down to the tom.

I am indebted for information on this point to B. P. Avery, esq.

The purpose of this trough was mainly to save the labor of carrying the dirt by hand from the claim to the tom; but the trough having been once built, its value in washing gold was soon apparent. It was, however, the ditch that gave opportunities for the general introduction of the tom and sluice, and in most districts they were unheard of until late in 1850 or 1851.

The tom is a trough about twelve feet long, eight inches deep, fifteen inches wide at the head and thirty at the foot.

A riddle of sheet iron punched with holes half an inch in diameter forms the bottom of the tom at the lower end, so placed that all the water and their mud shall fall down through the holes of the riddle and none pass over the sides or end. The water falls from the riddle into a flat box with transverse cleets or riffles, and these are to catch the gold.

A stream of water runs constantly through the tom, into the head of which the pay-dirt is thrown by several men, while one throws out the stones too large to pass through the riddle, and throws back to the head of the tom the lumps of clay which reach the foot without being dissolved.

12.—THE SLUICE.

The tom was a great improvement on the rocker, but it was soon superseded by a still greater, the sluice, which is a board trough, from a hundred to a thousand feet long, with transverse cleets at the lower end to catch the gold. With a descent of one foot in twenty the water rushes through it like a torrent, bearing down large stones and tearing the lumps of clay to pieces. The miners, of whom a dozen or a score may work at one sluice, have little to do save to throw in the dirt and take out the gold.

Occasionally it may be necessary to throw out some stones, or to shovel the dirt along to prevent the sluice from choking, but these attentions cost relatively very little time. The sluice is the best device heretofore used for washing gold, and is supposed to be unsurpassable. It has been used here more extensively than elsewhere, although it has been introduced by men who have been in our own mines, into Australia, New Zealand, British Columbia, Transylvania, and many other countries.

The sluice, though an original invention here, had been previously invented in Brazil; but it was never brought to much excellence there nor used extensively, and no such implement was known in 1849 in the industry of gold mining.

At first the sluices were made short, and afterwards lengthened, until some were a mile long, the length being greater as the gold was finer; that is, if the surface of the earth in the direction of the sluice was favorable. There were many little variations in the form of the sluice, to suit different circumstances.

The ground sluice is a mere ditch on a hill side or slope, and the miners dig up the bottom and dig down the banks, while the water carries away the clay and leaves the gold; but the dirt at the bottom of the ground sluice must afterwards be washed in a board sluice.

The ground sluice has been used to grade roads and to carry away snow from the streets of mining towns, as well as to wash gold.

In claims where many large stones were found in the pay-dirt, and had to be carried by the water through the board sluice, or where the sluice was to be used for a long period, they were paved with stones, because any wooden bottom was rapidly worn out. Sometimes the bed of a stream into which many sluices emptied was converted into a "tail sluice," which yielded a large revenue, with no labor save that of occasionally "cleaning up" or washing out the metal from the sand deposited in the crevices between the stones.

13.—PLACER LEADS TRACED TO QUARTZ.

The placer gold had originally been confined in rocky veins which were disintegrated by the action of chemical or mechanical forces, and the lighter material was swept away by the water, while the heavier remained near its primeval position.

The gold found in the bars of large streams far from the mountains, after having been carried a long distance, is in small smooth particles, as though it had been ground fine and polished by long attrition.

In small gullies in the mountains the gold is usually coarse and rough, as if it had suffered little change after being freed from the quartz by which it was once surrounded.

In hundreds of instances the abundance of gold in a gully has been traced unmistakably to an auriferous quartz lode in the hill-side above it, and the placer miners, following streaks of loose gold, have been brought to the rocky source from which it came.

In this manner the Allisen mine and the Comstock lode, not to mention other less celebrated mines or veins, were found. Such discoveries were made in 1850, and in the following year capitalists in New York and London, anxious to get their share of the marvellous wealth of the Sierra Nevada, formed companies to work the quartz mines at Grass valley and at Mariposa.

Millions of dollars were invested in machinery, and superintendents, with the wildest ideas, were sent to erect mills and to take charge of the precious metals. All these ventures proved complete failures. In most instances the machinery was utterly useless, and the superintendents utterly incompetent.

The castings for the mills lay about the wharves of San Francisco for many years, objects of curiosity for experienced miners, and of ridicule for the general public.

In one mill the metal was to be caught in a course sieve, and in another the quartz was to be crushed by a rolling ball. The mismanagement was so gross and the losses so severe that foreign capitalists became very shy of California quartz mines, and the development of that branch of industry was much retarded.

14.—A GOLD-DREDGING MACHINE.

It was not, however, in quartz mining alone that ridiculous blunders were made. Large sums of money were expended in the eastern States by men who had never seen a placer mine, and had no correct idea of the nature of the gold deposits, in making machinery to take gold more expeditiously from the river beds and bars than could be done by hand. One enterprising New York company sent a dredging machine to dig the metal from the bottom of the Yuba river, never questioning whether that stream was deep enough in the summer to float such a machine, or whether the tough clay and gravel in its bed could be dug up by a dredger, and entirely ignorant of the fact that the gold is mostly in the crevices of the bed-rock, where the spoon and knife of the skilful and attentive miner would be necessary for cleaning out the richest pockets.

15.—DECREASE OF WAGES.

With the introduction of the sluice, the ditch, and the hydraulic process, it became customary to hire laborers. The pan and the rocker required every man to be his own master.

In 1849 each miner worked for himself, or the exceptions were so few that they were almost unknown.

The method of working made it impossible for the employer to guard against the dishonesty of the servant, who could always make more in his own claim than any one could afford to give him. Men become servants usually because they have no capital, and cannot get into profitable employment without it; but there was no lack of profitable employment for the miner in 1849, nor did be need any capital, even if he had it.   But the sluice brought deep diggings, with large masses of pay-dirt, into demand, and the claims were held at high prices, so that their possession was in itself a capital.

There had been an abundance of rocker claims in 1849; but there were not enough good sluice claims three years later to supply one-third of the miners. The erection of a long sluice, the cutting of drains, often necessary to carry off the tailings, and the purchase of water from the ditch company, required capital, and the manner of cleaning up rendered it possible for the owner of a sluice to prevent his servants from stealing any considerable portion of his gold before it came to his possession.   Thus it was that the custom of hiring miners for wages became common in the placer diggings.

In 1852 the wages were $6 or $7 per day; the next year about $5, since which time they have gradually fallen, until now they are from $2 to $3 50 per day; the skilful quartz miner commanding the latter sum.

16.—GROWTH OF THE QUARTZ INTEREST.

The development of the quartz mining interest of the State has been slow and steady, unlike the placer mining, which, rising suddenly to gigantic proportions, soon reached its culminating point, and then began to decline rapidly.

The placers had been discovered by miners who were searching for them, and who spent much time and labor in the search; but in early years most of the richest auriferous lodes were found by men who were not looking for quartz.

Hunters, travellers, placer miners and road makers occasionally came, without thinking of it, upon valuable veins, which they immediately claimed, and proceeded to work or sell.

The first quartz miners in California were Mexicans, who knew how gold-bearing rocks were reduced in their native country.

They pounded up the quartz in mortars, or, if not rich enough to pay for reduction in that way, they made an arrastra or little circular stone pavement in the centre of which stood a post.   To an arm extending out from this was hitched a mule which dragged round a heavy piece of granite, between which and the pavement, the quartz was pulverized, and, when fine, the gold was caught with quicksilver and separated from the base matter by washing.

This process required neither capital nor skilled labor, nor delay, nor a number of laborers.   The owner of the arrastra could dig out his own rock one day, and reduce it the next.

As a matter of profit he usually selected only the richest pieces to work in the arrastra, throwing aside those portions that would not yield at the rate of $75 or more per ton.

With experience in the observation of quartz, and a mode of working in which failure was almost impossible, these Mexicans frequently did very well.

17.—FAILURE IN QUARTZ.

Their success excited the envy of the Americans, who would purchase the claims at high prices, and tell the Mexicans to see the wonders that would be done by American enterprise

The common result was that a large and costly steam-mill was erected; a multitude of laborers were employed; they did not know how to select the rich from the poor quartz; the mill was so large that it could not be kept going at its full capacity without receiving all the poor as well as the rich rock accessible in the vein; the amalgamator did not understand his business; the rich rock in which the Mexicans had been at work was soon exhausted; the creditors who had loaned money for the erection of the mill brought suit to foreclose their mortgage; the work stopped; the title of the property was insecure; and the people in the neighborhood said quartz mining was a very uncertain business. And so it is under that system of management; and that system, leading to failure, was followed in more than a hundred cases. Mills were built in places where only a little pocket of rich quartz had been found, and if the pay-quartz was abundant it was not properly selected; or, if selected, the amalgamation was intrusted to a man who knew nothing of the business, and the gold was lost.

Horace Greeley was near the truth when he said, "I am confident that fully three out of every four quartz mining enterprises have proved failures, or have at best achieved no positive success."[*]

And yet in nearly every case prudent and competent management would have secured success, perhaps on only a small scale, because in many instances the quantity of pay-rock was small. But the failure of three-fourths of the quartz mills built in early years did not prevent the continuous increase of mills, and of the yield of gold from quartz. When a miner found a vein yellow with gold, he could not turn his back on it because his neighbor's mill did not pay. Gradually more caution was used; competent miners and metallurgists became numerous, and the veins were carefully examined as to the quantity of pay-rock before mills were built.

As the placers declined the miners were compelled to turn their attention to quartz, and prospecting for quartz became a regular business.

18.—IMPROVEMENT IN QUARTZ MINING.

In the mode of pulverizing and reducing quartz comparatively few changes have been made. In some mills the same machinery and processes have been used without alteration or addition for ten years. There is, however, a general belief that the business has not been properly studied by any one, and it is certain that there is much difference of opinion in regard to the various important questions involved in the reduction of ores. The practice is not uniform either in regard to the fineness of pulverization, or the size and speed of the stamps, or the mode of amalgamation. Wood, as a material for the shafts of stamps, has given way to iron; the square form has been replaced by the cylindrical; and the stamps, instead of falling with a simple downward motion, now come down with a twist. The mortar into which the stamps fall is now always of iron, and the stamps stand in a straight line instead of forming a circle, as they did in some mills years ago.

Two of the main improvements in gold quartz mining have been in the concentration and the chlorination of sulphurets.

19.—THE HYDRAULIC PROCESS.

The sluice, though perfect as a device for washing the dirt, was not the last invention in placer mining.

The shovel did not furnish earth to the sluice fast enough, and the wages of a dozen workmen must be saved if possible. In 1852, Edward E. Mattison, a native of Connecticut, invented the process of hydraulic mining, in which a stream of water was directed under a heavy pressure against a bank or hill-side containing placer gold, and the earth was torn down by the fluid and carried into the sluice to be washed; thus the expense of shovelling was entirely saved.

The man with the rocker might wash one cubic yard of earth in a day; with the tom he might average two yards; with the sluice four yards; and with the hydraulic and sluice together fifty or even a hundred yards.

---

[*] An Overland Journey from New York to San Francisco, in the summer of 1859, by Horace Greeley, page 289.

The difference is immense. A stream of water rushing through a two-inch pipe, under a pressure of two hundred feet perpendicular, has tremendous force, and the everlasting hills themselves crumble down before it as if they were but piles of cloud blown away by a breath of wind or dissipated by a glance of the sun.

And yet even this terrific power has not sufficed. When the hills have been dried by months of constant heat and drought, the clay becomes so hard that the hydraulic stream, with all its momentum, does not readily dissolve it, and much of the water runs off nearly clear through the sluice, and thus is wasted for the purposes of washing.

The sluice could wash more dirt than the hydraulic stream will furnish when the clay is hard and dry.

To prevent this loss, the miner will often cut a tunnel into the heart of his claim, and by powder blast the clay loose, so that it will give way more readily to the water. There have been instances in which two tons of powder have been used at one blast in a hydraulic claim.

20.—HILL MINING.

As the introduction of the ditch led to the use of the sluice and hydraulic power, so the introduction of the latter led to a change in the mining ground.

The miners were now able and they even preferred to attack high hills of gravel, which afforded them an immense mass of auriferous earth, and furnished profitable employment to large streams of water for months or even years.

Those counties which contained the most extensive districts suitable for the application of hydraulic power were the most prosperous, while the towns dependent on river mining or on shallow placers fell into decay, and were partially and in some cases entirely deserted.

21.—DECLINE OF RIVER MINING.

From 1850 till 1856 river mining occupied a very important place in the industry of the State. The beds of all the streams in the auriferous regions were rich in gold, which could only be obtained by taking the water from its natural course by means of dams and ditches or flumes. The beds being deep, and the banks steep, rocky, and crooked, these enterprises to drain the rivers were very expensive, and they were also very dangerous pecuniarily, since only a brief portion of the year was suitable for the work, and an early rain might come and sweep away dam and flume before an ounce of gold had been obtained. The comb of the Sierra Nevada along nearly its whole length rises almost to the limits of perpetual snow, and the white caps do not disappear, or the rivers reach a low stage until late in the summer, so that three months may be considered as the limit of the period in which a river could be flumed, and the bed emptied of its gold.

Every perennial stream of much note in the auriferous districts has been flumed at some time in its history, but within the last seven years such enterprises have become rarities. One of the most costly and most remarkable river flumes in the State was erected in 1857 to drain the Feather river at Oroville. It was three quarters of a mile long and twenty feet wide ; the expenditures of the company during the season were $176,985, and their profits $75,000. They flumed the river again in 1858, and then lost $45,000.

Since that year no extensive fluming enterprise has been undertaken in any part of the State, and the little work done in the beds of rivers is mostly left to Chinamen, who are content to work for much less pay than white men expect for their labor.

In some of the diggings the auriferous clay is so hard and tough that the hydraulic stream and sluice are unable to dissolve it, and mills have been built to crush it fine, so that the water in the sluice can get an opportunity to dissolve all the earthy particles, and set free the metal.

The "cement mills," as they are called, are mostly of late construction.

The discovery of gold in Australia was made in 1851, by a miner from California, and it proved to be equal in magnitude to that in our own State; and, singular to say, it attracted little attention, and drew from us within two years only about a thousand of our residents, while many thousands were ready to rush to imaginary diggings in other directions.

22.—"RUSHES" TO AUSTRALIA.

Placer mining was at the height of its prosperity in 1852 and 1853. Wages were high, employment abundant for everybody that wished to hire out, and there was plenty of ground that would pay at least moderately for working with the rocker.

But the rich spots were few, and the miners who had shared the prosperity of 1849 were longing for the discovery of some new gold field that would again reward them with an ounce a day.

In the latter part of 1853, and the beginning of 1854, a series of newspaper letters and articles were published, asserting that there were very rich placers on the headwaters of the Amazon, in Peru.

These articles probably came from the same source, and must have been written with the deliberate purpose of throwing trade into the hands of a few ship-owners and merchants.

Whatever the design of the writer or writers may have been, the result was that two thousand miners went from California and Australia to Peru, where they found no placers, nor could they learn of any such place as that mentioned in the articles.

23.—THE KERN RIVER EXCITEMENT.

The next year was marked by a greater rush to Kern river, in the southern part of the State. Some small placers had been found there, and they served as the basis or the suggestion of a multitude of false letters, asserting that the basin of Kern river was as rich in gold as those of the American and Yuba rivers had been in 1849. These statements were copied into the newspapers, which had no means of verification, and the entire industry of the State was thrown into confusion. Miners abandoned good claims, farm laborers and clerks left their employers, the rate of wages and the cost of mining implements rose in the market, and soon six or eight thousand men were on the road to Kern river, and as many more were ready to start, when the newspapers began to show the folly of such a rush to diggings that had as yet produced no considerable amount of gold.

The tide of migration was arrested, and soon it turned back, the disappointed adventurers returning with the satisfaction of knowing that every river between the Mariposa and the Feather, even after seven years' working, was richer than Kern river had ever been.

24.—ANCIENT RIVERS.

It was in October, 1855, that a very remarkable discovery was made near Columbia, in Tuolumne county.

In various parts of the State, the miners in following up rich deposits of gold had come upon what appeared to be the channel of ancient rivers, which had been filled up and covered over with beds of clay and gravel in some places a thousand feet deep.

The high banks, the bars, the bends, the rapids, the deep places, the tributary gullies and brooks, the water-worn gravel, the remains of fresh-water mollusks, the flat stones pointing down stream, the heaps of gravel formed by eddies, the drift-wood, and the deposit of coarse gold in the centre and deep places of the channel—unmistakable evidences of a stream that had existed for centuries—were all distinctly recognizable.

In these ancient rivers the gold was distributed in the same manner as in those of the present geological era, but in greater abundance and usually in larger particles, as though it had not been subjected to so much wear.

The primeval streams were intersected in places by water courses of our own day, and these latter were usually richer just below the points of intersection than at any other places.

The largest and most noted of the ancient river beds yet discovered in California, called the Blue lead, runs nearly through the middle of Sierra and Nevada counties, has a width varying from a hundred to three hundred yards, and has been traced nearly forty miles.

Its course is at right angles to that of the present streams in the same neighborhood. The amount of gold taken from its bed has never been ascertained, but it cannot be less than $25,000,000, and perhaps twice as much.

25.—THE TUOLUMNE TABLE MOUNTAIN.

The traveller in the mining districts frequently sees "table mountains;" that is, high rocky elevations, with flat surfaces and steep sides. They are evidently remains of lava floods, from which the earth, by which they were once surrounded, has been washed away, leaving the basalt towering above the adjacent country.

The most remarkable of these table mountains is in Tuolumne county, through which runs the Stanislaus river, and with the same general course.

Its length, with its bends, is about thirty-five miles, its height from three hundred to one thousand feet above the clay and gravel near it, and its width from a quarter to half a mile. The smoothness of its surface, the gradual inclination to the westward, the basaltic nature of the rock, its proximity to a centre of great volcanic activity, and various other circumstances which cannot be stated here in detail, leave no room for doubt that this table mountain is a solidified bed of lava.

Some miners, sinking a shaft at a place where the lava had been carried away, leaving the sandstone or gravel under it bare, found gold, and some other miners, working along the side of the mountain, found a rich streak of pay-dirt, which ran down in a deep rocky channel obliquely under the mountain. They attempted to follow it, but they soon met a body of water, which they could neither avoid nor pump out. This put them on nettles. Further examination showed that there were other little channels running under the mountain and on both sides, and all going deeper as they went further in, and nearly all tending westward, with a course oblique to that of the mountain, and all containing more or less gold.

There must, then, be an ancient river bed under the mountain. This opinion, advanced by a few men without education, who wished to induce wealthy men to undertake the exploration of the mountain by tunnels, was met by incredulity and ridicule. Nevertheless, the projectors of the scheme had got the idea fixed in their minds, and they were determined to see what the mountain was made of. The storekeepers, in accordance with the general custom of assisting in developing the resources of their own neighborhood, willingly trusted them for provisions, tools, and clothes, while they were cutting a tunnel to reach the bed of the supposed ancient river.

They commenced their work at some distance from the basalt, and after cutting through clay and gravel reached a slate rock, which seemed to have been the ancient bank, and then they came to a bed of gravel of such character that the theory of the primeval river was fully established. But the tunnel was not deep enough.

It was far above the bed rock, and the water stood, as before, between the miner and the gold. Months of labor had been lost, and it was uncertain whether the next tunnel would strike the right level, nor could it be known whether the bed would be rich enough to pay. Nevertheless, hope and confidence, the chief divinities of the miner, and he is happy in their smiles even when privation is his companion and when experience tells him that no gold fortune is in store, continued to sustain him.

The Table mountain prospectors, however, had reason and experience, as well as hope and confidence, to cheer them, and the second tunnel was undertaken with the encouragement of many men who had sneered at the first. The right elevation had been struck this time, the bottom of the river bed was reached and was drained by the tunnel, and the gravel was found to be extremely rich. Ten feet square of superficial area yielded $100,000. A pint of gravel not unfrequently contained a pound of gold. The whole mountain was soon claimed.

The State echoed with the discovery. A stream of lava had filled up the bed of an ancient river for thirty miles, and in the course of ages the earth and slate that once formed the banks were washed away, leaving the basalt to mark the position of the golden treasure. Other similar deposits were found elsewhere, and other explorations, as bold in their conception but less successful or less important in their results, were undertaken in nearly every county.

26.—THE FRASER FEVER.

The years 1856 and 1857 were marked by no peculiar excitement or sudden change. The working of the gullies and river bars and beds was gradually becoming less profitable and productive, the quartz and ditch interests continued to grow larger, wages kept their downward tendency, and the number of hired laborers increased.

In 1858 the State received a shock that was felt in every fibre of her political and industrial organization. Rich diggings were found in the spring on a bar of Fraser river, and it was asserted and presumed that there were large tracts of excellent placers in the upper basin of the stream. The presumption was not without its foundation in experience and reason, but after all it was but a presumption.

The miners, however, were not disposed to listen to any doubts; they were ready to sacrifice everything in the hope of finding and being the first to enjoy another virgin gold field like that of California.

In the course of four months, 18,000 men, nearly one-sixth of all the voters in the State went to Fraser river, and many thousands of others were preparing for an early start. The confident belief prevailed that "the good old times" of '49 were to come again.

Servants threw up their positions, farmers and miners left their valuable property, wages rose, houses and land fell in value, and many persons believed that California would soon be left without a tenth part of her population.

All this excitement was made before any gold had been received in San Francisco, and before there was any direct and trustworthy evidence of the existence of paying diggings beyond the limits of a few bars, which could not give occupation to more than a hundred men.

Suddenly, and with no material addition to the evidence, the conviction burst on the people that Fraser river would not pay, and five-sixths of the truant miners had returned before the end of the year.

* 27.—DISCOVERY OF THE COMSTOCK LODE.

A party of emigrants discovered placer diggings on Gold cañon, a little tributary of Carson river, east of the Sierra Nevada, in 1849, and a permanent mining camp was established there in 1852.

It was observed that the gold contained a large proportion of silver, in some claims nearly one-half in value, but this fact was not without precedent in the placers of California, and was regarded simply as a misfortune for the miner, who did not receive more than $10 or $12 an ounce for his dust, while that obtained on the western slope of the Sierra usually sold for $17 or $18.

The Gold cañon diggings had been worked for seven years, and gave employment to about fifty men, when, in the spring of 1859, the miners, following up a rich streak of placer gold, came upon a quartz lode in the place now known as Gold Hill.

A couple of months later, some miners, in following up a placer lead in which the gold was mixed with about an equal weight of silver, came on the lode from which the metal had been washed down.†

They were working here in a rude way, with no idea of the value of their claim, when James Walsh, an intelligent quartz miner from Grass valley, passed

---

* The credit of this discovery has been claimed by so many parties, and the testimony is so conflicting, that I am induced to give at least two of the popular versions. Substantially they agree upon the main points. (See section 4, Resources of Nevada.)

† S. H. Marlette, surveyor general of Nevada, in his annual report for 1865, gives the following history of the discovery of the Comstock lode:

"In 1852, H. B. and E. A. Grosch or Grosh, sons of A. B. Grosh, a Universalist clergyman of considerable note, and editor of a Universalist paper at Utica, New York, educated metallurgists, came to the then Territory, and the same or the following year engaged in placer mining in Gold cañon near the site of Silver City, and continued there until 1857, when, so far as I can learn, they first discovered silver ore, which was found in a quartz vein, probably the one now owned by the Kossuth Gold and Silver Mining Company, on which the Grosh brothers had a location.

"Shortly after the discovery, one of the brothers accidentally wounded himself with a pick, from the effects of which he soon died, and the other brother went to California, where he died early in 1858, which probably prevented the valuable nature of their discovery from becoming known. In the mean time placer mining was carried on to considerable extent in various localities, principally in Gold cañon.

"In 1857, Joe Kirby and others commenced placer mining in Six Mile cañon, about half a mile below where the Ophir works now are, and worked at intervals with indifferent success until 1859. On the 22d day of February, 1858, the first quartz claim was located in Virginia mining district, on the Virginia croppings, by James Finney, generally known as Old Virginia, from whom the city of Virginia and the cropping have taken their name. This must be considered the first location of the Comstock lode, unless we consider the Kossuth claim as upon one branch of the Comstock, which may not be impossible in case we adopt the one lode system, for the lode is about one hundred feet in thickness, and its strike would take it to the eastern slope of Mount Davidson, as explorations prove, as I have been informed, the Virginia croppings to be the outcrop of the western portion of the Comstock.

"The discovery of rich deposits of silver ore was not made until June, 1859, when Peter O'Reilly and Patrick McLaughlin, while engaged in gold washing on what is now the ground of the Ophir Mining Company, and near the south line of the Mexican Company's claim, uncovered a rich vein of sulphuret of silver in an excavation made for the purpose of collecting water to use in their rockers in washing for gold. This discovery being on ground claimed at the time by Kirby and others, Comstock was employed to purchase their claim, whereby Comstock's name has been given to this great lode, by which those entitled to the credit of its discovery have been defrauded—a transaction, to compare small things with great, as discreditable as that by which Americus Vespucius bestowed his name upon the western continent, an honor due alone to the great Columbus.

"From this discovery resulted the marvellous growth of Nevada. Immediately the lode was claimed for miles; an unparalleled excitement followed, and miners and capitalists came in great numbers to reap a share of the reported wealth. The few hardy prospectors exploring the mountains for hidden wealth soon counted their neighbors by thousands; soon walked along miles of busy streets, called into existence by the throng of adventurers, and soon the prospectors were ransacking almost every part of the (at present) State of Nevada in search of silver lodes."

their place and examined their mine. His attention was attracted by the dark gray stone which he suspected was silver ore, and as an assay of it he sent a ton and a half of it to San Francisco, where it was sold for $3,000 per ton. He and some friends then bought out four of the five partners, paying $22,000 for four-fifths of 1,800 feet, or at the rate of $14 per foot.

Some shafts sunk on the vein showed that the gray stone, a rich sulphuret of silver, could be obtained in large quantities. The lode was soon claimed as far as it could be traced, and the market value of the shares rose so rapidly that before the end of the year $1,000 a foot had been offered for a portion of the lode.

28.—THE WASHOE EXCITEMENT.

The excitement about the silver mines spread throughout California in the spring of 1860, and thousands of miners crossed the mountains to work in the newly-discovered mines or to seek for others.

In every town companies were formed to equip and send out prospectors, and the work was continued on a large scale for three years. Thousands of square miles, never before visited by white men, were explored and examined, and many thousands of metalliferous lodes were found and claimed.

It was in 1860 that the silver districts of Esmeralda, Bodie, Potosi, Coso, and Humboldt were discovered, besides many others of less note. The chief silver mining town grew up at the Comstock lode, and was soon the home of a large and excited population. Every man owned thousands of feet of argentiferous lodes, and considered himself either possessed of a fortune or certain of soon acquiring one.

The confidence in the almost boundless wealth of the country was universal, but many were bothered to convert their ore into ready cash. Men who considered themselves millionaires had sometimes not enough money to pay for a dinner, and in their dress they looked like beggars.*

* The following extract from a letter written at Virginia, in April, 1860, gives a vivid picture of the condition of society there at that time :

"Of a certainty, right here, is Bedlam broke loose. One cannot help thinking, as he passes through the streets, that all the insane geologists extant have been corraled at this place. Most vehement is the excitement. I have never seen men act thus elsewhere. Not even in the earlier stages of the California gold movement were they so delirious about the business of metalliferous discovery. Hundreds and thousands are now here, who, feeling that they may never have another chance to make a speedy fortune, are resolved this shall not pass unimproved. They act with all the concentrated energy of those having the issues of life and death before them. They demean themselves not like rational beings any more. Even the common modes of salutation are changed. Men, on meeting, do not inquire after each other's health, but after their claims. They do not remark about the weather, bad as it is, but about out-croppings, assays, sulphurets, &c. They do not extend their hands in token of friendship on approaching, but pluck from their well filled pockets a bit of rock, and, presenting it, mutually inquire what they think of its looks. During the day they stand apart, talking in couples, pointing mysteriously hither and yon; and during the night mutter in their sleep of claims and dips and strikes, showing that their broken thoughts are still occupied with the all-absorbing subject. I shall be able to convey to your readers some idea of the intensity of this mining mania, when I assure them that this portion of the American people do not even ask after newspapers, nor engage in the discussion of politics. Little care they whom you choose President; conventions and elections, wars and rumors of wars, are nothing to them. They have their own world here. Here, bounded by the Sierra and the mountains of Utah, spread over the foot-hills and the deserts, is a theatre beyond which their thoughts are not permitted to roam ; to this their aspirations and aims are all confined. Whatever of energy, ambition, and desire are elsewhere expended on love, war, politics, and religion, are here all devoted to this single pursuit of finding, buying, selling, and trading in mines of silver and gold. Everybody makes haste to be rich ; and so great is the mental tension in this direction, that it may well be questioned whether, if a sweeping disappointment should overtake them, many will not be reduced to a condition of absolute lunacy. What guarantee this wildly-excited multitude have against the happening of this fearful contingency, I am not fully prepared to say, having, as yet, not been able

29.—THE BARREL AND YARD PROCESSES.

There was much difficulty in extracting the metal even from the richest ore. There were no mills to crush the rock, no skilful metallurgists to reduce the ore, and no confident opinion in regard to the best means of extraction. The simple processes used for reducing auriferous quartz would not suffice. The gold exists in the metallic form, and so soon as the rock is pulverized can be obtained by washing or amalgamation. But silver is in chemical combination with baser substances, and must be separated from them by chemical influences before the metal will submit to unite with quicksilver, by which it must usually be caught.

All the silver produced in civilized countries was obtained by two processes, the Frieberg German barrel, and the Mexican yard or patio. In the German process three hundred pounds of the ore, finely pulverized, are mixed with water to the thickness of cream, and after the addition of some salt, iron pyrites, scraps of iron, and quicksilver are put into a strong barrel, and kept revolving rapidly for fourteen hours, at the end of which time the silver and quicksilver have united, and they can easily be separated from the mud by washing. The barrels are rapidly worn out, the amount of work done is little, and the labor required is much. In the Mexican process the pulverized ore is mixed with water, salt, iron pyrites, and quicksilver, and left out in an open yard for three weeks, the mass being stirred or trodden with mules occasionally. This mode of reducing is very slow, and is unsuited to the cool climate of Nevada, in latitude 38°, and at an elevation of 5,000 or 6,000 feet above the sea.

30.—THE PAN PROCESS.

There was a general belief that some mode of amalgamation better than either of these could and would be devised, so while one set of men were engaged in hunting and opening mines, another set were busy in studying a mode for reducing the ores. A satisfactory result was not reached for several years, but it came at last in the invention of the pan process, as distinguished from the barrel and yard processes.

The pan is of cast-iron, about five feet in diameter and eighteen inches deep.

Five hundred or a thousand pounds of ore are put in with salt, iron pyrites, quicksilver, and enough water to make a thin mud. A muller revolves on the bottom of the pan, and serves to grind the matter, which is not fine enough, and also brings all the particles of the ore into contact with the chemicals and the quicksilver. Besides the motion of the muller, various devices are used to keep up a regular current, so that all portions of the mixture are successively brought to the bottom, and exposed to the action of the quicksilver. In some pans heat is applied. The American process extracts silver from the common sulphuret ore as thoroughly as any other process, with much more rapidity, and with less expense. It is, therefore, in almost universal use in the American silver mines of the Pacific slope, and has been introduced into Mexico, where it will probably in time supersede the yard process. While the metallurgists were working away at their pans, the miners generally were afraid to erect mills lest buildings and machinery might be unsuited to the new modes of working. The mills that were built charged $50 and $60 per ton for crushing and

to give the subject much examination since my return. To attempt eliciting information from those now here, only tends to confuse and complicate what is already incomprehensible. If you talk with one man, he is only concerned lest the argentiferous metal be rendered worthless by the superabundance here met with; while another, with equal opportunities, and perhaps better ability for forming a correct judgment, derides the idea of there being any silver apart from the Comstock vein, telling you that the whole thing is an inverted pyramid, having that truly wonderful lead for a base."

amalgamating, though the same work was done at Grass Valley, only one hundred miles distant, for less than $5 a ton.

The amalgamation was so conducted that only the free gold was saved. All the silver and much of the gold were lost. Ore that contained $500 to the ton was sent to the mill if it yielded $70 or $80, leaving about $10 profit, and a loss of $400 of silver.

The value of the ore and the amount of silver lost were precisely understood, but there was no remedy. It was necessary to take some silver from the mines at any sacrifice to keep up the confidence of the shareholders. Although the ore in sight was worth millions, the bullion sent across the mountains from Nevada amounted to only $90,897 in 1860.

The next year, however, the export rose to $2,275,256; in 1862 to $6,247,074, and in 1863 to $12,486,238. This increased rate might well astonish the world, and dazzle people in the vicinity.

31.—GROWTH OF THE WASHOE EXCITEMENT.

The silver excitement which pervaded California in the spring of 1860 continued to increase steadily for three years.

Washoe, by which name the mining region near the Comstock lode was generally known, was the main topic of conversation, and the main basis of speculation. Everybody owned shares in some silver mine. High prices were paid to strangers for mines at places of which the purchaser had never heard until a day or two before the purchase. Men seemed to have discarded all the dictates of prudence. Their judgment was overwhelmed by the suddenly acquired wealth of a few and by the general anxiety of the many to buy any kind of silver shares. People acted as though there were so many rich silver mines that men who had been searching for them would not be so mean as to offer a poor one for sale. Three thousand silver mining companies were incorporated in San Francisco, and 30,000 persons purchased stock in them. The nominal capital was $1,000,000,000, but their actual market value never exceeded $60,000,000, and not one in fifty owned a claim of the least value. And yet the organization of each company cost $100 on an average, and that money had to be paid by somebody. Although the mines were in western Utah, which was organized afterwards into the Territory and then into the State of Nevada, the shares were mostly owned in San Francisco, and that place was the centre of speculation and excitement, of profit and loss. On every side were to be seen men who had made independent fortunes in stocks within a few months.

The share in the leading mines on the Comstock lode were the preferred security for loans by money lenders and banks.

The shares, or feet, as they were more commonly called, (for in most of the companies a share represented a lineal foot lengthwise on the vein,) of the Comstock claims advanced with great rapidity, in some cases as much as $1,000 per month.

A foot of the Gould and Curry mine, worth $500 on the 1st of March, 1862, was sold for $1,000 in June; for $1,550 in August; for $2,500 in September; for $3,200 in February, 1863; for $3,700 in May; for $4,400 in June, and for $5,600 in July. Other claims advanced with a rapidity less rapid but scarcely less startling. In the middle of 1863, Savage was worth $3,600 per foot; Central $2,850; Ophir $2,550; Hale and Norcross $1,850; California $1,500; Yellow Jacket $1,150; Crown Point $750; Chollar $900, and Potosi $600.

32.—VIRGINIA CITY.

Virginia City, the centre of the mining industry, rose to be the second town west of the Rocky mountains. It had a population of 15,000, and the assessed value of its taxable property was $11,000,000. The amount of business done was twice as great as in any other town of equal size in the United States. And well might the town be large and busy. It produced more silver within a year than any other one mining district of equal size ever did. Neither Potosi nor Guanajuato could equal it. The former town yielded $10,000,000 annually for a time, but with that yield supported a population of 160,000. Indeed, it may be doubted whether any town of 15,000 persons ever before produced an average of $12,000,000 annually, or an average of $800 to the person. Well might excitement run high, and money be flush.

33.—THE SILVER PANIC.

But though the silver yield kept up, distrust set in, and prices of stocks commenced to fall in the summer of 1863. The people began to count up how many millions they had paid as assessments on claims that had been worked for years and had never yielded a cent. Experts from other silver mining countries said that no rich and permanent deposits of silver had been opened, save on the Comstock lode, and that the management of the mines there was grossly wasteful.

It was a notorious fact that many companies had been organized for the purpose of swindling the ignorant by selling worthless stock to them.

Prices declined slowly until the middle of the next year, and then they were attacked by a panic which smote hundreds of the Washoe speculators with terror and bankruptcy. Gould & Curry fell from $5,600 to $900 per foot; Savage, from $3,600 to $750; Ophir, from $2,550 to $425; California, from $1,500 to $21; Hale & Norcross, from $1,850 to $310, and others in like proportion.

The wild-cat or baseless speculations were swept away to destruction by the thousand, and never heard of more.

The dray-men, the hod-carriers, the mechanics, the clerks, the seamstresses, the servant girls, who had cheerfully paid assessments for years, in the confidence that they would soon have a handsome income from their silver mines, were disenchanted.

The name of Washoe, which had once been blessed, was now accursed by the multitude, though still a source of profit to a few.

People wondered how they could have been so blind. It was found on examination that the most deliberate and most dishonest deception had been systematically practiced in many cases. Most of the mines had been managed not with the object of taking silver from the ore, but for the purpose of making a profit by the sale and purchase of stocks.

The officers, or some of them, combined to raise or depress the shares as suited their schemes. It was an easy matter to instruct the miners to take out the richest or the poorest of the ore, and the returns of the mill could be published as a fair indication of the value of all the ore within sight.*

In the erection of buildings the financial management of the companies was grossly extravagant. Money was thrown about almost as if it had no value. It was presumed that the rich and extensive deposits found near the surface, instead of being exhausted, would become still richer as the works advanced in depth. The ignorance of metallurgy and lack of experience in silver mining led to many costly mistakes.

Wages much higher than those of California were paid.

* We find the following paragraph in the report of S. H. Marlette, the surveyor general of Nevada, for 1865:

"When a bulling operation was in progress the superintendent would write glowing letters; rich rock, selected from a large mass of poorer material, would be sent to mill; debts would be incurred to be paid in the future, and large dividends would be declared.

"If a 'bearing' operation was in contemplation, the rich deposits would be avoided: the rock sent to mill would prove to be very poor; assessments would be levied to pay off the debts of the company; suits would be commenced against it, and every device that could discourage stockholders would be adopted."

34.—LITIGATION ABOUT THE COMSTOCK MINES.

The overestimate of the value of the mines was one of the causes of a great litigation, for which opportunities were given by the careless manner in which claims were located, recorded, and transferred in early times. The lawyers charged fees high almost beyond example. Witnesses who found that their testimony was necessary in important suits suddenly had business in the eastern States, or in some other remote place, and could not be persuaded to remain till the trial unless some large sums of money were paid to them.

Subornation of perjury became a profession in which many engaged. So much money was spent in a law suit that it materially affected business.

When the trial of the suit between the Ophir and the Burning Moscow was transferred from Virginia City to Aurora, property in certain parts of the latter town rose fifty per cent., so confident were the residents there that the attendants at the court would be numerous and flush of money. In several cases more money was spent in litigation than the entire mine is now worth. The surveyor general of the State, in his report for the year 1865, says :

"I have understood that $1,300,000 have been expended in litigation between the Chollar and Potosi companies, and $1,000,000 more have been expended in the Ophir-Moscow trials. * * * I believe one-fifth of the proceeds of the Comstock would not more than pay the expenses of litigating the title thereto."

The yield of the Comstock lode, up to the date of that report, had been about $45,000,000 ; so Mr. Marlette's estimate of the amount spent in litigation would be $9,000,000, and four-fifths of this was expended within a period of three years.

The sum paid as dividends to stockholders in many permanent mines was less than that expended in litigation.

35.—THE MANY-LODE THEORY.

One of the main sources of the lawsuits was the doubt whether the Comstock lode had at its side a number of branches, or whether it was one of a series of independent and parallel lodes within a distance of two hundred yards. At the surface several seams of ore were perceptible, and the first claimants had taken the seam which was largest and lowest on the hill, and they asserted that the seams above were mere branches. This assertion, however, did not prevent others from claiming the upper seams, and thus arose the suits between the Ophir and the Burning Moscow, that between the Gould & Curry and the North Potosi, and that between the Potosi and the Bajazet, which were all cases of much importance in their day. The people were divided between the one-lode and the many-lode parties, and elections turned more than once on that question. Most of the stock of the one-lode companies was held in San Francisco, while a larger proportion of the stockholders of the many-lode companies were residents of Virginia City, so it was argued that it was the interest of Nevada that the old companies should be defeated. But the latter had the evidence of geology, and what was, perhaps, still more important, the money on their side, and the many-lode theory was at last completely overthrown, but not until after a struggle that cost years of time and millions of money. The Comstock vein has a dip of 45° to the horizon, and while it was in the process of formation large bodies of porphyry split off from the hanging wall, fell down into the vein stone and were there suspended, leaving a seam of quartz above as well as one below. These pieces of hanging wall are usually long, narrow, and deep, but not large enough in any direction to make two lodes out of one.

36.—EXPENSES INCREASING WITH THE DEPTH.

Another source of disappointment to the mining companies was that as the works advanced in depth expenses increased in an unexpected manner. The immense excavations for the extraction of ore required vast quantities of timber ; as the forests are distant and transportation dear, the mines now pay three-quarters of a million dollars annually for timbering alone.

The water increased, and powerful engines, consuming much wood, were required to pump constantly at an expense of $100 per day to each of half a dozen companies. Foul air made it impossible for the miners to work rapidly in the deep drifts, and ventilation was expensive. These, and a multitude of other considerations, contributed to the panic and kept the general stock market down.

But such influences could not entirely govern the price of particular stocks. Gould & Curry, which was sold for $900 per foot in July, 1864, advanced to $2,000 in April, 1865, and fell to $600 in October, 1866. Savage was $2,000 in April, 1865, and $1,100 in October, 1866. Of stocks, which were not noticed in the stock boards in the summer of 1864, Yellow Jacket rose in April, 1865, to $2,590 per foot, and was sold in October, 1866, for $700; Belcher, worth $1,650 in April, 1865, was offered for $95 in October, 1866. Alpha, worth $2,100 in April, 1865, was worth only $50 in October, 1866, and Crown Point fell from $1,225 in April, 1865, to $900 in October, 1866. A fall of fifty per cent. or a rise of two hundred per cent. in the market value of a large mine within the space of six months has occurred in more than two score cases within the last five years, and it is easily understood that in such events fortunes are made and lost with great rapidity.

37.—SOME CHARACTERISTICS OF ESMERALDA, HUMBOLDT, AND REESE RIVERS.

The stocks in all the other districts of Nevada were affected, and, it might almost be said, governed by the influence of those of Virginia City. While shares in the Comstock lode were high, so were those in mines elsewhere. At Esmeralda large masses of rich ore were found in the Wide West and Real Del Monte mines, and the price of their stocks rose to $400 per foot; but there, too, litigation, bad management, and the speedy exhaustion of the rich deposits near the surface were followed by a general collapse.

Esmeralda district, which yielded $500,000 annually for a couple of years, seemed to have been worked out, and all the explorations undertaken since 1864 have failed to show anything to compare with the ore opened in 1861 and 1862.

Several other districts in the vicinity, however, were found, and these promised to more than surpass Esmeralda in its best days. Humboldt had a history somewhat like Esmeralda.

A large body of rich ore in the Sheba mines brought the price of that stock up to $400 per foot, but they contained antimony, and could not be reduced without roasting, and the expenses of reduction, and litigation and the exhaustion of the rich body of ore, soon left the company insolvent; and since then the Humboldt district has been under a cloud, although many of the veins will undoubtedly prove profitable in time.

The Reese River mines, discovered in June, 1862, include a number of districts, in which a great variety of veins and ores are found. The development has been slow, yet it is the opinion of intelligent men who have examined the lodes that several of them will take a high place in the production of silver after a few years.

The last of the silver districts of Nevada in the order of discovery is Pahranagat, in the southeastern corner of the State, which first attracted attention in the beginning of 1866. No bullion has yet been extracted there, but some fine ore has been found, and the quantity appears to be considerable.

38.—SUTRO TUNNEL PROJECT.

In 1865 it became evident that if the mining in the Comstock mines were to be continued for many years, it would be profitable, and even necessary, to have

H. Ex. Doc. 29——3

a tunnel to drain the vein to a depth of 2,000 feet. Of the continuation of the mining there could be no reason to doubt.

The lode has the main geological characteristics which mark the greatest silver-bearing veins of Spanish America. It is a fissure vein that extends across several different formations, and at the richest place it separates two different kinds of "country" rock. It is of great length and great width. The general thickness and dip remain about the same, so far as they have been examined. The walls are distinctly marked. The inclination is about 45° to the horizon. There are large seams of clay-like substances along the sides, as though the sides had rubbed and ground part of the vein-stone to powder. Bodies of porphyry, many of them large and others small, are found in the vein-stone, looking as though they had cracked off the upper or hanging wall and fallen down.

The vein-stone, so far as traced, is about the same in all places, though the color varies from white and gray to brown. The ore is distributed irregularly, being found in some places in large masses and in others in thin seams. The general features of the lode are like those other great argentiferous veins, and mining geologists say that the class are inexhaustibly rich in silver. It is presumed that they are rich in ore far beyond any depth which miners can reach.*

----

*39.—BARON RICHTHOFEN'S REPORT.

The following is a quotation from "The Comstock Lode, its character and the probable mode of its continuance in depth. By Ferdinand Baron Richthofen, Dr. Phil., San Francisco, 1866:"

"If we proceed to compare the Comstock vein with those best explored, it is evident that it differs in nature from a certain class of narrow veins, which, as those of Freiberg, Konigsberg, and Chañarcillo, in Chili, Pasco, in Peru, Catorce, in Mexico, and Austin, in Nevada, fill a number of small fissures, which are either parallel or intersect each other, and which exhibit in depth nearly the same character and richness as near the surface. It presents, on the contrary, all the characters of a second class of silver veins, which are prominent on account of their magnitude and unity, and exhibit, wherever they occur, one great mother vein, or 'veta madre,' surrounded, in most instances, by some smaller veins of little or no importance. To this class belong the veins of Schemnitz and Felsobanya, in Hungary, the Veta Madre, of Guanajuato, and the Veta Grande, of Zacatecas, while the veins of Potosi, in Peru, and the Biscayna of Real del Monte, in Mexico, have to be referred more to this than to the former class. Notwithstanding their small number, these great mother veins furnish by far the greater portion of the silver produced throughout the world. They resemble each other in many points. All of them fill fissures of extraordinary width and length, and appear to be of very recent origin, and also to be intimately related to volcanic rocks, by which they are accompanied. Although the laws which govern the distribution of ore differ more or less for each vein, yet all of them have been found to be highly metalliferous to whatever depth explored; and it appears that nearly an equal quantity of silver is with most of them contained in each level, the vein of Guanajuato being an exception to this rule. It may be inferred that this will continue to be the case to an indefinite depth. There is, however, a marked difference in the concentration of silver, ores of extreme richness being usually accumulated in limited bodies in the upper levels, while in depth similar bodies recur greater in extent, but consisting of lower grades of ores. This is one of the principal reasons why, on all the veins mentioned, mining in upper levels has been so highly remunerative compared with the profits derived from deep working. Each ton of ore costs there but little to extract, and yields a large amount of metal, while raising the same weight from greater depth is more expensive, and at the same time a smaller amount of bullion is realized. The history of the Mexican mines is the best illustration of these relations. In former centuries counts and marquises have been made by the king of Spain whenever fortune enabled a single individual to accumulate enormous wealth in a few years. Mining then was confined to rich ores within a few hundred feet from the surface. In the present century, since greater depths have been reached, the Spanish crown, if it had still the sceptre of Mexico, would scarcely have found an opportunity of bestowing equal honors on fortunate mining adventurers, notwithstanding the unabated enterprising spirit of the population and the increased facilities of raising the treasures. And yet the production of the Mexican mines has anything but decreased. It appears, on the contrary, that it has never been so high as at the present time. Humboldt states that vastly the majority of the annual production of Mexico has through all times been derived from the mother veins alluded to above, and still at this day they furnish at least three-fourths of it, though each of them has repeatedly been abandoned as unprofitable. They would be inexhaustible sources of wealth if the increase of expenses attending the growing depth did not put a limit to all profitable mining.

"The equality of produce of the Mexican mines is probably partly due to the prevalence of true silver ores through all levels. The Hungarian offer less favorable conditions, as the

The water which gathers in mines at Virginia City, although the deepest there is not half so deep as in many in Mexico, is very great, and a tunnel or adit-level is necessary to secure drainage and ventilation and procure a cheap mode of extracting the ore and of exploring the lode. Fortunately the lode is situated on a mountain side, and there is an opportunity of draining the lode to a depth of two thousand feet by cutting an adit three and three-fifths miles. The expense will be several millions of dollars, but the saving will be far more. Considerations like these led to the formation of the Sutro Tunnel Company, which received a franchise from the legislature of the State and a grant of land from

---

ores, on account of the previously mentioned increase of lead and copper in depth, undergo a real deterioration. Yet they have evidently had at upper levels their concentrated bodies of rich ore. Such have been extracted at Schemnitz within the time of historical record, while their former existence at Felsobanya may be inferred from the shape and character of the old Roman works near the out-croppings.

"Let us now return to the Comstock vein, the 'veta madre' of Washoe, and examine what conclusions as to its future we are justified in drawing from the present condition of the explorations. In the first place, we have mentioned the fact that the ores through all the levels explored retain their character of true silver ores which they had near the surface. The amount of lead, copper, iron, and zinc has never been large in the Comstock ores, and these metals preserve now, at the lowest level, nearly the same relative proportion as formerly. Their increase, especially of lead, would be the most unfavorable indication for the future of the Comstock lode, as, besides the growing difficulty of metallurgical treatment, the conclusion would be justified that lead ores would more and more replace those of silver, and the limits of profitable productiveness would soon be reached. But as it is, no deterioration is to be expected, even if an impoverishment takes place. It thus approaches in its ore-bearing character the great mother-veins of Mexico, and is different from those of Hungary. But even the reasons for an impoverishment are by no means so evident as might appear at first sight. There have been, it is true, bonanzas near the surface, which surpassed in richness all those worked upon in later times. As such may be mentioned the bonanzas of the Ophir, the Gould & Curry, and the western body of ore in Gold Hill. Their richness and the facilities of their extraction co-operated in making the latter exceedingly profitable. Yet the production of the Comstock vein did not, at the time when it was solely derived from these surface-bonanzas, reach the figure it attained after the exhaustion of their principal portion. One of the reasons is that then the ore was concentrated within narrow limits, while as the greater depth was attained the distribution of the ores was much more general, though their standard was lower. New bodies of ore had been discovered, commencing at a depth of from one hundred and fifty to three hundred feet below the surface, such as the continuous sheets of ore in the eastern part of the lode in the Gold Hill mines and the Yellow Jacket, and the similar-constituted one in Chollar-Potosi. None of them contain, excepting a few narrow streaks or bunches, ores of equal richness with those of which the surface-bonanzas were composed. But their extent so far exceeds that of the latter as to make up, by the increased amount of daily extraction, for the interior yield. The profits of working are of course greatly diminished. These bodies of ore have continued to the deepest levels reached in the Comstock mines, varying in width and extent, and also in their yield. The latter did not increase, but in some instances, as in the southern part of Gold Hill, decreased with the growing width of the deposit, while in others no material change is perceptible.

"Few new bodies of ore made their appearance below the level of three hundred feet. Foremost in importance among them are two bodies discovered at seven hundred feet below the surface of the Hale & Norcross works, one of which is on ground supposed heretofore to be unproductive.

"Considering these facts exhibited by the Comstock vein itself, and comparing with them what is known about similar argentiferous veins, we believe ourselves to be justified in drawing the following conclusions:

"1st. That the continuity of the ore-bearing character of the Comstock lode in depth must, notwithstanding local interruptions, be assumed as a fact of equal certainty with the continuity of the vein itself.

"2d. That it may positively be assumed that the ores in the Comstock lode will retain their character of true silver ores to indefinite depth.

"3d. That it is highly probable that extensive bodies of ores equal in richness to the surface-bonanzas will never occur in depth.

"4th. That an increase in size of the bodies of ore in depth is more probable than a decrease, and that they are more likely to increase than to remain of the same size as heretofore.

"5th. That a considerable portion of the ore will, as to its yield, not materially differ at any depth from what it is at the present lower levels, while, besides, there will be an increasing bulk of lower-grade ores. We are led to this supposition by the similarity in character of all the deposits outside of the rich surface-bonanzas and the homogeneous nature which almost every one of them exhibits throughout its entire extent.

Congress, and met with the encouragement of the great companies mining on the lode, all of which signed contracts with the company binding themselves to pay a certain sum for every ton taken from their mines after the completion of the tunnel. Although the work has not been commenced, the project has fair prospects, and it occupies an important place in the history of mining in Nevada. The miners at Virginia City will never be content to abandon that plan of drainage.

40.—COLUMBIA BASIN AND CARIBOO MINES.

The first mines in what is now Idaho Territory were found in the bars of Clearwater river in the spring of 1860, and those of the Salmon river were opened in a few months later. The placers of Boisé were struck in 1862, those of Owyhee in 1863, and the quartz veins of Owyhee and Alturas began to attract attention in 1864. In eastern Oregon the placers of Powder and Burnt rivers were discovered in 1861, and those of John Day's river in the following year.

None of the Idaho or Oregon placers have proved so rich, so extensive, or so durable as those of California, although they have yielded considerable amounts of gold. The deep diggings of Cariboo, 500 miles from Victoria, in the upper part of Fraser valley, were discovered in 1859, and the placers in the shallow bars and creeks at the Big Bend of the Columbia, in the territory of British Columbia, in 1865. California had to send miners to all these places.

The number who went to Idaho was, probably, 20,000; and in 1866 at least 5,000 migrated to Montana.

It was also in this year that a rumor became current that rich placers had been discovered at Barbacoas, in New Granada, and the result was the migration and bitter disappointment of about a thousand men, who found nothing to reward their trouble.

"6th. That the ore will shift at different levels, from certain portions of the lode to others, as it has done up to the present time. More equality in its distribution may, however, be expected below the junction of the branches radiating toward the surface, when the vein will probably fill a more uniform and more regular channel. Some mines which have been heretofore almost unproductive, as the Central, California, Bullion, and others, have therefore good chances of becoming metalliferous in depth. But throughout the extent of the vein, it is most likely that the portion which lies next to the foot-wall will continue unproductive, as it did from the surface down to the lowest works, while the entire portion between it and the hanging wall must be considered as the probable future source of ore. As remarked in the foregoing pages, it is also probable that repeatedly, in following the lode downward, branches will be found rising from its main body vertically into the hanging wall and consisting of clay or quartz. Many of them will probably be ore-bearing. Such bodies of ore should be sought for, at all the mines, in what is generally supposed to be the eastern country. Experience in upper levels would lead to the supposition that such eastern bodies might carry richer ores than the average of the main portion of the vein.

"7th. That the intervention of a barren zone, as is reported by good authorities to occur at the Veta Madre of Guanajuato at the depth of twelve hundred feet, is not at all likely to be met with in the case of the Comstock lode. The argument which we have to adduce for this conclusion has some weight from a geological point of view. It is a well known fact that the enclosing rocks have usually great influence on the quantity and quality of the ores of certain metals in mineral veins, and that a rich lode passing into a different formation frequently becomes barren or poor. At the Veta Madre of Guanajuato a sudden decrease in the yield of the ore at the depth of twelve hundred feet attends the passage of the lode into a different formation, which from thence continues to the lowest depth attained. No such change can be anticipated for the Comstock lode, since the structure of the country seems to indicate the continuity of the enclosing rocks to an indefinite depth.

"In winding up these considerations, we come to the positive conclusion that the amount of nearly fifty million dollars, which have been extracted from the Comstock lode, is but a small proportion of the amount of silver waiting future extraction in the virgin portions of the vein, from the lowest level explored down to indefinite depth; but that, from analogy with other argentiferous veins, as well as from facts observed on the Comstock lode, the diffusion of the silver through extensive deposits of middle and low grade ores is far more probable than its accumulation in bodies of rich ore."

SECTION 2.

GEOLOGICAL FORMATION, ETC., OF PACIFIC SLOPE.

REPORT OF MR. WILLIAM ASHBURNER, MINING ENGINEER, MEMBER OF THE STATE GEOLOGICAL SURVEY OF CALIFORNIA, &c.

1. Gold mining interest of California.—2. Characteristics of the gold-belt.—3. Northern mining districts.—4. Mining in the sierras; mills, expenses, &c.

I.—GOLD MINING INTEREST OF CALIFORNIA

SAN FRANCISCO, *November* —, 1866.

In accordance with the request you made me some time since, I beg leave to submit the following report upon the present condition of the gold mining interest of California, so far as it can be ascertained. The absence of all published documents of a reliable nature, with the exception of those recently issued by the geological survey of the State, make it a matter of considerable difficulty to arrive at results which shall have the merit of being perfectly trustworthy, and the only means of obtaining them is by personal examination by competent individuals of the various gold fields throughout the State. Everybody will acknowledge that accurate statistics of the results obtained throughout the extensive mineral regions of the United States, particularly those where the precious metals are found, and published under the official sanction of the government, would be of the greatest value. If properly compiled they in themselves alone would go far to remove the great ignorance which prevails in the public mind with regard to many important facts bearing upon the question of mining, and enable people to judge for themselves how far the great majority of those wild assertions which are so frequently made by amateur visitors and newspaper correspondents are likely to be true. It is from this class of writers—who, from their education, are not qualified to weigh and appreciate the value of statements made to them, generally by interested and enthusiastic persons—that nearly all the information which the public now possesses of the gold and silver mines of this country is derived.

It is universally conceded that the great objection to mining is its uncertainty, and that, while in some cases the profits are large, the risks are more than proportionably great, and the cautious capitalist hesitates before embarking upon a mining enterprise, feeling that a shroud of mystery envelops the whole question, and that he may be placing himself blindfolded in the hands of evil and designing persons.

The mineral resources of many of the States have been under scientific investigation since 1830; but it was in 1844 that the first district for mining other minerals than coal and iron was opened up upon the shores of Lake Superior. Then followed a wild excitement in mines, which seems to have continued periodically since that time, upon the discovery of new and valuable mines. In 1863-'64 attention was particularly directed to the silver and gold mines of Nevada and Colorado. No statements seemed too gross to be made, or too improbable to be believed. Tracts in the midst of the desert covered with sage brush, and miles distant from any mineral-bearing vein, were located, companies formed, prospectuses issued, and considerable sums of money actually expended in search of mines which by no possibility could exist in such places.

A thorough survey of the various mining districts which are now attracting so much attention both at home and abroad would confer incalculable benefit upon the country at large, and every means should be employed to bring before the public information of such a reliable nature that the capitalist may be guided in his investments, and the field of the prospector for new mines be restricted to those comparatively limited districts where there is any chance of their efforts being successful. Money and time uselessly expended in running, prospecting, tunnels, or in sinking shafts that can never be turned to any account, is so much loss of capital and labor taken from the productive industry of the country at large. It was estimated that in 1862-'63 there were some 30,000 persons in this State and on its immediate borders engaged in prospecting for gold, silver, and copper; and it is a notorious fact that not even one per cent. of the claims discovered by those persons have ever proved remunerative to those who invested money in their development. In 1861-'62 the excitement ran high on copper, induced by the discovery of the Union mine in Calaveras county, and in a few months the Sierra Nevada, from the foot-hills to their summits, were covered with miners fruitlessly occupied in attempting to discover new deposits which could be worked with a profit. A few months of scientific labor turned in this direction would have shown how utterly futile the efforts of most of them would prove, and how exceedingly limited in width is the copper-bearing belt of California.

The existence of gold in California was known long before the date commonly ascribed for its discovery. In several places along the Coast Range of mountains between Santa Cruz and Los Angeles there were small, inconsiderable "diggings" which were worked by the Mexicans, and some of them are said to have yielded as much as $6,000 per annum, which, at that period, was a considerable sum. The interest which is attached to these now is chiefly historical, and they were generally abandoned as soon as the more extensive deposits which lie in the Sierra Nevada were made known.

It was on the 19th of January, 1848,[*] that the first gold east of the Coast Range was discovered on the South Fork of the American river, at a place now called Coloma. It was the result of accident, and although attempts were made to preserve the fact a secret, the news soon spread far and wide, and by July of that year it is stated that the number of persons employed on the American river and its branches were as many as four thousand, who were obtaining from $30,000 to $40,000 a day, and by November it is thought that from four to five millions of dollars had been already extracted. It was not until a year subsequent to this discovery, or in the spring of 1849, that commenced the most extensive immigration that the world has ever seen. Adventurers poured into California from all quarters of the globe: first from Mexico, Chili, and Peru; then from the Sandwich Islands, China, and New Holland; lastly from the United States and Europe. During the six months between the first of July, 1849, and the first of January, 1850, it is estimated that 90,000 persons arrived in California from the east by sea or across the plains, and that one-fifth of them perished by disease during the six months following their arrival, such were the hardships they had endured and the privations to which they were subjected.

The western slope of the Sierra Nevada was soon covered with explorers, who, with their "pans" upon their shoulders, penetrated every ravine or gulch, "prospecting" the sands and washing the gravel wherever there was chance of finding the precious metal. Mining towns sprang up with almost incredible rapidity, and for several years they presented a scene of busy life. But the shallow "diggings" soon became exhausted, and in 1851 the yield of gold was higher than it has ever been since, amounting to at least $65,000,000. During the last four years California has produced an average of about $30,000,000 per annum of gold from the mines situated within her borders. At least ninety per cent. of the total production reaches San Francisco by public conveyance, and by some it is considered that even a larger proportion is transported in this manner. In order to arrive at the present production, and compare it with what has been produced in former years, we must take the amount of uncoined bul-

---

lion which is known to have arrived here from the various mining districts, and add say ten per cent. for that brought by private hands. At the same time that this means is far from affording all the accuracy desired, it will give a closer approximation to the truth than any other.

Referring to the San Francisco Mercantile Gazette, which obtains and publishes regularly the amount of coin and bullion received in San Francisco from all sources, we find that the receipts of uncoined treasure from the interior, inclusive of that from Nevada, have been as follows during the last four years:

Production of gold from California during the last four years.

	1862.	1863.	1864.	1865.
From the northern mines...........	$30,948,369	$33,936,771	$34,782,312	$36,649,337
From the southern mines...........	6,601,509	5,610,094	5,347,778	5,108,413
Total bullion receipts.........	37,549,878	39,546,865	40,130,090	41,757,750
Deduct bullion from Nevada........	6,000,000	12,433,915	15,900,000	15,800,000
	31,549,878	27,112,950	24,230,090	25,957,750
Add 10 per cent. for arrivals in private hands..................	3,154,988	2,711,295	2,423,009	2,595,775
	34,704,866	29,824,245	26,653,099	28,553,525

Probable production for 1866, based upon the receipts of the first nine months of the present year.

Northern mines, exclusive, of Nevada bullion $19,719,900
Southern mines....................................... 3,385,010

23,104,910
Add 10 per cent. for arrivals in private hands.............. 2,310,491

25,415,401

If we compare this production with that of the Australian gold fields during the last three years, we find that these latter have produced as follows:
1863 .... 1,627,066 ounces.
1864 .... 1,545,450 ounces.
1865 .... 1,556,088 ounces.

The Australian gold is of remarkable fineness, averaging about $\frac{921}{1000}$, and worth, consequently, $19 04 an ounce. This would be, in our currency, as follows:
1863.. $30,984,336
1864.. 29,425,368
1865.. 29,627,916

The mineral statistics which are published annually by the colony of Victoria give much valuable information concerning the present situation of the gold mining interest in Australia, and from them the above information has been gathered. The average earnings of the miners in this colony have been as follows during the last three years:

	Alluvial miners.	Quartz miners.
1863...............................	$487 45	$596 24 per annum.
1864...............................	296 69	632 44 per annum.
1865...............................	323 32	491 36 per annum.

We have for this coast no statistics which will enable us to arrive at the average earnings of the miners in California with the same degree of accuracy, but there does not seem any reason to suppose that they are greater here than in Australia.

During the year 1864, of 1,545,450 ounces of gold exported from this colony, about one-third, or 503,618 ounces, were supposed to have been derived from the quartz mines. This proportion of two to one must be very nearly the relation which the gold produced from the placer diggings of California bears to that from the quartz mines, which probably does not exceed $8,000,000 or $9,000,000 per annum.

2.—CHARACTERISTICS OF THE GOLD BELT.

The auriferous belt of California extends from the Tejon pass, in latitude 35°, to the northern extremity of the State, or for a distance of about five hundred miles. The principal gold fields, however, and that portion of the State which has produced most largely, lies between about latitude 37° and the North Fork of the Feather river, or over a distance not exceeding two hundred and fifty miles. Towards the south this gold-bearing range is narrow, rarely exceeding twenty-five miles in width. As we proceed north, however, it widens rapidly, and along the Feather and Yuba rivers it reaches from the lower foot-hills of the Sierra Nevada to the central axis of the mountains, or over a width of fifty miles from east to west. There are other diggings in the more northern part of the State, bounded by the Trinity, Upper Sacramento, and Klamath rivers, which at one time were valuable, and yielded largely, but now the principal interest attaches to those deep placers lying between the forks of the Yuba, those deposits which underlie the volcanic formation in many places on the auriferous belt as far south as Tuolumne county—what are known as the cement diggings—and the quartz mines which are to be found between Tulare county on the south and Plumas county on the north. The "shallow diggings," which were formerly so immensely rich, and which attracted the first attention of the miner, are now, for the most part, hopelessly exhausted; but, notwithstanding this, by far the greater proportion of the total gold production of California is still derived from the "washings," hydraulic and others; and this will undoubtedly continue to be the case until those immense auriferous deposits lying in the northern part of the State, principally in Nevada county, are exhausted. Nothing but an accurate survey will give anything like an approximation as to the length of time which will be required to work them out at the present rate. Now we have only the wildest conjectures and statements, the result of hasty examinations, as to their extent and the probable amount of gold contained in them. At the present time, about eighty per cent. of the gold produced from the mines of California is derived from those lying north of the Mokelumne river, and the production from the southern mines, or those situated between Mariposa and Calaveras counties, is decreasing every year. Probably only about one-third of the gold productions of California comes from the quartz mines, leaving two-thirds to be furnished by the placer and cement diggings, or those sources of supply other than veins. Unfortunately, too little of a reliable nature is now known with regard to these latter for me to venture upon an intelligent exposition of them; but enough is known concerning the former to predict that quartz mining will continue to be one of the most lasting, as well as profitable, interests of this State, and there now seems no reason to anticipate that California will cease to be one of the principal gold-producing countries of the world for many years to come. I will therefore confine myself entirely to a description of a few of the more noted quartz mines of the State, showing, when it is possible, the amount of profit realized from the working of the quartz, its average yield, the expenses attending the milling and mining, and giving such other facts as may be considered as illustrating the present condition of this industry.

The principal quartz mining districts of California are in Tulare county, about Clear creek ; in Mariposa county, on the Mariposa estate and its immediate neighborhood, and also round about Centreville, north of the Merced river ; in Tuolumne county, within a few miles of Sonora, at Soulesbeyville, and near Jamestown ; in Calaveras county, at Angels ; in Amador county, near Jackson and Sutter creek ; in El Dorado county at Logtown and vicinity ; in Nevada county at Grass valley and Nevada ; in Sierra county within a few miles of Downieville ; in Plumas county at Indian valley and on Jamieson creek. These localities were nearly all centres of placer diggings before quartz mining became so important an industry. The width of this quartz-bearing range is, however, much narrower than that occupied by the placer workings, and while rarely more than twenty miles in width, is generally much less.

The number of veins in this belt is almost innumerable, but the proportion of those which contain gold in sufficient quantity to pay is exceedingly small.

The most reliable publication which has recently appeared with regard to the quartz veins of California was issued by the State geological survey in April, 1866. The statistics were compiled by Mr. A. Rémond, and give several important particulars with regard to the mills and mines in the region between the Merced and Stanislaus rivers. The district embraced by this report is about thirty miles long by from fifteen to twenty in width. Seventy-seven mines and sixty-five mills were examined and reported upon, and of these fifty-six mines and twenty-three mills were being worked at the time of Mr. Rémond's visit. So far as the mere number of the veins is concerned this region probably contains as many with features sufficiently promising to warrant exploration as any other district of equal size in California. The actual amount of capital invested in the erection of the mills examined has been $430,300, and in addition to this a considerable sum has been spent in the construction of roads, flumes, and ditches, and by far the larger proportion of this whole sum has been expended since 1862, particularly in the years 1864-'65, and therefore several of the mills may be considered as experimental, and the veins upon which they are situated as not having been proved sufficiently to be able to state whether the yield as given to him by the proprietor will be lasting. It is certain that the gross production of this region from the quartz mines now being worked is not very large, nor does it as yet compare favorably with several other districts not nearly so extensive. The greater number of these veins vary in width from about one foot to two feet six inches, while in one case there is a vein noted which is twenty-five feet in width and another fifteen feet. The average width of all the veins examined would appear to be about three feet. The "country rock," or the rock in which the quartz veins of California are incased, is for the most part either slate, granite, or greenstone, and it is not yet determined which of these three formations can be regarded as furnishing the most prolific mines, for we have in each of them veins which have produced largely, and still are continuing to do so, though several of them have attained a considerable depth.

In Mariposa county, and particularly upon the Mariposa estate, the most noted veins are in the slate and have a direction and dip nearly coincident with the general stratification of the enclosing rock. The principal mine in the district is the Princeton, which has produced between two and three millions of dollars. It was first worked in 1852, and the quartz is said to have yielded as high as seventy-five dollars per ton for a short time, but this large return was probably owing to the various sulphurets contained in the quartz and associated with the gold having been more or less decomposed near the surface by atmospheric agencies, and the gold liberated by this means, so that the outcrops of the vein were far above the average richness of the quartz. Since 1861, and until within the last year, the rock from this vein has yielded an average of $18 34 per ton, while the expenses of mining have been about $6, and the cost of milling $3 25.

This would show a profit over and above the expenses of working of nearly 50 per cent.

In the latter part of 1864 the yield of the quartz from this mine fell, almost without giving any warning, from $40 to $6 per ton, and for some time ceased to pay expenses. During 1865 the yield was better, but it is still far from affording as satisfactory results as in former years. The depth of the main shaft is nearly 650 feet, and the length of the underground workings not far from 1,400 feet. It is by no means certain that this mine is exhausted, and that another sinking will not open up new bodies of valuable ore. There are too many examples throughout California of mines falling off rapidly in their yield, and meeting with barren zones of quartz, both in depth and on the longitudinal extension of the vein, for any one to state positively that a lode which possesses so many characteristics of permanence as the Princeton should be abandoned, and that it will never again prove remunerative as in past years.

Near the northern end of the Mariposa estate are two mines known as the "Pine Tree" and "Josephine," which have been worked for nearly sixteen years. When this property passed into the hands of General Frémont these mines were considered as being among the richest as well as most reliable in California, and it is perhaps to be regretted that the anticipations formed at that time have never been realized, for it is mainly owing to their failure that so much discredit has been cast upon the quartz mining interest both at home and abroad. These two mines are situated in close proximity to each other, and although they have never been connected by underground workings they probably are upon one and the same vein. The Pine Tree vein has a direction nearly the same as that of the slates in which it is encased, or about northwest and southeast, while the Josephine runs more nearly east and west, and the axes of these two veins would form at their junction an angle of about forty degrees. Work is just now abandoned upon this latter mine, but is being actively prosecuted on the former, and the quartz is said to be paying better than was formerly the case, owing to a more careful selection and thorough metallurgical treatment. The outcrops of these veins are at an elevation of about fifteen hundred feet above the Merced river, and can be observed from a long distance to the north. Neither of them can be followed or traced individually for any great distance upon the surface in such a manner as to preserve their identity, and in this respect they in nowise differ from the great majority of gold-bearing veins in California. In fact, the experience of mining in this State has all tended to prove the fact that the longitudinal extension of these veins is generally very limited, and that the metalliferous portion is always considerably less in length than that of the quartz itself. This remark applies equally to the numerous copper-bearing veins which have been recently discovered, some few of which are valuable, while their "extensions" are almost invariably worthless.

The outcrop of these mines is a very marked and noticeable feature in the landscape. They form part of what is known as the great quartz vein of California which can be traced by its prominent outcrops about seventy miles north from Mariposa county, in nearly a straight line, continuing through Tuolumne, Calaveras, and Amador. It cannot be proved positively that this is one and the same vein, on account of the many breaks and interruptions which occur in its course, but certain it is that throughout this distance it preserves its distinguishing characteristics, both geologically and lithologically in a most remarkable manner. It furnishes some of the best gold mines in California, which are conspicuous for the great regularity of their yield, and the depth which they have attained. Along its course and in its immediate vicinity are some of the most extensive placers, which, although now for the most part exhausted, have in times gone by produced so largely that while worked they were regarded as being among the richest deposits in California. It must not be presumed that this great vein is gold-bearing throughout its whole course, or that even a notable proportion of the quartz which rises into peaks and mountains between Mariposa and Amador counties is auriferous. It is only here and there at wide intervals that mines can be found which can be worked with a profit. Mr. Rémond enumerates twenty as being found in the region which he examined, many of which are undoubtedly still experimental enterprises, and may yet be abandoned.

The yield of the quartz from the mines situated on this great vein is generally low and somewhat under the average of the Calif rnia quartz, but the gold-bearing portion of the vein is always of greater width than elsewhere, and the quartz can be mined at less expense than in those veins which are narrow and encased in the harder varieties of metamorphic rock.

The gross production of the Pine Tree and Josephine mines has been, undoubtedly, very large, though it is utterly impossible to state, with any degree of approximation, what it was previous to 1860. Since June, 1860, the quartz from these two mines has been treated at the Benton mills, on the Merced river, and from the time they commenced running until March of the following year the gross yield was about $155,000. The quartz near the surface paid much better than that which has been worked at the Benton mills. Not only does it appear to have been absolutely somewhat richer, but, owing to the decomposition of the sulphurets which existed in the Josephine rock in large proportions, it lent itself to a more ready amalgamation. Also, as it was worked in a ten-stamp mill, of comparatively small capacity to the Benton mills, which have sixty-four stamps, the mining superintendent was able to select his quartz with much more ease, and send only the better quality to the mill. The quartz from these mines in 1860 averaged about $9 per ton, and gradually grew poorer as the richer portions of the vein were worked out. The cost of mining, milling, and transportation amounted to about $5 50 per ton. This amount of $9 per ton is what was actually obtained in the mill, although there seems every reason to suppose that much more gold than that was really contained in the quartz, and, in fact, more has been lost and allowed to run to waste than has been secured. On several occasions attempts have been made to ascertain what proportion was lost and what saved, and it would appear that in the case of this quartz not more than forty per cent. of the gold actually contained in it was saved in the process of milling. The cause of this appears to be almost entirely owing to the very fine state of subdivision in which it exists, for very few specimens show any gold visible to the naked eye. Experiments are now being conducted on the Mariposa estate which seem to confirm this view, for on treating the quartz which formerly only returned $10 or $15 per ton, by more careful methods of amalgamation, it has been made to yield between $40 and $50. It is not to be presumed from this statement that all the vein consists of quartz of this richness; but there is a large amount which will certainly yield, by improved processes of treatment, much more than it has ever been possible to obtain from it by the ordinary rough method.

3.—NORTHERN MINING DISTRICTS.

As we proceed northward from Mariposa county, the next most interesting mine we meet with, situated upon the "Great Vein," is the App, near Jamestown, a few miles from Sonora, the county seat of Tuolumne. This mine has been worked almost uninterruptedly for nine years. The average yield of the quartz has been at the rate of $15 52 per ton, and the expenses of mining and milling have not exceeded $7 47 per ton. The yearly yield during this period has varied from $13 26 to $19 47 per ton, and the lowest monthly return was at the rate of $12 15; but even then a considerable profit was realized over and above the expenses. The lower works of this mine now present as fine an appearance as they have ever done, and when we regard the length of time during which it has been successfully worked, the great regularity of the yield of the quartz, and the various characters of permanency which the vein preserves, we have strong reasons for arguing that it will prove as persistent in depth as almost any other mine in California. In its external characters the quartz from this mine resembles very much that taken from the Pine Tree mine. The greater proportion, however, of the gold which it contains is in such a fine state of subdivision that it rarely happens that any of it is visible to the naked eye, and undoubtedly a great deal escapes amalgamation and is lost. By more thorough treatment in the mill, there seems every reason to suppose that the yield could be largely increased. Experiments have been lately instituted—and they would appear to confirm this statement—most fully showing that by more careful amalgamation the quartz, in some instances, can be made to yield from 50 per cent. to 140 per cent. more gold without a corresponding increase in the expense of treatment. Attention is now being given to this important matter throughout California, and experiments are being made in several mills to ascertain to what extent the gold is lost in the process of treatment, and how far it will be economical to erect new machinery for the purpose of saving it. The gold which is contained in the auriferous quartz exists either in such minute particles as to be quite invisible, and not distinguishable from the quartz itself, else in pieces of larger size, which can be readily seen and separated by pulverization and washing, or by the simplest forms of amalgamation, or else combined, probably mechanically, with the sulphurets of iron, zinc, and lead. In the first and last cases it is amalgamated with great difficulty, and it rarely happens in any of the mills of California that more than a small proportion of the gold is saved. When, however, it is in the state of free gold, as in the second instance, a notable proportion is secured by the most simple methods, and it is not likely that additional machinery would increase the yield sufficiently to pay for its cost. In the quartz from a vein upon the Mariposa estate, known as the "Mariposa," there are but comparatively few sulphurets present, and from repeated assays made from the tailings from the mill it would appear that almost 90 per cent. of the gold contained in the quartz was secured, while at the Benton mills, working upon Pine Tree quartz, only between 30 or 40 per cent. was saved. In this connection it may not be uninteresting to show what has been done in this direction in other countries, and how far it is possible to increase the yield of very refractory gold-bearing ores by careful working and skilful treatment. One of the oldest, and, when we consider the rebellious character of the ores, one of the most successful gold mines in the world is that of St. John Del Rey, in Brazil. The company now in possession has been in operation thirty-six years, and though, like nearly every other mining company, it has had its full share of ups and downs, the general results obtained have been most satisfactory to the shareholders, and it was only through the most careful, economical management of both the mining and milling departments that this end has been arrived at. There is no quartz mine in California which has ores in any quantity of so complex a nature or of so difficult a treatment as those of St. John Del Rey. They consist principally of specular iron mixed with sulphuret of iron, magnetic pyrites and quartz. The auriferous mass at this mine is about forty-four feet in width, and, like most of the gold-bearing veins of California, dips with the rocks in the vicinity at an angle of about 45° to the southeast. *

The vertical depth upon which this deposit has been worked is now 1,668 feet. Before the present company came into possession it had been worked for a hundred years, and was considered exhausted.

A recent number of the London Mining Journal gives some interesting details

---

* Whitney's Metallic Wealth of the United States, p 112.

with regard to the present financial position of this company, and as these favorable results were only obtained by economy in the management and skilful treatment of the ores, which yield far less than the average of California quartz, I will give a condensed statement of their operations for the last thirty-six years. The effective capital of the company is £129,000, divided into 1,100 shares, and there has been paid in dividends £756,245, or £68 15s. per share. There is on hand a reserve fund of £41,506, and the value of the property of the mine is estimated at £209,743, showing a total profit during the thirty-six years' working of £1,007,494. The produce of the mine during this period has been £2,902,480, and the expenses £1,894,986, or 65 3 per cent. of the gross receipts. The average yield of the ore raised and treated has been at the rate of 4½ oitavas per ton of 2,240 pounds. This is equivalent to about $8 50, or $7 59 reduced to the usual Califorinia ton of 2,000 pounds. The yield for the last three years has been as follows:

1863, 5,787 oitavas per ton, at $1 89 per oitava, $10 94; 1864, 4,827 oitavas per ton, at $1 89 per oitava, $9 12; 1865, 5,479 oitavas per ton, at $1 89 per ton, $10 36.

During this period of the total amount of gold contained in the ore there was extracted the following percentage:

1863, 72.35 per cent.; 1864, 75 52 per cent.; 1865, 77.95 per cent.

The various processes heretofore employed in California for amalgamating gold have been of the simplest possible description, and, although probably in a majority of instances where the gold was clean, free and uncombined with the sulphurets of iron, lead, copper, and zinc with which it is so frequently associated, these methods worked well, and the erection of expensive machinery, which would necessitate slower working, would not be warranted by the facts of the case. Yet it has often happened, particularly in those mines situated upon the course of the "Great Vein," that quartz which has been known to contain gold in paying quantities has not yielded when treated in the mill more than sufficient to pay expenses, and sometimes has been worked at a loss. This would appear to be chiefly owing to the inefficiency of the apparatus employed to collect and save the gold, which may have been in a very fine state of subdivision, or coated with a thin film of oxide of iron arising from the decomposition of pyrites, which prevents the mercury from adhering to it without the use of more vigorous mechanical or chemical means than are usually employed.

At and near Sutter creek, in Amador county, there are several very excellent mines situated upon the course of the "Great Vein." The most noted of these is that belonging to Messrs. Hayward & Co., and known as the Eureka. This mine has been worked for about eleven years, and has produced probably nearly as much gold as any other in California. The quartz has never averaged very high, and the principal production has been from ores of a low grade, not yielding probably more than from $10 to $15 per ton. The mine is situated at the junction of the slates and greenstone, the hanging or eastern wall of the vein being of the latter material, hard and compact, while the foot-wall is of a dark and soft argillaceous slate. The depth of the lowest workings is now 1,213 feet on the incline of the vein, which makes this shaft the deepest in the United States. The length of the underground workings is about 600 feet, and at the north and south extremities the vein thins out rapidly. The richest portion of this vein appeared to be at a depth of between 1,000 and 1,100 feet, where the quartz is said to have yielded nearly $30 a ton. The great depth attained in this mine shows conclusively that we cannot draw any general conclusions with regard to exhaustion of quartz veins at an inconsiderable depth. It is true that in nearly every quartz mine of California the outcrop has been found to be much richer than the main body of the vein at even a short distance from the surface, but it must be borne in mind that many of the veins, and in fact a majority of them, contained gold associated with various mineral sulphurets, which were decomposed and the gold infiltrated down for some distance below the surface of the ground, causing the upper portion to appear abnormally rich. Thus the gold contained in the first few feet of the vein may be the result of the degradation of many tons of quartz and the decomposition of a large quantity of sulphurets. It is only by taking the results afforded by the treatment of quartz during a series of months that anything like a correct average of the value of the ore can be obtained, and although this Eureka mine has probably yielded as regularly as any other prominent mine in California, it has been subject to great irregularities, and frequently the quartz has barely paid expenses. The popular idea that mineral-bearing veins grow richer as they are worked upon in depth, is a fallacy, and has no truth either in theory or fact; nor can we say that true veins, as distinct from veins of segregation and mineral deposits, grow poorer as we proceed downwards. I do not suppose there is a metalliferous vein in the world that is equally rich for any considerable distance, either lengthwise or up and down, and the valuable portion is almost always very limited in extent compared with the main body of the vein. Some of the silver veins of Mexico, which have produced such enormous sums, have been traced for miles, and on their course have furnished many valuable mines, but by far the greater proportion of the vein has been barren and unproductive. The Comstock vein of Nevada, which has already produced upwards of $60,000,000 worth of bullion, has been productive only over about one-seventh of its explored length.

These remarks apply with great force to the gold quartz veins of this coast. The ore exists in bunches or else in shoots or chimneys which cut the axis of the vein at every conceivable angle between the horizontal and the vertical, and these are always less than the length of the vein itself and sometimes than its width also.

It frequently happens that these ore-shoots have distinct terminal lines, and in these cases the experienced miner is enabled to select his ore and avoid extracting that which he knows is too poor to pay. On other occasions, however, it would appear that the gold is distributed without any regularity and apparently in the most capricious manner. When we consider the richness of the veins, the length of time that some of the mines have been worked, and the amount of gold annually produced, the most important quartz mining region of California is without any doubt that of Grass valley, in Nevada county. Here mines have been worked uninterruptedly since 1851. It is true there have been periods when the interest was more than usually depressed and several of the mines, which are now regarded as being among the best, were thought to be exhausted, and abandoned for the time being, but in many instances when work was resumed new bodies of gold-bearing quartz were opened up which proved rich and valuable. The veins in this district, and particularly those which have been the most productive, are noted for their narrowness as well as for the richness of the quartz. They are incased in a hard metamorphic rock, and the expenses of mining are, as a general thing, higher here than anywhere else in California, amounting, as they do in some instances, to from $20 to $26 per ton. Within the last fourteen years the total production from the quartz mines of the Grass Valley district has not been far from $23,000,000. The most prolific vein has been that situated upon Massachusetts and Gold Hill, which alone has produced more than $7,000,000 worth of gold during this time from a lode which will only average a foot or fourteen inches in width.

The "Eureka" is another prominent and leading mine in this vicinity. One great feature of interest connected with it is the gradual improvement of the quartz as greater depth has been attained upon the vein, which varies in width from three to four feet. This mine was first worked in 1854, and more or less ever since that period. About one year ago the property changed hands, and since that time the yield of the mine has been greater than at any previous time. When this vein was first worked and down to a depth of about thirty-five feet from the surface, the yield of the quartz was from $6 to $12 per ton, which but little more than paid expenses. Below this level the value of the quartz rapidly increased from $14 to $21, and at the one hundred foot level the quartz paid at the rate of $28; at the two hundred foot level the average was about $37, and now, between the second, and third levels or three hundred feet from the surface the average yield has been during the last four months at the rate of over $60 per ton. The quartz contains from two to three per cent. of sulphurets of iron, which are said to assay generally about $300 per ton, and are regarded as being among the richest in Grass valley. These sulphurets are worked by parties in the neighborhood, who charge $50 per ton and return whatever gold is extracted to the proprietors of the mine. During the four months which preceded the first of October the mine produced 42,227¾ tons of quartz, which yielded $255,072 55, and the expenses of mining and milling were $67,320 83, leaving as profit $187,751 72. The average yield of the quartz during the period was at the rate of $60 33 per ton. During the whole year the amount of quartz worked was 11,375¾ tons, which produced $526,431 41, at an expense of $168,389 23, leaving as profit for the whole year $368,042 18. The average yield per ton was $47 15, and the average cost of mining and milling was $13 75, leaving a profit of $33 40 per ton.

4.—MINING IN THE SIERRAS; MILLS, EXPENSES, &c.

In thus dismissing the Grass Valley district with only a brief description of two of its leading mines, I do not intend to detract at all from its past, present, or future importance, for there is no region in California, or probably upon the Pacific coast, where, by a careful study of the numerous veins in this neighborhood, so much information could be obtained which would throw light upon the vexed questions relating to gold mining and the metallurgical treatment of the quartz.

As we proceed north from Nevada county, the next most important quartz mining district is in the mountainous region round about Downieville, the county seat of Sierra. The placer mines in this vicinity have been exceedingly rich, and surpassed only by those in Nevada county in extent and permanence. Quartz mining, however, has received but comparatively little attention until within the last few years, probably owing to the rugged nature of the country and the severity of the climate during the winter months.

The most noted mine in this county, as well as the one which has produced most largely, is that known as the Sierra Buttes. This mine is about fourteen miles from Downieville, at an elevation of probably not less than 7,000 feet above the sea. The vein is enclosed in a hard metamorphic slate, and varies in width from six to thirty feet. In the process of working, the whole thickness of the vein is not removed, and the richer portions, which lie next the foot-wall, are sent to the mill. The average width of this more productive streak is about twelve feet. The depth upon which this vein has been worked is not far from 750 feet, and the quartz in the lower portion of the mine is said to pay as well as that taken from the upper works. Quartz from near the surface of this vein was worked in arrastras as early as 1851, but the first mill was erected in 1853. The present owners have been in possession of the property since 1857, and the yield of the mine has been, during the last nine years, approximately as follows:

	Gross yield.	Expenses.	Profits.
1857	$51,000	$15,000	$36,000
1858	55,000	15,000	40,000
1859	88,000	20,000	68,000

	Gross yield.	Expenses.	Profits
1860	$120,000	$37,000	$83,000
1861	198,000	48,000	150,000
1862	166,000	54,000	112,000
1863	156,000	57,000	99,000
1864	90,000	75,000	15,000
1865	196,000	64,000	132,000
	1,120,000	385,000	735,000

The yield of the quartz varies generally from $14 to $17 per ton, and the cause of the falling off in the gross product during 1863–'64 was the great scarcity of water, which necessitated the erection of a flume at an expense of $40,000.

The principal expenses attending the working of auriferous quartz are the cost of extracting the quartz from the mine and its subsequent treatment in the mill. With regard to the first no general data can be given, for the amount paid for mining varies from $1 50 to $26 per ton. It is dependent upon the hardness of the quartz; the hardness of the country rock in which the vein is encased; the relation which the auriferous portion of the vein bears to that which is barren; the depth of the workings, and finally the amount of water in the mine, and whether it has been drained by adits or pumping. As a general rule, however, it may be assumed that in the case of large veins, or those which exceed five or six feet in width, that the cost of extraction will be from $1 50 to $6, and that the total cost of mining and milling will not be more than $7 or $8 per ton under any circumstances.

With regard to the milling expense, however, we have accurate data to follow, and these are not much affected by change of locality.

The mills are generally situated in close proximity to the mines, for the difference between the cost of running a steam and a water mill is almost always less than the cost of hauling the quartz for any distance by teams. The mills are of nearly all sizes and capacity, and vary from those which have only two or three stamps to those which have forty-eight. The weight of these stamps is from 400 lbs. to 1.000 lbs., and they are run at a velocity varying from 50 blows to 80 blows per minute and fall from 10 to 14 inches. The favorite weight would appear to be about 650 lbs., with a fall of 12 inches and a velocity of from 60 to 70 blows per minute. It is generally assumed that a ten-stamp mill, with stamp of 550 lbs., falling 12 inches and striking 60 blows a minute, will crush 12½ tons of ordinary quartz in the twenty-four hours.

The mills which are moved by water power alone are situated either on the banks of rivers and streams where the water is free, or else the water is conveyed to them by a flume from some neighboring ditch and sold at a price which is generally the result of special agreement.

In the case of steam mills the fuel is always a principal item of expense: Wood—either pine or oak—is universally employed, and costs from $2 to $4 50 and even $5 per cord. Oak, when the two can be obtained and are equally convenient of access, generally costs one-third more than pine and is regarded as being nearly twice as valuable for steam purposes. The mean amount of fuel consumed in the steam quartz mills of California is not far from 0.164 cord for each ton stamped. The prices paid for labor in the mining towns is still very high, and in many cases operates as an effectual barrier to the working of some quartz mines. First class miners receive from $3 to $3 50, and in some cases as high as $3 75 per day, while ordinary laborers receive from $2 to $2 50. In the milling of quartz the item of labor is generally from 60 per cent. to 75 per cent. of the total expense. In mining the proportion which this item bears to the whole cost is much greater, so that it is easy to perceive to what an extent a reduction of wages would operate in favor of the quartz mining interest of this coast.

The mercury that is used in the process of amalgamating is derived entirely from the California mines, and generally costs the miner about sixty-five cents per pound; very little, however, is lost in the mills when proper care is observed, and this item of expense is insignificant, for it rarely exceeds six ounces for each ton of quartz treated, and frequently falls below this amount.

The average cost of milling quartz in the various mills of California may be stated as follows:

In water mills, when water is free .... $1 22 per ton of 2,000 pounds.
In water mills, when water is purchased ...... 1 60 per ton of 2,000 pounds.
In steam mills .... 2 14 per ton of 2,000 pounds.

It is very difficult to state, even approximately, what is the present average yield of the quartz from the California mines. It is probable, however, that it has not varied much within the last five years, and in 1861, taking the returns from those mines which were at that time believed to be profitable concerns, it was at the rate of $18 50 per ton. The two extremes were a mine in Grass valley, which was yielding at the rate of $80 per ton, and another at Angels, in Calaveras county, where the quartz only paid $5, and was still being worked at a small profit.

I remain, very respectfully, yours,

WM. ASHBURNER,
Mining Engineer.

J. Ross Browne, Esq., *Statistical Commissioner.*

SECTION 3.

CONDITION OF GOLD AND SILVER MINING ON THE PACIFIC COAST.

1. Decrease of yield.—2. Export of treasure from California.—3. Receipts from northern and southern mines.—4. Comparison of receipts and exports.—5. Quartz yield increasing. —6. Uncertainty in quartz mining.—7. Professor Ashburner's statistics.—8. Rémond's statistics.—9. Pulverization of quartz.—10. Amalgamation of gold.—11. Sulphurets and concentration.—12. Chlorination.—13. Gold in loose state.—14. Placers.—15. Cement mining.—16. Hydraulic mining.—17. River mining.—18. The Haquard quartz mine.—19. Sierra Buttes mine. —20. The Allison mine.—20½. The Eureka mine.—21. Smartsville Blue Gravel Company's mine.—22. Profits of mining generally.—23. Difficulties of getting good claims.—24. Comstock lode, the most productive in the world.—25. Comstock mining companies.—26. Quartz mills in Nevada.—27. The pan.—28. The Wheeler pan.—29. The Varney pan.—30. Knox's pan.—31. Hepburn pan.—32. The Wheeler & Randall pan.—33. Estimated yield of various mines.—34. Assessments levied.—35. The Gould & Curry mine.—36. The Ophir mine.—37. The Savage mine.—38. The Yellow Jacket mine.—39. The Crown Point mine.—40. The Hale & Norcross mine.— 41. The Imperial mine.—42. The Empire mine.—43. Productive mines of Reese river. —44. Yield of various silver districts.—45. Improvements in silver mining.

1.—DECREASE OF YIELD.

The first fact in the condition of gold mining in California is that the yield is and for the last thirteen years has been decreasing. We know this by the concurrent testimony of the miner, by the decrease in the traffic of crude bullion, and by the decline of the exports of gold. No record is kept of the amounts taken from the mines, and our best evidence in regard to the produc-

H. Ex. Doc. 29——4

tion is furnished by the reports of the receipts and shipments by express and steamer. From these we can get an approximation sufficiently near to serve all general purposes. The gold yield of California reached its culminating point in 1853, and the exportation of treasure, which rose in that year to $57,000,000, gradually fell until 1861, when it was $40,000,000. Then the silver of Nevada and the gold of Idaho began to come in and the amount of the shipments rose again.

2.—THE EXPORTATION OF TREASURE FROM CALIFORNIA.

The following table shows the amount of treasure manifested for exportation from San Francisco:

Years.	Amount.
1849	$4,921,250
1850	27,676,346
1851	42,582,695
1852	46,588,434
1853	57,330,034
1854	51,328,653
1855	45,182,631
1856	48,880,543
1857	48,976,697
1858	47,548,025
1859	47,649,462
1860	42,203,345
1861	40,639,080
1862	42,561,761
1863	46,071,920
1864	55,707,201
1865	44,984,546
Total	740,832,623

It is well known, however, that this sum is far less than the total production of the coast. In the first place about $45,000,000 must be added for the amount of gold and silver now in use in the Pacific States and Territories for currency; that amount being the estimate made by experienced bankers.

A second allowance must be made for gold jewelry and silver plate made in the country, and for specimens of nuggets and rich ores, the value of which may be $5,000,000. Many of the miners in remote camps bury their gold dust until they are ready to return to the Atlantic coast, and $5,000,000 may be laid by in that manner. But the greatest variation between the production and the manifested export was caused by the custom, common among passengers bound eastward, of carrying their dust or coin on their persons, so that no one knew how much they took. Thus there is no manifested export for 1848, and less than $5,000,000 for 1849, and less than $28,000,000 for 1850, while the actual production and exportation of those years was about $100,000,000. We can safely put down the amount carried away in sixteen years unmanifested at $200,000,000, and by this calculation we shall have a total production of about $1,000,000,000, from the coast up to the end of 1865. Of this sum all has come from the mines of California, save about $100,000,000 contributed by Nevada, Idaho, Oregon, Arizona, Washington, and British Columbia. The accounts, however, of the contributions from these States and Territories have not been accurately kept, with the exception of Nevada, so it is impossible to give any precise statement of them.

3.—RECEIPTS FROM NORTHERN AND SOUTHERN MINES.

The express company of Wells, Fargo & Co. transport nearly all the treasure produced on the coast, and they could, from their books, show the shipments of coin and bullion from every large mining town west of the Rocky mountains; but they have considered it advisable to allow the publication of the receipts of treasure at San Francisco only from the principal districts since 1860.

The following table shows the receipts of treasure, coined and uncoined, from the northern and southern mines of California:

Years.	Northern mines, California.	Southern mines, California.	Total, California.
1861	$26,346,431	$9,363,214	$35,709,645
1862	28,138,021	8,154,702	36,292,723
1863	25,429,157	7,411,931	32,841,088
1864	22,804,677	6,858,153	29,662,830
1865	24,557,570	6,428,960	30,986,530

Of the treasure thus received at San Francisco, about $4,000,000 annually is in coin, leaving the remainder to indicate the value of the dust and bars.

The "northern mines," as mentioned in the above table, include all those districts which send their treasure to San Francisco by way of Sacramento, or, in other words, all the interior of the State north of latitude 38° 30', while the "southern mines" include those districts which send their treasure by way of Stockton. To express it differently, the term "northern mines," as here used, means the counties Siskiyou, Shasta, Trinity, Plumas, Butte, Lassen, Sierra, Yuba, Nevada, Placer, El Dorado, Sacramento, and parts of Calaveras and Amador; while the term "southern mines" means Tulare, Fresno, Inyo, Kern, Stanislaus, Mono, Mariposa, Tuolumne, and parts of Calaveras and Amador. The extension of the railroad from Sacramento to the vicinity of Placerville, in 1863 and 1864, drew to Sacramento some trade that previously went to Stockton. The receipts from the southern mines show a marked and steady decrease. During the first nine months of 1866 the receipts from the southern mines were $3,418,436.

Receipts from Nevada and the northern coast.

The receipts from other places are the following:

Years.	Nevada.	Northern coast.	Foreign ports.
1861	$2,275,256	....	$1,702,683
1862	6,247,074	$4,931,579	1,904,064
1863	12,486,238	4,970,023	2,156,612
1864	15,795,585	8,052,968	1,715,024
1865	15,184,877	7,495,766	1,709,390

The "northern coast" means those mines which send their treasure to San Francisco by ocean steamers plying to ports of Northern California, Oregon, and Vancouver island. The term "foreign ports" excludes Victoria, and includes Mazatlan, Guaymas, La Paz, Honolulu, China, and Japan. San Francisco stands on a long peninsula, and all the traffic with the gold and silver mining regions is done across water. The yield of the northern mines is brought by the Sacramento steamers; the yield of the southern mines by the Stockton steamers; the yield of the northern coast by the northern coast steamers, and the imports from foreign ports are brought by other vessels.

The sources of the receipts are classified according to the vessels in which they are brought. These receipts are, however, not all in the precious metals as they come from the mines and mills, but portions are in coin.

Thus the coin included in those receipts was $9,363,214 in 1861, $5,593,421 in 1862, $6,383,974 in 1863, $5,743,399 in 1864, and $4,961,922 in 1865. No accounts have been kept of the coin sent to the interior; but all this coin received must have gone from San Francisco, which has the only mint of the coast, and is the point at which nearly all the passengers and treasure arrive.

4.—COMPARISON OF RECEIPTS AND EXPORTS.

The following figures show the exports, the receipts, and the difference between exports and receipts for the last five years:

Years.	Exports.	Receipts.	Difference.
1861	$40,639,080	$43,391,760	$2,752,680 gain.
1862	42,561,761	49,375,462	6,813,701 "
1863	46,071,920	52,953,961	6,382,041 "
1864	55,707,201	55,228,907	478,794 loss.
1865	44,984,546	55,467,573	10,483,027 gain.

The total amount of coin receipts for the five years was $32,045,928; and the excess of receipts over exported during the same period was $25,952,655. A large part of the coin received must have belonged to the regular circulation of the country, going and coming with the current of trade. The receipts of treasure at San Francisco during the first nine months of 1866 were $3,000 less than in the corresponding period of 1865.

The year 1862 was unfavorable to mining in California because of a great flood, and 1863 because of a great drought; and some special unexplained influence may have operated to reduce the production and shipment in 1865; but the annual gold yield of California cannot now be safely estimated at more than $27,000,000. Several millions of each year's produce of the precious metals may be retained on the coast for purposes of currency, ornaments, and table-ware.

5.—QUARTZ YIELD INCREASING.

The yield of the quartz mines is increasing slowly, as we know by the general testimony of the miners and by the increase of quartz mills; but there are no statistics to show the rate of increase. Although some mines have paid steadily at about the same rate for the last ten years, the business generally is very uncertain. Thus it appears from a report made by Mr. Rémond, State geological surveyor, that of sixty-three mills built in Tuolumne and Mariposa counties, between the Merced and Stanislaus rivers, thirty-eight were not running when he visited them between August and November, 1865, and in many instances the veins had ceased to yield quartz rich enough to pay. And so it is in every part of the State where quartz mills have been built—a considerable portion of them have been abandoned as very unprofitable investments. And yet every week new and valuable veins are discovered, and they cannot be left unworked; and though many quartz miners fail, yet others are deriving princely revenues from their claims.

Grass valley, the chief centre of the quartz mining of California, is becoming richer every year. It is safe to estimate that the capital invested in quartz mines and mills is yielding an average profit of twenty per cent. per annum, and that the average yield is at least three dollars per day for the men regularly at work on mines which have been fairly opened. There are in the State a multitude of men engaged nominally in quartz mining who really spend much of their time in prospecting and lounging about, unwilling to work hard for ordinary wages, but preferring to ramble over the country in the hope of striking a fortune. As to the well known mines the yield on some of them is more than twenty dollars per day to the hand the year round.

6.—UNCERTAINTY IN QUARTZ MINING.

There are certain elements of uncertainty in quartz mining not found in farming or manufacturing. The farmer, on looking at the soil, knows that it will produce grain enough to support him; he can ascertain precisely what it will cost him to transport his grain to a market, and so can calculate how much money he will receive from an ordinary crop. There is a possibility of a great drought or a great blight, but he has, perhaps, a little capital as a reliance in such a case, and he makes his estimates on the basis of an average season. If he cannot afford to risk anything, he does all his work with his own hands, and he cannot lose more than his time.

The manufacturer is uncertain about the price which he must pay for the raw material, but he knows the world will have the goods, and will pay as much to him as to anybody else, and if he can manufacture a little cheaper than others he is certain of his profit. If he is incompetent to manage the business successfully, some one else can afford to buy him out at the cost of the building and machinery and make it pay. When a manufacturing establishment is once erected by a person of judgment and experience, it is presumed that the business will go on steadily for generation after generation. The supply of the raw material and the demand for the manufactured article, at least if the goods are not of the sort required by fickle fashion, will remain constant.

But with gold mining it is different. Auriferous quartz lodes have paying quantities of metal only in spots or streaks. The law of the distribution of the precious metals in veins is yet unknown. The quartz may be traced for miles, but only here and there will it pay to work. No mineral lode anywhere is worked, I believe, with much profit for more than two continuous miles, and it is seldom that the pay-rock extends more than one thousand feet along a vein. The great quartz lode of Mariposa, called sometimes the mother vein of California, has been traced, it is supposed, for thirty miles or more; at least croppings of a large lead of the same quality of quartz, nearly in a straight line, are seen at various points between Bear valley, in Mariposa county, and Angels, in Calaveras county; and it is assumed that these croppings all belong to the same lode. In some places this vein is very rich, but the rich spots are not long, and are far apart, and in the intervals the rock is nearly or entirely barren. The miner may find quartz containing ten dollars to the ton, and he knows if the supply is abundant he may make a fortune from his claim; but to explore the lode requires a large capital, and there is no certainty of any return. The rock is too poor to work without a mill, and there is not enough in sight to justify the erection of a mill. If he takes the risk, and the pay-rock is soon exhausted, his mill, in that position, becomes worthless, and he loses the cost of all his framework, roads, and ditches, which, with the transportation, is frequently greater than the cost of the machinery proper. The manufacturer knows that his supply of cotton, wool, iron, leather, or wood, will not fail altogether, and if it becomes scanty he can raise his price so that his work will still be profitable; and the farmer knows that his soil will produce grass and grain as long as he lives; but the quartz miner does not know that the supply of his pay-rock will keep steady, and if it runs short he cannot expect the price of the precious metals to rise so that he can sell his produce for a higher price per pound.

There is again a great diversity in the facilities for quartz mining at different places. The farmer or the manufacturer usually goes into a level country with open roads, and after ascertaining the distance to the market and the cost of transportation, he can decide whether he can afford to go into business. Perhaps he would find fifty places within a range of ten miles, all equally good for his farm or his factory. But with the miner the case is different. The mines are usually found in the mountains, where there are no roads, water is not conveniently accessible, and wood is scarce. The rock in one part of the lode is hard, in another soft; in one there is much sulphuret of iron, in another little. It is relatively cheaper to work a wide streak of pay-rock, other things being equal, than a narrow one. The mill may be far or near; it may be above the level of the mine, or below it; the water for washing the pulverized rock may be obtainable for only part of the year, and the gold may be found in thick masses so that the workmen can conveniently pilfer considerable quantities. Many of the mills are in secluded places, where men of wealth do not like to live, and thus the property is put in charge of hired men, who lack the zeal and care of a proprietor. These are some of the points in which there are serious variations. It may safely be said that a farmer owning a hundred acres of rich soil on a prairie within twenty miles of any large town of Illinois, is certain of being able to make a very comfortable living; but a miner with a vein of auriferous quartz yielding ten dollars to the ton, within ten miles of a California town, is not certain of anything until he has examined the vein, its position its size, the character of the vein-stone and accompanying minerals, and the proximity and quantity of wood, besides a number of other particulars.

These are some of the diversities of circumstances which beset quartz mining in different places, and render it impossible to give a statement of the expenses of taking out rock, building a mill, and reducing the ore, applicable to the majority of the mines. It is useless to attempt to convey any precise idea about matters in which the variations are so great between the workings of different mines, and between the workings of the same mine at different times. All that can be done is to collect the facts in regard to the operations of the mines and mills of which we have reports, so as to show the range.

7.—PROFESSOR ASHBURNER'S STATISTICS.

In 1861 Professor W. Ashburner, connected with the State geological survey, prepared a tabular statement of the operations of the principal quartz mills then running in California. Of these there were four in Mariposa county, eight in Tuolumne, three in Calaveras, seven in Amador, three in Eldorado, two in Plumas, two in Sierra, and nine in Nevada—thirty-eight in all.

It appears from his table that in seven of the mills the stamps 400 and less than 500 pounds each; in eight mills the weight was 500 and under 600 pounds; in eight the weight was between 600 and 700 pounds; in eight it was 700 and less than 1,000 pounds; in two it was 1,000, and in one 1,500.

The height to which the stamp was raised when allowed to fall varied from eight to fourteen inches. In ten mills the height was ten inches; in six, twelve inches; in five, fourteen inches; in four, thirteen inches; in one, eleven inches; in one, eight inches; in one, nine inches.

In thirteen mills the speed of the blows was from sixty to sixty-five inclusive per minute; in ten mills it was from fifty to fifty-eight; in three mills it was from forty to forty-eight; in three mills it was seventy; in three mills it was eighty; and in one mill it was thirty-two per minute.

In six of the steam-mills the consumption of wood for ten tons of ore crushed was from a cord to a cord and a half; in eight mills it was from a cord and a half to two cords; in two mills it was from two to three cords; in three mills it was less than a cord; in one mill it was over three cords, and in another five cords.

The loss of mercury is reported for twenty-nine mills, and in two the loss is less than a pound in working one hundred tons of quartz; in twenty-one the loss is less than a pound in working ten tons; and in six the loss is over one pound in working ten tons. The lowest loss is seven pounds in working one thousand tons, and the yield of the rock there is reported to be $25 per ton, and the highest is one hundred and ninety-eight pounds for one thousand tons; and in that case the rock is reported to yield $17 14 per ton. The general rule is, however, that the higher the yield of gold, the greater the loss of quicksilver per ton, because more must be used.

The cost of extracting the quartz is reported for twenty-eight mines. In eight, it is $2 and less than $3; in four mines it is $3 and less than $4; in two mines it is $4 and less than $5; in five mines it is $5 and less than $6; in three mines it is $6; in two mines it is less than $2; in three mines it is between $7 and $14; in one mine it is $15; in another $20; and in another $26.

The average yield per ton was $5 and less than $10 in four mines; $10 and less than $16 in eleven; $16 and less than $55 in five; between $25 and $40, inclusive, in seven; between $50 and $75 in four, and $80 in one.

In seven mills the cost of stamping per ton was 50 cents and less than $1; in seven $1 and less than $1 50; in five $1 50 and less than $2; in four $2 and less than $3; in three $3 and less than $4.

In thirteen mills the total cost of treatment (which includes crushing, amalgamation, and all the handling after the delivery of the quartz at the mill, and loss of quicksilver,) was $2 and less than $3 per ton; in seven mills it was $1 and less than $1 50 per ton; in four mills it was over $1 50 and less than $2; in two mills it was less than $1; in five mills it was between $3 and $4; and in three mills it was respectively $4 59, $6 27, and $8 31. The cheapest treatment was that of the Badger mine, in Amador county, where the cost was only 67 cents per ton.

8.—RÉMOND'S STATISTICS.

In the months of August, September, October, and November of the year 1865, Mr. A. Rémond, in the service of the State geological survey of California, visited all the quartz mines and mills in operation, or that had been in operation, in those portions of Tuolumne and Mariposa counties lying between the Merced and Stanislaus rivers. The following is a list of the mines and mills thus visited:

No.	Mine.	Mill.
1.	French Mary	No mill.
2.	Hope	Brichman's.
3.	Victor	Victor.
4.	Mount Hope	Mount Hope.
5.	Catherine	Catherine.
6.	Cranberry	Yosemite.
7.	Rutherford	No. 6.
8.	Ferguson's	Ferguson's.
9.	Cedar	Cedar.
10.	Empire	Empire.
11.	Mary Harrison	Old French Mill.
12.	Malvina	New French Mill.
13.	Adelaide	Crown Lead.
14.	McAlpine	McAlpine.
15.	Louisiana	Louisiana.
16.	Schimer's	Low Mill.
17.	Funk's	Funk's (2) Mills.
18.	Casabon's	Casabon's.
19.	Goodwin's	Eclipse.

20. Derrick's.....................................Derrick's.
21. Humbug....................................Humbug.
22. Blue Ledge................................Black's.
23. Heslep's...................................Heslep's.
24. App's......................................App's.
25. Morse's....................................No mill.
26. Orcutt's...................................Orcutt's.
27. No mine...................................Ryerson's.
28. Eureka....................................Eureka.
29. Summers's.................................Summers's.
30. Grizzly....................................Grizzly.
31. Excelsior..................................Excelsior.
32. Dagner....................................Dagner.
33. Mt. Vernon................................No mill.
34. Monitor...................................Monitor.
35. Green's....................................Green's.
36. Pirate.....................................Pirate.
37. Independence..............................Independence.
38. Great Eastern.............................No mill.
39. Comstock..................................No mill.
40. Soulsby...................................Soulsby.
41. Independent...............................No mill.
42. Gilson's, (old mine).......................Gilson's.
43. Jackson's.................................No mill.
44. Calder's..................................No mill.
45. No mine...................................Wheeler's.
46. Consuelo..................................Consuelo.
47. Waters's..................................Waters's.
48. Watts's...................................Watts's.
49. Union.....................................Union.
50. Alabama...................................Alabama.
51. Gilson's, (new mine)......................Gilson's, (No. 42.)
52. No mine...................................Washington.
53. Toledo....................................Labitour.
54. Raw Hide.................................Raw Hide.
55. Shanghai.................................Shanghai.
56. Columbia.................................Columbia.
57. Patterson's...............................Patterson's.
58. Valparaiso................................Valparaiso.
59. Turner's..................................No mill.
60. Preston's.................................Preston's
61. Italian....................................Occidental.
62. Old Whiskey Hill.........................Wood's Crossing.
63. Nyman's..................................Nyman's.
64. John Knox's..............................No mill.
65. No mine..................................Widow Hill.
66. Clio......................................Clio.
67. Shawmut.................................Shawmut.
68. Josephine................................Stetson's.
69. Eagle.....................................Eagle.
70. Italian....................................No mill.
71. Nonpareil................................Duprat's.
72. Burns....................................No mill.
73. No mine..................................Cross's.
74. Second Garote............................Pacific, (No. 75.)
75. Morkam..................................Pacific.

76. Kanaka............................ ....Pacific, (No. 75.)
77. Phœnix......................... ....Phœnix.
78. Mohrmann's................... ....No mill.
79. Kenney's......................... ....Kenney's.
80. Golden Rule........... ....Golden Rule.
81. Golden Rule, (No. 80)........ ......Golden Rule, (No. 80.)
82. Golden Rule, (No. 80).......... ....Golden Rule, (No. 80)
83. Brown's Flat................. ....Brown's Flat.
84. Zuckermann's.............. .... Zuckermann's.

Number.	Average width of lode.	Average yield per ton.	Cost of extraction per ton.	Cost of transportation to mill.	Cost of treatment.	Whether mill is running.	Cost of mill.	Power used: water or steam.	No. of stamps.	Kind of amalgamating machinery.	Cost of roads.	Cost of ditches and flumes.
	Ft. in.											
1	1 6	$12 00										
2	1	6 00	$3 00	$1 00	$1 50	Not running	$4,000	Water	10	!C.	$500	$500
3	1	10 60				Not running	3,000	Water	5	!C. & A.	100	1,000
4						Not running	3,500	Water	5	C.	100	1,000
5	1 2	32 50	14 00	1 25	3 00	Not running	3,000	Water	3	C. & A.	1,000	600
6	2 6	18 00	3 50	2 00	3 00	Running	3,000	Water	5	C.	1,000	1,200
7	1 6	25 00										
8	8	20 00				Running	6,000	Water	8	C.	500	1,000
9	1	40 00	4 00	2 50	2 50	Running	3,000	Water	5	C.	90	150
10	1 6	40 00				Ruined				*	None.	None.
11	3	14 00	4 00	1 00	2 00	Not running		Steam	15	*	330	None.
12	10	19 00	1 75	87½	2 00	Running		Steam	35	*	150	None.
13	2	6 00	1 00	1 25	75	Not running	42,000	W. & S.	25	*	500	18,000
14	1	37 50	4 00	2 00	2 00	Not running	10,000	Water	8	*	00	200
15	1 6	25 00	4 00	75	2 00	Running	6,000	Steam	5	*	5 0	None.
16	1	15 00	3 00	None.	2 00	Not running	6,000	Steam	8	C.		None.
17	1					Not running	5,700	Water	10	C.	100	None.
18	1 6	15 00				Not running	6,000	Water	8	C.	100	3,000
19	2	15 00	2 00	1 50	1 50	Not running	4,000	Water	8	C.	1,000	1,000
20	1 6	25 00	12 00	3 00	4 00	Not running	3,000	Water	6	C.	1,500	500
21		4 00	1 50	50	3 00	Not running	2,300	Water	4	C.	50	500
22		23 00	5 00	2 00	3 00	Not running	1,500	Water	4	C.	None.	500
23	10	12 00	2 50	40	2 00	Running	12,000	Water	10	C.	300	1,300
24	6	18 00	3 00	75	2 50	Running	4,500	W. & S.	10	*	500	500
25	1 6	27 50	2 00	50	6 00						50	None.
26	2 6	25 00	2 00	50	6 00	Running	3,000	Water	5	*	50	
27						Running	20,000	Water		*		
28	4	14 00	4 00	None.	2 75	Running	28,000	Water	20	*		1,500
29	3	15 00	2 50	50	2 50	Not running	6,000	Water	8	*	5	900
30	7	17 50	4 00	50	6 00	Not running		W. & S.	20	*	2,200	1,500
31	2 6	60 00	3 00	50	1 00	Not running	13,500	Water	10	*	2,000	500
32	1	40 00	4 50	None.	1 75	Not running	22,000	Steam	10	*	None.	None.
33	1											
34	1 6	30 00	10 00	None.	2 00	Running	7,000	Water	5	*	1,000	00
35	1	80 00	10 00	None.	3 50	Running	4,000	Steam	5	*	None.	None.
36	1	25 00	9 50	50	3 50	Running	10,000	Water	10	C. & A.		
37	4 6	40 00	4 37½	50	2 75	Running	15,000	Steam	10	*		None.
38	2	20 00										
39	1 6		2 50									
40	1 3	27 50	8 00	None.	3 75	Running	20,000	Steam	20	C.		None.
41	10	36 00										
42	1 6	52 50	12 00	None.	4 50	Not running	9,000	Steam	10	C. & A.	None.	None.
43	6	107 00										
44	1 2											
45						Not running	7,500	Steam	10	*		
46	3 6					Not finished		Water	20	C.		
47	9	6 00	2 00	25	1 75	Running	3,000	Water	6	C.	1,000	600
48	2	180 00	60 00	25	7 00	Not running	800	Water	3	§A.	None.	2,500
49	2	8 00	1 00	25	1 75	Not running	2,000	Water	8	C.	50	500
50	25	10 00	1 50	None.	1 00	Running	1,500	Water	4	C.	150	200
51	1 4	40 00	13 00	1 25	6 00						1,000	None.
52						Not running	1,200	Water	3	C.	None.	None.
53	3 6	10 00	2 00	None.	2 00	Not running	14,800	Water	15	C.	1,000	4,000
54	4	25 00				Running		Water	10	C.	None.	
55	2 6	40 00	5 00	None.	2 00	Running	4,000	Water	10	C.	None.	100
56	3 6	9 00	2 10	60	2 50	Not running	15,000	Water	15	C.	1,000	4,000

5

Number.	Average width of lode.	Average yield per ton.	Cost of extraction per ton.	Cost of transportation to mill.	Cost of treatment.	Whether mill is running.	Cost of mill.	Power used; water or steam.	Number of stamps.	Kind of amalgamating machinery.	Cost of roads.	Cost of ditches and flumes.
	Ft. in.											
57	4	$8 00	$2 00	$25	$2 50	Not running	$6,500	Water	10	C.	$100	$1,200
58	2	80 00		None.		Ruined	3,000	Water	6	C.	None	
59	2 6			None.	None.							
60	10		2 00	60	1 50	Not running	4,000	Water	10	C.	300	500
61	6 6	20 00	4 00	None.	1 50	Not running	6,000	Water	12	C. & A.	400	300
62	15	15 00	50	50	1 50	Running	2,000	Water	4	C.	1,000	1,200
63	4	17 00	3 00	90	1 00	Running	4,000	Water	10	C. & A.	1,000	1,000
64	1	65 00										
65						Running		Water	5	C.	None.	
66	5 6	15 00	3 00	75	2 00	Not running	5,000	Water	10	*	1,000	16,000
67	1 6	25 00	2 75	None.	1 50	Not running	8,000	Steam	10	*	2,000	None.
68	8	8 00	2 00	None.	1 50	Not running	7,500	Water		*	800	500
69	2	12 00	3 50	50	2 00	Running	11,000	Water	10	C.	2,500	3,000
70	8											
71			30 00			Not running		Water	5	*		
72	4	20 00	1 00	1 12	4 50			Water		*		
73						Running	4,500	Water	10	*		
74	1 6											
75	4	14 00	1 50	40	3 00	Not running	3,000	Water	5	C. & A.		
76		8 00	2 00	2 00	3 00							
77	2 6	15 00				Not running	200	Water		A.	None.	
78	2 6											
79	5	15 00				Not running	1,000	Water		A.	None	
80	8	40 00	5? 00		2 00	Running	2,000	Water	5	C.	50	400
81						Not running	1,300	Water	2	*		200
82						Not finished	12,000	Water	15	*	None.	
83	6	40 00	11 00	None.	1 50	Not running	3,500	Water	4	C. & A.	None.	1,500
84	1 6	40 00	5 00		4 00	Not running	4,000	Water	4	C.		

* The amalgamating apparatus in the mills marked with the asterisk is given below.
† C. copper-plate. ‡ C. & A. copper-plate and arrastra. ‖ W. & S. water and steam. § A. arrastra.

In numbers 5, 6, 11, 12, 14, 25, 30, and 40 the average yield is obtained by dividing the sum of two figures given by Mr. Rémond. For instance, the average yield of mine No. 5 is given above as $32 50, whereas Mr. Rémond says the yield is from $25 to $40. In the same manner the cost of extraction in No. 37 is given at $4 37½, whereas Mr. Rémond says it is from $2 75 to $6. Mines Nos. 59 and 70 yield coarse gold, which is taken from the rock after pounding it in a hand-mortar.

In mill No. 11 Hungarian pans are used, and in No. 12 Hungarian pans and an arrastra; in No. 13, Patterson's pans and separators; in No. 14, copper plates and amalgamating pans; in No. 15, Salmon's amalgamator and Salmon's separator; in No. 23, copper plates, an arrastra, a Beath's grinder and a Salmon's concentrator; in Nos. 26 and 37, copper plates andblankets; in No. 27, a centrifugal grinder, a Ryerson's pulverizer, a super-heated steam apparatus, and a shaking table; in No. 28, shaking pans and a Chili mill; in No. 29, copper plates, shaking pans, and an arrastra; in No. 30, cast-iron barrels; in No. 31, copper plates and a shaking pan; in No. 32, copper plates, arrastras, and a shaking table; in No. 34, an Ambler's concentrator, a shaking table, and arrastras; in No. 35, copper plates and a Beath's amalgamator; in No. 45, Varney's pans and a concentrator; in Nos. 66 and 67, copper plates and Knox's pans; in No. 71, copper plates, a Farrand's amalgamator, and a settler; in No. 73, Varney's pans and a settler, and in No. 82, copper plates, shaking tables, and an arrastra.

It appears that the average thickness of 21 lodes is from 1 to 12 inches, inclusive; in 20, from 13 to 24 inches, inclusive; of 9, from 25 to 36 inches, inclusive ; of 10, from 37 to 48 inches, inclusive; of 9, from 5 to 10 feet, inclusive ; and of 2, over 10 feet.

In 9 mines the average yield is under $10 per ton ; in 22 it is between $10 and $19, inclusive; in 14 it is between $20 and $29, inclusive ; in 14 it is between $30 and $49, inclusive ; in 3 it is between $50 and $69, inclusive, and in 4 it is over $70. Only one mine has a yield as low as $4 ; three have a yield of $6 ; 4 of $8, and 1 of $9.

The cost of extraction per ton depends, to a considerable extent, upon the thickness of the vein, or, rather, of the pay-rock in the vein. In mine No. 48 the vein is only two inches thick, and it costs $60 to get out a ton of ore, while in No. 62 it costs only 50 cents to take out a ton of rock from a vein 15 feet wide. In 1 mine the cost of extraction was under $1; in 8, between $1 and $1 90, inclusive ; in 14, between $2 and $2 90, inclusive; in 9, between $3 and $3 90, inclusive ; in 9, between $4 and $4 90, inclusive; in 7, between $5 and $9 90, inclusive, and in 7, $10 or more.

In 16 mines there is no cost of transportation of ore to mill, the extraction covering that expense ; in 23 mines the cost is less than 90 cents ; in 7 mines it is between $1 and $1 90, inclusive ; in 6 it is $2 or more.

In 1 mill the cost of treatment is 75 cents ; in 14 mills it is from $1 to $1 90, inclusive ; in 19 it is from $2 to $2 90, inclusive ; in 9 it is from $3 to $3 90, inclusive, and in 9 it is $4 or more. The richer the rock, as a general rule, the more expensive the treatment. The quartz of mine No. 48, yielding $180 to the ton, costs $7 for treatment

Of the mills visited by Mr. Rémond in 1865, 38 were not running, 25 were running, 2 were ruined, and 2 were unfinished. Of those not running, some were standing idle for want of water, others had exhausted the pay-rock within sight and were preparing for further explorations, and the owners of a third-class had no expectation of resuming work, having found it unprofitable, but hoped to sell or intended to move their machinery.

The cost of each of 11 mills was under $2,900 ; of 20 mills it was between $3,000 and $3,900, inclusive ; of 14 it was between $5,000 and $9,000, inclusive, and of 14 it was $10,000 or more.

The number of stamps in 10 mills was 4 or less ; in 22 mills, between 5 and 9, inclusive; in 20 mills, between 10 and 14, inclusive ; in 10 mills, 15 or more.

The power in 52 mills is water ; in 11 mills, steam ; in 3, water and steam.

In 31 mills copper plates were used alone for amalgamating, (outside of the battery ;) in 3 the arrastra was used alone ; in 7, copper plates and arrastra ; and in 26, other devices, with or without copper plates or arrastras.

At 25 mills the roads cost less than $1,000 for each ; at 12 mills, between $1,000 and $1,900, inclusive ; at 4 mills, between $2,000 and $2,500, inclusive ; at 1, $6,500 ; and at 15, nothing.

At each of 21 mills the ditches and flumes cost less than $1,000 ; at 13 mills the cost was between $1,000 and $1,900, inclusive ; at 3, between $2,000 and $3,900, inclusive ; at 3, $4,000 or more ; and at 14, nothing.

The county assessor of Nevada county, California, reported the statistics of the quartz mines and mills of Grass valley and Nevada for the year ending October 1, 1866, as follows :

List of quartz mines at Nevada City and Grass valley.

Name of company.	No. of men employed.	Engines.	Stamps.	Tons of rock.	Average per ton.
GRASS VALLEY TOWNSHIP.					
Eureka Mining Company	175	3	20	11,400	$50
Union Hill	100	3	20	1,000	40
Cambridge, (new)	75	3	10	....	40
Allison Ranch	175	5	12	7,000	30
Ione	70	2	10	3,000	20
Forest Springs	6	....	10	4,500	50
Empire	80	4	36	6,000	45
Hewston Hill	65	3	....	1,500	100
New Orleans Mill	5	1	8	1,700	Cust.
Norambagua	100	1	....	....	50
Lone Jack	25	1	....	......	40
Golden Rock, (new)	10	....	....	......	20
Atlantic Cable, (new)	4	....	....	......	20
Wisconsin	40	1	....	1,000	50
Laton Mill	5	1	8	5,000	Cust.
Lucky	50	2	15	5,600	25
Ophir Hill, (new)	20	2	....	......	......
Black Ledge	......	1	....	......	30
Sebastopol	4	1	12	2,000	Cust.
Hartery Mine	50	2	8	4,000	20
Central, (new)	4	1	....	......	......
Gold Hill Mill	6	1	20	2,000	Cust.
Gold Hill Mine	10	1	....	......	......
Frankfort	10	....	....	200	14
Perrin's Mill	15	....	5	400	8
Inkerman	10	....	....	100	25
Lamarque	4	....	....	......	40
Shanghae	20	....	....	200	60
Almaden	15	....	....	500	25
Independent, (new)	4	....	....	......	......
Pike Tunnel, (new)	10	....	....	......	......
Burdett	10	1	....	......	......
Badger	20	1	....	......	......
Osborn Hill	30	3	15	......	100
Spring Hill	20	1	....	......	......
Larimer Mill	4	....	8	......	1,000
New York Hill	40	2	....	500	60
Rocky Bar	60	4	16	3,500	28
North Star	140	3	16	7,000	30
Merrimac	25	2	10	2,000	20
Coe Mining Company	......	2	....	......	......
Town Talk Mining Company	10	1	8	......	......
Redan	35	1	....	......	......
Betsey	......	1	....	......	60
Alta Hill	......	1	8	......	20
Slate Creek	......	....	....	......	20
Smith Mining Company	......	....	....	......	40
Murphy Mining Company	5	....	....	......	......
Essex	15	1	....	......	......
Kate Hayes	......	1	....	......	......
Idaho	......	1	....	......	......
Pacific Ore Company	5	1	5	......	......
Stockbridge	......	1	....	......	......
Byers's Quartz Mill	2	....	4	......	......
Shamrock Company	5	....	....	600	25
Omaha	4	....	....	60	22
Hill and Farnam Metallurg	4	....	....	......	......
Total	1,601	67	284	71,420	......

List of quartz mines, &c.—Continued.

Name of company.	No. of men employed.	Engines.	Stamps.	Tons of rock.	Average per ton.
NEVADA TOWNSHIP.					
Palmer's Mill	4	1	4	....	Cust.
Banner	40	2	10	....	......
Nevada Quartz Mining Company	30	....	12	....	$6
Providence	8	1	12	1,200	8
Oriental	4	1	8	800	Cust.
Sneath & Clay	55	3	12	6,000	......
New York	35	3	....	3,000	......
Murchie Mill	13	....	8	....	......
French Mill	4	1	6	600	Cust.
Forest Hill Mill	4	2	5	....	......
California, (new)	20	1	....	....	30
Wigham Mill	....	2	20	....	......
Cornish Mill	4	....	6	100	30
Pennsylvania	....	2	4	....	......
Willow Valley	....	1	....	....	......
Mohawk	....	1	....	....	......
Gold Tunnel	....	1	6	....	......
Oro Fino	....	....	4	....	......
Cunningham	....	1	....	....	......
Federal Loan	....	1	2	....	......
Manzanita	....	....	15	....	......
Stiles's Mill	6	....	8	2,500	25
Total	230	24	142	14,200	......

Grass valley is the most productive gold-quartz mining district in the world. The annual yield of an area drawn by a radius of four miles is $3,500,000. The number of laborers employed in the mines and mills is 2,000, showing an average yearly production for each person of $1,750, and the average yield of the rock worked is $30 to $35. The lodes are narrow, none of them exceeding seven feet in width, and most being less than a foot. They contain much pyrites, and this fact contributes with the narrowness of the veins to make the average expense of extraction and reduction high—about $15 per ton. Some of the works have been sunk to a depth of 400 feet, but most of the pay-quartz is obtained within 200 feet of the surface.

9.—PULVERIZATION OF QUARTZ.

The main processes of quartz mining are extraction, crushing, and amalgamation. The extraction of auriferous quartz from the vein is like that of ores generally. Any person familiar with copper mining can in a few days learn to be a good gold miner. The quantity of copper ore can usually be discovered by a glance, but in auriferous quartz it is often necessary to pulverize a piece of the quartz, and wash the powder in a spoon or little basin to see whether it will pay to extract. The cost of tunnels and shafts for opening mines in such rock as is usually found about the auriferous lodes is from ten to fifteen dollars per lineal foot.

Ninety-five per cent. of all the crushing in California is done with stamps. The stamp is a block of iron, weighing from 300 to 1,500 pounds, fastened to a wooden or iron shaft, usually iron. A battery consists of several stamps standing side by side, and in most mills the number of stamps is five or a multiple of five. The stamps are successively lifted by machinery, and then allowed to fall on the quartz. The height to which they are raised is from ten to fifteen inches, and each stamp falls from forty to eighty times in a minute. It is calculated that each stamp should crush a ton of quartz of ordinary quality in twenty-four hours. The mills usually run night and day. Of course, the amount of quartz crushed depends to a considerable extent on the hardness of the rock, the weight of the stamp, the height of the fall and the rapidity of the blows.

The fineness to which the rock must be pulverized depends on circumstances. The particles of gold may be very fine, so that the quartz must be reduced to an impalpable powder before they can be liberated; but if the particles of gold and the grain of the rock are coarse, or if the pulp is to go through a grinding pan, the quartz may be allowed to escape when many of the particles are as coarse as sea-sand, or even coarser. The battery has on one side a screen of wire-cloth, or perforated sheet iron, with apertures of the size of the largest particles that must be permitted to escape. A steady current of water runs through the battery, so as to carry away the quartz dust as soon as it is fine enough. The sheet-iron screens are punched with needles, and are known by the numbers. No. 7 screen is punched with a cambric needle; Nos. 3 with a darning needle.

In Grass valley most of the mills use Nos. 3 and 4 screens; elsewhere Nos. Nos. 4 and 5 and 6 are preferred.

A multitude of crushers have been tried to break up the quartz before it is given to the stamps or other pulverizing apparatus, but the number in use is very small. Those principally in use consist of two heavy iron jaws, which are wide apart at the top, and close together at the bottom, and as they work back and forth, the quartz is smashed between them. The quartz is usually in pieces not larger than goose eggs when delivered to the battery, and it is broken this size either by sledge-hammers, or by a large stamp, kept for the purpose of breaking up the large stones.

The musket-ball pulverizer has been tried as a substitute for stamps, and the report is favorable, but the trial has not been sufficient to command the confidence of miners. It is an iron barrel which revolves twenty-four times per minute on a longitudinal, horizontal axis. Inside of the barrel are a number of chilled iron balls weighing an ounce each. The quartz is introduced in particles not larger than a grain of wheat, and in two hours it is reduced to an impalpable powder.

Another pulverizer, that has been tried without attaining favor, is an iron star or wheel without a rim, which makes 1,000 or 1,500 revolutions per minute in an iron casing. The quartz is thrown with great force by the arms against the casing and is dashed into fragments by the concussion. The casing is so made with little offsets that the quartz strikes at right angles.

10.—AMALGAMATION OF GOLD.

Much of the gold is caught or amalgamated in the battery. The stamps fall into an iron box or mortar, into which an ounce of quicksilver is thrown for every ounce of gold supposed to be in the quartz. If the rock is crushed fine in the battery, two-thirds or three-fourths of all the gold saved may be caught there, leaving one-third or one-fourth that escapes through the screen.

After leaving the battery, the pulverized quartz in most mills runs down over copper plate which has been washed over with diluted nitric acid, and then rubbed with quicksilver till the whole surface is covered with amalgam. The particles of gold running over this surface adhere and form amalgam; and when the plate is covered with gold it operates far more effectually than when the quicksilver is fresh. Gold unites more readily with gold amalgam than with pure quicksilver. The copper plate, which is the bottom of a trough or sluice, may be fifty or a hundred feet long. Küstel in his book on *Nevada and Cali-*

fornia processes of silver and gold extraction (page 16) says, copper plates as a means of amalgamation are "very imperfect and mostly abandoned." Imperfect they may be, but they are still used in most of the quartz mills of the State; and in some of the best, or at least in some of those which produce the largest amounts of bullion.

Between the copper plates in many mills are troughs in the bottom of which are laid coarse blankets, or gunny-bag, or even cow hide with the hair on and the grain against the stream. Gold amalgam and sulphurets are caught in the rough surface of the blanket, gunny-sack, or hide, which must be taken up and washed at intervals, which are usually not more than half an hour long.

The shaking table used in amalgamation is a long box with transverse divisions containing quicksilver. It is set horizontally and is shaken longitudinally, receiving from 100 to 200 short jerks in a minute. By these jerks the pulp is thrown back upon the quicksilver.

At the Hayward mine the pulp runs out from the amalgamating battery over a wide pine board, across the grain, and the appearance of the amalgam on this board is supposed to give the best indication whether the proper quantity of quicksilver is being used in the battery. If too much, most of the amalgam runs off, and the little caught on the board is in brilliant round globules, and if not enough, the amalgam has a rusty look.

The arrastra is extensively used for amalgamating, and it has the merits of cheapness, grinding well, adaptability to any place, kind of power, economy of water, and facility of working; but it is slow, and is therefore not in favor in large mills.

Atwood's amalgamator, used in many mills at Grass valley, consists of level troughs, with quicksilver at the bottom; and over the troughs are horizontal revolving cylinders with projecting spikes, which stir up the quicksilver and the pulp as the latter passes over the trough.

Pans are coming into use slowly in the gold quartz mills—at least in some of the new ones lately erected in Grass valley. Küstel says of pan amalgamation that it is "at present the most perfect gold manipulation," and by it "gold is extracted as close as ninety-five per cent. of the fire assay"—that is, if there are no sulphurets. (*Nevada and California processes, page 63.*) The general opinion is that from twenty to forty per cent. of the gold is lost in the ordinary processes. The pans used are mostly like those that will be described as being used in the silver mills of Nevada. There is, however, one pan not used for silver reduction that has found some favor with gold miners. This is Baux and Guiod's pan, which has a tight fitting cover. The pulp runs constantly with a stream of water down into the pan through a tube at the side, and the light matter after being ground runs up and out through a tube in the centre. There is thus a constant feed and discharge, while in nearly all the other pans a batch of ore is put in and worked, and then taken out to make room for another batch.

The Ryerson amalgamator is an air-tight chamber in which quartz that has been crushed very fine by some dry process is subjected to the influence of super-heated steam for half an hour as a preparation for the quicksilver, which is then introduced and converted by the heat into a vapor, in which form it is supposed to pervade the pulp and get access to all the gold. Cold water is injected to condense the quicksilver, and the pulp is drawn up to be separated.

II.—SULPHURETS AND CONCENTRATION.

But after the pulp has passed through all the amalgamating processes customary in gold quartz mills, it is found that in many ores much of the gold is lost because of the presence of sulphurets of iron and copper. The presence of the sulphurets appears to chill the quicksilver and prevent it from taking hold of the gold, and many particles of gold appear to be enveloped by them. The gold can be separated from the pyrites, but heretofore the separation has been affected mainly in establishments specially devoted to that purpose, and not in the ordinary mills. It is customary to save the sulphurets and sell them to the sulphuret works, or keep them until there may be a sale for them. But for the purpose of saving them, they must be separated from the earthy and rocky matter in the pulp, and this is called concentration. The sulphurets have a specific gravity of 4.5, while quartz has a specific gravity of 2.6. By this difference in density, it is possible to separate the two.

There are several patent concentrators in use, all made of iron, and shaped like shallow pans. The one more used than any other has a bottom that rises from the edge to the centre, where there is an outlet through which the lighter material runs away. This outlet is, of course, not so high as the rim. This pan turns on a perpendicular axis, and is shaken back and forth by two hundred short jerks per minute. A hole in the side is left open for the escape of the sulphurets, which flow out in a steady stream; and lower down is another hole, which is opened when the heavier matter is to be taken out.

One of the best cheap concentrators is a long and wide rocker with a flat-bottom and a slight inclination. A boy can work one of these concentrating rockers for a large mill, and the cheapness of the machine and the slight power required for it are great advantages. The sulphurets are arrested by cleets in the bottom of the rocker, and need to be taken out at intervals of half an hour.

Any sluice serves also, to some extent, for concentration.

12.—CHLORINATION.

The most approved method of reducing auriferous sulphurets is chlorination. As a preparation for this process the sulphurets are roasted. They are placed in an oven brought to a red heat, retained in that condition for about six hours, or until the smell of sulphur has disappeared. After they have cooled the sulphurets are sprinkled with water, shovelled over, and put into wooden tubs or boxes, so made that chlorine gas can be introduced at the bottom and made to rise all through the mass. The tub or box is kept closely covered, and chloride of gold, which is soluble in water, is formed. After the lapse of four or five hours water is let in, and the chloride of gold is dissolved by it; the solution is drawn off into glass vessels, and some sheets of iron are put in; the chlorine unites with the iron, and the gold falls as a purplish-brown powder to the bottom of the vessel.

13.—GOLD IN LOOSE STATE.

Gold mines are divided into the two main classes of quartz and placer, but at Whiskey Hill, near the town of Lincoln, in Placer county, about thirty miles from Sacramento, a large mass of loose slate rock is found, containing considerable pyrites and about six dollars of gold to the ton. The material is so soft that eight tons can be crushed by a stamp in a day. It is supposed that below the water-line a vein of hard auriferous copper ore will be found. The mass of auriferous slate in the hill is large, and the mine is considered very valuable, one-half of it having been sold for $175,000. Similar bodies of auriferous slate mixed with clay are found at Lander's ranch, Placer county, and at Telegraph City, in Calaveras county.

14.—PLACERS.

Placer mining is decreasing every year. Every month witnesses the exhaustion of some rich placer district, or its exhaustion at least for the present. It may be that in the future, when laborers can be employed for fifty cents per day, claims which cannot be worked now will be in demand.

There are large bodies of gravel that contain just gold enough not to pay, at the present rates of water and labor, and it is evident that both must be cheaper after the lapse of a few years.

But although land might pay the miner, it may pay the farmer still better, and the State should give every preference to the latter, who beautifies and enriches the soil, while the miner destroys it.

Notwithstanding the continuous decline of the placer mining interest for ten years past, there are yet, and long will be, very rich placers. Some of the deposits of gold in clay and gravel are so protected that a score of years may elapse before they can be reached. On the sides and near the base of the Sierra Nevada are innumerable hills that are destined to come down before the hydraulic pipe of the miner. One of these hills commences near the town of You Bet, in Nevada county, and extends sixteen miles up the mountain side, with a height of two hundred feet, and a width of a mile; and there is reason to believe that the foundation throughout its length is a bed of rich auriferous cement.

15.—CEMENT MINING.

The cement deposit is a stratum of very tough clay enclosing gravel and boulders; and the clay is so stubborn that it will not dissolve in a sluice-box, and it has been necessary to crush it in mills. The material is heterogeneous; the clay is soft under the stamp; some of the gravel is hard, and other soft. The gravel is not auriferous, but it must be crushed, so as to permit the crushing of the clay. Several attempts have been made to separate the stones from the remainder of the mass without crushing them, but without success. As the stones contain no gold, all the power spent in crushing them is lost; but at present there is no other way, nor is it probable that any mode of separation can be devised. One stamp will crush from four to six tons of cement per day, and the cement stamps are only about half as heavy as quartz stamps. The pulverization is not so fine as in quartz; the sheet-iron screen through which the cement pulp escapes is punched with holes that vary from a sixteenth to an eighth of an inch in size. The particles of clay that escape are so small that they are easily dissolved in the water. The gold is caught in the battery, and that which escapes through the screen is caught in the sluice. It is a singular fact that many of the hills of the present day stand upon the beds and precisely indicate the course of the streams of a former geological epoch. The existence of a layer of basalt or volcanic rock along the top of these hills indicates that currents of lava followed the streams, and after hardening protected the gravel under them from being washed away by the great aqueous agencies which wore down the rock and earth in the neighborhood to a depth of more than two thousand feet in some places. So common are auriferous channels under the hills that the term "rim rock" has long been in common use among miners to indicate that part of the bed rock which separates the lowest portions of the channel from the outside of the hill on both sides. In some districts it is taken for granted that if a tunnel is cut into a basalt-covered hill at the proper elevation the channel of the ancient river will be found.

16.—HYDRAULIC MINING.

Most of the placer gold of California is obtained by hydraulic mining; the most profitable placer claims, as a class, are those worked by the hydraulic process; and the most prosperous mining counties are those which have the largest areas suitable for piping. The yield in some of the claims is as $100 per day to the hand, and occasionally twice or thrice as much, but the average is probably $10 or $15, of which about half goes to pay for wages, water, and other expenses.

H. Ex. Doc 29——5

17.—RIVER MINING.

Nearly all the river beds have been washed, but they are washed over and over again. The rivers are to be regarded as large sluices into which all the fine gold that escapes from the adjacent mining operations is carried and deposited; and thus there are some river beds that pay for a short time to wash every year. The yield, however, is not large, and miners take to the rivers only as a last resort.

In Trinity and Klamath counties, California, there is a large area of ground that is comparatively undeveloped; and that is the best region in the State for the miner who wants to work on his own account, and on a small scale. The country is rugged, the climate wet and cold, the roads bad, and there is some danger of Indians; but on the other hand there is much gold to reward the skilful miner who is willing to face the hardships and dangers of the place.

18.—THE HAYWARD QUARTZ MINE.

The Hayward claim is one of the notable mines of California. It is situated on Sutter creek, Amador county. The vein is peculiar in its character.

The quartz is in places almost a powder, and is mixed with slate and clay. The length of the ground worked is about one hundred and sixty yards, and both north and south the vein seems almost to disappear. The average yield of the rock is not high, although some very rich and beautiful specimens have been found in it. The mine has been worked since 1851, and the rock has always given a good average yield, but it is during the last eight years that the mine has risen to much importance. The total product is stated to be $6,000,000.

The yield per ton and the width of the vein have been gradually increasing, and now at a depth of 1,200 feet the former is $25, and the latter twenty-five feet. The works are by far the deepest in the State, and as the mouth of the mine is estimated to be nine hundred feet above the sea, the lowest works must be three hundred below the surface of the ocean. Professor Whitney speaks thus of the mine, in the first volume of his geological report, written several years ago: "The vein is enclosed in a dark-colored, rather soft argillaceous slate. In the Eureka the mass of vein stone is from eight to twenty feet wide, but in the Badger it widens out suddenly to forty feet.

"The length of ground worked in both mines is about four hundred and seventy feet; to the south of the Badger shaft, which is on the south end of the mine, there is hardly any quartz to be seen, and the lode, which is eight feet wide on the north side of the Eureka, pinches out very rapidly in that direction, so that the body of quartz worked is very short in proportion to its great width, being almost a column, or chimney, rather than a vein. At the junction of the two veins there is a large mass of slate and soft clay mixed with a little quartz, which is often in a state of fine powder.   *   *   *   *

"Few if any mines in the State have been more uniformly and permanently successful, while the yield of gold to the ton of rock stamped is quite low."

19.—SIERRA BUTTES MINE.

The Sierra Buttes quartz mine is one of the most noted and most valuable mines in the State. It is situated at an elevation of 6,000 feet, on the southwestern slope of the Downieville Butte, and twelve miles from the town of Downieville. There are two lodes, but most of the auriferous rock is obtained from the cliff ledge, which averages about twenty feet in width, and of this about eleven feet in thickness on an average are worked. In some places the pay streak is only two feet wide, in others seventeen. The average yield of the quartz is about eighteen dollars per ton.

The quartz is bluish white in color, and is very hard when first taken out, but it crumbles after having been exposed to the air for a time. The gold is disseminated in small particles through the rock, and in most of the quartz the metal is scarcely visible to the naked eye. There are few sulphurets, and therefore amalgamation is easy. About two-thirds of the gold is caught with quicksilver in the batteries, after leaving which the pulverized quartz is carried by water over about a hundred feet of copper plate covered with quicksilver, and then over a blanket, below which are some arrastras which are owned by different parties who pay for the tailings and the water.

The following is an authentic statement of the annual yield, expenses, and dividends since the mine came into the possession of the present company :

Years.	Yield.	Expenses.	Dividends.
1857	$51,000	$15,000	$36,000
1858	55,000	15,000	40,000
1859	88,000	20,000	68,000
1860	120,000	37,000	83,000
1861	198,000	48,000	150,000
1862	166,000	54,000	112,000
1863	156,000	57,000	99,000
1864	90,000	75,000	15,000
1865	196,000	64,000	132,000

No assessments have ever been levied. The produce of the mine has paid for all the improvements. The yield in 1866 is better than ever ; and the character of the lode has remained almost the same wherever they have worked it, without notable difference between the surface and the deepest workings.

20.—THE ALLISON MINE, &c.

The Allison mine at Grass valley is one of the richest and most productive in the State. It has been worked with almost uniform profit for ten years. The average thickness of the lode is about eighteen inches, and the rock yields from $30 to $150 per ton. According to the best information obtainable by the State geological survey 14,858 tons were reduced between March, 1857, and December, 1861, and the average yield was $50 per ton or $942,900 in all. Since the summer of 1862 the mine pays better than before. The lowest workings are nearly 500 feet deep, and the lode at that depth is three feet wide, with rock that averages $100 to the ton. The owners refuse to give any statements of their receipts or expenditures, but the men employed in the mill say the yield is $40,000 per month, or $400,000 for ten months' work in a year ; and of this sum two-thirds or more is clear profit. The claim has been worked for a length of about 1,400 feet.

The Norambagua mine at Grass valley has yielded more than half a million dollars in the last five years. The average yield of the ore is about $75 per ton. The deepest workings are 500 feet from the surface, and drifts have been run 1,000 feet along the course of the lode.

The following is a statement of the operations of the Eureka mine at Grass valley for the year ending September 30, 1866 :

Receipts from bullion	$531,431 41
Total expenditure at mine	192,648 44
Dividends	90,000 00
Net profits	368,042 18
Tons of quartz crushed	11,375 00
Average yield per ton	47 15
Average cost per ton crushed	14 80
Average cost of 1,500 tons	18 00
Average cost of remainder per ton	13 75

The following is a statement of the operations of the same mine for four months ending September 30, 1866 :

Receipts from bullion	$248, 072 55
Dividends	90, 000 00
Total expenditure at mine	69, 430 04
Net product of mine	187, 751 72
Tons of quartz crushed	4, 227 00
Average yield per ton	60 33

The Rocky Bar claim on Massachusetts Hill, near Grass valley, has produced about $1,500,000 in the last six years.

The Princeton vein, in Mariposa county, has yielded $2,000,000 within the last twelve years, but lately it has produced very little, and for a time work on it was abandoned.

21.—THE SMARTSVILLE BLUE GRAVEL COMPANY'S MINE.

The richest placer mine in the State is that of the Blue Gravel Mining Company at Smartsville, in Yuba county. The yield since March, 1864, has been as follows :

1864. March	$9, 381		1865. May	$24, 000
May	24, 275		June	50, 118
June	7, 000		August	24, 679
July	22, 350		September	46, 500
August	3, 485		October	26, 660
September	49, 440		December	37, 000
October	24, 669		1866. February	23, 746
December	45, 093		April	43, 423
1865. January	2, 723		June	23, 880
February	24, 051		August	42, 494
March	44, 981			
			Total	599, 948

The gold is obtained only when the sluice is cleaned up ; and the cleaning up occurs sometimes at intervals of two or three months, and there is no yield for the intervening months. The claim will continue to pay for many years, and probably it will be richer than ever, for the miners have not yet reached the bed rock. The claim covers an area of about a hundred acres on a long hill or ridge that stands over the bed of an ancient stream. The hill is made up of numerous layers of gravel, sand and boulders, with a rim of rock at the bottom on each side of the hill. To get access to the auriferous deposit it was necessary to cut a tunnel 1,700 feet long through the rim rock. This work was commenced in February, 1855, by the company, which had a capital of $20,000. This sum was soon expended in cutting a tunnel, which in places cost $100 per lineal foot, and then money was borrowed and the debt ran up gradually to $60,000, so that at the end of 1859 the company had spent $80,000 and nearly five years of hard labor, with no certainty of any return. In 1857 they began to wash some of the gravel in the higher portions of the claim, and the expense was greater than the yield for more than two years; but in 1860 this washing commenced to yield a profit, and in three years more the debt was reduced from $60,000 to $20,000. In December, 1863, the tunnel reached the pay-dirt, and then it was necessary to sink an incline down from the top of the hill so that the dirt could be carried off by the water through the tunnel. It was a difficult matter to open this incline to so great a depth and get it into such condition that there was no danger of the earth falling in and choking up the channel or killing the miners ; but at last this was accomplished, and since then the company have reaped a rich harvest of gold. They are using 500 inches (miners' measurement) of water per day, under a head pressure of 150 feet, at a cost of $75 per day. They use 125,000 pounds of powder annually in blasting to loosen the earth so that the water can wash it away readily. A steady current, eight inches deep and three feet wide, of mud, estimated to contain four inches in depth of solid matter, runs through their sluice, and they use three tons of quicksilver at one time to catch their gold. They have sluiced away an area of twenty acres, 100 feet deep, and they have built in all four miles of fluming, much of which is not now in use. They expended $80,000 on their first tunnel and have commenced another lower down. It will cost $75,000 and will require three years for completion.

The flume now in use is 3,000 feet long, and is paved alternately with wooden blocks set on end and flat stones set on the edge. The sections of block paving extend across the flume, and seventeen inches longitudinally, and the sections of stone paving are two feet long. The flume has an inclination of six and one-half inches in twelve feet.

This company is the only one which has mined steadily for ten years in the Smartsville district, with a profit for the whole period. Many other companies have spent immense sums of money and obtained no return. Others have made a profit for a year or two, but the general result has been failure. The Blue Gravel company succeeded only by the extraordinary and, it might almost be said, the unbusiness indulgence of their creditors, who might at any time for a period of seven years have come and taken the claim. As late as 1862 the shares in the company were selling at the rate of $11,000 for the whole claim. When the enterprise, the patience, the perseverance, the privations, the risks of failure, the hard labor of nine unprofitable years, the faithful devotion of the stockholders to one another, and the generous trust of the creditors are considered, it must be admitted that the Blue Gravel company have abundantly merited all their success. Many other claims of less value have cost their owners proportionately as much in money, labor, and patience.

22.—PROFITS OF MINING GENERALLY.

The business of mining has not been in any branch a source of much profit to the majority of those who have undertaken it in California. The proportion of California miners who have made fortunes within the last fifteen years is much less than that of the Illinois farmers. One of the chief sources of wealth in the United States east of the Rocky mountains has been the increase in the value of land, but in the mining districts hitherto there was little land to which a fee-simple title could be obtained. The largest income in the State of 1865 is that of Jules Tricot, who made in that year $182,511 by quartz mining and the sale of quartz mines, and the third largest is that of James P. Pierce, who made $102,011 in placer mining. When, however, we come to examine the incomes of the miners generally, we find that they are small.

The following table shows the number of adult white men in some of the mining counties, and the number of those who pay tax on an income of $1,800 or more, reckoned in legal tenders :

Counties.	No. white miners.	No. incomes $1,800.
Del Norte	250	None.
Klamath	700	5
Trinity	700	10
Siskiyou	2,500	24
Shasta	1,000	17
Plumas	1,000	9
Butte	1,000	13

Counties.	No. white miners.	No. incomes $1,800.
Sierra	2,500	45
Nevada	3,000	148
Placer	1,800	66
El Dorado	2,000	33
Amador	1,200	18

An examination of the lists shows that most of those who have these incomes are not miners, and that the proportion of those who have large incomes is greater in the agricultural districts and in the towns than in the mines. As a matter of curiosity, the list of incomes of Nevada county for 1865 is here appended, with the names of those who derive their incomes from quartz marked with an asterisk, and those who derive their incomes from placers, marked with a dagger.

NEVADA COUNTY.

Anderson, John*	$2,063	Findler, Thomas*	$13,051
Alger, Moxtont	6,341	Faulkner, James	3,090
Alexander, D†	1,000	Ford, Marin*	3,546
Abbey, Richard†	2,515	Fahey, John*	9,561
Belden, David	4,868	Fogarty, Park*	40,058
Bates, C. M	2,580	Furtt, Simon	1,900
Bigelow. E. W	2,400	Furtt, Daniel	1,900
Bigelow, E. W	1,689	Felton, D†	1,913
Byrne, James	2,490	Gregory, A. B	1,900
Brady, A. B*	4,708	Gepeard, George	5,639
Binkleman, D	2,064	Gad, B	1,898
Bennett, John	2,058	Galaway, Phillip*	3,544
Boury, G†	3,756	Greenwell, J. W†	2,525
Brown, J. H	7,274	Greenwell, S. J†	3,275
Baylis, J. H*	2,234	Gaskill, J. L†	7,546
Black. R. C†	1,804	Hawley, T. P	4,298
Bell, V. G†	2,138	Hinds, J. W	3,131
Colley, James	1,983	Hamilton. M. S	5,960
Crawford, W. H	4,124	Hunt, R. M	4,825
Clark, Jonathan	4,291	Hodue, Thomas	2,458
Cashin, John	5,020	Hasken, William*	2,393
Cohn, Jacob	1,898	Hunter, John R†	1,328
Coleman, Edward†	7,790	Henry, Samuel T †	2,335
Coleman, J. C*	7,768	Henderson, H	2,000
Corbett, E. S	2,963	Henry, William†	2,294
Caldwell, J. J.	1,800	Johnston, Peter	2,528
Cliff, William*	5,280	Johnston, John	2,528
Connolly, Ellen*	33,119	Judson, Orin†	3,428
Corbett, John*	4,736	Judson, Harw'd†	3,558
Colbert, Michael*	4,735	Kidd, George W*	3,749
Curmack, H†	4,619	Keeney, George	2,275
Crull, S. M†	4,799	Leavitt, C. C	5,079
Crull, J. St	5,362	Loutgenhisee, W*	6,025
Cadwalader, N†	27,190	Larimer, John*	3,150
Deal, M. S	2,400	Lee, S. W†	1,834
Davenport, T. T	5,120	Lloyd, Thomas*	3,200
Delano, A	7,500	Leech, Charles*	4,900
Dorsey, S. P	2,150	Laney, Thomas†	13,784
Dibble, A. B	3,654	Mackie, H	8,731
Daniel, William*	6,024	Marvillus, E. P†	2,609
Dornin, George D	3,410	Marsh, M. L	2,650
Dikeman, S. H†	2,032	McFarland, T. B	5,260
Enright, Michael†	2,738	Marsh, Charles	4,475
Edwards, J. R*	2,654	Mason, James B	2,523
Eddy, A. H†	3,138	Maguire. Thomas	3,526
Everett, Henry†	13,829	McDonald, G†	1,900
Effinger, John H†	3,400	Mull, E. W†	1,960
Ennis, Frank. †	2,875	Morian, F*	7,908
Finninger, R	3,420	Northy, E†	10,610
Farquhar, R. H	5,400	Nathan, B*	2,113
Fricot, J*	182,511	Nickell, G. W	2,888

O'Connor, M. P	$3,548	Stone, J. P	$1,936
Pierce, A*	6,900	Smith, C. C	1,963
Perry, S. E	1,850	Swan, A. B†	6,889
Phillips, Henry	5,713	Shardin, Charles†	1,893
Pralus, A*	89,681	Spooner, G. C†	8,019
Pollnier, Henry†	3,150	Smith, Francis	3,275
Quine, Patrick†	14,313	Smith, Jacob	1,900
Richards, F	1,833	Sheets, L. F†	2,840
Roads, W. H*	5,168	Tisdale, W. L*	4,884
Ripert, S*	80,096	Torson, O	3,104
Roberts, D. G*	31,400	Tower, A. D	3,806
Remington, M. L*	2,278	Tully, R. W	2,840
Rosmussan, P*	2,434	Turner, G. E	1,900
Rosendale, C. E†	4,966	Trenherth, J*	3,428
Spence, E. F	2,650	Thomas, John†	2,025
Sargent, A. A	5,321	Willian, B†	4,363
Swithenback, J	2,465	Whastenby, J†	25,165
Scaddin, Henry*	2,951	Werte, E. G	2,494
Silvester, H*	4,000	Watt, Robert*	42,890
Shaffer, George	2,453	Watt, William*	42,794
Smith, C. W	2,400	Whiting, L. L*	2,750
Smith, John	2,588	Williams, E†	8,575
Smith, Robert	2,588	Weil, A	2,960

This list is marked by a gentleman well acquainted in the county, but a few of those whose names are not marked may be miners. It appears that out of 148 names, 42 are those of quartz miners and 40 of placer miners. It must be remembered, however, that Nevada is the most prosperous and the most productive mining county in California, and that the proportion of large incomes among the miners is greater there than elsewhere.

23.—DIFFICULTY OF GETTING GOOD CLAIMS.

A fact which should never be overlooked on the Atlantic slope by persons who speak of mining is, that a good claim cannot be had by merely making an effort to get one. It costs as much effort generally as it costs to get a good farm, or more. If the claim is open and its value is established, it can only be bought at a high price. If it is not open, years may be spent in opening it, and then it may prove to be barren at last. That has been the experience of thousands. A list of the expensive tunnels and shafts undertaken in California and Nevada would include numerous failures after years of time and scores of thousands of dollars had been devoted to the labor. These things are not written, because few want to publish their own failures or to read about those of others; and a number of those who own mines famous for their rich yields had to struggle along for years, barely paying expenses and exposed to the jeers or the pity of their acquaintances for their obstinacy in sticking to claims that could never, it was said, be made to pay. It is unjust to the miner to assume that he is taking the public property without compensation. In most cases he has more than paid for it by his labor, and although it may not yield him a good income, it is no more than a fair return for his enterprise and industry, and he should be allowed to enjoy it as a proper encouragement to others to devote themselves to the development of other mines. Many, indeed, think that even with unrestrained liberty to take the precious metals from the public lands, and with entire exemption from taxation, the pay of the miner is less than that of any other equally industrious and intelligent body of laborers in the country.

24.—COMSTOCK LODE THE MOST PRODUCTIVE IN THE WORLD.

Although some rich argentiferous veins have been discovered in California, Idaho, and Arizona, they have not been developed sufficiently to enable us to say much of them; and our remarks on the condition of silver mining on the coast must be based chiefly upon the business as conducted in Nevada. During the last three years there has been no increase in the production, but the general condition is very satisfactory. The Comstock lode is now the most productive mineral vein in the world. A strip of land six hundred yards wide and three miles long yields $12,000,000 annually. There is no parallel to that in ancient or modern times. The other richest silver mining districts of the present century, such as Guanajuato, Zacatecas, Sombrerete, Durango, Chihuahua Alamos, Real del Monte, Potosi, Cero Paseo, and Chañarcillo, do not produce more than about $20,000,000 each annually, and the Comstock lode is now contributing more silver to the commerce of the world than any other four lodes. The total number of men employed in the mines and mills to obtain this metal is about 5,000, giving an average annual yield of $2,500 for each. The ore is not so rich nor so abundant as it has been in some Mexican lodes, but a greater yield has been obtained by employing more machinery. The general custom of the Mexican mines has been to employ men to carry the ore up out of the mine on their backs, and to transport it from the mine to the mill on mules, to pulverize it by mule power, and to stir it during amalgamation by tramping with the feet of men or mules. If water invaded the works it was hoisted by hand or by horse whims. Thus a Mexican mine required a hundred men to do the work that can be done in a Nevada mine by twenty, and it was difficult to make room for a hundred men to work within such narrow limits. Either they were continually in the way of one another or most of them discharged, and the work advanced with corresponding slowness.

The leading mines at Virginia City are marvellous for the extent of their works and the rapidity with which they extract and reduce the ore. The chief gold mines of California, high as their product is, are small affairs when compared with the vast works of the chief silver companies of Nevada.

25.—COMSTOCK MINING COMPANIES.

S. H. Marlette, surveyor general of the State, in his official report for the year 1865, gave the following list of the mining companies on the Comstock lode, with the accompanying statistics and remarks

Companies.	Length in feet.	Greatest depth reached.	Length of lode explored.
Utah	1,000	260	300
Allen	925	200	300
Sierra Nevada	2,157	410	400
Union	302	80	(*)
Ophir, N. mine	1,200	428	400
Mexican	100	620	100
Ophir, S. mine	200	620	200
Central	150	428	150
California	300	428	300
Empire, N	55	600	55
Eclipse	30	†595	30
French	20	†595	20
Empire, S. mine	20	550	20
Piato	10	550	10
Bowers	20	550	20
Piute	20	550	20
Winters & Kutstel	30	585	30
Consolidated 21 feet	21	585	21
Central No. 2	100	360	100
Kinney	50	369	(*)
White & Murphy	210	369	210

* 1 cross cut.   † Evidently an error, and much too large.

List of the mining companies on the Comstock lode, &c.—Continued.

Companies.	Length in feet.	Greatest depth reached.	Length of lode explored.
Sides	500	500	200
Best & Belcher	222	469	222
Gould & Curry	921	821	921
Savage	768	496	768
Hale & Norcross	400	700	200
Chollar Potosi	1,434	700	700
Bullion	940	*455	430
Exchequer	400	*540	None.
Alpha	278½	620	278½
Apple & Bates	31½	600	31½
Imperial (Alta)	118	600	118
Bacon	45	600	45
Rice Ground	13½	550	13½
Imperial, (H. and L.)	65⅞	550	65⅞
Challenge	50	554	50
Confidence	130	544	130
Burk & Hamilton	40	544	40
Yellow Jacket	957	430	......
Kentuck	90	300	Shaft.
Crown Point	540	301	540
Belcher	940	520	940
Segregated Belcher	160	500	160
Overman	1,200	640	1,200
North American	2,000	300	......
Baltimore American	2,000	300	......
	22,264		
Deduct 6 feet in dispute between Imperial and Apple & Bates' Cos.	6		
Total	22,258		

"The 'dead work' (*i. e.*, shafts, wings, tunnels, and excavations not in pay ore) of the Gould & Curry company equals about 12,750 lineal feet, (about 2 42/100 miles,) with an average cross-sectional area of thirty feet, or about 14,167 cubic yards.

"The companies enumerated above have excavated about 28 miles of tunnels and drifts, and about 5¾ miles of shafts, wings, and inclines, exclusive of stopes on ore chimneys, which will amount at least to as much more, giving a total of at least 67½ miles.

"The longest tunnel penetrating the Comstock lode is the Latrobe, 3,200 feet in length in a straight line, besides various branches, which was commenced in February, 1861, and is still being driven ahead. The above-mentioned companies have forty-four hoisting and pumping engines, which will probably average between thirty and forty horse-power, and give an aggregate of more than 1,500 horse power. The mines of the Comstock employ seventy-six mills for reducing their ores, with an aggregate capacity for crushing 1,800 tons daily, some of which are fourteen miles from the mines, the ore being transported on wagons.

"There is consumed annually by these companies about 22,265 cords of wood, at a cost of not far from sixteen dollars per cord, and a total cost of more than one-third of a million of dollars; and they use about 15,540,120 feet, board

* Evidently an error, and much too large.

measure, of timber and lumber, all of which must be transported long distances on wagons, at a cost of about forty dollars per thousand, or a total cost of nearly two thirds of a million of dollars. Thus, for wood and timber, we have a total annual cost of one million of dollars."

26.—QUARTZ MILLS IN NEVADA.

Surveyor General Martlett, in the report for 1865, gives the following figures of the quartz mills in the State:

Counties.	Steam.	Water.	Total.	Horse-power of engines.	No. of stamps.
Churchill	......	......	......	......	......
Douglas	......	......	......	......	......
Esmeralda	12	1	17	497	169
Humboldt	1	......	1	......	......
Lander	16	3	19	......	163
Lyon	21	9	34	940	508
Nye	......	......	4	......	38
Ormsby	......	......	......	......	......
Roop	......	......	......	......	......
Storey	......	......	36	1,510	623
Washoe	9	1	10	......	60

Capacity and machinery of Comstock mills.

The Mining and Scientific Press published the following quartz mills in Virginia City and the vicinity, with the name, the number of tons reduced per month, the number of stamps, and the kind of machinery used in reduction.

Quartz mills in Virginia City and the vicinity, with the name, the number of tons reduced per month, the number of stamps, and the kind of machinery used in reduction.

Location and name of mill.	Tons per month.	Number of stamps.	Remarks.
Virginia City.			
Summit	900	20	11 Wheeler pans, 4 settlers, 1 small Varney pan and settler, 1 agitator.
Central	670	13	4 Hepburn pans and 4 settlers, working 500 tons, wet; 4 furnaces and 6 barrels, working 170 tons, dry.
Ogden	1,000	22	12 Wheeler pans and 4 settlers.
Empire	800	21	24 Knox and 2 Wheeler pans.
Hoosier State	400	8	24 Knox pans.
Seven Mile Cañon.			
Mariposa	600	12	6 Wheeler pans, prospecting battery, 2 Knox pans and 3 large settlers.
Chas. Land's	1,000	20	1 Blake's breaker, 19 Wheeler pans, 5 settlers, and 2 grinders for grinding amalgam and work'g slum.
Bassett's	700	16	4 improved Wheeler and 2 Hepburn pans, 2 tubs, and 3 settlers.

Quartz mills in Virginia City, &c.—Continued.

Location and name of mill.	Tons per month.	Number of star'ps.	Remarks.
Winfield, or Booth's ...	1,000	18	1 Blake's breaker, 8 Hepburn pans, 1 grinder, and 4 settlers.
Gould & Curry.........	3,502	80	39 Hepburn pans, 3 Varney pans, and 21 settlers.
Empire State	700	15	2 Hepburn, 2 Wheeler, and 20 4-feet Knox pans.
G. Atwood's, Fly Deland's	600	15	26 Knox pans, 2 Wheeler pans, and 2 settlers.
Gold Hill and Gold Cañon.			
Eclipse	700	15	8 Hepburn pans, 2 grinders, and 4 settlers.
Crown Point	200	8	13 Knox pans and tubs.
Rhode Island Cr. P't Co.	1,350	25	8 Hepburn and 10 7-feet Knox pans.
Union................	400	14	14 tubs and 1 agitator.
Gold Hill	475	14	24 Knox pans, 6 6-feet tubs, and 4 settlers.
Sapphire	800	16	56 Knox pans.
Petaluma	300	8	18 Knox pans.
Imperial	1,100	44	74 Knox pans.
Empire	900	16	12 Wheeler pans, 6 settlers, and 2 concentrators.
Marysville	500	9	30 5-feet plain pans and 2 agitators.
Douglass	450	10	26 plain pans and 1 agitator.
Atlas	750	15	8 Hepburn pans and 4 settlers.
Piute, Pinte Co......	1,200	20	12 Hepburn pans, 6 8-feet settlers, and 1 grinder.
Pacific, Alpha Co.....	1,300	30	15 Wheeler pans, 5 large settlers, and 2 grinders.
Succor...............	600	20	2 Hepburn pans, 24 Wheeler flat-bottom pans, 1 settler, and 1 agitator.
Confidence	650	12	8 Varney pans, 5 settlers, and 3 agitators.
G. C. Reduction	600	15	6 Hepburn and 4 5-feet flat-bottom pans.
Phœnix	500	16	6 pans and 4 settlers.
Eastern Slope	550	12	6 Hepburn pans and 3 large settlers.
Swansea..............	600	12	22 6-feet tubs, 3 settlers, prospecting battery, and pan.
Excelsior	530	10	18 Knox pans and 1 settler.
Sacramento	550	12	12 7-feet iron pans and 1 agitator.
Weston's	700	15	9 Wheeler pans, 5 settlers, and 1 agitator.
On Carson river, from Empire to Dayton.			
Mexican	1,260	44	12 Hepburn pans, 4 furnaces, and 10 barrels; by wet process, 1,000 tons; by dry process, 260 tons.
Yellow Jacket........	2,300	40	30 Hepburn pans, 15 settlers, 2 agitators, and 2 grinders.
Brunswick	600	8	8 Varney pans and 4 agitators.
Merrimac	2,350	20	15 Wheeler, 4 Knox, and 1 Varney pan, prospecting battery and pan, 6 large settlers, and 10 agitators.
Vivian...............	750	16	8 Wheeler pans, 4 settlers, and 1 agitator.
Santiago	1,100	24	1 Blake's breaker, 14 Wheeler and 4 Hepburn pans and 9 settlers.
Eureka	1,100	20	10 Wheeler pans, 5 settlers, and 2 agitators.
San Francisco	500	10	3 Hepburn pans and 7 tubs.
Franklin.............	500	10	2 Wheeler and 2 Hepburn pans, 5 tubs, and 2 settlers.
Island	500	10	10 Varney pans and 3 settlers.
Ophir Co.'s..........	1,200	24	12 Hepburn pans and 6 settlers.
Dayton, No. 1........	500	20	6 Wheeler pans, 2 8-feet settlers, and 2 agitators.
Dayton, No. 2........	800	15	8 Varney pans, 4 settlers, and 3 agitators.
Birdsall & Carpenter...	2,400	30	20 Wheeler pans, 10 large size Wheeler settlers, 5 agitators, 1 grinder, and 1 Blake's rock breaker.
Golden Eagle	500	10	24 Knox pans and 1 settler.
Illinois	500	20	6 Hepburn pans, 2 settlers and 3 agitators.

Quartz mills in Virginia City, &c.—Continued.

Location and name of mill.	Tons per month.	Number of stamps.	Remarks.
Imperial Co.'s, Black P't	2,400	56	Blake's breaker, large size, 14 Hepburn pans, 27 7-feet tubs, and 7 7-feet settlers.
American Flat.			
Bay State............	1,400	23	14 Wheeler pans and 7 settlers.
Bigby & Co..........	400	10	5 Varney pans and 4 settlers, 1 extra pan and settler for tailings, and 1 barrel.
Washoe Valley and vicinity.			
Temelec	800	15	12 Wheeler pans and 2 large settlers.
Manhattan N. Y. Co ..	1,300	24	16 pans, 8 settlers, and 1 grinder.
New York..............	1,300	24	16 Varney pans, 6 settlers, and 1 grinder.
Atchison Savage Co....	1,200	20	1 breaker, 16 Wheeler pans, and 8 settlers.
Minnesota Savage Co...	1,000	16	1 breaker, 12 Wheeler pans, 6 settlers, and 1 agita'r.
Buckeye..	700	10	1 breaker, 8 Wheeler pans, and 4 settlers.
Ophir Co.'s..	450	72	Working only 36 stamps, (Freiberg process,) 9 furnaces, 24 amalgamating barrels; work 43 men; full capacity of mill, 750 tons.
J. H. Ball's...........	1,725	60	2 Blake's breakers, 8 furnaces, 20 barrels, 6 Varney and 4 Wheeler and Randall pans.

It appears from this table that there are 331 Knox's pans, 226 Wheeler's pans, 190 Hepburn's pans, 58 Varney's pans, 94 plain pans, 24 Wakelee's pans, 213 settlers, 37 agitators, 12 grinders, 59 barrels, 77 tubs, and two concentrators in use at these mills. Under the head of amalgamating machinery, though not strictly in place, the breakers are mentioned. The list includes 62 mills, 1,226 stamps, 919 pans. The total amount of ore reduced per month is given at 53,787 tons, but the capacity is considerably greater.

27.—THE PAN.

The pan, which is the chief instrument used in the amalgamation of the silver ores of Nevada, is of cast iron, two feet deep, and from two to seven feet in diameter—usually four and a half; to the bottom are fastened dies or movable pieces of iron which form a false bottom, and can be replaced by others when worn out. A shaft rises through the centre of the pan, and to it are fastened shoes or pieces of iron which are to run round over the false bottom and grind the pulp. Many of the pans have chambers at the bottom for steam, which is to keep the pulp at a heat of about 200°.

28.—THE WHEELER PAN.

The above is a description of the general features of the plain pan, the Wheeler pan, and the Varney pan. The Wheeler pan has curved grooves in the bottom, running from the centre to the rim, to hold the quicksilver. To the sides above the mullers are fastened boards so shaped as to throw the pulp to the centre. But for these boards the pulp would move as fast as the muller, sixty revolutions per minute, and might run over at the sides, and would not be brought into proper contact with the quicksilver at the bottom; whereas by throwing the pulp to the centre the current is broken, the heavy matter sinks to the bottom to be ground, and be mixed with the quicksilver.

29.—THE VARNEY PAN.

The Varney pan has a flat bottom, and is made to grind as well as amalgamate. The speed is greater and the pulp thinner than in the Hepburn. Some vertical pieces of sheet iron, which run from the side of the pan with a curve towards the centre, and in a direction contrary to that in which the muller runs, bring all the pulp successively under the muller. Near the centre there are holes in the muller, into which the heavier matter sinks, and from there it is carried out under the muller, being ground as it passes along. The muller does not reach quite to the side of the pan, so a little space is left there for quicksilver.

30.—KNOX'S PAN.

Knox's pan, which is used more than any other, is the simplest of the pans. It is used to amalgamate only, not to grind. Four boards, crossing one another at right angles, are set vertically in the pan, over the mullers so as to keep the surface of the pulp still. If the boards were not there the pulp would run round with the mullers and the ore would not be brought so well in contact with the quicksilver. The mullers run slow, making ten or twenty revolutions per minute.

31.—HEPBURN PAN.

The "Hepburn pan," as it is commonly known, or, as it is styled by the patentees, the "Hepburn and Peterson pan," which ranks third in the extent of use, has a bottom shaped like an inverted cone, with sides sloping up from the centre at an angle of 45°. The muller sets on this slope, and the pulp, which is mixed with only a little water so as to make a thick paste, runs up under the muller, flows inward over the edge, runs down over its upper surface to the centre, where it again turns to run up under the muller. Thus a constant current is maintained, and every particle of the pulp is successively ground and brought into contact with the quicksilver. The Hepburn pan is made with hard iron mullers and false bottom so as to grind well, and if the ore goes in coarse it comes out fine. The muller makes from forty to sixty revolutions per minute, and a large pan will take half a ton of ore at a charge and amalgamate it thoroughly in three hours.

32.—THE WHEELER AND RANDALL PAN.

It is evident that the iron in Hepburn's pan must be ground as well as the ore, and that the grinding will be the greatest at the sides of the pan and least at the centre. Thus it is that in the flat-bottom pan it is frequently necessary to get new mullers and new false bottoms or dies. To remedy this evil, and to make a pan in which, however much the wear, the muller shall fit close to the bottom, the Wheeler and Randall pan was invented. The bottom of this slopes upwards from the rim; but the slope, instead of being straight, as in the Hepburn, curves inward on the line called the tractory curve. The muller has the same curve, and no matter how much it wears it always fits close to the bottom. The same inventors have another pan made on the same principle, but with the point turned down instead of up. These pans have not come into extensive use, but they are mentioned here to show what experiments have been tried in the mechanical construction of pans.

33.—ESTIMATED YIELD OF VARIOUS MINES.

According to the estimate of Mr. Marlette, the following companies had taken out before the 1st September, 1865, the amounts set opposite their respective names :

Gould & Curry	$14,000,000
Opbir	7,000,000
Savage	3,647,764
Imperial	2,500,000
Yellow Jacket	1,891,916
Belcher	1,462,005
Total for six companies	30,502,085

34.—ASSESSMENTS LEVIED.

The following table gives a few instances of the manner in which money has been put into mines on the Comstock lode:

Mines.	Feet.	Assessment per foot.	Total assessment.
Yellow Jacket	1,200	$400	$480,000
Sierra Nevada	3,000	116	348,000
Alpha	278	1,210	336,380
Savage	800	235	188,000
Crown Point	600	290	174,000
Best & Belcher	224	580	119,920
Hale & Norcross	400	875	350,000
White & Murphy	210	303	63,630
Imperial	184	270	49,680
North Potosi	2,000	140	280,000
Total			2,289,610

This list does not include one-half of the amount of assessments levied by well-known companies, and several millions have been advanced in cash by capitalists in San Francisco for prospecting and opening mines which never were heard of, except by a few who spent their money and their friends'. A Mexican proverb says, "It takes a mine to work a mine."

35.—THE GOULD AND CURRY MINE.

The following figures of the operations of the Gould & Curry Company are taken from official reports:

Years.	Receipts.	Dividends.	Tons extracted	Percentage of dividends.	Average yield of ore per ton.
1862	$900,743		8,427		$104 50
1863	3,917,937	$1,464,400	48,743	34	80 40
1864	4,898,060	1,440,000	67,443	29	73 48
1865	2,395,242	618,000	46,022	25	50 76
Half of 1866	908,119	156,000	17,890	17	36 90
Total	13,020,101	3,678,400	188,525	28	69 06

The mine was not opened until 1862, and before it began to pay its way the sum of $175,000, or $148 per foot, had been levied as assessments. The dividends commenced in 1863, and for that year alone amounted to more than $1,000 a foot; and also for the next year, although very large sums were expended in building a mill and in making other improvements. The average yield of the ore, however, and the percentage of the dividends, decreased with each year. The ore was nearly twice as rich in 1863 as in 1865, and the expenses in the former year were greater than the gross receipts of the latter.

The total number of tons extracted in four years was 173,000, or a mass of 165 cubic feet, and the bullion produced amounted to about 300 tons of 2,000 pounds of 12 troy ounces each. The expenses of the mine and mill in 1865 were the following:

Total expense at mine	$609, 135 97

Under this head come the following items:

Labor at mine	298, 055 62
Contracts for tunnels, drifts, &c	37, 323 50
Lumber and timber	147, 382 92
Freight from California	11, 357 86

Total expenses at the reduction works	$356, 865 81

Under this head come these items among others:

Labor	160, 260 22
Hauling ore to mill by contract	32, 489 83
Firewood	206, 749 32
Foundry work	33, 188 30
Hardware	12, 631 28
Sulphate of copper	12, 747 56
Quicksilver	9, 903 98
Salt	15, 885 54
Water	10, 416 84
Oil, candles, &c	8, 440 78
Freight from California	20, 993 89

The following are further figures from the president's report for 1864:

Cost of extracting ores from mine, per ton	$10 84
Cost of reducing third-class ore at Gould & Curry mill	14 46
Cost of reducing third-class ore at Custom mills	21 82
Cost of reducing second-class ore at Custom mills	50 00
Average yield of all ores reduced, per ton	50 76
Average yield of second-class ore	255 66
Average yield of third-class ore at Gould & Curry mill	44 26
Average yield of all ores reduced at Custom mills	45 12

The following is a statement of the operations and expenses of the Gould & Curry mill, (which, however, did not reduce all the ore produced by the mine) for the six months ending May 31, 1866:

The pay of officers, general laborers, watchmen, teamsters, &c., was $14,354 88.

The cost of the driving power was, $10,565 87 for labor; $85,996 for wood; $2,618 for sundries; $99,179 87 in all.

The cost of preparing ore for the batteries was, $8,913 23 for labor; $828 for sundries; $9,741 23 total.

The cost of the batteries was, $14,266 38 for labor; $4,546 for shoes, dies, &c.; $2,002 for sundries; total, $20,814 38.

The cost of amalgamating was, $15,421 13 for labor; $1,363 for retort wood; $12,037 for shoes and dies; $5,794 for salt; $12,256 for sulphate of copper; $17,822 for quicksilver; $2,232 for sundries; total, $66,925 13.

The cost of repairs was, $16,424 48 for labor; $15,402 for sundries; total, $31,826 48.

The total expense of the mill was $79,945 97 for labor; $162,896 for material; total, $242,841 97.

The amount of ore delivered at the mill was 20,744 tons; the amount amalgamated was 17,890 tons. The difference of 2,854 tons "shows the loss of ores carried off in slimes."

The value of the ore and of the bullion produced was the following:

	Gold.	Silver.	Samples.	Total.
Value of ore....................	$185,765 12	$639,598 21	....	$825,363 33
Bullion produced..............	211,712 69	448,036 76	$507 72	660,257 17

[The excess of gold in the "bullion produced" over that in the "value of ore," must be accounted for by supposing that the samples assayed did not fully represent the average value of the ore.]

The average assay per ton was $46 13; the average yield was $36 90; the amount lost was 20 per cent. The total cost of reduction per ton amalgamated was $13 57.

The cost of reduction per ton was $0 80.23 for officers, watchmen, and laborers; $5 54.37 for driving power; $0 55.04 for preparing ore for batteries; $1 16.33 for batteries; $3 73.50 for amalgamation; $1 77.88 for repairs, and $13 57 in all.

The expenses of the mine during the six months were the following:

The salaries of officers were $6,766, or 20 cents per ton.

The cost of extracting ore was $103,042 99, or $3 06 per ton.

The cost of prospecting and dead-work was $68,631 04, or $2 04 per ton.

The cost of accessory work, $56,308 38, or $1 67 per ton.

The cost of improvements was $19,876 52, or 59 cents per ton.

The total cost of salaries of officers, extraction of ore, prospecting and dead work, accessory work, and improvements was $254,624 93, or $7 56 per ton.

The amount of ore produced was 33,705 tons.

The amount of bullion produced from the Gould & Curry ore by outside mills was $227,085 81, and the total receipts of the company for six months, $908,119 25.

The expenses were $254,624 93 for the mine; $243,131 97 for the Gould & Curry mill; $7,777 61 for assays; $128,404 83 for reducing ores at outside mills; $27,285 53 for general expenses, and $6,375 76 for the boarding-house. Total, $667,600 63.

36.—THE OPHIR MINE.

The Ophir company has tried and compared the yard, the barrel, and the pan processes of amalgamation, and the general result of their experience is that the yard process costs $30 per ton, and loses 20 per cent. of the metal; the barrel process costs $28, and loses 15 or 20 per cent. of the metal; and the pan process costs $15 per ton, and loses from 35 to 40 per cent. of the metal. They have abandoned the yard process, as unsuited to the climate and having no advantages; the barrel is retained for ore yielding $90 per ton or upwards; and the pan is preferred for poor ore. Ore containing $150 per ton will yield, at 80 per cent., $120 to the barrel, leaving $92 after subtracting $28 in the cost of working; whereas the same ore would give, at 65 per cent., a gross yield of $97 50, and a net yield of $82 50 to the pan, showing an advantage of $9 50 per ton in favor of the barrel. By the same mode of calculation ore containing $50 to the ton will yield $12 net to the barrel, and $17 50 net to the pan. Ore containing $80 to the ton gives about an equal net yield to the barrel and the pan. The following are the figures of some of the operations of the Ophir company for the year ending November 30, 1864:

	Tons worked.	Value.	Yield.	Cost per ton.
Barrel	4,554	$601,653 99	$519,703 38	$32 05
Yard	3,336	299,825 85	248,947 65	32 37

Since 1864 the cost of barrel amalgamation has been reduced to $28 per ton. In 1865 the barrel and pan were used, and the following figures show the amount of bullion produced, and the sums and proportions of gold and silver in it:

	Gold.	Silver.	Total.	Ratio of gold.
Barrel	$64,816 27	$178,747 61	$243,563 88	26 per cent.
Pan	115,029 16	96,247 72	211,876 88	54 per cent.

The qualities of ore used in the two processes were different, but the proportions of gold and silver were about the same; and hence it appears that the barrel loses the gold and the pan loses the silver. The value of the ore submitted to the barrel process in 1865 was $332,273 61, and the total bullion obtained, including some not represented in the above table, was $269,327 94, showing a loss of $62,945 67, or 18 per cent. The bullion obtained from the barrels was worth $1 05 per ounce, and, therefore, must have contained a considerable proportion of base metal, since one-fourth in value was gold, and pure silver alone is worth $1 33 per ounce. The pan bullion was worth $2 31 per ounce, or more than twice as much as the barrel bullion.

37.—THE SAVAGE MINE

At the annual meeting of the stockholders of the Savage Mining Company, on the 10th of July, 1866, Alpheus Bull, president, submitted a report, in which he said: -

"By reference to the annual reports heretofore made I find the first ore taken from the mine was in April, 1863. The total number of tons extracted up to July, 1865, (26 months,) was 81,183, or 3,122 tons a month. The entire yield of bullion from the above number of tons amounted to $3,600,709 26, being an average of $44 35 per ton.

"During these twenty-six months there was disbursed $2,939,808 76, besides paying over $800,000 in dividends. For reduction alone there was paid $1,682,701 44, almost fifty per cent. of the gross yield of the mine.

"The total production of ores the past year was 30,653 tons, of which there were reduced 20,535 tons, yielding bullion of the value of $1,303,852 91, or an average of $44 14 per ton, at a cost for reduction of $16 74 per ton. Notwithstanding there was less ore extracted during the year just ended, and the average value per ton a little less than the preceding years, yet the net earnings of the company are in favor of last year's operations. The cost for extraction of ores the past year is certainly high, but this is justly chargeable to the extensive improvements in building machinery and explorations in the mine, the practical benefits of which will be derived by the stockholders at some future period."

H. Ex. Doc. 29——6

The superintendent's report for the year ending on the 1st of July, 1866, gives the following figures relative to the ore extracted:

	Extracted. Tons.	Total yield.	Yield per ton.
First class	435	$93,220 04	$224 09
Second class	26,338	1,096,449 23	42 04
Third class	3,879	62,084 54	20 43
Total	30,652	1,251,753 81	....

Average yield of all ore reduced, per ton, $42 38.

During the last four months preceding the date of the report the cost of reduction had varied from $11 69 to $12 95 per ton.

38.—THE YELLOW JACKET MINE.

The following statistics of the yield of the Yellow Jacket Silver Mining Company for the year ending July 1, 1866, are taken from the annual reports made by the officers of the company:

218 tons first-class ore worked, yielded, per ton	$172 05
53,307 tons second-class worked, yielded, per ton	31 00
1,479 tons sold, yielded, per ton	3 26
Average of all ore worked per ton	32 51

Gross product of bullion from ores worked	$1,690,394 82
Gross product of ore sold	4,833 88
Total product	1,695,228 70

Assessments to the amount of $300,000 were collected, and no dividends were declared during the year, but a debt of $379,771 was paid off and a surplus of $142,915 remained on hand at the end of the year. Among the expenditures are the following items:

Crushing ore at outside mills	$507,438 23
Crushing ore at company's mills	352,178 81
Total cost of crushing	859,617 04

The term "crushing" here must include all the process of reduction, and the cost is about half the total yield of the ore worked.

39.—THE CROWN POINT MINE.

It appears from the annual report of the Crown Point Mining Company for the year ending May 1, 1866, that the recepts from the mine in that period were $659,191 37; the number of tons reduced, 18,259½; and the average yield per ton $37 33. Excluding about $8,000 of assay chips and bullion sold, there was $243,967 86 in gold and $437,207 27 in silver. The average cost of extracting the ore was $8 97. The cost of reduction is not given precisely.

40.—THE HALE AND NORCROSS MINE.

The Hale and Norcross Silver Mining Company own 400 feet on the Comstock lode. They commenced operations in 1862, and worked on for four years, at great expense, before they found any considerable body of ore to reward them.

They levied and collected assessments to the amount of $875 per foot, making a total for the company of $350,000 invested before any return began to come in. In February, 1866, 1,261 tons were taken out, and the amount has since steadily increased. September yielded 2,152 tons, and the eight months from February to September, inclusive, 16,986 tons, which produced $736,394 32 in bullion; an average of $43 35 per ton.

41.—THE IMPERIAL MINE.

The total receipts of the Imperial Mining Company, from the beginning of its operations to the 31st of May, 1866, were $259,133 80, including $50,000 of assessments. The dividends paid amounted to $527,500. The following are certain figures for the years ending May 31, 1865, and May 31, 1866:

	1865.	1866.
Tons extracted	28,236	34,735
Total yield	$854,630 56	$1,019,275 91
Average yield per ton	22 14	29 90
Cost of extraction per ton	5 37	5 49

The bullion for 1866 was worth $2 02 per ounce on average, the fineness in gold being .039 and in silver .942.

The cost of reducing 11,404 tons of ore at the Gold Hill mill was $8 66 per ton, and at the Rock Point mill, (where 23,227 tons were reduced,) $10 15 per ton.

42.—THE EMPIRE MINE.

The following are extracts from a report made by Benjamin Lilliman on the Empire mine on the 2d of December, 1864:

"Up to this time (November 30) this company have crushed, since their organization on March 7, 1863, about 25,000 tons (of 2,000 pounds) of ores in their own and other mills, and have received from it, for the same period, in bullion, one million forty-three thousand seven hundred and twenty dollars and forty-eight cents ($1,043,720 43,) as appears by the bullion receipts which I have examined. The actual value received by the company in working their ores has been, therefore, $40 76 per ton of 2,000 pounds. The amount lost in tailings it is impossible to fix, but we are justified, from the general experience of the mills working on the Comstock ores, in assuming the loss to be at least one-third of the total value extracted." * * * * "There has never been an assessment on the mine, nor was there any capital stock paid in. The *nominal* capital was one million of dollars. But the mine has paid for every-thing, besides paying its fortunate owners $308,000 above all costs and charges."

"If from the balance of		$731,720 48
We deduct the cost of the mill in 1863	$60,000	
Mill in Virginia City	75,000	
New shaft and present improvements to 1864	70,000	
		205,000 00
There remains for the presumed cost of mining and milling		526,720 48"

The president of the company, in his report for the year ending November 30, 1865, says:

"The receipts of the year, from all sources, amount to the sum of $543,081 79, and the total disbursements to $525,129 79, of which $120,000 have been paid in dividends to stockholders." * * * * "At the mine, during the year, the main shaft has been sunk 133 feet, and drifts run, at various levels 965 feet, consuming 554,500 feet of timber."

During the year 20,500 tons were extracted from the Empire mine, and the bullion produced amounted to $485,542 49, including $185,452 30 in gold and $298,929 96 in silver. The bullion was worth $2 02½ per ounce; weighed 240,812.20 troy ounces before melting, and 239,707.95 ounces after melting.

43.—PRODUCTIVE MINES OF REESE RIVER.

The following statement of the amount of bullion produced by the mines of Lander county, Nevada, during the quarter ending September 30, 1866, is taken from a report by the county assessor:

Name of mine.	Tons.	Pounds.	Average per ton.
Great Eastern	412	659	$176 82
Fortuna	23	....	85 71
North River	29	536	217 56
Troy	2	1,000	83 82
Diamond	1	402	132 57
Blind Ledge	2	1,965	128 64
Semanthe	2	774	276 97
Othello	5	1,105	36 35
Idora	16	1,237	212 62
Eastern Oregon	1	....	86 46
Foster	26	1,212	48 47
La Plate	50	882	71 60
Chase & Zent	4	1,000	362 04
Canada	6	1,500	132 90
Eldorado	2	568	291 58
Magnolia	4	1,171	259 93
Washington	4	88	187 43
Morgan & Muncey	17	634	107 75
Diana	17	563	180 40
Detroit	14	1,800	116 18
Camargo	39	....	90 77
Timoke	28	253	167 92
Dover	2	450	161 64
Isabella	19	503	40 08
Harding & Dickman	1	1,233	87 19
Providential	79	1,000	39 04
Cortez Giant	227	....	65 07
Folsom	5	1,019	166 00
Savage Consol, No. 1	160	....	156 83
Savage Consol, No. 2	230	....	74 00

44.—YIELD OF VARIOUS SILVER DISTRICTS.

The total annual yield of Lander county, Nevada, (or, as it is often called, Reese River region,) is about $900,000, and the yield of the Owyhee district in silver is about $1,500,000; so that this latter is next to Virginia City among the silver producing districts of the United States, and it has the resources to increase its production greatly within a few years. The yield of Esmeralda was nearly $1,000,000 in 1863, but it is now not $100,000, and the Humboldt district does not produce more than $50,000.

45.—IMPROVEMENTS IN SILVER MINING.

Although the silver mining at the Comstock lode is not in a satisfactory condition, it is at least progressive, and there is a certainty of steady improvement for a long time. So far as the extraction of the ore is concerned, there is nothing better anywhere. The pumping and hoisting are done by machinery of unsurpassed excellence. A machine has been invented for lowering men with safety into the mine, and another for framing the timbers to be used in supporting the sides and roofs of drifts. It is in the reduction department that the chief defect exists. For a long time most of the ore was sent to custom mills, and as they were paid a certain sum per ton, it was their interest to reduce as much as possible without special regard to the thoroughness. For years this was the only method of obtaining any return from most mines; and besides, it was in accordance with the custom of the silver miners of Mexico, Peru, and Bolivia, where for centuries the mines and the reduction works have belonged to distinct classes. *

But in time it became evident that the most productive mines must have reduction works of their own, and now they are provided with magnificent mills, in which the processes of pulverization and amalgamation are carefully studied by many careful and competent men; and they will undoubtedly make valuable contributions to the metallurgy of silver within a few years. Although the expenditures in the large silver mines are immense, they are not extravagant. The general financial affairs are very carefully studied and strictly managed. The operations are so extensive, the amount of material consumed is so great, and labor is so high, no small sums of money suffice. The completion of the railroad from Sacramento to Virginia City will reduce the cost of wood, and of various other important supplies, nearly or quite fifty per cent. and will be followed by consequent reduction in the price of labor; and the completion of the Sutro tunnel will reduce the cost of draining and ventilating the mines and of extracting the ore. The railroad may be in running order within a year; the tunnel will not be finished for several years at least.

SECTION 4.

RESOURCES OF NEVADA, OREGON, WASHINGTON TERRITORY, UTAH, MONTANA, AND IDAHO.

1. Historical sketch of Nevada.—2. Geography and products of Nevada.—3. Mines and mineral resources of Nevada.—4. Mining property, &c.—5. General view of the mines of Nevada, Oregon, Washington Territory, Utah, Montana, and Idaho.

1. HISTORICAL SKETCH OF NEVADA.

Boundaries.—The State of Nevada, erected from the former Territory of Nevada, extends easterly and westerly from the 37th to the 43d meridian west from Washington, and from the 42d degree of north latitude to Arizona, having Oregon and Idaho on the north, Utah on the east, Arizona on the south, and

* H. G. Ward, in his book on Mexico, speaks there of the reduction works in the leading mining districts of that country: "The haciendas are mostly close to Guanajuato, and though now in ruins, their number and extent attest both the former importance of the mines and the opulence of the *rescatadores* (amalgamators,) by whom these extensive buildings were raised. Few or none of them possessed a sufficiency of water to work their machinery, for which purpose mules were employed, and 14,000 of these animals were in daily use (to work the arrastras and tread the ores in the *patio*) before the revolution. The *rescatadores* purchased their ores at the mouths of the shafts, relying entirely on their own powers of estimating by the eye the value of the *montones* (heaps) exposed for sale in such a manner as not to make a disadvantageous bargain. In this science they attained great perfection; for more fortunes were made in Guanajuato by amalgamation works than by miners themselves; while the extent to which the system was carried afforded to the successful adventurer the means of realizing instantly almost to any amount. During the great *bonanza* (rich yield) of the Valenciana mine, sales were effected to the amount of $80,000 in one day; and it is to this facility in obtaining supplies that the rapid progress of the works in that mine, after its first discovery, may be ascribed. Had it been necessary to erect private amalgamation works in order to turn his new born riches to account, many years must have elapsed before the first Count Valenciana could have derived any advantage from his labors; for when fortune began to smile upon them, the man who was destined in a few years to rank as one of the richest individuals in the world did not possess a single dollar."

California on the southwest and west; comprising within its limits an area of 80,239 square miles. This region was a portion of the territory acquired by the United States from Mexico under the treaty of Guadalupe Hidalgo, belonging previous to its transfer to the "department of Alta California." Prior to its acquisition by our government it was inhabited only by the aboriginal races, there being no settlements of civilized people, not even a mission, within its borders. At the time of the discovery of silver in 1859, ten years after its first settlement by the whites, it contained less than one thousand inhabitants, which number, two years later, had increased to nearly 17,000, as appears by the census returns taken in August, 1861; the estimated population of the State being at present between thirty-five and forty thousand, at which number it has remained nearly stationary for the past three years.

The aboriginal races.—These consist of three or four principal nations, divided into many small communities or families, sparsely scattered over the entire country. These nations are the Washoes, inhabiting a succession of small valleys along the western border of the State, the Pah-Utahs occupying the balance and greater portion of the western; while the third division, the Shoshones—hold the eastern part of the State. Some have considered, and perhaps properly, the Pannocks, a race dwelling in the northern and northeastern portions of the State, as a distinct nation. With the exception of the last named, these Indians, though often at variance among themselves, are naturally peaceful and inoffensive, being distinguished less for their warlike propensities than a good natured indifference as to what is going on around them. They have never manifested any great degree of hostility towards the whites, nor seriously objected to the latter entering and settling in their country, their opposition generally extending no further than an occasional protest against the destruction of their pine orchards, upon the fruits of which they are largely dependent for their subsistence. The Washoes, though the least numerous of these tribes, have always been remarked for their honesty and friendliness towards strangers. These Indians, though somewhat nomadic in their habits, have their favorite places of abode, these being generally along the rivers or about the sinks and lakes where fish and wild fowl are to be obtained. These localities usually form their winter homes, much of their time during the summer and autumn being spent in the mountains, where alone is found the pinon, a species of scrubby pine, the nut of which forms with them a staple article of food. These people cultivate no land, depending entirely on the natural products of the country for a livelihood, and as these are not numerous or abundant they sometimes suffer from want. They build no houses, scarcely even a wigwam; a few sage brush or willows put up to break the force of the wind, affording them, even in winter, ample protection. Few of them own horses, fire-arms, or other property of value, the whole race being distinguished for extreme poverty. Formerly they dressed in the skins of wild animals, as many of them still do, the skins of the hare being chiefly used for this purpose. Latterly they are becoming addicted to a more civilized but scarcely improved style of dress, clothing themselves with the cast-off garments of the whites. The women are by nature modest and chaste, and, as among most savages, have to perform the greater part of the labor necessary to their own sustenance as well as that of the men. Taken as a whole, these cannot be considered a bad race of Indians, exhibiting few of the savage and murderous traits that distinguish the tribes further in the interior; and though shiftless and indolent they are not averse to work where favorable opportunities offer. Many of them are now employed by the whites, being found very useful in various kinds of unskilled labor. Two reservations have been set apart in the State for the use of these Indians; but as yet no thorough and systematic measures have been adopted for retaining them at these places or for instructing them in the arts of civilized life, nor is it likely that much will be accomplished towards that end through the agency of these reservations. Since their intercourse with the whites these people have become demoralized, and the increase of physical maladies among those of them thus exposed has already sensibly diminished their numbers.

First settlements by the whites.—The first settlements within the limits of this State were made in 1848 by the Mormons, some of whom, in passing back and forth between California and Salt Lake, observing the excellence of the land, located in Carson and Washoe valleys. The following year they were joined by a few adventurers, who, attracted by the gold discoveries in California, had made the journey overland, but stopped on finding here the object for which they had set out. From this time the population gradually increased, until, in the summer of 1859, it had been swelled to the number already stated, notwithstanding most of the Mormons had meantime left, having, by a mandate of the church, been ordered to repair to Salt Lake. Up to this period the crossing of the Sierra Nevada, in the absence of wagon roads or even tolerable trails, was an arduous task; yet quite a good many came over from California, bringing provisions to exchange for the famished stock of the immigrants, and finding here good pasturage, some remained and finally became permanent settlers. Meanwhile a few were drawn from that State by the gold diggings or a mere love of adventure, a few also being added by the overland immigration, thus making up a population so considerable in a country difficult of access and otherwise possessing so few attractions.

The gold discovery.—This event occurred, as above intimated, in the summer of 1849, being the result of examinations made by a party just arrived on their way to California across the plains. The first gold found was at a point near Carson river where the emigrant road crosses Gold cañon, and where the town of Dayton now stands. This cañon is a deep ravine coming down from the high range of mountains six miles to the west, and along the eastern slope of which the Comstock, the great silver-bearing lode of Nevada, is located. The head branches of this ravine cut the Comstock lode at a number of points, the deepest of these cuts being at Gold Hill. A portion of this lode is distinguished for its auriferous character. The particles of gold having been released from the masses of quartz at this place by the process of disintegration, were subsequently washed down the cañon and deposited in its bed and along its banks, the finer portions being carried still further down and left upon the bar at its mouth; hence the origin of these placer mines. That this is the primary source of these deposits is apparent, not more from the nature of the case than the character of the dust, which is so far alloyed with silver as to be worth only from $10 to $12 per ounce, corresponding in this particular with the gold obtained by crushing the surface rock at Gold Hill. The pay realized in these diggings for the first few years was very good, averaging nearly an ounce a day to the hand; but it finally declined (until in the fall of 1859, when they were mostly given up) to less than a third of that amount. The number of men engaged here in gold washing varied from 20 to 100; a majority of them, towards the last, being Chinamen, who continued working in a small way for a year or two after the diggings had been abandoned by the whites. The total amount of gold dust gathered from these placers is estimated at between three and four hundred thousand dollars. Some rate it much higher, affecting to believe that the Chinese took out larger sums than they reported. At no other place, except Gold cañon, have placer mines of any extent or value been found as yet in the State of Nevada. In Six Mile cañon, a ravine running parallel to and a short distance below Gold cañon, some trifling deposits were found, the following up of which led to the discovery of the Comstock ledge. Some surface mines, of narrow extent but considerable richness, were also found in 1857 near Mono lake, then supposed to be within the limits of Nevada Territory, but afterwards ascertained to be in California. For several years these paid fair and in some instances large wages, and a town of over a thousand inhabitants sprung up at that point. The town, however, as well as the diggings, is now nearly deserted, but little having been done there for the past five years. There are in the vicinity several small quartz ledges, showing in the croppings much free gold. In 1860, some of these were worked by arrastras driven by water power, very good results being obtained, and it is thought by many these ledges could be worked on an extensive scale with profit, wood and water power both being convenient. At a number of other points, as on the forks of the Carson and Walker rivers, in Washoe valley, near Virginia City, and elsewhere, placer deposits have from time to time been met with, but in no case have they been lasting or remarkable for richness, none of them having been worked for more than a short period, and all being now abandoned; and though the most diligent research has been made during the past six years in nearly all parts of the State, no mines of this class, of any great extent or value, have yet been discovered. At the same time there are, as is well known, in almost every quarter of the country, lodes of auriferous quartz sufficiently rich to pay for reduction when worked for gold alone.

Discovery of silver.—Unlike the finding of gold, the discovery of silver in Nevada was a fortuitous event, having been brought about in this wise: The miners working up Six-Mile cañon, when near its head, and a little below where the Comstock lode crosses it, encountered, mixed with the auriferous earth, a black metallic substance, which gave them much trouble, being, on account of its weight, difficult of separation from the gold. This was in the year 1858, and, although they were thus led to notice this substance, being ignorant of its value, they did not inquire into its particular character or attempt to trace it to its origin. It was to them simply a cause of annoyance, and, as such, to be avoided or got rid of as easily as possible. Having finally, during the subsequent winter and spring, worked up this gulch until they were in the immediate vicinity of the Comstock lode, it became expedient to dig a reservoir to hold the water used in washing, this being obtained from the ravines above; and, although a line of rich surface earth had before been traced up to this point and considerably worked, it was not until this excavation was made that the deposit of silver ore in place was discovered and laid open. Nor did the magnitude of the event come to be appreciated and made generally known until the month of June following, when intelligence of it first reached California. What little merit attaches to the discovery, though claimed by divers individuals, would seem to belong chiefly to one James Fennimore, or Phinney, as he was usually called on this side the mountains, and who was the first to locate a mining claim on the Comstock ledge proper. This claim, made more than a year before, covered the exact point where the silver was first found, it being on the north end of the original Ophir ground, and near the south line of the Mexican Company's claim. Here a mass of rich silver sulphurets, mixed with free gold, came quite to the surface, this rich deposit, carrying an increased quantity of gold, having subsequently been found to extend for a considerable depth below, being especially rich in the ground of the Mexican, or, as it was then more commonly termed, Spanish Company. Phinney, who, like most of the pioneer miners of Washoe, as the country was then called, was of a generous and improvident disposition, wherefore, having gotten ahead a few dollars, and being ignorant withal of the great value of his ground, sold it to his companion, Henry Comstock, for a trifling consideration. The latter, though comprehending better than Phinney the value of this property, had so little appreciation of its real worth, that he congratulated himself on being able to dispose of it shortly after for a few thousand dollars, having, however, the further satisfaction of imparting his name to this remarkable lode. Nearly all the valuable claims on the Comstock ledge, as far south as Gold Hill, had, within a few months after the discovery of silver, passed from the possession of the original locators and owners into the hands of more intelligent or wealthy men, leaving the former class, who might so easily have become millionaires, generally quite poor.

Before proceeding to a more particular description of the Comstock ledge, and of the mines and mining operations generally of Nevada, it may be expedient, as contributing to a better understanding of what must be said in that connection, to give a brief outline of the physical geography of the State, its natural resources and productions, climate, agricultural capacities, &c.

2.—GEOGRAPHY AND PRODUCTS OF NEVADA.

Its system of mountains, plains, and valleys.—Viewed as a whole the State of Nevada, in common with the great American basin or desert of which it forms a part, may be considered an elevated plateau, having a general altitude of more than 4,000 feet above tide-water. Traversing this lofty plain are numerous chains of mountains, separated by valleys having a width varying from five to twenty miles, and usually about equal to that of the adjacent mountains measured through their bases. The course of these valleys is, as a general thing, parallel to the main axes of the mountains, which have, for the most part, a northerly and southerly strike. These mountains vary in height from 1,000 to 5,000 feet above the common level of the country, having, therefore, an absolute elevation of from 5,000 to 9,000 feet above the sea. For a distance of nearly 300 miles the Sierra Nevada form a natural barrier along its western and southwestern border, the boundary line between this State and California running partially upon its summit and partially along or near the eastern base of this range, which, though not here attaining its greatest altitude, has, nevertheless, within the limits of Nevada, a general height of more than 7,000 feet, a few of the loftier peaks reaching a height of 10,000. These mountains do not on this, as upon the California side, slope to the plains with a long and gentle declivity, but pitch violently down, having precipitous sides throughout their whole course. They are covered nearly everywhere from base to summit with a growth of terebinthine forests, consisting of a variety of pine, spruce, and fir; well adapted to make superior lumber. There are also a few other scrubby trees, of but little value, and at one or two points groves of tamarack. No oak or other hard wood of any size is found on this slope of the sierra, nor, indeed, in any other part of Nevada. The alternation of mountains and valleys mentioned is preserved with much regularity throughout the State, being most marked in the central portions thereof. Sometimes the former contract or are so broken up as to transform the valleys into broad plains or basins, some of which are open and unobstructed, while others are covered with isolated buttes or clusters of rugged hills. Sometimes, also, these mountains seem to lose all order, being grouped in confused masses, or have an axis at right angles or otherwise nearly transverse to the trend of the principal ranges. As in the Sierra Nevada, these interior chains contain many peaks upon which, in spots sheltered from the sun, the snow lies all summer; and while some of them are comparatively well watered, sending down perennial streams from their sides, others contain but little or are wholly without water. This is especially the case with those in the more western and southern portions of the State.

Among these ranges, sometimes at short intervals, gaps or low passes are met with, affording easy crossing places, some of them being so low and smooth as to offer no serious obstacle to the passage of loaded wagons, and through which railroads could be constructed with the greatest facility. In their geological structure these mountains, though varying somewhat, have many features in common, the mass of them being composed chiefly of sienites, slates, and granite; limestone and porphyry are also common rocks. In places, the evidences of volcanic action are abundant, though not apparently of recent date, though lofty, and in many instances having their sides deeply channelled by numerous ravines, or, as they are more commonly called, cañons. The mountains of Nevada are not remarkable for boldness of outline or a generally rugged aspect, the once jagged peaks having been rounded into dome-like shapes by the process of disintegration. In some cases, however, these still shoot up into splintered and spire-like summits, presenting a contour particularly sharp and striking. Most of these ranges are sparsely covered with bunch grass, and also with scattered patches of piñon and other scrubby trees, three-fourths of their surface being destitute of any kind of timber. Along some of the streams that flow down their sides are narrow strips of alluvial soil suitable for gardens, and which, sometimes spreading out at the points where these streams debouch upon the plains, afford a sufficiency of arable land for small farms. The mountains form, of course, the chief repositories of the mineral wealth of the country, though metalliferous deposits of apparent value have, in some instances, been met with in the valleys or out upon the plains. As the mountain chains o ten continue their course for a hundred miles or more without break or deviation from their general course, so also do the intervening valleys extend longitudinally for a like or even greater distance without interruption, and with an inclination so slight as to be imperceptible by the eye. These valleys, owing to the breaking up or recession of the neighboring mountains, sometimes spread out into plains of great extent, while in other cases they sweep around the ends of the mountain ranges and open into other valleys, being on the same level or having a plain but little different from their own. In some instances these adjacent valleys are separated only by a low ridge or swell of land, so trifling as to offer no serious impediment to the construction of wagon roads or railways, either of which might, if following a generally northern and southern course, run for hundreds of miles over an almost perfect level. But while these valleys are longitudinally so nearly level, they all have a gradual slope from the bases of the lateral mountains towards their centres, giving to their transverse sections a curved or basin-like shape. Through a few of them runs a stream of water supplied from the mountain rills on either hand or about its sources. Most of these mountain streams, being small, sink out of sight, being absorbed by the dry and porous earth as soon as they reach the margin of the valley, leaving the latter without any general stream flowing above ground through its midst. In cases where there is a sufficient accumulation of water to cause a stream to run above ground through the valley there is usually a strip of arable or meadow land along its margin, the quantity generally being proportioned to the magnitude of the stream; Carson, Reese river, Umashaw, Paradise, and Pahranagat valleys being examples of this kind. This strip of good land is often but a few rods wide, again spreading out to a mile or more in extent, while in many places, as where the banks of the stream are high, it disappears altogether. In some of the valleys, as Ruby, Big Smoky, Toquima, &c., there is much good land, though there is no open stream flowing through them. In these cases the rivulets from the mountains, though they disappear on reaching the valley, no doubt make their way underground to its centre, and percolating through the earth cause these fruitful spots by a system of natural irrigation. Other valleys, again, owing to an absence of these mountain streams, are destitute of even the smallest amount of good land, or at least of such as can be made available for agricultural purposes, much of the soil being rich but unproductive, because of its aridity and lack of means for irrigation. These valleys are nearly all treeless, not even a shrub larger than the artemisia being met with, except in a very few of them; the exceptions being confined to those having large streams of water running through them, such as the Carson, Truckee and Humboldt, along which are a few scattered cottonwoods and willow, the latter of very little use. Along many of the mountain streams a similar growth of timber is met with, as well as birch and other trees, all of a small size. The more extended plains are marked by a greater degree of sterility and dryness than other portions of the country, all of these being destitute of wood and most of them but scantily supplied with grass and wholesome water, much of the latter being so warm or highly mineralized as to be unfit for use. These plains are, in fact, for the most part, nothing but absolute deserts. This system of valleys, and plains so enclosed by mountains and sometimes connected with each other, constitutes a series of basins, each having a drainage of its own, but scarcely any of them an outlet to the sea. To this mode of drainage Nevada, as well as many other parts of the Great Basin, is entitled for some of its most peculiar topographical and geological features, this common receptacle of the gathered waters becoming, according to circumstances, a lake, a meadow, an alkali flat or a salt bed.

The sinks, sloughs and lakes.—As stated, but a small portion of the waters of Nevada are supposed to reach the ocean. That very little does so through surface channels is apparent, some holding to the rather questionable theory that much of it makes its way thither through subterranean passages. However that may be, certain it is the surface accumulations are by no means great. But it must be considered that the fall of rain and snow is limited, while, owing to the aridity of the atmosphere and earth, evaporation and absorption take place rapidly. The only considerable lakes in the State are those formed by the waters of the Carson, Walker and Humboldt rivers, and bearing the names of these streams, respectively, together with Pyramid lake, receiving the waters of the Truckee river. To Lake Tahoe Nevada can hardly lay claim, two-thirds of it being on the California side of the line. There are, besides the above, a number of smaller lakes in different parts of the State, the most of which are not only of limited area but extremely shallow, which latter is also the case with the Humboldt and Carson. Pyramid, the largest of the number, being thirty-three miles long and fourteen wide, has a great depth; the Walker, nearly as large, being also quite deep. Carson lake has a diameter of about twelve miles, being nearly circular; the Humboldt being somewhat smaller. The waters of these lakes are impregnated with alkaline and other salts to a degree that renders them unpalatable, and in the case of the Humboldt, especially at low stages, scarcely fit to drink. Flowing from several of these lakes are streams carrying their surplus water and discharging it into other and still more shallow lakes situate a short distance below; the former of these are, in popular language, called *sloughs*, the latter *sinks*, implying that here the water finally disappears or sinks, which is not really the case, the sink of the Carson, forming also that of the Humboldt, having a greater area than either of those lakes, and, though extremely shallow, never wholly drying up, as some of the smaller lakes often do. Honey lake, ordinarily quite an extensive body of water, in seasons of extreme drought, wholly disappears. The little lakes formed in the spring by the Wemissa, Umashaw, and similar streams, all dry up later in the season.

Alkali flats and mud lakes.—As geographical objects these are in some respects closely allied to each other, being identical locations existing under different conditions; the alkali flat is often the mud lake dried up, and the mud lake the alkali flat covered with water. Where, as frequently happens, the surface of a valley or plain is composed of clay or other substance impervious to water, the latter, after heavy rains, will collect upon these spots, and spreading out sometimes cover a large extent of country. These bodies of water generally dry up in a few days or weeks at furthest, though some of them that attain a greater depth remain for a longer period, in some cases, until quite late in the summer. The beds of these lakes being almost perfectly level, they are never more than a foot or two deep, generally but a few inches; yet usually being clear and calm, and reflecting the surrounding mountains with the greatest distinctness the stranger is led to believe them a very formidable body of water, an illusion that is effectually dissipated on seeing the wild fowl wading far out into them, or on riding through them and finding they rarely ever reach above his horse's knees. These places whether covered with water or not, unless the road be thrown up and trod hard during the dry season, are difficult of passage in wet weather, particularly to loaded teams. When the mud lake dries up, an argillaceous sediment is deposited on its bottom, often impregnated with alkaline matter or other salts, which, being white, and frequently hardening until it glistens in the sun, give to these spots a marked and desolate appearance; so hard do these surfaces sometimes become that a heavily loaded wagon fails to cut through them, and animals passing over scarcely leave a footmark behind them. In other cases, these flats, or a portion of them, remain soft the year round, the water coming within a few inches of the surface. In these cases a constant efflorescence of saline matter is going on, the sublimated particles being deposited upon the surface and on the surrounding shrubbery, if there be any near by, which is not apt to be the case, the soil being so much covered with water and so mixed with agents unfriendly to vegetation that the wild sage and greasewood, the least dainty of all plants, fail to get a foothold upon these flats. Not even a moss or lichen, or the most lowly fungus, ever lives there. While these alkali flats and mud lakes are found in nearly every section of Nevada, the most extensive are met with in the northwestern part of the State, where in wet seasons they cover hundreds of square miles.

Its rivers and streams.—Nevada, considering the extent of its territory, is remarkable for its lack of streams of any magnitude. It has not a navigable river—scarcely more than one or two streams that in most countries would be called a river, within its borders. The Humboldt, the longest and largest river in the State, is, at ordinary stages, fordable in many places, as are all the others, nearly everywhere along them. The habit, common on this coast, of designating so large a class of diminutive streams as rivers, is apt to give them an importance on the map which they do not deserve. Reese river, though having a length, traced from its source to its sink, of nearly one hundred and fifty miles, is not over ten or fifteen feet wide, with an average depth of about two feet; other streams, popularly termed rivers, being still smaller. As a general thing, the rivers have a hurried current, with occasional rapids, though nothing like a cataract or even a tolerably-sized cascade is known to exist in the State.

Flowing through broad valleys the immediate banks of the streams are apt to be low—in the case of the smaller ones, only a few feet above the water. Reese river, a good type of this class, flows through a canal-like channel, with parallel banks, composed of clay and sodded quite down to the water, which at ordinary stages is from two to ten feet below the adjacent plain. Except far down, it never dries up and scarcely ever overflows its banks. It disappears at one or two points along its course, there being here no channel above ground. At these places large meadows are formed, and having diffused itself throughout their whole extent, the water reappears below, sometimes at several points, and being again gathered into one channel, flows on as before. It is worthy of remark, however, that in its passage through this meadow the water, from being perfectly limpid as above, has been turned to a milky color, though not perceptibly altered in taste, the discoloring matter being probably a species of clay containing no deleterious or offensive properties. Reese river, after running with no other interruptions than these for nearly one hundred miles, begins to diminish, standing only in pools along its course, which are separated, often for a considerable space, by the more elevated portions of its bed or patches of meadow land. The stream only at high water continues to run along this part of its route, when it makes its way nearly to the Humboldt, finally disappearing in a tule fen that dries up in the fall and winter, the seasons of greatest drought, or at least of lowest water in this country. The Wemissa, Umashaw, and many other streams terminate in a similar manner; these marshy spots, like those where the larger rivers find a terminus, being commonly called *sinks.*

The water in most of the rivers and creeks is wholesome and palatable throughout their entire course, that of the mountain rills being always excellent. The lower the stage of water and the further we go down the stream the more impure it becomes; the water of the lower Humboldt being, late in the season, hardly fit to drink, owing to the accumulated impurities here diffused through a smaller volume. In consequence of the waste from evaporation and absorption, most of the larger streams lose as much water from these causes as they gain from their tributaries, of which they have very few, imparting to the rivers of this region the further peculiarity of being quite as large, and sometimes even larger, near their sources than they are at their points of termination. The Humboldt supplies a good example of this kind, it being considerably smaller where it enters the lake than it is two hundred miles above, throughout all which distance it can hardly be said to have a single tributary, not a stream of any size discharging directly into it, even in the wet season. As before stated, most of these streams, as well as the valleys through which they flow, are destitute of timber, the latter, with few and inconsiderable exceptions, being confined to the mountains. In the Reese River valley proper, nearly one hundred miles long, there is not a stick of timber large enough for a fence rail, many others, of equal extent, being quite as badly off in this respect. Without trees, and containing but little verdure, these immense valleys and plains present for the most part a very dreary and monotonous appearance, many of the latter justly meriting the appellation of desert, so often applied to them. The water in the creeks running from the mountains is always good, and, as in some of the ranges these are numerous and occasionally quite large, they become objects of importance, not only as supplying the ordinary wants of the inhabitants, but as furnishing the means for irrigation and a considerable amount of propulsive power, their descent being uniformly great. The narrow strips of alluvial land found along some of these mountain rills, as well as the bottoms at their mouths, are generally covered with a growth of scrubby trees, consisting of birch, willow, cottonwood, &c. All the lakes, as well as the larger and some of the smaller streams, contain fish, some of which, the mountain trout, are excellent. The fish taken in most of the lakes and along the lower portions of the streams, however, are of an inferior kind, or the better species deteriorated through the impurities of the water.

Springs—thermal, mineral, and otherwise.—In the matter of springs, Nevada is considerably better off than in regard to streams of running water, the former in some parts of the State being quite numerous, many of them, either as to size, temperature, or the composition of their waters, justly-accounted geological curiosities. They occur at all attitudes and under nearly every peculiarity of condition, large and small, deep and shallow, cold, hot and tepid; in a state of ebullition and quiescence, impregnated with every variety of mineral and metallic substance, and perfectly pure. Sometimes they are found isolated, and at others standing in groups. Some send off steam and emit a gurgling or hissing noise, while others do neither. Some of these groups contain as many as forty or fifty springs, varying from one foot to thirty in diameter, and in depth from two feet to a hundred or more. In shape they incline to be circular.

The mineral and thermal springs are usually situated upon a mound or tumulus formed from the calcareous or silicious particles brought up and deposited by their own waters. These mounds often cover several acres, their summits being raised to a height of forty or fifty feet above the adjacent plains. In some cases the sides of the springs are formed of these limy or silicious concretions, raising them in huge basins several feet above the level of the mounds themselves, while in others they are composed simply of earth or turf. The water in most of them is soft and agreeable to the taste when cold, and so transparent that the minutest object can be seen on the bottom of the deepest spring; even the small orifices through which the water enters being distinctly visible. Frequently a hot and a cold spring are situate so close together that a person placed between them may dip one hand into each at the same time.   From most of them a small stream issues, the water in many merely keeping even with the top, while in others it does not rise so high.   Occasionally one is met with that has already become extinct, a condition to which others seem rapidly, and perhaps all are gradually approaching.   These fountains, both the thermal and mineral, are much used by the Indians as a cleansing or curative means, and there is little doubt but some of them possess rare medicinal virtues.   Several of them have already become places of much resort with invalids, the sulphurous and chalybeate waters being found particularly efficacious in a variety of diseases. To the Steamboat springs, in Washoe county, the largest number have thus far repaired, more because of their greater accessibility than their superior sanitary properties.   A few of these hot springs are subject to a tidal action, belching forth at times large quantities of water, followed by a subsidence that may last for months or years.

A chemical analysis of the waters of Steamboat springs shows them to contain in various proportions the chlorides of sodium and magnesium, with soda in different forms, lime, silica, and a small per cent. of organic matter.   Similar tests made of the waters from other springs disclose nearly the same constituent salts, with the addition in some cases of sulphur and iron.   Some of the cold springs, especially those found in the larger valleys, are quite as remarkable for their depth and dimensions as the thermals.   It frequently happens that the streams from the mountains, after sinking, reappear in the form of springs along the sides or out in the middle of the valleys.   Some of these are of but ordinary size, while others are immense pools, from twenty to eighty feet in diameter, and over one hundred feet deep, some of them sending off considerable streams of pure cold water.   Not all the cold springs, however, are free from disagreeable or deleterious minerals; many of those found on the plains being highly offensive and injurious.   From some of them even animals, though suffering with thirst, refuse to drink.

The salt beds.—These constitute not only a notable feature in the chorography, but also an important item in the economical resources of Nevada.   There are a number of these salt fields in different parts of the State; they, like the alkali flats and mud lakes, being confined to the valleys and plains in which they cover the points of greatest depression, the most of them being adjacent to or encompassed by a belt of alkali lands.   The heavier deposits are, no doubt, of lacustrine origin, occupying what were formerly the basins of inland seas or extended salt lakes.   Their formation, it would seem probable, was brought about by the subsidence of these lakes through evaporation or other more violent causes, whereby the entire saline contents of their waters were collected and precipitated at these points, the strata of clay interposed between the different layers of salt being the result of floods occurring at various periods.   Situate, however, in valleys from which the waters, having no escape, spread out over large surfaces and soon evaporate, leaving the salt and other solid substances with which they are charged behind, the formation of these saliniferous beds may, perhaps, be sufficiently accounted for by the agents and operations now in action, without presupposing the existence of others about which less is known. Of the considerable number found in the State, three of these beds at least merit special notice, because of the abundance and purity of their product, and the facility with which it can be gathered.   That at Sand springs, Churchill county, seventy miles east of Virginia City, extends over several hundred acres, a portion of it being covered with water to the depth of a few inches.   Under this is a stratum of pure coarse salt nearly a foot thick, and which only requires to be gathered in heaps or thrown on a platform in order to drain off the water, which is soon accomplished, when it is ready for sacking.   Under this top layer is another composed of clay of equal, and, in places, of greater thickness beneath which again occurs another body of salt, but of what magnitude is unknown, the ascertainment of this point being of no practical moment, inasmuch as the salt taken out above immediately reforms, the space soon filling up with new depositions from the super-saturated water. This bed is owned by a company who take out from it over half a million pounds of salt per month, the mills and reduction works about Virginia City obtaining their supplies here, and consuming the most of this large quantity, a little being ground up for table use. The company dispose of this salt ready for sacking at $20 per ton on the ground, the freight to Virginia being about $30. Having their own teams, however, they are able to deliver it at the mills for $40 per ton, a sum considerably below what the freight alone would be for transporting the article from San Francisco, whence, for several years at first, it was wholly derived, the freights at that time varying from $120 to $180 per ton. At these prices, adding first cost—say $12 per ton—many thousand tons were consumed by the mills in Nevada prior to 1863, when they began packing it in from the salt pools situate forty-five miles southeast of Walker lake, whereby the price was somewhat reduced. These pools, like the water at Sand springs, being super-saturated with salt, deposit it to a depth of several inches about their borders, renewing it in a short time when taken away. After the discovery of the bed at Sand springs, it being much nearer Virginia, salt ceased to be brought to that place from these pools, though the mills about Aurora still continue to obtain their supplies there. To the cheapened price of this community is the present diminished cost of reducing silver ores in Nevada somewhat due, the annual saving thus effected being in some of the larger establishments equivalent to a hundred thousand dollars or more.

About fifty miles north of Sand springs, being also in Churchill county, though near the line of Humboldt, is another and still more extensive salt bed than that already described, its superficial area being nearly twenty square miles. It does not differ, except in extent, from that at Sand springs; the water here also, instead of covering, coming only to within a few inches of the surface. At this place there is first an inch of dry white salt on top, then six inches of wet, overlying a stratum of tough mud, or blue clay, a foot and a half thick, and filled with cubical crystals of salt, some of them several inches square and bearing a strong resemblance to ice. Under this clay comes another layer of clean, coarse salt, reaching downward to an unknown depth. This field is also owned by a company who have erected a railway for running out, a platform for drying, and a house for storing their salt. Owing to its distance from the chief point of consumption, Virginia City, but little of this salt has been sent to that place, though the Humboldt mills and those at Austin, in part, have drawn from here their supply. Large as is this bed, it is surpassed by another situate in Nye, or possibly in Esmeralda county, the location of the boundary between the counties being not yet well settled. This deposit is about one hundred and twenty miles S. SW. from Austin, and seventy miles in the same direction from Ione, the shire town of Nye county. This bed covers more than fifty square miles, over nearly all which the salt, clean, dry, and white, being the pure chloride of sodium, lies to a depth varying from six inches to two feet. This is the surface deposit, what there may be below never having been ascertained, nor does it matter, the amount in sight being ample to supply the wants of the whole world for centuries, could it but be readily furnished at the points where required; and though at present of so little avail, when railroads come to be extended into these regions, there is no doubt but salt can be shipped to California, and perhaps to more distant localities with profit. Though sold on the ground by the companies claiming these beds at one cent per pound, and sometimes for less, this salt should be afforded at a price scarcely more than the bare cost of gathering it up—in most instances a mere nominal sum. Upon the great saliniferous field of Nye county millions of tons could be shovelled up lying dry and pure upon the surface to a depth varying from six inches to three feet, with most likely still more heavy bodies below. This, like the more limited beds elsewhere, is claimed by private individuals, either under some of the various land laws of the United States, or enactments of the State of Nevada, or perhaps by virtue of certain regulations similar to those adopted by the mining community, and which hitherto have constituted the tenure of their mining properties. As a means of guarding against combinations that might unduly enhance the price of a commodity so largely used and so indispensable in the reduction of silver ores, it might be expedient for the general government to take measures to prevent these salt beds being so completely monopolized by private parties, as is otherwise likely to be the case. Besides these more extensive beds, there are numerous plains upon which the salt is deposited to the depth of an inch or more by the process of efflorescence, the soil being damp and impregnated with saline matters to a greater or less degree. At these spots the salt, generally mixed with a small percentage of foreign matter, such as soda, lime, or magnesia, is gathered by simply scraping it in heaps upon the surface, which operation must be performed in the dry season, the smallest amount of rain causing it to dissolve and wholly disappear. It reforms, however, with fair weather, and when removed is speedily replaced by new depositions, being in this respect like the heavier beds, practically inexhaustible. This admixture of foreign matter does not seem to impair its value for the reduction of ores, though rendering it unfit for culinary uses. From one of these plains, situate in Big Smoky valley, forty-five miles south of Austin, the mills at that place and elsewhere in the Reese river region obtain their principal supplies of salt, it being furnished on the ground at one cent a pound; and as the average cost of hauling to the mills is not over twenty dollars per ton, the latter get this article at a comparatively moderate price. Upon these salt fields there are no signs of animal or vegetable life, though it is a singular circumstance, that coming up through the saline incrustation, near the edge of the largest of them, is a fine spring of pure cold water; similar springs being found either upon or in close juxtaposition to others. The deposits of salt in this region are not confined to these beds or plains; it sometimes occurs in elevated positions, the strata often, in the aggregate many feet thick, being imbedded in hills and mounds of such extent as to almost justify their being called mountains. One of these, situate in the newly created but not yet organized county of Lincoln, in the extreme southeastern corner of the State, covers an area of several thousand acres, the layers being composed of cubical blocks of salt, often a foot square, nearly pure, and as transparent as window glass. There are elsewhere in the State other mounds of salt, the strata separated by layers of earth, similar to this, but none, so far as known, of equal magnitude.

Lumber and fuel.—The only timber in the State capable of making really good lumber is that growing on the eastern slope and along the base of the Sierra Nevada mountains. A species of white pine is found in scattered groves on some of the mountains in the interior and eastern part of the State, but the trees are comparatively small, not more than two or three feet in diameter and forty or fifty feet high, the wood being soft and brittle. As we have seen, there is but little timber of any kind in the valleys, most of them containing none at all, while many of the mountains are equally destitute. The prevailing tree, where there is any east of the Sierra Nevada, is the piñon—a species of scrubby pine, having a low, bushy trunk, from six to twelve inches through and from fifteen to thirty feet high. Having a close fibre and being full of resin, it is heavy and burns well even when green, being equal to most kinds of hard wood in the amount of heat it gives out, and constituting a very valuable kind of fuel. Mixed with these forests of piñon there are sometimes a few juniper trees and mountain mahogany—neither of any service for lumber, though the latter, when dry, is an excellent fuel. Along most of the larger streams, as stated, there are a few cottonwoods and small willows; while, in some of the mountain cañons, these, together with birch, ash, and cherry, are found, all, however, of a dwarfish growth, and, though serviceable for fencing, not of much use for making lumber. With such a scarcity of good timber the better qualities of lumber command high prices in most parts of Nevada. Thus, at Virginia City, though within eighteen miles of the best timber lands, the price varies from $40 to $60, according to kind and quality. The further we go east the higher the price rules; the same quality of lumber that can be bought at the mills in the sierra for $20, in Carson for $30, and in Virginia City for $45, per thousand, costs $120 in Austin, where, at the same time, that made from the white-pine growing in the vicinity can be bought for $60, and fire-wood for a little more than half the price it is in Virginia. Much of the lumber employed in the erection of mills and the construction of machinery about Austin, as well as a large proportion of that used on other buildings in that place, has cost from $120 to $200 per thousand, it being considerably cheaper now than it was several years ago. Worthless as this piñon is for the purposes of lumber, many of the houses in the smaller towns in the interior are built of it—a face being hewn upon two sides of the stick, which is then set on end, the houses being constructed on the stockade plan. It is also used, where easily obtained, for building corrals, and to some extent for fencing; but, being hard and knotty as well as of small size, it requires much labor to prepare it for even the most common use. Wherever this tree is at all abundant, fuel can be obtained, delivered at the mills, for from $4 to $5 per cord, and sometimes a little less. In most parts of Churchill and Humboldt counties the price is higher, owing to the greater scarcity of timber or the difficulty of getting it down from the mountains. In Star City and Unionville, Humboldt county, juniper—a very poor kind of fuel—costs from $10 to $12 per cord. Where timber is scarce, sage-brush and other resinous shrubs—these being found nearly everywhere in the country—are used for fuel; even some of the mills, as the Sheba in Humboldt, and several others, having employed them wholly or in part for generating steam, for which purpose they answer very well, save the trouble of keeping the furnaces supplied, because of the rapidity with which they are consumed. In Virginia City and vicinity wood now costs from $12 to $16 per cord, the price varying with the quality. These are about the rates that have obtained there since the settlement of the place, though at times much higher have ruled when the season was inclement or the article scarce. Coal, or rather lignite, has been discovered at several places in the State, yet none of these deposits have as yet furnished more than a few hundred tons of fuel, nor have they thus far been sufficiently developed to determine their capacity and value in this respect. At Crystal Peak, on the Truckee, near the California line, a considerable amount of work has been done in the exploration of coal-beds supposed to exist at that point; and the prospect for finding there a large deposit of at least a moderately good fuel, is by experts considered encouraging. Beds of peat that burns well have also been found at one or two places in the State. A railroad—which can now be counted on as likely to be built within the next two years, connecting the Virginia mining district with the heavy forests of the Sierra Nevada—must tend to greatly diminish the cost of fuel and lumber, both of which are required in enormous quantities in the business of raising and reducing the ores, the erection of buildings, timbering the mines, &c.; the sums annually expended on this account, though scarcely so large now as formerly, amounting to over $2,000,000, nearly one-half of which it is believed might be saved through the aid of a railroad. When the Central Pacific railroad, now in rapid progress of construction across the sierra, shall have been built down the Truckee river—as it is calculated it will be within a year and a half from this time—it will pass a point not more than sixteen or eighteen miles distant from Virginia City, which would be the length of a branch road required for connecting this place with the main trunk, and through it with the heavily

timbered mountains only six or eight miles west from the point of intersection
of the two roads. The suggestions made with reference to the propriety of
preventing a monopoly of the salt-fields by private individuals might perhaps be
extended also to the wood-lands, more especially in the interior mining districts,
where these lands are limited in extent, and where, although the requirements
for fuel will probably be great, large tracts have already been secured in the
manner alluded to by private parties or companies.

MINES AND MINERAL RESOURCES OF NEVADA.

Various minerals.—Not only the precious, but also many of the useful metals,
as well as a large variety of mineral substances, are met with in the State of
Nevada, nearly all of them widely diffused and some of the latter in such abundance as cannot fail to render them commodities of economic value when greater
facilities shall exist for transporting them to the points of manufacture or
consumption. Besides the saliniferous basins already described, ores of copper
and iron rich in these respective metals; beds of sulphur, from some of which
this mineral can be obtained quite pure, though generally mixed with calcareous or other foreign matter; deposits of lignite and possibly true coal, though,
so far as explored, Nevada is not a strongly marked carboniferous region;
cinnabar, gypsum, manganese, plumbago, kaoline and other clays useful for
making pottery and fire-brick; mineral pigments of many kinds, together with
many of the more important salts and varieties of alkaline earths; soda in all
its combinations, nitre, alum, magnesia, &c., being encountered in nearly all
parts of the State and frequently in great abundance. Platinum and tin have
been found in small quantities, the latter as yet only in stream-works and never
in place, galena, zinc, antimony, nickel, cobalt, arsenic, &c., frequently occurring in combination with silver and other metals. Limestone, granite, marble, and
many other kinds of stone suitable for building purposes, with slate adapted for
roofing, are common and in some instances easily obtained, the work of quarry-
ing them being carried on above ground. The most useful material of this
class consists of a species of sandstone and a volcanic rock, the former of a
light gray and the latter of a reddish drab color, both of which occur in masses
quite upon the surface, and when fresh from the quarry are so soft as to be
easily wrought, though afterwards becoming so hard as to resist not only the
influence of the atmosphere, but also a high degree of heat, some of this igneous
rock being employed for smelting and roasting works, and even the manufacture
of crucibles, with success. That iron could be manufactured to advantage in the
interior of the State where the freights are high and the consumption of this
article so considerable, is the opinion of those most conversant with the subject,
and there is a strong probability that works of this kind upon a limited scale, at
least, will be established there within a short time. One of the heaviest beds
of iron ore yet discovered in the State is situated in the western part of Nye
county, and though not far distant from an extensive body of piñon from which
an excellent article of charcoal could readily be made, there is but little water
and no good land or important mines in the immediate neighborhood; wherefore,
although the ore is abundant, rich, and of supposed good quality, it is much to
be questioned whether iron even of the more common kind, such as is used for
dies, shoes, castings, &c., could be made here with profit, and consequently
whether this ferruginous bed is at present of any practical importance. Upon
some of the alkaline flats, as well as about certain springs and other localities,
the carbonate of soda exists so pure and in such profusion that it, like common
salt and other similar substances, must yet become one of the staple exports of
the country. At present but a very limited use is made of this article, it being
employed only by the laundrymen and soap-makers. There is now a small
establishment at Carson City engaged in manufacturing sulphuric acid, the raw

material being procured from the sulphur bed near the Big Bend of the Humboldt river, about the centre of Humboldt county. That other salts and mineral substances, such as nitre, borax, alum, &c., will yet be found in this State in such quantities as will make them of practical value, seems probable, though not enough is yet known as to the extent of these deposits to warrant the expression of a positive opinion on this point. Nevada is rich in organic remains both animal and vegetable, some of the latter being of extraordinary size and beauty. Huge fragments of fossiliferous wood and even the entire trunks of large trees have been discovered lying upon the surface of the ground often in a state of high preservation. There are springs in different places, the waters of which being highly charged with silicious or ferruginous properties, are constantly carrying on this fossilizing process upon animal and vegetable matter immersed in or otherwise sufficiently exposed to their operation. No diamonds or other precious stones have, so far as is known, yet been discovered in Nevada, though opals and agates, the latter remarkable for variety and beauty, have been found at many places. Neither petroleum nor other mineral oil has thus far been met with in the country, nor do the indications, so far as observed, favor the supposition that they will ever be discovered in quantities hereafter, the bituminous, like the carboniferous signs throughout the State, being scanty and unsatisfactory.

Characteristic features of the Comstock ledge.—Taken as a whole, this ledge, discovered as already related, is not only by far the most valuable silver-bearing lode yet found in the State of Nevada, but equals, perhaps, any deposit of the precious metals ever encountered in the history of mining enterprise, its productive capacity, as now being developed, surpassing, if the mass of its ores do not in richness equal, those of the most famous mines of Mexico and Peru. Being then so important in itself, and holding such prominence among the mines of this State, a somewhat detailed description of its location, character, exploitation, and future prospects may not be out of place. This lode is situate in Story county, about twenty-five miles from the western border of the State. It is found cropping out along the eastern slope of Mount Davidson, a lofty eminence in the Washoe range of mountains, which form a lower spur of the main sierra, with which it runs parallel, being separated thereform by Washoe and Steamboat valleys. Mount Davidson, like most of the range of which it forms a part, is extremely dry and barren, containing but little water or grass, and at present no timber at all, the few scrubby pines that once grew upon its sides having long since disappeared. Its bulk, like that of the Sierra Nevada and most of the mountain ranges in this State, is composed of granite, though largely made up of serpentine, quartz, gneiss, sienite, talcose, calcareous and other primary rocks. Breccia, porphyry, trap, trachyte, argillaceous, and silicious, with nearly every kind of igneous and sedimentary rock, are common in the mountains of this State, some rich argentiferous lodes having been found in many of these formations. The summit of Mount Davidson is 7,827 feet above tide water, 1,600 feet above Virginia City and the Comstock lode, and more than 3,000 feet above the plain of Carson river at its base. The direction and comparative size of this lode, the length and relative position of the various claims upon it, and its situation with reference to Virginia City and Gold Hill, the principal towns in the neighborhood, will be more readily understood by consulting the accompanying diagram, illustrating these and other points of interest connected therewith. The strike of the principal or mother vein, the only one exhibited on this plat, is, as will be seen, about fifteen degrees west of south, the northerly and southerly extremities thereof bearing nearly due north and south. In width or thickness it varies on top from twenty to two hundred feet, the most of it ranging between thirty and seventy feet, with a uniform tendency to expansion as penetrated downwards. The ledge, at some points along its course, as in the grounds of the Savage and the Gould & Curry companies, and again at Gold Hill, spreads out beyond its average width, it reaching at the latter place its greatest thickness, something over one hundred and fifty feet. In a vertical direction it undergoes a similar contraction and expansion, pinching at points to a few yards, or even feet, and again extending to its usual size. Though in spots appearing in high rocky projections, it does not show itself above ground throughout its entire length, there being considerable stretches where no outcrop is visible. That it preserves its continuity, however, below, seems probable, it having been found wherever searched after to any great depth. Nor has it proven prolific in ores throughout all its parts, there being a number of barren spaces along it, as in the ground extending from the Central to the Gould & Curry claim, some 1,400 feet, and at other points further south, in none of which have any considerable bodies of valuable ores been found, though explored to depths varying from three to five hundred feet. It is the opinion of geologists that within these hitherto unproductive spaces paying ores will yet be reached, though not, perhaps, until much greater depths have been attained.

In this as in most large and fruitful silver-bearing lodes the valuable ores, though generally diffused throughout the mass of the gangue or vein-stone, are still found to be more abundant in certain portions thereof called bonanzas or chimneys, which latter, as they usually have a pitch lengthwise the lode, must, according to their position, often run out of the ground of one company into that of another adjoining, leaving the one comparatively poor and enriching the other. Under this arrangement it might happen that one of these barren spots, by a bonanza striking into it at a greater depth, should be rendered productive, it being, moreover, liable to become so without reference to this system of distribution of ores, not by any means a feature of all mines. In its upper portions the Comstock lode dipped to the west at an angle of about sixty degrees, this angle in places being much larger, and at some points approximating ninety degrees. At greater depths, varying from one to three hundred feet, the ledge after gradually assuming a perpendicular position is now, at the depth of seven hundred feet, found pitching to the east at an angle of about fifty degrees, the inclination varying somewhat at different points along its line. In the development of this lode, which is now conceded by all competent judges who have examined it to be a regular fissure vein of the largest size, the usual contractions, faults, and displacements common in this class of veins have been encountered, and though causing much hindrance and extra labor, and at times giving rise to no little doubt and discouragement, they have in no case destroyed the continuity of the vein or caused it to be wholly lost sight of. Dykes of trap and other indurated rock have interposed at many points to check the work of exploration, while elsewhere imbedded within the mass of the lode have been found immense fragments of wall rock or other foreign matter barren of ore, causing much trouble and tending to depreciate for the time being the value of the mines. But in nearly every instance such obstacles have been overcome, these rocky barriers being penetrated, and these bodies of worthless material disappearing before the persistent efforts of well-applied labor.

The Comstock ledge has now been clearly traced and identified for a space, measured in a straight line, of a little more than one mile and a half, throughout which it has been found continuous and sufficiently rich in the precious metals to render the entire body of the ore-bearing portions of the vein remunerative, with the exceptions already pointed out. This space extends from the larger section of the Ophir company's claim, on the north, to that of the Belcher, and possibly of the Uncle Sam, on the south, some of the rich silver sulphurates characteristic of the mother lode having been found in the latter, though not at the depth yet reached, in large quantities. As stated, the rich ores have been found in some cases, as in the Ophir and Mexican grounds, and at Gold Hill, quite upon the surface, while in others it has only been reached at depths varying from fifty to five hundred feet. In the Gould & Curry claim very fair, though not what was then considered pay-rock, was met with in the outcroppings of the ledge, the millable ores not being obtained until a depth of nearly one hundred feet was reached.

In the ground of the Savage company, adjoining on the south, they were not reached until a much greater depth had been attained, while in that of the Hale and Norcross company, lying next, nothing worth putting through the batteries was met with until their shaft had, at great expense, been sunk to a vertical depth of more than 500 feet. In the Alpha, Yellow Jacket, and Crown Point claims, no heavy masses of millable ores were met with until they had been penetrated downward from one to three hundred feet, while, as before intimated, in the space between the claim of the Gould & Curry and that of the Central company, as also throughout a stretch of some hundred feet adjoining the ground of the Chollar-Potosi company on the south, and perhaps, also, in a like space similarly situated with reference to the Belcher ground, no metalliferous deposits of magnitude or value have thus far been developed. Much labor and money have been expended in efforts to trace the prolongation of the Comstock ledge, both to the north and south, of what are considered, in a productive sense at least, its present termini; but only with the results heretofore indicated, nothing of permanent value having been struck along the supposed line of its course, or adjacent thereto, beyond these points. Quartzose ledges exist in abundance, both to the north and south within the belt the Comstock is presumed to occupy, if it have an existence outside its present known limits; but none of these, nor yet any of the numerous lateral ledges in close proximity to the developed section of the mother vein, and by some considered a portion of it, have yielded more than a very insignificant percentage of the precious metals, nor are the present prospects of these properties such as to command for them other than mere nominal prices in the mining share market, many, that a few years ago sold readily at high prices, being no longer salable at all. Most of the ledges running parallel with the productive portion of the Comstock, and within one or two hundred feet of the latter, have been the cause of much expensive litigation, the owners of the main lode claiming them as belonging to it under the theory that they would all unite at some point, probably at no great depth beneath the surface; a view that the courts have been inclined to sustain and that experience tends to sanction.

The greatest vertical depth to which the Comstock ledge has been developed is a little more than seven hundred feet, there being several shafts along it from four hundred to seven hundred feet deep, with many others varying in depth from two hundred to five hundred feet, while some tunnels now under way, and soon most likely to be completed, will strike it at a still greater depth. The Sutro tunnel already projected, with a good prospect of being finished in the course of four or five years, will strike it at an estimated depth of eighteen hundred feet below the croppings of the Gould & Curry company, the highest point upon it. This work, according to the plan proposed, is to be twelve feet wide and ten feet high, so as to admit of a double train-way. It will be nineteen thousand feet long, cost between four and five millions of dollars, and when finished will enable this lode to be worked with probable profit to a depth of three thousand feet or more. The proprietor of this tunnel, which it is believed will soon become an urgent necessity, proposes to tax the different companies upon the Comstock ledge at the rate of two dollars for every ton of ore raised after the work is completed, and they are actually enjoying the benefits of having their mines drained thereby. The work, though formidable, is greatly inferior, both in cost and magnitude, to several others of a similar kind already completed, or under way, for securing deep drainage to various mines in Europe. In the year 1850 surveys were made for a tunnel in the Harz mines. Brunswick, to be nearly fourteen miles in length, and which it was estimated it would require twenty-two years to finish. Work was commenced upon this tunnel in July, 1851, and completed in June, 1864, the time required for its construction being less than thirteen years. The product of these mines is only about half a

million dollars in gold and silver, per annum, and the additional drainage
secured by this work was but three hundred feet, items quite insignificant compared with the annual yield of the Comstock lode, and the depth of drainage to
accrue from the construction of the Sutro tunnel. A tunnel some fifteen miles
in length, designed to drain the principal mines at Freiberg, Saxony, has been
in progress of excavation for several years, forty more being expected to insure
its completion; nor does this work deepen the present drainage upon those
mines to anything like the extent attained by the Sutro tunnel. Already a
number of extensive tunnels have been commenced, designed to intersect the
Comstock lode at depths varying from five hundred to one thousand feet beneath the surface. Some of these, after being partially completed, have been
abandoned; upon others work has been suspended at different stages in their
progress; while upon a few operations are still being vigorously prosecuted, with
the prospect of an early consummation. Some of the shafts now being sunk it
is proposed to carry to a depth of twelve or fourteen hundred feet, powerful
pumping and hoisting works being provided for the purpose.

Character, quantity, value, and distribution of ores in the Comstock ledge.—
The great body of valuable ores contained in the Comstock ledge consists of the
black and gray sulphurets of silver, several other varieties having been met with
in small quantities, more especially near the surface. Native silver is found
diffused throughout all parts of the vein; and while no large masses have been
obtained, many handsome specimens have been gathered from the various
claims, the aggregate value of all the virgin metal taken out being quite large.
Combined with this ore is a small amount of the baser metals, such as the sulphurets of antimony, lead, iron, copper, &c. These are present, however, only
in limited quantities, this ore being remarkable for its freedom from these and
similar substances; hence one of the elements of its comparatively cheap reduction. Associated with the silver is a notable percentage of gold, the bullion extracted during the earlier working of the mines containing a larger portion of it than
at a later period when, through improved machinery and processes and a more careful manipulation of the ores, the silver was more closely saved. At Gold Hill the
bullion extracted at first was worth from six to eight dollars per ounce; now it
is reduced to between two and three dollars, that from most other points along
the Comstock lode being worth still less, owing to the heavy alloy of silver it
contains. The deeper the mines at Gold Hill are worked the more the metal
tends to silver. By simply crushing and amalgamating, from seventy to ninety,
on an average more than eighty, per cent. of all the precious metals contained
in the great mass of the Comstock ores can be extracted, thereby dispensing
with the troublesome and expensive process of roasting or smelting, to which
only a small quantity of the extremely rich or more obdurate ores are subjected.
The mass of rocky matter enclosed between the walls of this ledge is not found
to be ore-bearing throughout all its parts. In spots it is quite barren, the ores
being collected in streaks or bunches, leaving the balance so entirely destitute
of metal, or only so slightly impregnated therewith, as to render it not worth
raising. In other places the metalliferous ores are generally diffused throughout
the vein-stone, being here usually of a lower grade than where occurring in a
more concentrated form. This lode, having been found remarkably rich at two
or three spots quite upon the surface, and these happening to be the points
where practical operations were first initiated, led at the outset to very exaggerated notions of its probable wealth, and a consequent overrating of its prospective value; a circumstance to which much of the wild speculation, as well
as many of the misapprehensions and mistakes, that subsequently characterized
the management of these mines, as well as the financial operations connected
therewith, may be justly attributed. Under the excitement of the moment, and
through the general ignorance prevailing in regard to the nature of silver mines,
it was inferred that these bonanzas would not only be of frequent occurrence
and extend indefinitely downwards, but that the entire body of the lode would

become larger and more productive the further it was penetrated in that direction; a supposition which, it is needless to say, subsequent experience has failed to confirm, most of these rich accumulations of ore having been exhausted at no great depth, and the ledge generally, though increasing somewhat in thickness as descended upon, having undergone no corresponding increment in the volume of the ores, or in the average yield of the precious metals. From many of the mines along the line of the Comstock there is at present a much greater amount of ore being raised than formerly, because of greater facilities for hoisting, and because a much lower grade of ore is now being worked than aforetime. In the earlier stages of mining at this place large bodies of metalliferous rock were left untouched in the upper levels, being then thought too poor to justify removal. Many of these, as well as thousands of tons of rejected rock thrown upon the dump piles, have since been sent to the mills and, with the present cheapened means of reduction, found to pay a profit; and thus it is, that while the average yield of the precious metals to the ton of ore has been steadily diminishing, the aggregate annual product of bullion from these mines underwent a rapid increase until three years ago, since which time it has been maintained at about the same point, the amount being about fifteen million dollars per annum. For the first two or three years after they were opened, the argentiferous ores taken from this ledge yielded from one to three hundred dollars per ton; the average of all worked being over one hundred and fifty dollars, while some small lots carefully selected went much higher, ranging from five hundred to two and even three thousand dollars to the ton. But the quantity of this class was limited, and it is probable that nearly as much equally rich ore could now be procured by carefully culling the entire mass taken out. These rich parcels were generally sent abroad for reduction, or sold in San Francisco to the dealers in metalliferous ores, who carried them to Europe—mostly to Swansea—for treatment.

To illustrate more clearly the depreciation that has gradually taken place in the value of these ores, or, rather, the manner in which, through the agency of cheapened and more efficient modes of treatment, the working of those of lower grade with profit has been constantly increased, we may take the case of the Gould & Curry company, which fairly represents the experience of most others in this particular. This company, during the four years extending from 1862 to 1865, inclusive, extracted from their claim the following numbers of tons of third-class ore, being the bulk taken out, with the average results stated, viz: 1862, 8,427 tons; average yield per ton, $104 50; 1863, 43,907 tons; average, $80 44 per ton; 1864, 55,602 tons; average, $73 48 per ton; 1865, 46,745 tons; yield, $45 41 per ton. For the year 1866 the amount of ore raised will probably not differ much from that of last year, while the yield per ton will be somewhat less. During these four years this company took out, in addition to the foregoing, fifty-two tons first-class ore that averaged $1,800 to the ton, and 14,103 tons second-class that averaged $234 to the ton, while one or two mines are doing better. The average yield of the leading mines on the Comstock ledge will not at present go much if any above $40 per ton; while that from the more auriferous claims at Gold Hill will scarcely yield $30. With the poverty of the ores the profits of the mine, of course, diminish, it costing but little more to work moderately rich than it does poor ores. The total number of tons of ore raised from all the mines on the Comstock ledge will reach and perhaps exceed one million and a half. The amount of ore extracted from the various mines depends upon their magnitude, the facilities for raising them, and the energy with which they are pushed. Most of the larger claims are now taking out at the rate of from twenty to fifty thousand tons per annum, and one or two at a still larger rate. The total amount of ore extracted from all the claims situate on the Comstock ledge may be roughly estimated at something over one and a half million tons.

Cost of mining, hauling, and reduction of ores.—These several items of expense vary considerably with circumstances. In estimating the cost of raising or mining the ores it is customary to include that of constructing, hoisting, and pumping works, timbering the mines, &c., as well as of the actual labor of extraction. The cost of mining the ores on the Comstock ledge averages at present about $14 per ton, the price varying from $10 to $20. For transporting the ores from the mine to the mill the cost is at the rate about $1 per ton for every mile the ore is carried, unless the distance be long, when it is less. Hauling the shortest distance usually costs $1 per ton. Where contracted for in large lots, teamsters haul from Virginia City to Carson river, seven miles, for $4 per ton. Ores treated by simple crushing and amalgamation, as most of those taken from the Comstock ledge are, can be reduced at a cost varying from $10 to $16 per ton, the average price being about $14. The auriferous ores at Gold Hill, which require but few expensive chemicals, do not cost over $8 or $10 per ton. Where water-power is used instead of steam the expense is about $3 per ton less, these all being reductions of from thirty to seventy-five per cent. on the prices that prevailed a few years ago. Where dry-crushing with roasting or smelting is adopted the expense is two or three times as great as by the above method. Not more than one-twentieth, if at present so large a proportion, of the ores from the Comstock mines are treated by dry-crushing, though upon a larger share of those taken from the ledges in the interior this plan could be adopted with advantage, the most of them requiring roasting or smelting. To the above rates, except in the item of hauling ores to the mills, which is about the same, there must be added, where these several operations are carried on in the outside districts, from fifty to one hundred per cent., the price of labor as well as most kinds of material being that much dearer there than about Virginia City. Extracting the ores from some of the extremely narrow ledges in these localities often costs four times as much per ton as from the claims on the Comstock lode, so much dead work being required to secure a small amount of ore from the former.

Annual and total product of bullion extracted from the Comstock ledge.—Assuming the gross amount of ore taken from the Comstock lode to have been one and a half million of tons, a rather low estimate, and supposing it to have yielded at the rate of forty-four dollars per ton, the present average being less than $40, we have a total bullion product of $66,000,000, reckoning to the end of the present year. That this estimate of the gross product is not far out of the way, the following table exhibiting the annual yield of all the mines in Nevada tends to establish. These figures are for the most part derived from authentic sources, and although they embrace the yield of all the mines in the State, we have only to make a deduction of about five or six per cent for the outside districts, the balance being justly credited to the Comstock lead:

1859	$50,000
1860	100,000
1861	2,275,000
1862	6,500,000
1863	12,500,000
1864	16,000,000
1865	16,800,000
1866	16,500,000
	*70,725,000

* The above estimate as stated is derived from authentic sources, but it differs somewhat from the estimate made by the surveyor general of Nevada given in section 3, clause 33, with which it may be compared, as well as with the total yield reported by the principal companies on the Comstock lode as given in clauses 35, 36, 37, 38, 39, 40, 41, and 42 in section 3.

An allowance of five millions of dollars would undoubtedly cover the product of all the outside mines, making that of the Comstock vein to be, as above, nearly $66,000,000. The rate at which this lode has been yielding heretofore can, in all likelihood, be kept up for an indefinite period to come, there being no example in the history of silver mining of a vein of this magnitude and character being exhausted or giving out, though many have been worked steadily for centuries and in some instances to depths three or four times as great as that yet reached on any part of the Comstock lode. The yearly turn out of these mines could easily be enlarged, as it no doubt will be hereafter, when new levels shall be opened or new claims be brought to a productive condition, and additional works shall be supplied for raising and reducing the ores. That their annual product will be augmented to twenty millions or more, in the course of a few years, seems quite likely. It could even, with the present means for extracting the ores, be increased several millions yearly were the leading companies disposed to employ a larger number of custom mills and to adopt the rushing and exhaustive system in vogue a few years ago; but which, while it secured large aggregate returns, was found to be attended with great waste and to tend to a rapid depletion of the mines. As a return to this plan cannot therefore reasonably be looked for, the anticipated increase of bullion may be expected to grow out of the causes above mentioned, in conjunction with a more economical and perhaps efficient reduction of ores, whereby those of a lower grade than are now worked can be treated with profit. The annual yield of none of the older claims has been as large for the past two years as it was for two or three years previous to that time, the deficiency being supplied by several new claims that have since become productive, such as the Hale & Norcross, Crown Point, and others. Thus the Gould & Curry company, whose mine did not begin to turn out bullion in any quantity until 1862, produced that year $858,819, in 1863 $3,887,755, in 1864 $4,921,516, and in 1865 $2,401,060, the product the present year being about the same as last. The entire amount of the precious metals taken from this mine, calculating to the end of the year 1866, amounts to about fourteen and a half millions of dollars. From the Savage mine there has been extracted during the same time about $4,500,000, the total yield for the year ending July 10, 1866, having been $1,256,663. The Hale & Norcross, which only lately began to yield largely is now producing at the rate of about $1,500,000 per annum. The product of the Imperial mine at Gold Hill was, for the year ending May 31, 1865, $854,630. For the last year it has not yielded so largely, the same remark being applicable to most of the formerly highly productive mines near it, as well as to many others near Virginia City, such as the Ophir, Mexican, Central-Chollar, Potosi, &c., from none of which has there been anything like the amount of bullion extracted the last two years that there was for the two years preceding, while upon one or two of them labor has nearly ceased. The cause of this falling off is not so much in the poverty of the mines themselves, some of which have been amongst the most prolific on the Comstock lead, and are still known to be rich, as in a lack of energy on the part of the owners in failing to provide the means for draining them of water and a renewal of prospecting operations. On some of these mines work has been suspended until more powerful machinery for hoisting and pumping can be supplied, while in a few other cases it has been for want of adequate means to go on, or because the small amounts of good ore at one time obtainable in the mine having given out, the owners have become discouraged or concluded to discontinue operations until the adjacent mines have been drained and explored.

Accruing profits, dividends, losses, disbursements, &c.—Of the net profits that have accrued to the owners of the mines upon the Comstock ledge, taking them as a whole, it is impossible to make any accurate computation. In many of the more valuable claims but little capital was at first invested, the owners being the original locators, or purchasing them from the latter for small and often mere nominal prices. This was more particularly the case with the numerous small but extremely rich claims at Gold Hill, as well as the Ophir and Mexican near Virginia City. At first there were no taxes of any kind upon the product of these mines; the body of ore was large, exceedingly rich, easily extracted—thousands of tons being found in the croppings above ground—and the most of it capable of being reduced at a comparatively small cost; wherefore the profits to the owners, or at least to such of them as had come by these properties cheaply, were, during the first three or four years, not only steady, certain, and large, but in many cases enormous; and had better judgment been exhibited at that period in working the mines, and more caution in properly securing their titles, or had greater economy in the expenditure of their proceeds been observed by the owners, much of the disaster, loss, and, in some instances, final ruin that overtook both might have been avoided. For the development of these mines and the working of the ores few assessments were ever required, the most of them being not only self-sustaining but dividend-paying from the start. Prior to the erection of steam-mills the argentiferous ores were sold and sent out of the country for reduction, the auriferous rock at Gold Hill being worked by arrastras, a slow method, but one that answers well where the rock is rich, and simple crushing and amalgamating serves the purpose. Another advantage at this early day was, the mines were mostly owned by single individuals, or two or three at most, acting as partners, and not by large incorporated companies; and thus a source of much wastefulness and mismanagement, not to say peculation and fraud, was guarded against. So large was the income from some of these claims at Gold Hill during the period we are considering that they readily commanded from five to fifteen thousand dollars per foot, the net monthly profits derived from them varying from five hundred to three thousand dollars per linear foot. In some cases persons owning but ten feet enjoyed from this source an annual revenue of more than twenty and even approximating thirty thousand dollars. Nor were these princely revenues confined to the claims in Gold Hill, proper, (a mound of quartz some three or four hundred feet in length;) the proprietors of the Mexican and Ophir for a time fared nearly as well. This temporary productiveness of the mines, leading, as has already been observed, to the subsequent high prices and extravagant notions of their prospective value, which in turn caused the undue excitement and over-speculation that culminated, on several distinct occasions not far separated, in general disappointment and loss. How frequent and extensive these losses have been may in some measure be gathered from the following tables exhibiting the fluctuations in the prices of such mining stocks as have been generally dealt in by the board of brokers, and which, although they do not embrace all the productive mines in the State, sufficiently indicate the fate that at one time or another has overtaken a large majority of them.

Table showing the fluctuations in mining shares from July 10, 1864, to January 1, 1865.

Name of company.	July 10	July 20	July 30	Aug. 10	Aug. 20	Sept. 1	Sept. 10	Sept. 20	Oct. 1	Oct. 10	Oct. 20	Nov. 1	Nov. 10	Nov. 20	Dec. 1	Dec. 10	Dec. 20	Jan. 1
Gould & Curry ... per ft	$1,600	$1,550	$900	$1,600	$1,400	$1,475	$1,250	$1,100	$1,300	$1,380	$1,610	$1,650	$1,335	$1,450	$1,600	$1,425	$1,520	$1,590
Ophir .... do ..	725	670	435	450	550	490	460	300	350	355	433	415	433	420	425	285	420	375
Savage .... do ..	1,150	2,300	750	1,300	1,300	1,300	1,290	1,235	1,400	1,800	1,850	1,900	1,800	1,925	1,800	1,625	1,725	1,600
Potosi .... do ..	900	1,000	925	875	900	840	650	690	720	790	750	850	925	900	725	540	665	700
Chollar .... do ..	425	300	300	325	475	550	650	650	690	850	930	1,000	925	990	1,025	965	1,030	1,050
Hale & Norcross . do ..	350	300	210		380	430	495	75	350	330	463	490	1,000	545	400	345	390	960
Sheba .... do ..	70	50	40	25	20	80	95		70	67	65	64	53	49	19	11	8	36
Daney .... do ..	50	45	30	33		35	30	27	20	28	27	62	28	22	22	20	23	16
Wide West .... do ..	8	7	20	17	18	30	31	27	35	28	26	28	33	14	17	13	21	28
Burning Moscow .. do ..	15	13	28	15	18	30	19	2	6	6	7	37	40	50	55	30	33	
Pride of the West do ..	3	2				2		2	8		2	7	4	6		3		
Bullion .... do ..	50	50	40	30	18	14	40	40	55	80	110	145	155	168	162	162	118	115
Real del Monte .. do ..	15	12	11	15	12	5	15	19	35	23	23	34	23	20		80	25	13
El Dorado .... do ..			8	10														
Overman .... do ..	200	300	250	225	175	150	175	160		163	165	165	130	135	75	900	830	120
Sierra Nevada ... do ..	20	15	16	15	210	10	22	20		20	42	50	45	47	46		25	20
Yellow Jacket ... do ..	700	600	450	400	450	375	400	525	620	725	800	970	950	925	875	900	830	763
White & Murphy .. do ..																		
Sides .... do ..	400	359	210	190	210	200	200		200	250	210	190	180	200	150	145	150	170
Uncle Sam .... do ..				13		16	24	21	22	30	31	30	18	47	46	20	25	15
Baltic .... do ..	62	22	20		23	25	23	30	25	55	40						20	
North American .. do ..	42	54	34	32	20	20	15	25		23	26		40		28	55		
Baltimore American do..	10	35	9	13	17	13	13	20		13	12		8	10	10	60	15	16
Meloncs .... do ..		12				14	12			20	45	63	100		61	12		
Antelope .... do ..	65	70	50		50	60		20	15	75		70		10	63		70	28
Napoleon .... do ..	63	60	43															
Sacramento ...... do ..			18	13		5	5	6	9	5	6	3	8	5		5	3	5
Utah .... do ..	18	20	18	15	13			6		9	6	3		4		5	5	5
Lady Bryan ...... do ..	10	15	5	4	5		7											6
Imperial .... do ..										149	151	155	148	145	122	129	118	120

Table showing the fluctuations in mining shares from January 1, 1865, to June 20, 1865.

Name of company.		Jan. 1	Jan. 10	Jan. 30	Feb. 1	Feb. 10	Feb. 20	Mar. 1	Mar. 10	Mar. 30	Apr. 1	Apr. 10	Apr. 30	May 1	May 10	May 20	June 1	June 10	June 20
Gould & Curry	per ft.	$1,500	$1,480	$1,500	$1,530	$1,565	$1,625	$1,750	$1,960	$1,900	$2,010	$2,015	$1,075	$1,800	$1,480	$1,600	$1,525	$1,695	$1,645
Ophir	do	375	300	300	325	365		385	440	450	530	590	580	500	490	550	485	480	500
Savage	do	1,600	1,640	1,600	1,650	1,565	1,620	1,615	1,445	1,750	2,000	2,025	2,040	1,600	1,375	1,300	1,100	1,150	1,420
Potosi	do	700	700	700	710	750	910	750	885	900	705	915	870	640	425	337	292	319	437
Chollar	do	1,050	900	1,020	990	810	235	715	545	700	1,130	843	830	680	423	373	215	317	473
Hale & Norcross	do	960	960	1,220	945	990		240	330	350	472	625	600	430	400	455	440	400	630
Sheba	do	36	30						29	21	28			58		38	18		13
Desert	do		12	14	7	6		10	45	23	16	15	16	20	9	7	15	15	13
Wide West	do	16	12	8		66	64		14	10	13	17	10	10		7	13		3
Burning Moscow	do	28	22	24	35			53	49	34	37	39	50	47	41	43	40	46	57
Pride of the West	do				78	60	115		115	110									
Imlilou	do	115	105	75	10			110	115	16	110	135	151	150	133	152	135	130	105
Reul del Monte	do	15		12					12	3	12	14					12	10	
El Dorado	do		100	90	23	130	245		10		6								
Overman	do	120		35	975	13	17	200	357	300	303	325	330	245	240	130	215	100	150
Sierra Nevada	do	20						18	22	21	18	26	22	16	17	14	14	12	14
Yellow Jacket	do	765	810	865		1,480	1,475	1,780	2,330	2,630	2,570	2,500	2,400	2,070	1,515	1,550	1,400	1,320	1,150
White & Murphy	do								50	35	15								
Sides	do								100	50	25								
Uncle Sam	do	170	190	210	270	350	275	325	270	325	330	320	285	250	245	200	115	100	155
Baltic	do	15			22	13			29	22	30	15							
North American	do			8	15		29	31	44	41	32	34		20		25	30	28	25
Baltimore American	do			24					20	20	21								
Mejones	do								19	5	3	23							
Antelope	do	50							29	15	20								
Napoleon	do								50	33	30								
Sacramento	do								10	5	8								
Utah	do	5							5	8	3								
Lady Bryan	do	6	8	8				9	13	9	11	23							
Imperial	do	120	120	128	120	125	900	150	143	192	200	213	205	283	282	225	137	175	217
Crown Point	do		630	650	700	729		1,070	1,440	1,430	1,400	1,360	1,170	1,000	1,000	885	725	780	750
Belcher	do			975	980	1,025	1,180	1,250	1,650	1,600	1,600	1,800	1,620	1,210	1,500	1,105	923	620	600

Table showing the fluctuations in mining shares from June 20, 1865, to November 20, 1865.

[Name of company.]		June 20.	July 1.	July 10.	July 20.	July 30.	Aug. 10.	Aug. 30.	Sept. 1.	Sept. 10.	Sept. 20.	Oct. 1.	Oct. 10.	Oct. 20.	Nov. 1.	Nov. 10.	Nov. 30.
Gould & Curry	per foot	$1,645	$1,730	$1,750	$1,730	$1,500	$1,500	$1,475	$1,135	$1,300	$1,240	$1,250	$1,000	$1,015	$1,010	$1,100	$475
Ophir	do.	500	493	465	520	425	400	400	240	385	415	340	515	390	425	392	349
Savage	do.	1,425	1,375	1,400	1,310	1,175	1,220	1,300	1,390	1,225	1,213	1,340	1,075	930	880	765	625
Potosi	do.	467	332	350	365	480	465	460	440	430	410	472	455	335	350	398	270
Chollar	do.	473	345	370	410	500	480	500	475	455	620	590	480	370	375	308	270
Hale & Norcross	do.	630	569	555	570	525	530	510	489	520	550	750	475	325	395	205	155
Sheba	do.	18	14	8	14				43				30	15	10		8
Daney	do.	15	7		6		50	70		40	40	35				15	
Wide West	do.	3	14	8	23	29	25	34	23	30	5	6					
Burning Moscow	do.	57	34	29												57	38
Pride of the West	do.																
Balliea	do.	165	140	175	180	175	137	175	160	125	125	126	125	70	62	57	
Real del Monte	do.																
El Dorado	do.																
Overman	do.	130	180	342	305	590	241	213	190	335	170	175	150	100	95	62	42
Sierra Nevada	do.	14	15	10	14	25	20	18	19	22	21	17	22	12	10	12	8
Yellow Jacket	do.	1,150	1,090	1,015	1,105	1,220	1,350	1,355	1,429	1,460	1,405	1,343	1,110	720	780	670	620
White & Murphy	do.																
Sides	do.	155	185	75	60		240	215	190	165							
Uncle Sam	do.			345	307	190				16							
Baltic	do.	25	28	20	16	35	30	29	24								
North American	do.			35	42												
Baltimore American	do.																
Melones	do.																
Antelope	do.																
Napoleon	do.																
Sacramento	do.																
Utah	do.	217	228	245	6	227	6	3	252	250	221	232	210	174	180	157	150
Lady Bryan	do.	730	765	800	218	905	230	255	1,120	1,115	1,150	1,130	1,023	730	760	730	830
Imperial	do.	695	760	775	910	805	960	1,250	875	908	910	975	630	400	455	440	300
Crown Point	do.		1,450	1,400	1,470		1,425	1,500	1,925	1,930	2,100	2,250	1,700	1,000	1,010	750	930
Belcher	do.																
Alpha	do.																

Table showing the fluctuations in mining shares from November 20, 1865, to June 29, 1866.

Name of company.	Nov. 20	Dec. 1	Dec. 10	Dec. 20	Dec. 30	Jan. 10	Jan. 20	Feb. 1	Feb. 10	Feb. 20	Mar. 1	Mar. 10	Mar. 20	Mar. 31	Apr. 10	Apr. 20	May 1	May 10	May 21	May 30	June 9	June 20	June 29
Gould & Curry ..per ft	$875	$975	$940	$850	$925	$885	$865	$850	$825	$1,060	$925	$1,000	$1,050	$1,050	$950	$975	$950	$890	$850	$730	$745	$800	$700
Ophir............do	340	370	250	350	370	345	325	400	435	440	425	730	650	740	700	725	670	530	365	362	360	283	210
Savage..........do	635	670	650	960	830	700	635	930	920	900	890	1,060	1,020	1,055	1,100	1,050	1,000	1,010	900	900	675	970	900
Potosi..........do	270	249	130	125	176	139	224	363	278	322½	367	380	396	370	365	310	308	325	295	299	300	185	183
Chollar.........do	185	150	170	125	280	240	315	825	940	980	1,280	1,090	1,020	1,010	990	950	920	960	957	970	960	1,100	1,275
Hale & Norcross..do	8								8		7	13	13	10	9	10	10	9	10	10	8		
Sheba...........do																							
Daney...........do																							
Wide West.......do																							
Burning Moscow..do	8	35	32	22	37	33	32	62	52	64	60	90	100	115	117	70	83	80	67	72	60	55	57
Pr-de of the West..do																							
Bullion..........do	42	43	23	15	63	41	36	58	50	49	72	95	70	63	73	78	80	79	51	24	27	21	24
Real del Monte...do	8	61	9	3	10	10	9	6				12	11	8	9	8	5	5		2	2	3	2
El Dorado.......do	620	535	355	495	530	440	370	463	407½	393	420	700	730	880	933	805	750	712	630	622	640	635	700
Overman.........do																							
Sierra Nevada....do																								
Yellow Jacket....do													9										
White & Murphy..do																							
Sides...........do											3½												
Uncle Sam.......do						2½	10½	120	114	121	126	177½	156	140	150	109	134	128	120	121	112	93	106
Bullie...........do	120	150	85	100	130	113	350	690	835	925	1,080	1,350	1,300	1,390	1,380	1,380	1,250	1,350	950	1,000	1,050	940	900
North American..do	830	700	490	460	540	565	230	195	160	180	270	300	285	340	377	310	332	327	175	192	160	150	162
Baltimore American.do	900	740	245	140	175	145	300	370	290	270	271	310	329	410	430	305	280	329	193	280	300	245	206
Antelope........do																							
Lady Bryan......do																							
Imperial.........do																							
Crown Point.....do																							
Belcher.........do																							
Alpha..........do																							

Table showing the fluctuations in mining shares from June 29, 1866, to September 30, 1866.

Name of company.	June 29.	July 10.	July 20.	July 30.	Aug. 10.	Aug. 20.	Aug. 30.	Sept. 10.	Sept. 20.	Sept. 30.
Gould & Curry........per ft.	$700	$725	$720	$705	$715	$740	$700	$710	$600	$610
Ophir.................do....	210	235	280	245	272	220	210	210	200	207
Savage................do....	900	865	925	950	1,200	1,150	1,085	1,160	1,100	1,115
Chollar-Potosi.........do....	183	185	190	171	180	173	129	136	115	110
Hale & Norcross........do....	1,275	1,260	1,300	1,425	1,600	1,650	1,600	1,750	1,680	1,800
Sheba.................do....										
Daney.................do....					5½			4½		
Wide West.............do....										
Bullion...............do....	57	58	47½	47	25	27	20	23	20	15
Real del Monte........do....										
El Dorado.............do....										
Overman...............do....	24	50	47	38	39	27½	11½	14½	4½	4
Sierra Nevada.........do....	2	4½	5	4½	2½			6½	5½	2½
Yellow Jacket.........do....	700	580	590	945	722	630	730	770	685	682
White & Murphy........do....										
Baltic................do....										
North American........do....										
Baltimore American....do....										
Melones...............do....										
Sacramento............do....										
Antelope..............do....										
Lady Bryan............do....										
Imperial..............do....	106	104	94	94	94	90	95	96	84	82
Crown Point...........do....	900	700	850	875	925	950	935	880	825	875
Belcher...............do....	162	170	155	130	149	108	125	120	115	94
Alpha.................do....	206			100	95				50	
Empire Mill & MiningCo.do....					115	120	103		77½	80
Confidence............do....				55	50	51	43	59	49	55
De Soto...............do....								3½		

These tables cover but a comparatively short period and do not show the more extreme and violent fluctuations that took place during the earlier periods in the history of mining speculations. Thus in the early part of the summer of 1859 the Ophir ground could be bought for one hundred dollars, and the Gould & Curry for three dollars per foot. In less than eight months the former had risen to $1,000, and the latter to $600 per foot, and though the Gould & Curry stock, owing to assessments, and the fact that no ore was being taken out, fell during the summer of 1861 to $200 per foot, we find that in less than two years from that time it was selling currently at the rate of $5,000 per foot, and again but one year thereafter for less than $1,000, and though it subsequently rallied somewhat, selling in April, 1865, for a little over $2,000 per foot, it can at the present time be bought for about one-fourth that sum; nor is this an extreme case, most of the other claims on the Comstock ledge having undergone similar vicissitudes, while some at Gold Hill have fluctuated still more widely. At one time the Empire ground could not be bought at $10,000 per foot; now it can be had for a little more than $1,000. The Sheba, Daney, Wide West, Burning Moscow, Real del Monte, and others that might be named, though now selling for almost nominal prices, and some of them not salable at all, were once selling currently at $500 per foot, upon most of them expensive mills and hoisting works having since been erected. Hundreds of claims that during these periodical seasons of excitement were finding buyers readily at sums varying all the way from one to a hundred dollars per foot are now no longer heard of, being in fact of no value whatever. In the shares of the productive mines on the Comstock ledge it is believed no further depreciation will be likely to take place, but rather that most of them will advance in price, the payment of dividends suspended upon many of them during the past year being gradually resumed, and though not so large as formerly, with a prospect of being continued hereafter. The Hale & Norcross company are now making monthly dividends of $75 per foot; the Yellow Jacket, of $50; the Gould & Curry, of $25; and many other companies greater or less amounts, while a few, owing to extra expenses the past year, are not making any, but expect to do so in a few weeks or months. Previous to June 1, 1865, the Empire company had taken from their mine a sum total of $1,500,000, of which $287,500 were paid in dividends. Including the product of the present year, the Gould & Curry company have taken from their mine a grand total of $14,000,000, of which $6,500,000 have been paid out in general disbursements and improvements; a little over $3,000,000 for work done by custom mills; the balance, something over $4,000,000, having been paid to the stockholders in dividends, while the assessments levied have been comparatively small. The extent to which assessments have been levied upon the principal mines in various parts of the State recently, dividends, &c., can be readily seen by reference to the following tables:

Table exhibiting the extent, value, &c., of the principal mines in the State, with total amount of assessments thereon, prior to January 1, 1865.

Name of company.	No. of feet in mine.	Shares per foot.	Total No. of shares.	Incorporate value.	Bid per foot.	Asked per foot.	Last monthly dividend per foot.	Recent assessments. (date / per foot)	Recent assessments. (date / per foot)	Total assessments per foot.
WASHOE DISTRICT.										
Baltimore American	2,600	1	2,600	$500		$30 00		Jan. 18 $5 00	May 31 $5 00	$16 75
Baltic	1,800	1	1,800	240	$15 00	25 00		July 23 6 00	Oct. 12 10 00	45 00
Bajazett and Golden Era	4,000	1	4,000	300	27 00	20 00		July 20 5 00	Aug. 3 5 00	36 25
Best & Belcher	224	4	896	500		250 00		Sept. 21 10 00	Dec. 23 50 10	369 00
Harding Moscow	4,100	1	4,100	500	21 00	25 00		Jan. 29 15 00	June 24 7 00	56 31
Burnside	800	1	800	540	7 00	8 00		Feb. 16 2 00	Aug. 31 30	9 50
Belcher	1,040	3	3,120	1,000	775 00	800 00	$24 00			
Buckeye, G.	100	10	1,000	100		3 00		Oct. 21 3 00	Dec. 17 2 50	25 70
Bullion, G. H.	200	12	2,500	200	105 00	167 00		Sept. 13 10 00	Sept. 17 10 00	
California	300	4	1,600	300				July 46 150 00		
Central	150	4	600	400		10 00		Jan. 23 13 00		
Caledonia Tunnel	5,000	1	5,000	1,000	625 00	600 00		July 12 1 50	Dec. 24 4 00	19 50
Crown Point	630	1	630	630		10 10	40 00	Nov. 30 5 00	March 16 3 00	190 00
China Cañon	1,800	1	1,800	30		150 00		Jan. 25 60 00	April 15 30 00	25 00
Chollar	600	4	2,400	800	1,025 00	15 00		Sept. 13 10 00	Nov. 7 8 00	320 00
Daney	60	4	2,000	60	12 60	3,045 00		Jan. 30 1 00		66 00
Desert	100	1	200	100		15 00		March 2 00		
Eldorado	600	1	600	500			25 00	Nov. 2 00	Nov. 3 2 00	27 00
Empire M. and M. Co	75	16	1,200	75		525 00	75 00	Dec. 17 3 50	March 29 10 00	
Gould & Curry	1,200	4	4,800	1,200	1,463 00	1,470 00		Nov. 8 50 00	Dec. 28 30 00	225 00
Grass Valley	400	1	400	500		30 00	7 50	Dec. 12 12 50	per share	270 00
Hale & Norcross	400	2	800	300	235 00	280 00		Nov. 10 1 00	July 16 6 00	27 00
Imperial	164	1	164	1,000	120 00	123 00		Nov. 18 3 00	Nov. 1 5 00	25 00
Iowa	1,200	1	1,200	100	5 00	12 00		July 27 3 00	Feb. 16 1 00	35 00
Lady Bryan	5,000	1	5,000	500		6 00		Nov. 10 10 00	March 2 10 00	7 50
Lucerne	600	1	600	300		3 00		Feb. 23 12 50	Feb. 18 12 50	
Mount Hope, G. H.	600	1	1,500	100		17 00		Nov. 29 2 00	Dec. 12 2 00	57 00
Michigan	2,100	1	2,000	200	40 00	41 00		Oct. 6 2 00	Oct. 18 2 00	140 00
Nevada, J. O.	250	1	2,000	250		20 00		Aug. 25 1 00	Dec. 25 25	
North Potosi	300	1	1,600	540	8 00	9 00		Sept. 11 2 00	March 1 00	11 50
North American	4,100	1	4,100					Nov. 3 2 00	April	
North Ophir	1,600	1	1,600	600			48 00	Oct.		
Norton	50	1	600	300		8 00				
Ophir	600	12	16,800	600	300 00	320 00		July 7 30 00	Nov. 19 50 00	62 00
Overman	1,200	1	1,200	500		25 00				
Potosi	1,400	2	2,800	500	600 00	675 00				

Table exhibiting the extent, value, &c., of the principal mines in the State, &c.—Continued.

Name of company.	No. of feet in mine.	Shares per foot.	Total No. of shares.	Incorporate value.	Bid per foot.	Asked per foot.	Last monthly dividend per foot.	Recent assessments per foot.				Total assessments per foot.
								Date	Amount	Date	Amount	
Porter	600	4	2,400	350	$5 00	$30 00	$5 00	Jan. 12	$3 00	Dec. 16	$9 00	$10 00
Pride of the West	1,400	1	1,400	100		6 00	75 00	Oct. 16	9 00			9 00
Savage	800	1	800	2,000	1,000 00	1,625 00		Feb. 11	4 00	April 21	10 00	175 00
Sacramento and Meredith	3,600	4	14,400	2,195		12 00		Dec. 21	50 00	March 17	25 00	
Sides	500	2	1,000	500		175 00		March 8	5 00	March 16	30 00	96 00
Sierra Nevada	3,000	1	3,000	500		23 00		March 26	5 00	May 13	5 00	
Spanish No. 2	1,600	1	1,600	500		10 00		Aug. 25	100 00	Dec. 29	60 00	227 00
Uncle Sam	1,200	1	1,200	210	200 00	205 00		March 25	10 00	June 31	7 50	27 30
Whitman	1,800	4	1,800	1,000				Oct. 6	18 00	Dec.	6 00	904
White & Murphy	210	4	840	150		50 00		July 21	30 00	Aug. 4	110 00	250 00
Yellow Jacket	1,200	1	1,200	1,000	760 00	285 00						
ESMERALDA DISTRICT.												
Antelope	1,200	1	1,200	500	40	60 00		Feb. 19	25 00	Sept. 14	25 00	162 50
Bamboo	600	1	600	500				Sept. 18	5 00	June 20	2 00	21 50
Esmeralda	1,640	1	1,640	1,000		5 00		Nov. 20	30			12 25
Falls of the Clyde	6,000	1	6,000	100								9 72
Golden Age and Empire	250	2	500	250	14 00	15 00	5 00	Nov. 6	1 00	Feb. 9	50	
Nevada	400	1	400	250		25 00		March 8	20 00			44 50
Real del Monte	3,110	1	3,400	500		7 00		Nov. 18	20 00	Sept. 20	12 50	8 25
Silver Hill	400	1	400	500				Jan. 5	3 00	Nov. 21	5 00	
Ural	1,600	1	1,600	250	12 00	5 00		May 25	5 00			19 00
Wide West	2,000	1	2,000	500		15 00						90 00
COSO DISTRICT.												
Coso	26,000	2	3,600	600				Jan. 29	1 00	May 11	1 00	13 00
Josephine	2,600		4,800	250				July 31	50	Nov. 19	1 00	20 50
San Carlos		2	2,800	100	30 00			April 14	1 50	June 6	4 00	7 50
Willow Springs	2,100	1	700	100				Sept. 9	2 00	Jan.	1 00	
HUMBOLDT DISTRICT.												
De Soto	1,980	2	1,980	100	30 00	35 00		Sept. 17	2 50	Dec. 12	50	19 35
Sheba	1,800		3,000	500				Aug. 12	50 00	Nov. 25	30 00	92 35

REESE RIVER DISTRICT.												
Amador	1,400		1,400			May	3	5 00	June	21	4 00	20 00
Coral	1,000		1,000			Jan.	29	2 00	May	25	3 00	8 40
Florida	800	1	900	500								
Oregon	880	1	600	200	20 00	Dec.	8	50	Dec.	29	10 00	1 00
Union No. 2	1,000	2	800	300		Nov.	16	10 00				2 50
Whitlatch	1,200	3	1,200	500		Nov.	23	50				36 00
Willow	2,600	2	2,400	1,000								
Yankee Blade	1,400	1	1,400	200	60 00	March	28	1 00	Sept.	5	3 00	5 50
North Star	1,000	1	1,000	500								1 50
Governor Seymour	1,000	1	1,030	500								1 50
Diana	1,200	1	1,200	500								2 00
Blue Ledge	1,000	1	1,000	500		Jan.	18	50				1 50
Joe Lane	1,600	1	1,060	2,500		Jan.	18	50				1 00
Honest Miner	3,400	1	1,400	3,000					March	21	50	2
MEXICO.												
Dios Padre	2,220	1	1,020	500	40 00	Dec.	13	3 00	Dec.			50 00
Mina Prieta	2,200	1	2,200	1,000		Dec.	20	10 00				160 00
Padre Guadalupe	3,000	1	3,000	1,000	25 00							9 00
San Marcial	13,200	1	13,200	100		Sept.	10	2 00				
San Nicholas	1,300	1	1,200	200					Sept.		2 00	
MISCELLANEOUS.												
Blue Ledge	7,800	1	7,800	50	3 00	June	16	1 50	Oct.	5	1 25	
Fellows	2,540	1	2,540	100								
Melones	3,400	1	3,400	50		June	30	50	Oct.	27	2 50	13 00
Napoleon	2,700	1	2,700	600	65 00	Feb.	13	10 00	June	8	5 00	17 00
Truxto, L. C.	7,866	1	7,866	200	22 00	Dec.	13	2 00				

* November 16, $9.

Table exhibiting the extent, value, &c., of the principal mines in the State, with total amount of assessments thereon, prior to October 1, 1866.

Name of company.	No. of feet in mine.	Shares per foot.	Total No. of shares.	Incorporate value.	Bid per foot.	Asked per foot.	Last monthly divd. dead per foot.	Recent assessments per foot.						Total assessments per foot.
WASHOE DISTRICT.														
Alpha	278	$4	1,200	$1,000	$70 00			Feb.	20	$120 00	April	24	$200 00	$1,240 00
Becca M. and M. Co	45	20	900	800				Aug.	11	10 00				31 75
Baltimore American	2,600	1	600	500				March	10	2 00	May	12	3 00	43 00
Baltic	1,800	1	1,800	200										390 00
Best & Belcher	224	4	896	500										91 34
Burning Moscow	4,100	1	4,100	500										11 50
Bureau	2,800	1	2,800					Feb.	1	50	May	5	1 00	
Belcher	1,040	1	1,040	1,000	77 50	80 00		March	30	67 00	July	21	45 00	36 70
Buckeye	3,600	1	800	160				Sept.	6	3 00	Dec.	1	3 10	
Bullion, O. H.	2,500	1	800	500	5 00	8 00		April	23	10 00	July	12	10 00	
Calif-ruia	300		2,000	300										
Central	150	10	1,800	280				July	19	5 00	Dec.	21	2 00	27 00
Caledonia Tunnel	5,000	12	2,400	400	300 00	300 00	$80 00	Nov.	8	2 00				390 00
Crown Point	600	4	1,500	1,000	93 00	953 00		April	5	25 00	Aug.	10	3 00	443 00
Confidence	130	12	1,800	500	30 00	51 00		Dec.	16	100 00				87 00
Chollar-Potosi	2,400	4	8,000	600	109 00	118 00	6 00	June	12	3 00				
Daney	60	1	60	60	5 00	5 50								
Desert	200	2	100	100		1 50								
Exchequer	400	20	300	300	68 00	75 00		Dec.	13	2 00	June	30	2 00	
Empire M. and M. Co	75	16	800	800		300 00	100 00							$25 00
Gould & Curry	1,200	4	1,200	1,200	1,675 00	1,600 00	6 00	Dec.	13	50 00				270 00
Grass Valley	4,200	2	4,800	500	73 00	80 00								27 00
Hale & Norcross	400	2	800	500										27 75
Imperial	184		4,000	1,000										35 00
Iowa	1,200	1	1,200					March	5	1 00	May	18	1 00	
Lady Bryan	5,000	1	5,000	100										
Lucerne	1,810	4	1,800	500										
Minerva	890	1	3,600	500										
Michigan	1,500	1	1,500	100				July	24	10 00	Oct.	4	7 00	74 00
Nevada, J. O.	2,100	1	2,100	200				Aug.	6	12 50	Oct.	18	12 50	140 00
North Potosi	2,000	1	2,000	250				Aug.	12	10 00	Nov.	16	6 00	
North American	4,190	1	4,100	300										
North Uphir	1,600	1	1,600	500										
Norton	1,600	1	1,600	50										
Ophir	1,400	1	16,800	300	160 00	125 00		Aug.	31	100 00	Aug.	24	15 00	11 50
Overman	1,200	12	3,200	500				May	5	10 00				

Name														
Porter	600	600	1	600	500			Oct.	24	100 00	May	12	20 00	10 00
Pride of the West	1,400	1,400	1	1,400	100									9 00
Savage	800	800	1	800	2,000	1,185 00	75 00							233 00
Sacramento and Meredith	14,100	3,600	4	14,100	125	1,300 00								
Skira	500	560	2	500	540	1 30								
Sierra Nevada	3,100	3,100	1	3,100	500			Feb.	7	20 00	May	12	20 00	116 00
Spanish No. 2	1,600	1,600	1	1,600	500	1 75		Aug.	2	4 00	Oct.	2	2 50	
Whitman	1,530	1,530	1	1,530	1,000									
White & Murphy	210	840	4	210	150			June	18	7 50				27 50
Yellow Jacket	1,200	1,200	1	1,200	1,048	715 00	50 00	Oct.	30	22 50	Feb.	12	120 00	303 50
						720 00		Nov.	14	100 00				400 00
ESMERALDA DISTRICT.														
Antelope	1,200	1,200	1	1,200	500			Sept.	18	5 00	June	20	2 00	162 50
Humboo	600	640	1	640	500									21 50
Esmeralda	1,640	1,640	1	1,640	1,000									12 25
Falls of the Clyde	6,000	6,000	1	6,000	100			Nov.	20	50				9 72
Golden Age and Empire	2,600	2,600	2	2,600	250									
Nevada	600	600	1	600	250									
Real del Monte	4,400	4,400	2	4,400	400			Jan.	5	2 00				44 50
Silver Hill	3,040	3,040	1	3,040	500			Nov.	18	20 00				8 25
Ural	400	400	1	400	500									19 00
Utah	1,600	1,600	1	1,600	230									111 50
Wide West	2,000	2,600	1	2,000	540			Oct.	3	5 00	Oct.	18	5 00	
COSO DISTRICT.														
Coso	26,000	3,600		26,000	600			March	2	1 30	Sept.	20	1 00	14 00
Josephine	9,600	4,800	2	9,600	250									20 50
San Carlos		4,640			110									7 50
Willow Springs	2,700	2,700	1	2,700	100									
HUMBOLDT DISTRICT.														
De Soto	1,980	1,980	1	1,980	100			June	17	2 50				96 85
Sheba	1,800	3,640	2	3,640	500									112 35
REESE RIVER DISTRICT.														
Amador	11,200	1,400		1,400	1,000			Feb.	28	5 00				96 50
Coral	1,000	1,400	1	1,400	500									8 40
Florida	800	800	1	800	200									
Oregon	800	1,600		1,600	300									1 00
Union No. 2	1,000	1,000		1,000	500									2 50
Whitlatch	2,800	1,200	2	1,200	1,000			April	29	10 00				56 00
Willow	1,000	2,400	1	2,400	200									
Yankee Blade	1,400	2,400	1	2,400	500									
North Star	1,000	2,000	1	2,000	500			May	1	5 00				5 50
Governor Seymour	1,000	2,000	1	2,000	500									1 50
Diana	1,300	1,300	1	1,300	500									1 50
Blue Ledge	1,000	1,000	1	1,000	1,200									2 50

* Per share.

Table exhibiting the extent, value, &c., of the principal mines in the State, &c.—Continued.

Name of company.	No. of feet in mine.	Shares per foot.	Total No. of shares.	Incorporate value.	Bid per foot.	Asked per foot.	Last monthly divid'd per foot.	Recent assessments per foot.	Total assessments per foot.
Joe Lane	1,000	$1	1,000	$500					$1 00
Honest Miner	1,400	1	1,400	1,000					2 00
MEXICO.									
Dios Padre	2,900	1	1,920	500				Dec. 20 $10 00	52 00
Mina Prieta	2,280	1	2,280	1,000					160 00
Padre Guadelupe	3,000	1	3,000	1,000					9 00
San Marcial	13,290	1	13,290	100					
San Nicholas	1,300	1	1,200	200				Sept. 10 2 00	
MISCELLANEOUS.									
Rice Ledge	7,890	1	7,890	50				Oct. 5 1 25 July 12 $1 50	
Fellows	2,500	1	2,500	100				March 22 1 00 Oct. 6 2 50	
Melones	3,000	1	3,000	50				June 30 5 00 Dec. 20 7 05	
Napoleon	3,700	1	3,700	600				May 18 2 00 July 6 3 00	
Triunto, L. C.	2,866	1	7,866	200					

From the foregoing tables it will be perceived that several mines upon which heavy assessments have been paid are now worth nothing at all, the Baltic, North Potosi, and the White & Murphy, in the Washoe district, the Antelope and Wide West in Esmeralda, and the Sheba in Humboldt, being cases in point. It will also be seen that in other cases of this kind though the assessments per foot are much less, the total amount collected and expended upon these now worthless mines is large, owing to the great number of feet they contain, the Baltimore American, Amador, Buckeye, Burnside, &c., being examples of this class. The Alpha is quoted as worth only $70 per foot, while the assessments amount to $1,240 per foot, from which, if this quotation is to be accepted as indicating its true value, it would appear that the stockholders of this mine have sunk over $325,000, besides the original cost of their grounds; a view that the actual facts in this particular case will hardly justify, the company owning a valuable hoisting works and the prospects of their mine being far from desperate.

The above tables contain the names of only a small portion of the companies that have been organized, generally incorporated at considerable expense, for the purpose of mining, or rather perhaps it should be said dealing and speculating in mine in this State; nor do they indicate more than one in a hundred of the ledges that at some time between the summers of 1860 and 1864 were supposed to possess some considerable value, and upon which more or less work was during that period performed. These ledges were not confined to the so-called Washoe district, meaning the central western portion of the State, but were scattered all over it except the extreme northern, eastern, and southern parts, which had not then been much explored. The amount of money expended upon or about these ledges in various ways, the most of it in attempts at opening them with shafts or tunnels, varied from the smallest sum to $100,000, being in the aggregate very large, not less perhaps, labor included, than three or four millions of dollars, nearly all of which, though not illegitimately applied—the prospecting of these mines being a necessary measure—was practically lost, very few of them having exhibited a sufficient quantity of pay ores to impart to them any value. It must be remembered, however, that but few of them have been opened to any great depth, leaving a chance for the finding of more metalliferous ores, should they ever be more thoroughly explored, as many of them undoubtedly will be. In speaking of this class of lodes on which more or less labor has been expended, no allusion is made to the still larger class, numbered by thousands, which were located under the laws of the various districts, and after being held for a short time were abandoned, being forfeited for want of the requisite improvements, and upon which, fortunately, no work was done at all. But even this class did not fail in seasons of excitement to possess at least a nominal value in the mining-share market, some of them being disposed of to the ignorant or credulous for considerable sums of money. Fortunately this mode of procedure is now pretty much over with, never, it is hoped, to be again reinstated. It will be seen by these tables that while the losses from the depreciation of mines upon which assessments have been paid have been heavier in the Washoe district, they have been quite as frequent, considering the entire number, and even more complete, in the outside districts, where, so far as the stock reports indicate, all values would seem to have been extinguished for this species of property. Of the seventy millions of dollars extracted from the mines in Nevada, it is questionable whether even one-third has been paid to the shareholders in the shape of dividends—not enough in many cases to cover the assessments they have been called upon to pay; while it is well known the mines, taken as a whole, with all improvements, would not sell for anything like what they cost. Yet at present many of these properties are depressed in price far below their intrinsic value, as the experience of the future will undoubtedly show.

Extent and cost of underground work.—Including tunnels, shafts, adits, drifts, and actual stopings excavated in the business of exploitation, prospecting, and ventilating the Comstock vein, it is estimated that the various companies owning mines along it have executed an amount of subterranean work equal to nearly forty miles in linear extent. The expense attending this kind of work depends so wholly upon their size, length or depth, the material to be removed or penetrated, and other circumstances surrounding each particular case, that it would be difficult to fix upon a figure indicating their average cost. The price for excavating shafts and tunnels ranges from five to fifty dollars per running foot, many of the larger tunnels having cost throughout more than twenty dollars per foot. These prices, as are all the other money estimates in this report being based on specie values. The sinking of the larger and deeper shafts, including timbering, has generally cost from twenty to forty dollars per foot. The large shaft intended for both working and prospecting purposes now being put down jointly by the Empire and Imperial companies at Gold Hill, estimated throughout, will cost at the rate of fifty-eight or sixty dollars per foot. This is, however, of extra large dimensions, being seven feet four inches by thirty feet eight inches, and to be carried down 1,200 feet. It will call for twelve months' time and an expenditure of about $80,000 to complete it. Short tunnels and shafts of moderate depth, where the ground is tolerably favorable, can be excavated for six or seven dollars per foot, and sometimes for less. In this kind of work on and about the Comstock ledge there has been expended between two and three millions of dollars, exclusive of the expense attendant on the removal of the ores and the timbering up of the mines.

4.—MINING PROPERTY, ETC.

Number and capacity of mills, hoisting works, &c.—There are at this time 170 mills for the crushing and reduction of ores in the State of Nevada. This number embraces only such establishments as are now completed and ready for running or nearly so, there being several, some of them of large capacity, in course of construction, but not sufficiently advanced to warrant speaking of them as being already in existence. These mills carry 2,564 stamps, weighing from 400 to 800 pounds each, the average being about 600 pounds, and have an aggregate capacity equal to 6,322 horses. Their average cost has been about $60,000, or an aggregate of $10,000,000, one of them, the Gould & Curry, carrying 80 stamps and supplied with two large engines, has cost, with grounds, alterations, and surroundings, over $1,000,000; several others have cost from $150,000 to $250,000, the Ophir, in Washoe valley, having cost much more. Of this number 35 are driven by water and the balance by steam, a few of each class using both water and steam. Of these mills 36 are in Story county, 34 in Lyon, 10 in Washoe, 8 in Ormsby, and 1 in Douglas, a total of 89, all of which are running on Comstock ore; Esmeralda county contains 21 mills, Nye 8, Lander 22, Humboldt 5, and Churchill 4. Some of these structures are very substantial, being built of brick and granite or other stone; some, on the contrary, being cheap and fragile; the machinery, however, is in most cases good. At the time many of them were erected labor, freights, and material were much higher than at present, wherefore they cost a great deal more than equally good establishments would now do. Attached to most of these mills are shops, ore and timber sheds, and, in some cases, boarding-houses, &c., the cost of which is generally included with that of the mill. Twenty per cent. or more of these mills are not at present running, most of those lying idle being in the outside districts. Those employed upon the Comstock ores are mostly kept running, except a few that may be stopping for repairs. Of all the mills in Esmeralda county not more than one-half are at work, nor have they been for the past two years. In Lander county there are also many unemployed, particularly about Austin. The causes of these stoppages are various; in a few cases the mills are imperfect and not fit to do good work. In others they have been tied up with litigation, or perhaps been unable to run steadily for want of water. The principal trouble, however, in both Lander and Esmeralda has been an insufficiency of pay-ores to keep them running, the ledges about Austin being so extremely small that although in some cases rich, they can supply only a very inconsiderable quantity of ore, while in Esmeralda, where the ledges are large, the good ores found upon the surface appear to have run out. A number of deep prospecting shafts have lately been undertaken there, and it is generally believed by those best acquainted with the mines that bodies of remunerative ores will yet be found at greater depths.

Most of these mills run day and night, stopping only on Sundays; at which time machinery is examined and such temporary repairs as may be needed are made. They employ from five to fifty hands each, the usual number being from ten to fifteen, though the Gould & Curry mill requires over a hundred. In a majority of cases the mill-owners also own mines and crush their own rock, while some do custom work, reducing ores for others at so much per ton, or buy and crush it on their own account. A few crush the ores dry, though nearly all adopt the wet method. It is generally calculated that each stamp will crush a ton of ore every twenty-four hours. Some do less and others do more, according to the weight of the stamp and the character of the ore. Besides these mills there are in the State six smelting works, the most of them on a small scale, and twenty-five or thirty arastras—some driven by water, but the greater number by horse or mule power. There are also in the State about fifty steam pumping and hoisting works, many of them structures of a costly and massive kind. There are also in the State a number of large foundries and machine-shops, and over fifty saw-mills, mostly propelled by water, with one small flour-mill now running, and another being erected.

Roads, ditches, &c.—A number of toll-roads, several of them extending over the sierra and others quite into the interior of the State, have been built under the charters from the present State or former Territorial legislature. The length of these roads, some of which have been very expensive and formidable works, is not less in the aggregate than three hundred miles, the entire cost of their construction having been over $500,000. One of these, the Kingsbury road, crossing the sierra near Genoa, has cost, with alterations and improvements, $150,000; the amount of tolls it has taken in being more than double that sum. As a general thing, however, these roads have not proved lucrative, the amount of tolls received barely sufficing to keep them in repair and pay a moderate interest on the investment, some failing to even do this. The water ditches of this State, built either for milling or irrigating purposes, and generally for both, are numerous, but not, with the exception of two or three, of great magnitude. The Humboldt ditch, nearly one-half built, taking water from that river and conveying it to the vicinity of the principal mines, is seven feet wide on top, five on the bottom, and two deep. It will be over sixty miles long, and will cost when completed nearly $100,000. Preparations are now being made for constructing a large aqueduct, to be built of wood, for taking the entire body of water running in the west branch of Carson river from its cañon and conveying it to Empire City, a distance of nearly thirty miles. The work as projected will cost over $200,000. Other ditches and flumes, not of such magnitude, but still quite extensive, are to be found at Empire City, Dayton, in Washoe and Truckee valleys, and elsewhere throughout the State, the number of small ones along the eastern slope of the sierra and among the mountains of the interior, built mainly for irrigating purposes, being quite large; and gradually, as population and improvements increase, the running waters of the State will be diverted from their natural into artificial channels, to be used for irrigation and propulsive power. There are about thirty saw-mills in the State, all but one driven by water. With the exception of three or four of limited capacity in the Reese river country, they are all situated in the foot-hills along the eastern base of the sierra, where water-power is abundant, and where alone any really good timber is to be found. The price of lumber at these mills is about $20 per thousand, the cost increasing rapidly with the distance it has to be hauled.

Number of companies formed for mining purposes; districts erected, ledges located, &c.—The number of mining companies incorporated for the purpose of prospecting for locating, working, or dealing in mines in the State of Nevada, amounts to over one thousand. Many of these never proceeded to actual operations beyond the act of organizing, and most of them cannot be said to have a present existence. Besides these incorporated companies three times as many minor associations, though often consisting of the same parties, were organized under the laws of the several mining districts for similar purposes; most of these, like their more pretentious neighbors, having since been disbanded and ceased as companies to have any existence. Of the number of districts erected or ledges located by these numerous parties during the three or four years that the mining excitement raged, no accurate statement can be made, new districts being formed and after a short time disbanded, to be again followed by others covering in part or perhaps the whole of the same territory; and ledges being located by the thousand, to be in like manner given up, being forfeited from failure to do the requisite amount of work or otherwise comply with the laws of the district. In size these districts varied greatly, as they still do, being from ten to a hundred miles square, and having as a general rule natural objects, such as mountains, valleys, ravines, &c., for boundaries. The number of mining districts in the State regularly organized and having a recognized legal existence, with records and officials, may be set down at about one hundred; the number of ledges worked sufficiently to hold them under the local laws of the district where they are situated, may be roughly estimated at between four and five thousand. Upon some of these a large amount of work has been done, though upon nine-tenths of them but very little. Of the adult population of the State about two-thirds are engaged in the various branches of mining. Wages of miners vary from $3 50 to $5 per day, or from $60 to $100 per month. The prices of labor, like almost everything else, are from fifty to seventy-five per cent. higher in this State than in California.

Taxes and legislation.—The only measures adopted by the general government looking to a realization of revenue from the mines on this coast are the laws passed by Congress in the years 1864 and 1865. The first of these, which took effect August 29, 1864, provided for the levying of a tax of one-half of one per cent. on all bullion assayed, and prohibiting, under severe penalties, the sale, transfer, exchange, transportation, exportation, or working of any bullion not having first been assayed. The other law requires every miner whose receipts amount to over one thousand dollars per year, and every person, firm or company employing others in the business of mining, to take out a license for which they shall pay the sum of ten dollars. Neither of these measures can be considered impolitic, unjust or oppressive, nor are they the subject of complaint by the great mass of those most affected by them. In addition to these acts the legislature of the State of Nevada enacted a law two years since, by which it is provided that from the gross returns or assayed value per ton of all ores, quartz or minerals in that State, from which either gold or silver is extracted, there shall first be deducted the sum of twenty dollars per ton, and upon seventy-five per cent. of the remainder a tax of one per cent. ad valorem shall be levied for State and county purposes, provision also being made for collecting a like tax upon any of this class of ores transported from the State. The revenue derived from this source for the year 1865 amounted, in Story county, where the principal mines are situated, to $40,145, to which may be added two or three thousand for outside districts. The State also taxes the mills, hoisting works, and all other above-ground fixtures and properties, real and personal, but not the mines proper. The mineral land law passed at the last session of Congress, providing for the sale of mines upon the public domains, though exciting some apprehension among miners at first, and perhaps somewhat imperfect in its details. is now generally approved, and will, no doubt, result in benefit to both the government and those most affected by its operations.   By enabling the present claimants to secure titles to their mines, it will increase the confidence of capitalists in this species of property, and thus greatly enhance its value and tend to promote its more rapid development.   The only title heretofore enjoyed or obtainable by these claimants has been one of possession, held under sufferance from the general government and by virtue of the local laws, rules, and regulations of the several mining districts, and which latter, though generally wholesome and just in their provisions, were always brief and insufficient, considering the momentous interests constantly growing up under them, and not unfrequently contradictory and obscure, or otherwise imperfect and objectionable.   The laws of the various districts, though similar in their general features, often differ in some of their provisions.   They are, however, so nearly alike in all essential particulars that the few examples hereunto appended will serve sufficiently to illustrate their common character.

5.—GENERAL VIEW OF THE MINES OF NEVADA, WASHINGTON TERRITORY, UTAH, MONTANA, AND IDAHO.

General view of the mines of Nevada.—In considering the mines and the metalliferous territory of Nevada it has been customary to divide the State into several sections designated as follows, viz: the Washoe, the Esmeralda, the Humboldt, and the Reese River districts, each of which covers a large area of country and contains a number of those smaller subdivisions known as mining districts.

The Washoe region.—This embraces all the central and western portion of the State, and includes the counties of Douglas, Ormsby, Washoe, Story, and Lyon, which, united, contain only as much territory as Roop, scarcely half as much as either Esmeralda or Churchill, and not one-quarter that embraced within the limits of either Humboldt, Nye, or Lander county.   Notwithstanding its comparatively diminutive size, Story county contains more than one-third of the taxable property as well as of the inhabitants of the State.   The only mines of any considerable and well-established value in the Washoe region, those upon the Comstock lode, being also in this county, and from which is extracted more than ninety per cent. of all the bullion produced in the State.

Upon the discovery of the Comstock ledge a large population was drawn over the mountains, the number of inhabitants within the boundaries of the present State of Nevada being somewhat larger in 1863 than at this time.   Prospecting— that is, exploring the country for metalliferous veins—was at once commenced and pushed with vigor; a good proportion of the Washoe, Esmeralda, and Humboldt regions having been subjected to a pretty thorough inspection during the first three years following the discovery of silver.   Within this time thousands of ledges were located throughout all parts of this extensive Territory. Many of these were of large size, well defined, and frequently prospected well, sometimes largely, in both gold and silver upon the surface.   Others were of less magnitude, lacked the features of true veins, and were quite or nearly barren of the precious metals.   In some cases free gold abounded in the croppings. but the preponderating metal, so far as any existed, was silver, the most of these being located as argentiferous veins.   Upon a few of the larger and more promising a large amount of work was performed, while upon a majority but little or nothing was done; the sums expended upon them, however, could not in the aggregate have been less than eight or ten millions of dollars, some estimating it much higher.   All this large sum of money was spent in the mere preliminary business of prospecting and exploring a class of mines which, with but few exceptions, have thus far proved unproductive, and may be set down as possessing no present market value, many, even of those upon which large sums had been expended, being now abandoned. The total amount of bullion extracted from all the mines in the Washoe, Esmeralda, and Humboldt regions, apart from those on the Comstock lode, will not this year amount to half a million dollars, a sum considerably less than what was realized from them during several preceding years. It is not to be inferred, however, that all these mines will ultimately prove worthless. A considerable number only require more careful management and a sufficiency of means to secure for them deeper and a more thorough exploration to render their working almost certainly remunerative and perhaps largely profitable. Excluding eighty per cent. of all the ledges located as belonging to a class so manifestly worthless that no work should ever have been performed upon them, one-half of the remainder may be set down as possessing such signs of value as would warrant a moderate expenditure to prove more fully their character, while the balance may justly be considered as being lodes that with judicious management and the application of a moderate sum can speedily be developed into productive and paying mines, many of them being already in an advanced stage of exploration, a few having steam hoisting works attached to them, and a still smaller number mills also for reducing their ores. The great mistakes made in these earlier efforts at silver mining, as displayed both in the regions under consideration and elsewhere, consisted in locating and attempting to open so many worthless ledges, and in the superficial character of the work performed generally. Through this means vast sums were uselessly thrown away, and by so much scattering the work applied, nothing was done effectually. Had this labor been concentrated upon a few of the more promising lodes, many of these would no doubt now have been yielding large quantities of millable ores, whereby the annual yield of bullion would have been much increased, and the useless expenditure of millions of dollars have been saved, besides our actual knowledge of the metalliferous resources of the country been greatly extended. These were mistakes honestly made through ignorance, and are not to be confounded with those growing out of the spirit of cupidity and speculation that at one time prevailed, and of which sufficient has been said elsewhere. They are, moreover, mistakes that, having abundantly evinced their mischievous effects, are now being generally avoided. One cause that led to the expectation that this superficial style of working should suffice, was the fact that the accumulations of rich ores that led to the discovery of the Comstock vein were found quite upon the surface; hence it was thought that in all cases bodies of pay ores should in like manner be met with, if not in the croppings, certainly at no great depth below them, a supposition contradicted by the experience of silver miners nearly all the world over, these rich masses upon the surface being of rare occurrence. A partial excuse can also be found for this indiscriminate practice of locating ledges in the additional fact that many of them were as large and often much larger, and to all appearance equally as valuable as the Comstock; the difference, generally speaking, only being made apparent where, after reported trials of the ores taken from different and often from great depths, they were found to be valueless. In many of these ledges the walls were as regular, the mass of vein-stone as great, and, judging by the eye, as likely to be metalliferous as that of the Comstock; hence, many companies operating in the contiguous as well as in the more remote districts, encouraged by the resemblance of their ledges to the great mother vein, persevered in their efforts until large sums were expended, yet without reaching the hoped-for deposits of rich ores. In many of these cases operations, after being suspended for several years have again been resumed with the purpose that they shall be carried on to a point determinate of the probable value of the lode in process of exploration. At present several of these deep prospecting shafts are being sunk in the Washoe section of country, and, as it is reported, with the most hopeful prospects. There are, moreover, in this region many ledges on which work has been steadily kept going since their commencement four years ago, the method of opening being by means of tunnels which have not yet reached the vein; some of these are to be several thousand feet in length, and will yet require a year or two for their completion; the owners remaining, meantime, in ignorance of the precise character of their ledge. In Alpine county, which, though in the State of California, is situate entirely on the eastern side of the sierra, and generally considered as belonging to the Washoe region, there are, beyond any question, many argentiferous lodes of great magnitude and undoubted value. Upon several of these heavy works of exploration have been in progress for three or four years, and which, as they approach completion, begin to reveal many valuable features in these ledges. Owing to the protracted nature of these works but little bullion has yet been produced in this county, though it is likely a handsome sum will be turned out the coming year, as a number of mills and smelting works are being erected in that section.

Of the one hundred and seventy mills in the State, eighty-nine, carrying 1,440 of the 2,564 stamps, are in the Washoe district. These mills have a capacity equal to 3 841 horse-power, and cost, in the aggregate, over five and a half million of dollars, all the other mills in the State having but 2,481 horse-power, and costing but $5,500,000. Here, too, are most of the water-mills, thirty in number, that are running in Nevada. Of these eighty-nine mills, thirty-six, carrying 625 stamps, 1,500 horse-power, and costing $3,000,000, are in Story county. Two of them are driven by water; the balance by steam. There are also in this county ten arrastras driven by water, and one smelting establishment. In Lyon county there are thirty-four mills, having 489 stamps, 1,286 horse-power, and costing $1,705,000. Eleven of these mills are propelled by water. There are five arrastras in this county, and one metallurgical works. Washoe county contains ten mills, 200 stamps, 610 horse-power, costing $520,000; seven of them are driven by water, and several by water and steam combined. Ormsby county contains eight mills, 123 stamps, 435 horse-power, costing $375,000. Nine of these mills are driven by water, and three partly by water and partly by steam. Douglas county has but one mill, five stamps, ten horse-power; cost $5,000; driven by water.

The Esmeralda region is generally considered as coextensive with Esmeralda county, and as also covering a contiguous strip of mineral territory on the California side of the line. It is, for the most part, an elevated, dry, and barren country, containing but little agricultural or grass land, and no timber except the scattered patches of piñon, heretofore described, much of it being destitute of even this. It embraces within its limits over twenty mining districts, some of which contain mines of much importance. Esmeralda district, the earliest settled portion of this region, contains two-thirds of all the population, they being residents of Aurora, the principal town in the county. Upon the mines in this district also has most of the heavy work been done, and here are located three-fourths of all the mills that have been erected in that section of country. Several of these, being very extensive and complete in their appointments, cost large sums of money; but, as yet, none of them have accomplished much in the way of turning out bullion, partly because some have been grossly mismanaged, or their operations suspended by protracted and costly litigation, but chiefly because the ledges first opened, and which were generally considered the best in the district, prospecting largely upon the top in silver, and often also in free gold, grew barren, or pinched out as descended upon, or suffered such interruption and displacement as to render it impossible longer to identify or follow them. Hence, for the past two or three years most of the mills about Aurora have been idle, and chiefly because they could not get a sufficiency of pay ore from the mines in the vicinity to keep them running. It is the opinion of geologists that most of these disturbances are confined to the first few hundred feet beneath the surface, and that below that point these ledges, which promised so well, and some of which really were so rich above, will again be found regular, compact, and, most likely, highly metalliferous. At all events, confiding in this theory, several companies have resolved to test this question by sinking deep prospecting shafts on a number of the largest and most promising lodes at this place, powerful hoisting and pumping works having been provided for this purpose, and some of the shafts having been sunk several hundred feet lower than any level before attained. This work is to be prosecuted till some definite results are arrived at, and it is now believed by those most conversant with the subject that in the course of the next year quite a number of the mills about Aurora will be able to run on ore obtained from these deep workings, and that the whole of them will be able to do so, running full time, in the course of a couple of years more at the farthest. With the general disappointment in the character of the mines at large, the suspension of work upon those esteemed as of the better class, and the stoppage of the mills erected at so much cost, business of all kinds has greatly declined, population has fallen off nearly one-half, and real estate has so declined that it will not sell for one-quarter the prices readily commanded, three or four years ago, the depreciation of mill and mining properties being more marked than any other. Mills that cost a quarter million of dollars would not now sell for a third of that sum, while mines that were selling currently, under the stimulus of popular excitement and the artful machinations of speculators, at three and four hundred dollars per foot would not now sell for one dollar, the most of them being considered of so little value that their prices are no longer quoted on the lists of mining stocks dealt in by the brokers. Some mines in this region, however, of more recent location, and situate mostly in the outside districts, exhibit, as before stated, many satisfactory evidences of permanency and wealth, the most noted of these being in Silver Peak and Red Mountain districts, on the eastern margin of Esmeralda county. The Silver Peak mine in the former contains a large body of argentiferous ores lying very near the surface. A ten-stamp mill running upon this extracted, during the few months it was in operation, a large amount of bullion, the entire mass of the ore yielding by the most simple process over one hundred dollars per ton. This mine having been sold to an eastern company, nothing has been done upon it for the past six or eight months, the ten-stamp mill having been removed to Red mountain, a few miles west, where it is to be run in conjunction with a small three-stamp mill put up there two years ago, and which has also been running with success ; the ore at that place abounding in free gold to such an extent that it merely requires crushing and running over blankets. It is the intention of the Silver Peak company to put up a large first-class mill the coming year upon their mine. In the Columbus district, lying between Silver Peak and Esmeralda, there are a number of un-mistakably rich ledges, but they have not yet been much developed, and it would be too soon to pronounce an opinion upon their probable permanency. No mills have yet been built at this place, though one is talked of as likely to be taken in next summer. The number that could be kept running would, in any event, be limited, the district being but scantily supplied with wood and water. In the Volcano district, near Columbus, a great variety of metals and minerals have been found, there being here, besides veins seemingly rich in gold and silver, immense reefs of magnetic iron ore, numerous cupriferous lodes, large and highly impregnated with copper ; also saline pools surrounded with heavy deposits of salt, and, according to Dr. Blatchley, generally esteemed good authority, veins of true coal of the bituminous variety, two of these, varying from three to four feet in width, having lately been found by him while on a tour of extended research throughout the southeastern part of the State. In the Montgomery, Hot Springs, and Bodie districts, lying mostly in California, there are also many ledges of favorable aspect, some of them of well-ascertained value, there being in the last-named district two large mills, one of which is running successfully, and the other nearly ready for operations. In Lake district, also in this county, and situate on the west side of Walker lake, a large number of gold-bearing ledges were discovered in the summer of 1865, and though prospecting extremely rich in this metal on the surfaces, they have not yet been opened to a sufficient depth to fully establish their value as permanent mines. Two small mills are in course of erection in this district, and there is no doubt but they can obtain enough ore to give them profitable employment for some time at least.

In view of the many promising mines scattered over all parts of the Esmeralda region—the long and varied experience enjoyed by the inhabitants in every department of mining enabling them to avoid the mistakes of the past and to conduct the business hereafter with greater efficiency and economy—it is but reasonable to predict that this interest will soon undergo a revival, and the country meet, in part at least, the expectations entertained of it at an early day.

The mills built in Esmeralda county, twenty-one in number, carry in the aggregate 241 stamps, have a propulsive capacity equal to 672 horse-power, and cost $1,150,000. Only two of them are driven by water. There are also ten arrastras and two small smelting works in this region. These mills are distributed over the country as follows : One of ten stamps and one of three at Red mountain, three of small capacity in Hot Spring, Blind Spring, and other districts south of Aurora, two in Bodie district, and the balance on Walker river and in the Esmeralda district proper.

The Humboldt region.—This section occupies the northwestern corner of the State, covering the counties of Humboldt and Roop, and, for the sake of convenience rather than from its geographical position, also that of Churchill, lying south of the former. The appearance of the country, as well as the general character of the mines, is very similar to those of Esmeralda ; nor does the history of operations here differ materially from that of the latter. The same difficulties were encountered and the same mistakes made here as there. Owing to the careless manner in which many of the claims were located, the obscurity and imperfection of the laws, and the still more imperfect manner in which they were enforced, a majority of all the titles, more particularly those to what were considered the better class of mines, became involved in litigation, thereby retarding their development and destroying confidence in them generally. Millions of feet of unprospected ledges were sold, sometimes fairly, but oftener through misrepresentation and chicanery, and the proceeds, amounting in the aggregate to vast sums, were spent usually in every manner of extravagance and folly, and rarely in any persistent and well-directed efforts at opening the mines. Towns were built, hotels and saloons of luxurious style were erected, real estate in these embryo cities went up to enormous prices, everybody seeking to get rich from speculating in city lots or "feet," as these mining properties were designated, but little being done meantime towards advancing the business that should have first been looked after, the opening up and proving of the mines. Mills were also procured and put up at heavy expense before it had been ascertained that enough ores could be had to keep them running, this latter mistake not having been committed to the same extent in Humboldt as in the Esmeralda and some parts of the Reese River regions, where more than two-thirds of the mills have remained constantly idle from the causes set forth. It is also true that an equal proportion of the entire number of mills put up in Humboldt have been doing nothing much of the time ; the principal advantage here being that only a small number of mills, and these mostly of an inexpensive kind, were erected.

In the Black Rock country, lying in the western part of Humboldt county, many ledges claimed by the finders to be good were discovered during the past year. These veins are large, and some fair tests have been obtained from them by mill process, yet they are not enough opened to afford any decisive clue as to their ultimate value. A small mill has been forwarded to the district, and a more thorough trial of the ores will no doubt soon be had. These mines lie in the midst of a hideous desert, and unless excessively rich can possess no present value, the country for more than fifty miles in every direction being almost wholly devoid of wood, water, and grass.

In the Pueblo mountains, sixty miles northeast of Black Rock, a district was organized, and many ledges located five years ago. A small water mill erected there, and afterwards burnt by the Indians, has not since been rebuilt, nor have the mines showing fine surface indications been at all opened; wherefore, little or nothing is known as to their real character. The ores are an argentiferous galena, abounding in both silver and lead, and may possibly require reduction by smelting. If so, this mode could be adopted with a fair prospect of success, as wood and water are tolerably plentiful in the neighborhood of the mines, there being also much good hay and farming land in the extensive valley adjacent.

In Humboldt county proper mining operations, as well as population, have diminished considerably during the past two years, nor will the shipments of bullion this year equal those of either of the three years immediately preceding. The work now being done, however, is more thorough, being confined to a smaller number of ledges than before, and will no doubt prove more satisfactory in its results.

In Churchill county there are three districts that have attracted some notice, because of the supposed valuable ledges they contained. These are severally named the Silver Hill, the Mountain Well, and the Clan Alpine, and to them most of the work performed in the county has been confined. There are in this county four quartz mills, carrying 55 stamps, and having a driving power equal to that of 165 horses. The total cost of these mills was $395,000. Three of them are in Mountain Well, and one not quite finished in Clan Alpine district. They have produced but a few thousand dollars' worth of bullion all told, none of them having been able to run for more than a few days at a time, from an insufficient supply of pay ore, but few of the ledges here having been opened to even the superficial depths common to most other districts. In the higher strata of some of them small aggregations of very rich ores have been found, and the chances favor the supposition that when properly developed they will afford enough ore to keep the present and perhaps additional mills running. Very few additional mills, however, can ever be operated in the western half of the county, owing to the limited supply of wood and water.

The Reese River region, embracing within its boundaries the extensive counties of Lander and Nye, covers more than one-half of the entire State of Nevada. The geology of this region differs somewhat from that in the western part of the State, limestone of the silurian epoch abounding here, and other sedimentary rocks being more common. Carboniferous signs are also more frequent. The ledges throughout this region are mostly encased in granite or granitic rock, such as gneiss, sienite, &c., in limestone, and the several varieties of slate, a few only being found in rocks of volcanic origin. Most of the large and well-defined veins lie in silurian limestone, a formation highly favorable to the existence of deep-fissured and permanent mines. The lodes about Austin, Lander county, occur wholly in granite, both walls as well as the country rock being of this character. They are for the most part very narrow, varying from six to eighteen inches in width on top, and expanding to two or three feet at the depth of 300 feet, the greatest vertical depth to which any have yet been opened. Besides being narrow, these ledges are apt to suffer much from faults, and occasionally contract to a mere seam of quartz, or disappear altogether. Where these faults have occurred the experienced miner is generally able to place them again sometimes without much labor. Most of these veins run in a northerly and southerly direction, and stand at an angle varying from 45 to 60 degrees, very few of them having a more vertical position. Owing to the firmness of their walls very little timbering is required, though their extreme narrowness compels the performance of much dead-work in the course of their development. There are 36 steam hoisting works employed on the mines in the neighborhood of Austin. They are mostly of small capacity, from 20 to 25 horse power, but owing to the small amount of ore as well as water required to be raised they will meet all the demands for hoisting until the mines reach a depth of four or five hundred feet. The ores in this vicinity are the sulphurets and the red antimonial sulphurets of silver, though in the top rock, and in some instances for a considerable distance beneath the surface, these have been changed by decomposition into chlorides, bromides, and iodides of silver. These ores, being impregnated with antimony and arsenic, all require roasting. Though small in quantity, not more than 35 or 40 tons being raised daily from all the mines in the Reese River district proper, these ores are extremely rich, yielding by mill process from one to two hundred dollars per ton, the average yield being nearly one hundred and fifty dollars, while selected lots often go as high as four or five hundred dollars. There are in the several districts immediately around Austin seventeen steam mills, carrying nearly two hundred stamps, and capable of crushing and amalgamating one hundred and fifty tons of ore daily. Owing, however, to an inadequate supply of ore not one-quarter of these mills have been kept running during the past year, nor is even so large a proportion now in operation. With a more thorough exploration of the veins, however, upon which they are dependent for their supplies of ore, it is thought an additional number will soon be running, and that all will be able to do so in the course of a year or a year and a half at the furthest. The cost of reducing ores about Austin is now $45 per ton; the expense of raising them is about $15 per ton.

In several of the outside districts mines of not only undoubted, but very great value, some of them to all appearance not inferior to the Comstock ledge, have been discovered within the past two years. The most remarkable of these is the ledge known as the High Bridge, in the Philadelphia district, seventy-five miles south-southeast of Austin, the entire mass of vein-stone in which, varying from five to fifteen feet in thickness, pays under the stamps over one hundred and fifty dollars per ton. A small five stamp mill erected at the place and running on this ore turns out over a thousand dollars worth of bullion per day, the ore taken indiscriminately and worked in a very imperfect manner yielding over two hundred dollars per ton. This is beyond dispute an immensely valuable deposit of silver, and it is the intention of the companies claiming it to erect one or more large mills for reducing the ore the coming summer. In the Northumberland, Hot Creek, Danville, Reveille, and Pahranagat districts, all situated to the east and southeast of the Philadelphia district, in may ledges of great promise have been discovered within the past year, some of them to all appearance quite as good as the High Bridge, showing beyond peradventure that a great silver producing region exists in this part of the State. Several small mills have been taken into this section, and many more of large capacity will soon follow, and it will be cause for surprise if the annual bullion product of the Reese River region, now about $1,000,000, is not more than doubled within the next two years. These districts, as also the Murphy ledge, fifty miles south of Austin, a decidedly valuable mine, are all in Nye county, which contains a number of districts abounding in argentiferous lodes of great magnitude and prospective value.

The Reese River region contains thirty-two mines, of which twenty-two are in Lander and ten in Nye counties. These carry three hundred and ten stamps, have a capacity of four hundred and twenty-five horse-power, and cost $1,500,000, the expense of erecting mills here being much greater (owing to cost of freight and lumber) than in the western part of the State.

Oregon.—The yield of the mines in this State the present year will not exceed $2,000,000, nearly the whole being the product of placer diggings, and mostly taken from the mines on John Day river and its tributaries. Several auriferous veins have been worked with arrastras for a number of years past at Althouse and State creek, in southern Oregon, paying, for the means invested, very largely; and there is no doubt but these mines, with ample facilities for reducing the ores, would turn out considerable amounts of bullion annually. Some attempts were made during the present year to work the quartz lodes, of which there are quite a good many in the Santian district, situated in the Cascade mountains, but the results obtained have not thus far been encouraging.

Washington Territory.— As in the State of Oregon so in this Territory, the only class of mines that have yet proved productive are the placer diggings, of which there is here a considerable extent; the best paying mines heretofore discovered being those about Fort Culville and in the Pend d'Oreille country, the Kootenai mines and those near the Big Bend of the Columbia, generally spoken of as being in Washington Territory, being in fact in British Columbia. The product for the present year from this quarter may be set down at about $1,000,000, though this must be understood as embracing the yield of the last-mentioned districts, that of Washington alone not reaching one quarter this amount.

Utah.—This Territory is known to abound in many of the useful and, it is believed, also in the precious metals. Coal of fair quality and in considerable quantities has been found in various parts of the Territory, and both lead and iron have been produced for many years past by the Mormons living in the southern counties. That so little is known of its wealth in the precious metals is owing to the fact that the leaders of this people discouraged the searching after them, it being contrary to the policy of the church to have its subjects engage in mining pursuits, wherefore but little was known of the mineral resources of Utah until the soldiers stationed at Salt lake brought them to light. No placer mines of any extent have yet been found in this Territory, but a number of large lodes heavily charged with argentiferous galena have been opened at Rush valley, a short distance southwest of Salt Lake City, and, being tested by the smelting process, proved rich in both lead and silver. A number of furnaces were erected here two years ago, since which they have been kept part of the time in operation, and with suitable appliances it is thought a considerable amount of silver bullion might be produced from these mines. With the influx of gentile population Utah is destined to be thoroughly explored, and whatever mineral riches it may contain to be brought to light; and we may reasonably look for some important discoveries to follow in that section before long. At Egan cañon several rich silver-bearing lodes were located over two years ago. Three mills have since been put up at this point, two of which have produced quite a large amount of bullion.

The principal silver-bearing lode at this point, known as the Gilligan Ledge, has been tested to the depth of three hundred feet, and is considered to contain one of the richest veins in the State of Nevada. It has a width of eight feet, and has produced by ordinary process of mill-working at the rate of $345 per ton, for fifty tons. The average of ore rates at something over $100 per ton.

This valuable mine belonged, until recently, to a San Francisco company, consisting of seven private individuals, who worked it on their own account, under the superintendency of Mr. John O'Dougherty, who, by a careful system of operations, not only developed the mine, but built a five-stamp mill without expense to the company. It is one of the few mines in the county which has paid its own expenses from the first crushing of the ores.

During the past summer the mill has been idle owing to the departure of the superintendent, who went east for the purpose of procuring capital sufficient to erect a mill of the first class, with capacity to work all the ores that can be obtained from the ledge.

The Steptoe Company, of New York, have also large interests here, and own a number of ledges, which, however, have not yet been developed sufficiently to furnish an absolute test of their value.

A consolidation has been formed between the Social or Gilligan company and the Steptoe, which will probably result in mutual benefits. The Steptoe company have capital, and have already made provision for the erection of a large mill; the Social company have a developed ledge already tested, and unquestionably productive.

This consolidation owns, in addition, some fine copper mines on the line of the proposed trans-continental railway. No work of any importance has yet been done upon them.

Egan cañon is situated one hundred and sixty miles from Salt Lake City, and already forms the nucleus of quite a thriving little mining town. The overland stage and telegraph lines pass through this cañon on the route to Salt Lake. Preparations are being made for the vigorous working of all the valuable mines in this district, and it is believed they will yield profitable results during the coming summer.

Montana.—The productive mines in this Territory have thus far mostly consisted of placer diggings, the principal of which, being situated east of the summit of the Rocky mountains, are without the province of these reports. The amount of gold dust taken out the present year has been large, but in the absence of any authentic data no accurate computation can be made thereof. According to the public press of that region it will reach the sum of $15,000,000, though this is probably a rather high estimate. During the past summer a large number of quartz lodes have been taken up and opened, some ten or fifteen mills, varying in capacity from five to twenty stamps, having meantime been brought in and some of them gotten in operation. The quartz is easily worked, and yields largely, the product being chiefly gold. All the goods and machinery destined for the eastern part of Montana are freighted up the Missouri or across the plains. Most of the gold dust and bullion produced in this Territory is sent east, very little of it reaching California. Those best acquainted with the country have a high opinion of its mineral resources, and believe it will in a few years rival Idaho and Nevada, if it do not surpass them, in its product of the precious metals.

Idaho.—The product of the placer mines in this Territory has been gradually diminishing for the past two years, though this falling off, if it have not already been, will soon be more than made up by the yield of the quartz mines, which are beginning to be worked quite extensively. The product from both sources the present year will probably not fall short of $10,000,000, some estimating it much higher. It should be observed that there are no means of arriving at accurate estimates of the precious metals taken out in this Territory, many of the millmen not caring to make known the results of their operations, and large quantities of dust being brought out of the country in private hands. Of the total sum produced, from one-fourth to one-fifth is taken from the placers, of which some virgin diggings of considerable extent and value have been found the past summer; and as ditches have been constructed for bringing water into the mines on quite an extensive scale, and hydraulic washing is being introduced wherever practicable, the probability is that the present quota from this source will be kept up for some time to come. There are now twenty-four quartz mills completed and running in this Territory, with eight others in course of erection. They carry a total of nearly four hundred stamps, cost in the aggregate $1,000,000, and have a united capacity equal to five hundred horses. Besides these mills, about one-fourth of which are driven by water, there are a large number of arrastras running in the Territory, the most of which are also propelled by water. Of the quartz mills eight are supplied with one hundred and thirty-four stamps, are situate in Atturas county, ten in the Owyhee district, and the balance in the counties adjacent; the whole being in the southern section of the Territory. The Poorman ledge, so-called, situate in the Owyhee district, is, perhaps, for its size, the richest deposit of silver ores ever discovered, immense masses of pure sulphurets, and even pieces of virgin silver weighing many pounds, having been extracted from it. Unfortunately, it is now closed up by litigation, and has not for several months produced any bullion. There are also several other rich silver-bearing claims in this vicinity, though the mines of Idaho consist mainly of auriferous quartz, of which there are great quantities that will yield by the most cheap and expeditions modes of working from $20 to $30 to the ton. Considering the abundance of these ores, the facility with which they can be treated, and the ample supplies of wood and water in the vicinity of the principal mines, it may fairly be concluded that the bullion product of Idaho will in a few years be more than doubled, and that the yield of her mines will hereafter be steady and rapid.

REPORT OF DR. A. BLATCHLY, MINING ENGINEER, TO J. ROSS BROWNE, SPECIAL COMMISSIONER FOR THE COLLECTION OF MINING STATISTICS.

SOUTHEASTERN NEVADA.

This portion of the State of Nevada, owing to the hostility of the Indians, was almost totally unexplored until last spring. About that time, observing that the Indians in the vicinity of the mining towns were able to feed and clothe themselves much better than those who lived out in the mountains, they changed their tactics, and instead of opposing exploration, offered every facility in their power to promote it, and nearly all of the mineral discoveries in this region have been made by means of their assistance.

The volcanic rocks which so greatly predominate in the northern and western portions of the State are not found to any considerable extent in the southeastern. Hence, there is a much larger amount of metalliferous country accessible in the same compass than in other portions of the State.

These volcanic rocks are the despair of the experienced prospector, for he knows full well that they enclose neither metal nor mineral of any value in this country, and where they abound water is generally wanting. Their geological age is comparatively recent, and undoubtedly more than one-half of the metalliferous veins in the State of Nevada are covered by rocks of volcanic origin.

In this part of the State limestone predominates, but granite, slate, and sandstone occur at intervals. All of these rocks enclose valuable metalliferous veins in equal abundance.

This limestone affords better exemplifications of the geology of the sedimentary rocks than any other sections west of the Rocky mountains yet discovered. With the slight and hasty examinations already made, the silurian, triassic, and jurassic have been positively determined, and considerable evidence has been found of the existence of the Devonian and carboniferous epochs. In the territory of the United States no finer field exists for the researches of a geologist.

Trap dykes of porphyry and green-stone are abundant, and enormous veins of quartzite of three or four hundred feet in thickness can be traced for forty or fifty miles.

Compared with the veins found in California, Oregon, Idaho, and the other portions of Nevada, the metalliferous veins in this portion of the State are large, and usually can be traced on the surface for a long distance.

As this country has been but recently explored, all of the ores so far obtained have been taken from near the surface; consequently, only surface ores have been obtained. These consist of chloride and carbonate of silver, associated with small amounts of native silver, and nearly all contain gold. Besides the precious metals, ores of copper, lead, iron, antimony, and arsenic are abundant, and when railroads traverse the country, will be of great value.

So far as observed all of the geological formations contain valuable metalliferous veins, from the azoic up to the triassic.

As this portion of the State is about two hundred miles east and west by three hundred north and south, and contains a great number of districts, each of which has a very considerable extent, and contains a great number of metalliferous veins, it will be impossible in a brief space to do more than briefly notice some of the most important districts.

Silver bend, or Philadelphia.—This district, which was discovered by an Indian, is about seventy-five miles southeast from Austin. It was one of the first discoveries in this part of the State, and its mines have been more developed than those in the other districts.

One of the principal veins is the High Bridge, which crops to the surface for the distance of about a mile, and has been opened at a number of different points, and at one to the depth of about fifty feet. It appears to be composed of a number of different strata, all of which contain rich ore; their aggregate thickness varies from five to twenty feet.

The country rock is slate, and it has every indication of being a true fissure vein, and consequently will be found deep and permanent. It contains a large amount of good milling ore at the surface.

A small ten-stamp mill has been erected for reducing the ore, and the average yield is about one hundred dollars per ton, the mill saving about sixty per cent. of the silver contained in the ore. Its daily production is a trifle over one thousand dollars, provided it were fully opened; with suitable mills for the reduction of its ores the production of bullion could be increased tenfold.

The Silver Champion has produced richer ore than any other vein in the district. It is smaller than the High Bridge, and has not been opened but to a small extent. Besides this, there are a number of other veins in this district of great promise, as the Green and Oder, Silver Top, Minerva, and many others.

The metalliferous veins are found in slate and limestone, the greater number being in the slate, while the veins in the granite, so far as they have been examined, are entirely barren.

Northumberland district.—This district is about twenty miles north from Silver Bend, and on the same slope of the same range of mountains. Here the metalliferous veins are found in slate and granite.

Rich ores are found near the surface, and, when opened, there is no doubt that it will prove to be a valuable district.

Wood and water are moderately abundant, sufficient for the wants of the district for years to come.

It is singular that the granite at Silver Bend should enclose only barren veins, and at this district, which is only twenty miles distant, and in the same range of mountains, with granite apparently of the same lithological character, should contain some of the richest veins in this district. This shows the fallacy of the notion that some particular rock is, in all cases, more favorable for enclosing metalliferous veins than another of azoic or sedimentary rocks—experience showing that, in Nevada, all of the rocks, except the volcanic, contain valuable mines.

Hot creek —This district was named from a group of hot springs, the waters of which uniting form a creek of some magnitude, retaining its heat for a long distance below. This furnishes an abundant supply of water for the use of the district. Along the banks of the stream the warmth of the water induces a growth of vegetation of tropical luxuriance, and many plants grow here that are not found in other parts of the State.

The country rock is chiefly limestone, with small amounts of slate and granite traversed by numerous trap dykes.

The metalliferous veins are large, rich, and numerous, and many of them show large amounts of valuable ore at the surface.

As this is one of the most recent discoveries, but little work has been done in developing and proving the mines. But the results of the workings of a number of tons of ore from different mines have been very satisfactory.

A small mill is nearly completed and will soon be in running order, and from the richness and abundance of the ores, and the experience of the managers, there is do doubt that the enterprise will be successful.

Wood is very abundant near the mines, being mostly nut pine, which is excellent for fuel, but very indifferent for lumber.

Reveille district.—This district is about forty miles southeast from Hot creek, and about the same distance northwest from Pahranagat. This is a more recent discovery than Hot creek, which it greatly resembles, having the same country rock, with veins of equal or larger size, containing the same ores, and the district is probably of equal value.

Pahranagat district.—This is the only mining district in the State that was discovered by Mormons or people from Salt Lake. It was found about a year before any other district in this part of the State. It is situated in the southeast corner of the State, about two hundred miles from the head of navigation on the Colorado river, according to what is believed to be the best authorities, although many others make the distance much less.

The mineral belt is long and narrow, and contains a great number of veins in a small compass. They are usually of fair size and well impregnated with ore, and when developed will no doubt prove valuable.

The country rock is the same as in Hot creek and Reveille, and the general characteristics are the same. The laws of this district are very liberal to the original discoverers, but almost entirely exclude later prospectors. They require no work on the mine except to pile a heap of stones, and that holds the mines perpetually. Hence no work has been done, and none probably ever will be done, by a majority of the present holders. A New York company have recently commenced operations, and no doubt will thoroughly prove their mine.

Silver Peak.—This district is about one hundred and twenty miles south from the city of Austin. The country rock consists of granite, slate, and limestone, the greater number of veins being in the slate. They are usually large, and contain both gold and silver, besides copper and lead.

A mill has been erected and run for a considerable time, but the workings were not very satisfactory, owing to the large amount that was lost in the tailings.

The Vanderbilt and Pocatilla are the two most noted veins in this district. They are of large size, and with a mill capable of saving the gold and silver would yield a fair profit.

A large number of other districts have been formed in this part of the State, as the Danville, Palmetto, Red Mountain, Pawdit, Columbus, and Volcano. From all of these specimens of rich ore have been obtained, but their true value can be determined only after they have been fully developed.

In Columbus district a few of the veins have been partially opened, and ore worked from them with most satisfactory results. In another year a mill will probably be erected, and with proper management ought to be successful.

Volcano district has veins which contain gold and silver, but is remarkable for croppings of larger copper veins than any others yet found in California or Nevada. These veins have not been opened, but the outcrop is of enormous magnitude, and the ore, besides copper, contains a small amount of silver. When this country has proper railroad facilities this copper ore will be of great value.

Although this mining region has been too recently discovered to admit of definitely proving its value by working on a large scale, still sufficient has been learned to prove that it contains vast deposits of ore rich in gold and silver.

Salt is found abundantly in nearly all of the valleys, in marshes or as an incrustation on the soil at the bottom of the basins. From these sources is derived all the salt that is used in the reduction of the silver ore throughout the State, the annual consumption for this purpose in the State being very great. But at Pahranagat salt is found in a mine in vast quantities. It is in large transparent crystals, and also beautifully colored, green, blue, &c., as in the Cordana mine in Spain. This variety is much purer and stronger than that found in the valleys. This latter variety was deposited by evaporation, and contains much soda and other impurities.

Coal has been found at Volcano and Pahranagat and near Salt Lake, and from the geological structure of this part of the State it is highly probable that, when full explorations have been made, coal will be found in abundance, and of good quality. That found near Salt Lake has been worked to a considerable extent, and has been pronounced to be of excellent quality. At Pahranagat and Volcano no work has been done to prove the quality or extent, except what has been done by nature. This is a very fine field for exploration in a country like this, where, in the course of a few years, fuel will be a very important consideration.

As this region has been until recently infested by bands of hostile Indians, rendering it dangerous for small parties of prospectors to remain long in the country, considerable irregularities have been observed in the formation of new districts and in the framing of laws.

At Silver Bend a district was formed, and called the Philadelphia district, with laws and regulations as is usual in such cases. From a variety of causes the founders of the district were obliged to leave, when another set of prospectors came in, formed another district, and claimed the mines by virtue of their laws. The result has been vexatious and expensive litigation.

At Pahranagat the laws exclude new comers, and do not require the owners to do any work on the mines.

A general law by Congress regulating the formation of new districts, and making them a matter of record, so that after a district is once organized its existence can be easily proved, would prevent troubles of this nature from arising in the future; also a clause setting forth precisely the conditions under which a claim becomes forfeited. In many of the mining districts if no work is done on a claim for the space of one year the claim is considered to be abandoned. This clause in mining laws is pretty general, but in many courts it has been decided that miners by their laws have a right to prescribe the mode of possession, but not the mode of dispossession. As the mines in each district differ, and in one it is advisable to claim ground on each side of the vein, and in others it is not, these points can be better regulated by the miners themselves than by any general law, but in the formation of districts, and provisions for the forfeiture of a claim, some general law is requisite.

A. BLATCHLY,
Mining Engineer.

AUSTIN, NEVADA, *November* 26, 1866.

[From Governor McCormick's message, October 8, 1866.]

ARIZONA.

Finances.—The total territorial indebtedness, as audited to this time, amounts to twenty-one thousand and fifty-one dollars and forty-one cents, and there is a balance of two hundred and forty-nine dollars and fifty cents in the treasury to the credit of the general fund. Of this indebtedness, fifteen thousand five hundred and ninety dollars are payable in gold, being the amount of bonds (and interest on the same to January 4, 1867) issued under the act of the first assembly, approved November 9, 1864, and entitled "An act to provide for the contingent expenses of the territorial government." In view of the fact that until the present year but two of the counties were fully organized, and that

now, although all contribute to the revenue, the total receipts, owing to the
limited amount of taxable property in the Territory, are small, this is no more
than a reasonable debt.   Compared with that of neighboring Territories, containing a larger population and far better sources of revenue, it is insignificant,
and will be complained of only by those singular individuals who expect the
wheels of government to move without cost.

Still I would advise that no expenditure of the territorial funds, however
earnestly it may be asked, or necessary it may seem, be authorized by your
honorable bodies without the most careful consideration; and if you can impress
upon the counties the importance of economy in their affairs, it will be well to
do so.   In the matter of promptly and thoroughly collecting the revenue they
should be urged to increased vigilance, not only for their own benefit but for
that of the Territory at large.

Some seven thousand dollars of the gold bonds before referred to will become
due in a little more than a year from this date, and although another legislature
may meet before that time, it is not too early to make provision to insure their
payment, and thus to sustain the territorial credit.

There is a balance of about five hundred dollars in the treasury from the
special fund created by the sale of territorial mining claims, which I would suggest be assigned to the general fund; also, that all further receipts from such
sales be so disposed of.

The Treasury Department having made the Territory an internal revenue
district, and appointed an assessor and collector, we may soon expect to be called
upon to contribute directly to the national revenue.   I had hoped, in view of our
comparatively small population, and the drawbacks with which we have to contend, that we should escape other than territorial taxation for the present.   But
it becomes us, as loyal citizens of the great republic, cheerfully to do our part,
however humble it may be, towards cancelling the sacred debt incurred in pre-
serving the national integrity.

The mines.—If there is less excitement over our mining interests there is
more confidence in their excellence, and a strengthened belief that their development will surprise the world.   Ten quartz mills will have been erected in this
county alone before the close of the present year.   Those already in operation
afford a gratifying evidence of the value of the gold ores, and as the lodes are
sunk upon they show permanence and size.   The appearance of sulphurets and
refractory elements at a certain depth may involve the necessity of more elabo-
rate machinery, but no obstacles will, I think, be sufficient to baffle the enterprise of our miners, who, depending more upon their own energies and capital
than upon help from abroad, are determined to know no such word as fail.

The rare advantages of wood, water, and climate are more than sufficient to
offset the costs of living and the heavy expense of transporting machinery here,
and I believe, as I have often asserted, that there are few localities upon the
Pacific coast where quartz mining may be so economically, agreeably, and
profitably pursued.

Those of the silver mines below the Gila, and on the Colorado, that are
judiciously worked, with scarcely an exception, show great wealth, and fully
maintain the traditional reports of the metallic opulence of the country.

The considerable capital now devoted to the development of the copper lodes
on the Colorado and Williams Fork is but an earnest of that which this important work will soon command.   The uniform richness of the ore, the
quantity of the same, and the facilities for its extraction and shipment combine
to make the mines among the most desirable of the kind upon the continent.

Mining laws.—The act of Congress to legalize the occupation of mineral
lands, and to extend the rights of pre-emption thereto, adopted at the late session, preserves all that is best in the system created by miners themselves, and
saves all vested rights under that system, while offering a permanent title to all

who desire it, at a merely nominal cost. It is a more equitable and practicable measure than the people of the mineral districts had supposed Congress would adopt; and credit for its liberal and acceptable provisions is largely due to the influence of the representatives from the Pacific coast, including our own intelligent delegate. While it is not without defects, as a basis of legislation it is highly promising, and must lead to stability and method, and so inspire increased confidence and zeal in quartz mining.

As, in the absence of necessary legislation by Congress, the act gives authority to the legislature of any State or Territory to provide rules for the location and working of mines to their complete development, it will be your duty to prepare such rules, either by amending the present mining law of the Territory so as to conform to the law of Congress, or by its repeal, and the substitution of an entirely new statute. Whatever your preference in this particular, I would suggest that care be taken to make the required rules as intelligible and comprehensive as possible, and that the recording and preservation of titles, both for the security of the miner and the capitalist, and to obviate future litigation, be entrusted only to the most responsible officers. It is also important that, excepting in districts where active hostility on the part of the Indians absolutely prevents, the actual occupation and improvement of claims be made a requisite to their possession, unless pre-empted under the congressional law. The lack of such a requirement hitherto has seriously retarded the development of our mineral resources and the general prosperity of the Territory, and proven discouraging to new comers, especially in the counties on the Colorado river, where hundreds of lodes, taken up in years past by parties now absent from the Territory, are unworked, and yet, under the existing law, no one has a right to lay claim to them, be he ever so able or anxious to open them.

Agriculture.—The valleys of the Territory, more extensively cultivated this year than ever before, have produced an abundant harvest. The yield of corn, vegetables, and small grain is such as to prove that henceforth we need not look abroad for food; and I make no doubt that if assured that their crops will be bought and promptly paid for, and they are properly protected from Indian incursions, our ranchmen will, during the ensuing year, by the favor of Heaven, raise all the breadstuffs that may be required to subsist the military force in the Territory. Here in central Arizona, even in the mountain districts, where comparatively little was expected in the way of agricultural success, the pursuit of the husbandman is likely to be one of the most profitable. The heavy rains of the present season indicate that irrigation will seldom be necessary, and the fertility of the soil is remarkable. It seems as though every thing planted attained the most luxuriant and complete growth in the shortest possible time. The grains, vegetables, and melons taken promiscuously from any of the ranches, and raised without fertilization of any kind, or other than the simplest care, would command a premium if placed in competition with the products of the richest and most expensive farms and gardens of the Atlantic States.

Land district.—By the seventh section of the act of Congress, approved July 22, 1854, the pre-emption privilege was extended to lands, whether settled upon before or after survey, within the region of country comprehended by the present Territories of New Mexico and Arizona. Hitherto pre-emption declarations, in virtue of this act and that of July 2, 1864, have been filed with the surveyor general, but Congress having made Arizona a land district, they will, so soon as the district is organized, be received here.

The congressional mining law provides that wherever, prior to the passage of the act, upon the lands heretofore designated as mineral lands, which have been excluded from survey and sale, there have been homesteads made by citizens of the United States, or persons who have declared their intention to become citizens, which homesteads have been made, improved, and used for agricultural purposes, and upon which there have been no valuable mines of gold silver, cinnabar, or copper discovered, and which are properly agricultural lands, the said settlers or owners of such homesteads shall have a right of pre-emption thereto, in quantity not to exceed one hundred and sixty acres; or said parties may avail themselves of the provisions of the homestead act of Congress, approved May 20, 1862. It further provides that upon the survey of the so-called mineral lands, the Secretary of the Interior may designate and set apart such portions of such lands as are clearly agricultural lands, which lands shall thereafter be subject to pre-emption and sale as other public lands of the United States, and subject to all the laws and regulations applicable to the same.

This favorable action, and the establishment of a land office, whereby all delay in perfecting titles will be obviated, must encourage our people in the cultivation of lands in immediate proximity to the mines—a matter of the first importance to the prosperity of our mining interests.   •

SECTION 5.

1. Copper resources of the Pacific coast.—2. Various copper districts.—3. Geological formations in which copper is found, &c.—4. Reduction of ores, quantity, &c.

1.—THE COPPER RESOURCES OF THE PACIFIC COAST.

Introductory remarks.—The comparatively recent date when the importance of these resources first attracted any attention; the extent of territory over which they have been traced; the absence of any correctly compiled statistics con-nected with them in either the State or federal offices; the indisposition of influ-ential parties to give any information, under the plea that it would expose the secrets of their business, and the efforts of others to make mines in which they are interested appear of greater or less value than well-known facts would war-rant; the vague and unreliable nature of most of the articles which from time to time appear in the local papers on the subject, as well as many minor impedi-ments, render it exceedingly difficult to convey a clear idea of the proportions and actual value of these resources in a hastily compiled report. Even were the fullest details of information available, many interesting facts must unavoidably be crowded out of such a report. Sufficient may be presented here, however, to demonstrate the extent and value of the copper mines of the Pacific coast, and to prove that under a more judicious system of development they may be made much more profitable to their owners as well as to the federal government, and that an important means towards the accomplishment of this end will be attained by the collection and proper arrangement of statistical and general information on the subject.

The discovery of copper on the Pacific coast.—The existence of copper on the Pacific coast was well known for many years before California became a State in the great American republic. The ores of this metal are known to have been found in Mexico, at various points, in great abundance for centuries past. In the territory within the limits of this State they were found as far back as 1840, near the Solidad pass, about ninety miles north of Los Angeles.

The first officially recorded discovery of copper in California, since it has be-come a State, was made by Dr. J. B. Trask, who acted as State geologist from 1851 till 1854. During that time, in the course of his travels, he found copper in nearly every county in the State—the first discovery being made near a place then called Round Tent, in Nevada county.

As but little attention was paid to the report of these discoveries, and the notes and specimens of the ores collected by Doctor Trask were soon after lost or de-stroyed, they exercised but little influence.

In the summer of 1855 public attention was again called to the fact of the existence of copper in this State, by the discovery of a body of beautiful ore at Hope valley, Amador county, by an old prospector, known as Uncle Billy Rodgers. The ore from this place, being rich in garnets, attracted great attention. About the same time a party of prospectors in El Dorado county found a large body of green and blue carbonates on a side of a hill a few miles from Placerville, and, attracted by the brilliant colors of these minerals, collected several sacks full of them and sent them to San Francisco, where, by assay, they were found to contain 40 per cent. of copper, and worth about $140 per ton.

These discoveries were mentioned in nearly all the papers published in the State at the time, but were soon forgotten in the more exciting search for gold which occupied almost everybody's attention, and the now great copper resources of the Pacific coast remained without an effort being made for their development till November, 1860, when Mr. Hiram Hughes, returning from a trip to Washoe, whither he had gone to search for silver, while prospecting for that metal among the foot-hills that margin the valley of San Joaquin, without being aware of the fact discovered the gossan or cap of a copper lode, on what is now known as Quail Hill, No. 1—an insignificant mound among the Gopher hills, in the southwestern portion of Calaveras county, about 35 miles southeast from Stockton, and six miles from Central ferry, on the Stanislaus river. This gossan, which presented much the appearance of a body of iron-rust held together by a frame-work of quartz, was found to be very rich in gold, and it was for this metal that Hughes worked his claim. Soon after, while making further explorations for "iron-rust," he discovered the croppings of what is now known as the Napoleon mine, about three miles southwest of his first discovery. As there was less gold, and considerable of what was then, to him, an unknown mineral, in this place, he sent a lot of the ore to San Francisco, where it was pronounced 30 per cent. copper ore, and worth about $120 per ton. As soon as this fact became known there was a great excitement, and everybody began prospecting for "iron-rust," and as the indications of copper were to be found almost at every point among the Gopher hills, hundreds of claims were speedily marked out and recorded— the favorite direction being along the course of the lode on which the Napoleon was located, as this was easily traced for miles; the most important "extensions" on the original lode being the Josephine on the west, the Lotus, Magnolia, and Collier on the east. But as none of these mines, except the Napoleon, ever produced much marketable ore, work on all of them very soon ceased. Hughes and his partners, after partially developing the Napoleon mine, which contained 2,700 feet on the lode, in 1862 sold eleven-eighteenths of it to a company for $22,000. This company, in October, 1862, was incorporated under the title of the Napoleon Copper Mining Company, which, after taking out of the mine and shipping about 4,000 tons of good ore, sold the mine, in 1864, to Martin & Greenman, dealers in ores, of San Francisco, who at present own and work it.

Notwithstanding the great amount of prospecting that followed Hughes's discoveries, it was not till some time in June, 1861, that the lode on which the mines at Copperopolis are located was discovered, though it is only about six miles from the Napoleon, and the locators of the Union, Keystone, and other mines were all old residents and miners in the vicinity. W. R. Reed, Dr. Blatchly, and Mr. McCarty located 11,250 feet of the Copperopolis lode in July, 1861. This location embraced the ground now owned by the Union, Keystone, Empire, Calaveras, and Consolidated companies. Many interesting and instructive facts might be here introduced to exhibit the ignorance of the parties who first discovered these important mines as to the value of their property. The following will be sufficient to illustrate this curious fact:

J. W. Bean, esq., who built the first hotel at Copperopolis, had been mining for years among the Gopher hills and in the vicinity of Salt Spring valley;

and though such was the abundance and beauty of the specimens of copper ores all around him that he collected nearly a cart-load of them as curiosities to decorate his rude cabin, he afterwards threw them away as useless. In 1855 he had collected so many of these specimens that his partner would not have any more of them brought into the cabin.

Mr. Hughes, whose blindly-directed enterprise led to the discovery of the value of the copper resources of the Pacific coast, had also been mining for years among the Gopher hills; and although his observant attention had been attracted to the peculiarities of the rocks that form these hills, he had no idea of the stores of wealth that lay scattered so lavishly all around him till he had made a trip to Washoe during the excitement which followed the discovery of silver there. When in that Territory, being forcibly struck with the great resemblance between the rocks near the Comstock lode and those that he was so well acquainted with about the Gopher hills and Salt Spring valley, and not being successful over there, he returned to the old familiar field of his labors and commenced prospecting for silver, and did not know for many months after his return that he had acquired a fortune by discovering a copper mine. So with Mr. McCarty, one of the present owners of the great Union mine. He had lived in Salt Spring valley nearly ten years, mining and ranching by turns. As early as 1852 he had sunk a deep prospect-hole on the ground now belonging to the Keystone company, and threw away the rich copper ores as worthless, while seeking for gold, which he never found. So with Mr. Hardy, another of the original locators of the Union. This gentleman, a keen, intelligent man of business, who was for a long time the superintendent of that mine, and afterwards became senator for Calaveras county, resided for years within two miles of where Copperopolis now stands without having any idea of the immense wealth that lay stored up for him in the hard, sterile banks of the little creek that meandered past his homestead.

The limits of this report will not admit of any further digression on this very interesting history.

As soon as the magnitude and importance of the discovery made by Mr. Reed and his party became known, the rush of prospectors to the locality became tremendous, and in a few days claims were staked off extending for nearly twenty miles in all directions along the lode, or rather lodes, (for there are more than one of them,) across and parallel to them. Large sums of money were in many instances expended in the purchase and development of claims which were located miles away from all indications of any lode whatever.

One of the effects of this great excitement was the creation of the now thriving town of Copperopolis, the first house in which was built by Mr. Reed in September, 1861. In less than two years after it contained a population of nearly 2,000, which supported three schools, two churches, a weekly newspaper, four hotels, with stores and workshops of all kinds sufficient for an active, thrifty community. It now has three lines of stages running to and from it daily, and has a costly railroad in course of active construction to connect it with the navigable waters of the San Joaquin river, which, when completed, will more than double its wealth and population.

To give the names of all the claims that were located in and around Salt Spring valley during the first great excitement would serve no useful purpose, as most of them, after the expenditure of more or less labor, have either been abandoned altogether or are held till labor and transportation shall become cheaper or copper ores become more valuable. The most important mines in the valley at present—the only ones that are being developed—are the Calaveras, Empire, Union, Keystone, Consolidated, and Kentucky, which range from south to north in the order in which they are here written, and the Inimitable, which is located on the east side of and parallel with the Union. The developments in this and other mines located parallel with the original claims leave little room to doubt that there are at least two—some persons say four—distinct lodes, or very large consecutive bodies of ore, identical in composition, independent of the main lode. The question of whether there is one or more lodes promises to be as fruitful a point for the lawyers to settle as a similar question was among the owners on the Comstock lode, in Nevada.

The thousands of persons from all parts of the State who were attracted to the Salt Spring Valley mines by the reports of their value, thus becoming acquainted with the general appearance of copper ores, on returning to their several districts soon discovered these ores almost everywhere, so that before the close of the year 1861 a well-defined belt of copper ore, containing several distinct lodes, was traced and partially developed from a point about thirty miles north of Los Angeles, at La Solidad, through Mariposa, Merced, Fresno, Tuolumne, Stanislaus, El Dorado, Placer, Nevada, Yuba, Trinity, Sierra, Plumas, and Shasta counties, to a point about twenty miles west of the town of Yreka, in Siskiyou county, where it enters the State of Oregon in a northern spur of the Siskiyou mountains, the most western branch of the Sierra Nevadas. As will be more fully explained in another portion of this report, there is a most remarkable uniformity in the direction and dip of the lodes in this great copper belt, as well as in the geological formations in which they are found, in the character of their ores, and in several other features, all which point to a simultaneousness of origin over very large tracts, many portions of which have been much disturbed and shifted by subsequent subterranean action.

Other extensive deposits of copper ores have been discovered in the coast range, particularly around the base of a spur of Mount Diablo, at the low divide in Del Norte county; in Hope valley, Amador county; at Whiskey Hill, in Placer county, and at several other points which it is not necessary to particularize at this time.

The results of all these discoveries were the location of thousands of claims, some of them of considerable importance, in nearly every county in the State, and the incorporation of a countless number of copper mining companies, whose certificates of stock were bought and sold at the public boards and by private merchants by thousands; and for about a year the development of the copper resources of the Pacific coast was prosecuted with great zeal. But a few months' experience taught those most deeply interested in the business that, with unskilled and expensive labor, uncertain and costly transportation, and a great distance from a market for the final disposal of the ore, it is unprofitable to work the richest and most extensive copper mines in the world.

The excitement attending the discovery of so much copper in California, as may well be supposed, soon spread through the adjoining States and Territories, and it was not long before many important lodes were discovered in Oregon, Nevada, Colorado, Sonora, and Lower California. As it will be quite impossible to even mention all these discoveries in detail, only a few of the most important will be referred to at this time.

In 1860 a miner named Hawes, who had long been working in that vicinity, having his attention attracted to the quantity of metallic copper found in the sluices of the miners who were engaged at Placer mining for gold, commenced a search, and soon discovered a valuable lode of copper ore in a small gulch about six miles from Waldo, Josephine county. On this lode was subsequently located the Queen of Bronze mine, the most important copper mine in Oregon. Soon after the discovery made by Hawes, other parties found an extensive copper district on the Illinois river, near the junction of that river and Fall creek, about eighteen miles north-northwest from Waldo. Another district was about the same time discovered at Rockland, in Josephine county, in which more than twenty mines of importance were subsequently located.

Copper has also been found in Wasco county; on the John Day river, and at several other points in the State of Oregon. The districts in Josephine county being near the dividing line between that State and California, and the lode having been examined from Waldo to near Crescent City, Del Norte county, in the latter State, where an extensive district known as the Alta has since been developed, leaves no room to doubt that they are all located on the same great belt of copper ores referred to above.

The largest masses of metallic copper found on this coast have been obtained from these Oregon mines. One piece reported to have weighed half a ton was taken from the "Diamond" mine; another piece weighing four hundred pounds was taken from the "Cruikshank" mine, and a great many pieces weighing from one hundred to three hundred pounds each have been found in this vicinity.

In 1862 several valuable deposits of copper ore were discovered on Williams's fork of the Colorado river, in Arizona Territory, near where Aubrey City has been since located. But it was not till November, 1863, when Mr. Robert Ryland, of San Francisco, commenced work on the "Planet" mine, at this place, that the true value of these Arizona copper mines was ascertained. There are undoubted proofs of the existence of exceedingly valuable copper mines in this Territory, at various points convenient to the navigable waters of the Colorado and its tributaries. Mr. Pompelly, a scientific geologist and mineralogist, who subsequently was appointed mineralogist to the Japanese government, made an extended examination of the mineral resources of Arizona, and in the published report of his observations he refers particularly to the extraordinary richness and extent of the copper resources of the Territory. Other parties, who have travelled extensively through it since Mr. Pompelly, fully corroborate all that gentleman reported on this subject. Important mines have been discovered, and districts organized at many points in the Territory, among which are the Iretaba district, about twenty-five miles southwest from Fort Mohave; the Freeman district, about sixty miles south of Williams's fork; the Chimewawa district, on the west bank of the Colorado, nearly opposite La Paz; the Salaza district, about thirty-five miles northeast of La Paz, and the Castle Dome district, about thirty miles north of the Gila. The formations in which the copper is found in this Territory are altogether different from those in which it is found in Oregon and California. The ores themselves are also quite distinct, and far more valuable than those found in these States. The details of these peculiarities will be given hereafter.

About the time the Colorado mines were discovered, a singular but quite extensive lode of copper ore, containing considerable metallic copper and silver, was discovered near Loretto, in the province of Comondu, Lower California. Several tons of exceedingly rich ore, which averaged sixty per cent., was brought to San Francisco in 1862, from the "Favorita" mine, also in Lower California.

In 1864 a number of valuable deposits of copper ores were discovered in various places in the State of Nevada. Among the most important of these discoveries are the "Peavine" district, near the Hennep pass, but a short distance from the line of the Central Pacific railroad. The completion of this road to the neighborhood of this district has given it much importance of late, the railroad company offering to deliver the ore in Sacramento at nine dollars per ton. Other copper mines have been located on Walker's river, in Esmeralda county, and on the south fork of the Carson river, in Ormsby county, and at other points in this State, the ores from which will be profitable to ship as soon as the completion of the Pacific railroad shall afford the means for sending them to a market.

■ The above hurriedly compiled notes, though giving the merest outlines of the extent of the copper resources of the Pacific coast, are sufficient to convey an idea of the magnitude and importance of these resources, which, under a judicious system of encouragement by the federal government, may be made to produce many millions of dollars annually.

The locality of the most important mining districts.—It will be impossible under this heading to mention any except those in which well-known mines are located, and of these only to give the merest outline description. To avoid expansion, as the materials are very abundant, only those from which ores are known to have been exported will be referred to. These are the following:

The Copperopolis, Table Mountain, Napoleon, Lancha Plana, Campo Peco, and Copper Hill, in Calaveras county.

The Newton, Cosumnes, and Hope Valley, in Amador county.

The La Victorie and Birdseye, in Mariposa county.

The Buchanan, in Fresno county.

The Osos, in San Luis Obispo county.

The Solidad, in Los Angeles county.

The Genessee Valley, in Plumas county.

The Alta, in Del Norte county.

The Mount Diablo, in Contra Costa county.

The Rockland, in Oregon.

The Peavine, in Nevada.

The Favorita and Sauce, in Lower California.

The William's Fork, in Arizona.

Copperopolis mines.—The Copperopolis mines are located in Salt Spring valley, in the southwestern portion of Calaveras county, about thirty-five miles nearly east from Stockton, at the head of navigation on the San Joaquin river. This valley is large, beautiful, and well sheltered, and very fertile, producing all descriptions of fruits, grain, and vegetables, in the greatest perfection. Its peculiar excellence in these respects has caused it to be more or less under cultivation since the settlement of California by the Americans. It is bounded on the east by the Bear mountains, a lofty branch of the foot-hills lying between the Stanislaus and Calaveras rivers, which nearly divide Calaveras county into two parts. On the west it is bounded by a range of low broken hills which skirt the eastern side of the valley of San Joaquin. It extends nearly to the Calaveras river on the north. The most famous copper mines on the coast are located on the west of this valley, near the head of what is called Black creek, a small tributary to the Stanislaus.

The lode on which the Union, Keystone, Empire, Calaveras, and Consolidated mines are located passes through this valley in the direction of north 30° west. It has been more or less developed for about fifteen miles, and found to curve slightly towards the north, at its western extremity.

There are other lodes in this valley on which are located many mines known to be of great value, though they have not been as extensively developed as those on the main lode. It is claimed that there are four of these lodes, which range from a few feet to six miles in distance from the main one, but all follow the same direction. This cupriferous belt has been traced with comparatively slight interruptions from this valley to the American river, its general course being about north 15° west.

The most important mine in the valley is the Union. This contains 1,950 feet on the main lode, which was originally divided into thirteen shares of 150 feet each. But at present it is nearly all owned by Meader, Lalor & Co., merchants, of San Francisco, Mr. McCarty, one of the original locators, being the only one retaining any portion of their claim.

The owners of this mine never formed themselves into an incorporated company, as nearly all other mining companies generally do. Probably no necessity arose to compel them, as no assessments were ever levied on their shares, the mine paying well from the very commencement of their operations. It gave them a dividend of $11,000 per share in December, 1862, and during the year 1863 the dividends amounted to $20,000 per share, clear of all expenses. It is not possible to tell how much the mine has paid since, in consequence of

Meader & Co. having purchased it soon after the last dividend in 1863 was declared, and they have their own reasons for not making its revenue public. It is alleged that in the winter of 1863 that firm paid Mr. Reed, the locator of the mine, $65,000 in cash for 975 feet. In 1864 Mr. Hardy, another of the original locators, it is stated sold his interest in the mine to the same firm for $650,000.

There is but little doubt that this mine contains the largest body of yellow sulphurets of copper ever discovered. Some scientific gentlemen have expressed doubts as to whether this body of ore is a true vein, or merely a local surface deposit, as it does not present some of the characteristics of veins of similar ore found in other counties. The fact that it has been explored to the depth of upwards of 500 feet without any symptoms of its giving out, and that it has been examined for many miles consecutively, presenting the same general appearance throughout, is, to say the least, a stronger proof in support of the opinion that it is a continuous, regular vein, than any *theory* can be that it is not.

The work on this mine is carried on by means of three shafts, which have been sunk from 300 to 500 feet on the lode, from which several levels or drifts have been run along its course. For the purpose of hoisting the ore there is a fourteen horse-power steam-engine at the mouth of each of the two outer shafts. At the main shaft, from which the mine is drained, there is an eighty horse-power engine, which is used for both pumping and hoisting. Another shaft is in progress, and nearly completed, which is being sunk for the purpose of striking the lode at a depth of between 400 and 500 feet, at a point where it is known to dip considerably to the east. All the other shafts having been commenced on the lode, passed through it on reaching a limited depth, going further from it as the depth increased, involving an increased expense in running tunnels to strike it at each succeeding level.

The dimensions of this body of ore have been ascertained with tolerable accuracy, for a length of nearly 600 feet, and to a depth of upwards of 400 feet, by shafts and levels which have been made in it. Near the surface, for, say 150 feet in depth, the lode varied in proportions very much, ranging from one foot to twelve feet in width. At the depth of 200 feet in the main shaft it was nearly 21 feet wide; at 250 feet deep, it was nearly 30 feet wide; and continued of nearly the same width to 300 feet in depth, when it became less uniform, and began to decrease in proportions, till at the depth of about 400 feet at the north, near the Keystone line, it had decreased to about 6 feet in width, while for 200 feet north from the main shaft it is nearly 28 feet wide. As the Keystone company have recently struck the lode on their ground, within 100 feet of the dividing line between the two mines, at a depth of 360 feet, where it is 10 feet wide, it is presumable that its contraction in the Union, at nearly the same level, is not permanent.

It would be difficult to obtain correct information as to the product of this mine, from its opening up to the present time, as its proprietors seem averse to furnishing particulars. It is known, however, that the exports of ore from this State amounted to 5,553 tons in 1863, and to 10,234 tons in 1864, at least one-half of which was obtained from the "Union." The company's books show that from the 10th March to the 31st December, 1865, 25,542 tons of ore were actually shipped from the mine. As the firm owning it state that the average of all its ores shipped is 15 per cent., and estimate it to be worth $75 per ton, it follows that its products for 1865 exceeded $1,500,000 in value. The shipments for 1866, as will be seen by reference to the table of exports, will exceed those of 1865—the quantity shipped being only limited by the number of vessels available for carrying it away. The above figures will convey a slight idea of the importance of developing such a fruitful source of national wealth as is presented in the copper mines of the Pacific coast.

The Union company employ about 250 men about the mine, in the various departments of its operations. None of the companies at Copperopolis employ any Chinese coolies.

. The Keystone is next in importance to the Union, which it adjoins on the north. It contains 3,300 feet on the lode. It is owned by an incorporated joint-stock company, the shares in which are one hundred and fifty in number. It was on this claim that the first work of development on the lode was done, in what is still called the discovery shaft, on the north end of the claim, and which is still used by the company in their operations.

The shareholders in this mine have not been as fortunate as those of the Union. The Keyston ehas never yielded them a dividend since its discovery; on the contrary, it has cost them $100,000 in assessments over and above the receipts from its whole product of ore, which up to October 1, 1866, amounted to 5,719 tons, worth, at $75 per ton, $428,925. The enormous expenses incurred in the development of this mine have probably been caused by mismanagement, and costly, useless experiments for concentrating the low-grade ores, of which the mine produces very large quantities.

The best informed among the stockholders in this mine estimate that it has produced sufficient ore to defray all the expenses of working. The $100,000 collected as assessments have been expended in experiments and machinery. The company have very fine and powerful hoisting, pumping, and concentrating machinery. The latter is only used during the winter and spring, when there is an abundance of water available. The ores in the Keystone are identical with those in the Union, but they are not found in as large a body, or as compact. The lode in this mine has at no time exceeded ten feet in width, and it is usually so much divided by the containing slate that the cost of its separation by hand-labor causes it to be not very profitable to the company. At the depth of 260 feet in the main shaft the lode was only six feet wide, and contained a body of iron pyrites nearly a foot thick through the centre of it for nearly 150 feet in length, and it was further divided by seams of slate into irregular masses from one inch to six inches thick.

The greatest depth reached on this mine is about 400 feet. Quite recently, in the sixth level, at a depth of about 360 feet in the Houghton shaft—that is, the shaft nearest to the dividing line between this mine and the Union—a body of ore nearly ten feet thick was struck while drifting within 150 feet of this dividing line. In this body of ore there is only about four feet sufficiently rich to pay for shipping; the remainder is so divided by the containing slate, or contains so large a proportion of iron pyrites, as to fall below the average of 12 per cent. the present lowest grade of paying ore.

There are six shafts in this mine, only two of which, the discovery shaft and that nearest the Union, are in use—the cost of sinking and timbering the others being nearly a total loss to the company. In fact, the first two years' work done on the mine was wasted through the inexperience of those who were intrusted with its management.

The annual product of the Keystone, according to the books of the company, has been as follows:

1862	596 tons of 2,376 pounds.
1863	758 tons of 2,376 pounds.
1864	1,506 tons of 2,376 pounds.
1865	1,743 tons of 2,376 pounds.
1866, (till October 1,)	1,386 tons of 2,376 pounds.
Total production	5,719 tons.

The company employ about one hundred men in the various departments of their works.

The Empire mine is located next to the Union, on the south. It contains

1,800 feet on the same lode. It is owned by an incorporated company, the majority of the stockholders in which are capitalists who reside at New York. This company have expended a very large amount of money in developing their mine. The greater portion of this expenditure, as has been the case with the Keystone company, has been wasted through incompetent management. Great improvements in this respect have been made recently, and the prospects of the company are promising. The explorations now in process show considerable good ore, and there are indications of an increase in the dimensions of the lode.

The ore in this is similar to that in all the other mines on the lode; but in the croppings on this claim there was considerably more quartz than there was upon any other claim on the lode. In this quartz, which was of a milky whiteness, there was metallic copper, crystallized in leaf and fern-like forms, which were exceedingly brilliant and beautiful when first taken out of their stony matrix.

The Calaveras is located next south of the Empire, on the same lode, of which it contains 3,000 feet. The croppings on this claim were exceedingly rich, but the lode has not proven to be so below the surface. Several shafts have been sunk and many drifts and cuttings made without finding any body of ore of importance. The company are not working this mine at present.

The Consolidated is located on the same lode, north of the Keystone. It contains 3,000 feet.

The Webster is the name of another important mine in this valley. It is located about one and a half mile east of Copperopolis, on a massive body of ore nearly twenty-eight feet wide. This ore is of a different character to that in the main lode, and is much less valuable; for, though quite solid and compact, it does not average more than eight per cent., in consequence of the larger percentage of iron it contains.

The Inimitable is another important mine in this valley, located on a different lode altogether. This mine is situated parallel with the Union, and but a few feet apart from it, on the east side. So close are these two mines together that the owners of the Inimitable had some intentions of suing the Union company for damages for taking out some of their ore on some of the lower levels, which they claimed was on the Inimitable's ground. The Napoleon mine, which is located four miles south from Copperopolis, is on the eastern end of a lode which runs through this valley, parallel with the main lode, but about six miles apart from it, which has been located upon for nearly fifteen miles. The Scorpion, Swansea, Massachusetts, Pacific, and other valuable mines, are located on this parallel lode. These lodes are easily traced to near the banks of the river, where they all disappear, and are not again visible till near the town of Montezuma, in Tuolumne county, six miles from the other side of the river. Gopher Hill, where the first discovery of copper was made, is supposed to be the extreme west of the main lode.

The above is not by any means a complete list of the mines in Salt Spring valley. There are scores of others, but these are the most important.

At present about one thousand men are employed in various capacities among the mines in this district, the larger proportion of whom are foreigners, chiefly English and Irish. No Chinese are employed about the mines except as cooks, washermen, and servants.

The Table Mountain mine is located about five miles southeast from Copperopolis, and about one mile from the Stanislaus river. It is the last claim on the main lode on this side of that river. It contains 2,150 feet on the lode, which is here about six feet wide, and much divided by the containing slate. This mine is owned by a joint-stock company of twenty-one shareholders. It has been considerably developed, and about one thousand tons of ore have been shipped from it.

The Campo Seco, Lancha Plana, and Copper Hill mines are located on a continuation of the main Copperopolis lode, where it makes its appearance between the Calaveras and Mokelumne rivers. All these mines were discovered in 1861, shortly after the discovery of the Union and Keystone mines. They have been extensively developed, and the lode has been well tested by shafts and drifts. It presents the same peculiarities as were noticed at Copperopolis. It is quite large on the Campo Seco claim, being twenty feet wide at one hundred feet deep. It is scarcely as large in the Lancha Plana, and in the Copper Hill it is only about six feet. The character and composition of the ores are identical with those at Copperopolis, and they are contained in the same description of rock, and present many other features of similarity. Large quantities of ore have been shipped from these mines; but the present low price of ores, which is lower than it has previously been for the past fifteen years, leaves so small a profit after paying expenses that the companies are storing most of their ores in anticipation of an improvement in the market. About one hundred and fifty men are employed among these mines, about forty of whom are Chinese, who perform much of the labor above ground, such as separating and bagging the ores, &c.

Quite extensive concentrating works are being put up on the Campo Seco mine. The company intend to concentrate most of their ores into about fifty per cent. matte or regulus.

The Napoleon mine is located about four miles south of Copperopolis, in what are called the Gopher hills, a range of low, broken hills, very irregular in form and direction, on the east of the San Joaquin valley. They are the first hills met with after leaving Stockton and travelling east. As has already been mentioned, this was the first copper mine opened in California. As such, Mr. Hughes, who discovered both the Napoleon and the Quail Hill mines, claimed the latter as a silver or gold mine.

The Napoleon contains 2,700 feet on two well-defined lodes of ore, similar in composition to those at Copperopolis. It was located in November, 1860, and in October, 1862, was owned by an incorporated company; each foot in the mine representing a share of stock. In 1863 these one-foot shares were selling at $100 each.

In consequence of the country through which the Napoleon lode traverses having been much disturbed by subterranean forces, it is extensively dislocated. The "faults," as the miners call these dislocations, are so numerous that all the other mines on this lode had to cease operations because they could not trace it far enough consecutively to obtain any extensive body of ore. This misfortune has happened to the Napoleon. At the depth of about 400 feet the lode, after narrowing from twenty to less than six feet, finally was lost altogether by a shift in the containing rock. The company have been engaged for more than a year in attempting to rediscover it. They have sunk a new shaft nearly 400 feet deep, some distance to the south of the old one. The prospects are that they will meet with a large body of good ore in this new shaft.

The Napoleon is located on the eastern extremity of a lode which has been traced to San Domingo gulch, twenty-five miles distant, where the Noble mine, owned by Pioche & Beyergue, French merchants of San Francisco, is located on it. The Napoleon commenced shipping ores in May, 1863.

The following statement, compiled from the books of the company, furnishes full particulars of the product of the mine:

Shipment of ores from the Napoleon copper mine.

Date.	First class.	Second class.	Concentrated ore.
1863.	*Pounds.*	*Pounds.*	*Pounds.*
May	36,826	45,302	....
June	137,930	108,420	....
July	185,498	61,014	....
August	73,037	98,172	....
September	250,234	230,873	....
October	232,100	507,810	....
November	187,480	284,920	....
December	69,060	234,110	....
Total	1,172,165	1,507,621	
1864.			
January	42,240	170,930	....
February	44,330	367,020	....
March	91,960	386,640	....
April	30,470	334,940	....
May	28,970	205,740	....
June	17,160	232,100	....
July	49,720	252,070	....
August	6,820	159,750	....
September	....	134,410	420,835
October	....	238,370	190,540
November	....	192,216	164,025
Total	351,570	2,674,226	775,400
1865.			
March	....	8,100	....
April	20,250	115,950	....
May	....	78,150	158,600
June	....	48,450	132,000
July	....	....	323,120
August	....	....	159,460
September	....	6,420	170,305
Total	20,250	257,070	943,485
Grand totals	1,543,985	4,501,917	1,718,885

Seven million seven hundred and sixty-four thousand seven hundred and eighty-seven pounds altogether, or nearly four thousand tons.

In September, 1865, the company sold the mine to Martin & Co., dealers in ores, of San Francisco. Since it has been in the hands of this firm, for reasons explained above, the yield of ore has nearly ceased. The total shipments from the mine since the purchase have not exceeded 150 tons, of which about one-half has been second class, and the other concentrated ore.

With reference to the classification of the ores in the above table, as the same method for that purpose is followed in all mines producing the same description of ores, it may be as well to explain that method in this part of the report.

The heavy costs for labor, bags, transportation, commissions, &c., causing all ores below 10 per cent. to be valueless on this coast, none are shipped below that grade; but as there is a considerable advantage gained by separating the ores which vary more than 5 per cent. in richness, the plan generally followed is to class all above 15 per cent. as first, and from 10 per cent. to 15 per cent. as second. There is some difference in the grade of the ores from the various mines. The Union ores are the lowest. The owners of that mine, being extensive shipping agents, have facilities for shipping ores of less value than will pay to ship from any other mine. The average of all the ores shipped from the Union does not exceed 15 per cent. From the Napoleon they were above 16 per cent., causing a difference in value of nearly $5 per ton. The Keystone ores are about 1 per cent. higher than the Union.

The concentrated ores above referred to were prepared by the following very economical process: A pit of about two feet deep was cut in the soft soil, about twenty feet square, in which was laid as evenly as possible about four cords of dry pine wood; over this was piled, in the form of a truncated cone, one hundred tons of ore. There was nothing more done, except to ignite the wood, which soon set the sulphur in the ore on fire, and it continued to burn for six or seven weeks, when the greater portion of the sulphur having been evaporated, the fire went out and the ore was concentrated about 6 per cent, or 10 per cent.; poor second class was converted into 16 per cent., or first class.

The machinery used on this mine consists of a small six-horse power steam-engine, for hoisting and pumping. There are usually about thirty hands employed on this mine, about one-third of whom are Chinese.

Quail Hill, No. 1, where Hughes made the first discovery of copper, is about three miles east from the Napoleon mine, and about seven miles west from Copperopolis. Quite a town, called Telegraph City, has sprung up between these two discoveries of Hughes's.

2.—VARIOUS COPPER DISTRICTS.

Forest Hill district.—The most important mines in Amador county are the Cosumnes, in the Forest Hill district, near Jackson, the county seat, and the Newton, on the same lode, about three miles to the west, near Ione valley, a beautiful and fertile valley, separated from the great valley of the Sacramento by low, irregular hills, as Salt Spring valley is divided from the valley of the San Joaquin. The Cosumnes was located in January, 1862. A company to work it was incorporated in February, 1863. It contains 5,000 feet on the main lode and the same quantity on the Oriental lode, which runs parallel and close to it. This Oriental lode, which is quite extensive, was discovered by the Rev. J. B. Fish, in January, 1863. It appears that the reverend gentleman was returning from a trip to Copperopolis, when he observed the croppings of the lode as he was riding past, the location being near the road. Getting off his horse, he satisfied himself that what he saw was copper ore, and located the claim for himself and friends. The parson's mine has produced nearly one hundred tons of good ore.

The Newton was located early in 1863, by Dr. J. Newton, of Jackson, in the names of himself and six members of his own family, who at present control it. Dr. Newton was the first person in this county who worked a copper mine in it.

Quite a town, called Copper Centre, has sprung up between these two districts. Two years ago it was one of the most active copper mining camps in the State—hundreds of claims having been located on the two copper belts, which can be traced for miles on both sides of the original claims. One of these belts is about six miles northeast of the other, and follows the same course as the parallel lodes at Copperopolis—north about 50° east. These lodes also dip from 10° to 20° to the east, as do those at Copperopolis; are in the same geological formation, and the ores are so much alike in appearance and composition that the best judges cannot tell one from the other. There is no doubt but that the Amador county mines are located on the same lodes as the mines at Copperopolis. There are many valuable copper mines in this vicinity, but though the great distance from a market, and the want of capital and experience of those who own them, work on all except the Cosumnes and Newton has ceased. Probably these would also have remained undeveloped had not Meader & Co., copper merchants of San Francisco, become interested in them.

A great deal of work has been done on the Newton, which has been sufficiently tested by shafts and drifts to prove that it is of great value, and this value would be fourfold greater if there were proper means for bringing the ore to tide-water. The lode on this mine is not so large as it is at Copperopolis, but the ore is less divided by the containing slate than it is in the Keystone. At one hundred feet deep the lode here was only three and half feet wide. It increased considerably as the depth of the shafts increased. Most of the ore from this mine will average 15 per cent. In 1864 it shipped about one hundred tons per month, averaging 16 per cent.

On the Cosumnes ground the lode is about ten feet wide at one hundred and twenty-five feet deep, and averages about 16 per cent. This company shipped about two hundred and fifty tons per month during 1864, averaging 12 per cent.

Hope valley.—The Rodger's mine, in Hope valley in this county, is located a few miles west of Carson cañon, on the borders of the State of Nevada, only a few miles from some of the highest peaks of the Sierra Nevadas. It was discovered in 1855, but has never been worked to any extent, though the ore is very valuable and of great beauty. It is not a regular lode, but a sort of chimney, which makes its appearance, about two feet wide and nearly perpendicular, in the face of a lofty bluff of solid, hard, white granite, at the eastern end of the valley. The only sign of this body of ore is confined to its exposure in the face of the bluff, and for about thirty feet on the top of it. A great deal of prospecting has been done in the vicinity, in the hope of finding a continuation of it, but in vain. The ore is accompanied on the south side by a body of hard, grayish, crystaline limestone, the only sign of that mineral for many miles around—the whole country being composed of bare, rugged cliffs and peaks of felspathic granite. On the north side of the ore there is a seam, of about a foot wide, of dark brown quartz, of a peculiar cellular structure. There is a great abundance of brilliant lime garnets in this ore, which, together with the peculiar combination of sulphurets, oxides, and carbonates of which it is formed, render it exceedingly interesting for cabinet specimens; though it is very doubtful whether it will ever pay to extract it for commercial purposes.

Mariposa county mines.—The existence of important lodes or deposits of copper ores of considerable commercial value in Mariposa county was known for several years before any attempt was made to turn them to profitable account. The croppings of a series of large bodies of the ore are seen protruding through the surface all through the county, from where it unites to Merced county on the one side to where it joins Fresno county on the other. It was not until the summer of 1863 that any attention was paid to copper mining in this county. The distance from a market and want of roads, as well as the broken and disturbed condition of the geological formation in which the ore is contained, prevented men of experience and capital investing time or money in their development.

There are two extensive districts in which copper mining is carried on in this county. One is on the south side of it, on the Chowchilla river, near the dividing line between this county and Merced. This is called the Hamilton district. It embraces mines in both these counties. The other is the Hunters' Valley district. This is located west of the Bear Valley mountains and south of the Merced river. The La Victoire, the most important copper mine in Mariposa county, is in this district.

A good many companies are working in the Hamilton district; but thus far the developments have not been of much importance, as no shaft of any considerable depth has been sunk, and no permanent lode has been discovered. There is but little doubt that the mines in this county are located on portions of the great cupriferous belt referred to in the introductory remarks to this report as passing through the State; but the shifting and dislocation to which it has been subjected since its formation have so broken it up that it is exceedingly doubtful whether any permanent mine will be discovered in the southern district of this county. Some activity has been imparted to this district during the past year by the erection of several smelting furnaces on a small scale, which, operating on the silicates, oxides, and carbonates of the metal, which are found in great abundance for miles around, make large quantities of regulus and black copper from 60 per cent. to 96 per cent. of fineness. The owners of these furnaces pay a fair price of all the ores of a suitable character the miners can bring. This will account for the activity in the district and for the shallowness of the explorations, as the ores cease to be of the class required at a few feet below the surface.

One of these furnaces has been erected on James's ranch, and another, about six miles distant, on the border of Fresno county, at Buchanan Hollow. From this latter place about one hundred and fifty tons of copper, in bars ranging from 80 per cent. to 96 per cent. of metal, have been exported from San Francisco to New York by Coffee & Risdon, the proprietors of the works.

The furnaces at James's ranch are constructed on the French plan, introduced on this coast, on the Queen of Bronze mine, in Oregon, by M. De Hierry, a French metallurgist of considerable ability. They are capable of operating on about eight tons of ore in twenty-four hours. The class of ores operated on have averaged about 12 per cent., the greater portion of which has been obtained from the Green Mountain and Lone Tree mines, near the works.

The company obtain plenty of pine wood charcoal at $70 to $80 per ton. All the smelting is done with this description of fuel. About a ton of this charcoal is required to produce a ton of marketable regulus. There are about a dozen men employed at each of these works.

The furnaces used at Buchanan Hollow are what are known as Haskell's water-lined, a brief description of which will be found under the head of "Processes," &c. They are of about the same capacity as those mentioned above, and consume about the same quantity of the same description of fuel. There are several of this latter description of furnaces in use in this State; one on the Cosumnes mine, in Amador county; another on the La Victoire mine, in Mariposa county, and several others are in an advanced state of construction in various localities.

About six miles south of these smelting works at Buchanan Hollow there are several of the best mines in this county; among them is the Bachman. In the shaft on this mine, at a depth of sixty feet, the lode is ten feet wide, composed of yellow sulphurets, identical in appearance and composition with those found at Copperopolis and Campo Seco, and accompanied with all the characteristics of the lodes in those districts, and affording many facts to prove a connection in the origin of all of them.

Near the smelting works on James's ranch there is a series of lodes, traceable for about ten miles, and ranging N. 24° W., corresponding very closely with those already noticed in Salt Spring valley. In a shaft sunk on the Dozer lode, one of this series, at a depth of eighty feet it was found to be six feet wide, composed of nearly solid yellow sulphuret. But, as was explained above, the disturbance of the containing rock does not hold out a reasonable hope of the permanence of any body of ore in the district.

Mr. Haskell, the proprietor of the Buchanan lode, has recently sold it and the smelting works above described to a firm at Stockton for $22,000. This will afford a basis on which to estimate the value of the best mines in the district.

The "La Victoire" mine, in Hunter's valley, is a most valuable property, being second in importance to scarcely any copper mine in the State. It is located in a section of this county which has not been affected by those disturbing causes which have broken up the lodes in all the other sections. It also possesses the very great advantage of having an immense body of very good ore above the level of the surrounding country, which enables the company to extract it without the use of expensive hoisting and pumping machinery. The lode runs through a hill several hundred feet in length and nearly three hundred feet high, cropping out on the very summit of it, and traceable, unbroken, through its entire length, at an average width of nearly five feet. The proprietors, who are mostly Frenchmen, have sunk shafts on the lode at both ends of the base of this hill to the depth of nearly two hundred feet, without discovering any material difference in its appearance, the only important change being that, while the lode dips to the east at an angle of 45° at twenty-five feet below the surface, at the base of the hill, at one hundred feet lower, it dips at an angle of 68°; but, as it increases nearly a foot in thickness at the point where the dip changes, it is evident that the change has not been the effect of dislocation. A great deal of very rich ore has been taken out of this mine, much of it containing sufficient gold to pay for working it for that metal only.

It may be proper in this connection to state that the copper bars made in this county by the furnaces described above contain a very large per cent. of gold. Some of it, assayed by Kellogg & Hueston, of San Francisco, was found to contain as high as $450 to the ton. Much of this copper contains $50 in gold to the ton; none of it less than $20.

There is a small smelting furnace on this mine, but it is not in use. For the past year but little work of any kind has been done on the mine in consequence of disagreements among the owners, one portion of whom are playing the game of "freeze out" upon the others.

There are several other good copper mines in this district, but those who own them do not appear to have either the means or disposition to develop them, and capitalists from abroad are afraid to invest very extensively in such mines in this county till they have been better examined.

San Luis Obispo county mines.—The Osos mines in San Luis Obispo county were discovered in the spring of 1864. They are situate about eight miles west of the Old Mission of San Luis Obispo, on the Osos ranch, near the south end of a wide belt of cupriferous ores that is traceable for more than twenty miles to the north, among the range of mountains which lay between the town of San Luis Obispo and the Old Mission of Santa Marguerita. This belt of ore, on which there are a great number of mines, presents very much the same peculiarities as are mentioned in the description of the Hamilton district, in Mariposa county. The disturbance of the lode by subterranean causes has broken it up to such an extent as to render it unprofitable to mine. The Osos district, as is the case with Hunter's valley, in Mariposa, appears to have been less affected by these disturbing causes. A shaft one hundred and ten feet deep has been sunk on the Osos lode, which was from four feet to twelve feet wide. One hundred tons of ore, averaging eighteen per cent., have been shipped from this mine direct to Boston and Swansea, and there are several hundred tons more ready for shipment. Ex-congressman Phelps is extensively interested in these mines.

Los Angeles county mines.—The Solidad district, in Los Angeles county, is located about thirty miles due north from Los Angeles. The knowledge of the existence of copper in this locality was published by M. Duflot de Mofras nearly twenty years ago, as it was somewhere in the neighborhood that placer mining for gold was carried on as far back as 1840. Mr. Bidwell, member of Congress for California, saw these early gold miners at work, and probably saw the croppings of the copper lode, which are quite extensive and conspicuous for a long distance. In 1854 a Frenchman named Maris discovered the mines in what is now known as the Solidad district, but the discovery attracted no attention till the excitement about copper, which followed the discovery of the mines at Salt Springs valley, in 1861 and 1862, when great activity in prospecting raged in this locality, and a great amount of work was done during the following two years. At present, and for more than a year past, none of the claims have been worked. Among the few important mines in this district are the La Solidad, Copper Hill, and Occidental. On the first named, at the depth of one hundred feet, the lode was found to be about seven feet wide. This is the deepest shaft in the district.

The geological formations and ores in this district are precisely the same as those already described in San Luis Obispo and Mariposa counties, and the same disturbing causes have broken up the lodes, which range in the same direction within a few degrees.

Plumas county mines.—The copper mines in Genessee valley, Plumas county, are the highest on this coast; the valley in which they are located being a small basin of a few miles in circumference, embosomed high up among some of the loftiest peaks of the Sierra Nevadas, which are clustered together in the northeast of this county. This portion of Upper Plumas contains some of the most magnificent scenery to be found on the coast. Immense granite ridges are seen rising bare and bleak two and sometimes three thousand feet above the densely wooded ridges at their base, while below, cañons thousands of feet deep form courses for the waters, which look like silver threads as they go meandering through the black gorges that lead them to unite with the waters of the Feather river, thousands of feet still further below. Nature appears to have performed some of her mightiest labors in this locality. Subterranean fires have piled up the molten rocks thousands of feet high, for the highest peaks are composed of lava, while the floods of water have worn the frightful cañons which furnish the bed for the present insignificant streams. Amid the very centre of so much ruggedness, caused by nature's greatest forces, Genessee valley forms a beautiful contrast, with its grassy fields and the curling smoke of its smelting furnaces and other evidences of the power of man. The belt of copper ores already referred to passes through this valley in a course ranging north twenty-five degrees west. As may well be imagined, in such a country, the lode has been extensively dislocated; but by examining the unshifted bodies of the containing slates, which may be traced for many miles, as well as the form and composition of the lodes, it is proved that this is part of that great belt. The chief copper mines, the Cosmopolitan, are located about five miles from the village of Taylorville, and three-fourths of a mile from a ranch which was originally located in the valley by a Mr. Gifford. They were discovered in the beginning of 1862. The inaccessibility of the place and the broken character of the country preclude the possibility of this ever becoming a very important copper mining locality. Nevertheless, parties interested in these mines have erected smelting works which have cost upwards of $30,000, and made several tons of good regulus by a process invented by a farmer named J. C. Chapman, who never had any knowledge or experience in copper smelting till the discovery of these mines. As long as the parties interested in this enterprise could obtain plenty of oxides, carbonates, and silicates of the metal, which were quite abundant and very rich at the commencement of their operations, they obtained regulus sufficient to pay expenses; but as soon as they reached the sulphurets in the lode the works had to stop, as they were not adapted to operate on this class of ores. At the present time they are not in operation. These works were put up by Bolinger, Blood & Co.

At a depth of sixty feet the lode on the Cosmopolitan mine was found to be about fourteen feet wide, containing about ten per cent. of metal. It lies between the granite and limestone on this claim. The metamorphic slates and serpentine, which accompany the copper all through this State, are here a few hundred feet to the south.

Del Norte county mines.—The Alta district, in Del Norte county, is situated on what is known as the "low divide," an extensive plateau on the summit of a lofty range of mountains which divide the valley of the Illinois river from the

Pacific ocean. These mountains run through the northern portion of California and the south of Oregon, for more than one hundred miles, and cross the western branch of the Sierra Nevadas at nearly right angles.

Altaville, the centre of this district, is about fifteen miles northeast from Crescent City, Del Norte county. There are a great number of mines in the district; many of them have been extensively worked, and probably one thousand tons of good ore has been shipped from them since their discovery, in 1860. Among those which have shipped ore are the Alta, Union, Pacific, Lady Belle, Chrysopolis, Comstock, Diamond, Express, Pearl, Copper Hill, Excelsior, and a number of others. The Alta was the first mine worked in the district, and is the only one worked at present.

The mines in this district are not connected with the great copper belt so frequently alluded to in this report. This runs several miles to the east, where the Siskiyou mountains connect the counties of Yreka, in California, with Josephine, in Oregon. The ores in the Alta district are quite distinct in deposition, appearance, and character from those found in the mines on the great belt. The deposits are separate and distinct; of probably the same age and origin, as they are similar in other respects to those found around the base of Mount Diablo, and in the coast range further south. The first forty-two tons of ore shipped by the Alta company averaged forty-five per cent., and sold in San Francisco for $7,000 cash, the cost of their extraction and delivery not exceeding $2,000. They were red oxides, chiefly, of which there was a large body nearly three feet wide and fifty feet long, near the surface, but this was soon exhausted, as there is no well defined lode on the ground. In fact it is doubtful whether there is a consecutive body of ore of fifty feet in length in the whole district. The croppings of what are supposed to be lodes—nearly a dozen of them—are seen ranging nearly north and south for many miles, but the body of ore beneath these croppings is so irregular in position, owing to the distortion of the serpentine in which they are contained, that it is almost impossible to tell in what direction the average of them do lie.

The Alta Company have sunk a shaft on their mine to the depth of nearly four hundred feet without finding a regularly defined lode. They meet with bunches of ore, chiefly yellow sulphurets of a very low grade, varying in size from a mere film to ten feet thick, but not sufficiently connected to make the mine profitable to work under the existing state of the copper market. This mine is exceedingly well situated for obtaining its ore cheap, if a large body of it should be found, as drifts could be run into the hill at a great depth at comparatively little cost.

The Rockland district is located about fifteen miles east of the Alta district, above described, and about thirty miles from Crescent City, Del Norte county, California. The mines in this district are located on the great copper belt, which may easily be traced in the vicinity for nearly twenty miles, in the direction of N. 28° W., the general trend of this belt, by which it may be followed from where first noticed, north of Los Angeles, to about twenty-five miles west of this district, which is a few miles within the limits of the State of Oregon. There are several other districts within this State in which important copper mines have been located on this belt; but time will not admit of any reference being made to them. The Queen of Bronze, near Waldo, Josephine county, the most valuable copper mine in Oregon, is located on this belt, about sixteen miles west from this point. Extensive smelting works have been erected on this latter mine, and thousands of tons of ore have been exported from these mines, which, as has been already stated, have been discovered since 1860.

There are some peculiarly interesting features connected with the copper mines of this district, which have a tendency to throw considerable light upon the subject of the action of volcanic forces on metallic ores, because in this vicinity an enormous volcanic dyke, nearly one hundred feet wide, approaches the copper belt at an obtuse angle, within a hundred feet, and it is within this point of proximity that the large masses of metallic copper mentioned above were discovered. Another point in the same connection may be here mentioned. The age of the rocks containing the copper, throughout the whole extent of the great belt, has been tolerably well ascertained to be between the triassic and tertiary eras, and as this volcanic force, which has caused the conversion of the ores into metals from one end of it to the other, must have been exerted subsequently, the opportunity here afforded to examine the largest and most clearly defined dyke on the coast is very important.

Mount Diablo district.—The principal copper mines in the Mount Diablo district are located about the northern base, and up the side of a spur of Mount Diablo, called Mount Zion, and along the north side of Mitchell's cañon, near the town of Clayton, Contra Costa county. The first discovery of these mines was made in 1860, and considerable work was done on several of them for about two years, in efforts to discover the lode, but without success, as there is no lode in the mountain. The copper found here is not connected with the great cupriferous belt, but exists in detached bunches and masses, as is the case in the Alta district, in Del Norte county, described above. The croppings of the patches of ore here run north and south, as they do at Del Norte. Some metallic copper has been found on the north side of Mitchell's cañon, but in every case, after reaching a few feet below the surface, the ore, when found in bodies sufficiently large to take out, has been found of a very low grade; ten tons of selected ore shipped by the Keokuk company did not yield more than eight per cent. It is doubtful whether the mines in this district will ever pay to work.

Peavine district.—The Peavine district was discovered in 1864. It is located a few miles east of the Henness pass, in Washoe county, Nevada, one portion of it being within three miles of the line of the Central Pacific railroad. The district embraces an era of ten miles square, in which there are a great number of claims of considerable importance. The ores in all these mines are entirely distinct from those found in California, as well as the containing rocks. They are usually much contaminated with quartz, but they contain a large per cent. of gold and silver. The completion of the Central Pacific railroad to within a few miles of the district has given considerable impetus to prospecting, and a great number of companies are preparing to take out ore, the railroad company having informed those interested that it would carry ores to Sacramento, from any point in the Henness pass, for $9 per ton. The ores of most of these mines being silicates, carbonates, and oxides, are very easily concentrated, a fact which the owners of the Bay State mine appear to be aware of, as they are putting up a small furnace, on Haskell's plan, to operate on all the ores they can purchase, as well as what they can obtain from their own mine. No ores of any consequence have been shipped from this district, in consequence of the distance to a market; but in 1864 a Doctor Landszwert made a number of large bars of fine copper from them, which were exhibited at the State fair, at Carson City, in that year. These bars contained $150 per ton in gold, and about $250 per ton in silver, according to the doctor's assay.

Lower California mines—Of the copper mines in Lower California but little of an authentic character is known. The Sancè mine, as described by Mr. W. Thompson, an old Cornish miner, who was superintendent of it for three or four years, is located near Loretto, a place in the province of Comondu, about thirty miles from the coast, where there is a good harbor. The lode is described as being from eight to ten feet wide, enclosed between walls of slate and granite. It has been extensively explored by shafts and levels, and about five hundred tons of ore have been shipped to Europe, where it sold for about five hundred dollars per ton. This ore, specimens of which have been brought to San Francisco, is of a very peculiar character, being a sort of talcose gangue, containing flattened scales of metal of various sizes, from several feet in length and breadth, to small specks like fine gold dust. Many of the larger masses of this copper are covered with an incrustation of metallic silver, the only similar combination of these two metals found on this coast, though the combination of metallic copper and silver is quite common at the Lake Superior copper mines. This mine has not been worked for nearly two years.

Arizona mines.—The mines in Arizona, from which ores have been sent to San Francisco, are located on both banks of Williams's Fork of the Colorado river, where, there is but little doubt, will very soon be one of the most important copper mining districts on this coast. The existence of the deposits of ore now in course of development at this point was well known for several years before the discovery of the mines in California. A quantity of the ore from some of the mines about Mineral Hill was sent to Boston, as early as 1858, and examined by Doctor Jackson, the distinguished mineralogist of that city, who pronounced them of extraordinary richness. But a variety of causes, among which the want of means for transporting the ore was the chief, prevented any advantage being gained by the discovery till 1862 when the owners of the Planet mine shipped about one hundred tons of their ore to San Francisco, where it sold for a price that left a profit of upwards of $100 per ton over and above all expenses for its extraction and transportation, the land carriage from the mine to the river, about twenty miles, having been done by pack-mules. A good road has been cut to connect the mines with the river since that time.

There are nearly fifty good mines in this district on both banks of the river. The Planet is the most important on the south, and the Mineral Hill on the north. The greatest activity has prevailed among these mines during the past year, and about 1,500 tons of ore have been shipped from them all collectively ; the principal shippers being the Planet, Great Central, Mineral Hill, Philadelphia, Mountaineer, Mammoth, Copper Hill, and Occidental. Ten times the quantity shipped might have been sent had there been means for taking it away. Gentlemen just returned from these mines state that there are upwards of 1,000 tons of ore that will average 40 per cent., now lying on the river bank ready for shipment. The steamers and two or three schooners employed in the trade are wholly inadequate for the purpose.

Some of the mines in this district have been extensively explored by means of shafts, tunnels and drifts, and in nearly every case the body of ore has increased in importance in proportion to the extent to which it has been developed. The Mineral Hill company have run a tunnel on their mine for the length of 350 feet, out of which, while cutting, they took nearly 1,000 tons of ore of an average of 30 per cent., the whole work from the surface being in a body of ore. The ore in none of the mines in the district is found in a regular lode, as in the mines in California, but the whole country appears to be formed of the ores of iron and copper, the hills for miles around being colored red by the iron, or green and blue in patches where waters containing carbonate of lime in solution have percolated through the copper.

In running the tunnels and drifts through this extraordinary material, the miners run considerable risk of injury by being crushed by heavy masses of ore, which, having been held in place by large quantities of powdery oxide of iron, drop out when they are undermined in cutting the drifts. When such blocks fall out, in some cases hundreds of tons of this dry powder, which is nothing more nor less than iron rust, will come rushing down and block all further work till the opening can be timbered up.

The great body of ores found in the district being black and red oxides, silicates and carbonates, all of a character that admit of conversion into regulus by the application of heat alone, and by a single process, several of the companies have erected extensive smelting works. Martin & Greenman, who are largely interested in the Mineral Hill mines, are putting up works that will cost nearly $100,000 when completed.

Some of the ore taken from this extraordinary hill are so exceedingly rich in gold, that a 10-stamp battery is being erected to crush the ore and work it for the gold, by the ordinary processes adopted for saving gold from quartz ; the tailings will be afterwards smelted for the copper they contain, nearly 40 per cent.

The gangue rock of nearly all these Arizona ores is composed of spathic iron, heavy spar and quartz ; the ores found in California being free from gangue rock, though they are generally mixed with the containing slate or serpentine.

Knowles & Lightner, another firm, extensively engaged in these Arizona mines, are also putting up smelting works on their ground. The Great Central company have a set of such works in active operation, and turning out large quantities of good regulus of about 80 per cent.

Most of the labor done about these mines is performed by natives, Mexicans and Chinamen. Not more than one-fourth of the workmen are Americans or Europeans.

Aubery City is located on the north side of the fork, and would soon become quite an important place of business if sufficient tonnage could be obtained to carry away the ore that could be furnished by the mines in its neighborhood.

3.—THE GEOLOGICAL FORMATIONS IN WHICH COPPER IS FOUND.

Peculiarities of formations.—There are peculiarities about the geological formations in which the copper ores are found on this coast, which derive an interest from the great extent of country over which they can be traced. For instance : Not a single important body of such ore has been found on this coast, either among the coast range, the foot-hills, or among the Sierra Nevadas, except in the immediate vicinity, if not actually in serpentine or other magnesian rocks or matamorphised slates. This is the case in all the districts above described, the only exception being at Hope valley, Amador county. For the hundreds of miles over which the great belt of copper ores can be traced, it is never found except in one or the other of these rocks, and invariably without any gangue rock, except this containing slate or serpentine. This great belt of copper ore is never formed except in the immediate vicinity of the auriferous slates and quartz. As has already been mentioned, all the copper found on this coast contains a large per cent. of gold, and many of the most important auriferous quartz lodes contain a considerable per cent. of copper ore. In some sections of the State the gold itself is so much alloyed with copper that it is not more than half as valuable as that obtained from other sections. The numerous fossils that have been discovered in both the auriferous slates and in the vicinity of the great copper belt, prove that both formations belong to the same geological era. It may therefore be reasonable to suppose that the same causes which produced the one, at the same time produced the other. The nature of these causes has not been sufficiently studied to be of any practical use ; though the subject involves many important practical and scientific points, such as the compilation of facts and the observations of practical men in the department you have just inaugurated may throw much light upon.

The costs of working the copper mines.—The cost of working the copper mines on this coast is, under the present system, a great impediment to the development of this source of national wealth. Expenses of copper mining are much influenced by three conditions : the convenience of the mine to the market for its product, the kind of labor employed, and the position of the mine in reference to facilities for working it.

The mines at Copperopolis, which are most favorably located with reference to the convenience for sending their ores to market, pay, on an average, about $8 per ton to carry their ore from the mine to the ship which carries it to the furnaces, about $15 per ton as freight charges by these ships, and about $4 per ton for bags in which to carry it; or $27 per ton for carrying the ore to the nearest market, a sum nearly equal to the average value of all the copper ores obtained from the mines in England and the continent of Europe. Such mines as are located further inland, or in localities removed from main travelled thoroughfares, have to meet additional costs for transportation.

This expensive transportation compels a closer examination of the ore than would otherwise be necessary, and this work has all to be done by hand, in order to select only such of it as may be sufficiently rich to warrant the expense, requiring considerable skill on the part of the laborers employed. This operation costs, at a very low estimate, $1 per ton for such ore as may be selected, and causes a waste, in some classes of ore, amounting to ten per cent. by mixing the crumbled rich ore among the slate and refuse, which is thrown on the dump pile, for want of a ready means for its separation.

The costs for bags alone, unavoidable under the present system, has been the cause of the stoppage of the work on several good mines. These bags are an enormous tax on the copper resources of this coast. There are no means, under this system, of avoiding this expense, as shipowners will not carry the ore to New York or Boston unless it is in bags. Occasionally, a cargo of one grade ore has been shipped to Swansea in bulk; but as it is very rarely that an entire cargo belongs to one party, or is of one grade, it is very rarely that this method of shipment is adopted. These bags are scarcely ever returned, and consequently are nearly a total loss. Meader & Co., who are largely connected with the shipping business, secure the return of a small portion of their bags, but as they have undergone the wear and tear of a six months' voyage round the Horn in a damp hold of a ship, and been subjected to the rough handling in scores of movings, they are of comparatively small value when returned.

The class of laborers employed, and the wages paid for their services, are another material condition greatly influencing the costs of copper mining on this coast. The average wages of copper miners, American or European, in California, except at Copperopolis, is about $3 per day. The Keystone and Union, the two largest companies at that place, pay $2 60 per day to all their laborers, whether they work above or below ground. Other companies in the valley pay $3 per day for drifters, and $2 50 per day for all other laborers. Many of the companies in other portions of the State employ Chinamen almost exclusively for all work done above ground, who work for $1 per diem. As these Chinamen, under proper supervision, do as much work, and as well as any other class of laborers, it follows that those companies that employ them effect an important saving of expense. The owners of the Copperopolis mines have not introduced this class of labor in that locality lest it might create disturbances among the miners, of whom there are about eight hundred in the valley. These men, as is usual with their class, have an intense hatred to the Chinese, a feeling which is not by any means allayed by the knowledge that their presence and employment would insure a reduction in the rate of wages. It is quite probable the introduction of Chinamen to work on these mines would create considerable disturbance. But it is scarcely to be expected that proprietors of mines costing millions of dollars, the returns on which depend on the economy with which they are worked, will be deterred from availing themselves of the services of the cheapest labor in the market, through fear of the acts of any class of citizens. It being so much to the interest of the State that every facility should be afforded to those engaged in developing its mineral resources, any interference on the part of individuals or combinations to prevent the introduction of cheap labor for that purpose would be severely punished.

The mines in Oregon and in the northern portion of California pay from $2 to $3 per day for laborers.

At the mines in Arizona most of the work is done by Mexicans, who are satisfied with about $30 per month and a certain quantity of provisions. There are a good many Chinese employed at these mines, who are paid $30 per month and board themselves. The Americans and Europeans employed are paid from $50 to 60 per month in addition to their board.

The position of the mine, the facilities it possesses for working, is another important condition connected with the costs. Mines located in the lower level of broad valleys, such as those at Copperopolis, where they have to hoist everything taken out of the mine and to lower everything put into it by machinery, and to pump the seepage water of an extensive district from a sump hole five hundred feet in depth, labor under the greatest possible disadvantage. The costs of engines, their wear and tear, and the expense of their superintendence and repair, imposes a cost of more than $5 per ton on all the ores extracted from these mines. It is a fair estimate to calculate that every ton of ore taken from the Union and Keystone mines costs $16 per ton as it reaches the surface. This calculation includes the division of all the expenses attending the conduct of the business of the mine by the quantity of ore actually shipped. These figures, explaining the costs of working the copper mines when compared with those showing the value of their products, show why so many good mines have stopped work during the past year.

The present price of fifteen per cent. ore at Swansea and New York is less than $50 per ton. To obtain this it costs the mines at Copperopolis—

For extraction from the mine	$16
Freight to San Francisco	8
Freight to Swansea or New York	15
Bags	4
Sorting	1
Total	44

This does not include any allowance for loss by broken bags or carelessness in handling after shipment, or expenses for commissions, &c. It must also be remembered that not one-half of the ore extracted from these mines will average fifteen per cent. It is known that Meader, Lalor & Co. have shipped thousands of tons of ore which did not exceed twelve per cent. These Copperopolis mines, exporting nearly three-fourths of the ore, furnish unmistakable data on which to base a calculation of the very slight margin of profits that arise from copper mining on this coast as at present conducted.

There are some mines, such as La Victoire, in Mariposa county, and those in some of the northern counties and in Oregon, in which the costs of extraction of the ore does not exceed $4 per ton, as they are worked by tunnels and require no hoisting or pumping. But the cost of transportation is much greater from all these mines than it is from Copperopolis, and the quantity of fifteen-percent. ore costs more for selecting. The quantity of carbonates, silicates, and oxides obtainable in any locality in California and Oregon is so unimportant as not to come within range of calculations concerning the costs of regular mining.

It cannot be possible that this present condition of affairs connected with the copper resources of the Pacific coast is without remedy, as the annexed table will show. The mines on this coast within five years of their discovery, in spite of every disadvantage of inexperience in the work of their development and want of knowledge of the nature of their ores, have exported nearly eighty thousand tons of ore, valued at the very lowest estimate at upwards of $5,000,000. A national source of wealth so productive in its infancy will not be left to die of inanition for want of the fostering care of the general government. As will be explained anon, to smelt the ores on this coast, with the present price of fuel and the metal when made, would be but a partial and temporary remedy, the final success of which is involved in doubt. The recommendation of the chairman of the national revenue commission on this very point explains the only effectual plan that will secure the extended development of the copper resources of this coast. The following is a copy of the commissioner's recommendation referred to : "The commission therefore recommend that all excise duties on domestic copper be repealed ; and that the duties on imported copper ores and copper be advanced to a moderate extent, or sufficient to relieve the copper mining interests of the United States from the depressing effects of the internal taxes upon their supplies, and to give to it as good a standing in our own markets, with reference to foreign competition, as they had before the present taxes were imposed."

4.—REDUCTION OF ORES.

Processes in use for smelting and concentrating the ores.—Numerous plans have been proposed and tested for the purpose of smelting and concentrating the copper ores found on this coast, none of which, for causes to be stated, have been entirely successful, though several of them have been partially so. A detailed description of all these various processes, and of the furnaces and apparatus used, while it might be both interesting and instructive, would be out of place in this report. Most of these plans which have been tested, on the large scale, have possessed some novel principle, which might be of advantage if employed in combination with old established processes, by those who possess the necessary skill, experience, and judgment to admit innovations upon systems under which they may have been educated. This seeming digression is intended to explain the principal cause of the failure of some of the most costly works that have been erected for the purposes to which this portion of the report refers. In not a few cases, those having charge of these works appeared to labor under the impression that it was so absolutely necessary to follow the old patterns introduced from their native land, that some German, French, and Cornish operatives seemed to attribute their failure to the fact that the laborers employed, and the materials used, did not understand the German, French, or Cornish language.

Early in 1862, works of an experimental character were erected at Antioch, on the banks of the San Joaquin river, near the base of Mount Diablo, for the purpose of testing the adaptability of the coal obtained in that vicinity, for smelting purposes; many persons, supposed to be authorities on the subject, expressing the opinion that such coal was unsuited for the purpose.

These works were erected under the direction of Mr. Thomas Price, an experienced Welsh copper miner, who has for several years been acting as agent for the Swansea smelters, for the purchase of copper ores on this coast—a gentleman of considerable scientific attainments and a first-class practical chemist and metallurgist. It may be proper to state further, that this gentleman, whose opinions on this subject of fuel should have much weight, is also professor of chemistry at the most famous college on this coast, and superintendent at the assaying and refining works of Kellogg, Hueston & Co., the most extensive private establishment in that business in the United States.

These works put up by this gentleman at Antioch consisted of a reverberatory furnace and roasting kiln, built on the plan of those in use at Swansea, but on somewhat smaller scale, and with a slight change in the form of the grate, to adapt it to the fuel. The furnace has a base of thirteen feet six inches long, by nine feet four inches wide, with a chimney-stack, for the purpose of creating sufficient draft and carrying off the fumes, sixty-five feet high. All these works were built of the best available materials.

As stated above, this furnace was built as an experiment, chiefly to test the adaptability of the Mount Diablo coal for smelting purposes—to ascertain the quality and quantity of heat it generates.

It would occupy too much space to enter into any extended details of the nature of this coal; but it may be necessary, to make the subject plain to those who have never paid any attention to the study of such matters, to state that in a reverberatory furnace the fire in its passage up the chimney strikes the roof, and is forced down upon the ore by means of a "bridge," built between it and the burning fuel. In all flames, no matter how generated, there is one portion more intensely hot than the others. This is called the "reducing flame" because of its action in reducing ores, under certain conditions, into metals. All coals do not produce a flame of the same nature or length, and the operation of the reverberatory furnace depends, in a great measure, upon its being so constructed that the "bridge" is placed so that the reducing portion of the flame is caused to strike the ore at the proper point.

After this explanation it will not require any technical or scientific knowledge of the principles of combustion to understand that a furnace to use fuel, which burns with a short flame and little smoke, requires great modifications in its construction when it is to be used to burn fuel which produces a long flame and much smoke. The experiments at Antioch settled this point clearly, if not satisfactorily, to those interested, and proves, for general information, that furnaces built on the plan of those used at Swansea, in which the short-flamed Welsh coal is used, are not adapted for the use of the long-flamed coals of the Pacific coast. But the question whether this long-flamed coal could not be used for smelting purposes, in a suitably constructed furnace, remains still unsettled. Mr. Price states this Mount Diablo coal could be economically used for that purpose in a properly constructed furnace, but thinks no attempt should be made to proceed any further than in the conversion of the ores into regulus. The price of all descriptions of coal being so much higher on this coast than a better article can be obtained in other countries, the refining of the metal can be more profitably done in those countries.

It is much to be regretted that the company, which expended nearly $50,000 in making these experiments at Antioch, did not carry them out to a full conclusion, by permitting Mr. Price to make such changes in the form of the furnace as his skill and experience may have suggested. But in California, where money commands from 18 to 24 per cent. interest, such experiments are not considered profitable.

The first bar of metal from the Antioch smelting works was received at San Francisco on the 14th of September, 1863, and created almost as much interest as the first bar of bullion from Washoe. During the time these works were in operation they produced about 200 tons of matt, or regulus, of an average of about 50 per cent., the balance being iron, sulphur, silica, &c. This was obtained from about 2,000 tons of ores from various parts of the State, but chiefly from Copperopolis, of an average of about 10 per cent., which the company advertised to purchase at the following prices:

7½ per cent................................	$15 per ton of 2,376 pounds.
9 per cent.................................	17 per ton of 2,376 pounds.
10 per cent.................................	19 per ton of 2,376 pounds.
11 per cent.................................	21 per ton of 2,376 pounds.
12 per cent.................................	25 per ton of 2,376 pounds.

None were accepted below 7½ per cent.

The coal used in the operations cost about $7 per ton delivered on the grounds of the company. One ton of this coal, it was estimated, would reduce two tons of ore, after the furnace had become thoroughly heated; but in consequence of the difficulty in obtaining good materials for lining it the furnace was not kept steadily heated. The best imported fire-bricks, in consequence of the action of the sulphur in the ore, would not endure more than about fifteen days. Work had consequently to be stopped within that period, and everything cooled off, in order to re-line the furnace. This entailed a great loss in the cost of fuel and labor, as well as of metal, and as the works were only calculated to operate on about eight tons of ore in twenty-four hours, these stoppages absorbed all the profits.

A Mr. Henry Davis, another practical Welsh copper smelter, who had been in charge of an extensive smelting establishment in Chili previous to his arrival on this coast, has made a number of experiments at the works at Antioch since they were closed by the original owners. This gentleman also expresses the opinion that the Mount Diablo coal, used in a properly constructed furnace, ould be profitably employed in the reduction to regulus of such ores as will not pay to ship in bulk.

The smelting works erected at the Union mine, at Copperopolis, are on a more extended scale than those at Antioch. They cost nearly $75,000, and consist of two cupola blast furnaces, and other buildings, which were erected under the superintendence of M. Desermeaux, a French engineer, on the plans introduced on this coast by M. D'Heirry, a very skilful French metallurgist, who has erected similar works on the Queen of Bronze mine, in Oregon. The whole establishment consists of four large kilns for roasting the ores to deprive them of a portion of their sulphur, two large blast furnaces on the most approved German plan, with a powerful blast set in motion by a 20-horse power steam engine. The kilns are each capable of roasting 500 tons of ore at a batch, which required from 7 to 12 weeks to burn, according to the weather and the care taken in laying them. After burning in these kilns the ore was placed in the blast furnaces, which are capable of operating on eight tons of such materials, each, in twenty-four hours. The only flux used in any of the operations was a portion of the slag from previous meltings, or silica in the form of quartz. The ore came from the furnaces, after the first operation in them, in the form of two qualities of regulus, the one containing about 80 per cent. of copper, the other about 40 per cent. This regulus was afterwards broken up and re-melted three or four times, in order to deprive it of all the sulphur, and to oxidize the iron as much as possible. No attempts were made to refine this matt into tough copper. The costs for fuel in these operations were exceedingly heavy, as charcoal, costing from 37 to 50 cents per bushel, had to be used. This, together with the necessity for handling the materials so many times by expensive and unskilful laborers, rendered the operations so unprofitable that the works were discontinued after a few months' trial—not before some 5,000 tons of ores, averaging about 8 per cent., had been converted into regulus, which sold from $200 to $250 per ton, showing that these waste ores may be rendered valuable if they can be operated upon by some cheap process.

The smelting works at the Cosmopolitan mine, at Genesee valley, Plumas county, cost about $30,000. These are constructed on the plan described by Piggott, in his work on copper, somewhat modified by Mr. J. C. Chapman, one of the proprietors of the mine, under whose directions the works were built. The blast here is generated by two double-action piston bellows, four feet in diameter, set in motion by a large water-wheel. No ores have been operated on at this place except oxides, carbonates and silicates, and as long as plenty of such ores were attainable, this company was able to obtain respectable quantities of good matt and inferior copper; but when the supply ceased, they had to close up their establishment, as it was not adapted to operate on sulphurets.

At these works the molten materials were not drawn off into rough bars and remelted, as at Copperopolis, but they were run into a sort of cauldron built in front of the furnace, in which they were kept sufficiently liquid to allow the copper to fall to the bottom by its superior specific gravity; and as the slag, being the lightest, floated on the surface and cooled quickest, it was scraped off and thrown away ; the copper, on cooling, readily separating from the regulus which was allowed to cool above it. The latter was remelted and the former was ready for market. The fuel used at these works was pine wood charcoal, costing about thirty-seven cents per bushel.

Other smelting works, of a novel and very economical and useful character, have been erected on the La Victoire mine, at Hunter's valley, Mariposa county ; at the Buchanan mine, in Merced county; at the Campo Seco mine, in Calaveras county, and at several other mines in various portions of the coast, on a plan introduced by Mr. Nathaniel Haskell, a California mechanic, and called by him the "water-lined cupola furnace." These furnaces are capable of reducing twenty tons of oxides, carbonates, or silicates to good regulus in twenty-four hours.

The peculiar feature of this useful invention is a "water lining," which may be described by stating that the cupola consists of two parts, one within the other, like the divisions of an onion. These parts are formed of stout iron boiler plates, strongly riveted at the joints. Between the two there is a space of about six inches ; this is kept constantly filled with cool water, by means of a tank above. This cool water saves an immense quantity of heat that would otherwise be lost by radiation, and, as a matter of course, affects a corresponding saving in fuel. No fire bricks are used in these furnaces, which, besides being a great saving in the consumption of this costly article, affects an additional saving by requiring no time, labor, or heat to be lost in replacing these bricks every few days, as they become destroyed by the heat. A very powerful and even blast is kept up in these furnaces by a large cylinder bellows, set in motion by a small steam-engine. One of these furnaces, used at the Buchanan mine, has produced upwards of 100 tons of good marketable copper during the past year, which has sold at San Francisco for from $300 to $320 per ton of 2,000 pounds. That at the La Victoire mine, has only recently been put into operation, but is producing 80 per cent. of regulus at the rate of 24 tons per week.

It may be quite proper to state that these furnaces are not adapted to operate on ores containing a very large proportion of sulphur, unless they have been thoroughly calcined, and are combined with a large proportion of other ores or suitable flux. The sulphur has a very damaging effect on the iron of the cupola when both are heated to the necessary temperature to melt the ore.

These furnaces will be of great benefit to the owners of mines containing large bodies of oxides, silicates, and carbonates, which are of too poor a quality to ship to market in bulk. They are very cheap and portable, the cupola, blast, engine, and boiler only costing about $3,000, and all combined only weighing about five tons.

In 1862 a lady, a Mrs. Hall, invented a novel description of furnace for smelting copper ores, by means of jets of superheated steam being passed into the cupola during the time the fuel and ore were in an incandescent state. To the cupola of this furnace was attached an apparatus for condensing the fumes, previous to their passage into the chimney. This invention was very much lauded at the time by Colonel Charles Harazthy, in a letter published over his own name in the papers at San Francisco.

The concentrating works erected by the proprietors of the Keystone mine at Copperopolis are on the principle adopted by some of the large copper mining establishments in Cornwall, England. The ores in these works are operated upon by water. The object sought to be obtained is the separation of the gangue rock by means of the difference in the specific gravity and hardness in it and the ores. There are conditions in which this process is quite simple, cheap, and effective. It is so where the ore is contained in a silicious gangue, or in hard spar, in a locality where there is an abundant supply of free water, constantly running, and where there are plenty of cheap laborers to be had who understand the details of the operations.   But as none of these conditions exist at Copperopolis, the experiment, which cost about $50,000, if not an absolute loss, has been only so far successful as only to be of use, at a very heavy expense, during a few months in the winter, when the rains fill the company's reservoirs.   And then, in consequence of the ore being free from gangue rock, and the containing slate, from which it is sought to separate it, being of nearly the same specific gravity and hardness, it is not possible to save more than three-fourths of it, at a cost of more than it is worth.

These works have been erected in the best manner and of the best materials, under the directions of Mr. Pawning and his brother, two thorough, practical machinists.   In the operation of these works the ore is brought between two heavy iron rollers, where it is crushed as fine as possible, and afterwards led, by means of an endless belt, on to five "jiggers," or shaking tables, which are each contained in a large tank of water.   The motion of these tables causes all the lighter particles to float off in the stream of water passing through the tanks. These fine particles are collected in "settlers," dried and saved.   The coarser grains which do not float off are retained in sieves arranged beneath the tables, and are returned to the rollers to be reduced to the proper fineness.   The machinery of this cumbrous contrivance is set in motion by a sixty-five horse-power steam engine.

Many other companies concentrate their ores, to a slight extent, by the process described in the description of the Napoleon mine, given in another portion of this report, with such modifications as the judgment of the parties carrying on the work may suggest, or the necessities of the case may compel.

The above will probably not be considered a flattering account of the various processes that have been introduced for concentrating and smelting the copper ores found on this coast.   But the many failures therein recorded are not of a character to discourage so energetic a people as those of the Pacific coast.

The want of success is in so many instances so clearly traceable to the want of skill and experience on the part of the operators that it is evident a plan for profitably working the lowest of these ores will be devised when experience shall have taught those engaged in the business the defects and advantages of the various processes now in use.

The few observations contained in this division of the report should be sufficient to convince any reasonable person that the manufacture of refined copper on this coast, with profit, is an impossibility under the present state of affairs.

In reviewing the above remarks on these processes, it will be observed that the furnace erected at Antioch was erected as much to test the coal as to smelt the ore.   It was made of only sufficient capacity to operate upon eight tons of ore in twenty-four hours.   This was a serious error and a material source of loss.

The furnace should have been made of a capacity sufficient to have operated upon at least ten tons.   Twelve or fourteen tons would have been better, as it requires nearly the same quantity of fuel and the same amount of labor to operate upon eight tons of ore as it would to operate on ten or twelve tons.

The furnaces at the copper mines in Chili, which are built on the same general plan, and operate upon ores very similar to those found on this coast, and use a fuel very much like that used here, are constructed of a capacity to work from twelve to fourteen tons of ore in the twenty-four hours.

The Chilian copper smelters have no better indigenous coal than is to be found on this coast.   They are compelled to import the greater portion of the coal used in their works from England.   As good an article, and at as low a price, may be obtained here from Sydney, if it is absolutely necessary to import any coal at all.

• In California, in consequence of the absence of readily available quantities of oxides, carbonates, and silicate ores, and the preponderance of ores containing a large percentage of sulphur, smelting will always be more expensive than it is where a different class of ores are used, because it is necessary to put such sulphur ores through the preliminary process of roasting, which is costly, slow, and sometimes causes much loss. The object of this process is to expel the sulphur, arsenic, antimony, phosphorus, or other deleterious element that the ore may contain, and to oxidize the iron as much as possible. But if this process be carried too far, or the ore contains a very large proportion of the sulphuret of iron, or when the heat becomes excessive, a fusion takes place, which makes the separation of the metal from the sulphur much more difficult. This action in the roasting process caused the loss of many thousands of dollars to the proprietors of the Union mine, by requiring the regulus produced at their smelting works to be roasted three or four times to expel the fused sulphur from it.

With Sydney coal, which may be landed at San Francisco at $9 per ton, the reduction of low grade ores to 50 per cent. regulus could be made a very profitable investment for capital. The necessary works, if erected on sufficient scale to afford a market for, say, 8 per cent. ores, would give an immense impetus to the development of the copper resources of the Pacific coast; because, without some such market, all the ores of that standard will be valueless for many years to come, and they form about seven-eighths of all the ores on this coast.

To prove that such works would yield a large profit on the capital invested, the following calculation is here given:

Costs attending the conversion of ten tons of 10 per cent. ore into 45 per cent. regulus:

Ten tons of ore, at $16 per ton..............................	$160 00
Roasting in heaps, at $1 per ton.............................	10 00
Six tons of Sydney coal, at $9 per ton........................	54 00
Labor of four men.........	15 00
Incidental expenses..	10 00
Total costs.......	249 00

Per contra:

Ten tons of the above ore produced two and three-quarter tons of regulus of 45 per cent. This is worth $4 per unit, or..........	$495 00
Deduct freight and expenses attending export....................	100 00
Leaving balance.......	395 00
From this deduct cost of ore and reduction....................	249 00
There is a clear profit of..........................	146 00

This profit would be fully 20 per cent. larger if one thousand tons of ore were operated upon.

The Bristol copper mine, in Connecticut, when under the management of Mr. H. H. Sheldon, the present superintendent of the Keystone mine, at Copperopolis, paid a very large revenue to its proprietor from ores that did not exceed 3 per cent. in value, on an average. Such a person, after a reasonable amount of experience on this coast, will certainly be able to devise a plan by which ores of three times that value may be worked to a profit.

Among the principal causes of the failure of the smelting works tried on this coast have been—

1st. The uniform character of the ores operated on.

2d. The want of experienced and steady, skilled laborers.

3d. The misconstruction of the furnaces.

At Swansea the smelters have the advantage of purchasing ores of all or any classes, as all are brought there from many different districts. With this assortment of ores at their command, they can arrange the charges of their furnaces to suit their fuel. On this coast there are no established means for obtaining such a wide selection of ores as will admit of their being combined so as to be worked with advantage. Most of the smelting works which have been tried on this coast operate on the ores from generally the one mine on which they were erected, and these are generally of one class.

The furnaces built on this coast have generally been copies of such as are used in England, Germany, or France, where fuel of a totally different character is used. The impatience of the parties interested in such works to obtain from them immediate profitable results has prevented the necessary experiments being made to adapt these imported furnaces to our local fuel.

No smelting works have been carried on long enough on this coast to discipline a sufficient number of workmen to conduct the details of the operations with the care necessary to insure success. The few good workmen who have come here from England, France, or Germany, all aspire to be superintendents, or to own a mine themselves, without possessing the ability to impart their knowledge to the more intelligent laborers placed under their direction.

All these obstacles to success would be in a great measure removed if extensive works were to be erected at some convenient central point, where those having ores to dispose of could always find a fair market. Such works, properly conducted, would yield a liberal return on the money invested in their erection, and would be of incalculable benefit to the copper interests of the Pacific coast.

The export of copper ores from the Pacific coast.—It is difficult to obtain a correct return of all the copper ores exported from this coast, as the custom-house authorities have not kept anything more than an approximating account of such as have been shipped through that department; the manifests of the vessels in which it has been shipped in many cases not specifying the quantity of ore taken, only giving its value; in some cases entering it as so many packages of unspecified merchandise of a stated value. This makes it difficult to estimate the quantity, because at the commencement of this exportation the ore was shipped in barrels, casks, and boxes, some of which contained nearly half a ton each, and as the value of the ore differs so much, the value given, if correct, would furnish no basis for calculating the quantity.

It is through this cause that the published reports of the exports of ore given in the leading commercial papers of San Francisco at stated intervals differ so much with one another. The reports of the exports for the nine months of the present year, published in these papers, are as follows:

The Alta, 15,174½ tons; the Bulletin, 15,350¾ tons; the Commercial Gazette, 20,848½ tons.

There is considerable discrepancy in these reports, the Gazette being probably nearest correct.

The following list, compiled from every available source, gives the names of mines which are known to have sent ore to San Francisco, and the quantity purchased from each. There are several firms in that city which purchase or make advances on copper ores. Among those most extensively engaged in this business are Meader, Lalor & Co, Martin & Greenman, Mr. Price, Conroy & O'Conner. None of these parties appear disposed to give information relating to their business, under the impression, perhaps, that such information might in some way or other injure them, and it was not through them directly that this list was made out:

List of mines that have shipped ore.

Name of mine.	Where located.	Quantity shipped.
		Tons.
Union	Copperopolis, Calaveras county	56,542
Keystone	........do...............do.....................	5,719
Copper Hill	Near Campo Seco, Calaveras county	1,500
Calaveras	Copperopolis, Calaveras county	100
Campo Seco	Campo Seco, Calaveras county	1,300
Lancha Plana	Lancha Plana, Calaveras county	250
Napoleon	Gopher hills, Calaveras county	4,000
Newton	Near Jackson, Amador county	3,000
Cosumnes	........do............do..................	1,500
Table Mountain	Calaveras county	250
Birdseye	Mariposa county..................................	25
	Regulus.	
Buchanan...............	Mariposa county	200
Superior	Mt. Diabolo, Contra Costa county	12
Keokuk................	........do...........do...................	10
Alta....................	Del Norte county	100
Osos	San Luis Obispo county	100
Arroyo Seco............	Los Angeles county...............................	15
La Solidad	........do......do.....................	50
Copper Creek Company .	....	26
Trinity Company	Trinity county	20
Pueblo Company	....	25
La Victoire	Mariposa county..................................	2,000
Del Pino................	Lower California, (belongs to Capt. Winder, U. S. A.).	20
Philadelphia............	Arizona	100
Mountaineer............	Arizona, (belongs to Captain Winder, U. S. A.)......	75
Grand Central..........	........do..........do..........do........	100
Planet	........do.......... do ....do..........	700
Mineral Hill............	........do.......... do ....do..........	500

A total of 78,239 tons, not including any shipments from the Queen of Bronze, or any of the mines in Oregon or Lower California, or any of the many small lots that were shipped as experiments by the mines worked in all parts of California during the excitement about copper that prevailed during the years 1860, 1861, 1862, and 1863. It is quite within limits to estimate the ores received from all unnamed sources since 1860 at 1,761 tons. This, added to the quantities given in the list above, makes a total of 80,000 tons received at San Francisco and exported since the discovery of the mines at Copperopolis.

The following table, giving the exports of copper ores from San Francisco from January, 1860, to October, 1866, compiled from the records at the custom-house and the shipping lists, shows a difference of upwards of 22,000 tons when compared with the list above. This discrepancy can only be explained on the grounds above stated. The books of the principal mines given in this list show that the quantities set opposite their respective names have been actually shipped from them. The ores shipped from the leading mines is calculated according to English weight, 2,376 pounds to the ton. Some of the smaller companies may have estimated their ore by the United States weight, or only 2,000 pounds to the ton; but this would not account for so large a discrepancy.

Exports of copper ores from San Francisco from January, 1862, to October, 1866.

Year.	To New York.	To Boston.	To Swansea.	Total for year.
	Tons.	*Tons.*	*Tons.*	*Tons.*
1862	86	3,574 16/20	....	3,660 16/20
1863	1,337	4,208 18/20	7 15/20	5,553 13/20
1864	4,905 16/20	5,064	264 7/20	10,234 3/20
1865	4,146 2/20	9,050	2,591 16/20	17,787 18/20
1866	7,676 19/20	3,415 4/20	10,384 15/20	21,476 18/20
Totals	20,151 3/20	25,312 18/20	13,248 13/20	58,712 18/20

The above table includes concentrated ores and regulus, when shipped in bags or barrels, but not metallic copper in pigs or bars, of which there was shipped about 25 tons in 1865 and 3,787 bars, of unknown weight, in 1866. In this quantity is included 120 tons from the smelting works at Buchanan Hollow, Mariposa county, shipped by Coffee & Risdon, of San Francisco. As this metal averages 80 per cent., one ton of it is equal to five tons of 16 per cent. ore. The export of this metal is consequently equal to 1,725 tons of such ore, making a total, when added to quantity in the first table, of 79,964 tons—in round numbers, say 80,000 tons; in addition to which there are upwards of 2,000 tons of ores at Stockton and San Francisco ready for shipment, awaiting vessels to carry it away, and nearly 20,000 tons are ready for shipment at the various mines, where it is retained in consequence of the very low price of such ores in this market at present; the whole showing that upwards of 100,000 tons of copper ore have been taken out of the mines of California since their discovery in 1860. Estimating this ore at an average value of $50 per ton, which is very much below its actual value, the products of these copper mines since their discovery have added $5,000,000 to the material wealth of the country, and opened a wide field for the employment of the enterprise, capital, and labor of thousands of its citizens.

A comparison of the product of the copper mines of the Pacific coast with those in other countries may be instructive in this place. Sir Henry De La Beché, the head of the department of mines in England, stated in a lecture given at the great exhibition in London, in 1861, that the average of all the ores of copper produced in Cornwall and Devonshire did not exceed 8 per cent. when dressed, and that the supply was constantly becoming less, and more costly to obtain as the working in the mines became deeper. These two counties are the chief sources of copper in all Europe. Here, on this coast, there are absolutely inexhaustible sources of ores ranging from 10 per cent. to 12 per cent., which may be obtained within a couple of hundred feet of the surface of the ground.

In the parliamentary returns published by order of the British government, it appears that in the year 1861 the gross yield of copper ores in Great Britain, including England, Ireland, and Wales, amounted to 231,487 tons of the value of $6,800,000, or a little over $29 per ton. On this coast, under the present system, ore of that value would not pay to take it out of the ground. As has already been explained it costs between $40 and $50 per ton to place the ores obtained on this coast in a market. The rates for freight to New York and Liverpool are more than double as high as they were two years ago, in consequence of the great demand for first class vessels to carry grain to those places.

Concluding remarks.—None of the metallic copper made on this coast is suitable for castings or for rolling into sheets, owing to defects in the processes for refining it. It is too brittle for rolling, in consequence of containing traces of sulphur. It is too hard for casting, turning, and polishing, and too liable to tarnish and turn nearly black in color, in consequence of containing more or less iron in alloy.

The present depression in the copper mining interests on the Pacific coast has been much increased by the excessive cost of freight to New York and Swansea, which, falling at a time when the ores are of less value than they have been for the past fifteen or twenty years, causes it to be unprofitable to ship those that heretofore have formed the great bulk of the exports. The price of freight at this time is nearly double what it was in 1861 and 1862. To illustrate this fact, it may be stated that the ship Haze, in 1861, was chartered to carry a cargo to New York for $5,000 in gold. Within the past few weeks the same vessel has been chartered for the same destination for $16,660 in gold, or $25,000 in currency. In 1861 freight to Liverpool was offering at $11 per ton; at present it is not procurable at less than $17 per ton.

It will be readily understood that an article, the exports of which, though amounting to two millions of dollars annually, the profits of which are limited to such a slight margin, as already explained is the case with copper ores on this coast, must cease to be a source of revenue to the government, or of employment and profit to the people, when the cost of its production and export exceeds the value of the product. This is a question deserving the most serious consideration.

The products of the copper mines on the Pacific coast might be greatly increased if the legislation of Congress were so framed as to make them profitable to procure. This would increase the taxable property of the country, while the products of the mines, now far below their capacity, would add materially to its absolute wealth; for if we do produce our own copper, it must be purchased from other nations, for money or produce, as it is indispensable in the arts and manufactures.

Under our form of government, with such an extent of territory as we possess, and such an intelligent and enterprising people as inhabit our mineral regions, it should be a paramount object so to regulate the scale of taxes and duties on the products of any branch of national industry as to encourage the labor engaged in its development. A sound policy would dictate that so great an interest as copper mining is destined to become in the United States should be encouraged by every possible means in its infancy, and until the skill and experience of those interested in its development shall enable them to compete with a reasonable hope of success with the copper miners and smelters of other countries in which the business has been conducted for centuries. This they cannot do at present, nor ever will be able to do, unless they are assisted for a few years by favorable legislation. The duties and taxes, direct and indirect, on copper, under the present system, amount to $4 63 on each 100 lbs. of American-made metal, while that imported from other countries only pays $2 50 on each 100 lbs. It is this invidious distinction that is crippling the energies of those interested in developing the copper resources of the Pacific coast. A reversal of this state of affairs, the levying of a duty of about $2 50 on each 100 lbs. of foreign copper, over and above what is levied on our home-produced copper—a duty that would inflict no injury on any American interest—would immediately revive the now languishing copper interests of the whole country.

Measured by the facts and figures contained in this report, it requires no stretch of the imagination to comprehend the great national importance of the copper resources of the Pacific coast; already, within five years of their discovery, exporting sufficient ores of unusual richness to produce 10,000 tons of metal annually—a quantity nearly equal to one-half of the supply of the whole world twenty-five years ago, and five times as large as the produce of the whole United States only ten years ago! It requires but experience and the advantages it gives, and a slight protection on the part of the general government, to make the Pacific coast occupy the same prominence as a copper-producing country that it now occupies as the producer of gold and silver.

SECTION 6.

QUICKSILVER MINES OF CALIFORNIA.

1. New Almaden mines.—2. Products and exports.

1.—NEW ALMADEN MINES.

The ore of quicksilver.—Cinnabar is the principal and only valuable ore of the mercury of commerce, which is prepared from it by sublimation.

It is a sulphide (sulphuret) of mercury, composed, when pure, of quicksilver 86.2, sulphur 13.8, in which case it is a natural vermilion, and identical with the vermilion of commerce; but it is sometimes rendered impure by an admixture of clay, bitumen, oxide of iron, &c. Cinnabar is of a cochineal red color, often inclining to brownish red and lead gray, with an adamantine lustre, approaching to metallic in dark varieties, and to dull in friable ones. It varies from subtransparent to opaque, has a scarlet streak, and breaks with a subconchoidal uneven fraction. $H = 2$ to 2.5, specific gravity $= 8.99$. In a matrass it entirely sublimes, and with soda yields mercury with the evolution of sulphurous fumes. When crystallized it belongs to the rhombohedral system.

Cinnabar occurs in beds in slate rocks. The chief European beds are at Almaden, near Cordova, in Spain, and at Idria, in Upper Carinthia, where it usually occurs in a massive form, and is worked on a thick vein belonging to the Alpine carboniferous strata. It also occurs in China, Japan, Pluanca Vilica, in South Peru, and at New Almaden, in California, in a mountain east of San José, between the bay of Francisco and Monterey, where it is very abundant and easy of access.—*Ure's Dictionary.*

Classes of cinnabar ores.—Gruesa is the best quality or first class, in pieces eight to twelve inches or more in diameter; mostly pure ore of cinnabar, with little or no admixture of refuse rock.

Granza is the second quality, in pieces of three to eight inches, generally containing a considerable proportion of rock. It is either taken from the mine in such pieces or is broken off from larger pieces of rock in the yard.

Tierras—earth or dirt—is the lowest quality, and is not taken into account in the *ores* produced at the mine; neither are the miners paid for it. It is made into bricks and sun-dried previous to being reduced in the furnaces. Each adobe or brick weighs about twelve and a half pounds.

The "carga" or load of ore is considered to be three hundred pounds.

Extracts of a report by Professor B. Silliman, jr., from the American Journal of Science and Arts for September, 1864.

The New Almaden quicksilver mines are situated on a range of hills subordinate to the main Coast range, the highest point of which at the place is twelve to fifteen hundred feet above the valley of San José. Southwest of the range which contains the quicksilver mines, the Coast range attains a considerable elevation, Mount Bache, its highest point, being over thirty-eight hundred feet in height.

New Almaden is approached by the railroad running from San Francisco to San José, a distance of forty-five miles. In the course of it there is a rise of one hundred feet, San José being of this elevation above the ocean. From San José to New Almaden the distance is thirteen miles, with a gradual rise of one hundred and fifty or perhaps two hundred feet.

The rocks forming the subordinate range, in which the quicksilver occurs, are chiefly magnesian schists, sometimes calcareous and rarely argillaceous. As a group they may be distinguished as steatitic, often passing into well-characterized serpentine. Their geological age is not very definitely ascertained, but they are believed by the officers of the State geological survey to be not older than cretaceous. But few fragments of fossils, and these very obscure, have yet been found in these metamorphic rocks. At a point just above the *dumps*, behind the reduction works at the hacienda (or village,) there is an exposure, in which may be clearly seen in projecting lines the waving edges of contorted beds of steatite and serpentine, interspersed with ochrey or ferruginous layers, more easily decomposed; and the partial removal of the latter has left the steatitic beds very prominent.

The mine is open at various points upon this subordinate range over a distance of four or five miles, in a northeast direction. The principal and the earliest workings of the mine were in a right line, but little more than a mile distant from the hacienda. The workings are approached, however, by a well-graded wagon road, skirting the edges of the hills, which is two and three eighths miles in length.

It appears, partly from tradition, and partly from the memory of persons now living, that the existence of cinnabar upon the hill was known for a long time prior to the discovery that it possessed any economic value. In fact, upon the very loftiest summit of this subordinate range, cinnabar came to the surface, and could be obtained by a slight excavation or even by breaking the rocks lying upon the surface. In looking about for physical evidences such as would aid the eyes of an experienced observer in detecting here the probable presence of valuable metallic deposits, one observes on the summit of the hill, at various points along the line of its axis for two or three miles, and also beyond, toward the place called Bull Run, occasional loose boulders of drusy quartz, with more or less well-characterized geodes and combs; accompanying which is an ochraceous or ferruginous deposit, such as frequently forms the outcrop of metallic veins. There is, however, no such thing as a well-characterized vein, the quartz and its associated metals occurring rather in isolated masses or bunches segregated out of the general mass of the metamorphic rocks, and connected with each other, if at all, somewhat obscurely by thread veins of the same mineral.

The main entrance to the mine at present is by a level about eight hundred feet long, and large enough to accommodate a full-sized railroad and cars. This level enters the hill about three hundred feet from its summit, and is driven into a large chamber, formed by the removal of a great mass of cinnabar, leaving ample space for the hoisting and ventilating apparatus employed in working the mine.

At this point a vertical shaft descends to an additional depth of nearly three hundred feet, over which is placed a steam "whim" with friction gearing and wire rope, worked by a steam-engine, and by means of which all the ore from the various workings of the mine is conveniently discharged from the cars, which convey it out of the level to the dressing floors.   *   *   *   *   *

In order to reach the lower workings of the mine, the observer may employ the bucket as a means of descent, or he may, in a more satisfactory manner, descend by a series of ladders and step, not in the shaft, but placed in various large and irregular openings, dipping for the most part in the direction of the magnetic north, and at an angle of thirty to thirty-five degrees. These cavities have been produced by the miner in extracting the metal, and are often of vast proportions; one of them measures one hundred and fifty feet in length, seventy feet in breadth, and forty feet in height; others are of smaller dimensions; and they communicate with each other sometimes by narrow passages, and at others by arched galleries cut through the unproductive serpentine.

Some portions of the mine are heavily timbered to sustain the roof from crushing, while in other places arches or columns are left in the rock for the same purpose.

The principal minerals associated with the cinnabar are quartz and calcareous spar, which usually occur together in sheets or'strings, and in a majority of cases penetrate or subdivide the masses of cinnabar. Sometimes narrow threads of these minerals, accompanied by a minute coloration of cinnabar, serve as the only guide to the miner in re-discovering the metal when it has been lost in a former working.

Veins or plates of white massive magnesian rock and sheets of yellow ochre also accompany the metal. Iron pyrites is rarely found, and no mispickel was detected in any portion of the mine; running mercury is also rarely, almost never, seen.

The cinnabar occurs chiefly in two forms, a massive and a sub-crystalline. The first is fine granular, or pulverulent, soft, and easily reduced to the condition of vermillion; the other is hard, more distinctly crystalline, compact and difficult to break; but in neither of these forms does it show any tendency to develop well-formed crystals. It is occasionally seen veining the substance of greenish white or brown compact steatite or serpentine.

The ores are extracted by contract, the miners receiving a price dependent upon the greater or less facility with which the ore can be broken. By far the larger portion of the work-people in the mines are Mexicans, who are found to be more adventurous than Cornishmen, and willing oftentimes to undertake jobs which the latter have abandoned. The price paid for the harder ores in the poorer portions of the mine is from three to five dollars per carga of three hundred pounds. This weight is obtained after the ore is brought to the surface and freed by hand breaking from the superfluous or unproductive rock; by this arrangement, the company are secured from paying for anything but productive mineral. All the small stuff and dirt formed by the working of the " labors," are also sent to the surface to form the adobes used in charging the furnaces.

It has often happened in the history of this mine, during the past fifteen years, that the mine for a time has appeared to be completely exhausted of ore. Such a condition of things has, however, always proved to be but temporary, and may always be avoided by well-directed and energetic exploration. Upon projecting, by a careful survey, irregular and apparently disconnected chambers of the mine in its former workings in a section, there is easily seen to be a general conformity in the line of direction and mode of occurrence of the productive ore-masses. These are found to dip in a direction toward the north, in a plain parallel, for the most part, to the pitch of the hill, but at a somewhat higher angle. An intelligent comprehension of this general mode of structure has always served hitherto in guiding the mining superintendent in the discovery of new deposits of ore.

Since the settlement of the famous lawsuit, which has so long held this company in a condition of doubt, the new parties, into whose hands the property has now passed, have commenced a series of energetic and well-directed explorations at various points upon the hill, with a view to the discovery of additional deposits of ore. At one of these new openings, distant at least five hundred feet from the limit of the old workings, and not more than two hundred feet from the summit of the hill, a deposit of the richest description of the softer kind of cinnabar has been discovered, which, so far as hitherto explored, has a linear extent of at least seventy or eighty feet, and in point of richness has never been surpassed by any similar discovery in the past history of the mine. A charge of one hundred and one thousand pounds, of which seventy thousand were composed of this rich ore, thirty-one thousand pounds of "granza" or ordinary ore, and forty-eight thousand pounds of adobes, worth four per cent., making a total charge of one hundred and five thousand eight hundred pounds, yielded, on the day of our visit, four hundred and sixty flasks of mercury at seventy-six and a half pounds to the flask. This yield is almost without parallel in the history of the mine. The only preparation which the ores undergo, preparatory to reduction, consists of hand-breaking or "cobbing" for the removal of the unproductive rock.

The small ores and dirt hoisted from the mine are made into "adobes" or sun-dried bricks, sufficient clay for the purpose being associated with the ore. The object of these "adobes" is to build up the mouths of the furnaces to sustain the load of richer ores. No flux is employed, there being sufficient lime associated with the ores to aid the decomposition of the sulphurets.

The furnaces are built entirely of brick, in dimensions capable of holding from sixty thousand to one hundred and ten thousand pounds, according to the character of the ores employed. The chambers are fired from a lateral furnace, fed with wood, and separated from the ore by a wall pierced with numerous openings by the omission of bricks for that purpose.

Connected with the furnace is a series of lofty and capacious chambers, also of masonry, through which the whole product of combustion is compelled to pass alternately above and below from chamber to chamber, until all the available mercury is condensed. The draught from these furnaces is carried by inclined stacks up to the top of a lofty hill several hundred feet distant; and here the sulphurous acid and other effete products of the furnace are discharged. Formerly no precautions were taken to prevent the escape of mercury through the foundations of the furnace to the earth beneath; now the furnaces stand upon double arches of brickwork, and plates of iron are built into the foundations, so as to cut off entirely all descending particles of the metal and turn them inward. To be convinced of the importance of this precaution, it is sufficient to watch the operation of the furnace for a few moments, when an intermittent stream may be seen to flow into a reservoir provided for it, and which by the former process was completely lost in the earth.

On taking up the foundations of some of the old furnaces, within the last two years, the metal was found to have penetrated, or rather permeated, completely through the foundation and clay of the substructure down to the bed-rock beneath, a depth of not less than twenty-five or thirty feet. Over two thousand flasks of mercury were thus recovered in a single year from the foundations of the two furnaces. This loss is entirely avoided by the improved construction which has been adopted.

The whole process of reduction is extremely simple, the time occupied from one charge to another being usually about seven days. The metal begins to run in from four to six hours after the fires are lighted, and in about sixty hours the process is completed. The metal is conducted through various condensing chambers, by means of pipes of iron, to a "crane-neck," which discharges into capacious kettles. It undergoes no further preparation for market, being quite clean from all dross.

Property of the company.—The landed estate of the Quicksilver Mining Company consists, therefore, of seven thousand eight hundred acres, or a fraction over twelve square miles, of which more than one-third is mineral ground, traversed by veins of cinnabar which have been traced for miles and tested in more than a dozen places, and of which the celebrated New Almaden mine, which has produced, prior to its possession by this company, more than fifty thousand tons of ore, yielding about twenty-four million pounds of quicksilver, is but a single development.

The permanent improvements upon the property of the company consist of—

Dwelling-houses, workshops, and stores at the hacienda.................... 61
Dwelling-houses, workshops, and stores at New Almaden mine.......... 276
Dwelling-houses, workshops, and stores at Enriqueta mine............. 55
Dwelling-houses on the farms....................................... 13

Total.. 405

The buildings cost over $160,000.

There are six furnaces at the Hacienda, costing about $100,000.

The railway from the mouth of the New Almaden mine to the furnaces, one and one-quarter mile in length, was completed in December last, and cost about $12,000.

The population located upon the lands of the company, and nearly all in its employ, are as follows:

At the Hacienda 286
At New Almaden village... 1,396
At Enriqueta village.. 176
On the farms... 85

Total.. 1,943

The inventory of personal property at the several mines, exclusive of ores on hand, amounts to the sum of $113,876.

2.—PRODUCTS AND EXPORTS.

Produce of quicksilver at New Almaden, from July 1, 1850, to August 31, 1863.

Dates.	No. of months.	Ore consumed.	Percentage.	Furnaces.	Washings.	Total.
		Pounds.		*Flasks.*	*Flasks.*	*Flasks.*
July, 1850, to June, 1851.	12	4,970,717	35.89	23,875	....	23,875
July, 1851, to June, 1852.	12	4,643,290	32.17	19,921	....	19,921
July, 1852, to June, 1853.	12	4,839,520	27.94	18,035	....	19,035
July, 1853, to June, 1854.	12	7,448,000	26.49	26,325	....	26,325
July, 1854, to June, 1855.	12	9,109,300	26.23	31,860	....	31,860
July, 1855, to June, 1856.	12	10,355,200	20.34	28,183	....	28,183
July, 1856, to June, 1857.	12	10,299,900	18.93	26,002	....	26,002
July, 1857, to June, 1858.	12	10,997,170	20.05	29,347	....	29,347
July, 1858, to Oct., 1858.	4	3,873,085	20.05	10,588	....	10,588
Nov., 1858, to Jan., 1861.	....	Mine	closed	by injunction.	......	......
Feb., 1861, to Jan., 1862.	12	13,323,200	18.21	32,402	2,363	34,765
Feb., 1862, to Jan., 1863.	12	15,281,400	19.27	39,262	1,129	40,391
Feb., 1863, to Aug., 1863.	7	7,172,660	18.11	17,316	2,248	19,564
Total	10 yrs. and 11 mos.	102,313,442	....	302,916	5,740	308,756

General average from furnaces 22.20 per cent.   Produce of quicksilver 23,519,834 pounds.

NOTE.—By the terms of the compromise with Messrs. Barron & Co., in August, 1863, the New Almaden mine was to be held and worked by them for the benefit of this, the Quicksilver Company, during the months of September and October, and the company was to assume the entire control on the 1st of November.

During these two months the product was as follows: September, 2,371 flasks; October, 3,149; total product, 5,520, or 422,280 pounds.

Tabular statement showing the product of all the furnaces from November, 1863, to December, 1864, inclusive.

Months.	Charges.	Total quantity of ore reduced.			Total pounds of ore of all qualities reduced.	Total quicksilver.	
		Grueso.	Granza.	Tierras.		Flasks.	Pounds.
Nov., 1863..	13	16,200	628,100	347,200	999,500	1,604	120,300
Dec., 1863..	18	38,600	958,400	371,800	1,369,000	2,436	182,700
Jan., 1864..	19	27,000	432,800	302,800	1,462,600	2,381	178,575
Feb., 1864..	16	4,500	1,042,800	166,400	1,213,700	1,979	148,425
Mar., 1864..	20	46,100	1,318,500	172,600	1,607,200	3,443	358,975
April, 1864..	17	259,500	1,012,900	189,400	1,389,800	3,252	243,900
May, 1864..	21	174,700	1,155,300	272,500	1,604,500	3,022	226,650
June, 1864..	25	38,800	1,567,200	312,700	1,918,500	3,377	253,275
July, 1864..	28	160,800	1,838,500	288,100	2,287,400	4,801	360,075
Aug., 1864..	28	161,600	1,806,600	273,600	2,231,800	4,674	350,550
Sept., 1864..	26	115,700	1,841,300	273,200	2,230,700	3,947	296,025
Oct., 1864..	31	133,800	1,828,600	286,400	2,314,300	4,004	300,300
Nov., 1864..	34	45,400	2,115,500	326,200	2,488,100	3,511	263,385
Dec., 1864..	34	93,000	2,018,700	424,000	2,535,700	3,775	283,125
Totals	332	1,314,200	20,326,000	4,005,900	25,646,100	46,216	3,566,200

```
Total product from furnaces ........................................    46,216 flasks.
Total product from washings.........................................       720 flasks.
                                                                       ─────────────
            Total .......................................................    46,936 flasks.
```

Average per cent. of all ore reduced, tierras deducted, 16.49.

Tabular statement showing the gross product monthly for 1865.

	Flasks.	Pounds.
January...	3,768	288,252
February	3,512	268,668
March	3,427	262,165½
April	4,050	309,825
May	4,501	344,326½
June..	3,961	303,016½
July..	3,671	280,831
August..	4,470	341,955
September	4,598	351,747
October	3,010	230,265
November	3,839	293,683
December	4,271	326,731
	47,078	3,604,465½
Product from washings	116	
	47,194	

[From official report of Mr. Bond, the vice-president, for 1865.]

"The quantity of ore mined and reduced was 31,948,400 pounds, or about 16,000 tons, and the general average of all the ore reduced, allowing 3 per cent. for tierras, was 12.43 per cent.

"It will be noticed that while the production of quicksilver during 1865 has been in excess of any previous year, yet it has not increased in proportion to the increased quantity of ore mined. The average percentage of 1864, as shown by the last year's report, was 16.40 per cent., and for the ten years preceding was 22.20 per cent."

Tabular statement showing the gross product monthly for 1866.

	Flasks.
January	3,950
February	3,703
March	3,043
April	1,000
May	2,900
June	2,700
July	3,173
August	3,180
September	3,190
October	3,190
Total	30,029

Comparative statement of quicksilver exported from California to various countries from 1859 to 1864.

To—	1859.	1860.	1861.	1862.	1863.	1864.
	Flasks.	Flasks.	Flasks.	Flasks.	Flasks.	Flasks.
New York	250	400	600	2,265	95	1,695
Great Britain			2,500	1,500	1,062	1,609
Mexico	103	3,886	12,061	14,778	11,590	7,483
China	1,068	2,725	13,788	8,725	8,889	18,908
Peru	571	750	2,804	3,439	3,376	4,300
Chili	930	1,040	2,059	1,746	500	2,674
Central America			110	40	40	30
Japan			50	25		262
Australia	325	100	1,850	800	300	103
Panama	133	130	57	424	120	45
Victoria, V. I	19	327	116	5	42	21
Total	3,399	9,448	35,995	33,747	26,014	36,918

And the exports previously have been—

	Flasks.		Flasks.
In 1858	24,142	In 1855	27,165
In 1857	27,262	In 1854	20,963
In 1856	23,740	In 1853	18,800

Exports to January 1, 1866.

At the commencement of the year 1865, the company had under consignment and on hand 20,396 flasks of quicksilver, in addition to the quantity, 7,396 flasks, consigned through Messrs. Alsop & Co., which was distributed as follows:

	Flasks.
Consigned to China	7,000
Consigned to Mexico	4,250
Consigned to Peru	1,000
Consigned to Chili	600
Consigned to New York	1,200
Consigned to London	1,600

Consigned to Oregon.. 30
Consigned to Australia... 100
On hand in Nevada.. 1,854
On hand in California.. 2,762

     Total flasks.................................. 20,396

The product for 1865 has been distributed as follows:

Consigned to China... 14,250
Consigned to London.. 10,400
Consigned to Peru.. 5,500
Consigned to Chili... 2,000
Consigned to New York.. 6,800
Consigned to Mexico.. 2,650
Consigned to Australia... 200
Consigned to Oregon.. 280
On hand in Nevada.. 4,641
On hand in California.. 473

     Total flasks.................................. 47,194

Total number of flasks to be accounted for...................... 67,590

The number of flasks sold from these consignments during the year, and accounts therefore closed and settled, were 19,756, as follows:

Sold in China.. 4,000
Sold in New York... 4,500
Sold in Mexico... 450
Sold in Australia.. 100
Sold in London... 1,600
Sold in Peru... 1,000
Sold in Nevada... 6,495
Sold in California... 1,350
Sold in Oregon... 261

     Total flasks.................................. 19,756

Flasks remaining on hand January 1, 1866, and to be accounted for.. 47,834

  This quicksilver was distributed as follows:

Consigned to China... 17,250
Consigned to Mexico.. 6,450
Consigned to New York.. 3,500
Consigned to London.. 10,400
Consigned to Chili... 2,600
Consigned to Peru.. 5,500
Consigned to Australia... 200
Consigned to Oregon.. 49
On hand in California.. 1,885

     Total flasks.................................. 47,834

H. Ex. Doc. 29——12

The quantity consigned through Messrs. Alsop & Co , on hand January 1, 1865, 7,396 flasks, has been sold, making the total sales for account of the company, during the year 1865, 27,152 flasks.

The foregoing statement includes only the shipments and sales of quicksilver which have been closed and finally settled.   In addition to the above, the company have received advices of the sales in China and London of about 10,000 flasks.

Products of other quicksilver mines in California during the year 1866.

Guadalupe, average flasks per month.............................   150
New Idria, average flasks per month..................................   500
Knox & Redington, average flasks per month..........................   300

SECTION 7.

BORAX, SULPHUR, TIN, AND COAL.

1. Principal borax countries.—2. Manufactured borax.—3. Discovery of borax in California.—4. Product of borax in California.—5. Process of working.—6. Deposits of sulphur.—7. Tin.—8. Coal.—9. Iron.

1.—PRINCIPAL PLACES WHERE BORAX IS FOUND.

Prior to the discovery of borax in California, the principal localities in which the borates were found were at Halberstadt, in Transylvania, at Viquentizoa and Escapa, in Peru, in the mineral springs of Chambly, St. Ours, &c., Canada West, and in certain salt lakes of India, Thibet, and other parts of Asia, whence the greater part of the borax of commerce was formerly obtained.

* "The salt separated from these waters by evaporation, either natural or assisted by artificial contrivances, is sent to Europe as crude borax or tincal, sometimes in large regular crystals, but more frequently as a white or yellowish white mass, which is very impure, containing lime, magnesia, and alumina, and likewise covered over with a greasy substance, (said to be added to diminish the risk of breakage during transport.)   According to analysis by Richardson and Bronell, crude Indian borax contains :

Boric acid, (anhydrous).........................	22.88	40.24	24.41
Soda...	12.59	11.11	11.71
Chloride of sodium.............................	0.92	0.11	0.21
Sulphate of sodium............................	0.13	0.49	2.84
Sulphate of calcium...........................	1.36	68	1.36
Insoluble matter..............................	17.62	1.37	20.02
Water..	44.50	46.00	39.45
	100.00	100.00	100.00

2.—MANUFACTURE OF BORAX.

"The purification or refining of this crude Asiatic borax has been carried on from very early times in various seaport towns in Europe, especially at Venice, and more lately at Amsterdam."

*   *   *   *   *   *

* Dictionary of Chemistry, by Henry Watts, vol. 1, p. 646.

"The greater part of the borax used in the arts is now* prepared in France by treating the native boric acid of Tuscany with carbonate of sodium, according to a method first practiced by Payen and Cartier."

3.—DISCOVERY OF BORAX IN CALIFORNIA.

The following extracts from a report by Dr. John A. Veatch, dated June 28, 1857, give a succinct and very interesting history of the discovery of borax in California:

"Since the demonstration of the existence of boracic acid and the borates in California in quantities sufficient for commercial purposes, a history of the discovery and a description of some of the more important localities of these useful products become matters of some interest.

"I believe I was the first to detect the borates in mineral waters in this State, and perhaps, as yet, the only observer of their localities. My attention was first drawn to this subject by noticing crystals of bi-borate of soda in the artificially concentrated water of a mineral spring which I chanced at the time to be examining for other matters. This water was from one of the several springs since known as the Tuscan springs, and which have gained some fame, and very justly, I believe, as medicinal waters. The spot has been described by Dr. Trask under the name of the Lick Springs, and is so designated on Britton and Rey's late map; lying on the north part of Tehama county, eight miles east of Red bluff. The crystals alluded to were observed on the 8th day of January, 1856. Several pounds were subsequently extracted by evaporating the water to a certain degree of concentration and allowing the borax to crystallize. The pioneer specimens of this product were deposited in the museum of the California Academy of Natural Sciences, as an evidence of the existence of a new and important link in the chain of our mineralogical productions, showing that along with the rich productions of the noble and useful metals, we have also the mineral substance so essential to their easy application to the purposes of man.

"The water, holding in solution so valuable a product, was thought worthy of a critical analysis; and consequently at an early period the aid of a chemist of this city was invoked. The reported result, which I placed at the disposition of Dr. Trask, was thought worthy of a place in his geological report of that year, and appears in it. My mind being now alive to the subject, I learned, upon inquiry, of other localities which I supposed might yield the borates. One of these, near the mouth of Pitt river, forty miles north of the Tuscan springs, I had the pleasure of visiting in company with Dr. Wm. O. Ayres, in April, 1856. Specimens there obtained yielded the borate salts; and, from a subsequent examination of the intermediate country, several similar localities were found. The quantity was too small to be of any practical importance, but the prevalence of the salt gave encouragement to further search. A reconnoissance of the "coast range" of mountains, from the neighborhood of Shasta over a length of some thirty miles towards the south, brought to light borates in the numerous small springs abounding in that region, but only in minute quantities. These springs were found almost exclusively in the sandstone, or in the magnesian limestone overlaying it; and the borates seemed to abound in localities bearing indications of volcanic disturbance. Thus a kind of guide was obtained in the prosecution of further explorations. I began to entertain hopes of finding streams with stronger impregnations, or accumulations, of the borates in salt lagoons said to exist in Colusi county, where the sandstone formation was largely developed, the adjacent foot-hills presenting volcanic features. Hunters told tales of mineral springs of sulphurous and bitter waters; of lakes of soda, and alkaline plains, white with efflorescent matters, in that region. Not being in a

* Prior to the discovery of borax in California.

situation immediately to visit those inviting localities, I had, for the time, to content myself with pointing out to the hunters and others occasionally passing through that country such appearances as I wished particularly to be noted. Their reports, together with specimens sometimes furnished, were all corroborative of the correctness of my theory. Colonel Joel Lewis, of Sacramento City, who occasionally visited the coast range on hunting excursions, and to whom I explained the object of my search, and who, although not a scientific man, is an intelligent observer, had the kindness to look, in his peregrinations, for certain indications. He subsequently informed me by letter that he had met with an Irishman, living in Bear valley, who had found a 'lake of borax,' as it was pronounced by an Englishman who lived with the Irishman, and who had been at one time employed in a borax manufactory in England, and therefore assumed to speak knowingly on the subject. He also informed me in the same letter that a Major Vanbibber, of Antelope valley, had discovered large quantities of nitre in the same neighborhood. These glowing reports led me to hasten the excursion I had so long contemplated. In a personal interview with the colonel he told me of an enormous mass, of a white, pulverulent substance, he had himself observed near the margin of Clear lake, of the nature of which he was ignorant. Mr. Charles Fairfax, who was with the colonel at the time, stated to me that a small rivulet running at the base of the white hillock was an intensely impregnated mineral water, totally undrinkable, as he had accidentally discovered by attempting to slake his thirst with it. From the meagre information gathered from these gentlemen, I was led to hope the ' hill of white powder,' as they termed it, might prove to be borate of lime. I determined to satisfy myself by a personal examination at once, and I finally induced Colonel Lewis to act as my guide by furnishing him with a horse and paying expenses. It was some time in the early part of September of last year that he and I left Sacramento for the localities that had so much excited my hopes. At the town of Colusi, which we reached by steamer, horses were obtained, and we proceeded in a westerly direction across the Sacramento valley to the foot-hills of the coast mountains, a distance of about twenty miles. That portion of the plains skirting the hills gave unmistakable evidence of a heavy charge of mineral salts, and the exceedingly contorted and interrupted state of the hill strata enabled me at once to predict the presence of the beloved borates, which chemical trial on some efflorescent matter taken from a ravine proved to be the case in a slight degree. At this point we entered 'Fresh-water cañon,' which cuts the hills and forms a passway into Antelope and Bear valleys. Here I received information from a settler of a hot sulphur spring a few miles south of Bear valley, on one of the trails leading to Clear lake. This spring we succeeded in finding on the following day. It was with no small pleasure that I observed the outcropping magnesian limestone in the hills surrounding the valley of the springs. The strong smell of sulphureted hydrogen, and the appearance of a whitish efflorescence on the rocks, manifested, even at a distance, almost the certainty of finding the mineral I sought. The indications were not deceptive. The efflorescence proved to be boracic acid, in part, while the hot, sulphurous water held borate of soda in solution, together with chlorides and sulphates. There are three hot springs at this place, and several cold ones, all alike strongly impregnated with common salt and borax. The quantity of water yielded in the aggregate is about one hundred gallons per minute—the hot and cold springs yielding about equal quantities. The temperature of the hot water is 200° Fahrenheit, and that of the cold 60° Fahrenheit. The same phenomenon occurs here that is observed at the Tuscan springs, viz., free boracic acid in the efflorescence on the margin of the springs, while the water itself shows a decided alkaline reaction. A careful examination proves that the efflorescent matters come directly from the waters of the spring—taken up by capillary attraction of the soil and evaporated by the air. The singular fact may be accounted for by the decomposition of the borates by the sulphuric acid generated by atmospheric action on the sulphur in which the soil abounds; or the same decomposition may be produced by the hydrosulphuric acid passing up in gaseous form from the laboratory nature has established beneath. The same action, doubtless, takes place in the water, but the boracic acid set free is at once taken up by the excess of alkaline matter, while, in the efflorescence, no fresh supply of alkali offering, the acid remains in its free state when once displaced by more powerful acids.

" These springs seem to be identical in the character of their waters with the Tuscan springs, and therefore doubtless possess the same extraordinary medicinal virtues. As a source of borax these springs could be made available, but as the owners of this locality possess others of superior richness, it is not likely to be ever called to yield its mineral treasure. The situation is a pleasant and romantic one. The distance from the town of Colusi is thirty-five miles, over mostly a smooth and pleasant road. From Clear lake it is eighteen miles, and over rather a rough country. The Indian name of the place is Co-no-to-tok, a generic word having reference to the white appearance of the ground. Mr. Archibald Peachy located a three-hundred-and-twenty-acre school land warrant on this place in behalf of the borax company. After satisfying myself with the examination of this interesting spot, noting nothing of interest save a ' soda spring,' the water being impregnated to a remarkable degree with carbonic acid gas, about eight miles from the lake. A chemical test also detected boracic acid in small quantity. The following day we reached the ' Hill of White Powder,' the goal of our hopes, on the margin of Clear lake. This ' White Powder Hill,' the goal of our hopes, proved an illustration of how little the recollections of mere casual observers are to be depended upon. The hill, in place of consisting of materials in a state of disintegration, so as to admit of being ' shoveled up,' as my friend supposed, proved to be a concrete volcanic mass, bleached white by sulphurous fumes, and looking, at a little distance, like a huge mass of slaked lime, which the inattentive observer might readily suppose to be a ' hill of white powder.' The hope of a treasure in the form of borate of lime vanished forever.

" The road had been rather toilsome, the weather exceedingly hot, and my guide not very well; and as he had gone the full length of the contemplated journey, and felt somewhat disgusted at the result so far, and had nothing more to draw his attention in this direction, he proposed to return at once by the way of the Irishman's ' borax lake ' and Vanbibber's nitre placer. This was agreed upon; so, collecting a few specimens of efflorescent matters from the ground, and filling a bottle with the water in the ravine, I closed the examination of the ' Hill of White Powder.' The ravine I afterwards called the " boracic acid ravine," and the white hill is now called ' Sulphur Bank.' Of these I shall have occasion to speak hereafter.

" Before leaving the neighborhood I determined, however, to know something more of its surroundings. I learned, upon inquiry of Mr. Hawkins, who lives near the spot, that a place not far off, known by the name of ' Alkali lake,' presented a rather peculiar appearance. Hawkins consented to act as my guide. After travelling a short distance, and clambering to the narrow edge of an almost precipitous mountain ridge, we looked down the opposite slope, equally steep, on a small muddy lake that sent up, even to our elevated position, no pleasant perfumes. Thus, on one of the hottest days September ever produced, without a breath of air to dilute the exquisite scent exhaled from two hundred acres of fragrant mud, of an untold depth, I slid down the mountain side into ' Alkali lake,' waded knee-deep into its soapy margin, and filled a bottle with the most diabolical watery compound this side the Dead Sea. Gathering a few specimens of the matter encrusting the shore, I hastened to escape from a spot very far from being attractive at the time, but which I have since learned to have no prejudice against. Of this place I shall have occasion to say more. On my return to Hawkins's, who had the kindness to entertain me with the genuine hospitality of a frontiersman, I looked to my last specimens and found encouraging results in the partial chemical examination I was able to give them. I now again placed myself under the guidance of my friend Lewis, and we started for the Irishman's house in Bear valley. We found the owner of the 'borax lake,' but the borax had evaporated with the water and left nothing but common salt, tinged of a beautiful bluish red color, which I suppose had given the notion that it was something out of the usual way. It was the only specimen of salt I remember to have seen in the coast range that contained no boracic acid in any form; it was guiltless of even a trace. The next step was to examine the nitre region. Major Vanbibber, the reputed discoverer, being a grandson of Daniel Boone, ought to possess, one would suppose, an hereditary knowledge of one of the essential constituents of gunpowder; and as Colonel Lewis had shown me a specimen of very pure nitre, which he said the Major had given him, I rather expected to find a few more left. This, however, was rather worse than the 'borax lake' disappointment; the major had actually forgotten where the lake was, and whether there were any more specimens than those he gave Lewis. The major, I believe, must really have forgotten, for upon subsequent examination the specimen proved to be refined saltpetre that undoubtedly came from some shop or drug store.

"There was certainly a mistake about its origin; but I felt amply repaid for a hard day's ride in spending a night under the hospitable roof of a direct descendant of the renowned 'Backwoodsman of Kentucky.' I observed near the major's house a small pond. Some salt crystals I picked up had the peculiar bevelled angles indicating the presence of borax. The quantity was inconsiderable. Thus ended my first expedition to Clear lake. We here set our faces direct for Colusi, as there seemed nothing more to be seen; and as I had engaged the horses we rode at rather a high per diem, I felt anxious to terminate the trip. From Colusi my guide returned to Sacramento and I to Red Bluff; from there I came again to San Francisco, for the purpose of testing my specimens more critically than I was able to do in the country.

"Convinced of the richness of my 'Alkali lake' specimens, it remained to be seen whether the quantity was sufficient to justify the hope of making it available for practical purposes. A further and more strict examination was necessary. I felt, too, the propriety of a thorough exploration betwixt the Bluff and Clear lake, and more thence to the bay of San Francisco, thus rendering continuous the reconnoissance from Pitt river to the last-named point, a distance, in a direct line, of two hundred miles. After a hard struggle for the funds requisite, I returned to Red Bluff; and from thence, in company with my son, commenced a pretty thorough examination of the coast range and the adjoining edge of the Sacramento valley.

"Nothing of much importance presented itself until reaching a saline district, about eighty miles south of Red Bluff. It is one of the branches of Stony creek. Valuable salt springs exist here. The water contains the borates in minute quantities; and one spring was remarkable for the enormous proportion of iodine salts held in solution. In our slow, onward progress borax now and again manifested itself; but as it had grown familiar, I no longer went into ecstacies over a mere trace. I still treated, however, the slightest indications with due deference, and noted their localities.

"In due time I again reached the 'white hill.' The disgust of the first disappointment had worn off, and I felt disposed to re-examine the locality more critically. I now discovered, for the first time, that the 'white hill' was mostly a mass of sulphur, fused by volcanic heat. The external dust, composed of sulphur, mixed with sand and earthy impurities, and formed a concrete covering of a whitish appearance, hiding the nature of the mass beneath. On breaking the crust, numerous fissures and small cavities, lined with sulphur crystals of great beauty, were brought to light. Through the fissures, which seemed to communicate with the depth below, hot aqueous vapors and sulphurous fumes constantly escape. The fused mass, covering many acres and exhibiting a bluff front some forty feet high, is exceedingly compact and ponderous in structure; of various shades, from yellow to almost black. It seems to be very pure sulphur. The quantity is enormous, and at no distant day may be made available.

"From the 'sulphur bank' I again turned my attention to the ravine. The water, as I had before ascertained, was strongly impregnated with boracic acid, in a free state. The stream is small, yielding only about three gallons per minute, and is soon lost in the sandy soil, in its progress toward the margin of the lake. From the porous nature of the ground surrounding the spring, and saturated with the same kind of acid water, it is probable a large quantity escapes without making its appearance on the surface. The soil for some yards on either side of the ravine is, to the depth of an inch or two impregnated with boracic acid in summer. Sulphuretted hydrogen escapes in continued bubbles through the water, a feature common to all the borax localities I have yet found; in some places, however, the carburetted takes the place of the sulphuretted hydrogen. The head of this ravine is about three hundred yards from the margin of Clear lake, winding around the base of the 'sulphur bank,' receiving some small springs in its course, which seem to have their origin beneath the sulphur. The flat land bordering the lake, some eight acres in extent, through which the ravine runs, shows a strong impregnation of boracic acid in its soil. The point where the ravine enters the lake is marked by a large quantity of water of a boiling temperature, issuing through the sand, a little within the margin of the lake. This percolation of hot water covers an area of one hundred and fifty by seventy-five feet. This fact I observed on my second visit, but not until the third or fourth visit did I ascertain that the water contained a considerable quantity of borax, along with an access of boracic acid. From a gallon I obtained four hundred and eighty-eight grains of solid matter, consisting of borax, boracic acid, and a small portion of silicious and other earthy impurities. On digging to a slight depth just outside the lake, the hot water burst up and ran off freely. From one of these places a stream issued of sixty gallons per minute. I have estimated the entire quantity at three hundred gallons per minute, and feel very confident of being largely within bounds. The stream seems to come from the direction of the sulphur bank, and it would probably be easy to intercept it before it enters the lake, by digging a little above high-water mark. It may be well to note here, that the difference between high and low water marks in Clear lake is never more than three feet.

"The enormous amount of borax these springs are capable of yielding would equal half the quantity of that article consumed both in England and America. The large quantity of water in which it is dissolved would, of course, involve the necessity of extensive works for evaporation. Graduation, as a cheap and effective method of evaporation, would be exceedingly applicable here, from the continued prevalence of winds throughout the entire year. These winds blowing almost unceasingly from the west, form a peculiar feature of the country about Clear lake.

"There is nothing to hinder the manufacture of many million pounds of borax per annum, at a cost but little beyond that of producing salt by graduation. Fuel for final evaporation could be had in any quantities from the extensive oak forest in the immediate vicinity. With these observations I dismiss this locality, adding, however, that Mr. Joseph G. Baldwin located this with a four hundred and eighty acre school land warrant, for the benefit of a borax company.

"Having wandered from my story of my second visit to the 'sulphur bank,' and blended with it observations made in several subsequent examinations, I now turn to my second visit to 'Alkali lake, or Lake Káysa, as the Indians call it. I need only say, however, I became fully satisfied of the great value of the locality, the extent of which has only been recently developed. I observed that the lake itself contained but little water, but that wells dug anywhere near its margin immediately filled with the same kind of water; the conclusion, therefore, was, that an almost inexhaustible supply was obtainable. I learned, too, that what seemed to be mud at the margin and shelving off and covering the entire bottom to the depth of some feet, was a peculiar jelly-like substance of a soapy feel and smell. This matter I found to be so rich in borax, that I supposed it might be advantageously used for the extraction of the mineral. Thus satisfied of the value of the lake, I little thought that within a few yards of me lay an additional value in the form of millions of pounds of pure borax crystals, hidden by the jelly-like substance I was then contemplating. This important fact was not observed until some six months afterwards.

"This locality is by far the most important of any I have yet discovered. It is situated, as may be seen by reference to the accompanying map, in the angle formed by the two prongs into which Clear lake is divided at its eastern extremity. The elevated hill land that fills the angle separates into two sharp ridges, each following its division of the lake and leaving a valley between, of a triangular shape, near the apex of which lies Alkali lake. Clear lake is, therefore, on two sides of it, distant to the north about a mile, and to the south about half the distance. The open part of the triangular plain looks to the east, and expands into an extensive valley, from which it is cut off, partially, by a low volcanic ridge running across from one hill to the other, and thus enclosing the triangle.

"This ridge is composed of huge masses of rock resembling pumice-stone, which float like cork in water. A thin stratum of ashy-looking soil, scattered over with obsidian fragments, covers the ridge and affords root to a stunted growth of manzanita shrubs.

"The whole neighborhood bears marks of comparatively recent volcanic action. Indeed, the action has not ceased entirely yet; hot sulphurous fumes issue from several places on the edge of the ridge just named, on the side next Alkali lake.

"The 'lake,' as it is called, is rather a marsh than a lake. In winter it covers some two hundred acres, with about three feet depth of water. In the dry portion of the year it shrinks to some fifty or sixty acres, with a depth of only a few inches. The 'soapy matter' covers the entire extent with a depth of nearly four feet, the upper part, for a foot in depth, being in a state of semi-fluidity, the lower having the consistency of stiff mortar. Beneath this is a rather tenacious blue clay. This water was nearly as highly charged with solid matter as that of the lake in its highest summer concentration; the proportion of borax to other substances being greater. The soapy or gelatinous matter, however, presents the greatest feature of attraction, being filled with the prismatic crystals of pure borax. They vary from a microscopic size up to the weight of several ounces. These crystals are semi-transparent, of a whitish or yellowish color. The form is an oblique rhomboidal prism, with replaced edges and truncated angles. In some cases the edges are bevelled, and in others the unmodified hexahedral prism exists. Beneath the gelatinous matter, and on the surface of the blue clay, and from sixteen to eighteen inches in it, crystals of a similar form, but much larger, are found. They weigh from an ounce, and seem to have been formed under different circumstances from the other crystals. My first impression was that they had been formed in the upper stratum, and, sinking by their own gravity, had found their present position. An examination proves, however, that they were formed where they lie, as particles of the blue clay are found enclosed in their centres, which could not have been the case had the upper crystals been their nuclea, for no blue matter is ever found in them.

"The first inquiry of practical interest relates to the quantity of borax already formed. On this subject I cannot speak with perfect confidence. The quantity is very considerable, but I do not look on the experiments heretofore made to test this matter as conclusive. The area covered by the crystalline deposit is not coextensive with that of the lake, but has been found over a space of about twenty acres in the examination made so far. A very valuable collateral product, iodine, with the compounds of which the water seems to be exceedingly rich, could be made a source of revenue with but little additional expense. With regard to the quantity of iodine I cannot speak positively, not having isolated the product; but from the brilliant reaction with the qualitative tests, there can be no doubt of its being great. Should this article be manufactured largely the sulphuric acid required might be made on the spot from the products of the 'sulphur bank,' one and a half mile distant. With this I leave 'Alkali lake.' I would state that I located this place in my own name for the company.

"There is yet another important borax locality in the same vicinity, resembling much the foregoing in its more prominent features. It consists of a pond of water of about twenty acres. The bottom is covered with the same soap-like substance, but seems to contain no crystals. The water contains less solid matter in solution, but the percentage of borax is greater in proportion to the other substances than in the Alkali lake. The borax separates readily by crystallization, and forms about thirty-three per cent. of the whole matter. Like the foregoing, this pond has no outlet and no visible source of supply; yet it is said never to be dry, although the water is never more than three feet deep. It would perhaps be a profitable source of borax if the millions of pounds the before-described localities are capable of yielding be not enough to supply the demand. It is in the midst of a magnificent grove of pines and oaks. This place was taken by Mr. Archibald Peachy, by the location of a three-hundred-and-twenty-acre school land warrant. The borates are also known to exist in other localities between Clear lake and Napa City. In Siegler valley there is a hot spring, in the waters of which I detected borate of strontia and other borate salts. Near Napa there is a borate spring, and one in Suisun valley, near the marble quarry. None of these places are important. The foregoing are the only borax localities known in the northern part of this State; and I feel confident there are no others in that quarter that can ever compete with the inexhaustible stores of the Alkali lake and the hot springs. I had expected to find something worthy of attention at or in the neighborhood of the geysers, but there was no trace of borates in the hot waters of those springs, nor anywhere totally in the surrounding district. The geological features of the country were so different from those of that where I had theretofore found the borates, that I was able to predict as soon as I saw it that nothing of the kind existed. In a hasty reconnoissance of the great Tulare valley I found traces, but nothing more, of these substances. I have reasons for doubting the existence of any large quantities in that region. That portion of the valley bordering on the Coast range might be worth examining further. It is there, if anywhere, valuable deposits may be looked for.

"There probably are as many as three districts in the lower part of the State presenting the borates. One or more valuable localities may probably be found among them."

4.—PRODUCT OF BORAX IN CALIFORNIA.

Up to this date but one borax company has been formed in California. There was some talk of organizing another company eight or nine months since, the parties interested having discovered on the shores of Owen's lake, in the southern part of the State, a substance resembling the borate of lime of South America but an analysis of some specimens and of the waters of the lake showing no trace of borax, the project was abandoned. The California Borax Company is the only company on this coast of which I have any knowledge. This company produces at present about two tons of crude crystals daily. Their process is simple, the entire machinery consisting of six small coffer-dams, six feet square each, open at top and bottom. By means of floats these coffer-dams are sunk in the mud; the water is then bailed out, and the finer crystals extracted by washing, as in placer gold-washing.

5.—PROCESS OF WORKING.

The mud taken from different parts of the lake after the crystals have been extracted in this primitive way give, by analysis, from 11.9 to 18.7 per cent. of prismatic borax, and from virgin mud, partially dried, from which the borax has not been extracted, a result of $31\frac{5}{10}$ crystallized borax is obtained. Several tons of the mud, which had been worked over by the coffer-dams, were treated practically by lixiviation, and gave the following results:

Fine prismatic borax, 15 per cent.; carbonate of soda, $28\frac{1}{2}$ per cent.; common salt, $8\frac{1}{4}$ per cent.; equal to $51\frac{3}{4}$ per cent. Thus yielding in the three salts more than one-half the weight of the whole. The mud partially dried lixiviates easily, and the salts are separated without difficulty.

When the company's works are completed the present mode of production will be discontinued.

The fine crystals are found in the upper layer or stratum of soft mud to the depth of about six feet. They dissolve easily, and are subsequently reformed in large crystals by the process of boiling and crystallization. Below the first stratum is a stiff, blue mud containing the largest crystals, which are picked out by hand, the mud being too stiff to be treated by washing. The quantity obtained by the present process could be increased by increasing the number of coffer-dams. This has not been done for the reason that the company have been engaged during the summer in the erection of expensive works for the treatment of the mud by lixiviation, having found by analysis and by actual experiment that for every pound taken out by the coffer-dam washing process fourteen or fifteen pounds go back into the lake, where it is held in solution or in minute crystals by the liquid mud. It is expected that they will be in successful operation by next spring, when, it is confidently anticipated, the capabilities for production will be practically unlimited.

Borax lake covers two hundred and nineteen acres in the latter part of the summer.* At other seasons it covers quite four hundred acres. of which about three hundred acres may be considered as borax ground. The average depth of the water is about two and a half feet. It is the mud, however, which contains the borax in large quantities. The first eight and a half feet average 15 per cent. borax, 28 per cent. carbonate of soda, and $8\frac{1}{4}$ per cent. common salt. Below the depth of eight and a half feet the smallness of the coffer-dams has prevented their working, hence it is not known how much further down this high average will continue. At the depth of sixty feet the mud brought up by an artesian borer give by analysis but 3.51 per cent. of borax. The intermediate points between eight and a half and sixty feet have not yet been tested. The artesian borer was sent up for the purpose of testing the ground at all depths, but, being worked by inexperienced hands, was broken on the first trial after having reached the depth of sixty feet.

An estimate of average workings shows that twenty cubic feet of mud will yield one ton, so that taking the number of square feet to the acre, the number of feet already tested, and the percentage of borax contained in the mud, an approximate idea may be formed of the value of this deposit.

The company estimate that if the crystallization which is going on all the time were to cease suddenly, they would still have a deposit of at least two thousand tons of borax and eight thousand tons of carbonate of soda to the acre.

Besides the innumerable boracic springs which find an outlet in the bed of the lake, there are other springs on the same property which deposit boracic acid over a large surface of ground. These are not worked for the reason that the lake furnishes the borax itself in such great abundance.

Under the impression that the total consumption of borax in Great Britain was less than 2,500 tons per annum, the company proposed limiting the capacity of their works to about eight tons a day. Recent information, however, satisfies them that the actual consumption in Great Britain is upwards of 11,000 tons. They profess to be able to place borax in London cheaper than it can be manufactured there, which, at the lowest estimate, is five cents per pound. The carbonate of soda will pay the cost of production.

The cost of labor at borax lake is $31 per month. The laborers employed are Chinese, and they find themselves. Fuel is abundant all over the hillsides. Transportation to the bay of San Francisco is $15 per ton.

In 1865 this company exported 1,707 cases of borax, valued at $38,765; and during the first nine months of 1866 they have exported 1,998 cases, valued at $42,235, and there is a steadily increasing demand for it in the markets of the Atlantic States, as its great purity is becoming known. The imports of this article on this coast have nearly ceased since this California product has been introduced. The superintendent of the mint, all the assayers and manufacturers who use this article in their operations, combine in stating that it is far better than any imported.

There are several lakes among the Sierra Nevadas in the States of California and Nevada, the waters of which contain large quantities of boracic acid in solution. But the only place on the coast, if not in the world, where it is found in a crystalline form in such abundance, is in the coast range.

6.—DEPOSITS OF SULPHUR.

There are sulphur deposits in many parts of the State, but only one thus far has been worked successfully—that belonging to the Borax Company, near Clear lake, which has been in operation about four months. The capacity of the present refinery is from six to ten tons per day, depending on the variable quality of the material worked.

Along the entire base of the sulphur hills flow innumerable boracic acid springs. Near the shores of the lake are boiling springs of borax.

7.—TIN.

[From the Geological Survey of California, vol. I, p. 180, by Prof. J. D. Whitney.]

The Temescal range was, in 1860 and 1861, the scene of a great excitement on the subject of tin, which metal was supposed to occur here in large quantity, hundreds of claims being taken up, covering all the hills and ridges for miles around. Tin ore was undoubtedly found at one locality in these hills and in considerable quantity, as specimens of it have been seen in various collections from San Francisco to New York. The ore, which appears to be a mixture of cassiterite, (tin stone, or oxide of tin,) with more or less earthy or mineral matter, resembling a mixture of hydrous oxides of iron and manganese, is quite unlike in appearance to any previously seen, and its true character would hardly have been recognized by the most practiced mineralogist. Some specimens, assayed in New York and Boston, gave as much as 60 per cent. of the metal.

The locality from which this ore was obtained was the so-called Cajalco mine, about three miles north of the Temescal ranch-house. Here a shaft had been sunk, in the winter of 1860–'61, to the depth of thirty-six feet; but it was partly filled with water and inaccessible at the time of our visit. A great number of the claims taken up in this vicinity were visited. They seemed nearly all to be located on seams or streaks of dark hornblende running irregularly through the granitic and highly metamorphic rocks. Although there was no appearance of tin about any of these, or any signs of regularity in the "leads," a great many specimens were collected and carefully assayed for tin, without there being a trace of that metal found in any one of them. The excitement has undoubtedly long since died away, and it is not probable that the mass of the ore in the Cajalco mine was very extensive, or more would have been heard of it before this time.* At all events, it is a singular and interesting occurrence of this metal, and we know of no other locality on the Pacific coast north of Mexico where tin ore has been found in place. A single fragment of this substance was given us, apparently under circumstances justifying credence in the discovery, as having been found loose in the soil in the northern part of the State, near Weaversville; but the vein from which it was derived has probably never been discovered, as such a fact could have hardly failed to become widely known.

A belt of limestone crosses through Temescal valley, as was recognized from the occurrence of numerous fragments of this rock on the surface. The bed itself we were unable to discover. It is of a light brown color, semi-crystalline in texture, and contains minute organic bodies, of which the exact nature could not be made out.

8.—COAL.

SIR: In accordance with your request, I herewith submit a report on the coal mines of the west coast of North America, the character of the coal, the present condition of the mining interests, and a table of statistics of the amount consumed in San Francisco during the last six years. The latter item is practically a statement of the actual yield of our domestic mines, inasmuch as San Francisco is almost the only market, the outside consumption barely amounting to ten per cent. of the amount used in this city.

I remain, very respectfully, your obedient servant,

W. M. GABB.

J. ROSS BROWNE, Esq.

Mr. Gabb's Report.

The great coal-bearing formations of the world, those from which the coals of Pennsylvania and the Mississippi valley are obtained, are not represented on the Pacific slope of the North American continent. It is not to be understood, however, that the carboniferous formation is the only one in which valuable deposits of coal have been found. Every one of the great groups of rocks has been found to yield coal in workable quantities in some part of the world. The brown coal of Germany, of nearly the same geological age as that of the Oregon mines, has been worked for many years with profit. So also the cretaceous coal of California has its analogue in New Zealand. In the older formations, the jurassic, triassic, and permian rocks, intermediate in age between the coals of California and those of the great coal-fields of the Atlantic slope, all yield their stores of carbonized plants to the miner, whether under the name of coal or lignite.

The coal deposits of the Pacific may be divided into two distinct groups,

---

* The cause of the suspension of operations on these mines, as alleged by persons living in Los Angeles county and familiar with the circumstances attending the discovery, is that the claims are in litigation.   J. R. B.

geologically. The older, including all of the workable coals of California, as well as that of Washington Territory and Vancouver island, belongs to the cretaceous formation, the analogue of the white chalk of England. This formation consists here of two members, the older of which contains the northern coal deposits; and, although it exists in California, making a large portion of the coast range, it is, so far as known, in this State entirely barren of coal. The upper group, on the other hand, is not found outside of the limits of California, is confined almost exclusively to the coast range, and is the coal-bearing formation of this State.

The other group is the miocene or middle tertiary formation. This group of rocks is one of the most widely spread on this side of the continent, and is known, so far, to exist from the Russian possessions on the north to Cape San Lucas on the south. In a thousand places along this vast extent it contains small seams of coal, well marked enough to deceive the ignorant prospector, but never of sufficient extent to be practically valuable, except in a single locality in the State of Oregon.

Before proceeding further, it would, perhaps, be well to glance in detail at the several localities on this coast that have yielded coal in profitable quantities. The number of these localities is small, though, doubtless, an increased demand, combined with a diminished cost of labor, will increase their number.

Bellingham bay, in almost the extreme northwestern corner of Washington Territory, is the site of one of the largest and best mines on this side of the continent. The deposit consists of about fourteen feet in thickness of coal and slate, of which I was informed that about nine feet were available for mining. The coal itself, as compared with other coals of the coast, is of fair quality, the greatest drawback being the occasional presence of sulphur, rendering it unpleasant for domestic purposes. The position of the mine, with reference to the harbor, is excellent. The mouth of the mine is barely over a fourth of a mile from the vessels in the harbor in which the coal is shipped. The coal is, therefore, only handled in the mine and while being picked in the coal-house, thereby avoiding much of the breakage to which soft coals are subjected by repeated handlings. The vein dips at a high angle, and all of the coals and the water have to be extracted by expensive machinery.

At Nanaimo, on Vancouver island, about seventy miles above Victoria, there is a deposit of the same geological age as that at Bellingham bay, and which has been worked extensively. This mine was originally owned and worked by the Hudson Bay Company. About 1863 it was sold to a company called the Vancouver Island Coal Company. The appliances about the mine are of the most substantial and convenient kind, and the working of the mine was, at the time of my visit, a model of good engineering. The coal is claimed to be superior to any other produced on the coast, and commands a higher price in the San Francisco market than any other west coast coal.

Many other deposits of coal exist along the shores of the Straits of Fuca and Puget sound. Most of these are, however, either so inaccessible or so small that, with the present costs of labor and transportation, they can hardly prove profitable. An exception to this remark may exist in the Straits of Fuca mine, near Clallam bay, Washington Territory, opened within the last year or two. It is claimed that this is a really good mine. It will certainly need to have an extensive deposit of good coal to be of the slightest value on that inhospitable coast.

Coming southward, the next region of any importance is Coos bay. As stated above, the coal of this locality is of tertiary age. The deposit does not seem to be very extensive, and it is so located that but a small portion of it can be worked. Most of the coal lies under heavy rolling hills at a great depth from the surface. One mine—the Newport or Flanagan mine—has been worked in a small way for eight or nine years with very satisfactory results. Upwards of thirty thousand tons of coal have been shipped to San Francisco, and sold there at a price above the current average price of west coast coals. The deposit consists of three veins, separated by only a few inches of soft claystone, and making an aggregate thickness of eight to nine feet of good compact coal, with almost no slate or bone coal.

The deposit is nearly horizontal, dipping towards the mouth of the mine with only sufficient angle to permit unassisted drainage, and the running out of the cars by gravity. No hoisting or pumping gear has ever been or ever will be used in this mine. The coal is carried seven-eighths of a mile in cars to a wharf, where it is shot into lighters and carried a mile thence to the vessel in which it is shipped to San Francisco. Were the railroad extended so as to avoid lighterage, and the expense and loss consequent on the repeated handlings of the coal, and were the coal shipped in steam vessels devoted exclusively to this trade, instead of being carried by the one or two hundred tons at a time in lumber vessels, this mine might be made the most profitable, as well as the most popular, on the coast.

Many localities of coal are known in interior Oregon—as, for instance, on the McKenzie fork of the Willamette river; the vicinity of Eugene City; several places in the valley of the main Columbia, &c., &c.; but interior coal mines can never be of practical value in California or Oregon at a distance from railroads and navigation, unless for local manufacturing purposes, especially in the vicinity of the heavy forests which clothe so much of the surface of Oregon.

In California the coal formation is found over a large area. I have identified it in the coast ranges from the vicinity of Round valley, Mendocino county, to New Idria, Monterey county. In the former locality the coal forms a bed about ten feet thick, very impure, but with one or two seams, of about a foot thick, of excellent quality. The locality is so inaccessible, however, that it can never be of any value. At New Idria, about four miles from the Idria mine, the same beds occur again, and have been "prospected" to some extent for coal. Here they exist as beds of clay slates, barely impregnated with a little carbonaceous matter. Impure as these strata are, they are nevertheless, without doubt, the exact equivalent of the coal beds of Monte Diablo.

The Monte Diablo mines are located in a range of hills lying north and northeast of the mountain, along a nearly east and west outcrop. The coal has been found for five or six miles in a nearly continuous line, although not more than three miles of this extent has as yet proved of sufficient value to render mining profitable. The veins have been somewhat disturbed by faults, and I have reason to believe, from some examinations I made in 1862, that beyond certain limits they thin out rapidly. This is markedly the case to the west of the Peacock mine.

The deposit in this region consists of two veins, the lower of four feet thick, known as the "Peacock" or "Cumberland" vein; the other, of three feet thick, called the "Clark" vein. These two veins, named after the first mines in which they were first well explored, are separated by about three hundred feet in thickness of sandstones.

A number of mines have been opened at various points along the outcrops of the two veins, the principal of which are the Cumberland and Black Diamond, the Clark, Cruikshanks, Adams, Independent, Manhattan, and Peacock. In some of these veins work has been suspended, as, for instance, in the Peacock mine, where the vein was found so much disturbed as to be of little value. In others, work has been prosecuted with considerable vigor, and, as the shipments to San Francisco show, with some success. The greatest drawback to the profitable working of these mines has been the cost of land carriage from the mines to a shipping point on the San Joachim river. Formerly the coal was hauled from the mines to a shipping point on the river, a distance varying from six to nine miles. Recently, however, two railroads have been completed, one terminating at New York, the other near Antioch, thereby very materially diminishing the most important expenses to which the proprietors of the mines were subjected.

High hopes were at one time built on the coal discoveries in Corral Hollow, some thirty miles south of Monte Diablo, on the east face of the Coast range. Several mines were opened and much money expended. In fact a small quantity of coal was carried thence to San Francisco, but inasmuch as it has been ascertained by careful and reliable estimates that every ton of coal thus delivered in San Francisco had cost the proprietors of the mines over one hundred dollars, ($100,) the presumption is that the mines are of but little commercial value. There is here at least one bed of coal of considerable size, but of very poor quality and variable thickness. Furthermore, it is so broken and twisted by the disturbing forces to which the rocks of the vicinity have been subjected that, even were the coal good in quality, the vein could not be relied on.

On the southern slope of the San Gabriel mountains, about thirty-five miles northeast of Los Angeles, is a locality from which some coal has been obtained. I saw a ton or more in a blacksmith shop in that city a year ago. It is apparently a little below the average of west-coast coals in quality, is soft, and somewhat impure. So far as I am aware the locality has never been visited by a geologist, and we have no definite information about it, though the general features of the region appear to point to the same geological age for this as for the Monte Diablo beds.

The distance of this mine from water transportation must render it valueless at least to the present generation.

About seven miles northeast from Oroville is a small bed of very impure coal. The material contains so much earthy matter that it is almost a question of doubt whether it would not be more proper to describe it as carbonaceous shale rather than as coal. Of course it is valueless for fuel, though I was informed in 1864 that it was used successfully in the Oroville gas-works for the manufacture of illuminating gas.

On Eel river, about three or four miles southwest of Round valley, Mendocino county, is a bed of coal about ten feet thick, striking directly across the bed of the river and forming a little cascade. The deposit is of the same geological age as that of Monte Diablo, and although most of it is very impure, it contains one or two seams, of about a foot thick each, of excellent quality.

It is, however, so far inland and so completely surrounded by high and rough mountains that it is extremely doubtful if it will ever become practically available.

In addition to the above localities, which have already yielded or can be made to yield coal in quantity, there are hundreds of places scattered all over California, especially in the Coast range, where small quantities of coal have been found, and where, at the same time, there is no possible chance of finding it in such quantity as to be of value. The miocene rocks contain everywhere small seams of coal of an inch or more in thickness, which, like the *ignis fatuus*, have led on the unfortunate miner by holding constantly before his eyes the dazzling promise of a fortune as soon as the "veins come together," or when he shall have gotten "below the water line"—prospects always in the future, often implicitly believed in, and never realized. The little inch-veins, often very numerous and quite close together, never unite, but have been known to run parallel for many yards—in fact, as far as the patience and money of the "prospector" would extend.

The coals of the west coast are, like all coals of the later geological formations, soft, more or less friable, and contain considerable water. Compared with true carboniferous coal, such as Pennsylvanian or English, they give less heat, and the loss is far greater by breakage in handling.

The following table of analyses of various coals on this coast is extracted from the report of Professor Whitney, State geologist of California. The professor

remarks that these analyses were made in 1861 and 1862, and are from specimens taken at no very great depth:

| | Mount Diablo, California. | | | | | Bellingham bay, Washington Ter. | Nanaimo, Vancou-ver's island. | Coos bay, Oregon. |
	Clark mine.	Black Dia-mond.	Cumberland.	Peacock.	Corral Hol-low.			
Water	13.47	14.69	13.84	14.13	20.53	8.39	2.98	20.09
Bituminous substances...	40.36	33.89	40.27	37.38	35.62	33.26	32.16	32.59
Fixed carbon	40.65	46.84	44.92	44.55	36.35	45.69	46.31	41.98
Ash	5.52	4.58	0.97	3.94	7.50	12.66	18.55	5.34

It will be observed that there is a great similarity between all of the coals
produced on this coast. There is probably, however, one weak point in the
table. The Nanaimo coal is here shown to have a very large quantity of ash as
compared with the California and Oregon coals. It is not improbable that the
analysis may have been based on a poorer specimen than the average, though
Professor Whitney assures me that it looked like a fair sample.

The subjoined table exhibits the amount of coal received in San Francisco
since the year 1860. It does not, however, give the full yield of all the mines,
inasmuch as small quantities of our domestic coals are shipped to inland towns
and used in the vicinity of the mines. It will be seen, however, that, small as
the figures are, the demand is steadily increasing, and the facilities are good for
supplying this demand for many years to come:

Imports of coal into San Francisco since 1860.

	1860.	1861.	1862.	1863.	1864.	1865.	1st 9 months 1865.		1st 9 months 1866.	
	Tons.	Tons.	Tons.	Tons.	Tons.	Tons.	Tons.	Casks	Tons.	Casks
Foreign coals—										
Sydney	7,850	23,370	12,390	16,290	21,190	17,610	9,144	......	34,484	......
Vancouver.......	6,635	6,475	8,870	5,745	12,745	16,190	8,551	......	7,280	......
English..........	6,640	23,565	16,055	14,660	18,330	9,655	5,959	......	5,131	......
Chili	1,900	12,495	5,110	1,790	2,323	1,410	......	......	1,480	......
Unspecified......	......	......	......	......	......	810	......	......	......	......
	23,045	65,905	42,625	39,085	54,600	45,675	23,654	......	48,375	......
Eastern—										
Anthracite.......	34,985	26,060	36,685	38,660	41,680	22,585	20,638	......	6,293	......
Cumberland.....	5,970	2,975	4,970	5,670	7,275	4,230	20	2,858	6,834	3,604
	40,955	29,035	41,655	44,330	48,955	26,815	20,658	2,858	13,127	3,604
Domestic—										
Bellingham bay.	5,490	10,055	10,050	7,750	11,845	13,700	8,000	......	9,590	......
Coos bay........	3,145	4,630	2,815	1,185	1,200	1,500	1,300	......	2,500	......
Monte Diablo....	......	6,620	23,400	43,200	37,450	58,560	39,848	......	54,087	......
	8,635	21,305	36,265	52,135	50,495	74,760	49,148	......	66,177	......
Grand total..	72,635	116,245	120,545	135,550	154,050	147,250	93,460	2,858	127,679	3,604

9.—IRON.

In consequence of the present high price of fuel and labor, the development
of the iron resources of the Pacific coast has not received as much attention as
their magnitude and importance demands. There are numberless extensive deposits of all descriptions of iron ores in all the States and Territories on the
coast. Thus far there has been but one furnace erected for the reduction of

this ore to metal. This establishment is located near St. Helena, within a short distance of the Columbia river, in Oregon, where there is an exceedingly fine body of ore, conveniently located with reference to fuel and water transportation. Arrangements are in progress for the erection of similar works in other places. One is in course of construction in Sierra county, California, about fifteen miles above Downieville, where there is a very large body of ore, which assays from 60 to 75 per cent. There is some talk of erecting a smelting works in the vicinity of San Francisco for the purpose of reducing the grains of specular iron ore found in great abundance among the sand on the shores of the bay.

The consumption of pig-iron in California is rapidly increasing, as the demands for machinery multiply.

In 1859 the foundries at San Francisco consumed 5,000 tons.

1860	do	do	6,500 do.
1861	do	do	6,500 do.
1862	do	do	5,000 do.
1863	do	do	10,000 do.
1864	do	do	14,000 do.
1865	do	do	20,000 do.
1866	do	do	20,000 do.

There is probably as much more used in the interior of that State, Nevada, and Oregon.

LIST OF THE ORES OF METALS FOUND ON THE PACIFIC COAST.

Copper, silver, antimony, manganese, iron, lead, arsenic, magnesium, tin, zinc, bismuth, molebdenum, chromium, tellurium, mercury, nickel, cobalt.

NON-METALLIC MINERALS.

Marble, alabaster, sulphate of lime, carbonate of lime, kaolin, pipe-clay, fullers' earth, sulphur, borax, fire-clay, soapstones, asbestos, lithographers' stone, petroleum, asphaltum, salt, alum, emery, coal, blacklead.

BUILDING MATERIALS.

Granites, sandstones, limestones and marbles, slates, brick clays, &c.

GEMS AND PRECIOUS STONES.

Diamonds, rubies, emeralds, amethysts, garnets, beryl, topaz, agates, jaspers, cornelians, opals, sapphires, egmarin, &c.

SECTION 8.

MINING REGION, POPULATION, ALTITUDE, ETC.

1. Mining region and mining population.—2. Main divisions.—3. Altitudes.—4. Climate.—5. Capacity to maintain a large population.—6. Number of miners.—7. Timber.

1.—THE MINING REGION AND THE MINING POPULATION.

All that portion of our continent west of the Rocky mountains is, we may say in general terms, rich in minerals, and especially in gold, silver, and copper. The western slope of Mexico has produced more silver during the last three hundred years than all the rest of the world. Arizona has rich placers and valuable veins of silver and copper; Nevada has silver; California, gold, silver, and copper; Oregon, gold; Idaho, gold and silver; Montana and British Columbia, gold. The lower part of the basin of the Columbia and the upper

H. Ex. Doc. 29——13

part of the basin of the Colorado are comparatively poor. The richest mines n
the interior basin are of silver; the richest in the basins that open to the sea
are of gold.

2.—MAIN DIVISIONS.

The American territory on the Pacific slope has an area of 900,000 square
miles, and is divided by well marked topographical features into four main
divisions :

1. The coast, which includes a strip about 150 miles wide, west of the Sierra
Nevada and Cascade mountains.

2. The basin of the Colorado, which includes all of Arizona and the eastern
and southern parts of Utah.

3. The basin of the Upper Columbia, which includes nearly all of Idaho and
portions of Oregon, Washington Territory, Utah, and Montana.

4. The interior basin, which includes most of Nevada and Utah and parts of
Oregon and Idaho.

These divisions, or basins, are separated from one another by high mountain
ranges, but the only divide which has been carefully traced and laid down on
the maps is that east of the coast basin. The ridges which separate the interior basin from the Columbia on the north, and from the Colorado on the south,
have not been precisely laid down. The interior basin is divided up into a
number of independent minor basins, all of which are high, arid, and, in their
natural condition, desolate; although there are a few valleys which by the hand
of man have been irrigated and cultivated. Along the coast considerable quantities of rain fall; the surface of the earth is, in the low lands, covered by a
deep mould, and there is a luxuriant vegetation, especially in Oregon and
Washington, where the forests on the mountains are so dense that there is little
hope for the discovery of minerals among them. But in the basins of the interior, the upper Columbia and the Colorado, there is little mould or vegetation ;
the mountains are steep, the rocks are bare, and mineral veins are readily found
and traced.

The poverty of the country in agricultural resources is the cause of one of
its great advantages for mining.

3.—ALTITUDES.

The American mining regions of the Pacific slope, like most of those elsewhere, are mountainous. The gold mines of California are at various elevations—from 500 to 6,000 feet above the level of the sea. The Sierra Nevada
rises in many places to a height of 9,000 feet, or even more ; and from the
comb of the ridge to the level land of the valley, the distance in a direct line
is from forty to fifty miles ; and the descent of the streams, with all their bends,
is more than a hundred feet to the mile. With the rapidity of current consequent on such a descent, they have worn very deep channels, leaving steep and
high intermediate hills. It is on the side of the mountains thus cut into great
cañons that most of the mining of California is done. The average elevation
of the placers of the Sacramento basin may be estimated at 2,000 feet. The
lowest mining towns never have snow or ice for more than a day or two at a
time, while in the highest the snow lies every year four or five months; and
racing on snow-shoes is one of the common winter amusements. The mines in
the valley of Klamath river are at an elevation of about 2,500 feet. The silver
mines of Kearsarge, in California, are 10,000 feet above the sea. The silver
mines of Alpine county are 6,000 feet high. The mines on the Comstock lode
are from 5,500 to 6,500 feet high. The Reese River mines have an elevation
of about 7,000 feet. The Idaho mines vary in height from 3,000 to 6,000 feet.
The mines of Arizona are at various elevations—from 300 to 3,000 feet. Those

on the banks of the Colorado river are probably as near the level of the sea as any in the world. The quicksilver mine of New Almaden is 1,000 feet above the sea.

The following are the elevations in feet above the sea of some of the principal mining towns :

Placerville..	1,800
Auburn	1,200
Dutch Flat	2,943
Nevada, California..	2,573
Brandy City	3,592
Eureka, Sierra county	5,223
Sierra Buttes mine	7,000
Nelson's Point..	3,858
Quincy	3,500
Shasta City...	1,159
Murphy's..	2,201
Silver Mountain	6,516
Markleville	6,306
Mogul	8,650
Silver City	4,911
Virginia City, Nevada.....................................	6,205
Como, Nevada	6,600
Colorado, at Mohave crossing..............................	356
Great Salt Lake city	4,351

Herschel lays down the rule that the temperature sinks one degree of Fahrenheit for each 350 feet of elevation.*

4.—CLIMATE.

In the coal mining districts of Monte Diablo, and at the quicksilver mine of New Almaden, the climate is very mild and equable. The sea breeze is felt nearly every summer day, and a temperature of 90° is rare. The heat of the sun's rays is broken by the cool winds and fogs from the ocean, and the evenings are invariably cool, so that though light cotton garments may be pleasant for wear at noon, woollen are in demand before sunset, and every night, even in July and August, good blankets are prized.

In winter ice is seldom formed, and not once in a year does it last through a day, and if snow falls it is only on high peaks. Skating, snow-balling, and sleigh-riding are amusements which cannot be enjoyed here. Fogs are not uncommon in the summer, but they always disappear after the sun has been up a few hours, and two-thirds of the days of the year are cloudless. There is no rain from May to November, and during the rainy season the amount of water that falls is twenty-two inches, or about half of the quantity that falls at New York or Philadelphia in a year. Thunder and lightning are very rare, and such violent electric storms as are frequent every summer in the Mississippi valley are unknown on the coast of California. It may safely be said that no climate in the world is more favorable to the health and activity of man, or more conducive to the comfort of the laborer.

As we leave the coast the moderating influences of the sea breezes are lost, and the winters are colder and the summers warmer. At the lowest mining camps east of Sacramento, although the winters are very mild, yet ice and snow in small bodies are often seen for two or three consecutive days, and the summers are intensely hot ; and, indeed, in all the mining districts of California the summers are warm, even at high elevations, especially in the deep cañons,

---

*Physical Geography, by Sir J. F. W. Herschel, page 226.

where the breezes are not felt, and where the heat of the sun is caught by steep rocks and reflected down upon the mining camps below.

In the valleys and lower part of the mountains the heat is excessive from May to October, the thermometer standing as high as 85° or 90° nearly every day for month after month. There is no rain usually in that part of the year; the sky is almost cloudless; the bare earth appears to be perfectly dry during the summer and fall; heats are therefore higher than in many other countries blessed with abundant vegetation and frequent showers throughout the year in the same latitude. But the nights are always cool, especially after midnight; and as we rise in altitude on the mountain sides, we find neither frosts nor snows, and the summers are shorter and cool days more frequent. At Yreka, with an latitude of two thousand five hundred feet, frosts come even in July; and in the latitude of San Francisco, frosts occur every month at an altitude of about five thousand feet, and snow lies on the ground for seven or eight months of the year. In the higher mining camps of Sierra county the snow lies from five to ten feet deep, every winter, for months, and the miners shovel the snow from the roofs of their cabins to save them from being crushed by the weight; and cut tunnels under the snow from cabin to cabin, and provide snow shoes so they can travel over the surface of the snow if necessary. During a large part of the year the country is arctic in its appearance, and the climate is arctic in its temperature.

In the lower mining districts of the southern part of Sacramento basin the heat is almost torrid. At Millerton, in the San Joaquin foot-hills, the mean temperature for three summer months has been as high as 106°, and occasionally there are winds so hot that they blister the skin. The amount of rain in California increases as we rise in altitude and latitude. That is a general rule. Thus at San Diego, in latitude 32°, the annual rain-fall is 11 inches; at San Francisco, in latitude 37° 48', it is 22 inches; and at Humboldt Bay, in latitude 4° 46', it is 34 inches. Those places are all at the level of the sea and on the sea-coast; five additional inches of rain may be added for each thousand feet of altitude. So it may be said that in the latitude of San Francisco places at the height of 2,000 feet on the sierra have 32 inches of annual rain-fall; places 4,000 feet high have 42 inches; those 6,000 have 52 inches; and those 8,000 feet 62 inches. These are general deductions from numerous observations taken at different points; but they must not be regarded as precise and invariable. The higher the altitude the greater the difference in the rain-fall of different years, and the stronger the influence of topographical features in determining the amount of fall within a limited area.

Much more water usually falls on that side of a mountain from which the storm comes than on the other. At an altitude of 3,000 feet, and higher, large quantities of snow fall; but in the estimate of the amount of rain on the mountains given above, a foot of snow is equivalent to a little more than an inch of water. But north of California, or east of the Sierra Nevada, we come into other climates. At Fort Yuma, 100 miles east of San Diego, only one-third as much rain falls as at the latter place, and most of the rains come, not in the winter, but in the summer. The rainy season of Arizona and the Colorado valley is the dry season of the coast of California. All through Arizona the climate is dry and the summers hot, but the winters are exceedingly cold in some of the higher mining districts.

Nevada and Utah are high, dry, arid, and desolate. The evaporation equals the rain-fall, and therefore no water can be spared for the ocean, but all is swallowed up in sinks or lakes, in basins surrounded by mountains on every side. If the fall exceeded the evaporation, the waters would rise until the basin would overflow, and at the outlet a channel would be worn through the mountains until much of the inner lakes were drained, and at the bottom of that lake large bodies of sand, gravel and loam would be deposited, suitable for the support of vegetation, when at last it should rise above the water in consequence of the increasing depth of the channel at the gap in the mountains. The valley of the upper Colorado looks as if it had once been converted into a great lake by the elevation of the Cascade mountains, but the river cut a channel at the Dalles before a sufficient quantity of soil had been deposited over the basin, and so the greater part of it is desolate. There is much resemblance between the climates of Idaho and Nevada. The summers are very warm, the winters are cold, and the fall of rain scanty, but the rain-fall is greater in Idaho than in Nevada.

The following figures show the temperature for each month and for the year at various towns in or near mining districts :

	Latitudes.	January.	February.	March.	April.	May.	June.	July.	August.	September.	October.	November.	December.
Benicia	38.03	47	52	53	57	59	67	67	66	64	62	54	47
Fort Miller..........	37.	47	53	56	62	68	83	90	83	76	67	55	48
Fort Reading	40.28	44	49	54	59	65	77	82	79	71	62	52	44
Fort Yuma..........	32.43	56	58	66	73	76	87	82	90	80	76	64	55
Fort Jones	41.36	31	37	43	49	54	61	71	68	62	57	41	32
Sacramento	38.34	45	43	51	59	67	71	73	73	66	64	52	45
Grass valley	....	27	37	38	44	49	52	63	58	53	43	36	46
Meadow valley	39.56	34	32	41	....	61	66	71	68	57	52	44	32
Fort Wall	43.04	24	24	25	42	....	....	....	63	59	48	22	....
Dalles..............	45.36	33	40	46	53	59	67	73	70	61	53	41	33
Salt Lake City	40.46	27	35	39	50	65	71	81	....	....	....	41	34
Lapwai	46.27	31	38	42	52	59	68	70	72	64	48	41	40
Fort Defiance	35.44	26	30	38	46	51	64	69	67	56	46	35	29

The following table shows the rain-fall at a few points and in inches :

	Spring.	Summer.	Autumn.	Winter.	Total.
Sacramento	7.01	0.00	2.61	12.11	21.73
Fort Yuma.......................	0.27	1.30	0.86	0.72	3.15
Fort Miller......................	9.57	0.02	2.80	9.79	22.18
Fort Miller......................	11.30	0.39	4.89	12.44	29.02
Fort Jones.......................	5.38	0.89	5.30	5.20	16.77
Fort Defiance	2.91	6.45	4.84	2.97	17.17
Dalles	2.63	0.42	3.78	6.98	13.81

The cost of living is high in all the States and Territories west of the Rocky mountains. Flour and beef are usually sold in San Francisco for about the same price demanded in New York ; but transportation to the mines is very expensive, and the commissions and profits of traders are large. To Austin the freight in summer by wagon is seven to ten cents per pound from Sacramento ; to Virginia city, three and one-quarter cents ; from Marysville to Quincy, two and one-quarter cents ; to Grass valley, one-half of a cent ; to Downieville, one cent and a third. The freight from San Francisco to La Paz, on the Colorado, about one and a half cent per pound ; and to the Idaho mines, about seven cents per pound. In the winter freights rise, and there is then no limit to them, save the needs and the purse of the shipper. The mining counties of California now grow nearly all the fruits and vegetables, and some of the grain, consumed by the miners ; but all the clothing, fine tools, fine furniture, and many articles of food are brought from the valleys or chief seaport.

In consequence of the bad condition of the roads in the winter and the unsettled character of the population the supply is frequently unequal to the demand, and then prices go to high figures, especially in the remoter districts. The cost of the necessaries of life generally for laboring men is three times as great in the mining counties of California as in the interior counties of New York, and from four to six times, in Nevada, Idaho, and Arizona.

5.—CAPACITY TO MAINTAIN A LARGE POPULATION.

California can maintain a large population. In many respects the State resembles Spain. It has a similar climate, soil and size, and should support as many inhabitants. The population of Spain is at present fourteen millions, and under the Moorish dominion many valleys which are now bare and desolate were well tilled and densely populated. Spain has 188,000 square miles, and California 160,000, and our State has sources of wealth which the Spanish peninsula has not. The Sacramento basin bears a strong resemblance to Lombardy, which has the densest population and most thorough tillage of Europe. In an area of 6,000 square miles three millions of people are collected ; and they are noted for physical beauty and intellectual activity ; hence it does not appear that their crowded condition has done them harm. A large part of the wealth of the Lombards is derived directly and indirectly from irrigation. which they have carried further than any other nation. The Alps there rise to an average height of 6,000 feet, from their northern boundary along a line one hundred and twenty miles, and the snow which falls in these mountains furnishes the water for many of the most valuable canals. The Sacramento basin has an area of 25,000 square miles, lying along the foot of a mountain range 400 miles long and 10,000 feet high on an average. The low land of the basin has a soil as fertile and a climate as genial as that of Lombardy. The amount of moisture from rain is not so great in the valley, but that obtainable from the mountains is greater. The Lombards have natural lakes that serve as admirable reservoirs ; but the Californians can make lakes by throwing dams across the cañons. The vine, the silk-worm, and rice, which contribute much to the wealth of the valley of the Po, will thrive at least as well in the valley of the Sacramento. When, in addition to these agricultural resources, we consider the mineral wealth of the Sierra Nevada, and the commercial advantages of the terminus of the Pacific railroad, the central position between China and New York, and between Oregon and Mexico, we are justified in the conclusion that California can well support a population of ten or fifteen millions.

6.—NUMBER OF MINERS.

The following table shows the number of miners of different classes in certain counties of California, as estimated by well-informed persons in those counties, the limited time for the preparation of this report not permitting more than an estimate on this point:

	Total number of white miners.	Total number of Chinese miners.	Number of gold quartz miners.	Hydraulic miners.	Other placer miners.	Silver miners.	Copper miners.
Del Norte	250	300	......	100	350	......	100
Klamath	700	300	100	50	850	......	100
Trinity	700	1,500	100	500	1,600	......	....
Siskiyou	2,500	500	300	200	2,500	......	....
Shasta	1,000	300	500	100	1,000	100	100
Plumas	1,000	400	300	300	700	......	100
Butte	1,000	1,500	200	300	2,000	......	....
Sierra	2,500	1,500	500	500	2,700	......	....
Nevada	300	1,500	2,000	1,000	1,100	300	100
Yuba	1,000	1,000	300	300	1,300	......	100
Placer	1,800	1,500	300	600	2,350	......	50
El Dorado	2,000	3,000	300	500	4,150	......	50
Alpine	400	......	......	......	......	400	....
Amador	1,200	1,500	400	200	1,600	......	500
Calaveras	2,500	2,000	500	500	2,500	......	1,000
Tuolumne	2,000	1,500	500	300	2,400	......	300
Mariposa	1,000	1,500	500	100	1,600	......	300
Merced	50	100	......	......	150	......	....
Stanislaus	200	100	......	......	300	......	....
Fresno	150	300	50	......	400	......	....
Mono	200	......	......	......	100	100	....
Kern	400	......	200	......	......	200	....
Ingo	200	......	......	......	......	200	....
Total	25,750	20,800	7,150	5,850	29,550	1,300	2,700

7.—TIMBER.

The mining counties of California are generally supplied with abundant timber for present uses. The forests, from 3,500 to 5,500 feet above the level of the sea, on the western slopes of the Sierra Nevada, are very dense, and are composed of magnificent conifers, many of which have a diameter of five feet or more, and a height of 200 or 250 feet. The sugar pine and the Douglas spruce, both valuable for lumber, are large and abundant. These dense forests are, however, higher up than most of the mining districts, which are found among hills covered with scattered oak and nut pine. In the vicinity of the chief mining towns the trees have been destroyed in a ruthless manner, and many hills that were once well timbered are now bare. There was no private owner for the land, and the timber was wasted in many cases; trees were cut down for firewood, and only the branches were taken because by that means the wood-chopper could cut more wood than if he split up the tough trunk. This course was profitable to the woodman, but bad for the State; and numerous complaints were made until 1864, when the legislature made it a criminal offence to destroy the timber in this manner, although permitting any one to cut the timber on the public land for firewood or other useful purposes in an economical manner.

In the northwestern corner of California and the southwestern corner of Oregon the forests are so dense in several of the mineral districts that they interfere greatly with mining, and will prevent the exhaustion of the auriferous deposits for many years. In eastern Oregon and in Idaho there is enough timber to supply the miners for many years. In Nevada and in western Arizona there is a great scarcity, and wood can be obtained in few places without high expense. Good firewood costs from two to four dollars per cord in most of the mining towns of California, and from ten dollars upwards in Nevada.

˙SECTION 9.

Annotated catalogue of the principal mineral species hitherto recognized in California, and the adjoining States and Territories: by William P. Blake. March, 1866.

Actinolite.—Occurs with garnets in steatite at Petaluma.

Alabaster.—In Los Angeles county. Specimen in cabinet of the author, received from Mr. Tyson, of Arizona.

Andalusite.—Mariposa county. In the drift of the Chowchillas river, near the old road to Fort Miller, there is a great abundance of fine crystals of andalusite which show the dark lines or crosses in a remarkably perfect and interesting manner. They are found also in the stratum of conglomerate which caps the hills along the stream, and are doubtless in place in the slates a little higher up the river.

Smaller and less perfect "macles" occur in the slates at Hornitos, on the road to Bear valley. Some of the specimens from the Chowchillas river resemble those from Lancaster, Massachusetts.

Antimony, (sulphuret of.)—(See *Stibnite.*)

Antimony ochre.—San Amédio mountain, with antimony-glance.

Agates and carnelian.—Beautiful pebbles of agate and carnelian are abundant along the beach and near Crescent City. They are much water-worn, and are generally of light colors. Larger pebbles and more highly colored are abundant in the pebbly drift along the Colorado river. Small but very smoothly worn specimens of agate and jasper may be picked up on the shores of Lake Tahoe.

Arsenic.—Monterey county, at the Alisal mines, twenty-five miles from the Mission of San Carlos.

Arsenical antimony—Ophir mine, Nevada Territory. In reniform, finely crystalline, somewhat radiated masses, of a color between tin-white and iron-black, on a fresh fracture, but grayish black from tarnishing; associated with arsenolite, calcite, and quartz.—(*F. A. Genth, Am. Jour. Sci.,* (2) *xxxii,* 190.)

Arsenolite.—Occurs in large masses, with native gold, at the Armagosa mine, Great Basin. It is also reported from the Ophir mine with arsenical antimony.—(*Genth.*)

Asbestos.—Calaveras county, Salt Spring valley, at the Kentucky claim. Los Angeles county (?) in large masses. (From Major Strœbel.)

Azurite, (blue carbonate of copper.)—In fine crystalline groups and masses, with malachite, at Hughes's mine, Calaveras county. (1861.)

Biotite.—From the vicinity of Grass valley. (Cabinet of C. W. Smith.)

Bitumen.—Occurs abundantly in numerous places in the Coast mountains, south of San Francisco, but especially south of San Luis Obispo, and in the vicinity of Los Angeles. It is frequently seen floating in the Santa Barbara channel. It is abundant in Tulare county, on the west side of the Tulare valley, near Buena Vista and Kern lakes, and at this and other localities is associated with petroleum, (which see.)

Blende occurs sparingly in many of the gold-bearing quartz veins of the State, especially when lead is present, as, for example, at the Princeton mine, Mariposa estate ; the Adelaide mine, Hayward & Chamberlain's mine, and in several of the Grass valley mines in Nevada county ; at Meadow lake, in considerable masses, with galena, iron pyrites, and copper pyrites. It is associated with yellow copper in the Napoleon mine and the Lancha Plana ; in Sacramento county, at Michigan bar, associated with galena, oxide of iron, and copper ore. (Cabinet of Dr. Frey.) Placer county, fifteen miles from Lincoln, towards Nevada, with galena and gold ; at the Bloom claim, near Angels' camp, Calaveras county ; also in a quartz vein in Coulterville.

Borax.—Lake county, in large crystals in the clay of the Borax lake.

Boracic acid.—Clear lake, Lake county.

Carbonate of magnesia.—(See *Magnesite.*)

Carbonate of soda.—San Bernardino county, at Soda lake, sink of the Mohave river ; in Tulare county, along the borders of the smaller lakes, when drying up ; at the borders of the Santa Anna river, near San Bernardino.

Cassiterite.—San Bernardino county, at the "Temescal tin region," about sixty miles from Los Angeles. Occurs in many veins associated with schorl (?) traversing granite. In most of the ores the tin oxide is found only by crushing and washing. At the "Gun lode" a peculiar drab colored oxide is found in considerable quantities. It appears to be liberated by the decomposition of an arsenical ore, arsenic being abundant in the samples. The oxide, as collected in that region for examination, is in various degrees of purity, and exhibits different colors. Some of the samples obtained by washing are black, others brown, and some red and drab colored.

Idaho Territory, on Jordan creek, in placers, in beautiful rounded masses, from one-eighth to half an inch in diameter, very pure and clean—the variety known as wood tin.—(Cabinet of the author, specimens received from Charles T. Blake, esq., of Idaho City.)

Mexico, State of Durango : wood tin of great purity and beauty occurs abundantly in this State. It closely resembles the stream tin of Idaho.

Cerusite, (carbonate of lead.)—In large crystals resembling those from Siberia, in the Russ district (?) Great Basin, near the Mojave river ; Arizona, in heavy incrusting masses upon the galena of the Castle Dome district.

Chalcedony.—Large masses of white chalcedony, delicately veined, and in mammillary sheets, occur in Monterey county, near the Panochés ; on Walker river, Washoe ; and of a fine pink color near Aurora, Esmeralda. In pear-shaped nodules in the eruptive rocks between Williamson's Pass and Johnson's river, Los Angeles county.

Chalcopyrite, (yellow copper ore.)—This is the chief ore of the copper mines of California, as it is likewise of the mines of Cornwall, England. It is therefore found at a great number of localities, along the copper-bearing belt which stretches in a nearly unbroken zone from Mariposa county northwesterly to Del Norte county, parallel with and on the western side of the chief gold-producing belt of the State.

In Calaveras county, the chief localities (for the massive ore) are : The Union, Keystone, Empire, Napoleon, Campo Seco, and Lancha Plana mines. In good crystals, implanted on and among clear quartz crystals, at the Noble copper claim on Domingo creek. (Collection of Dr. Jones, Murphy's.) In Mariposa county, the La Victoire mines in Hunter's valley, and Haskell's claims, below Mariposa town, and claims along the Chowchillas river. Amador county, at the Newton mine ; Eldorado county, at the Cosumnes mine, Hope Valley mine, at the Bunker Hill mine, El Dorado Excelsior, and other claims at and near Pilot Hill. Plumas county, at the Genessee and Cosmopolitan mines. It occurs, also, in small quantities in Contra Costa county, in the rocks of Mount Diablo and in those of the Coast mountains south and north of San Francisco. In Los Angeles county, at Richmond district, and at Big Meadow district, both on the interior slope of the mountains at the margin of the Great Basin.— (*Vide Geol. Rec., Cal., p.* 290.)

Lower California, a few leagues south of San Diego, at the Winder claims.

Arizona, at the Apache Chief mine, after getting below the "surface" ores. At the San Pedro mimes, near Fort Buchanan. Near Caborca, in northwestern Sonora.

Chloride of silver.—At the mines about Austin, Lander county, Nevada, this species is abundant in the surface ores, being derived from the decomposition of the mixed sulphurets of silver below the water level. It was also found in the decomposed ores of the upper portions of the Comstock lode, and is common to all the silver veins of the Great Basin. Some remarkably fine specimens were obtained at the ———— mine in Slate Range district, California. Occurs also in the Willow Springs district, and in the veins of El Dorado cañon, Arizona.

Chrysocolla, (silicate of copper.)—Not common in California, where the sulphurets in decomposing give carbonates and oxides; but in Arizona, along the Colorado river, very common at and near the surface where the veins containing copper glance are decomposed. Fine specimens were taken from the Great Central claim, about twenty miles from La Paz and at the Blue lode.

Chromic iron.—Monterey county, in masses, with green crusts and coatings of emerald nickel. Santa Clara county, near the North Almaden mine.

Chrysolite.—In serpentine, near San Francisco, and at New Almaden, Santa Clara county.

Cinnabar, (sulphuret of mercury.)—This is the characteristic mineral of the coast mountains, from Clear lake on the north to San Luis Obispo on the south. It appears to be connected chiefly with the secondary rocks, though at San Luis Obispo Prof. B. Silliman collected a group of fossils which appear to be miocene tertiary. (See a notice by Mr. Gabb, Proc. Cal. Acad. Nat. Sci.) The principal locality is the well known mine of New Almaden, in Santa Clara county, and the adjacent mines of the Enriqueta and the Guadalupe. The ore occurs massive, in large bunches and "strings," and is associated with calc spar, bitumen, and pyrites. The total production of quicksilver, chiefly from the New Almaden, up to January, eighteen hundred and sixty-five, was three hundred and seventy-one thousand eight hundred and eighty-three flasks, valued at about fifteen million of dollars in gold. At the North Almaden, on the east side of the San José valley, and nearly opposite the New Almaden, considerable quantities of cinnabar have been taken out of prospecting pits at this place, at several different points. A heavy ferruginous outcrop shows the general course of the metalliferous belt. The rock is hard and flinty, and is frequently beautifully streaked with brilliant red cinnabar, the whole sufficiently compact to give fine specimens for polishing by the lapidary. It occurs abundantly, and in very handsome cabinet specimens, at the New Idria mines, in Monterey county, at which work has recently been resumed. There are many localities in Napa county, and in the vicinity of Clear lake, and the Geysers. In small crystals in hornstone, at Buckhorn ranch, north of Berreyesa valley.

In Mariposa county, near Coulterville, in finely colored crystals in quartz in a gold vein. Nevada county, about four miles from Grass valley, washed out of sluice boxes, and entirely different from the New Almaden ore in appearance. Arizona, about eighteen miles from the Colorado river; at Olive City, at the Alma claim, and the Eugenie, located by Mr. Ehrenberg; associated with silver. Reported to exist in Idaho, on the Owyhee river.

Corundum.—Los Angeles county, in the drift of the San Francisquito Pass, in small crystals. (Baron Richthofen.)

Copper, native.—This species is common in small quantities in the surface ores of the principal copper mines of the State, but is not found below the permanent water level. No veins of this metal like those of Lake Superior are known upon the Pacific coast, but the abundance of large drifted masses of solid copper in one or more streams upon the northwest coast, (Russ. Poss.) leave little doubt that such veins do exist in that high latitude. Calaveras county, at the Union mine, some very fine masses of dendritic or moss copper have been taken out.—(Cabinet of J. B. Meader.) The Keystone mine, adjoining the Union, also produced some good specimens in 1861. Found also at the Napoleon and the Lancha Plana mines; and in Sacramento county, at the Cosumnes mine. In Santa Barbara county, occurs disseminated in grains in the midst of serpentine rock. Arizona, on the Gila river, about ninety miles from Fort Yuma, at the Arizona Copper Company's mine; associated with red oxide of copper and green carbonate, and spread in crystalline masses through a gangue of calc spar.—(Cabinet of the author.) For the ores of copper, see *Chalcopyrite, Red Copper, Vitreous Copper,* &c.

Copper glance.—Los Angeles county, at the Maris mine, Soledad district, in grains and irregular masses in a sienitic granite. It contains silver. The decomposition of this ore at and near the surface gives metallic copper, and metallic silver, incrusting the surfaces of the granite where fissured. This locality was known and worked as early as 1853. In Arizona this is the most common ore of copper, especially in Weaver district, near La Paz, or Olive City. It is usually argentiferous, and is there associated with gold in quartz veins. Found also in the Chahuabi valley, the Tajo, and the San Pedro mines, and near Caborca, in northwestern Sonora.

Derbyshire spar.—Castle Dome district. (See *Fluor spar.*)

Diamond.—Butte county, Cherokee Flat, ten miles from Oroville. In well formed, highly modified crystals, from one-eighth to three-sixteenths of an inch in diameter, and generally of a pale straw yellow color. Crystallization tetrahedral, like figure 267, page 24, Dana's System of Mineralogy.

Idaho.—Reported to exist on the Owyhee river.

Diallogite, (carbonate of manganese.)—Occurs abundantly in the silverbearing veins about Austin, Nevada. By decomposition it becomes black, and discolors the upper parts of the vein, but at and below the water line, with the unchanged ores of silver, it has a delicate flesh-red or pink color.

Dolomite—Amador county, in narrow, snow-white veins, traversing a talcose chloritic rock, and bearing coarse free gold.—(Cabinet of the author, specimen presented by Mr. James.) Calaveras county, Angel's Camp, in the Winter, Hill's and other mines, massive, with the quartz veins, and bears gold. Sometimes in fine crystals, lining cavities. San Bernardino county, at the Armagosa mine, bearing coarse gold.

Embolite.—Is believed to occur in the surface ores of Lander county, Nevada, near Austin, and of Washington district, further south, but has not been certainly identified.

Emerald nickel.—Monterey county, with chrome ore.

Feldspar.—San Diego county, in crystals. (See *Orthoclase.*)

Fluor spar.—In crystals and large cleavable masses of various tints—white, pink, and purple and green, like the specimens from Derbyshire, England, in the veins of galena and blende, Castle Dome district, Colorado river, Arizona. Sparingly, in small white cubes, with the copper ore, at Mount Diablo.

Galena, (sulphuret of lead.)—This common ore of lead has not yet been found in finely crystallized cabinet specimens on the Pacific coast. The localities of the massive or granular ore are numerous, it being found in small quantities in many of the gold-bearing veins of the State, especially at the following: Mariposa county, at Marble Springs mine; Princeton mine; Adelaide. Calaveras county, at the Barnes and Silver Elephant claims, at Murphy's; at the

Star of the West, Blue Mountain district, and the Good Hunter claims, with gold. In Sacramento county, at Michigan bar, with blende and pyrites. Nevada county, at Meadow lake, with blende. Tuolumne county, at the Soulsby mine, with blende and iron pyrites and gold. In Nevada county, in several of the veins at Grass valley, with free gold. In Tehama county, on Cow creek; and abundantly in veins on the island of Santa Catalina. In Arizona it is abundant in the veins of the Castle Dome district, twenty five miles from Fort Yuma, and in the Eureka district on the same river, about twenty-five miles further north; also in the Piccacho district, and in the Weaver district, near La Paz; at the Santa Rita mine, with gray copper ore; in the Tajo vein, with copper glance, blende, tetrahedrite, and gold; in the Santa Cruz mountains, south of Fort Buchanan; at the Mowry and Patagonia mines; at San Xavier, on the Santa Cruz, (Pumpelly.) In Nevada it is abundant on Walker's river, north of Esmeralda, and at Steamboat Springs, Galena district. It is also found in portions of the Comstock lode, Washoe, associated with the silver sulphurets; but where it is associated in that vein with much blende and copper pyrites, it is not rich in silver—forming the ore commonly known there as "base metal."

Garnet.—El Dorado county, at Fairmount mine, three miles from Pilot Hill, in large blocks and masses two feet thick or more. Associated with specular iron, calc spar, iron pyrites, and copper pyrites, with actinolite in steatite, near Petaluma, Sonoma county; in large semi-crystalline masses, weighing ten to twenty pounds, and of a light color, from the Coso mining district. (Specimens of this were brought to San Francisco under the supposition that it was tin ore.) A beautiful green garnet, grossular, is found with the copper ore of the Rogers claim, Hope valley, El Dorado county, and similarly in copper ore at the Mountain Meadows, Los Angeles county. In Russian America, Stickeen river, in finely formed trapezohedral and dodecahedral crystals imbedded in mica slate, and much resembling specimens from Monroe, Connecticut.

Gold, (crystalline.)—Placer county, at Irish creek, three miles from Coloma, in arborescent and crystalline masses covered with octahedrons. (Eighteen hundred and fifty-four, cabinet of author.) At Forrest Hill, in the same county, in the placer claims of the Messrs. Deidesheimer, in flattened and distorted octahedra. One crystal is a partially formed octahedron, with a rectangular base one inch long by seven-eighths of an inch wide. At Mameluke Hill, near Georgetown, in jagged crystalline masses, in a quartz vein. In El Dorado county, at Spanish Dry Diggings, in large masses of irregular dendritic crystallizations. One mass recently obtained weighed about sixteen pounds, and was purchased by Mr. Dickinson, of New York, for preservation. Calaveras county, a large partly formed crystal with octahedral edges; if perfect would be two inches in diameter. Tuolumne county, flattened, distorted, octahedrons from the Whiskey Hill mine Mariposa county, octahedrons from the placers near Coulterville, but very rare. At the Princeton mine, rarely, in nests and bunches of octahedrons, with brilliant faces.

Small delicate microscopic prisms of gold have been found in the vicinity of Sonora. They appear to be terminated with crystalline planes at both ends, and probably are elongated octahedrons. (From the collection of Doctor Snell.)

Crystals of spongiform gold, from one-eighth to one-quarter of an inch in diameter, and as light almost as cork, were washed out by Doctor Hill from a claim near Angel's. This is a condition of native gold which, it is believed, has not been hitherto noticed.

In Plumas county, Sherman lode, Light cañon, on coatings of green and blue carbonates of copper, proceeding from the decomposition of variegated copper pyrites or vitreous copper in part. This gold was apparently deposited after the deposition of the carbonate of copper. The specimens are beautiful. (Cabinet of Mr. Waters, Sacramento.) Mariposa county, in a narrow vein of calcite or dolomite, two inches wide, cutting slates; precise locality not known. The gold was in coarse masses and strings in the middle of the vein. Amador county, near Drytown, in a vein of pearl spar, which is very pure and white, and without admixture with quartz or pyrites. The gold is in coarse masses in the midst of the pearl spar. (Specimens collected by Mr. James, and presented to the author.)

Gold in small quantities occurs at many places in the Coast mountains, and associated with cinnabar. Some specimens of coarse gold have been found in the cinnabar veins of Colusa county. In Excelsior district gold occurs with molybdenite. In San Bernardino county, at the Armagosa mine, in feldspar and in calc spar, in a granitic rock, associated also with arsenolite.

Many large masses of gold have been taken from the placers of California at various times, of which no authentic record or description has been kept. In 1864 a large mass, one hundred and eighty-seven ounces, (fifteen and seven-twelfths pounds,) was taken from the middle fork of the American river, about two miles from Michigan bluffs, Placer county.

The Carson Hill quartz claim, in Calaveras county, is celebrated for the size and weight of the masses of gold taken from it, some of which weighed six and seven pounds. (For further observations upon gold, its geology and distribution, see an article at the end.)

Gold and tellurium.—(See *Tellurium*.)

Gray copper ore.—With gold in the Pine Tree mine, Mariposa grant, and similarly at the Iona Company's claim, and others upon the same belt near Coulterville. (See *Tetrahedrite*.)

Graphite.—About twenty miles above the Big Tree Grove, in crystalline scales; also at the mine of the Eureka Plumbago Company, (locality not known.)

Gypsum—Los Angeles county, in the Great Basin, near the entrance to the Soledad or " New Pass." San Diego county, along the banks of Carizzo creek, and on the slope of the desert. Tulare county, at the vein of stibnite, in crystals. Nevada county, near the Truckee Pass, in beautiful stellar radiations, from one-half of an inch to three inches in diameter. (Cabinet of C. W. Smith, Grass valley.)

Hematite, (specular iron ore)—This is a very abundant ore in California, and Arizona, on the Colorado river, near Williams's Fork. Some of the dry arroyos or cañons in that region are crowded with blocks of the pure ore, from one to two feet in diameter. It is broken from beds and seams in an impure metamorphic limestone. The structure is granular, passing into micaceous, and freshly broken surfaces are extremely brilliant. Specimens of similar ore were brought in by Jules Marcou, in eighteen hundred and fifty-three, from the valley of Williams's Fork, further north. This ore occurs also in Humboldt valley, and abundantly on the coast of Mexico, south of Acapulco.

Hessite.—El Dorado county. (See *Telluret of silver*.)

Hornblende.—At San Pablo. At Soledad, in sienite. At Vallecito, near Murphy's.

Hyalite.—Associated with semi-opal, in the Mount Diablo range, about thirty miles south of Mount Diablo. (In cabinet of J. B. Meader, Stockton.)

Idocrase.—Siegel lode, El Dorado county. (?)

Iodide of mercury—Santa Barbara county. (?)

Ilmenite.—El Dorado county, near Georgetown, from the gold washings; a very fine crystal, about an inch in diameter, with brilliant planes.

Iron ores.—(See *Magnetite* and *Hematite*.)

Iridosmine.—With platinum and gold in the beach sands of the northern counties. An analysis by C. Kurlbaum, jr., in Dr. Genth's laboratory, of a sample of the residue from gold washing and amalgamation obtained by the author in eighteen hundred and fifty-four, gave 48.77 per cent. of iridosmine. Found also as a residue in melting large lots of placer dust.

Iron pyrites.—Found in most of the gold-bearing quartz veins, either crystalline or massive; usually from one to five per cent. of the whole weight of the ore. The value for gold varies greatly. At Grass valley the concentrated sulphurets are worth from one hundred dollars to three hundred dollars per ton. Cabinet specimens of this mineral may be had in very large crystals, cubes, at the Fairmount claim, three miles from Pilot Hill, Eldorada county. It is there associated with garnets, brown spar, and specular iron. Found in brilliant druses lining fissures in the rocks of the E Pluribus Unum tunnel, three miles from Murphy's, Calaveras county. In brilliant but small cubical crystals in the gold ore of the Mameluke claim, near Georgetown, Eldorado county. Mariposa county, in large and perfect crystals in the slates near the Deville mine, south of Princeton Hill. Placer county, in large crystals, near the Grizzly Bear House, between Auburn and Forest Hill.

Jasper.—Very fine masses of brown and yellow jasper are abundant near Murphy's, Calaveras county, in the quartz veins, and in the debris from them.

Kerargyrite.—(See *Chloride of silver.*)

Lignite.—San Francisco county, Contra Costa county, Monterey county; in Amador county, in thick beds at the base of the Sierra Nevada; used in Ione City for steam boilers; Santa Barbara county, Humboldt county, along the Eel river; Klamath county, at Gold Bluff, four hundred feet below the surface. (Lieutenant Tuttle, U. S. army.) Del Norte county, at Point St. George. (Professor Sherman Day.) In Nevada, Washoe county, along the Truckee river; in Lyon county, at the "Whitman mines."

Limonite.—Mariposa county, at Burns's creek, near the old road to Fort Miller, in a heavy outcrop of quartz; solid blocks of limonite, from two to four feet thick, are found there. (See Geol. Rec. Cal., p. 290.) Oregon, sixteen miles from Portland, in an extensive bed; specimens were sent by Governor Gibbs to the Mechanics' Fair exhibition in 1864.

Macle.—Mariposa county. (See *Andalucite.*)

Magnesite, (carbonate of magnesia.)—Tulare county, near Visalia, between Four creeks and Moore's creek, in the foothills, in solid beds of pure white, massive carbonate of magnesia, hard, fine grained, and like unglazed porcelain in texture. The beds are from one to six feet thick, and are interstratified with talcose slates and serpentine. Similar beds are described to me as existing in the Diablo range. Alameda county, about thirty miles south of the mountain. Mariposa county and Tuolumne county: a heavy bed of magnesian rock, chiefly magnesite, charged with crystals of iron pyrites, accompanies the chief gold-bearing quartz vein of those counties. This rock is charged also with nickel and chrome talc in green films, like the magnesite of Canada.

Magnetite.—In large beds, massive, and of superior quality, in Sierra county; also in octahedral crystals, forming beautiful cabinet specimens. In Plumas county, near the line, fine groups of octahedrons associated with garnet (?) and epidote. (?) Mariposa county just east of the Mariposa estate, on the trail to Yosemite. Placer county, at Utt's ranch, six miles from Auburn. At the Cañada de las Uvas, Los Angeles county, in a vein about three feet thick, in limestone; in the sienitic granite of the mountains between the Great Basin and Los Angeles; seen in drift fragments in the valley of Soledad, or "Williamson's Pass." Elderado county, at Volcanoville, on the middle fork of the American river, near the great quartz vein. This locality was noted by the writer in eighteen hundred and fifty-three. This ore is, perhaps, titaniferous, but specimens are not at hand for examination. Trinity county, near Weaverville, in small veins. (Trask, 3d report, 1865, p. 56.) Nevada county, three miles from Grass valley. Eldorado county, fine octahedral crystals, in slate, near the Boston copper mine; in small brilliant crystals, with quartz, pyrites, and calc spar; at the El Dorado Excelsior copper claim.

Malachite, (green carbonate of copper.).—In remarkably fine specimens, associated with crystalline blue carbonate, at Hughes's mine, Calaveras county, (1861.)

Manganese, oxide.—(See *Pyrolusite.*)

Manganese, carbonate of.—(See *Dialogite.*)

Mercury.—Native quicksilver is found in Napa (?) county, near the Geysers, at the Pioneer claim, in a silicious rock.

(For sulphuret of mercury, see *Cinnabar.*)

Mercury, iodide of.—Santa Barbara county, (Mr. G. E. Moore.)

Mispickel.—Grass valley, Nevada county, at Betsey mine, with gold. This mineral is a common associate of gold in the quartz of the State. Crystals of mispickel are sometimes penetrated with gold.

Molybdate of lead.—State of Nevada, Comstock lode, in the upper part of the California mine, in the "rusty lode," in small yellow crystals; in good crystals in the ——— (?) mine, Weaver district, Arizona.

Molybdenite.—Occurs in fine specimens at several localities in the gold region; Nevada county, at the Excelsior mine, Excelsior district, abundantly with gold.

Mountain cork.—Tuolumne county.

Nickel.—(See *Emerald nickel.*)

Orthoclase.—San Diego county, in granite veins along the road between Santa Isabel and San Pasquale, associated with tourmalines and garnet. Fresno county, at Fort Miller, in coarse-grained granite, under the edge of the lava plateau.

Opal—semi-opal.—A white milky variety of opal is found in Calaveras county, at Mokelumne Hill, or on the hill near that place, known as Stockton Hill, on the west side of Chile gulch. A shaft has been sunk there three hundred and forty-five feet, and the opals are found in a thin stratum of red gravel. They vary in size from a kernel of corn to the size of walnuts. Many of them contain dendritic infiltrations of manganese oxide, looking like moss. About a bushel of these stones are raised in one day, and are said to have a market value. A white milky variety, similar to the above, and without "fire," is found with magnesite in Mount Diablo range, thirty miles south of the mountain; also in the foot-hills of the Sierra Nevada, at the Four Creeks.

Pearl Spar.—(See *Dolomite.*)

Petroleum.—Abundantly distributed throughout the coast counties from San Diego in the south to Crescent City in the north. The purest and most limpid natural oils have thus far been obtained from the localities north of San Francisco, in Humboldt and Colusa counties. These oils are green by reflected light, and resemble the best samples from Pennsylvania. No abundantly flowing wells have yet been found. In Humboldt county there are many springs, giving both oil and gas, and numerous wells are in progress. So also in Colusa county, at Bear valley, about twenty-five miles west of Colusa, several springs, giving a fine quality of lubricating oil and much gas; also at Antelope district, nineteen miles west of Colusa. In Contra Costa county, ten miles from Oakland, there are petroleum springs, and a very superior oil has been obtained from the region of Mount Diablo. In Tulare county there is an extensive region where oil and gas springs abound. The localities are numerous in the counties of San Luis Obispo, Santa Barbara, Tulare, and Los Angeles.

Platina.—With iridium and iridosmine, on the coast at Cape Blanco, southern Oregon. Analysis of a sample of the mixed metals from Port Orford, in eighteen hundred and fifty-four, gave forty-three and fifty-four one-hundredths per cent. of platina.

Proustite, (light red silver ore.)—In the veins about Austin, Lander county, Nevada. At the Daney mine, and occasionally in the ore of the Comstock lode.

Pyrargyrite, (dark red silver ore.)—(See *Ruby silver.*)

Pyrolusite.—Red Island, Bay of San Francisco, in vein or bed 3' to 4' wide, in the metamorphic jaspery shales—the "prasoid" rocks. This is a remarkably pure ore of manganese, and has been extensively mined for shipment.

Pyrophyllite occurs in the gold region; locality not known.

Pyroxene.—In fine crystals, dark green, near Mud springs, Eldorado county.

Pyromorphite, (phosphate of lead.)—In Nevada, in the outcrops of the Comstock lode, especially the back ledges of the Ophir ground, giving green coats and crusts on the surface of the quartz.

Pyrrhotine, (magnetic pyrites.)—Mariposa county, at the Iona Copper Company's tunnel, north side of the Merced river, on the trail from Bear valley to Coulterville.

Quartz.—This abundant mineral is obtained in fine crystals in the quartz veins in various parts of the State, and in the mines of Washoe. Some large and well-formed crystals, from three to four inches or more in diameter, have been found at Red Hill, in Placer county, (cabinet of C. W. Smith, Grass valley,) and in the placer claims in the vicinity of Placerville, where, also, a fine large crystal of smoky quartz was found. Mariposa county, on Whitlock's and Shirlock's creeks, in the quartz veins, in fine groups of crystals; also at the Mariposa mine, and in the eastern parts of the Princeton vein. Calaveras county, at the Noble claim, on Domingo creek. Nevada county, in the Grass Valley mines, often supporting gold between the crystals, and at the "French lode," (Eureka?) crystals of a light greenish tinge, like that of datholite.

Red oxide of copper occurs sparingly in thin crusts and sheets with the surface ores of the principal copper mines in Calaveras county, especially the Union and Keystone. In Mariposa county, at La Victoire mine, with green and blue carbonates of copper. Del Norte county, at the Evoca, Alta, and other mines, in very good cabinet specimens, the cavities being lined with crystals. In Plumas county, and in the upper parts of most of the copper veins of the State. Arizona, at the Arizona Copper-Mining Company's claim, near the Gila river, in large masses, with native copper and thin crusts of green carbonate. At the claim known as No. 15, Yavapais district, with native copper.

Ruby silver, (pyrargyrite.)—This beautiful ore of silver was first discovered in the Daney mine, Washoe, by the writer, in eighteen hundred and sixty-one, and has since been found sparingly in the Ophir and the Gould & Curry. In the latter mine some very fine specimens were obtained by Mr. Strong, and are deposited in the cabinet of the company, at the office in Virginia City. This ore is abundant in the veins about Austin, Reese river, and is often so thoroughly spread through the quartz of the gangue as to give it a decided reddish color. It is generally associated with sulphuret of silver. No good crystals have yet been found.

Salt—rock salt.—Abundant in the dry season as an incrustation throughout California. Found in large quantities in Nevada, in the beds of desiccated lakes at numerous places. About twelve miles north of Armagosa mine, in large masses. In the Wasatch mountains, southeast of Lake Timpanogos, on the headwaters of a small creek tributary to Utah lake, in thick strata of red clay. (Frémont's Geog. Mem., 67.) This is said to be the same locality mentioned by Father Escalante in his journal, and noted by Humboldt on his map as "*Montagnes de Sel Gemme.*" Salt crystallizes from the spray of the waters of the Great Salt Lake, and is found abundantly on its shores, and on twigs and shrubs. The Great Salt Lake is a saturated solution of common salt. The shores in the dry season are incrusted with salt, and shallow arms of the lake present beds of salt for miles. Plants and shrubs are incrusted to a thickness of an inch or more with crystallized salt deposited by the spray. Five gallons of the water taken in the month of September, and evaporated by Colonel Frémont over a fire, gave fourteen pints of salt, which analysis showed to have the following proportions (Frémont's Memoir, 9 :)

Chloride of sodium	97.80
Chloride of calcium	0.61
Chloride of magnesium	0.24
Sulphate of soda	0.23
Sulphate of lime	1.12

Schorl, (see *Tourmaline.)—Selenite.*—In beautiful stellar crystallizations on the crossing of the Little Truckee, Henness Pass road. The blades composing these aggregates are from half an inch to two inches in length, and from one-eighth to one quarter of an inch in width. They are perfectly clear, and most of them hemitroped so as to form arrow-headed crystals. (Cabinet of C. W. Smith.)

Selenid of mercury —In large masses from the vicinity of Clear lake.

Silver, native.—This metal, in its native state, is rare in the State of California. At Silver Mountain district (formerly Eldorado county) it occurs in the decomposed surface ores. Los Angeles county, in the decomposed parts of the Maria vein, Soledad, covering surfaces of syenite. Sonora, at the celebrated Planchas de la Plata, just south of the Arizona line, and near the meridian of Tubac. According to the best Mexican and Jesuit authorities, large masses of native silver were discovered there in 1769. One mass is reported to have weighed three thousand six hundred pounds. No vein has been found; the deposit is a placer. (Pumpelly.) Nevada — Story county, in the Comstock lode, in filaments, and matted, hairy masses—"wire silver," usually closely associated with silver glance and stephanite. At the Burning Moscow claim (Ophir) some large masses of ore were taken out in 1864 completely charged with the metal. Occurs also at the Daney mine, with native gold and sulphuret of silver. Lander county, in the veins about Austin, associated with the surface ores, such as the chloride and bromide of silver, and green and blue carbonates of copper. Idaho Territory, in large masses at the "Poor Man's lode," or "Candle-box mine," where it was said the lumps of silver were as large as candle boxes. That a great quantity of large masses of the metal was taken out there is no doubt. It is common in the silver lodes of the Owyhee, and is usually very filamentous and finely divided and embedded in granular quartz.

Silver, (telluret of.)—A single specimen was obtained by the author in 1854, near Georgetown, in Eldorado county. It had been washed out from the gold drift, and the parent vein has never been found.—(Rep. Geol. Rec. Cal., 302.)

Smoky quartz.—A large crystal about six inches in diameter, from Placer county, and in the cabinet of Dr. White, Placerville.

Sphene.—In small hair-brown crystals in the granite of the Sierra Nevada.

Stephanite, (brittle sulphuret of silver.)—Very fine crystals of stephanite were obtained from the Ophir and Mexican mines, Nevada, soon after they were opened. These crystals were from half an inch to two inches in length, but were generally imperfectly formed. They greatly resemble the crystallizations of vitreous copper from the Bristol mine in Connecticut. A large collection of these was made by R. L. Ogden in 1859 and 1860, and were noticed by the writer in the Mining Magazine. They are now more rare, but have been found in nearly all the principal claims upon the Comstock lode. Some very good specimens were taken from the Gould & Curry, preserved in the cabinet by C. L. Strong, in 1864. They are frequently implanted among quartz crystals in nests or geodes, and are covered with a hairy growth of wire silver.

Crystals of silver ore from Silver Mountain district are probably this species.

Stibnite.—Tulare county, in a large vein near the Pass of San Amédio (vide Rep. Geol. Rec Cal., pp. 292-3.) It occurs in large, solid masses, boulders of which are numerous in the beds of the arroyos leading from the vein. In Nevada, at or near the Gem mine, Dunglen; at the Sheba mine, in beautiful needle-like crystals, and at the De Soto and other mines in that vicinity; in Russ district, Great Basin.

Stroymeyerite.—Arizona. Heintzelman mine.

Sulphur.—Colusa county; Napa county, at the Geysers. In Nevada, in extinct solfataras, Humboldt valley.

Sulphuret of silver—Nevada, Comstock lode; occurs with stephanite in the Ophir, Mexican, Gould & Curry, and other mines upon that line of claims. It is also present in the ore of the vein at Gold Hill, and appears to be the chief source of the silver in those ores. It has not been observed in crystals. In the large chamber of the Ophir mine, in eighteen hundred and sixty-one, it was very abundant, in irregular masses ramifying through the fragmentary white quartz so as to hold it together in hand specimens. Large masses of vein-stuff could be broken down, in which the sulphuret of silver constituted at least half of the whole weight. Native gold was commonly associated with it in that part of the mine. It is now more frequently found associated with copper pyrites and galena. This species is also found in small crystals in the ore of the Daney mine, associated with native silver, gold, and ruby silver. It is common in the ores of Reese river, associated with ruby silver and manganese spar. It is probably the chief ore of silver in the Cortez district.

Sulphuret of iron—(See *Iron pyrites.*)

Telluret of silver.—El Dorado county. (See *Silver.*)

Tetrahedrite, (*gray copper.*)—Mariposa county, with the gold in the Pine Tree vein; also with the gold in the same or similar vein at the Crown lode, Emily Peak, and at Coulterville in several claims. Calaveras county, at Carson Hill, in the large vein, and associated with gold. This ore, in decomposing, leaves a blue stain of carbonate in the quartz, and where it is found the rock is generally rich in gold. In Nevada it occurs abundantly in the Sheba mine, Humboldt county, massive and rich in silver. It is associated with the following species, which were noted from time to time by Mr. Moss, the superintendent, and in part by the author: Ruby silver, argentiferous galena, antimonial galena, iron pyrites, blende, cerusite, calcite, quartz with acicular antimony, sulphuret of antimony in delicate needles and massive native silver, bournonite. Found also in Lander county, with the silver ores of the veins near Austin; at the Comet lode, Veatch cañon, south of Austin. Los Angeles county—at the Zapata claim, San Gabriel mountains. Arizona—at the Heintzelman mine, containing from one to one and a half per cent. of silver. (Pumpelly.) Also, at the Santa Rita mine, associated with galena.

Tellurium and gold, (*tetradymite?*)—At the Melones and Stanislaus mines, one mile south of Carson Hill, Calaveras county. Very beautiful specimens of native gold, associated with tellurium, were taken out of a vein from six to eighteen inches thick, and at a depth of two hundred feet from the surface. This telluret has a tin-white color, and is not foliated like the tetradymite from the Field vein in Georgia. Its exact specific character is not yet determined.

Tin ore, (*oxyd of tin.*)—(See *Cassiterite.*)

Topaz.—In clear, colorless crystals, finely terminated, from one-eighth of an inch to half an inch in diameter, found in the tin washings of Durango, Mexico. (Cabinet of the author, 1864.) Noticed by C. F. Chandler, American Journal of Science, 1865.

Tourmaline.—San Diego county, north side of the valley of San Felipe, in feldspathic veins, (for description and figures see Rep. Geol. Rec.Cal., Blake, p. 304;) Tuolumne county.

Tremolite.—White and fibrous in limestone, Columbia, Tuolumne county.

Tungstate of manganese.—With tungstate of lime, in the Mammoth mining district, Nevada. (C. T. Jackson, Proc. Cal. Acad., iii, 199.)

Variegated copper ore, ("*Horseflesh ore.*")—Sigel lode, in Plumas county.

Vitreous copper.—(See *Copper Glance.*)

Zinc.—(See *Blende.*)

Principal public and private mineralogical and geological collections in California, known to the author.

I.—PUBLIC COLLECTIONS.

STATE GEOLOGICAL COLLECTION—Sacramento and San Francisco; not arranged, and in part destroyed by fire in eighteen hundred and sixty-five, at the Pacific warehouse.

STATE AGRICULTURAL SOCIETY'S—At Sacramento; partly in cases, but not classified or arranged.

SAN JOAQUIN AGRICULTURAL SOCIETY—At Stockton; collected chiefly by Dr. Holden; not large, nor well arranged.

CALIFORNIA ACADEMY OF NATURAL SCIENCES—At San Francisco; not arranged; in boxes, and stored, awaiting a suitable room or building for their display. This collection was made in great part by and through the exertions of Dr. J. G Trask, and has many valuable specimens taken from our mines soon after their discovery.

COLLEGE OF CALIFORNIA—At Oakland. A collection of minerals and fossils of California; partly arranged.

SANTA CLARA COLLEGE. (No particulars known.)

ODD FELLOWS' LIBRARY ASSOCIATION—At San Francisco. A valuable miscellaneous collection of minerals, ores, fossils, and curiosities, chiefly the donation of the members of the Order; arranged in cases, at the Hall. The Order is indebted, chiefly, for this valuable addition to their rooms, to the zeal and enthusiasm of their president, S. H. Parker, esq.

OCCIDENTAL HOTEL—Lewis Leland, San Francisco. A collection containing many very choice and valuable specimens of ores and precious metals of the Pacific coast.

II.—PRIVATE COLLECTIONS.

W. P. BLAKE—At San Francisco and Oakland. A collection of minerals, ores, geological specimens, and fossils, from California, Nevada, Arizona, Idaho, Mexico, the eastern States, Japan, and China, with some European minerals. About sixty boxes of this collection were destroyed in the Pacific warehouse, by fire, in eighteen hundred and sixty-five. A portion, stored at the college and elsewhere, was uninjured. It is now partly in boxes, and partly in cases, in San Francisco, and at the College of California, Oakland. There are probably five thousand to six thousand specimens, a great part of them selected by the owner at the localities. It contains a valuable and extensive suit of crystalline gold.

Dr. J. M. FREY—Sacramento. A large and valuable miscellaneous collection of Pacific coast minerals, including a fine suit of gold in crystals. Arranged in part, in cases, in Sacramento

Dr. JOHN HEWSTON, Jr.—San Francisco. Miscellaneous collection.

Dr. JONES—Murphy's, Calaveras county. A miscellaneous collection, chiefly local.

A. P. MOLITOR—San Francisco. Miscellaneous collection.

R. L. OGDEN—San Francisco. A miscellaneous collection of copper and gold ores. A large collection made by this gentleman up to eighteen hundred and sixty-one, was purchased by W. P. Blake, in eighteen hundred and sixty-one.

AUGUSTE RÉMOND—San Francisco . (No particulars known.)

Dr. SNELL—Sonora, Tuolumne county. A rich and valuable collection of fossils and aboriginal relics from the auriferous gravel under Table mountain, and of minerals and ores from that region. This is the richest collection of relics of the mastodon and the mammoth in California.

T. J. SPEAR—San Francisco; formerly at Georgetown, in eighteen hundred and sixty-two and three. A small miscellaneous collection, which included an ammonite, from the gold slates of the American river; valuable to science as one of the evidences of the secondary age of the gold-bearing rocks of California.

Dr. STOUT—San Francisco. A miscellaneous collection of Eastern and European specimens, arranged in cases.

C. W. SMITH—Grass valley, Nevada county. An interesting collection, arranged in cases, and containing some choice specimens from the mines of Grass valley.

Dr. WHITE—Placerville, El Dorado county. A miscellaneous collection, containing many interesting specimens from that region,.and some foreign minerals, by exchange.

W. R. WATERS—Sacramento. Miscellaneous collection of minerals and ores, arranged in case.

Notes on the geographical distribution and geology of the precious metals and valuable minerals on the Pacific slope of the United States.

If we attempt to delineate by colors upon a map the geographical distribution of the gold, silver, copper, and quicksilver localities of the Pacific slope, we obtain a series of nearly parallel belts or zones, following the general course or trend of the mountain chains and of the coast. So, also, if we enter the Golden Gate and travel eastward across the country to the Rocky mountains, we pass successively through zones or belts of country characterized mineralogically by different metals and minerals.

In the Coast mountains, for example, quicksilver is the chief, and the highly characteristic economical mineral. The localities of its ore are strung along the mountains through the counties north and south of the Golden Gate. We have also petroleum, sulphur, and calcareous springs, nearly coincident in their distribution. Passing from this grouping of minerals eastward over the coal beds of Mount Diablo, and crossing the great interior valley of California, (probably underlaid by lignite,) we rise upon the slope of the Sierra Nevada, and reach the copper-producing rocks. These form a well marked zone, which has been traced almost uninterruptedly from Mariposa to Oregon, following the lower hills of the Sierra Nevada.

East of the copper belt, (and in the central counties, over a chain of hills known as "Bear mountains,") we find the great gold-bearing zone, characterized by lines of quartz ledges, following the mountains in their general northwesterly and southeasterly course. This gold belt is composite in its character—the veins traversing either slates, limestones, sandstones, or granite.

Crossing the snow-covered crest of the Sierra, where in some parts iron ores have been found, we leave the region of gold and enter that of silver, mingled with gold, extending up and down the interior eastern slope of the Sierra throughout California, into Arizona and Mexico on the south, and Idaho on the north.

At the Reese River mountains, further east, towards Salt Lake, the gold is replaced by silver, associated with copper, antimony, and arsenic; and this grouping is in its turn replaced by the gold-bearing sulphurets of the Rocky mountains. This is the *general* distribution of the precious metals. There are, doubtless, local exceptions.

It is evident that this distribution of the metals and minerals in zones has been determined by the nature of the rocky strata, and by their condition of metamorphism. It is worthy of note that the minerals of the coast ranges are chiefly the more volatile and soluble, such as cinnabar, sulphur, petroleum, and borax, distributed in rocks ranging from the tertiary to the cretaceous, inclusive.

The longitudinal extension of the gold-bearing zone is yet undetermined. The metal has been traced through the whole length of California, through Oregon and Washington, into British Columbia, and beyond, along the Russian possessions, towards the Arctic sea. Southward, it is prolonged into Sonora and Mexico, and there is every reason to believe that its extension is coincident with the great mountain chain of North America in its course around the globe, into and through Asia.

After years of laborious search for fossils by which the age of the gold-bearing rocks might be determined, I had the pleasure, early in 1863, to obtain a specimen containing *Ammonites* from a locality on the American river, preserved in the cabinet of Mr. Spear. This fossil was of extreme importance, being indicative of the secondary age of the gold-bearing slates, and was therefore photographed, and copies of it sent to the Smithsonian Institution at Washington, for description. It was subsequently noticed in the proceedings of the California Academy of Natural Sciences, September, 1864. The same year, when at Bear valley, Mariposa county, upon the chief gold-bearing rocks of California, I identified a group of secondary fossils from the slates contiguous to the Pine Tree vein, and noticed them at a meeting of the California Academy, October 3, 1864, announcing the jurassic or cretaceous age of these slates. The best characterized fossil was a *Plagiostoma,* (or *Lima,*) to which I provisionally attached the name *Erringtoni.** The attention of the geological survey having been directed to this locality by my announcement and exhibition of the fossils in San Francisco and at the academy, Mr. Gabb, the palæontologist of the survey, visited the locality and obtained specimens. These fossils were of such interest and importance to science, and to the geological description of the State, that an extra plate was engraved for them and published in the appendix to the volume on the geology, recently issued.†

Fossils of the secondary age from Genesee valley, in the northern part of the State, were common in collections in 1864, and are described by the State Geological Survey, volume one, "Palæontology." It appears also, from the same source, that Mr. King, a gentleman connected with the survey, had obtained *belemites* from the Mariposa rocks in 1864, but no figures or description are given.

We may thus regard the secondary age of a part, at least, of the gold-bearing rocks of the Sierra Nevada as established, a result of no small importance practically, for it destroys the dogma, which has been very generally accepted, that the Silurian or Palæozoic rocks are the repositories of the gold of the globe. We may now look for gold in regions where before it was generally presumed to be absent, because the formations were not Silurian or Palæozoic.

The Silurian age of the gold rocks of California has not always been assumed. It has been repeatedly questioned. In the preface to the writer's "Report of a Geological Reconnoissance in California," it is stated that a considerable part of the gold-bearing slates of California are probably carboniferous. The absence of all evidence of Silurian fossils west of the Rocky mountains is also distinctly noted. (p. 276.) The opinion of the comparatively modern age of the gold

---

* In honor of Miss Errington, a lady residing on the estate, who drew my attention to some impressions on the slates which she had picked up on the English trail, which proved to be fossils.

† I regret to observe that in this publication, as well as in Mr. Gabb's notice of the fossils, no mention is made of my previous announcement, and that my part in the discovery and publication of the secondary age of the Mariposa gold rocks is studiously and wholly ignored.

rocks has been steadily gaining strength and support for years past, and has been the subject of discussion in the daily journals.

The prevalence of gold in the Coast mountains, in or in close proximity to rocks of *tertiary* age, leads us to question whether it may not occur in the rocks of this late period also. The fact, recently ascertained, that gold is very generally associated with cinnabar, makes it more than probable that the metal has been deposited in formations as recent even as the Miocene, (or middle tertiary,) for, according to the best evidence we now have, this is the age of a part, at least, of the quicksilver-bearing rocks.

Such a result need not surprise us, although so far in opposition to generally existing views of the geological association of gold. The geological age of the rocks has manifestly nothing to do with the deposition of gold; it is only necessary that the rocks should have a favorable mineral composition and a suitable degree of metamorphism. On this general view, we may be prepared to find gold in rocks of any geological period, from the tertiary to the Laurentian or Huronian rocks, inclusive.

The lithology of the chief gold-bearing zone or belt of rocks of California is interesting. The chief or "mother vein" extends through several counties, with occasional breaks or interruptions; and throughout its course preserves its distinguishing characters. It follows also the same geological horizon or zone, keeping between well-marked geological and geographical boundaries, so that a description of the strata adjoining it at one place will serve to give a general view of them throughout. A cross-section in considerable detail was made on the Mariposa estate in eighteen hundred and sixty-four. This estate includes the southern end of the "Great Vein," there known as the "Pine Tree." It also includes several veins lying west of the line of the Pine Tree, of which the most important is the "Princeton," noted for its richness and large production of gold. This group of veins follows a long valley between two high ridges — Bear Mountain on the west, and Mount Bullion on the east. These ridges are formed of hard rocks; the rocks of the valley are argillaceous and sandy slates and sandstones. The stratification of these slates is remarkably regular and distinct; their thin outcrops standing sharply out at intervals in long lines in the ravines and on the hillsides, mark their trend, and show that they are nearly vertical, or have a slight inclination northeast or easterly. The general direction of the outcrops and of the valley is northwest and southeast; but there are several local variations.

These slates are generally light colored or drab at the surface; but in depth they are black, like roofing slate, and break up into rhomboids. This is particularly well shown at the Princeton vein. There are numerous intercalations of sandy layers passing into sandstones — sometimes into coarse grits, and even pebbly beds, and beds of slaty conglomerate. The softer and most finely laminated portion of the group is generally found near the medial line of the valley, and is the point at which the Princeton vein occurs. It is near this part of the series, at the northern end of the estate, that the jurassic fossils occur.

The following is an approximate geological section of the estate, at right angles to the course of the rocks, and nearly over the Princeton vein. It is a composite section, being made up of three distinct portions where the observations had extended, but all near together, so as to present a fair view of the sequence of the formations. The whole embraces a distance of about four miles, according to the scale of the small published map of the estate. The southwestern end is taken along Bear creek, the middle portion across the Princeton vein, and the remainder on a line near Upper Agua Fria, northeasterly to Bullion ridge. The following is the sequence of formations from west to east:

SECTION ACROSS THE MARIPOSAS.

1. Coarse, heavy conglomerates, metamorphosed—Bear mountains.
2. Compact crystalline slates; crystalline cleavage.
3. Conglomerate; slaty.
4. Argillaceous slates, regularly stratified; thick series.
5. Sandstone and sandy beds, (thin.)
6. Princeton gold vein; quartz three feet thick.
7. Argillaceous slates and quartz veins; the horizon of the jurassic fossils.
8. Magnesian rock and quartz veins.
9. Pine Tree, or "Mother Vein," or its extension.
10. Argillaceous slates.
11. Conglomerate; slaty.
12. Compact slates.
13 Greenstone, limited in extent; probably a metamorphosed sandstone.
14. Sandstones and sandy slates.
15. Serpentine and magnesian rocks—the northern extension of Buckeye ridge.
16. Compact slates, crystalline and much metamorphosed.
17. Conglomerates and sandstones, heavy and massive; the so-called "greenstone" of Mount Bullion range.

This is the general outline of the formations. Both of the bounding ranges of the valley are formed by the heavy metamorphic conglomerates, so much altered and changed as to be scarcely recognizable. They are generally supposed to be formed of greenstone, and in some places they do not give any evidence of their sedimentary origin; in others, the outlines of the pebbles and boulders are distinct. These boulders are remarkably large and heavy. From the general similarity of the rocks of these two ranges—Bear mountain on the west, and Bullion range on the east—together with the succession and character of the formations between, I am led to regard the whole series as a fold or plication, and the valley as either synclinal or anticlinal—probably the former.*

Bear Mountain range is prolonged far to the north into Calaveras county, and there forms the separation between the valley of Copperopolis, traversed by the Reed or Union copper lode, and the gold quartz region of Angel's camp and Carson Hill. The whole belt of formations from Amador county, southeastward, through Calaveras, Tuolumne, and Mariposa counties, is an interesting field for a geologist to work up, to show not only the geographical extent of the rocks and the veins, but the structure or folding of the whole. The two lines of hard conglomerate forming the high ridges are distinct for nearly the whole distance. The serpentine rocks which accompany the gold formation are probably the result of local metamorphic action, for they often occur in lenticular or elipsoidal patches in the other rocks. So also the greenstone, in places, appears to be an altered portion of rocks, which at other points are distinctly sedimentary, and exhibit slaty stratification.

---

* The above section of the gold formation of the estate, and the substance of the observations upon it, were given in a report to F. L. Olmsted, esq., in eighteen hundred and sixty-four. Inedited.

SECTION 10.

LAWS AND CUSTOMS OF FOREIGN GOVERNMENTS IN RELATION TO THE OCCUPANCY OF MINERAL LANDS AND THE WORKING OF MINES.

1. The crown right.—2. Permanent titles to the mineral lands of the United States.

I.—THE CROWN RIGHT.
[Compiled from references in the New Almaden case.]

By the civil law all veins and mineral deposits of gold and silver ore, or of precious stones, belonged, if in public ground, to the sovereign, and were part of his patrimony; but if on private property, they belonged to the owner of the land, subject to the condition that if worked by the owner he was bound to render a tenth part of the produce to the prince, as a right attaching to his crown; and that, if worked by any other person by consent of the owner, the former was liable to the payment of two-tenths, one to the prince, and one to the owner of the property. Subsequently it became an established custom in most kingdoms, and was declared by the particular laws and statutes of each, that all veins of the precious metals, and the produce of such veins, should vest in the Crown, and be held to be part of the patrimony of the King or sovereign prince. That this is the case with respect to the empire of Germany, the electorates, France, Portugal, Arragon, and Catalonia appears from the laws of each of those countries, and from the authority of various authors.

And the reason is, that the metals are applicable to the use of the public, who ought not to be prejudiced by any impediments being thrown in the way of the discovering and working of their ores; besides which their products rank, not among those of an ordinary description, but among the most precious the earth affords; and, therefore, instead of being appropriated to individuals, are proper to be set apart for the sovereign himself, whose coffers being thus enriched, he will be enabled to lighten the burdens of the people; all which is set forth at length by the authors above referred to.

This question, as is observed by the great Cardinal de Luca, has not received any general or uniform determination, but is decided by the laws and customs of each particular kingdom or principality; for upon the breaking up of the Roman empire the princes and states which declared themselves independent appropriated to themselves those tracts of ground in which nature had dispensed her more valuable products with more than ordinary liberality, which reserved portions or rights were called rights of the Crown. Among the chief of the valuable products are the metallic ores of the first class—as those of gold, silver, and other metals proper for forming money, which it is essential for sovereigns to be provided with in order to support their warlike armaments by sea or land, to provide for the public necessities, and to maintain the good government of their dominions. And such is the course mentioned in the first book of Maccabees to have been pursued by the Romans with regard to the mines of Spain, and such also is the plan adopted by our sovereigns with regard to those of the Indies, some of which they have reserved to themselves, and the remainder they have left to their subjects, charged with the payment of a fifth, tenth, or twentieth part of the produce.

According to the law of England the only mines which are termed royal, and which are the exclusive property of the Crown, are mines of silver and gold; and this property is so peculiarly a branch of the royal prerogative that it has been said that though the King grant lands in which mines are, and all mines in them, yet royal mines will not pass by a general description.

This prerogative is said to have originated in the King's right of coinage, in order to supply him with materials. It may be observed, however, that the

right of coinage in the earlier periods of European society was not always exclusively exercised by the Crown ; that the same reason might apply to other
metals—as copper and tin—and that in those rude times the prerogative was
perhaps as likely to have its origin in the circumstance of those rare and
beautiful metals having always been among the most cherished objects of ambition, and which were, therefore, appropriated to the use of the Crown, like
the diamonds of India, in order to sustain the splendor and dignity of its rank.

Whatever reason may be assigned for this right of the Crown, and of whatever value the right may be, it has been long decided not only that all the mines
of gold and silver within the realm, though in the lands of subjects, belong exclusively to the Crown by prerogative, but that this right is also accompanied
with full liberty to dig and carry away the ores, and with all other such incidents thereto as are necessary to be usual for getting them.

This right of entry is disputed by Lord Hardwicke, in a case where there
was a grant from the Crown of lands with a reservation of all royal mines, but
not of a right of entry. The lord chancellor said he was of opinion that there
was by the terms of the grant no such power in the Crown, and that by the royal
prerogative of mines the Crown had given no such power, for it would be very
prejudicial if the Crown could enter into a subject's lands, or grant a license to
work the mines ; but that when they were once opened it could restrain the
owner of the soil from working them, and could either work them itself or grant
a license for others to work them.

In the days of Queen Elizabeth the rights of miners were discussed in a legal
controversy, in which some of the ablest men in England participated. Two
men, named Howseter and Thurland, went, without permission, upon the lands
of the Earl of Northumberland, and commenced digging for copper ore. The
earl warned them off. They made complaint to the Queen's attorney general,
stating that the ores contained some silver or gold, and he prosecuted the earl
for resisting the efforts of these miners in extracting the precious metals from
the earth, for the reason that all the gold and silver in the earth within the
realm belonged to the Queen and not to the owner of the land. All the justices
of England heard the argument and took part in the discussion.

The question principally debated was, whether by the prerogative of the
Crown all ores containing silver or gold belonged to the Crown as a part of
regalia.

The judges decided that all gold or silver ores belonged to the Crown,
whether in private or public lands; that any ores containing neither gold nor
silver belonged to the proprietor of the soil ; that the King could grant away
mines of gold or silver, but not without express words in his patent demon-
strating his intention to sever the mines from his royal patrimony.

Some of the reasons upon which the arguments were based were expressed in
felicitous though quaint language, and are worthy of being reproduced :

1. "And the reason is that metals are applicable to the use of the public,
&c.;   *   *   *   besides which, their products rank, not among
those of an ordinary description, but among the most precious the earth affords, and, therefore, instead of being appropriated to individuals, are proper to
be set apart for the sovereign himself, whose coffers, being thus enriched, &c.
*   *   *   Among the chief of the valuable products are the metallic
ores of the first class, as those of gold, silver, and other metals proper for forming money, which it is essential for the sovereign to be provided with in order
to support their warlike armaments by sea and land, to provide for the public
necessities, and to maintain the good government of their dominions," &c., &c.
—(And. Plowdin, 315.)

2. "As to the first of these three points Onslow alleged three reasons why
the King shall have the mines and ores of gold or silver within the realm in
whatever land they are found. The first was in respect to the excellency of the

thing;   *   *   *   and the common law, which is founded upon reason, appropriates everything to the person whom it best suits, as common and trivial things to the common people, things of more worth to persons in a higher and superior class, and things most excellent to those persons who excel all others; and because gold and silver are the most excellent things which the soil contains, the law has appropriated them (as in reason it ought) to the person who is most excellent, and that is the King."

3. " For the same reason, he says, it has given him "whales and sturgeons " which are in the sea in England—that is, "in the arms of the sea or water within the land, so that the excellency of the King's person draws to it things of an excellent nature. The second reason was in respect of the necessity of the thing; for the King is the head of the public weal, and the subjects are his members, and the office of the King, to which the law has appointed him, is to preserve his subjects; and their preservation consists in two things, viz: in an army to defend them against hostilities, and in good laws. And an army cannot be had and maintained without treasure, for which reason some authors, in their books, call treasure the sinews of war.   *   *   *   *   And, therefore, as God has created mines within this realm as a natural provision of treasure for the defence of the realm, it is reasonable that he who has the government and care of the people, whom he cannot defend without treasure, should have the treasure wherewith to defend them. The third reason was in respect of its convenience to the subjects in the way of mutual commerce and traffic; but one has need of the things which another has, and they cannot sell or buy together without coin. It belongs to the King only to fix the value of coin, and to ascertain the price of the quantity, and to put the print upon it; for if he (a subject) makes coin, it was high treason by the common law."

Act of Congress for the occupation and sale of the mineral lands of the United States.

In the annual report of the Secretary of the Treasury for the year 1865, the substitution of an absolute title in fee for the indefinite possessory rights or claims under which the mines were held by private parties was earnestly recommended.

The following extracts from the Secretary's report embody the main considerations by which Congress was governed in the passage of the act approved August, 1866:

"The attention of Congress is again called to the importance of early and definite action upon the subject of our mineral lands, in which subject are involved questions not only of revenue, but social questions of a most interesting character.

" Copartnership relations between the government and miners will hardly be proposed, and a system of leasehold, (if it were within the constitutional authority of Congress to adopt it, and if it were consistent with the character and genius of our people,) after the lessons which have been taught of its practical results in the lead and copper districts, cannot of course be recommended.

"After giving the subject as much examination as the constant pressure of official duties would permit, the Secretary has come to the conclusion that the best policy to be pursued with regard to these lands is the one which shall substitute an absolute title in fee for the indefinite possessory rights or claims now asserted by miners.

" The right to obtain a 'fee simple in the soil' would invite to the mineral districts men of character and enterprise; by creating homes, (which will not be found where title to property cannot be secured,) it would give permanency to the settlements, and, by the stimulus which ownership always produces, it would result in a thorough and regular development of the mines.

"A bill for the subdivision and sale of the gold and silver lands of the United States was under consideration by the last Congress, to which attention is respectfully called. If the enactment of this bill should not be deemed expedient, and no satisfactory substitute can be reported for the sale of these lands to the highest bidder, on account of the possessory claims of miners, it will then be important that the policy of extending the principle of pre-emption to the mineral districts be considered. It is not material, perhaps, how the end shall be attained, but there can be no question that it is of the highest importance, in a financial and social point of view, that ownership of these lands, in limited quantities to each purchaser, should be within the reach of the people of the United States who may desire to explore and develop them.

"In this connection it may be advisable for Congress to consider whether the prosperity of the treasure-producing districts would not be increased, and the convenience of miners greatly promoted, by the establishment of an assay office in every mining district from which an annual production of gold and silver amounting to ten millions of dollars is actually obtained."

Mr. Conness, chairman of the Committee on Mines and Mining of the Senate, made the following report, May 28, 1866 :

The Committee on Mines and Mining, to whom was referred Senate bill No. 257, "An act to regulate the occupation of mineral lands, and to extend the right of pre-emption thereto," have had the same under consideration, and beg leave to report a substitute, and to recommend its passage.

By this bill it is only proposed to dispose of the vein mines, and to provide for the segregation of the agricultural lands lying within the mineral regions. The proposition contained in it is to transfer the title of the United States to the possessors at a reasonable rate, and as a part of that rate to secure the payment of a percentage of the net proceeds of the vein mines into the treasury, until the present burdensome public debt shall be paid ; this percentage to be in lieu of all tax imposed upon bullion at the mints and assay offices under existing laws.

It is not proposed to interfere with, or impose any tax upon, the miners engaged in working placer mines, as those mines are readily exhausted, and not generally remunerative to those engaged in working them.

Your committee, in arriving at the conclusions they have, and recommending the passage of an act to provide for investing the miners of the country with the fee-simple to their vein mines, have not been unmindful of what the country owes to the enterprising men who have gone into the forests and recesses of the western States and Territories, and who have developed to the commerce of the world the heretofore hidden treasures therein ; they who, by patient and often ill-requited toil, without aid from the government in any manner whatever, have shown the ample foundation of the national credit in the mineral resources of the public domain. That policy by which the greatest amount of the precious metals shall be produced, and the greatest individual and aggregate wealth amassed by our own people, must be the wisest and best.

There has been constant fear felt by those who are engaged in promoting these results that some disturbance and interference with vested rights of property would occur. Measures for the sale of the mines and for the taxation of those engaged in working them have, from time to time, been proposed, creating the deepest apprehensions and most seriously affecting mining property. It is a first duty that all such doubts and fears shall be set at rest by the promulgation of a policy which shall give full and complete protection to all existing possessory rights upon liberal conditions, and with full and complete legal guarantees, and to provide the most generous conditions looking toward further explorations and developments.

There are widely differing opinions as to the course proper to be pursued between the population of the mining regions and the people of the east, whose representatives in Congress too often, without exact knowledge on the subject, propose heavy burdens upon the mining industry. The mass of people living in the mines feel that the mines should be left free and open to and within the reach of the hardy explorer and adventurer without tax or impost whatever; nay, feeling the many disappointments and failures to which they are subject in their efforts to acquire wealth from this source, they believe that the government of the United States, which they love, should rather offer rewards from the public treasury for the discovery of mines, than that such discovery should be but the signal for measures of taxation.

They also fear all systems of sale, lest any which should be adopted might result in a monopoly of the mines and their concentration into few hands. They are jealous of all systems for the disposition of the mineral lands which shall allow the lands to be bought by the fortunate possessors of large capital, in extensive bodies, to the exclusion of the men whose only capital consists in their labor. They, nevertheless, will readily acquiesce in any plan which shall confirm existing rights at reasonable rates, and which shall be safe against the evils to which your committee have referred.

The amount proposed is five dollars per acre for the vein mines and all the land adjoining necessary for working them, and the payment of three per cent. of the net product of all such mines into the treasury of the United States, which shall be in lieu of the present impost.

It will be remembered that the present tax was adopted in preference to the five per cent. tax on the *gross proceeds* of the mines proposed by the House of Representatives in 1864. Any tax on the gross product of mines must be purely a tax upon effort, and must result, as the recent tax on crude petroleum did, in the ruin of those engaged in the business, and a serious limit on production.

Another feature of the bill recommended is, that it adopts the rules and regulations of miners in the mining districts where the same are not in conflict with the laws of the United States. This renders secure all existing rights of property, and will prove at once a just and popular feature of the new policy. Those "rules and regulations" are well understood, and form the basis of the present admirable system in the mining regions: arising out of necessity, they became the means adopted by the people themselves for establishing just protection to all.

In the absence of legislation and statute law, the local courts, beginning with California, recognize those "rules and regulations," the central idea of which was *priority of possession*, and have given to the country rules of decision so equitable as to be commanding in its natural justice, and to have secured universal approbation. The California reports will compare favorably, in this respect, with the history of jurisprudence in any part of the world. Thus the miners' "rules and regulations" are not only well understood, but have been construed and adjudicated for now nearly a quarter of a century.

It will be readily seen how essential it is that this great system, established by the people in their primary capacities, and evidencing by the highest possible testimony the peculiar genius of the American people for founding empire and order, shall be preserved and affirmed. Popular sovereignty is here displayed in one of its grandest aspects, and simply invites us not to destroy, but to put upon it the stamp of national power and unquestioned authority.

This should be done generously, for the nation's sake. Those brave men who have established a high civilization on the far-off Pacific, whose hearts, in the nation's trials, beat so true, and who are now fast closing in upon the civilization of your own west, should be made to feel, not that you are masters, but brethren and friends.

By their loyalty they gave you peace where your power was scarcely felt; by their industry they gave the solid base of silver and gold to the national issues and the national credit, and it is left to history to balance and to tell how, without that peace their patriotism so well preserved, and that silver and gold which their industry gave the nation, the national cause could have been equally benefited. From their earnings, too, came those contributions which will forever form so beautiful a chaplet around their own brows. They set the highest example of a Christian people, patriotic and peaceful, sturdy and loyal to freedom, industrious and charitable. It is for such a people that we legislate.

The necessity for the segregation of the agricultural part of the public domain from that which is purely mineral is of the first character. It will be remembered that mining alone cannot supply a single human want, and no community would eventually be so poor as a mining community purely. But the miner is nearly always the pioneer of society where mines exist—shortly, however, to be followed by the agriculturist and the artisan. Mutual production and exchange result, and society is established. Nothing renders society so stable as giving to the people the title to the land upon which they live. They learn to love it, and are the first to find out its greatest value, and consequently to employ it for the highest uses. Homes of a permanent character are thus established, and the school-house and church follow to light the path and to cheer the way through life. To these ends the earliest ownership should be given to him who, by patient and virtuous toil, proposes to become a cornerstone to community. Every wise consideration demands that the segregation of the agricultural lands from those purely mining should be made, and this bill makes such provision.

Your committee are aware that they tread new ground, but they bring many years of experience to the task, and the light has been used to reach the end which will promote the greatest happiness of the citizen and the glory of the republic.*

The following is a copy of the act of Congress approved August —, 1866, to legalize the occupation of the mineral lands, and for other purposes :

SECTION 1. That the mineral lands of the public domain, both surveyed and unsurveyed, are hereby declared to be free and open to exploration and occupation by all citizens of the United States, and those who have declared their intention to become citizens, subject to such regulations as may be prescribed by law, and subject also to local custom or rules of miners in the several mining districts, so far as the same may not be in conflict with the laws of the United States.

SEC. 2. *And be it further enacted,* That whenever any person or association of persons claim a vein or lode of quartz, or other rock in place, bearing gold, silver, cinnabar, or copper, having previously occupied and improved the same according to the local custom or rules of miners in the district where the same is situated, and having expended in actual labor and improvements thereon an amount not less than one thousand dollars, and in regard to whose possession there is no controversy or opposing claim, it shall and may be lawful for said claimant or association of claimants to file in the local land office a diagram of the same, so extended laterally or otherwise as to conform to the local laws, customs, and rules of miners, and to enter such tract and receive a patent therefor, granting such mine, together with the right to follow such vein or

---

* See Congressional Globe for debates on this bill.

lode, with its dips, angles, and variations, to any depth, although it may enter the land adjoining, which land adjoining shall be sold subject to this condition.

SEC. 3. *And be it further enacted*, That upon the filing of the diagram as provided in the second section of this act, and posting the same in a conspicuous place on the claim; together with a notice of intention to apply for a patent, the register of the land office shall publish a notice of the same in a newspaper published nearest to the location of said claim, and shall also post such notice in his office for the period of ninety days; and after the expiration of said period, if no adverse claim shall have been filed, it shall be the duty of the surveyor general, upon application of the party, to survey the premises and make a plat thereof, indorsed with his approval, designating the number and description of the location, the value of the labor and improvements, and the character of the vein exposed; and upon the payment to the proper officer of five dollars per acre, together with the cost of such survey, plat, and notice, and giving satisfactory evidence that said diagram and notice have been posted on the claim during said period of ninety days, the register of the land office shall transmit to the General Land Office said plat, survey, and description; and a patent shall issue for the same thereupon. But said plat, survey, or description shall in no case cover more than one vein or lode, and no patent shall issue for more than one vein or lode, which shall be expressed in the patent issued.

SEC. 4. *And be it further enacted*, That when such location and entry of a mine shall be upon unsurveyed lands, it shall and may be lawful, after the extension thereto of the public surveys, to adjust the surveys to the limits of the premises according to the location and possession and plat aforesaid, and the surveyor general may, in extending the surveys, vary the same from a rectangular form to suit the circumstances of the country and the local rules, laws, and customs of miners : *Provided*, That no location hereafter made shall exceed two hundred feet in length along the vein for each locator, with an additional claim for discovery to the discoverer of the lode, with the right to follow such vein to any depth, with all its dips, variations, and angles, together with a reasonable quantity of surface for the convenient working of the same as fixed by local rules : *And provided further*, That no person may make more than one location on the same lode, and not more than three thousand feet shall be taken in any one claim by any association of persons.

SEC. 5. *And be it further enacted*, That as a further condition of sale, in the absence of necessary legislation by Congress, the local legislature of any State or Territory may provide rules for working mines involving easements, drainage, and other necessary means to their complete development; and those conditions shall be fully expressed in the patent.

SEC. 6. *And be it further enacted*, That whenever any adverse claimants to any mine located and claimed as aforesaid shall appear before the approval of the survey, as provided in the third section of this act, all proceedings shall be stayed until a final settlement and adjudication in the courts of competent jurisdiction of the rights of possession to such claim, when a patent may issue as in other cases.

SEC. 7. *And be it further enacted*, That the President of the United States be, and is hereby, authorized to establish additional land districts, and to appoint the necessary officers under existing laws, wherever he may deem the same necessary for the public convenience in executing the provisions of this act.

SEC. 8. *And be it further enacted*, That the right of way for the construction of highways over public lands, not reserved for public uses, is hereby granted.

SEC. 9. *And be it further enacted*, That whenever, by priority of possession, rights to the use of water for mining, agricultural, manufacturing, or other purposes, have vested and accrued, and the same are recognized and acknowledged by the local customs, laws, and the decisions of courts, the possessors and owners of such vested rights shall be maintained and protected in the same; and the right of way for the construction of ditches and canals for the purposes aforesaid is hereby acknowledged and confirmed. *Provided, however:* That whenever, after the passage of this act, any person or persons shall, in the construction of any ditch or canal, injure or damage the possession of any settler on the public domain, the party committing such injury or damage shall be liable to the party injured for such injury or damage.

SEC. 10. *And be it further enacted,* That wherever, prior to the passage of this act, upon the lands heretofore designated as mineral lands, which have been excluded from survey and sale, there have been homesteads made by citizens of the United States, or persons who have declared their intention to become citizens, which homesteads have been made, improved, and used for agricultural purposes, and upon which there have been no valuable mines of gold, silver, cinnabar, or copper discovered, and which are properly agricultural lands, the said settlers or owners of such homesteads shall have a right of pre-emption thereto, and shall be entitled to purchase the same at the price of one dollar and twenty-five cents per acre, and in quantity not to exceed one hundred and sixty acres; or said parties may avail themselves of the provisions of the act of Congress approved May 20, 1862, entitled "An act to secure homesteads to actual settlers on the public domain," and acts amendatory thereof.

SEC. 11. *And be it further enacted,* That upon the survey of the lands aforesaid, the Secretary of the Interior may designate and set apart such portions of the said lands as are clearly agricultural lands, which lands shall thereafter be subject to pre-emption and sale as other public lands of the United States, and subject to all the laws and regulations applicable to the same.

2.—PERMANENT TITLES TO MINERAL LANDS IN THE UNITED STATES.

In glancing back over the history of California for the last eighteen years, we cannot overlook the fact that the State has, for the want of a permanent mining population, lost what would be worth more than a hundred millions of money. The work has been done mostly by men who had no homes, and who did not intend to remain in California. Their enterprises generally were undertaken for the purpose of making the most profit in a brief time. There was no proper care for a distant future; and without such care no society is sound, no State truly prosperous. If a claim could, by hastily washing, be made to pay $10 per day to the hand for three months, or $6 for three years by a careful washing, the hasty washing was preferred. If a fertile valley that would have yielded a revenue of $5 per acre for century after century to a farmer could be made to yield $5 per day to a miner for one summer, its loam was washed away, and a useless and ugly bed of gravel was left in its place. The flumes, the ditches, the dwellings, the roads, and the towns were constructed with almost exclusive regard to immediate wants. The good turnpike roads were private property, on which heavy tolls were levied, so that not unfrequently a gentleman in a one-horse buggy would have to pay $5 or $10 toll in a day's travel. The claims were made small, so that everybody should have a chance to get one; but the pay-dirt was soon exhausted, and then there must be a move. In such a state of affairs miners generally could not send for their families or make elegant homes. Living alone and lacking the influences and amusements of home-life, they became wasteful and wild. Possessing no title to the land, they did nothing to give it value, and were ready to abandon it at any moment. The farmers, merchants, and other fixed residents of the mining counties are agitated and frightened nearly every year by the danger of a migration of the miners to some distant place. One year it is Peru; another it is British Columbia, Idaho, Reese river, Pahranagat, or Arizona; and it may next be Brazil, Liberia, or Central Africa, for all we know.

The losses to individuals and to the State have been so great from these migrations that for years past there has been an increasing desire for some change in the tenure of mining lands, so that the mining population shall be attached to the soil, and thus have an opportunity and a motive for establishing permanent homes and a personal interest in improving and enriching the country. The act of Congress passed at the last session for the granting of fee-simple titles to lode mines, and to the agricultural lands in the mineral districts, is the beginning of a new and better era in the history of the Pacific coast. So soon as the necessary surveys can be completed, many applications will be made for patents, and in a few years great and beneficial changes will result. Such is the general opinion among the more intelligent miners and public men of the coast. As an indication of the manner in which the news of the passage of the act was received, the following passages are quoted from leading editorials in influential newspapers :

The San Francisco Bulletin, in its issue of July 31st, said :

"No measure of equal consequence to the material, and, we may add, to the moral interests of the Pacific States, was ever before passed by Congress. * * * The passage of the bill, whatever defects it may develop when more critically examined and enforced, marks a change in the public land policy equal in importance to the adoption of the pre-emption and homestead system ; indeed its practical effect will be to extend the now unquestionable benefits of that system to the vast field of the mineral regions which have hitherto been largely excluded from those benefits. * * * It was one of the greatest evils of the negative policy of Congress regarding the mineral lands that, while it prevented our own people from acquiring titles to them, it opened their treasures freely to the transient adventurers from abroad, who only came to take them away without leaving any equivalent. As a measure calculated to give homogeneity and fixedness to our population, security to titles, and encouragement to investments of capital and labor, the new mining law is full of promise. We believe it will have the effect also to stimulate exploration and production in the mining districts. Its good features are apparent ; its bad ones will appear in time and can be easily remedied."

The Alta Californian of the same date, said :

"The passage of the bill will be regarded in future times as an epoch in the history of the State. It offers a patent to every lode miner who desires it ; it opens all the agricultural land in the mineral districts to pre-emption and homestead claims, and it will give secure titles, build up comfortable homes, and fix a large permanent population in the rich mining country of the Pacific slope."

The Mining and Scientific Press, in its issue of the 14th of July, 1866, spoke thus, editorially :

"The papers generally throughout the State (California) and Nevada appear to approve the bill ; and so far as we can judge there is a general feeling favorable to its passage, as a necessity for quieting the public mind upon this vexatious question."

The Stockton Independent of January 8, 1866, spoke thus of some of the evils which this bill was designed to cure :

"There are now over one hundred thousand adult men and women in the mines of California and Nevada without homes or the possibility of acquiring them. Shall we let this preposterous rule go on from generation to generation, until from hundreds of thousands this nomadic population amounts up to millions and tens of millions? From the twenty-seventh to the forty-seventh meridian of longitude, and from latitude thirty-four to the extremest northern line of the

United States, all is mineral land—all has been prospected and proven to be such.

Is it the part of wise statesmanship to adopt as a permanent law the rule that the millions who are in the next quarter of a century to occupy this vast area —over one-third of our territory—shall be without homes? Such a thing is horrible to contemplate. Compared with it the anarchy and social demoralization which have reigned in Mexico, Peru, and other Spanish American countries for the last half century are as nothing. The policy is wholly opposed to the instincts and habits of the Anglo Saxon race—opposed to the idea of law and government. It invites the nation to anarchy and offers a premium to crime and pauperism.

It is high time that the rule were changed. All the mineral lands ought to be surveyed in small lots and sold, or at least given away in fee to the occupants.

These people should have homes and the means of acquiring permanent property and status as citizens."

The Sacramento Union of the 23d of June said:

"There are many miners who feel as deep an interest in the matter as others who devote themselves exclusively to farming, for prosperous miners, who do not wish to abandon the hills and valleys where they have harvested fortune, have a passion for pretty homes and a blooming ranch. Upon the whole, this bill has been framed with a more intelligent regard for the interests of the people of the Pacific coast than any other previous measure that we can now recall, and it is probable that its provisions can be executed without inflicting injury upon the rights which accrued under the policy hitherto pursued by the government. It is a great stride towards the final adjustment of a dangerous question, and a vast improvement upon the measures broached at Washington at various periods during the past three years."

Governor McCormick, of Arizona, in his annual message delivered to the legislature on the 8th of October, 1866, said:

"The act of Congress to legalize the occupation of mineral lands, and to extend the rights of pre-emption thereto, adopted at the late session, preserves all that is best in the system created by miners themselves, and saves all vested rights under that system, while offering a permanent title to all who desire it, at a mere nominal cost. It is a more equitable and practicable measure than the people of the mineral districts had supposed Congress would adopt, and credit for its liberal and acceptable provisions is largely due to the influence of the representatives of the Pacific coast, including our own intelligent delegate. While it is not without defects, as a basis of legislation it is highly promising, and must lead to stability and method, and so inspire increased confidence and zeal in quartz mining."

The Virginia Enterprise, the leading journal of the State of Nevada, in its issue of July 13, advocating the passage of the bill, said:

"The bill proposes nothing but what already exists,except giving a perfect title to the owners of any mine who may desire it. But the effect of this single title clause, if the bill becomes a law, will be of wonderful benefit to our State. Domestic, and especially foreign capitalists, who have been restrained from investing in our mines on account of the uncertain tenure by which they were held, and the general insecurity of title, will not hesitate to invest when they are guaranteed unmolested and permanent possession by the government. It will give an impetus to prospecting, for discoveries will be salable; to developments and heavy operations generally, for titles will be quiet and secure. It will create an unprecedented demand for labor, and inaugurate enduring prosperity throughout the State. The poor and the rich, the workingman and the capitalist, will be equally benefited by it."

It may be useless to regret past mistakes, and there is some difference of opinion among miners whether any serious mistake has been made, but it is evident that if the mining population could have been made permanent residents of the various counties as early as 1849, California would now be thrice as rich, in a pecuniary point of view, as she is at present. Her gold produce alone has been $900,000,000; and the produce of her agriculture and other branches of industry has been nearly as much, and yet the total assessed value of the taxable property of the State is only $180,000,000, of which nearly half is land alone; so it seems California, with all her wonderful wealth, intelligence, and industry, has made only five per cent. profit on her business in a period of twenty years of such an abundance of gold and comparative cheapness of the necessaries of life as were never witnessed elsewhere in the world.

SECTION 11.

1.—MINING LAWS.

Mining for gold and silver is a business new in Anglo-Saxon life, and not provided for in our laws. Suddenly the American government has found itself in the possession of the richest deposits of the precious metals in the world, with the certainty that the mining industry based upon them will be one of the greatest and most permanent interests of the country. It is necessary now to foster this industry, to protect it, to frame a code of laws that will leave every possible liberty to the miner who wishes to work fairly in extracting the metal from the earth, and will throw every possible obstruction in the way of the drones and swindlers who wish to defraud the honest laborer by compelling him to pay for the right of working mines that should be open to him without charge.

And, first, let us look at the regulations adopted by the miners and the statutes adopted by certain States and Territories in regard to mining for gold and silver.

It is impossible to obtain, within the brief time allowed for this preliminary report, a complete collection of the mining regulations, and they are so numerous that they would fill a volume of a thousand pages. There are not less than five hundred mining districts in California, two hundred in Nevada, and one hundred each in Arizona, Idaho, and Oregon, each with its set of written regulations. The main objects of the regulations are to fix the boundaries of the district, the size of the claims, the manner in which claims shall be marked and recorded, the amount of work which must be done to secure the title, and the circumstances under which the claim is considered abandoned and open to occupation by new claimants. The districts usually do not contain more than a hundred square miles, frequently not more than ten, and there are in places a dozen within a radius of ten miles. In lode mining, the claims are usually two hundred feet long on the lode; in placers the size depends on the character of the diggings and the amount of labor necessary to open them. In hill diggings, where the pay dirt is reached by long tunnels, the claim is usually a hundred feet wide, and reaches to the middle of the hill. Neglect to work a placer claim for ten days in the season when it can be worked is ordinarily considered as an abandonment. The regulations in the different districts are so various, however, that it is impossible to reduce them to a few classes comprehending all their provisions. The States of Nevada and Oregon and the Territories of Idaho and Arizona have each adopted statutes in regard to the size and tenure of mining claims, and these statutes, so far as they conflict with the district regulations, probably supersede them, although the act of the last session of Congress to legalize the occupation of the mineral lands provides for the issue of patents to only the holders of those lode claims which are occupied and improved according to the local custom or rules of miners in the district where the same is located.*

Question might arise whether the statute of the State or Territory is to be recognized as of any force in determining the right of claimants to patents. The congressional act mentions only "the local custom or rules of miners in the district;" and those words certainly do not describe a statute; and yet the statute should be preferred, because it is uniform, clear, preserved in unquestionable records, accessible to all, and of precise jurisdiction; whereas the local customs and rules are various, and in many districts indefinite, unrecorded, almost inaccessible, and conflicting in their jurisdiction.

The evils of the system of local customs and rules are well stated in a report made to the senate of Nevada on the 23d February last by the committee on mines and mining. The subject under consideration was the adoption of a general statute to supersede these local customs and rules. The committee say:

"In the establishment of a code of mining laws in this connection there are certain self evident principles which should be adopted—

"First. The interest in question being coextensive with the area of the State, and intimately blended with every part of it, the laws which seek to regulate it should be general in their character, uniform in their application, and universal in their dissemination.

"Second. It being a vital and permanent interest, the laws which govern it should have the vitality and stability of legislative enactment.

"Third. It being an interest pertaining to our own people, but valueless to them without foreign aid, the aim of the laws should be twofold, to give protection to our citizens and encouragement to capital."

Does the present system answer all or any of these requirements?

1. As to uniformity: there is now nothing approaching it. There never was confusion worse confounded. More than two hundred petty districts within the limits of a single State, each one with its self approved code; these codes, differing not alone each from each other, but presenting numberless instances of

* Section 2. *And be it further enacted,* That whenever any person or association of persons claim a vein or lode of quartz, or other rock in place, bearing gold, silver, cinnabar, or copper, having previously occupied and improved the same according to the local custom or rules of miners in the district where the same is situated, and having expended in actual labor and improvements thereon an amount not less than one thousand dollars, and in regard to whose possession there is no controversy or opposing claim, it shall or may be lawful for such claimant or association of claimants to file in the local land office a diagram of the same, so extended laterally or otherwise as to conform to the local laws, customs, and rules of miners, and to enter such tract and to receive a patent therefor, granting such mine, together with the right to follow such vein or lode with its dips, angles, and variations to any depth, although it may enter the land adjoining, which land adjoining shall be sold subject to this condition.

contradiction in themselves. The law of one point is not the law of another five miles distant; and a little further on will be a code which is the law of neither of the former, and so on *ad infinitum*, with the further disturbing fact superadded that the written laws themselves may be overrun by some peculiar "custom" which can be found nowhere recorded, and the proof of which will vary with the volume of interested affidavits which may be brought on either side to establish it.

Again, in one district the work required to be done to hold a claim is nominal; in another, exorbitant; in another, abolished; in another, adjourned from year to year. A stranger, seeking to ascertain the law, is surprised to learn that there is no satisfactory public record to which he can refer; no public officer to whom he may apply who is under any bond or obligation to furnish him information or guarantee its authenticity. Often in the newer districts he finds there is not the semblance of a code, but a simple resolution adopting the code of some other district, which may be a hundred miles distant. What guarantee has he for investment of either capital or labor under such a system?

Again, under the present loose organization of districts, with their vagueness of boundary, it is often impossible to determine by which code of laws a location is governed. Cases of this kind have already arisen in several districts, and are liable to do so again in any part of the State; and, under the present system, there is no means of guarding against it, except by an actual survey of the boundaries of every district—an incalculable expense.

2. As to permanency of regulations, even such as they are, there is now no guarantee even of that. A miners' meeting adopts a code; it apparently is the law. Some time after, on a few days' notice, a corporal's guard assembles, and, on simple motion, radically changes the whole system by which claims may be held in a district. Before a man may traverse the State, the laws of a district, which by examination and study he may have mastered, may be swept away, and no longer stand as the laws which govern the interest he may have acquired; and the change has been one which by no reasonable diligence could he be expected to have knowledge of. But if the laws be uniform, and registered upon the statute book of the State, he will have security in his tenure, and reasonable notice of any change therein.

3. As to protection to the miner and encouragement to the capitalist, the present system, or lack of system, affords neither. The cause of uncertainty of titles to land in our sister State did not, through fifteen years of her history, more paralyze her progress than the uncertainty of mining titles in the outside districts now retards our development. Five years ago a horde of greedy prospectors from every part of the Pacific coast swept over our State, leaving their notices of location on every "dip, spur, and angle," "thick as leaves in Vallambrosa;" and, after a year or two of feverish unrest, swarmed away again to the newer fields of Idaho and Montana, leaving nothing to mark their passage but their faded "notices" mouldering on the hillside, their pitiful burlesque of development in the way of assessment-work, and the threatening terrors of the common-law doctrine as to "vested rights." This is what the true citizens of Nevada, those who, never losing faith in her future, have adhered to her fortunes in sunshine and gloom, now reap from the ruinous system of unlegalized district laws. They see thousands of claims in which capital would be eager to engage, could satisfactory title be given, now lying neglected because there is no system of abandonment as yet, or sufficient legislative or judicial sanction to gain the confidence of business men. Such will not be satisfied with a "general belief," or an "evident tendency of decisions;" they insist on definite enactment or positive adjudication. In vain do our people relocate abandoned mines in accordance with the only laws which govern the matter. When such titles are presented to the capitalist his first inquiry is: "What is the authority for so

doing?   Has your legislature authorized it?   Has your judiciary sanctioned it?
If not, where is the security for investment?"

As an instance of the manner in which the mining regulations are changed
and the mining records neglected, the experience of North San Juan, one of
the most prosperous and permanent mining towns, may be given here.

The Sweetland mining district was organized and a series of regulations
adopted for it in 1850, when claims were restricted to thirty feet square   In
1852 the size was enlarged to eighty by one hundred and eighty feet, and the
regulations were changed several times in other respects.   In 1853 the Sweetland district was subdivided into three smaller districts, of which North San
Juan is one.   This latter adopted a set of regulations at the time of its organization, and adopted the set now in force a year later.   A mining recorder was
elected in 1854, but he has been absent from the district for five years, and no
one has been chosen to fill the place   The regulations are treated by many
persons as if they were no longer in force—at least, as regards certain points;
and in many cases it would be difficult to ascertain whether there is any good
title to claims under the regulations.

2.—NEED OF CONGRESSIONAL MINING LAW.

I would suggest that the act of last session should be so amended that, in
the granting of patents, State and territorial statutes in regard to the size,
possession, working, and abandonment of claims should be regarded as of
higher authority than the "local custom or rules;" and I venture to recommend
further that a congressional act should be passed prescribing the manner of
taking up, recording, working, and abandoning mining claims so long as the
title remains in the United States, so that uniformity shall prevail throughout
the whole country.   Such an act, based on the laws and regulations of which
copies are given on subsequent pages, would, I am confident, give general satisfaction to the miners, as securing their equal rights.   As it is now, there is
great diversity.

The following list shows some of the differences in the size of the claims:

Arizona, under statute, 600 feet square.

Oregon, under statute, 300 feet on the lode by 150 feet wide.

Idaho, under statute, 200 feet on the lode by 100 feet wide.

Nevada, under statute, 200 feet on the lode by 200 feet wide.

Nevada county, California, miners' regulations, 100 feet.

Tuolumne county, California, miners' regulations, 150 feet on the lode and
150 feet on each side.

Sierra county, California, miners' regulations, 250 feet on the lode and 250
feet on each side.

Copperopolis district, California, miners' regulations, 150 feet on the lode and
250 feet on each side of the lode by 300 feet wide.

In most districts of Nevada and in many of California a miner may claim for
each person in his company 200 feet on the lode, but he acquires no exclusive
right of possession to the adjoining land, except in so far as he may have to
occupy it in his mining operations.   In Arizona, Oregon, Idaho, and some districts of California and Nevada, the mine may take a considerable tract on the
sides of the lode.   If we compare the size of the claims simply in relation to
the length on the lode, we see that, taking the space allowed to the miner in
Nevada county, California, as the unit of measurement, the miner in the State
of Nevada gets twice as much, in Oregon thrice as much, and in Arizona six
times as much.   There is no good reason why the claims should not be of the
same size in all these places.   The act of Congress provides in section 4 "That
no location hereafter made shall exceed two hundred feet in length along the
vein for each locator, with an additional claim for discovery to the discoverer

of the lode, with the right to follow such vein to any depth, with all its dips, variations, and angles, together with a reasonable quantity of surface for the convenient working of the same as fixed by local rules : *And provided further,* That no person may make more than one location on the same lode, and not more than three thousand feet shall be taken in any one claim by any association of persons." These provisions reduce the length of the claims to be located hereafter in Arizona and Oregon to two hundred feet for each person ; but they do not authorize any enlargements of the claim in the districts where the limit is less than the two hundred feet. And yet justice and sound policy require that a miner should be permitted to take up as large a claim in Nevada county or in Tuolumne county, California, as in Oregon or Arizona.

3.—THE CUSTOMARY LIMITATION OF SIZE.

The limitation is, however, more apparent than real. If John Smith supposes a lode to be rich, he selects a portion three thousand feet long, puts a stake at each end, with a notice, and files with the recorder of the district or county, a notice that he and fourteen associates have taken up that claim. If he imagines that there is some rich ground outside of the three thousand feet, he takes another claim of three thousand feet, in the names of fifteen friends not mentioned in the first notice. He may have no authority from those persons to take claims for them, but no one objects in such a case. If John Smith now desires to own more than his two hundred feet, he goes to the men whose names he has put down, and requests them to give him a bill of sale for one hundred feet, or one hundred and fifty feet each, and as they owe their claims to him, they cannot refuse. Then, instead of being the owner of only two hundred feet, he can become, with little trouble or expense, the owner of three or four thousand feet. He can hold as many feet by purchase as he pleases. There is no limitation in any county to the amount of mining claim that can be held by one person by purchase ; but in Mexico no company can locate more than four times as much as the claim of a single individual, and there is less opportunity for the abuse of which mention has been made. It would be advisable, in my opinion, to amend the act of last session so that no claim for any company shall exceed sixteen hundred or two thousand feet in length. The Mexican law fixes the limitation at two hundred varas, or about twenty-two hundred feet. I would recommend further that, in the proposed change in the length of claims, each individual should be entitled to hold by location not more than five hundred feet. The valuable claims are usually found by solitary miners, or by small parties of not more than three. When such, or a miner or party, finds a place in a rich lode, there is no good reason why he or they should be compelled by the law to give most of it away to friends, as is done under the present law and custom. Three locators get only six hundred feet out of three thousand, or one-fifth. They may request their friends to convey to them one-half of the remaining four-fifths, but oftentimes they fear that such request would give offence, and if the claim turns out to be valuable, most of the benefit goes to persons who have done nothing to discover the mine. It would be better to offer a larger reward to the miner, and not compel him to give so much to his friends. Two hundred feet is not enough on ordinary lodes for a mining enterprise ; the pay-streak of rock may run down obliquely lengthwise in the vein, and the miner wants to know that he can follow it for a considerable distance in his claim. If two miners should find a rich place in a quartz lode, and could trace it for eight hundred feet along the lode, and were satisfied that the mine would prove profitable from the start, and were doubtful whether any part of the lode beyond the eight hundred feet would pay, it is evident that they would rather own the eight hundred feet by location than be compelled to give half of it to other persons. The knowledge that location could acquire more than two hundred feet by location would encourage prospecting. If, on the other hand, the lode contained only a moderate quantity of valuable ore, and could not be made to pay until after an investment of more capital than the two had at their command, then they could make up the original company of eight persons, with one hundred feet to each ; or they could take up the claim in their two names, and each could sell or give away portions of his share to friends who would furnish money. By increasing the amount that each individual can hold by location, the miner has everything to gain and nothing to lose. If the mine will pay from the start, the profit goes to the man who deserves it ; if the mine requires outside capital for its development, the miner can obtain it as readily as at present. The Spanish law which was framed in 1783, after an experience of two hundred and fifty years, and is now in force throughout Spanish America, allows each locator to hold two hundred varas, or five hundred and fifty feet. The quartz regulations of California were most of them framed about 1852 and 1853, with no experience, and under the influence of persons familiar only with the small claims customary in the placers. It is true that many of the regulations have been re-enacted at later dates, but the old influences have not been broken up. There is now a disposition to find fault with the California regulations, and to prefer the provisions of the Mexican law, as to the size of claims.

4.—PROPOSED WIDTH OF CLAIMS.

A claim should cover not only the lode but a certain area on both sides. The act of Congress allows a reasonable quantity of surface for the convenient working of the same, as fixed by "local rules." Here again the "local rules" alone are recognized. What is a "reasonable" quantity of surface ? In Arizona it is three hundred feet on each side of the middle of the lode ; in Oregon it is twenty-five feet on each side of the lode ; in Idaho it is a tract one hundred feet wide ; in Tuolumne county, California, it is one hundred and fifty feet on each side of the lode ; in Sierra county, California, it is two hundred and fifty feet wide on each side ; in the Copperopolis district it is three hundred feet wide ; in the State of Nevada, Nevada county, California, and in many other counties of California, it is all the land that is actually occupied by the works of the company or miner, and no more. Under the customs in those districts in which the miner obtained no fixed quantity of surface, he never laid claim to any portion outside of his lode, except as he occupied it for his tunnel, shaft, mill, dwelling, ditch, dump, reservoir for tailings, or something of the sort ; if he had all his works at one end of his claim, he had no title to any of the surface of the other end ; any other miner might then take up another lode within ten feet of his and work it. The law of Mexico, the statutes of Arizona, Oregon and Idaho, and the regulations of Tuolumne and Sierra counties, authorize the miner to occupy a specific amount of surface, and all the minerals within that area belong to him, whether he has discovered all the lodes within it or not. It often happens that large veins have branches or spurs, which at the surface appear as if they were parallel veins, and when the main vein is opened and found to be rich, outsiders, if not forbidden by the laws or regulations, make a custom of claiming the spurs and branches, in the hope that they may prove to be independent lodes, or in the expectation of making money out of them before the connection can be proved, or for the purpose of compelling the owner of the main lode to buy them out, and thus save the expense of litigation. Such claims upon spurs, and the litigation resulting from them, have been among the most important facts in the history of Virginia City, and they have been common in many of the quartz districts of California. They are among the greatest evils that beset lode mining in certain counties. It was mainly to prevent this kind of fraud, for it is scarcely possible to give any other name to it as generally practiced, that the law of Mexico authorized the miner to hold a tract five hundred and fifty feet wide at right angles to the course of the lode, and thus he could cover any ground which he found interlopers might want to claim. The purpose was not so much to give him room for working, as to secure his title and protect him from litigation and troublesome neighbors. Under every set of regulations, customs, or local rules, and under every code of mining law, the owner of the main vein under the first location owns all the spurs; but he may not be able to prove for years that it is a spur. This was the case in several important suits in Virginia City, where the spur was not traced to its union with the main vein until the miners had gone down five hundred feet, and they did not reach that depth till after years of working. There may be, and no doubt are, cases in which two valuable and independent lodes are found within two hundred feet of each other; and in such instances it would perhaps be injurious to the mining interest to let the first claimant have both lodes, but such cases would be very rare. As a matter of fact there is no complaint among miners of any evil caused by giving a claim to a fixed area of surface, whereas there is great complaint about the license of taking claims on spurs within a few feet of the main lode. The latter evil is common; the former is almost unknown; the general sentiment among the miners favors the recognition of a surface claim at least two hundred feet wide across the lode.

5.—WORK REQUIRED TO HOLD CLAIMS.

One of the greatest evils that besets lode mining at present is that a vast number of claims are held without being worked, and without any expectation on the part of the claimants of working them. Most claims are taken up merely as a matter of speculation, and not for the purpose of mining; and many of the claimants are persons who have never done any regular work at quartz mining. When a rich vein is found, a multitude of persons rush to the place, and each one gets a claim, if possible, in every vein in the district. He puts down the names of enough associates to make up a claim a thousand or two thousand feet long, and thus all the lodes of the district are soon appropriated. Two or three of the associates may be present with him or perhaps not one of them has ever been near the place. He has taken his claims and he now waits for others to develop the district and prove that they are valuable. If by the opening of the adjacent mines, his claims are proved to be rich, he sells out at a handsome profit; if not, he has lost little. Then if a miner goes into one of the quartz mining districts and wishes to prospect a vein thoroughly, he will find that most of these lodes which he would prefer to work are held as claims, though no substantial work has been done in them. He cannot afford to buy, because he might have to buy dozens before finding one that would yield anything before being examined; and he cannot afford to prospect before buying, because any discovery that he might make would enhance the price, and be to the profit of the claimant. The system that recognizes the validity of unworked claims is a great check to mining industry and to the development of mineral wealth. The individuals who profit by it are usually of a class who thrive at the expense of the industrious and enterprising. The miner desiring to get a claim with the intention of working it has everything to lose and nothing to gain by the system. It is true that the local regulations require the claim-holder to do a certain amount of work every year to secure his title, but this requirement is in most districts a mere form,* and it is evaded by sham work, or the require-

---

*The San Francisco Mining and Scientific Press, a recognized authority among miners, says in its issue of the 14th of July, 1866:

" With regard to the performance of labor to perfect a title, every miner knows that the rule, as at present established, is a mere farce."

†Governor McCormick of Arizona, in his message delivered to the territorial legislature on the 8th of October, 1866, says:

ment is a nullity because no provision is made for ascertaining whether the work has been done, and the title is held to be good until, when some adverse claim is made, the first claim is pronounced invalid by a court, after a trial in which the result does not necessarily go with justice. The presumption is always with the first claimant in such cases. A considerable portion of the community being interested in similar sham claims, it is difficult to get a jury to give a verdict against them, even if the testimony were against them; but the law is so framed that usually if one witness swears that a certain amount of work has been done to hold a claim, the adverse party cannot disprove it. Now let us see what amount of work is necessary to hold a lode claim in various districts.

In the course of the year 1866, eighty miles of quartz claims were taken up in Nevada county, and most of these claims are held to-day by a good title under the mining regulations, though not five miles of the eighty to-day are worked, and the owners of the remaining seventy-five have no intention of working their claims soon.

The Nevada Transcript, (Nevada county, California,) in a number published in October, 1866, said :

"It is safe to estimate the mining locations of the past two years in this county, including water privileges, gravel and quartz claims, at about 373 miles. The locations of the present year amount to over 177 miles. Of these fully one-half are quartz claims. This estimate will suffice to show the great importance to which quartz mining has grown within a very short period. Very few of the many ledges located have yet become yielding mines, and a large number are now unworked, the owners, having done work enough to hold them, are waiting for more enterprising men to develop the neighboring claims"

Under the statute of Nevada a claim may be held for one year by the excavation of fifty cubic feet of rock for each two hundred feet, or by the payment of two cents per foot.

Under the statute of Oregon a claim may be held for a year by work to the amount of fifty dollars for each three hundred feet, or for the share of each original locator.

In Idaho, under the territorial statute, work to the amount of one hundred dollars for the claim of each original locator gives a perpetual title.

According to the territorial statute of Arizona the claimant or claimants must sink a shaft thirty feet deep, or cut a tunnel fifty feet long, within the first ten days, to establish a claim, which may then be held for two years without further work by filing an annual affidavit of intention to work the claim; and after two years the claim, no matter how many feet it contains, may be held by thirty days' work annually.

Under the local regulations of the Virginia district, three days' labor would secure the title to two hundred feet for one month, or work to the amount of forty dollars for six months.

The local regulations for Reese River district do not provide for any forfeiture for lack of work.

The local regulations of Nevada county, California, require twenty days' work or labor to the amount of one hundred dollars to secure a claim for one year.

"It is also important that, excepting in districts where active hostility on the part of the Indians absolutely prevents, the actual occupation and improvement of claims shall be made requisite to their possession, unless pre-empted under the congressional law. The lack of such a requirement hitherto has seriously retarded the development of our mineral resources and the general prosperity of the Territory, and proved discouraging to new comers, especially in the counties on the Colorado river, where hundreds of lodes, taken up in years past by parties now absent from the Territory, are unworked; and yet, under the existing law, no one has a right to lay claim to them, be he ever so able or anxious to open them."

In the Copperopolis district seven days' work holds a company's claim for a year.

Under the local regulations of Tuolumne county, California, one day's work will hold a claim for a month, or labor to the value of one hundred dollars will hold it for six months.

6.—PROPOSED CHANGE AS TO WORK REQUIRED.

There is no uniformity here, nor is the same amount of labor required by any two codes. Diversity implies injustice to individuals and injury to the State. If it were wise to give a perpetual title in Idaho, after labor to the value of one hundred dollars had been done, it cannot be wise to require labor worth fifty dollars annually in Oregon, or one hundred dollars in Nevada county, California. All the statutes and regulations require some work, except the State of Nevada, which enables the claimant by paying two cents per lineal foot annually, to hold his claim forever. The two cents are to go into the State treasury, and the commutation, if maintained, will have a very prejudicial effect on the mining interest. It will enable men to hold claims without working them, and that is precisely the result which the laws should prevent. One of the evils with which lode mining has now to contend is that the miners who are willing and anxious to work lodes lying idle on public land cannot get possession of them. The law should be strict against those who hold claims without working them. Every presumption should be against titles that are not founded on continued occupation and work. The statutes should be so framed that the miner who desires to work, and who does work in good faith, shall have every advantage over the drone who takes claims and tries to hold them until their great value is proved by others, so that he can sell them out, after having incurred little expense or risk.

In Mexico it is expected that the miner will keep at least four men employed continually at his mine, and if he omits to have so many as four for a period of four months, except in time of war, famine, or pestilence, he forfeits his title. The constant labor of one, two, or three men, or the employment of a dozen during the year, is not enough. The Mexican law, however, is too strict on this point for the present wants of the American mining districts. Wages are so high that many companies, which really intend to open the mines, and are at work in good faith with one or two men, would abandon their claims rather than undertake to pay four men continuously. Nevertheless, severe as Mexican law is on individuals, it is admirably fitted to develop the mining interest. The Spanish maxim is that the man who does the most work in the mine has the most right to it.

7.—LAW NEEDED FOR CENTURIES OF MINING.

It is evident to all who have made themselves familiar with the history of mining in other countries, and who have examined the mineral resources of the Pacific States, that our gold and silver mining industry will last for centuries, and will grow to be far more important and to employ many more laborers than at present. It is evident, too, after the consideration of the various statutes and local regulations that some further legislation is necessary to protect and foster the development of this great industry. If further legislation be necessary, wisdom suggests that action should not be postponed for a time. The mining industry is too important to the interests of individuals and to the wealth and growth of the State to be neglected. It is now, while the business is still in its infancy, that the proper principles should be laid down, so as to secure the miner in the safe enjoyment of the treasures which he brings to light. The land on which the mining industry is based belongs to the Union, and Congress has the exclusive jurisdiction over the tenure of claims until the time when they become private property.

The act of the last session is an excellent foundation on which to build up gradually a code suited to our wants, and the local mining regulations suggest many important provisions. The interests involved, both public and private, are so great that much caution is necessary; and yet the necessity of some uniform and comprehensive system is undeniable. It is better to legislate too little than too much, and the first statutes should be confined to a few general and fundamental principles, to which additions can be made as experience is gained and the wants of the miners are better understood. The main purpose of legislation, in mining, should be to protect the working miner, and encourage him in the development of the mineral resources of the country. His interest in this matter is intimately associated with the prosperity of the nation.

8.—CONGRESS ALONE CAN ESTABLISH UNIFORMITY.

Congress alone can establish uniform rules, applicable equally to all the mining districts. Experience has shown that if the matter be left to the several States and Territories in which the mineral deposits are found, each will have its own system. Local, personal, and immediate interests have far more influence in local legislatures than in Congress; which last, from the manner in which it is constituted, must pay more regard to general, permanent, and public interests. It is therefore in every respect to be desired that Congress should exercise its power and fix by a comprehensive act the terms upon which claims to mines on the public land may be held. A wise and generous basis for such legislation was laid by the act of last session. The equity of the miner's title was acknowledged; the courts were directed to protect him in his possession; and the validity of the local rules was for the time recognized. The subject was too extensive to dispose of it all at once. It is better to do the work slowly than to do it ill. Step by step we shall advance to have a superior law, worthy of the superior energy, intelligence, and industry of our miners, and the superior richness and extent of our mineral deposits.

The following are the miners' regulations in some of the principal mining districts:

9.—MINERS' REGULATIONS.—QUARTZ REGULATIONS OF NEVADA COUNTY, CALIFORNIA.

ARTICLE 1. The jurisdiction of the following laws shall extend over all quartz mines and quartz mining property within the county of Nevada.

ART. 2. Each prospector of a quartz claim shall hereafter be entitled to one hundred feet on a quartz ledge or vein, and the discoverer shall be allowed one hundred feet additional. Each claim shall include all the dips, angles, and variations of the vein.

ART. 3. On the discovery of a vein of quartz, three days shall be allowed to mark and stake off the same in such manner, by name of the owner and number of the claim, or otherwise, as shall properly and fully identify such claims. Parties having claims may cause a map or plan to be made and a copy filed with the recorder, if deemed requisite to more particularly fix the locality.

ART. 4. Work to the extent of one hundred dollars in value, or twenty days' faithful labor, shall be performed by each company holding claims, within thirty days of the date of recording the same, as provided for in article sixth of these laws; and the duly authorized representative of a company making oath that such money has been expended, or that such labor has been performed, shall be entitled to a certificate from a county recorder or deputy, guaranteeing undisputed possession of said claim for the term of one year; and a like sum of money or amount of labor expended or performed within twenty days of each succeeding year, duly acknowledged as herein named, shall entitle the claimant or company, from year to year, to further certificates of undisputed proprietorship and possession ; and a company having a mill contracted for in good faith, to the amount of five thousand dollars, for the working of its claim or claims, the proper representatives of the company making oath of the same, shall be entitled to receive from said county recorder a title-deed to said claim or claims, guaranteeing to the claimant or company, their successors and assigns, undisputed possession and proprietorship forever under these laws; provided that nothing in this article shall at any time be inconsistent with the laws of the United States.

Art. 5. Whenever the requisite amount of money or labor has not been expended within thirty days from the adoption of these laws, the claim or claims thus neglected shall be considered abandoned and subject to be relocated by any other party or parties.

Art. 6. Any person a citizen of the United States, or any person having taken the necessary steps to become a citizen of the United States, shall be entitled to hold one quartz claim as provided for in article first, and as many more as may be purchased in good faith for a valuable consideration, for which certificates of proprietorship shall be issued by the county recorder.

Art. 7. The regularly elected county recorder of Nevada county shall serve as recorder of this county in quartz claims, authenticating his acts by the county seal. He shall appoint as his deputy such person for Grass valley as may be elected by the district of Grass valley, and he shall pass his records to his successor.

Art. 8. The fees of the recorder and deputy shall be the same as the statute fees for recording per folio.

Art. 9. No title to a claim hereafter taken up or purchased shall be valid unless recorded in the books of the aforesaid county recorder or deputy within ten days of its location or purchase.

Adopted December 20, 1852, and still in force.

10.—QUARTZ REGULATIONS OF SIERRA COUNTY, CALIFORNIA.

Article 1. A claim on any quartz ledge in this county may have a length of two hundred feet along the same, and a width of two hundred and fifty feet at right angles with the ledge, on each side of the same, to include all quartz found within the above-mentioned limits.

Art. 2. Any person discovering a gold-bearing ledge, not previously located, shall be entitled to two claims, being one claim for discovery.

Art. 3. No person but a discoverer shall be entitled to hold more than one claim by location, in a company.

Art. 4. No one but an American citizen, or a foreigner who has and exhibits his foreign miner's tax receipt, shall be allowed to hold a claim by location on any quartz ledge in this county.

Art. 5. It shall be necessary for claimants to post a notice on some conspicuous place on the claims located, setting forth the number of feet claimed, and from what point, upon which the real names of the locators shall appear in full. Said notice shall hold good for ten days, at the expiration of which time a copy of said notice shall be placed upon the records of this county. The notice and record as above shall hold said claims, without further improvements, from and after the first day of November until the first day of May following, if recorded after said first day of November. But upon all claims located between the first day of May and the first day of November following, labor to the amount of eight dollars per claim shall be expended toward the prospecting or developing the same in each thirty days after such location.

Art. 6 To hold quartz claims for the first twelve months after location, it shall be required of each claimant to expend at least ore hundred dollars upon each claim of two hundred feet in such improvements as may be required in the development of the same.

ART. 7. Quartz claims, which have been duly located in accordance with the foregoing rules and regulations, persons are entitled to hold without limit as to number, by afterwards conforming to the requirements set forth in these by-laws.

ART. 8. All quartz claims in this county heretofore located, upon which no permanent improvements have been made, will be declared forfeited within thirty days after the publication of these by-laws, unless the notice of location is renewed and recorded, if not already upon the records of the county, and labor expended upon the same in accordance with the foregoing regulations for holding quartz claims.

II.—QUARTZ REGULATIONS OF TUOLUMNE COUNTY, CALIFORNIA.

The following are the quartz regulations of Tuolumne county :

ARTICLE 1. The jurisdiction of the following laws shall extend over and govern all quartz mining property within Tuolumne county :

ART 2 Each proprietor or locator of a quartz claim shall be entitled to one hundred and fifty (150) feet in length of the vein, including all its dips and angles ; also one hundred and fifty (150) feet on each side of said vein, together with the right of way on either side of said vein, to run tunnels and drifts any distance that may be necessary in order to work said vein; provided that the right to one hundred and fifty (150) feet herein granted on each side of the vein shall not be deemed to conflict with or detract from the right of any subsequent locator who may discover a vein *outside* of said one hundred and fifty (150) feet, to follow *his vein* through said ground.

ART. 3. The original dicoverer of a vein shall be entitled to hold three hundred (300) feet in length on said vein, by virtue of discovery.

ART. 4. No man shall, by virtue of pre-emption, be entitled to hold more than one claim on the same vein, except as provided in article third.

ART. 5. All quartz claims hereafter taken up or located shall be plainly marked by notices posted, containing the claimants' names and the number of feet claimed

ART. 6. The parties locating a quartz claim shall put at least one full day's work on said vein in every thirty days, in order to hold the same. A day's work shall be eight hours' labor ; provided, however, that the sum of one hundred dollars ($100) expended on said claim shall hold the same for six months from the date of its expenditure.

ART. 7. Any individual, company, or companies erecting machinery for working quartz shall, by virtue of said machinery, hold the vein or veins belonging to said individual, company, or companies.

ART. 8. These laws shall be in full force and effect from and after the first day of September, A. D. 1858.

III.—QUARTZ REGULATIONS OF SACRAMENTO COUNTY.

ARTICLE 1. The jurisdiction of the following laws shall extend over all quartz mines and quartz mining property within the county of Sacramento.

ART. 2. Each proprietor of a quartz claim shall hereafter be entitled to two hundred feet of a quartz ledge or vein, and the discoverer shall be allowed two hundred feet additional. Each claim shall include all the dips, angles, and variations of the vein.

ART. 3. On the discovery of a vein of quartz, three days shall be allowed to mark and stake off the same, in such manner, by name of the owner, and number of the claim, or otherwise, as shall properly and fully identify such claims. Parties having claims may have a map or plan made and a copy filed with the recorder, if deemed requisite to more particularly fix the locality.

ART. 4 Work to the extent of sixty dollars in value or twenty days' faithful labor shall be performed by each company holding claims, within thirty days from the date of recording the same, as provided in article six of these laws, and the duly authorized representative of a company making oath that such money has been expended, or that such labor has been performed, shall be entitled to a certificate from recorder guaranteeing undisputed possession of such claims for the term of one year; and a like sum of money or amount of labor expended or performed within twenty days of each succeeding year, duly acknowledged as herein named, shall entitle the claimants or company, from year to year, to certificates of undisputed proprietorship and possession; and a company having a mill contracted for in good faith to the amount of five thousand dollars for the working of its claim or claims, the proper representative of the company making oath of the same, shall be entitled to receive from said county recorder a title-deed of said claim or claims, guaranteeing to the claimants or company, their successors or assigns, undisputed possession and proprietorship forever under these laws; provided that nothing in this article shall be at any time inconsistent with the laws of the United States.

ART. 5. Whenever the requisite amount of money or labor, as provided for in article four, has not been expended within sixty days from the adoption of these laws, the claim or claims thus neglected shall be considered abandoned, and subject to be located by any other party or parties.

ART. 6. Any person, a citizen of the United States, or any person having taken the necessary steps to become a citizen of the United States, shall be entitled to hold one quartz claim, as provided for in article second, and as many more as may be purchased in good faith for a valuable consideration, for which a certificate of proprietorship shall be issued by the recorder.

ART. 7. The discoverer of a new ledge or vein of quartz shall be entitled to two hundred feet for his discovery, and one claim additional, even though he is already in the possession of another claim taken up by himself, and the same benefit may be claimed for each and every discovery, although many discoveries may be made by one person.

(The above regulations were adopted by a meeting of the quartz miners of Sacramento county, held at Ashland, January 22, 1857, and are still in force. There are, however, very few quartz claims of any value in the county.)

12.—PLACER REGULATIONS OF COLUMBIA DISTRICT, CALIFORNIA.

The following regulations for the placer mining district of Columbia, Tuolumne county, California, are considered to be as good as any in the State:

ARTICLE 1. The Columbia mining district shall hereafter be considered to contain all the territory embraced within the following bounds: Beginning at the site of M'Kenny's old store, on Springfield flat, and running in a direct line to a spring on a gulch known as Spring gulch—said gulch running in a southern direction from Santiago Hill. Thence, in a direct line from said spring, to the angle of the road leading from Saw-mill flat to Kelly's ranch, near Wood's creek. Thence, running along the ridge on the west of Wood's creek, to the southern bounds of Yankee Hill district. Thence, following the ridge, to the high flume between Columbia and Yankee Hill. Thence, following the New Water Company's ditch, to Summit pass. Thence, in a direct line to the head of Experimental gulch—including said gulch. Thence, following the upland, to a point opposite Pine Log crossing. Thence, following the upland, to the head of Fox gulch, and including said gulch. Thence, following the upland around, the head of Dead Man's gulch, to the site of the Lawnsdale saw-mill. Thence in a direct line to the place of beginning.

ART. 2. A full claim for mining purposes, on the flats or hills in this district, shall consist of an area equal to that of one hundred feet square. A full claim on ravines shall consist of one hundred feet running on the ravine, and of a width at the discretion of the claimant, provided it does not exceed one hundred feet.

ART. 3. No person or persons shall be allowed to hold more than one full claim, within the bounds of this district, by location; nor shall it consist of more than two parcels of ground, the sum of the area of which shall not exceed one full claim; provided nothing in this article shall be so construed as to prevent miners from associating in companies to carry on mining operations, such companies holding no more than one claim to each member.

ART. 4. A claim may be held for five days after water can be procured at the usual rates, by distinctly marking its bounds by ditches, or by the erection of good and sufficient stakes at each corner, with a notice at each end of the claim, followed by the names of the claimants, and by recording the same according to the provisions of article 10.

ART. 5. When a party has already commenced operations upon a claim, and is obliged to discontinue for want of water, or by sickness or unavoidable accident, the presence upon the ground of the tom and sluices, or such machines as are employed in working the claim, shall be considered as sufficient evidence that the ground is not abandoned, and shall serve instead of other notice; the bounds of the claim still being defined, except so far as the marks may have been obliterated by the work which has been done, or by other causes.

ART. 6. Claims shall be forfeited when parties holding them have neglected to fulfil the requirements of the preceding articles, or have neglected working them for five days after water can be procured at the usual rates, unless prevented by sickness or unavoidable accident, or unless the miners have provided by law to the contrary.

ART. 7. Earth thrown up for the purpose of washing shall not be held distinct from the claim from which it was taken, but shall constitute part and parcel of such claim.

ART. 8. Water flowing naturally through gold-bearing ravines, shall not be diverted from its natural course without the consent of parties working on such ravines; and when so diverted, it shall be held subject to a requisition of the party interested.

ART. 9. No Asiatics shall be allowed to mine in this district.

ART. 10. Any or all claims, now located, or that may be located and worked, can be laid over at any time, for any length of time not to exceed six months, by the person or persons holding the same appearing before the recorder of the district, with two or more disinterested miners, who shall certify over their own signatures that the said claim or claims cannot be worked to advantage, and by having the same recorded according to the laws of the district, and by paying a fee of one dollar; provided each claimant shall sign the record in person or by a legal representative, stating at the same time that said claim is held by location or by purchase.

ART. 11. There shall be a recorder elected, who shall hold the office for one year from the date of his election, or until his successor be elected, whose duty it shall be to keep a record of all miners' meetings held in the district; to record all claims, when requested by the claimants, in a book to be kept for that purpose, according to article 10; and to call miners' meetings, by posting notices throughout the district, when fifteen or more miners of the district shall present him with a petition stating the object of the meeting, and paying for printing notices; provided that, in the absence of the recorder, the above-named number of miners shall not be disqualified to call a meeting, at the place specified in article 16. He shall at all proper times keep his record book open for inspection.

ART. 12. No company or companies of miners, who may occupy the natural channel through any gulch or ravine for a tail-race or flume, shall have the exclusive right of such channel, to the exclusion of any company of miners who may wish to run their tailings into the same.

ART. 13. Any party or parties locating claims in gulches or ravines where such flumes or tail-races exist, shall first confer with the party or parties owning said tail-races or flumes, for the use of the same on such conditions as they may agree upon; and in case of a disagreement, each party shall choose two disinterested miners, and the four shall choose a fifth, who may determine the matter or matters in dispute.

ART. 14. Any company or companies of miners shall have the right to run their water and tailings across the claim or claims below them, if it can be done without injury to the lower claims.

ART. 15. The limits of this district shall not be changed without the consent of a regularly called mass meeting of the miners of the district.

ART. 16. No miners' meetings held outside of Columbia, for the purpose of making laws to govern any portion of the district, or to amend these laws in any manner, shall be considered as legal.

ART. 17. All mining laws of this district, made previous to the foregoing, are hereby repealed.

13.—PLACER REGULATIONS OF NORTH SAN JUAN DISTRICT.

ARTICLE 1. The boundaries of the district of San Juan shall be as follows: On the east the public road leading to Hess's crossing; on the south the road leading from the village of San Juan to Kentz's tavern, and the ravine extending thence to Hatfield's crossing on the Middle Yuba; and on the west and north the Middle Yuba

ART. 2. The dimensions of a mining claim in this district shall not exceed one hundred and eighty feet in length by eighty feet in breadth.

ART. 3. No person shall be entitled to more than one claim by location, but the right to hold by legal purchase shall be unlimited.

ART. 4. To indicate possession of any claim or claims it shall be the duty of the owner or owners thereof, if not habitually at work thereon, to post on some conspicuous part of such claim or claims a notice stating the boundaries and dimensions thereof, and his or their intention thereon; and also to designate the prominent lines or corners thereof by suitable stakes or blazes. But in a claim or set of claims whereon work is being regularly performed, the presence of the owners thereof, or their representatives, shall be deemed a sufficient excuse for the absence of the notice hereinbefore specified.

ART. 5. It shall be the duty of the owners of all that class of claims specified in the first clause of article 4 (i. e., those wherein work is not being regularly performed) to renew their notices once in every thirty days, except in the absence of water from the diggings, when it shall not be necessary.

ART. 6. If a person or persons in prospecting any claim or set of claims shall have expended thereon the sum of five hundred dollars in money or labor, (labor to be estimated at the rate of wages current at the time,) his or their right to such claim or claims shall be secure for the period of two years from the time such expenses were incurred; but after the expenditure of the said two years said rights shall be subject to the restrictions specified in articles 4 and 5 of these laws.

ART. 7. It shall be the duty of a recorder to be elected annually by the miners of the district; to make a record on application of the owners of the boundaries and dimensions of each and every claim or set of claims in the district, for which he shall be entitled to a fee of fifty cents for each record. On the sale or transfer of any claim in this district it shall be the duty of the purchaser to have such sale or transfer recorded.

ART. 8. It shall be the duty of all owners of claims that have been located or purchased previous to the date of this meeting to have such claim recorded on or before the first day of December, A. D. 1854, and all claims located or purchased after the date of this meeting shall be recorded within one week from the time of said location or purchase.

The above regulations were adopted on the 5th November, 1854. North San Juan is the largest hydraulic mining district in California.

14.—PLACER REGULATIONS OF PILOT HILL.

The following are the regulations of the placer district of Pilot Hill, Calaveras county, California:

Section 1. Each tunnelling and shafting claim shall consist of one hundred feet in width to the man, and running through the hill on a parallel line with the commencement of the tunnel.

Sec. 2. That each company holding tunnel or shafting claims, in order to hold the same, shall be required to perform work to the amount of twenty-five dollars each week for a period not to exceed twelve months.

Sec. 3. That each gulch claim shall consist of one hundred and fifty feet in length by fifty in width to each man.

Sec 4. That each surface claim shall consist of two hundred feet in length by one hundred feet in width to the man.

Sec. 5. That each gulch and surface claim shall be worked within three days after the date of location, if water can be obtained.

Sec. 6. That each tunnelling, shafting, gulch, and surface claim shall be marked off by stakes, or other marks, so that the boundaries of each claim can be distinctly traced.

(Pilot Hill and Kanaka Camp are not important districts, but their regulations are peculiar in some respects, and are therefore given here.)

15.—REGULATIONS OF NEW KANAKA CAMP.

The following are the regulations of New Kanaka Camp, in Tuolumne county:

Article 1. [This article describes the boundaries of the district.]

Art. 2. Creek claims shall be two hundred feet in length, and from bank to bank.

Art. 3. Gulch or ravine claims shall be two hundred feet in length and fifty in width.

Art. 4. All claims on bars or flats shall be two feet in length and fifty feet in width.

Art. 5. It shall be required that all claims be worked one full day in three, when permanent water can be had, except in cases of sickness or legal cause.

Art. 6. All miners are entitled to one claim by pre-emption and one by purchase; provided such claims purchased shall be, on investigation, found to have been obtained in a legal or *bona fide* manner.

Art. 7. Chinamen shall not be allowed to own claims in this district, either by purchase or pre-emption.

Art. 8. All persons who find it necessary to cut a tail-race to their claims shall have the privilege of cutting through any ground below them, owned by other parties, provided it will not result to the injury of such parties.

Art. 9. It shall be required of all persons owning claims in this district to designate the boundaries of said claims by digging a trench around the same.

Art. 10. All disputes arising in regard to mining shall be left to arbitration, each party to choose one man, and, in case of disagreement, they to choose an umpire.

Art. 11. Arbitrators in all cases, for services, shall be paid for all time consumed at the rate of three dollars per day.

ART. 12. All claims may be laid over, by having the same recorded, from the time ditch-water fails until it can be obtained again.

ART. 13. A recorder shall be chosen, whose duty shall be to keep a book of records, with the number of each claim recorded, from one to an unlimited number. It shall also be the duty of said recorder to go on to each and every claim recorded and post at either end of each claim a piece of tin, with the number stamped thereon, corresponding with the number on the book of record.

16.—REGULATIONS OF THE COPPEROPOLIS (COPPER) DISTRICT.

ARTICLE 1. This district shall be known as the Copper Cañon district.

ART. 2. The boundaries of this district shall be as follows, viz: Bounded on the north by the Angels' trail, east by Empire district, south by the O'Byrne Ferry district, and west by Black Oak, Four Spring Run, and Four Spring district.

ART. 3. A miner shall be entitled to one claim by location on a lead of one hundred and fifty feet in length and three hundred feet in width. Any miner discovering a new lead or vein shall be entitled to an extra claim of the above extent.

ART. 4. Claims shall be duly staked at each end, with at least one notice posted in a conspicuous place on the claim, with all the claimants' names therein, and such a notice shall be posted up as aforesaid once a year at least, and during the month of August, in the presence of witnesses.

ART. 5. Companies of miners having adjoining claims, and working together only one of such claims, shall hold good the balance of claims.

ART. 6. All claims, whether obtained by location or purchase, shall be represented in person or by proxy whenever they can be worked in conformity with the laws hereby prescribed.

ART. 7. There shall be one day's work done on each claim, or company's claim, once a month, commencing on the 1st of May and terminating on the 1st of December.

ART. 8. No claim shall be forfeited by sickness or legal inability of the claimant.

9. There shall be a recorder elected, whose duty it shall be to keep a correct copy of all claims in the district. It shall be the recorder's duty to visit the claims in person, and give an accurate description, landmarks, and also names of company occurring therein. His fee shall be fifty cents per claim.

ART. 10. When any dispute shall arise respecting claims in the district, each party shall select a disinterested miner to act as arbitrator to settle the matter in dispute, and if said arbitrators shall be unable to agree they shall choose another miner or referee, whose decision shall be final. All arbitrators and referees shall be chosen from the miners of this district.

Adopted August 3, 1860.

17.—STATUTE OF NEVADA CONCERNING MINING CLAIMS.

The following are the main sections of a statute of the State of Nevada approved February 27, 1866:

SECTION 1. Any six or more persons who are males of the age of twenty-one years and upwards, holding mining claims in any mining district, or who hold mineral lands not within the boundaries of any established mining district, may form a new mining district embracing said claims, at a meeting of such persons to be called by posting for five days in at least five conspicuous places within the limits of such proposed new district notices in writing stating the place and time for holding such meeting, describing as near as may be the limits of such proposed new district, and signed by not less than five of such persons. At said meeting all males of the age of twenty-one years and upward holding mining claims, or any interest therein, within said limits, may vote, and by a majority vote determine whether said new mining district shall be established, and its boundaries, which shall be within the limits named in said notices; and thereafter the persons so qualified and holding mining claims in such newly established district shall proceed to select a name therefor and elect a district recorder, who shall be qualified as aforesaid. He shall perform all the duties required of him by law, and shall, within thirty days after qualifying, file and record in his office a record of the proceedings of said meeting. No district formed under the provisions of this act shall be divided by any county line. Mining districts now existing may be continued.

SEC. 22. On and after the second Saturday of July, 1866, all locations of mining claims shall be made in the following manner: On a monument not less than three feet high, firmly established in a conspicuous place on the claim, there shall be placed a plainly-written notice embracing a description of the ground claimed, the date of location, the name of the claim, the name of the company, and the names of the locators, with the number of feet claimed by each, and a copy of said notice, accompanied by a written request for a survey of said claim by the district recorder, shall, within thirty days after the making of such location, be filed in the office of the district recorder of the district in which said claim is located; and in case there be no legally authorized district recorder in and for the district, or the claim be outside of the limits of an organized mining district, then, and in that case, said notice may be filed in the office of the county recorder of the county in which said claim is located; and a written request for a survey by the county surveyor shall be served upon the county surveyor within a reasonable time thereafter; the county surveyor, or his deputy, shall perform all the duties required of a district recorder by the provisions of this act. He shall keep a record of all his transactions in such cases, and for such services he may charge and receive the same fees allowed by law for his services in like cases. Within thirty days after the making of such location there shall be done on said claim, as assessment work, to hold the same up to and including the day preceding the first Saturday of the then following August, excavation involving the removal of fifty cubic feet of earth or loose material, or five cubic feet of solid rock, for each two hundred feet in the claim; and, as soon as may be thereafter, said district recorder shall survey the same and record the notice of survey as provided in section 14 of this act; and said district recorder shall file and record a certificate in regard to the assessment work, which shall be substantially in the following form:

—— DISTRICT, —— COUNTY, NEVADA, —— DAY OF —— MONTH OF —— YEAR.

This is to certify that on the —— claim governed by the —— company, surveyed on —— date, there has been done by or on behalf of said company sufficient work to hold said claim up to the first Saturday of August next.

——, *District Recorder.*

SEC. 23. Any person may locate mining claims in favor of others, but no person shall be entitled to hold by location more than two hundred feet of any one ledge, except by virtue of discovery of the same, for which he shall be entitled to hold two hundred feet additional. In the case of locations made as extensions, the location of two hundred feet by virtue of discovery is allowed. No claim shall, in the aggregate, exceed in extent two thousand feet on any one ledge.

SEC. 24. Any location made on a ledge by authority of this act shall be deemed to include all the dips, spurs, angles, and variations of said ledge. The locators of any ledge shall be entitled to hold one hundred feet on each side of the same, not interfering with the mining rights previously acquired by others' and all dips, spurs, angles, variations, veins, cross-ledges, strings, and feeders within such area of two hundred feet, by the extent of the claim on the supposed line of the ledge as located, shall be considered as claimed and held by said locators as a part of said ledge, and no ledge in any claim subsequently located shall be followed and worked within the said area without the permission of the holders of said area. All measurement of boundaries shall be horizontal air-lines. Nothing in this act shall be so construed as in any manner to change the amount of ground that may be held in any mining claim located and held in accordance with district mining laws, but on and after the first Saturday of August, 1866, all such claims shall in all other respects be subject to the provisions of this act. Locations may be made on blind ledges in the same manner as on cropping ledges, and any person, company, or corporation finding a blind ledge in any excavation made by him or them shall, for ten days after finding the same, have the exclusive privilege of locating the same.

Sec. 25. No person shall become a locator in more than one claim on the same ledge, and any second location made on the same ledge by or in the name of a party already located on such ledge shall be void.

Sec. 26. The holders of any claim shall have the right to use so much of the land in the vicinity thereof as may be requisite for dumps, for the erection of the necessary buildings, machinery, and other works connected with said claim, and for the convenient development and working of the same. And in the development and working of the said claim they may sink shafts and inclines, and run drifts, tunnels, and cuts on any lands in said vicinity, but the prior owner of such lands shall be entitled to reasonable compensation for all damages sustained by reason of such dumps, the erection of such works, or the conducting of such operations. If the prior owners of any such lands have duly claimed the same as mining ground, they shall be entitled to all the ores taken out in the course of such operations, and shall not be interfered with in the conducting of their own mining operations on their own claims. The amount of such compensation shall be determined by a majority of three commissioners, one of whom shall be appointed by such prior owners, one by the party engaged in such development or working, and one by the two thus selected. The amount so fixed shall, within fifteen days after the fixing of the same, be paid to said prior owners, or deposited in the county treasury, subject to the order of said prior owners. Said commissioners shall, before entering upon their duties, take and subscribe to an oath, before some person duly qualified to administer the same, to make a true appraisement thereof according to the best of their knowledge and belief.

Sec. 30. For the purposes of this act the term "foot," when used without qualification in relation to mining ground, is hereby declared to mean twelve lineal inches, horizontal air line measurement, on the line of the ledge as located; the term "assessment work" is hereby declared to mean the work done partly, in order to hold a claim, and involving the excavation of fifty cubic feet of earth or loose matter, or five cubic feet of solid rock, for each two hundred feet in the claim; the term "assessment dues" is hereby declared to mean two cents for each foot in a claim, to be paid for the purpose of holding the same one assessment year; and the term "assessment year" is hereby declared to mean the period extending from and including the first Saturday of August of one year to and including the day immediately preceding the first Saturday of August of the following year. The doing of assessment work or the payment of assessment dues shall be regarded as evidence of intention to hold the claim on which or with reference to which the same was done or paid, for the period for which the same was done or paid. The payment of assessment dues shall be in lieu of the assessment work heretofore usually required as an evidence of intention to hold a mining claim for a specified period; and such payment shall not be required in any case where the holders of a mining claim are in good faith, and to the extent specified in section thirty-two of this act, engaged in developing or working the same.

SEC. 31. On the first Saturday of August, 1866, at which time the first assessment year shall begin, this act shall supersede all district mining laws, and thereafter said laws shall be considered as repealed: *Provided*, Any and all rights heretofore acquired under and by virtue of such district mining laws shall be determined in accordance with said mining laws existing at the time when said rights were acquired. During the period extending from and including the first day of May, 1866, to and including the day immediately preceding the first Saturday of the following August, no claim shall become subject to relocation by reason of the non-performance of assessment work. Locations may be made under this act at any time on and after the second Saturday of July, 1866, at which time the district recorders elected under this act shall, if qualified, enter upon the discharge of their duties, and on and after said second Saturday of July no location shall be made under district mining laws.

SEC. 32. The doing of assessment work, or the payment of assessment dues, shall not be required in order to hold a claim during any assessment year, if during the year next preceding such assessment year there has been done on said claim, by or on behalf of the claimants thereof, an amount of work costing at a fair valuation not less than fifty cents for each foot in said claim; but in all other cases assessment work shall be done or assessment dues shall be paid as provided in this act. Assessment dues shall be paid for every assessment year by the parties holding the claim to the district recorder elected under this act, before the first Saturday of August commencing the assessment year for which they are paid, except as otherwise provided in this section.

SEC. 33. Except as otherwise provided in section 32, every mining claim located and held under district mining laws, on which before the first day of May, 1866, there has been work done involving the excavation of fifty cubic feet of earth or loose matter, or five cubic feet of solid rock, for each two hundred feet in such claim, shall be subject to assessment dues. On every mining claim located and held under district mining laws, on which such work has not been done before the first day of May, 1866, assessment work shall be done on or before the day immediately preceding the first Saturday of August, 1866. The doing of such assessment work or the paying of such assessment dues shall enable the owner of said claim to hold the same for the next ensuing assessment year, commencing on the first Saturday of August, 1866.

SEC. 34. The assessment work done within the thirty days after the location of a claim under this act, as provided in section 22, shall hold the same only up to the beginning of the assessment year following the date of said location, and for such next ensuing assessment year and for every year thereafter, except as provided in section 32 of this act, such claim shall be subject to assessment dues.

SEC. 45. The extraction of gold or other metals from alluvial or diluvial deposits, generally called placer mining, shall be subject to such regulations as the miners in the several mining districts shall adopt.

18.—REGULATIONS OF THE VIRGINIA DISTRICT, NEVADA.

The following are the regulations of the district of Virginia City, Nevada, adopted September 14, 1859:

ARTICLE 1. All quartz claims hereafter located shall be two hundred feet on the lead, including all its dips and angles.

ART. 2. All discoverers of new quartz veins shall be entitled to an additional claim for discovery.

ART. 3. All claims shall be designated by stakes and notices at each corner.

ART. 4. All quartz claims shall be worked to the amount of ten dollars or three days' work per month to each claim, and the owner can work to the amount of forty dollars as soon after the location of the claim as he may elect; which amount being worked shall exempt him from working on said claim for six months thereafter.

ART. 5. All quartz claims shall be known by a name and in sections.

ART. 6. All claims shall be properly recorded within ten days from the time of location.

ART. 7. All claims recorded in the Gold Hill record and lying in the Virginia district shall be recorded free of charge in the record of Virginia district, upon the presentation of a certificate from the recorder of the Gold Hill district certifying that said claims have been duly recorded in said district; and said claims shall be recorded within thirty days after the passage of this article.

ART. 9. Surface and hill claims shall be one hundred feet square, and be designated by stakes and notices at each corner.

ART. 10. All ravine and gulch claims shall be one hundred feet in length, and in width extend from bank to bank, and be designated by a stake and notice at each end.

ART. 11. All claims shall be worked within ten days after water can be had sufficient to work said claims.

ART. 12. All ravine, gulch and surface claims shall be recorded within ten days after location.

ART. 13. All claims not worked according to the laws of this district shall be forfeited and subject to relocation.

ART. 14. There shall be a recorder elected, to hold his office for the term of twelve months, who shall be entitled to the sum of fifty cents for each claim located and recorded.

ART. 15. The recorder shall keep a book with all the laws of this district written therein, which shall at all times be subject to the inspection of the miners of said district; and he is furthermore required to post in two conspicuous places a copy of the laws of said district.

19.—REGULATIONS OF REESE RIVER DISTRICT, NEVADA.

The following are the regulations of the Reese River district, Nevada:

SECTION. 1. The district shall be known as the Reese River mining district, and shall be bounded as follows, to wit: On the north by a distance of ten miles from the overland telegraph line, on the east by Dry creek, on the south by a distance of ten miles from the overland telegraph line, and on the west by Edward's creek, where not conflicting with any new districts formed to date.

SEC. 2. There shall be a mining recorder elected on the first day of June next for this district, who shall hold office for one year from the 17th of July next, unless sooner removed by a new election, which can only be done by a written call, signed by at least fifty claim-holders, giving notice of a new election to be held, after said notice shall have been posted and published for at least twenty days in some newspaper published in or nearest this district; and the recorder shall be a resident of this district.

SEC. 3. It shall be the duty of the recorder to keep in a suitable book or books a full and truthful record of the proceedings of all public meetings; to place on record all claims brought to him for that purpose, when such claim shall not interfere with or affect the rights and interests of prior locators, recording the same in the order of their date, for which service he shall receive one dollar ($1) for each claim recorded. It shall also be the duty of the recorder to keep his books open at all times to the inspection of the public; he shall also have the power to appoint a deputy to act in his stead, for whose official acts he shall be held responsible. It shall also be the duty of the recorder to deliver to his successor in office all books, records, papers, &c., belonging to or pertaining to his office.

SEC. 4. All examinations of the record must be made in the full presence of the recorder or his deputy.

SEC. 5 Notice of a claim of location of mining ground by any individual, or by a company, on file in the recorder's office, shall be deemed equivalent to a record of the same.

SEC. 6. Each claimant shall be entitled to hold by location two hundred feet on any lead in the district, with all the dips, spurs, and angles, offshoots, outcrops, depths, widths, variations, and all the mineral and other valuables therein contained, the discoverer of and locator of a new lead being entitled to one claim extra for discovery.

SEC 7 The locator of any lead, lode, or ledge in the district shall be entitled to hold on each side of the lead, lode, or ledge located by him or them one hundred feet; but this shall not be construed to mean any distinct or parallel ledge within the two hundred feet other than the one originally located.

SEC 8 All locations shall be made by a written notice posted upon the ground, and boundaries described, and all claimants' names posted on the notice.

SEC. 9. Work done on any tunnel, cut, shaft, or drift, in good faith, shall be considered as being done upon the claim owned by such person or company.

SEC. 10. Every claim (whether by individual or company) located shall be recorded within ten days after the date of location.

SEC 11. All miners locating a mining claim in this district shall place and maintain thereon a good and substantial monument or stake, with a notice thereon of the name of the claim, the names of the locators, date of location, record, and extent of claim. It is hereby requested that owners in claims already located do comply with the requirements of this section.

SEC. 12. The recorder shall go upon the ground with any and all parties desiring to locate claims, and shall be entitled to receive for such service one dollar for each and every name in a location of two hundred feet each.

SEC. 13. It is hereby made the duty of the mining recorder, upon the written application of twenty-five miners, to call a meeting of the miners of the district by giving a notice of twenty days through some newspaper published in the Reese River district, which notice shall state the object of the meeting and the place and time of holding the same.

SEC. 14. The laws of this district passed July 17, 1862, are hereby repealed.

SEC. 15. These laws shall take effect on and after the fourth day of June, 1864.

20.—QUARTZ STATUTE OF THE STATE OF OREGON.

SECTION 1. That any person, or company of persons, establishing a claim on any quartz lead containing gold, silver, copper, tin, or lead, or a claim on a vein of cinnabar, for the purpose of mining the same, shall be allowed to have, hold, and possess the land or vein, with all its dips, spurs, and angles, for the distance of three hundred feet in length and seventy-five feet in width on each side of such lead or vein.

SEC. 2. To establish a valid claim the discoverer or person wishing to establish a claim shall post a notice on the lead or vein, with name or names attached, which shall protect the claim or claims for thirty days; and before the expiration of said thirty days he or they shall cause the claim or claims to be recorded as hereinafter provided, and describing, as near as may be, the claim or claims, and their location; but continuous working of said claim or claims shall obviate the necessity of such record. If any claim shall not be worked for twelve consecutive months it shall be forfeited and considered liable to location by any person or persons, unless the owner or owners be absent on account of sickness, or in the service of their country in time of war.

SEC. 3. Any person may hold one claim by location, as hereinafter provided, upon each lead or vein, and as many by purchase as the local laws of the miners in the district where such claims are located may allow; and the discoverer of any new lead or vein, not previously located upon, shall be allowed one additional claim for the discovery thereof. Nothing in this section shall be so construed as to allow any person not the discoverer to locate more than one claim upon any one lead or vein.

SEC. 4. Every person, or company of persons, after establishing such claim or claims, shall, within one year after recording or taking such claim or claims, work or cause to be worked to the amount of fifty dollars for each and every claim, and for each successive year shall do the same amount of work, under penalty of forfeiture of said claim or claims: *Provided*, That any incorporate company owning claims on any lead or vein may be allowed to work upon any one claim the whole amount required as above for all the claims they may own on such lead or vein.

SEC. 5 It shall be the duty of the county clerk of any county, upon the receipt of a notice of a miners' meeting organizing a miners' district in said county, with a description of the boundaries thereof, to record the same in a book to be kept in his office as other county records, to be called a "book of record of mining claims;" and, upon the petition of parties interested, he may appoint a deputy for such district, who shall reside in said district or its vicinity, and shall record all mining claims and water rights in the order in which they are presented for record; and shall transmit a copy of such record at the end of each month to the county clerk, who shall record the same in the above-mentioned book of record, for which he shall receive one dollar for each and every claim. It shall further be the duty of said county clerk to furnish a copy of this law to his said deputy, who shall keep the same in his office, open at all reasonable times for the inspection of all persons interested therein

SEC. 6. Miners shall be empowered to make local laws in relation to the possession of water rights, the possession and working of placer claims, and the survey and sale of town lots in mining camps, subject to the laws of the United States.

SEC. 7. That ditches used for mining purposes, and mining flumes permanently affixed to the soil, be and they are hereby declared real estate for all intents and purposes whatever.

SEC. 8. That all laws relative to the sale and transfer of real estate, and the application of the liens of mechanics and laborers therein, be and they are hereby made applicable to said ditches and flumes: *Provided*, That all interests in mining claims known as placer or surface diggings may be granted, sold, and conveyed by bill of sale and delivery of possession, as in cases of the sale of personal property: *Provided further*, That the bills of sale or conveyances executed on the sale of any placer or surface mining claim shall be recorded within thirty days after the date of such sale, in the office of the county clerk of the county in which such sale is made, in a book to be kept by the county clerk for that purpose, to be called the record of conveyances of mining claims.

SEC. 9. Mortgages of interests in placer or surface mining claims shall be executed, acknowledged, recorded, and foreclosed as mortgages of chattels.

SEC. 10. The county clerk shall be entitled to a fee of one dollar each for every conveyance or mortgage recorded under the provisions of this act.

21.—QUARTZ STATUTE OF IDAHO.

The following is the statute of Idaho in regard to quartz claims:

SECTION 1. That any person or persons who may hereafter discover any quartz lead or lode shall be entitled to one claim thereon by right of discovery, and one claim each by location.

SEC. 2. That a quartz claim shall consist of two hundred feet in length along the lead or lode by one hundred feet in breadth, covering and including all dips, spurs, and angles within the bounds of said claim, as also the right of drainage, tunnelling, and such other privileges as may be necessary to the working of said claim.

SEC. 3. The locator of any quartz claim on any lead or lode shall, at the time of locating such claim, place a substantial stake, not less than three inches in diameter, at each end of said claim, on which shall be a written notice specifying the name of the locator, the number of feet claimed, together with the year, month, and day when the same was taken.

SEC. 4. All claims shall be recorded in the county recorder's office, within ten days from the time of posting notice thereon : *Provided*, That when the claim located is more than thirty miles distant from the county seat the time shall extend to fifteen days.

SEC. 5. Quartz claims recorded in accordance with the provisions of section 4 of this act shall entitle the person so recording to hold the same to the use of himself, his heirs and assigns : *Provided*, That within six months from and after the date of recording he shall perform, or cause to be performed, thereon work amounting in value to the sum of one hundred dollars.

SEC. 6. Any person or persons holding quartz claims in pursuance of this act shall renew the notice required in section 3 at least once in twelve months, unless such claimant is occupying and working the same.

SEC. 7. The conveyances of quartz claims heretofore made by bills of sale or other instruments of writing, with or without seals, shall be construed in accordance with the local mining rules, regulations, and customs of miners in the several mining districts, and said bills of sale or instruments of writing concerning quartz claims without seals shall be *prima facie* evidence of sale, as if such conveyance had been made by deed under seal.

SEC. 8. Conveyances of quartz claims shall hereafter require the same formalities and shall be subject to the same rules of construction as the transfer and conveyance of real estate.

SEC. 9. The location and pre-emption of quartz claims heretofore made shall be established and proved when there is a contest before the courts, by the local rules, customs, and regulations of the miners in each mining district where such claim is located, when not in conflict with the laws of the United States or the laws of this Territory.

SEC. 10. This act to take effect and to be in force from and after its approval by the governor.

Approved February 4, 1864.

23.—STATUTE OF ARIZONA.

The following is the statute of Arizona on the registry and government of mines and mineral deposits, with the exception of the sections providing the manner in which the rights of miners shall be enforced by the courts :

SECTION 1. All mining rights on the public lands of the United States, as well as rights acquired by discovery on the lands of private individuals, are possessory in their character only, and such possessory rights shall be limited, regulated, and governed as hereinafter provided.

SEC. 15. Every mining claim or pertenencia is declared to consist of a superficial area of two hundred yards square, to be measured so as to include the principal mineral vein or mineral deposits, always having reference to and following the dip of the vein so far as it can or may be worked, with all the earth and minerals therein. But any mining district organized in accordance with the provisions of this chapter may prescribe the dimensions of said mining claim or pertenencia for such district : *Provided*, That in no case the dimensions so prescribed shall exceed the number of yards allowed by this section ; *and further provided,* That no such mining district shall diminish the extent of the territorial claim to one pertenencia, as defined in this section.

SEC. 16. Any person discovering or opening a vein or other mineral deposit in this Territory, not actually worked or legally owned by other parties or registered in accordance with this chapter, shall by properly denouncing and registering the same be entitled to claim and hold a possessory right to a tract of land to the extent of two mining claims or pertenencias, including the said vein or mineral deposit, and conforming as nearly as possible to the general direction thereof, each to be measured two hundred yards long by two hundred yards wide, the direction of the lines to be determined by the person claiming.

SEC. 17. If two or more persons are associated, and have formed a company for the exploration and working of mines, and one or several shall make discoveries of mineral deposits in consequence thereof, said company so engaged in exploration shall be entitled to denounce and register one discovery claim only upon each lode.

SEC. 18. It shall be lawful for the claimants of a mine or mineral lands to locate and take possession of public lands for a mill site and other necessary works connected therewith, which shall not exceed one quarter section, containing a stream or other water suitable for the purpose. They shall have a right to place a dam or other obstructions on such stream, and to divert its waters for the above uses and purposes. They shall, within the time and in the manner prescribed in this chapter for the registration and denouncement of mines, proceed to denounce and register the same with the clerk of the probate court, and they shall be known as auxiliary lands. And if within three years from the day their notice of claim is so recorded, they shall expend in fitting the same for a mill, or in placing a mill or reduction works thereon, the sum of one hundred dollars, they may cause the record of such work to be made and proceedings for confirming their title to be instituted as provided in section 29 of this chapter, with like effect, and receive a certificate of title as therein provided, conforming as nearly as they can to the requirements of that section. Instead of the work required by section 32 of this chapter they shall use the machinery or other works erected upon said land for mining purposes at least thirty days in each year. Such claims shall be subject to all the provisions of this chapter which are applicable to mining rights, and may be abandoned and relocated. All rights to auxiliary lands acquired under the laws of any mining district before this act takes effect shall be valid, and the owners of the same, upon complying with the provisions of this section, may take the like proceedings to confirm their titles, with a like effect.

SEC. 19. It shall be the duty of all claimants of mining claims, mineral lands, and auxiliary tracts, to at once define the extent and boundary of them as nearly as possible, by good substantial monuments or other conspicuous marks, in the presence of the recorder of the mining district, or of some witness who shall prove to the satisfaction of the recorder that the same has been done, and to post up a public notice of their claim at the opening of the principal vein, and to have them properly registered and recorded within three months from the time of first claiming them at the office of the mining district recorder according to the provisions of this chapter. Such record shall give a faithful description of the veins, mineral deposits, and tracts of lands, the character and bearing of the veins or deposits, and their connection with natural monuments or conspicuous objects in the vicinity.

SEC. 20. No person shall change his original monuments or boundaries of mineral or other lands, but if a subsequent investigation makes this convenient or necessary, and it can be done without prejudice to other parties, then such change shall take place by the sanction of the judge of the probate court, provided they are properly recorded, and the new boundaries and monuments fixed at once when the original ones are removed.

Sec. 21. All minerals, woods, waters, earths, and vegetation found within the boundaries of any tract of land registered and claimed for mining shall be exclusively used by him or them who are legally entitled to the possession of the land wherein or whereon they are situated, so long as they are used for mining purposes only : *Provided*, That no one shall have the right to prevent transient persons from using the waters along the public highways, where they were provided by nature in natural tanks, springs, streams, or otherwise, nor from making such equitable disposition of the waters as the legislature shall prescribe.

Sec. 22. No person shall have the right to impede or inconvenience travelling by fencing up the public roads, filling them up with rubbish, or undermining them so as to endanger their safety, neither shall any one change their established direction without sanction of the proper authorities.

Sec. 23. Whenever two or more persons or parties explore and prospect one and the same vein, and at or about the same time but at different places, and without knowledge of each other, then he or they who shall prove first occupancy shall have the right of first location, taking the principal point of excavation as the centre of their claim or claims on each side along the general direction of such vein or deposit. The other parties shall proceed by the same laws after the others have fixed their boundaries. Should there be left vacant ground between the different parties, then it shall be at the option of the first discoverers so to change their boundaries as shall best suit them, and have them recorded accordingly Any other parties shall locate in the order of the time of their arrival on the vein or mineral deposit.

Sec. 24. Whenever two or more parties shall select the same mine or mineral deposit for exploration, and the parties first on the ground, knowing the other parties to be at work, shall fail to give warning, either verbally or in writing, of their priority claim on such vein or deposit, then that portion of the mine situated between the main excavations of the two parties shall be equally divided between them, irrespective of the number of members each company may have : *Provided*, That the intervening portions shall not exceed the quantity of land allowed by the provisions of this chapter.

Sec. 25. The laws and proceedings of all mining districts established in this Territory for the denouncement, registration, and regulation of mines, mining claims, mineral lands, and auxiliary lands, prior to the day this act takes effect, are hereby legalized and declared to be as valid and binding in all courts of law as if enacted by this legislative assembly, to the extent and under the conditions and restrictions herein contained.

I. All rights, claims, and titles to any veins, mineral lands, or mineral deposits, and auxiliary lands, acquired before this act takes effect, under, by virtue of, and in conformity to the laws of said mining districts, are hereby declared to be valid and legal, and shall be respected and enforced in all courts of this Territory, when sustained by the evidence herein provided; but no amount of work done thereon shall be construed to give a perpetual title thereto, but shall give such title only and such rights and privileges as is provided in section 29 of this chapter.; and no person who was at the time of the location of his claim an inhabitant of this Territory shall forfeit his claim because he was not a resident also of the mining district in which his said claim was located. And no such right, claim, or title shall be considered as abandoned provided the claimant shall within six months from the day this act takes effect file with the clerk of the probate court of the county in which his claim is situated a brief description of the same, giving the name of the district in which the lode is situated, and of the lode or lodes, and the extent of his claim thereon, with a declaration that he intends to retain and work the same according to law, unless such claim has been forfeited and subject to relocation under the laws of such mining district before this act takes effect.

II. All records and all papers required by the laws of said mining districts to be deposited with the recorders of said districts for record shall be received as evidence of their contents in all courts of this Territory, and shall not be rejected for any defects in their form, when their contents may be understood, but shall be valid to the extent provided by said mining laws, except as hereinbefore restricted: *Provided*, That such records and papers are deposited with or recorded by the clerk of the probate court of the county in which said mining district is located, and within three months from the time this acts takes effect; and if said records or papers are lost or mutilated, or if such recorder of a mining district shall neglect or refuse to deposit the same as aforesaid, an affidavit of their contents made by any person interested therein, or certified or sworn copies thereof, may be so recorded, and shall have the like effect.

III. All conveyances of mines, mining rights, mineral and auxiliary lands made prior to the time this act takes effect shall be valid and binding to pass the title of the grantor thereof, although defective in form and execution, if their contents can be understood, and as such shall be received and regarded in all courts of this Territory; *Provided*, That such conveyances shall be deposited with or recorded by the clerk of the probate court of the county where said mines are situated, within three months from the time this act takes effect, and if lost or mutilated, copies or affidavits of their contents, executed as aforesaid, may be recorded as provided above.

Sec. 26. Every recorder, register, clerk, or other recording officer, of every such mining district, or who has at any time acted as such recording officer, within three months after this act takes effect, shall deposit with the clerk of the probate court of the county in which said district or greater part thereof is situated, all records which he has so kept, and all papers deposited in his hands for record, and papers so made or deposited with his predecessors in said office, which are in his hands as aforesaid, or he shall so deposit certified copies of the same. And such records and other papers shall be securely kept by such clerk, open in office hours to public inspection, and copies of the same duly certified by him shall be received in all courts of justice, and have the same effect as the originals. And any such recorder, register, or other recording officer of each mining district who shall neglect or refuse to comply with the provisions of this section shall be liable in damages to the party injured thereby, and shall be liable to be punished by the judge of probate of the county in which said mining district, or the greater part thereof, is situated, for contempt, by fine not exceeding five thousand dollars and imprisoned not more than one year, and shall be incapable of holding any such office and mining claim.

Sec. 27. Mining districts now existing may be continued, or new mining districts may be established in the manner and for the purposes hereinafter provided.

I. The recorder of every mining district now existing shall at the same time that he deposits the records of said districts with the clerk of the probate court, as the last preceding section requires, take an oath before the judge of said court that he will faithfully perform the duties of his office until another recorder shall be elected and qualified in his place, which oath shall be recorded by the clerk of the probate court. He shall record in a book to be kept by him for that purpose all notices of claims or rights to veins, mineral deposits, mineral lands, and auxiliary lands which may be left with him to be recorded, and shall note on all papers which may be received by him to be recorded, the time when they were so received by him, and they shall be considered as recorded from that time. He shall, when requested by any such claimant, go with him to his claim and see that the same is measured by metes and bounds, and marked by substantial monuments on the surface of the earth, and shall make a record of the same, and of the time when it was done, and certify it to be correct, or shall make a record and certificate of the same on the evidence of a credible witness, who was present when the same was done, and is cognizant of the facts, and whose name shall be entered on the record. He shall, when requested by any such claimant, go with him to his claim and examine any shaft that may be sunk by him, or tunnels that may be opened to the same, and make measurements of the same, and a record and certificate as aforesaid; and he shall in like manner examine, measure, or estimate, and make and record a certificate of any work which is required by law to be done by a claimant. And the said recording officer shall, quarterly, file with the clerk of the probate court of the county in which said district is located a copy by him certified of all records made by him for the three months last preceding, which shall be duly recorded by said clerk, and a copy of said record duly certified by him shall be evidence of its contents in all courts of this Territory. And such recording officer shall be liable to all the penalties provided in the preceding section if he shall neglect or refuse to perform any of the acts and duties required of him by this section, but shall not be required to perform any such service until his fees for the same, to be fixed by the mining districts, are paid him, if he requests it. And if any paper deposited with him for record is required to be recorded by the clerk of the probate court, he shall at the time said paper is so deposited with him take and receive the fee fixed by law for recording such paper by said clerk, and pay the said clerk said fee when he deposits said paper with him to be recorded as aforesaid. All such mining districts may make laws not inconsistent with the laws of the Territory, may elect officers for the government of such districts, and fix their compensation, but all such acts and proceedings shall be recorded, and all records and papers thereof filed with the clerk of the probate court as aforesaid.

II. Any number of persons, not less than twelve, owning mining claims in any mining district, or in any contiguous mining districts, or who have discovered and may wish to denounce a mine or mineral lands, not within the limits of any established mining district, may proceed to make a new mining district at a meeting of persons holding claims in such district so to be established, and of claimants in any districts to be divided or to be included therein. They shall cause a notice in writing, and specifying the limits of said contemplated district, signed by them, to be posted in three conspicuous places in said district, and if any part of an established district is to be included therein by leaving a copy of said notice with the recorder of said district at least ten days before the day of said meeting. At said meeting all persons holding claims as aforesaid may vote, and may determine by a majority vote of those present whether said new district shall be established, and its limits, but within the boundaries named in the notice for said meeting, and thereupon the persons holding claims in such newly established district shall proceed to select a name, and make laws therefor, and elect a recorder, who shall be qualified as aforesaid, who shall perform all the duties and be subject to all the liabilities provided in this chapter for such officers, and shall file with the clerk of the probate court as aforesaid a record of the proceedings of this and all subsequent meetings at the time and in the manner herein provided.

SEC. 28. It shall be the duty of all claimants of mineral tracts to sink at least one shaft of thirty feet in depth, or to run a tunnel of fifty feet in length, in the body of the vein or in the adjoining rock, so as to test the vein from the surface, for the purpose of ascertaining the character and capacity of such mineral deposit, within the space of one year from the day of first taking possession thereof, and they shall notify the recorder of the mining district that said shaft or other work is completed, and that they intend working the vein or mineral deposit. And the recorder shall examine said work in person, and make and record a certificate of the result of such examination, which shall contain a statement of the condition and quality of the vein or mineral deposit, the amount of labor performed, and a general view of the results obtained. Said report shall be accompanied by three specimens taken from different parts of the work, which said specimens, with a copy of the record so made by him, shall be filed by him within the time required by this act in the office of the clerk of the probate court. And said clerk shall make a record of the same. Such specimens shall be numbered and described by him, and be preserved for the use of the mineralogical professorship of the University of Arizona.

SEC. 29. The judge of the probate court, at any time within thirty days after the record made by the clerk of said court, as provided in the preceding section, upon complaint in writing made to him by such claimants, describing fully their claims, stating the labor performed by them, and the certificate thereof, and that the registration of the same has been made as required by law, and requesting that their title thereto may be confirmed, shall cause a summons, under the seal of his court, to be issued, requiring all persons interested to appear at a day named therein, and which shall not be less than sixty days from the day the same was issued, and show cause why the title of such complainants and claimants should not be confirmed, a copy of which complaint and summons, duly attested by the clerk of the probate court, shall be published twice in the Territorial newspaper, and be kept posted in the office of said clerk from the day of issuing the same to the return day thereof; and if no person shall appear on such return day to contest the right of the claimants to such claims the judge of probate shall examine all the records filed in the office of his clerk relating to such claims, and if he finds that the said claimants have in all respects complied with the provisions of this chapter, he shall make a decree in substance that the complainants having complied with the laws of this Territory relating to the denouncement and registration of mines have acquired a perfect title to their claims (describing the same) until the 1st day of January, A. D. 1868, and forever after unless abandoned by them. And the said clerk shall give the said claimant a copy of such decree, under the seal of the court, which shall be conclusive evidence of title in any proceedings relating to such claims, until they are abandoned. And unless the persons adversely interested and contesting the title of the complainants shall appear on the day named in said complaint, and proceed as hereinafter provided, they shall be forever barred from contesting the title of said complainants to such claims. And if the contestants shall so appear they shall on that day or some day to be fixed by said judge proceed to file an answer, setting forth their claim and case, and the proceedings shall then be conducted in conformity to the provisions of this chapter and the code of civil practice. And whenever a final decree is made thereon, determining the title to said claim or mine, by said judge, or by any other court on appeal, the said judge shall cause a record to be made in the office of his clerk of such decree, and a certified copy thereof may be made as aforesaid, with the like effect. And any claimants of mineral lands who before this act takes effect have in any way or under any law acquired a title to such mineral lands, after filing with the clerk of the court their evidence of title and description of claim as required by this chapter, may cause an examination of the shaft sunk by them or other work done by them to be made as aforesaid, and take the like proceedings for the confirmation of their titles, with the same effect : *Provided,* This section shall not apply except when the complainants are in possession of such mine or mining rights, claiming title thereto.

SEC. 30. By reason of the Indian wars and unsettled condition of the country, the time within which a shaft is required to be sunk, or other labor performed on a claim, shall not commence until two years from the day this act takes effect, and all the provisions of this chapter relating thereto are suspended for that time ; but any claimant may sink a shaft or do such other labor, and at any time after the record of their claims with the probate court, and thereupon institute proceedings to confirm their titles, and be entitled to all the rights and privileges provided for in this chapter.

SEC. 31. No single person or company shall be compelled to sink shafts or make other improvements on more than one of the tracts of land claimed by him or them for the same vein or mineral deposit; and any number of claimants on the same vein or mineral deposit, who may unite for said purpose, shall be allowed to concentrate labor, capital, and energy to any one single point which to him or them shall be best suited to ascertain to the best advantage the general character, quality, and capacity of that particular vein or mineral deposit, and may take the like proceedings to confirm their titles.

SEC. 32. After the work required by section 28 of this chapter has been performed, and the record thereof made as therein provided, two years shall be allowed the claimants of mineral lands to develop the same, and procure machinery and provide for working the same; and during that time the same shall not be considered abandoned, although no work be done thereon: *Provided*, That, in such an event, they shall annually, and before the first day of June in each year, file with the clerk of the probate court an affidavit signed by them that they have not abandoned such claims, but intend, in good faith, to work them; and said term of two years shall not commence until the first day of January, A. D. 1868. And after the expiration of said term of two years, it shall be obligatory upon claimants to such mineral lands to hold actual possession of them and work the vein, which obligation shall be considered as complied with by doing at least thirty days' work thereon in each year; but if such claimants are prevented from working such vein by the hostility of Indians or other good cause, rendering said working difficult or dangerous, they may, by authority of the judge of probate first obtained, be relieved from performing labor thereon from time to time, but for not more than one year at any one time, during the continuance of such cause.

SEC. 33. Any person who may discover a mineral vein or deposit as aforesaid, which is not included within a mining district, or which may be in a mining district in which there is no legally authorized recorder, may acquire title thereto, and to auxiliary lands, by giving notice as aforesaid, and recording the same with the clerk of the probate court of the county in which the same is situated, and may take the same proceedings, with the like effect, with the clerk of the probate court that are required to be taken with the recorder of a mining district.

SEC. 34. Discoverers of mines on lands in the legal ownership or possession of others, and not public lands, before doing the work of sinking the shaft required by section 28 of this chapter, shall pay to such parties such compensation for the use of the same as may be awarded by the judge of probate upon complaint of either party, or shall give bond to such parties for payment of the same, and sureties to be approved by said judge; and whenever it becomes necessary or advantageous to construct tunnels for the purpose of drainage, ventilation, or the better hauling of ores or other subterraneous products or mining materials, it shall be lawful for any party or parties to construct such tunnel or drift through all private and public property: *Provided*, That all damages arising from such subterranean works to the other parties, to be determined as provided above, shall be paid by the parties for whose benefit such tunnelling is done, to be paid before such work is commenced, or security given to the satisfaction of the judge of probate for the payment of the same; but no damages shall be paid on public lands when claims for such lands shall be set up after such tunnel shall have been projected or actually in process of construction: *Provided*, That the lapse of time between projection and actual work shall not exceed ninety days, and that the tunnelling parties give timely notice of their project to any new claimant of the so affected ground.

SEC. 35. Whenever such tunnel as mentioned in the preceding section shall intersect or traverse mineral deposits, or run along lodes claimed and held by other parties, then it shall be at the option of the owners of such other mineral deposits either to pay one-half of the expense of excavation for the distance that such tunnel runs through their mineral deposits, and secure the whole of the ores excavated, or to divide the ores with the tunnelling parties, the latter paying all expenses of excavation; or it shall be optional with either party to abandon all claim to the ores excavated.

SEC. 36. If, in the construction of such subterranean works, new veins or deposits are encountered in ground not claimed or owned by other parties, they shall become the property of the party for whom such tunnel is constructed, and shall be denounced and registered as is required of new mines, and shall be governed by the same laws as are prescribed in this chapter.

SEC. 37. Any claimant or claimants not complying with any of the foregoing conditions and obligations shall forfeit all right to any such recorded or unrecorded claims to mineral and auxiliary tracts; and it shall not be lawful for him or them to register such claims anew within a period of three years after such forfeiture. All such tracts shall be free for working and registry to any but those excepted in this section.

SEC. 38. All veins and mineral deposits situated on public lands, which have not been worked and occupied from the time of the acquisition of the Territory by the United States up to the time of the passage of this chapter, except as herein provided, shall be considered as abandoned and subject to registry and denouncement.

SEC. 39. All veins and mineral deposits that have been or may be abandoned hereafter shall, in all cases and respects, be governed by the laws regulating the opening and working of new veins and deposits, as prescribed in this chapter.

SEC. 40. Whenever any mine, vein, or mineral deposit shall have been abandoned or forfeited in accordance with the provisions of this chapter, and registered anew by other parties, it shall be obligatory upon such parties to give the former owners warning thereof, so as to remove from the tract within the space of three months anything he or they may claim valuable or useful. Such warning shall be given in the nearest newspaper published in the Territory, and by posting it at three of the most conspicuous places in the county where the mine is situated. Three months after the expiration of such warning, any and all buildings, furnaces, arrastras, metals, and every other species of property which may still remain on the ground of such mine, vein, or mineral deposit, shall become the undisputed property of the new claimant, without compensation of any kind to any person whatever.

SEC. 41. Any person taking possession of or entering upon a mining claim or auxiliary lands, registered according to the provisions of this chapter, and before it is abandoned, shall be ousted therefrom in a summary manner by the order of the probate judge, and the malfeasor shall be adjudged to pay all damages and costs consequent thereon.

SEC. 51. It shall be the duty of persons who may discover and claim mining rights or mineral lands, at the same time that they may define the boundary of their claim or claims to any lode or mine as required by the provisions of this chapter, to lay off and define the boundary of one pertenencia as required by the provisions of this chapter, adjoining their claim or claims, which shall be the property of the Territory of Arizona. And at the same time that they present their notice of claim or claims to be recorded by the recorder of the mining district, they shall also present to such recorder the claim of said Territory. And if said discoverers and claimants shall neglect or refuse to present to such recorder the claim of said Territory as aforesaid, they shall forever forfeit all claim to the mine or ledge so discovered by them. Any recording officer recording the claim or claims of such discoverers and claimants, when the claim of said Territory is not filed therewith as aforesaid, shall be subject to all the penalties provided in section 26 of this chapter. Such claim shall be recorded as provided in this chapter for like claims, but no work shall be required to be done thereon, nor shall it be considered to be abandoned so long as it is the property of the Territory; and if sold, the time within which the purchaser shall be required to work said claim shall commence from the day of sale, except when the time is suspended as before provided. Every clerk of the probate court, as soon as he records the said claim, shall send a copy of his record to the treasurer of the Territory, and no fees shall be charged by any recording officer in any matter relating to said claim. And the territorial treasurer may at any time after six months from the day he receives such record as aforesaid, and at such time and place as in his opinion will be most for the interest of the Territory, cause such claim to be sold at auction to the highest bidder, but every such sale shall be at least twice advertised in the territorial newspaper, and be held at his office, or the office of the clerk of the probate court, or recorder of the mining district of the county where the claim is situated. And the treasurer is authorized to make a deed of the same to the purchaser in the name of the Territory; and the amount received by him shall be added by him to any fund now or hereafter provided for the protection of the people of the Territory of Arizona against hostile Indians, and be expended as provided by law. And after all expenses as are incurred by the territorial authorities for the purpose of destroying or bringing into subjection all hostile Indian tribes in this Territory are liquidated, then all remaining or accruing funds, out of all or any sales of territorial mining claims, shall be applied as a sinking fund for school purposes.

SEC. 52. The extraction of gold from alluvial and diluvial deposits, generally termed placer mining, shall not be considered mining proper, and shall not entitle persons occupied in it to the provisions of this chapter, nor shall any previous section of this chapter be so construed as to refer to the extraction of gold from the above mentioned deposits.

SEC. 53. This chapter shall be in force and take effect from and after the 1st day of January, A. D. 1865.

23.—THE MINING LAWS OF MEXICO.

The following are extracts from the royal ordinance of the King of Spain, published in 1783, and ever since in force in Mexico. The translation is by Rockwell.* Only those portions of the ordinance are copied relating to the location, size, and tenure of claims. The sections not quoted are devoted mainly to a statement of the manner in which the miners are to enforce their legal rights:

CHAPTER IV.

SECTION 1. As it is most just and proper to reward with particularity and distinction those persons who devote themselves to the discovery of new mineral places and metallic veins found therein in proportion to the importance and utility of such discovery, I order and command that the discoverers of one or more mineral mountains, wherein no mine or shaft has been open before, acquire in the principal vein as much as three portions, together or separate, where it best pleases them, according to the measures hereafter signified; and that, on having discovered more veins, they shall acquire a portion in each vein, fixing on and marking the said portions within the term of ten days.

SEC. 2. The discoverer of a new vein in a mountain known and worked in other parts may hold in it two portions, together or separated by other mines, on condition that he specifies them within ten days, as mentioned in the preceding section.

SEC. 3. He who proposes for a new mine in a vein already known and worked in part is not to be considered a discoverer.

* A compilation of Spanish and Mexican law in relation to mines and titles to real estate in force in California, Texas, and New Mexico, and in the countries acquired under the Louisiana and Florida treaties when annexed to the United States. By J. A. Rockwell. New York, 1851.

SEC. 4. The person referred to in the preceding sections must present a written statement to the deputation of miners in that district, or in case there should not be one in that district, to the nearest thereunto, specifying in it his name, those of his associates, (if he has any,) the place of his birth, his place of habitation, profession, and employment, together with the most particular and distinguishing features of the tract, mountain, or vein of which he claims the discovery; all which circumstances, as well as the hour in which the discoverer shall present himself, must be noted down in a register kept by the deputation and clerk, (if they have one;) and after this the said written statement shall, for his due security, be restored to the discoverer, and notices of its object and contents shall be affixed to the doors of the church, the government houses, and other public buildings of the town for the sake of general notoriety.

And I ordain that within the term of ninety days the discoverer shall cause to be made in the vein or veins so registered a pit of a yard and a half in diameter or breadth and ten yards (varas) in depth, and that immediately on the existence of the vein being ascertained one of the deputies in person shall visit it, accompanied by the clerk, (if there is one,) or if there be no clerk, by two assisting witnesses and by the mining professor of that territory, in order to inspect the course and direction of the vein, its size, its inclination on the horizon, called its falling or declivity, its hardness or softness, the greater or less firmness of its bed, and the principal marks and species of the mineral; taking exact account of all this in order to add the same to the entry in the register, together with the act of possession, which must immediately be given to the discoverer in my royal name, measuring him his portion, and making him enclose it by poles at the limits as hereafter declared; after which, an authentic copy of the proceedings shall be delivered to him for the security of his title.

SEC. 5. If during the above-named ninety days any one should appear asserting a right to the said discovery, a brief judicial hearing shall be granted, and judgment given in favor of him who best proves his claim; however, if this should happen after the stated time, he (the new claimant) shall not be heard.

SEC. 6. The restorers of ancient mines which have been abandoned and left to decay shall enjoy the same privileges as discoverers, of choosing and possessing three portions in the principal vein and one in each of the others, and both revivers and discoverers shall, as an especial reward, be on all occasions preferred to other persons under parity of circumstances.

SEC. 7. If there arises any question as to who has been the first discoverer of a vein, he shall be considered as such who first found metal therein, even though others may have made an opening previously; and in case of further doubt, he who first gets it registered shall be considered as the discoverer.

SEC. 8. Whoever shall denounce in the terms hereafter expressed any mine that has been deserted and abandoned shall have his denouncement received, if he therein sets forth the circumstances already declared in section four of this chapter, the actual existence of the mine in question, the name of its last possessor, if he is acquainted with the same, and those of the neighboring miners, all of whom shall be lawfully summoned, and if within ten days they do not appear, the denouncement shall be publicly declared on the three following Sundays; this meeting with no opposition, it shall be signified to the denouncer that within sixty days he must have cleared and reinstated some work of considerable depth, or at least of ten yards perpendicular and within the bed of the vein, in order that the mining professor may inspect its course and inclination and all its peculiar circumstances as is declared in the above-named section four. The said professor should, if it is possible, examine the pits and works of the mine and see if they are decayed, destroyed, or inundated; whether they contain a draft pit or adit or are capable of such; whether they have an outer court, a whim, machines, rooms for habitation, and stables; and an account and register of all these circumstances must be entered in the corresponding book of denouncements, which should be kept separately. And the said examination being made, the portions being measured and bounded by stakes in the ground, as shall hereafter be explained, possession of them shall be given to the denouncer, without regard to any opposition, which cannot be attended to unless made within the term before described; however, if during that time any opposition is brought forward, the parties shall have a brief judicial hearing and the cause be determined accordingly.

SEC. 9. If the former mine owner should appear in order to oppose the denouncement when the three public proclamations are over and when the denouncer has commenced the sixty days allowed for reinstating the pit of ten yards, he shall not be heard as to the possession, but only as to his right in the property; and if he succeeds in establishing this, he must make good the expenses incurred by the denouncer, unless the latter is proved to have acted fraudulently, in which case he must lose such expenses.

SEC. 10. If the denouncer does not make or complete the shaft as prescribed, nor take possession within the sixty days, he loses his right, and any other person has the power of denouncing the mine. If, however, from the ground being entirely broken up or otherwise difficult and impracticable, or for any other real and serious obstacle he has been unable to complete the same within the said sixty days, he must have recourse to the respective territorial deputation, when, his difficulties being examined and proved, the period may be prolonged for as long a time as the deputation may think necessary for the purpose, and no more; no opposition to his claim being admitted after the ordinary term of sixty days.

SEC. 17. I prohibit any one (not being the discoverer) from denouncing two contiguous mines upon one and the same vein; but I permit any person to acquire and possess one by denouncement, and another or more by purchase, gift, inheritance, or other just title. And I further declare that if any one desires to attempt the re-establishment of several inundated or decayed mines, or other considerable enterprise of this kind, and for this purpose claims the grant of several portions, although they be contiguous and upon the same vein, such claim must be laid before the royal tribunal general of Mexico, in order that, the circumstances and importance of the undertaking being ascertained, they may acquaint the viceroy therewith, who, on finding therein nothing prejudicial to the body of the miners, the public, or my royal treasury, shall grant him this and other privileges, exemptions, and aids, on condition that my royal approbation is previously obtained to all such favors, which cannot be granted by the ordinary authority of the viceroy.

SEC. 18. Beds of ore and other depositories of gold and silver, on being discovered, shall be registered and denounced in the same manner as mines or veins, the same being understood of all species of metal.

CHAPTER VII.

SECTION 1. To all the subjects in my dominions, both in Spain and the Indies, of whatever rank and condition they may be, I grant the mines of every species of metal under the conditions already stated, or that shall be expressed hereafter, but I prohibit foreigners from acquiring or working mines as their own property, in these my dominions, unless they be naturalized or tolerated therein by my express royal license. (See decree of President Comonfort.)

SEC. 2. I also prohibit regulars of religious orders, of both sexes, from denouncing, or in any manner acquiring for themselves, their convents, or communities, any mines whatever; it being understood that the working of the mines shall not devolve upon the secular ecclesiastic, as being contrary to the laws, to the orders of the Mexican consul, and to the sanctity and exercise of their profession; and, therefore, in consequence of this prohibition, all such secular ecclesiastics shall be expressly obliged to sell or place in the hands of lay subjects the mines or establishments for smelting ore, and reducing establishments which have devolved on them by inheritance or other cause, the same being completed within the term of six months, or within such time as may be considered necessary to insure a useful result, which is to be fixed by the viceroy, with a previous intimation to the royal tribunal general of the mines; provided, that if it is ascertained that by artifice or fraud the effects of this article are attempted to be eluded, to the prejudice of the working of such mines and establishments, in which the state is so much interested, they shall be denounced and disposed of in the same manner as mines in general.

Sec. 3. Neither shall mines be held by governors, intendents, mayors, chief judges, nor any other public officers whatever, of the mine towns and districts, nor their clerks; but I permit such persons to hold mines in any territory out of their own jurisdiction.

Sec. 4. Neither shall administrators, stewards, overseers, keepers of tallies, workers or watchers of mines, nor, in general, any person in the service of mine owners, whether of superior or subordinate class, be permitted to register, denounce, or in any other manner acquire mines within the space of a thousand yards round those of their masters, but I allow them to denounce any mine for their said masters, even though not authorized by them to do so, provided the aforesaid masters make good the denouncement in the terms prescribed by section eight of chapter six of these ordinances.

CHAPTER VIII.

Section 1. Experience having shown that the equality of the mine measures established on the surface cannot be maintained under ground, where in fact the mines are chiefly valuable, it being certain that the greater or less inclination of the vein upon the plane of the horizon must render the respective properties in the mines greater or smaller, so that the true and effective impartiality which it has been desired to show towards all subjects, of equal merit, has not been preserved; but, on the contrary, it has often happened that when a miner, after much expense and labor, begins at last to reach an abundant and rich ore, he is obliged to turn back, as having entered on the property of another, which latter may have denounced the neighboring mine, and thus stationed himself with more art than industry. This being one of the greatest and most frequent causes of litigation and dissension among the miners, and considering that the limits established in the mines of these kingdoms, and by which those of New Spain have been hitherto regulated, are very confined in proportion to the abundance, multitude, and richness of the metallic veins which it has pleased the Creator of his great bounty to bestow on these regions, I order and command that in the mines where new veins, or veins unconnected with each other, shall be discovered, the following measures shall in future be observed.

Sec. 2. On the course and direction of the vein, whether gold, silver, or other metal, I grant to every miner, without any distinction in favor of the discoverer, whose reward has been specified, two hundred yards, (Spanish yards or varas,) called measuring yards, taken on a level, as hitherto understood.

Sec. 3. To make it what they call a square, that is, making a right angle with the preceding measure, supposing the descent or inclination of the vein to be sufficiently shown by the opening or shaft of ten yards, the portion shall be measured by the following rule.

Sec. 4. Where the vein is perpendicular to the horizon, (a case which seldom occurs,) a hundred level yards shall be measured on either side of the vein, or divided on both sides, as the miner may prefer.

Sec. 5. But where the vein is in an inclined direction, which is the most usual case, its greater or less degree of inclination shall be attended to in the following manner.

Sec. 6. If to one yard perpendicular the inclination be from three fingers to two palms, the same hundred yards shall be allowed for the square, (as in the case of the vein being perpendicular.)

* Sec. 7. If to the said perpendicular yard there be an inclination of—

Two palms and three fingers, the square shall be of 112½ yards.

Two palms and six fingers, the square shall be of 125 yards.

Two palms and nine fingers, the square shall be of 137½ yards.

Three palms, the square shall be of 150 yards.

Three palms and three fingers, the square shall be of 162½ yards.

Three palms and six fingers, the square shall be of 175 yards.

Three palms and nine fingers, the square shall be of 187½ yards.

Four palms, the square shall be of 200 yards.

So that if to one perpendicular yard there correspond an inclination of four palms, which are equal to a yard, the miner shall be allowed two hundred yards on the square on the declivity of the vein, and so on with the rest.

Sec. 8. And supposing that in the prescribed manner any miner should reach the perpendicular depth of two hundred yards, without exceeding the limits of his portion, by which he may commonly have much exhausted the vein, and that those veins which have greater inclination than yard for yard, that is to say, of forty-five degrees, are either barren or of little extent, it is my sovereign will that although the declivity may be greater than the above-mentioned measures, no one shall exceed the square of two hundred level yards; so that the same shall be always the breadth of the said veins extended over the length of the other two hundreds, as declared above.

Sec. 9. However, if any mine owner, suspecting a vein to run in a contrary direction to his own, (which rarely happens,) should choose to have some part of his square in a direction opposite to that of his principal vein, it may be granted to him, provided there shall be no injury or prejudice to a third person thereby.

Sec. 10. With regard to the banks, beds, or any other accidental depositories of gold or silver, I ordain that the portions and measures shall be regulated by the respective territorial deputations of miners, attention being paid to the extent and richness of the place and to the number of applicants for the same, with distinction and preference only to the discoverers; but the said deputations must render an exact account thereof to the royal tribunal general of Mexico, who will resolve on the measures which they in their judgment may consider the most efficacious, in order to avoid all unfair dealing in these matters.

Sec. 11. The portions being regulated in the manner described above, the denouncer shall have his share measured at the time of taking possession of the mine, and he shall erect around his boundaries stakes or landmarks, such as shall be secure and easy to be distinguished, and enter into an obligation to keep and observe them forever without being able to change them; though he may allege that his vein varied in course or direction, (which is an unlikely circumstance;) but he must content himself with the lot which Providence has decreed him, and enjoy it without disturbing his neighbors; if, however, he should have no neighbors, or if he can, without injury to his neighbors, make an improvement, by altering the stakes and boundaries, it may be permitted him in such case, with previous intervention, cognizance, and authority of the deputation of the district, who shall cite and hear the parties, and determine whether the causes for such encroachment are legitimate.

CHAPTER IX.

Sec. 6. If any mine owner, in consequence of the great richness of the metallic substance in his vein, is desirous of substituting for the pillars, beams, or *sufficient and necessary supports, made of the metallic substance itself, others constructed of mason work of stone and mortar, he may be permitted to do so under the inspection of one of the deputies of the district, assisted by his clerk' and with the approbation of the mining professor.

SEC. 7. I strictly prohibit any one from taking away or in any degree weakening and diminishing the pillars, beams, and necessary supports of the mines, under pain of ten years' imprisonment, to be inflicted according to the form prescribed by chapter three of these ordinances, by the respective judge in each case, upon any workman, searcher, or investigator who shall have committed such offence, and the same upon the miner or mine watcher who has permitted it; and the master of the mine shall lose the same, together with half of his property, and be forever excluded from all mining employments.

SEC. 8. I ordain and command that the mines shall be kept clean and unobstructed, and that the works necessary or useful for the circulation of air, the carriage and extraction of the metal or other purposes, although they may contain no more metallic matter than such as may remain in the pillars and partitions, shall not be encumbered with rubbish and clods of earth, but that all these must be carried out and thrown by each person on the earth-mound of his own property, but on no account upon that of another person without his express leave and consent.

SEC. 9. In the mines there must be proper and safe steps or ladders, such and as many as are considered necessary by the mining surveyor, for the purpose of ascending and descending to the farthermost works, so that the lives of persons employed in the mines may never be endangered by their being weak, insecure, rotten, or much worn.

SEC. 10. In order to avoid the violation of the provisions of any of the sections contained in this chapter, it is my sovereign will that the deputies of the miners, accompanied by the mining professor of the district, and by the clerk, if there be one, or, in default of him, by two witnesses in aid, who shall once in every six months, or once in every year, in places where the former is impracticable, visit all the mines in their jurisdiction which are in a course of actual working; and if they find any failure in the points referred to in the above-mentioned sections, or in any others whatever, which regard the security, preservation, and better working of the mines, shall provide immediately a remedy for such defect, and take means to assure themselves that such remedy is carried into effect. And if the remedy be not applied, or if the same failure shall occur again, the proper penalties must be exacted, multiplying and aggravating them even to the extent of dispossessing the person so offending of the mine, which shall then belong to the first person who may denounce it, provided the deputies proceed in the form prescribed by chapter third of these ordinances.

SEC. 11. I most rigorously prohibit all persons from piercing through adits, or cross levels, or other subterraneous passages, from works which are higher and full of water, or from leaving between them and others such slight supports as may allow the water to burst through; on the contrary, persons owning such works must have them drained by engines before they shall attempt to communicate with new ones, unless the mining professor should judge that such piercing through will not be attended with danger to the workmen engaged in it.

SEC. 12. Also I prohibit all persons from introducing workmen into any works containing noxious vapors, until they have been properly ventilated, according to the rules of art.

SEC. 13. Whereas the mines require incessant and continual working, in order to procure the metals, certain operations being indispensable, which cannot without much time be accomplished, and which, if interrupted, generally require as great expenses in their re-establishment as they did in their original undertaking; wherefore, to remedy such inconvenience, and also to prevent masters of mines, who either cannot or will not work them, from keeping them in a useless state for a length of time, by pretending to work them, and thus depriving them of the real and effective labor which others might bestow on them, I ordain and command, that whosoever, during four successive months, shall fail to work any mine with (at least) four paid workmen, occupied in some exterior or interior work of real utility, shall, by so doing, lose all his right in said mine, which shall belong to any person denouncing it, upon his satisfactory proving, according to the provisions of chapter six, such act of desertion on the part of the owner.

Sec. 14. Experience having shown that the provisions of the preceding section have been eluded by the artful and fraudulent practice of some owners of mines, who cause their mine to be worked during some days in each [period of] four months, keeping them in this manner many years in their possession, I ordain that whosoever shall fail to work his mine in the manner prescribed by the said section during eight months in the year, counting from the day of his coming into possession, even though the said eight months should be interspersed with some days or weeks of labor, shall by such labor forfeit the mine: and it shall be adjudged to the first person who denounces the same, and satisfactorily proves this second species of desertion; unless for this, or the one mentioned in the preceding section, there be just cause assigned, such as pestilence, famine, or war, in that same mining place, or within twenty leagues thereof.

Sec. 15. Considering that many mine owners who have formerly worked their mines with ardor and diligence, expending large sums in shafts, adits, and other undertakings, may often be obliged to suspend their operations while soliciting supplies, or for want of workmen, or necessary provisions, and other just and sufficient causes, which, combined with their former merit, render them worthy of equitable consideration, I declare that any such mine owner keeping his mine in disuse in the manner and for the time above mentioned shall not forfeit it at once in the manner described above, but his mine shall nevertheless be liable to denouncement before the respective new tribunals of miners, in order that, both parties having been heard, and alleged merits and causes considered and proved, justice may be done between the parties.

Sec. 16. Since many mine owners abandon their mines either for the want of the capital necessary for carrying on operations therein, or because they do not choose to consume that which they may have already acquired from them, or because they have not spirit to venture on the difficulties of those undertakings, from which they may have conceived great hopes, or for other causes, and since persons are not wanting who might be desirous of taking such mines if they were informed of their intended abandonment, and as it is much easier to maintain a mine when in a course of working than to reinstate it after it has suffered the injuries of time, it is my will that no person shall abandon the working of his mine or mines without making the deputation of the district acquainted therewith, in order that the deputation may publish the same by fixing a notification on the doors of churches and other customary places for the information of all persons.

Sec. 17. In order to avoid the false or equivocal reports which are often spread concerning deserted mines, the consequence of which reports is to augment the distrust in which this profession is ordinarily held, deterring many persons from engaging therein who do not otherwise want inclination to follow it, I ordain:

Sec. 18. That no one shall abandon the working of his mine without giving notice to the respective deputation in order that an inspection may immediately be had thereof by the deputies, accompanied by the clerk and surveyors, who must examine and measure the mine, particularizing all its circumstances, and draw up a map describing its plan and outlines, which, together with all the necessary information, must be preserved in the archives, with liberty of access to all persons who may wish to see it, or to take a copy thereof.

CHAPTER XI.

SECTION 1. Inasmuch as mines are often worked by miners joined in companies, from the time of the denouncement of such mine, or according to contracts entered into subsequently in various ways, to the great advantage and improvement of the operations in mines, since it is much easier to engage therein when many persons concur, each subscribing a part of his capital; and as where the wealth of one alone is not sufficient for great undertakings, that of a united company may be ample; in such cases I desire and command that such companies, whether public or private, may be encouraged, promoted, and protected by all convenient measures, my viceroy granting to those who may form themselves into such companies every favor, aid, and exemption which can be granted them, according to the judgment and discretion of the royal tribunal of miners, and without detriment to the public or my royal treasury.

SEC. 2. Although by these ordinances I prohibit any individual mine-owners, working within the ordinary limits, from denouncing two adjoining mines on the same vein; yet, notwithstanding, to those who work in companies, although they be not the discoverers, and without prejudice to the right which they might derive from becoming discoverers, I grant the right of denouncing four new portions, or four deserted mines, even though they should be contiguous and on the same vein.

SECTION 12.

Books on California.—2. Table of distances.

1.—BOOKS ON CALIFORNIAN MINES.

California has been the subject of hundreds of books written since the discovery of gold; but most of them were notes of personal adventure, with a few rambling and vague remarks about the mineral resources and mining industry of the Pacific coast.

Nevertheless, although only a small proportion of the works published about the land of gold, the Californian contributions to mining literature are not unimportant; and when the State geological survey shall have completed its labors and published all its reports, it may safely be said that few countries have done so much in so brief a space of time to illustrate the metallurgy, mineralogy, and geology of the precious metals.

The following are titles of some of the books that treat of the mineral resources and mining industry of the coast:

Geology and Industrial Resources of California. By Philip T. Tyson. To which is added the official reports of General Persifer F. Smith and B. Riley, including the reports of Lieutenants Talbot, Ord, Derby, and Williamson, of their explorations in California and Oregon, and also of their examination of routes for railroad communication eastward from those countries. Baltimore: 1851. 8vo., pp. 160.

Professor John B. Trask's Report on the Geology of the Sierra Nevada or California Range. Document No. 59, Senate of California. 1853. 8vo., pp. 30.

Report on the Geology of the Coast Mountains and part of the Sierra Nevada, embracing the Industrial Resources in Agriculture and Mining. By John B. Trask. Document No. 9, Senate of California. 1854. 8vo., pp. 90.

Report of a Geological Reconnaissance in California, made in connection with the expedition to survey routes in California to connect with the surveys of routes for a railroad from the Mississippi river to the Pacific ocean, under the command of Lieutenant Williamson, corps topographical engineers, in 1853. By William P. Blake, geologist and mineralogist of the expedition. New York. H. Bailliere, 1858. 4to, pp. 600.

Geology of North America, with two reports on the Prairies of Arkansas and Texas, the Rocky Mountains of New Mexico, and the Sierra Nevada of California, originally made for the United States government by Jules Marcou. Zurich, 1858. 4to, pp. 144.

General Report upon the Geological Collections of the Pacific Railroad Survey, by William P. Blake, geologist of the office of the United States Pacific railroad explorations and surveys. 4to, pp. 50. (In vol. iii of Explorations and Surveys for a Railroad Route from the Mississippi River to the Pacific Ocean.)

Report upon the Geology of the Route from San Francisco Bay to the Columbia River, by J. S. Newberry, M. D., geologist and botanist of the expedition. 4to., pp. 84. (In vol. vi of Explorations, &c., as above.)

Geological Report on the Route from San Francisco to Santa Fé, by way of the Coast and the Gila, by Thomas Antisell, M. D., geologist of the expedition. 4to., pp. 204. (In vol. vii of Explorations, &c., as above.)

Mining on the Pacific States of North America, by John S. Hittell. San Francisco, 1861. 18mo., pp. 224.

The Resources of California, comprising agriculture, mining, geology, climate, commerce, &c., and the past and future development of the State, by John S. Hittell; second edition, with an appendix on Oregon and Washington Territory. San Francisco, 1866. 12mo., pp. 494.

The Comstock Lode, its character, and the probable mode of its continuance in depth, by Ferdinand Baron Richthofen. (Dr. Phil.) San Francisco, 1866. 8vo, pp. 83.

Nevada and California Processes of Silver and Gold Extraction, for general use, and especially for the mining public of California and Nevada, with full explanations and directions for all metallurgical operations connected with silver and gold, from a preliminary examination of the ore to the final casting of the ingot; also a description of the general metallurgy of silver ores. By Guido Kustel, mining engineer and metallurgist, former manager of the Ophir works, &c. Illustrated by accurate engravings. San Francisco, 1863. 8vo, pp. 330.

2.—TABLE OF DISTANCES.

FROM SAN FRANCISCO.

BY OCEAN; NAUTICAL MILES.

Up the coast.

	Miles
Tomales, Cal	45
Mendocino City, Cal	128
Humboldt bay, Cal	223
Trinidad, Cal	239
Crescent City, Cal	290
Port Orford, Oregon	338
Umpqua river, Oregon	402
Columbia river, Oregon	550
Astoria, Oregon	559
Portland, Oregon	642
Vancouver, W. T	682
Cape Flattery, W. T	691
Port Angeles, W. T	738
Port Townsend, W. T	773
Seattle, W. T	807
Steilacoom, W. T	836
Olympia, W. T	855
San Juan island, W. T	765
Bellingham bay, W. T	798
Victoria, V. I	759
New Westminster, B. C	823

Down the coast.

	Miles
Half Moon bay, Cal	46
Santa Cruz, Cal	80
Monterey, Cal	92
San Luis Obispo, Cal	200
Point Conception, Cal	250
Santa Barbara, Cal	288
San Pedro, Cal	374
San Diego, Cal	456
La Paz, Mexico	1,305
Mazatlan, Mexico	1,480
Guaymas, Mexico	1,710
San Blas, Mexico	1,470
Manzanillo, Mexico	1,570
Acapulco, Mexico	1,840
Panama, C. A	3,280
Callao, Peru	3,900
Valparaiso, Chili	5,210
Cape Horn	6,380

Via Panama.

New Orleans	4,680
New York	5,140
Southampton	7,800

Via Cape Horn.

Rio Janeiro	8,323
New York	13,140
Liverpool	13,100

Across the ocean.

Honolulu, H. I	2,100
Jeddo, via H. I	5,550
Shanghai, via H. I	6,450
Hongkong, via H. I	6,980
Sydney, via H. I	6,720
Melbourne, via H. I	7,200
Calcutta, via H. I	10,460

INLAND; STATUTE MILES.

Vicinity of San Francisco bay.

San Quentin	12
Petaluma	48
Geyser Springs	105
Vallejo	24
Napa City	50
White Sulphur Springs	67
Benicia	30
Suisun	50
Martinez	33
Diablo coal mines	44

Northern towns.

	Miles
Sacramento	117
Marysville	171
Downieville	236
Oroville	197
Red Bluff	264
Weaverville	365
Yreka	401
Jacksonville, Oregon	463
Salem, Oregon	710
Portland, Oregon	760
Olympia, W. T	850
Folsom	138
Nevada	182

Overland route.

Placerville	165
Carson City, N. T	253
Humboldt mines, N. T	420
Great Salt Lake City	784
South Pass	1,035
St. Joseph, Mo	1,975
St. Louis, Mo	2,279
New York City	3,417

Southern towns.

Stockton	117
Copperopolis	153
Mokelumne Hill	176
Big Trees	198
Sonora	197
Mariposa	211
Yosemite Valley	217
Visalia	384

Coast road.

Redwood City	31
San Jose	51
San Juan	94
Monterey	130
San Luis Obispo	234
Santa Barbara	344
Los Angeles	444
San Diego	576

Butterfield route.

San Bernardino	594
Port Yuma	732
Tucson, Arizona	1,013
Mesilla, Arizona	1,396
St. Louis, via Arizona	2,881

SAN FRANCISCO TO SACRAMENTO.

By steamer.

San Francisco to—

Opposite Alcatraz island	2	
South end Angel island	4	6
North end Angel island	1½	7½
Red Rock	5	12½
Brothers	2	14½
Pinole	4	18½
Mouth of Straits	6½	25
Benicia	5	30
Navy Point	1	31
Point Edith	3	34
Seal island	1	35
Point Gillespie	3	38
Point Roe	1	39
Snag Point	2	41
New York Slough	5½	46½
Point Hanson	2½	49
Montezuma island	2	51
Tree island	4	55
Twin Houses	3	58
Sacket Hog Bend	6	62
San Joaquin Slough	1	63

		Miles
End of Wood Island	5	68
Rio Vista	5	73
Cache creek	1	84
Hog's Back	4	78
Mouth of Steamb't slough	6	84
Head of Steamboat slough	6	90
Head of Randall's island	4	96
Grape Vine ranch	5	101
Embarcadero	8	109
Sutterville	9	118
Sacramento	3	121

SAN FRANCISCO TO SAN DIEGO.

Via coast road.

San Francisco to—

San Mateo		21
Redwood City	10	31
San Jose	19	50
Gilroy	32	82
San Juan	12	94
Monterey	36	130
San Antonio	75	205
San Luis Obispo	43	248
Santa Inez	68	316
Santa Barbara	42	358
San Buenaventura	30	388
Los Angeles	100	488
San Gabriel ranch	10	498
Anaheim	15	513
Aliso ranch	22	535
San Juan mission	7	542
San Mateo ranch	11	553
Las Flores	11	564
San Luis Rey	10	574
Las Enotnitas	18	592
Soledad ranch	15	607
San Diego	13	632

SACRAMENTO TO RED BLUFF.

Via Sacramento river.

Sacramento to—

Russian Crossing		12
Fremont	14	26
Charleston	10	36
Knight's landing	10	46
Eagle Bend	8	54
Old Eagle Bend	5	59
Three Rivers	5	64
Poker Bend	5	69
Howell's	5	74
Big Eddy	5	79
Dry Slough	8	87
Eddy's	8	95
Twenty-Mile Island	10	105
Font's ferry	7	112
Butte creek	6	118
Colusa	7	125
Sherman's	7	132
Snyder's	4	136
Nine-Mile house	5	141
Bogg's	5	146
Princeton	5	151
Butte City	7	158
Cut Off	7	165
Pike's	5	170
Plaza City	9	179
Jennings	9	188
Monroeville	3	191
Big Chico	8	199
Bidwell's	6	205
Soule Landing	7	212
Snadon's	8	220
Gazelle shoot	6	226
Moon's	6	232
Maybew's	8	240
Tehama	8	248
Doll's ranch	11	259
Red Bluff	11	270

2.—Table of distances—Continued.

SACRAMENTO TO VIRGINIA CITY.

Via Dutch Flat.

Sacramento to—		Miles.
Auburn		40
Illinoistown	18	58
Dutch Flat	12	70
Wilson's ranch	14	84
Summit valley	16	100
Donner Cabins	9	109
O'Neal's bridge	21	130
Steamboat Springs	15	145
Virginia City	12	157

Via Henness Pass.

Sacramento to—		
Colfax		55
Madlen's		61
Dutch Flat		69
Zeus		72½
Polly's		84½
Jones's		100
Donner lake		110
Prosser creek		129½
Chamberlin's		128½
Brown's		135½
Hunter's		145½
Virginia City		157½
Virginia City to the Humboldt mines		150
Virginia City to Aurora		116

SACRAMENTO TO SALT LAKE CITY.

Via Austin, (Reese river,) Nevada.

Sacramento to—		
Folsom		22
Latrobe	15	37
Shingle Springs	8	45
Placerville	8	53
Sportsman's Hall	11	64
Riverside station	10	74
Webster's	9	83
Strawberry valley	11	94
Summit	3	97
Yank's	8	105
Lake Tahoe	9	114
Genoa	10	124
Carson City	14	138
Virginia City	16	154
First well	13	167
Second well	7	174
Third well	12	186
Eighteen-Mile post	8	194
Ragtown	12	206
Slough bridge	16	222
Sand Springs	16	238
West Gate	22	260
Cold Springs	14	274
Edward's creek	12	286
Mount Airy	15	301
Jacobsville	13	314
Austin	6	320
Simpson's park	16	336
Dry creek	21	357
Robert's creek	29	386
Diamond Springs	25	411
Ruby valley	24	435
Butte station	19	454
Shell creek	30	484
Antelope Springs	19	503
Deep creek	24	527
Willow Springs	42	569
Fish Springs	21	590
Simpson's Springs	39	629
Rush valley	23	652
Fort Crittenden	17	669
Great Salt Lake City	41	710

SACRAMENTO TO PORTLAND.

Sacramento to—		
Nicolaus		25
Marysville	20	45
Oroville	26	71
Chico	26	97
Tehama	26	123
Red Bluff	13	136
Horsetown	29	165
Shasta	8	173
French gulch	15	188
Trinity Centre	27	215
New York house	14	229
Callahan's	13	242
Fort Jones	22	264
Yreka	18	282
Henly	20	302
Mountain house	17	319
Jacksonville	23	342
Grave creek	41	383
Canyonville	26	409
Roseberg	26	435
Oakland	17	452
Hawley's	30	482
Eugene City	25	507
Corvallis	39	546
Albany	10	556
Salem	24	580
Oregon City	37	617
Portland	13	630

STOCKTON TO VISALIA AND OWEN'S VALLEY.

Stockton to—		
Heath & Emory's		28
Dickinson's ferry	21	49
Seeling	13	62
Hornitos	16	78
Chowchilla	25	103
Fresno	16	119
Millerton	15	134
King's river	25	159
Visalia	28	187
Tule river	25	212
Deer creek	8	220
White river	15	235
Linn's valley	9	244
Kern river	20	264
Walker's Pass	25	289
Little lake	30	319
Owen's lake	35	354
San Carlos	41	395

LOS ANGELES TO LA PAZ, ARIZONA.

Los Angeles to—		
San Gabriel		12
El Monte	2	14
San Jose	12	26
Cocomungo	12	38
San Bernardino	25	63
Old S. B. mission	8	71
Frink's	7	78
Dr. Edgar's	8	86
Chapin's ranch	6	92
Antonio creek	4	96
Grant's creek	3	99
Indian run	5	104
White river	2	106
Agua Caliente	10	116
Sand Hole	11	127
Old rancheria	6	133
Toro's	9	142
Martinez	5	147
Palma Seco	12	159
Dos Palmes	7	166
Brown's Pass	10	176
Tabasseco	8	184
Chucolwalla	18	202
Slough	15	217
La Paz	16	253

La Paz to Fort Mohave		140
La Paz to Walker's diggings		146
La Paz to Pimo villages		200
La Paz to Tucson		280
La Paz to El Dorado canon		190

PORTLAND TO LEWISTON.

Portland to—		Miles.
Lower Cascades		50
Portage	5	55
Dalles	38	93
Celilo	13	106
Five-Mile rapids	5	111
John Day	11	122
Indian rapids	3	125
Squally Hook	3	128
Rock creek	7	135
Chapman's woodyard	6	141
Big Bend	6	147
Willow creek	9	156
Castle Rock	8	164
Long Island (foot)	5	169
Long Island (head)	7	176
Grand Ronde landing	10	186
Umatilla rapids	8	194
Windmill rock	7	201
Wallula	15	216
Snake river (mouth)	11	227
Rapids	6	233
Fish Bend	10	243
Jim Fort's island	10	253
Pine Tree rapids	7	260
Pelouse crossing	30	290
Fort Taylor	5	295
Penawawa creek	25	320
Almota creek	14	334
Alpowa creek	26	360
Smith's ferry	3	363
Lewiston	7	370

DALLES TO LEWISTON.

Dalles to—		
Deschutes		15
Mud Springs	12	27
John Day's river	12	39
Juniper spring	12	51
Willow creek	18	69
Well's spring	16	85
Butter creek	18	103
Umatilla river	9	112
Umatilla crossing	18	130
Wild Horse creek	18	148
Walla-Walla	20	168
Dry creek	7	175
Reed creek	15	190
Tucanon	17	207
Patapha	11	218
Alpowa	14	232
Smith's ranch	8	240
Craig's ferry	9	249
Lewiston	1	250

Lewiston to Pierce City		90
Lewiston to Elk City		145
Lewiston to Florence		110
Lewiston to Idaho City		190

DALLES TO IDAHO CITY.

Via John Day mines.

Dalles to—		
Fifteen-Mile creek		12
Todd's bridge	10	22
Salt spring	8	30
Bake Oven hollow	14	44
Thorn hollow	6	50
Antelope valley	12	62
Potato hills	10	72
Pyramid rocks	4	76
Cherry creek	10	86
Bridge creek	7	93
Foot of mountain	11	104
Rock creek	12	116
John Day	17	133
South Fork	7	140
Canyon City	35	175
Dixie creek	11	186
Burnt river	35	221
Malheur river	18	240
Emigrant road	20	260

2.—*Table of distances*—Continued.

	Miles.			Miles.			Miles.
Old Fort Boise	16	276	St. Joseph river crossing.	5	169	Rock creek	7	431
Boise City	25	301	Cœur d'Alene river	11	180	Deer Lodge creek	8	439
Idaho City	29	330	Cœur d'Alene crossing	11	191	Livingston's creek	9	448
			Cœur d'Alene mission	8	199	Little Blackfoot river	8	456
WALLA-WALLA TO FORT BENTON.			Three-Mile prairie	4	203	Mullan's Pass	13	469
			Ten-Mile prairie	5	208	Great Prickly Pear	4	473
Via Mullan's military road.			Johnson's Cut-off	20	228	Silver creek	6	479
			Summit Steven's pass	8	236	Little Prickly Pear	16	495
Walla-Walla to—			St. Regis Borgia river	5	241	Medicine Rock	3	498
Dry Creek		9	Prairie	9	250	L. P. P. Upper Camp	7	505
Touchet	11	20	Prairie	13	263			
Reed creek	15	35	Bitter Root crossing	10	273	LEWISTON TO KOOTENAI MINES.		
Tucanon	12	47	Prairie	10	283			
Snake river	3	50	Brown's prairie	13	296	Lewiston to—		
l'alouse river	15	65	Nemote creek	8	304	Palouse crossing		40
First crossing	4	69	West foot of mountain	6	310	Pine creek	10	50
Second crossing	4	73	Point of Rocks	9	319	Lottow	7	57
Third crossing	2	75	Skahotay creek	9	328	Forks of trail	2	59
Fourth crossing	2	77	Kulkullo creek	4	332	Willow prairie	5	64
Moealisia	7	84	Hell Gate Ronde	6	338	Rock creek	10	74
Orntayouse	13	97	Observatory creek	13	351	Spokane River ferry	15	89
Tcho-tcho-oo-seep	15	112	Big Blackfoot river	12	363	Soltesu's	6	95
Clel-ch-l-pow-vet-sin	9	121	Hell Gate river, 1st cross'g	5	368	Pen d'Oreille slough	23	118
Camas Prairie creek	17	138	HellGate river,11th cross'g	25	393	Pen d'Oreille crossing	24	142
Loocheoutiz	12	150	Creek	7	400	Big bend of lake	15	157
Iuchatzkan spring	8	158	Flint creek	11	411	Kootenai crossing	50	207
Poun Luke bridge	6	164	Gold creek	13	424	Elk creek	123	330

APPENDIX 1.

Address on the history of California, from the discovery of the country to the year 1849, *delivered before the Society of California Pioneers, at their celebration of the tenth anniversary of the admission of the State of California into the Union. By Edmund Randolph, esq. San Francisco, Sept.* 10, 1860.

PIONEERS : From the importunities of the active present which surrounds us, we turn for a brief space to the past. To-day we give ourselves up to memory.

And, first, our thoughts are due to those who are not here assembled with us; whom we meet not on street nor highway, and welcome not again at the door of our dwellings; upon whom shines no more the sun which now gladdens the hills, the plains, the waters of California—to the pioneers who are dead. To them, as the laurel to the soldier who falls in the battle for that with his blood he has paid the price of victory, you will award the honor of this triumph, marked by the marvellous creations which have sprung from your common enterprises. To them you will consecrate a success which has surpassed the boldest of the imaginations which led you forth, both them and you, to a life of adventures. Your companions died that California might exist. Fear not that you will honor them overmuch. But how died they, and where do they repose—the dead of the pioneers of California?

Old men amongst you will recall the rugged trapper. His frame was strong; his soul courageous; his knowledge was of the Indian's trail and haunts of game; his wealth and defence, a rifle and a horse; his bed, the earth; his home, the mountains. He was slain by the treacherous savage. His scalp adorned the wigwam of a chief. The wolf and the vulture in the desert feasted on the body of this pioneer. A companion, wounded, unarmed, and famishing, wanders out through some rocky canon and lives to recount this tale—lives, more fortunate in his declining years, to measure, perhaps, his lands by the league, and to number his cattle by the thousand. And the sea, too, has claimed tribute; the remorseless waves, amid the terrors of shipwreck, too often in these latter days have closed over the manly form of the noble pioneer. The monsters of the deep have parted amongst them the flesh of our friends, and their dissevered members are floating, suspended now in the vast abysses of the ocean, or roll upon distant strands, playthings tossed by the currents in their wanderings. And here, in San Francisco, exacting commerce has disturbed the last resting place of the pioneers. Ten years and a half ago, pinched by the severities of a most inclement winter, under the leaky tent which gave no shelter, they sickened and died (and then women and children were pioneers, too) by scores, and by hundreds they sickened and died. With friendly hands, which under such disastrous circumstances could minister no relief, you yet did bury them piously in a secluded spot upon the hill-side or in the valley, and, planting a rude cross or board to mark the grave, did hope, perhaps, in a more prosperous day, to replace it with a token in enduring stone. But the hill and the valley alike disappear hourly from our sight. The city marches with tremendous strides. Extending streets and lengthening rows encroach upon the simple burial-ground not wisely chosen. The dead give place to the living. And now the builder, with his mortar and his bricks, and the din of his trowel, erects a mansion or store-house for the new citizen upon the same spot where the pioneer was laid and his sorrowing friend dreamed of erecting a tombstone. Meanwhile, by virtue of a municipal order, hirelings have dug up and carted away all that remained of the pioneers, and have deposited them in some common receptacle, where now they are lying an undistinguishable heap of human bones.

Pursuing still this sad review, you well remember how, with the eager tide along and up the course of rivers, and over many a stony ascent, you were swept into the heart of the difficult regions of the gold mines; how you there encountered an equal stream pouring in from the east; and, in a summer, all the bars, and flats, and gulches, throughout the length and breadth of that vast tract of hills, were flooded with human life. Into that rich harvest Death put his sickle. Toil to those who had never toiled; toil, the hardest toil, often at once beneath a torrid, blazing sun, and in an icy stream; congestion, typhus, fevers in whatever form most fatal; and the rot of scurvy; drunkenness and violence, despair, suicide, and madness; the desolate cabin; houseless starvation amid snows: all these bring back again upon you in a frightful picture many a death-scene of those days. There fell the pioneers who perished from the van of those who first heaved back the bolts that barred the vaulted hills, and poured the millions of the treasures of California upon the world!

Wan and emaciated from the door of the tent or cabin where you saw him expire; bloody and mangled from the gambling saloon where you saw him murdered, or the roadside where you found him lying; the corpse you bore to the woods and buried him beneath the trees. But you cannot tell to-day which pine sings the requiem of the pioneer.

And some have fallen in battle beneath our country's flag.

And longings still unsatisfied led some to renew their adventurous career upon foreign soils. Combating for strangers whose quarrels they espoused, they fell amid the jungles of the tropics and fatted that rank soil there with right precious blood; or, upon the sands of an accursed waste, were bound and slaughtered by inhuman men who lured them with promises and repaid their coming with a most cruel assassination. In the filthy purlieus of a Mexican village swine fed upon all that murder left of honored gentlemen, until the very Indian, with a touch of pity, heaped up the sand upon the festering dead, and gave slight sepulture to our lost pioneers.

Though from the first some there were who found in California all they sought; and as they lived so died, surrounded by their children and their newly made friends, and were buried in churchyards with holy rites; and although those more lately stricken repose in well-fenced grounds, guarded by society they planted, and whose ripening power they have witnessed, and are gathered to a sacred stillness, where we too may hope that we shall be received when full soon we sink to our eternal rest.   Alas! far different the death and burial of full many a pioneer.

In deeds of loftiest daring of individual man, encounters fierce and rudest shocks, too often has parted the spirit of the pioneer, and left his mortal body to nature and the elements.   Thus wilds are conquered, and to civilization new realms are won.

Upon his life and death let them reflect who would deny to the pioneer the full measure of the rights of freemen.

For us we behold the river or the rock, the mountain's peak, the plain—whatever spot from which his eyes took their last look of earth.   There, as he lies, one gentle light shining athwart the gathering darkness, still holds his gaze.   Guided by that light we will revisit the distant home of the dying pioneer.   In imagination we will there revive the faded recollections of the intrepid boy who, in years long past, disappeared in the wilderness and the west, and for a lifetime has been accounted dead.   We will renew, while we console, the grief of the aged father and mother.   To the fresh sorrows of the faithful wife we pledge the sympathy and love of brothers.   To the sons and daughters of our friends we stretch forth our hands in benedictions on their heads.   To ancient friends we too are friends, until with our praises, and the eventful story of his life, we make to live again in his old peaceful home him who died so wildly.   What though, to mournful questioning, we cannot point their graves?   They have a monument—behold the State; and their inscription, it is written on our hearts.

Thus, as is meet, we honor our dead pioneers with severe yet pleasing recollections, grateful fancies, and tears not unmanly.   With an effort we turn from ourselves to our country.

Of populous Christian countries Upper California is among the newest.   Her whole history is embraced within the lifetime of men now living.   Just ninety-one years have passed since man of European origin first planted his footsteps within the limits of what is now our State, with purpose of permanent inhabitation.   Hence all the inhabitants of California have been but pioneers.

Cortez, about the year 1537, fitted out several small vessels at his port of Tehuantepec, sailed north and to the head of the Gulf of California.   It is said that his vessels were provided with everything requisite for planting a colony in the newly discovered region, and transported four hundred Spaniards and three hundred negro slaves, which he had assembled for that purpose, and that he imagined by that coast and sea to discover another New Spain.   But sands and rocks and sterile mountains, a parched and thorny waste, vanquished the conqueror of Mexico.   He was glad to escape with his life, and never crossed the line which marks our southern boundary.   Here we may note a very remarkable event which happened in the same year that Cortez was making his fruitless attempt.   Four persons, Alvar Nunez Cabeza de Vaca, Castillo, Dorantes, and a negro named Estevanico, arrived at Culiacan, on the Gulf of California, from the peninsula of Florida.   They were the sole survivors of three hundred Spaniards who landed with Pamfilo Narvaez on the coast of Florida for the conquest of that country, in the year 1527.   They had wandered ten years among the savages, and had finally found their way across the continent.   The same Nunez was afterwards appointed to conduct the discovery of the Rio de la Plata, and the first conquests of Paraguay, says our authority, the learned Jesuit Father Miguel Venegas.

The viceroy Mendoza, soon after the failure of Cortez, despatched another expedition, by sea and land, in the same direction, but accomplished still less; and again in 1542, the same viceroy sent out Juan Rodriguez Cabrillo, a courageous Portuguese, with two ships to survey the outward or western coast of California.   In the latitude of 32 degrees he made a cape which was called, by himself, I suppose, Cape Engaño, (Deceit;) in 33 degrees, that of La Cruz, and that of Galera, in 36½ degrees, and opposite the last he met with two large islands, where they informed him that at some distance there was a nation who wore clothes. In 37 degrees and a half he had sight of some hills covered with trees, which he called San Martin, as he did also the cape running into the sea at the end of these eminences. Beyond this to 40 degrees the coast lies NE. and SW., and about the 40th degree he saw two mountains covered with snow, and between them a large cape, which, in honor of the viceroy, he called Mendocina. The headland, therefore, according to Venegas, was christened three hundred and eighteen years ago. Cabrillo continued his voyage to the north in midwinter, and reached the 44th degree of latitude on the 40th of March, 1543. From this point he was compelled by want of provisions and the bad condition of his ships to return, and on the 14th of April he entered the harbor of Natividad, from which he had sailed.

In 1578, at midsummer, Sir Francis Drake landed upon this coast, only a few miles northward from this Bay of San Francisco, at a bay which still bears his name. Sir Walter Raleigh had not yet sailed on his first voyage to Virginia. It will be interesting to know how things looked in this country at that time. After telling us how the natives mistook them for gods, and worshipped them, and offered sacrifices to them, much against their will, and how he took possession of the country in the name of Queen Elizabeth, the narrative goes on: "Our necessaire business being ended, our General with his companie travailed up into the countrey to their villiages, where we found heardes of deere by 1,000 in a companie, being most large and fat of bodie. We found the whole countrey to be a warren of a strange kinde of connies, their bodies in bignes as be the Barbarie connies, their heads as the heads of ours, the feet of a Want, (mole,) and the taile of a rat, being of great length; under her chinne on either side a bagge, into the which she gathered her meate, when she hath filled her bellie abroad. The people do eat their bodies and make great accompt of their skinnes, for their king's coat was made out of them. Our General called this countrey Nova Albion, and that for two causes: the one in respect of the white bankes and cliffes which lie toward the sea; and the other because it might have some affinitie with our countrey in name, which sometime was so called.

" *There is no part of earth here to be taken up, wherein there is not a reasonable quantitie of gold or silver.*"

Every one will at once recognize the burrowing squirrel that still survives to plague the farmer, and who it will be seen is a very ancient inhabitant of the fields he molests; and no one but will dwell upon the words in which he speaks of the gold and silver abounding in this country. Were they but a happy guess in a gold-mad age, a miracle of sagacity, or a veritable prophecy? Before he sailed away, "our General set up a monument of our being there, as also of her Majestie's right and title to the same, viz: *a plate nailed upon a faire great poste, whereupon was engraven her Majestie's name, the day and yeare of our arrival there, with the free giving up of the province and people into her Majestie's hands, together with her highness' picture and arms, in a piece of sixpence of current English money under the plate, whereunder was also written the name of our General.*"

These mementoes of his visit and the first recorded landing of the white man upon our shores, I think have never fallen into the possession of any antiquary. And it would also appear that Sir Francis Drake knew nothing of Cabrillo's voyage, for he says: "It seemeth that the Spaniards hitherto had never been in this part of the country, neither did discover the lande by many degrees to the southward of this place."

There were other expeditions to Lower California and the western coast, after the time of Cortez and Cabrillo, but they all proved fruitless until the Count de Monterey, viceroy of New Spain, by order of the King, sent out Sebastian Viscayno. He sailed from Acapulco on the 5th day of May, 1602, with two large vessels and a tender, as captain-general of, the voyage, with Toribio Gomez, a consummate seaman, who had served many years in cruising his Majesty's ships, as admiral; and three barefooted Carmelites, Father Andrew de la Assumpcion, Father Antonio de la Ascension, and Father Tomas de Aguino, also accompanied him.   And that Viscayno might not lack for counsellors the viceroy appointed Captain Alonzo Estevan Peguero, a person of great valor and long experience, who had served in Flanders; and Captain Gaspar de Alorçon, a native of Bretagne, distinguished for his prudence and courage; and for sea affairs, he appointed pilots and masters of ships; likewise Captain Geronimo Martin, who went as cosmographer, in order to make draughts of the countries discovered, for the greater perspicuity of the account intended to be transmitted to his Majesty, of the discoveries and transactions on this voyage.   The ships were further supplied with a suitable number of soldiers and seamen, and well provided with all necessaries for a year.   This expedition was therefore, in every respect, a notable one for the age.   Its object, the King of Spain himself informs us, was to find a port where the ships coming from the Philippine islands to Acapulco, a trade which had then been established some thirty years, might put in and provide themselves with water, wood, masts, and other things of absolute necessity.   The galleons from Manila had all this time been running down this coast before the northwest wind, and were even accustomed, as some say, to make the land as far to the north as Cape Mendocino, which Cabrillo had named.   Sebastian Viscayno with his fleet struggled up against the same northwest wind.   On the 10th of November, 1602, he entered San Diego and found, on its northwest side, a forest of oaks and other trees, of considerable extent, of which I do not know that there are any traces now or even a tradition.   In Lower California he landed frequently, and made an accurate survey of the coast, and to one bay gave the capricious appellation of the 'Bay of eleven thousand Virgins.'   Above San Diego he kept further from the shore, noting the most conspicuous landmarks.   But he came through the canal of Santa Barbara, which I suppose he so named, and, when at anchor under one of the islands, was visited by the king of that country, who came with a fleet of boats and earnestly pressed him to land, offering as proof of his hospitable intentions to furnish every one of his seamen with ten wives.   Finally he anchored in the bay of Monterey on the 16th of December, 1602—this was more than four years before the English landed at Jamestown.   The name of Monterey was given to this port in honor of the viceroy.   On the 17th day of December, 1602, a church, tent or arbor, was erected under a large oak close to the seaside, and Fathers Andrew de la Assumpcion and Antonio de la Ascension said Mass, and so continued to do whilst the expedition remained there.   Yet this was not the first Christian worship on these shores, for Drake had worshipped according to a Protestant ritual at the place where he landed twenty-five years before.   The port of Monterey, as it appeared to those weary voyagers, and they were in a miserable plight from the affliction of scurvy, seems to have been very pleasing.   It is described in the narrative of Father Andrew as an excellent harbor, and secure against all winds.   " Near the shore are an infinite number of very large pines, straight and smooth, fit for masts and yards, likewise oaks of a prodigious size for building ships.   Here likewise are rose trees, white thorns, firs, willows, and poplars; large clear lakes, fine pastures and arable lands," &c., &c.   A traveller of this day, perhaps, might not color the picture so highly.   Viscayno sent back one of his ships with the news, and with the sick, and with the other left Monterey on the 3d of January, 1603, and it was never visited more for a hundred and sixty-six years.   On the 12th, having a fair wind, we are told that he passed the port of San Francisco, and that losing sight of his other vessel he returned to the port of San Francisco to wait for her.   Father Andrew de la Assumpcion (as reported in Father Venegas) on this interesting point uses the following language : " Another reason which induced the Capitania (flag-ship) to put into Puerto Francisco was to take a survey of it and see if anything was to be found of the San Augustin, which, in the year 1595, had, by order of his Majesty and the Viceroy, been sent from the Philippines to survey the coast of California, under the direction of Sebastian Rodriguez Cermenon, a pilot of known abilities, but was driven ashore in this harbor by the violence of the wind. And among others on board the San Augustin was the pilot Francisco Volanos, who was also chief pilot of this squadron. He was acquainted with the country, and affirmed that they had left ashore a great quantity of wax and several chests of silk; and the general was desirous of putting in here to see if there remained any vestiges of the ship and cargo. The Capitania came to anchor behind a point of land called La Punta de los Reyes."

Did Vizcayno enter the Bay of San Francisco? I think it plain that he did not. Yet exceedingly curious and interesting it is to reflect that he was but a little way outside the heads, and that the indentation of the coast which opens into the bay of San Francisco was known to him from the report of the pilots of the ships from the Philippines, and by the same name. In the narratives of the explorers the reader is often puzzled by finding that objects upon the shore are spoken of as already known, as for example in this voyage of Vizcayno the highlands a little south of Monterey are mentioned by the name of the Sierra de Santa Lucia, so named at some previous time: the explanation follows in the same sentence where they are said to be a usual land-mark for the China ships—i. e., undoubtedly the galleons from the Philippines. Vizcayno could reach no further north than Cape Mendocino, in which neighborhood he found himself with only six men able to keep the deck; his other vessel penetrated as far as the forty-third degree; and then both returned to Acapulco. In those days there was a fabulous story very prevalent of a channel somewhere to the north of us which connected the Atlantic and Pacific oceans, and it seems that some foreigner had actually presented to the King of Spain a history of a voyage he had made directly across from Newfoundland to the Pacific ocean by the straits of Anian. The King is said to have had an eye to the discovery of this desirable canal at the same time that he was making provision for his trade from the Western Islands.

In 1697 the Jesuits, with patient art and devoted zeal, accomplished that which had defied the energy of Cortez and baffled the efforts of the Spanish monarchy for generations afterwards. They possessed themselves of Lower California, and occupied the greater portion of that peninsula, repulsive as it was, with their missions. In 1742, Anson, the English commodore, cruising off the western coast of Mexico, watched for the Spanish galleon which still plied an annual trip between Acapulco and Manila. This galleon was half man-of-war, half merchantman, was armed, manned, and officered by the King, but sailed on account of various houses of the Jesuits in the Philippines, who owned her tonnage in shares of a certain number of bales each, and enjoyed the monopoly of this trade by royal grant. She exchanged dollars from the Mexican mines for the productions of the east, and we read that at that day the manufacturers of Valencia and Cadiz, in Spain, clamored for protection against the silks and cotton cloths of India and China thus imported—by this sluggish craft which crept lazily through the tropics, relied upon rain to replenish the water jars on deck, and was commonly weakened by scurvy and required about six months for the return voyage—into Acapulco, thence transported on mules to Vera Cruz, and thence again after another tedious voyage to Europe. Anson watched in vain; the prudent galleon thought it best to remain under the shelter of the guns of Acapulco, in the presence of so dangerous a neighbor. He sailed away to the west, stopped and refreshed his crew at a romantic island in the middle of the Pacific ocean, went over to Macao and there refitted, and then captured the galleon at last, with a million and a half of dollars on board, as she was going into Manilla, after a desperate combat with his ship, the Centurion. He then returned to China, extinguishing a great fire in Canton with his crew, sold the galleon in Macao, and got back safe to England with his treasure. His chaplain, Mr. Richard Walter, the author of the admirable narrative of this celebrated voyage, goes on, after relating the capture, to say : " I shall only add, that there were taken on board the galleon several draughts and journals. * * Among the rest there was found a chart of all the ocean, between the Philippines and the coast of Mexico, which was that made use of by the galleon in her own navigation. A copy of this draught, corrected in some places by our own observations, is here annexed, together with the route of the galleon traced thereon from her own journals, and likewise the route of the Centurion from Acapulco through the same ocean."

Here we may look for information. We have at least one log-book and chart of the old Manilla galleons. What if we could have access to the books of account of those venerable old traders in their monasteries at Manilla! Examining this chart we find that the coast of California, from a little further north than Punta de los Reyes, is laid down with remarkable accuracy. We have a great indentation of the coast immediately below Punta de los Reyes, a large land-locked bay with a narrow entrance, immediately off which lie seven little black spots called Los Farallones—in short, a bay at San Francisco, but without a name. The Farallones, I think, were named by Cabrillo, in 1542, two hundred years before Anson's time. Was this our port of San Francisco as we know it, or that which Vizcayno entered when he anchored on the 12th of January, 1603, under a point of land called La Punta de los Reyes? Lower down we have Point Año Nuevo and Point Pinos, and a bay between, but not the name of Monterey, then a great many islands, then Point Conception, then San Pedro, and then the Port of San Diego, and Lower California to Cape San Lucas. The outward track of the galleon lies between 12 and 15 degrees north, and on her return she goes up as high as about 35 degrees, and there being off Point Conception, but a long way out to sea, she turns to the south and runs down the coast to Cape San Lucas, where the Jesuit fathers kept signal fires burning on the mountains to guide her into port, and expected her return with the fruits and fresh provisions which the exhausted mariners so much needed. Such was the strange precursor of the steamship and clipper on the waters of the Pacific, and the first great carrier of the commerce between its opposite shores ! You will observe how nature brings this commerce to our doors. The outward run of the galleon so near the equator was to take the eastern trade-winds, which wafted her without the necessity of changing a sail directly to the Philippines ; China and the Indies—and her returning course was to avoid these trade-winds and to catch the breezes which to the north blow from the west. And this great circle of the winds touches our shores at the Bay of San Francisco. This chart was drawn for the use of the Spanish generals, (for such was the title and rank of the commanders of the Spanish galleons,) and " contained all the discoveries which the Manilla ships have at any time made in traversing this vast ocean."

It was these discoveries that gave names to so many points upon our coast undoubtedly, and prompted so many explorers, after Cabrillo, and both before and after Vizcayno. Knowing so much, the wonder is that these navigators did not know more. They named, and noted on their chart, yet did not know our Bay of San Francisco. Yearly for centuries they coasted by. A priest or soldier standing upon the deck of this old-timed ship, might gaze upon a glorious land that overhung the western sea ; with hills on hills a swelling pile, glowing in sunsets that had gilded them through countless ages. But, save in the casual visits of the earliest navigators, we know not that foot of white man yet had pressed the soil of California. The world was busy in commerce and in war. But the breeze still ruffled the vacant waters, dimpled the idle grass, and fanned the sultry sides of the solitary mountains of California. These slopes and plains pastured but the deer and elk. A despicable type of man, in petty groups, wandered through these valleys, of which the bear was more the lord than he. No other human tenant occupied the most delightful of the habitations of man, nor had from the creation down.

The Spaniards were at best but feeble navigators. Witness the galleons making a tedious progress in the latitude of calms. Anson says that the instructions to their commanders were, in his day, to keep within the latitude of 30 degrees, if possible, as if they feared to encounter the stiffer breezes further north, an instruction, however, not always followed, as their chart demonstrates. To vessels such as then were built or to be found in Mexican or South American ports the daily winds from the northwest, which in summer roughen the sea all along the coast to Cape San Lucas, were gales against which it was dangerous and almost hopeless to attempt to make head. This labor had not diminished from the days of Cabrillo and Vizcayno. These most beneficent northwest trade-winds cut off California from Spanish America by sea. By land the desert tracts of the Gila and Upper California, both unexplored, barred the approach from the south; and to the east the human imagination had not yet traversed the interval from the Atlantic ocean. In 1769 the history of mankind may be said to have begun upon this coast. In this wise it begun.

Charles the Fifth, on the 17th day of November, 1526, addressed these words to his Indies:

"The kings, our progenitors, from the discovery of the West Indies, its islands and continents, commanded our captains, officers, discoverers, colonizers, and all other persons, that, on arriving at those provinces, they should, by means of interpreters, cause to be made known to the Indians that they were sent to teach them good customs, to lead them from vicious habits and the eating of human flesh, to instruct them in our holy Catholic faith, to preach to them salvation, and to attract them to our dominions."

The same spirit breathes through every part of the laws of the Indies, as they were issued for successive centuries, which may be seen by reference to the code in which they are compiled.

The ministers who executed these pious purposes of the king were mainly the soldiers of the cross. Christian priests converted our savage ancestors in the forests of the north of Europe, and laid the foundations of the great republic of European states, of which the cement is modern civilization. Christian priests endeavored to repeat that grand achievement in America. A sublime contemplation! They interposed the cross and staid the descending sword and the still swifter destruction of private greed. Their powerful protector was the King of Spain, when both continents were almost entirely Spanish. Their dusky converts who acknowledged the dominion of Christ were saved as subjects of the king, were admitted to civil rights, and mingled their blood with that of the descendants of the Visigoths. In the lineaments and complexion of the Spanish American we still behold the native Indian whom the church preserved. Exalted charity! at least in motive; and although the teacher could not foresee that the same lesson would not effect the same result in pupils so diverse, it was not their fault that they did not raise the crouching Indian to the level of the conquering German.

In 1767 the Jesuits being banished from the Spanish dominions, Lower California was transferred to the charge of another celebrated order, the Franciscans. Into this field, when it had been wrested from the Society of Jesus, the Franciscans were led by one who was born in an island of the Mediterranean, the son of humble laborers. From his infancy Father Junipero Serra was reared for the church. He had already greatly distinguished himself in the conversion and civilization of heathen savages in other parts of Mexico; and afterwards had preached revivals of the faith in Christian places, illustrating, as we are told, the strength of his convictions and the fervor of his zeal by demonstrations which would startle us now coming from the pulpit—such as burning his flesh with the blaze of a candle, beating himself with a chain, and bruising his breast with a stone which he carried in his hand. Further, this devout man was lame from an incurable sore on his leg, contracted soon after his landing in Mexico; but he usually travelled on foot none the less. You have before you the first great pioneer of California! His energies were not destined to be wasted in the care of missions which others had founded. He entered immediately upon the *spiritual conquest* of the regions of the north. Josef de Galvez, then visitor general, a very high officer, (representing the person of the king in the inspection of the working of every part of the government of the province to which he was sent,) and who afterwards held the still more exalted position of minister general for all the Indies, arrived at this time in Lower California, bringing a royal order to despatch an expedition by sea to re-discover and people the Port of Monterey, or at least that of San Dieogo. Father Junipero entered with enthusiasm into his plans, and after consulting with him and learning the condition of the missions and the latitude of the most northern, Galvez, the better to fulfil the wishes of his majesty, determined, besides the expedition by sea, to send another which should go in search of San Diego by land, at which point the two expeditions should meet and make an establishment. And he further resolved to found three missions; one at San Diego, one at Monterey, and another mid-way between these, at San Buena Ventura. A fleet, consisting of two small vessels, at this time came over to Lower California from San Blas; the San Carlos and the San Antonio, otherwise the Principe. Of these the San Carlos was the capitania or flag-ship. Galvez, a really great man, labored with great diligence and good nature to get them ready for sea; with his own hands assisting the workmen, such as there were to be found in that remote corner of the world, in careening the vessels, and the fathers in boxing up the ornaments, sacred vases, and other utensils of the church and vestry, and boasting in a letter that he was a better sacristan than Father Junipero, because he had put up the ornaments, &c., for his mission, as he called that of San Buena Ventura, before that servant of God had those for his of San Carlos, and had to go and help him. Also, that the new missions might be established in the same manner with those of Sierra Gorda, where Father Junipero had formerly labored, and with which he was much pleased. Galvez ordered to be boxed up and embarked all kinds of household and field utensils, with the necessary iron-work for cultivating the lands, and every species of seeds, as well those of old as of new Spain, without forgetting the very least, such as garden-herbs, flowers, and flax, the land being, he said, in his opinion, fertile for everything, as it was in the same latitude with Spain. For the same purpose, he determined that from the furthest north of the old missions the land expedition should carry two hundred head of cows, bulls, and oxen, to stock that new country with large cattle, in order to cultivate the whole of it, and that in proper time there should be no want of something to eat.

Father Junipero blessed the vessels and the flags, Galvez made an impressive harangue, the expedition embarked, and the San Carlos sailed from La Paz, in Lower California, on the 9th day of January, 1769. The whole enterprise was commended to the patronage of the Most Holy Patriarch St. Joseph. On the San Carlos sailed Don Vicente Villa, commander of the maritime expedition; Don Pedro Fages, a lieutenant commanding a company of twenty-five soldiers of the Catalonian volunteers; the engineer, Don Miguel Constanzo; likewise Dr. Pedro Pratt, a surgeon of the royal navy, and all the necessary crew and officers. With them for their consolation went the Father Friar Fernando Parron. Galvez, in a small vessel, accompanied the San Carlos as far as Cape San Lucas, and saw her put to sea with a fair wind on the 11th day of January,

1769. The San Antonio, the other vessel, went to Cape San Lucas, and Galvez
set to work with the same energy and heartiness to get her ready. She sailed
on the 15th day of February, 1769. The captain of the San Antonio was Don
Juan Perez, a native of Majorca, and a distinguished pilot of the Philippine
trade. With him sailed two priests, Fathers Juan Vizcayno and Francisco
Gomez. The archives of this State contain a paper of these times which cannot
but be read with interest. It is the copy of the receipt of the commander, Vin-
cente Villa, containing a list of all the persons on board the San Carlos, and an
inventory of eight months' provisions. It reads thus:

OFFICERS AND CREW, SOLDIERS, ETC., OF THE SAN CARLOS.

The two army officers, the father missionary, the captain, pilot, and
    surgeon .... 6 persons.
The company of soldiers, being the surgeon, corporal, and twenty-
    three men .... 25 persons.
The officers of the ship and crew, including two pages, (cabin boys
    doubtless) .... 25 persons.
The baker and two blacksmiths .... 3 persons.
The cook and two tortilla makers............................ 3 persons.

Total .... 62 persons.

Dried meat, 187 arrobas, (25 pounds,) 6 libras; fish, 77 arrobas, 8 libras;
crackers, (common,) 267 arrobas, 3 libras; crackers, (white,) 47 arrobas, 7 libras;
Indian corn, 760 fanegas; rice, 37 arrobas, 20 libras; peas, 37 arrobas, 20 libras;
lard, 20 arrobas; vinegar, 7 tinajas, (jars;) salt, 8 fanegas; panocha, (domestic
sugar,) 43 arrobas, 8 libras; cheese, 78 arrobas; brandy, 5 tinajas; wine, 6 tin-
ajas; figs, 6 tinajas; raisins, 3 tinajas; dates, 2 tinajas; sugar, 5 arrobas; choco-
late, 77 arrobas; hams, 70 arrobas; oil, (table,) 6 tinajas; oil, (fish,) 5 tinajas;
red pepper, 12 libras; black pepper, 7 libras; cinnamon, 7 libras; garlic, 5
libras; 25 smoked beef tongues; 6 live cattle; 70 tierces of flour, each of 25
arrobas, 20 libras; 15 sacks of bran; lentiles, 23 arrobas; beans, 19 arrobas,
20 libras; one thousand dollars in reals (coin) for any unexpected emergency.
Besides 32 arrobas of panocha (domestic sugars,) 20 for the two missions of San
Diego and Monterey, one half to each, and the remaining 12 arrobas for the gratification of the Indians, and to barter with them. 16 sacks of charcoal; 1 box
of tallow candles of 4½ arrobas; 1 pair of 16-pound scales; 2 pounds of lamp
wick.
    The original of this simple and homely document, but which enables us to
realize so clearly these obscure transactions, yet so full of interest for us, was
given unquestionably to Galvez, and this copy we may presume brought to
to California on this first voyage of the Santa Carlos to serve as her manifest. It is dated the 5th of January, 1769. Of the same date we have the
instructions of Galvez to Villa and Fages, addressed to each of them separately—that is, the original is given to Villa under the signature of Galvez
and a copy to Fages. They are long and minute. The first article declares
that the first object of the expedition is to establish the "Catholic religion
among a numerous heathen people, submerged in the obscure darkness of paganism, to extend the dominion of the King our lord, and to protect this peninsula
from the ambitious views of foreign nations." He also recites that this project
had been entertained since 1606, when it was ordered to be executed by Philip
III, referring to orders which were issued by that monarch in consequence of
the report made by Vizcayno, but which were never carried into effect. He
enjoins that no labor or fatigue be spared now for the accomplishment of such
just and holy ends. San Diego, he says, will be found in latitude 33 degrees,

as set forth in the royal cedula of 1606, (one hundred and sixty-three years before,) and that it cannot fail to be recognized from the landmarks mentioned by Vizcayno. At the conclusion in his own handwriting we have the following :

"Note.—That to the fort or presidio that may be constructed, and to the pueblo (village) of the mission which may be established at Monterey, there shall be given the glorious name of San Carlos de Monterey.—Joseph de Galvez," (with his rubric.)

When the San Antonio sailed she seems to have carried a letter from Galvez to Pedro Fages, who had gone in advance on the San Carlos, for we have it now in the archives. It is dated cape San Lucas, February 14, 1769. The body of the letter is in substance : That the San Antonio arrived at the bay (San Lucas) on the twenty-fifth of last month, (January ;) that she was discharged and cleared of barnacles ; that he examined the vessel with his own eyes, and found the keel thereof as sound as when it was placed in the vessel ; that the necessary repairs had been made, and her cargo again placed on board, and that to-morrow, if the weather permit, she will sail, and that he trusts in Providence she will come safely into Monterey and find him (Fages) already in possession of the country.

So far it is in the handwriting of a clerk. He then adds a postscript with his own hand, addressed as well to Father Parron and the Engineer Constanzo as to Fages. I read it, for it is pleasant to have, as it were, a personal acquaintance with the eminent personage who directed the foundation of Upper California, and to find him a gentleman of such manifest abilities, generous temper, and enthusiasm :

"My Friends : It appears that the Lord, to my confusion, desires infinitely to reward the only virtue I possess, which is my constant faith, for everything here goes on prosperously, even to the mines abounding in metals. Many people are collecting, with abundance of provisions.

"I hope you will sing the Te Deum in Monterey, and in order that we may repeat it here, you will not withhold the notice of the same an instant longer than is necessary.

"This is also for the Reverend Father Parron.
                                     "JOSEF DE GALVEZ," (Rubrica.)

Just as active was he in getting off the land expedition. The chief command was given to Don Gaspar de Portala, captain of dragoons, and then governor of Lower California ; the second rank to Don Fernando Rivera y Moncada, captain of a company of foot soldiers who carried leathern bucklers. And in imitation of Jacob, Galvez, in view of the dangers of the route through savages and an unknown country, divided the force into two parts, to save one if the other was lost. Rivera was to lead the first and the governor to follow after. Rivera sets out towards the north as early as September, 1768, collecting mules and muleteers, horses, dried meat, grain, flour, biscuits, &c, among the missions ; encamps on the verge of the unexplored regions, and sends word to the visitor general that he will be ready to start for San Diego in all of March. Father Juan Crespi there joins him, and on the 24th day of March, which was Good Friday, he begins the journey. This party consisted of the Captain Rivera, Father Crespi, a pilot who went to keep a diary, twenty-five foot soldiers with leathern bucklers, three muleteers, and a band of Christian Indians of Lower California, to serve as pioneers, assistants to the muleteers, and for anything else that might be necessary, and who carried bows and arrows. They spent fifty-two days in the journey, and on the 14th day of May arrived, without accident, at San Diego. Father Junipero Serra, president of the missions of Lower California, and of those that were to be founded, marched with Portala. The season of lent, the dispositions to be made for the regulation of the missions during his absence, and the preparations for the expedition in its spiritual part, detained him, so that it was May before he joined Portalà at the same encampment from which Rivera had set out. The reverend father president came up in very bad condition. He was travelling with an escort of two soldiers, and hardly able to get on or off his mule. His foot and leg were greatly inflamed, and the more that he always wore sandals, and never used boots, shoes, or stockings. His priests and the governor tried to dissuade him from the undertaking, but he said he would rather die on the road, yet he had faith that the Lord would carry him safely through. A letter was even sent to Galvez, but he was a kindred spirit, and agreed with Father Junipero, who, however, was far into the wilderness before the answer was received. On the second day out, his pain was so great that he could neither sit nor stand, nor sleep, and Portala, being still unable to induce him to return, gave orders for a litter to be made. Hearing this, Father Junipero was greatly distressed on the score of the Indians, who would have to carry him. He prayed fervently, and then a happy thought occurred to him. He called one of the muleteers and addressed him, so runs the story, in these words: "Son, don't you know some remedy for the sore on my foot and leg?" But the muleteer answered, "Father, what remedy can I know? Am I a surgeon? I am a muleteer, and have only cured the sore backs of beasts." "Then consider me a beast," said the father, "and this sore which has produced this swelling of my legs, and the grievous pains I am suffering, and that neither let me stand nor sleep, to be a sore back, and give me the same treatment you would apply to a beast." The muleteer, smiling, as did all the rest who heard him, answered, "I will, father, to please you;" and taking a small piece of tallow, mashed it between two stones, mixing with it herbs, which he found growing close by, and having heated it over the fire, annointed the foot and leg, leaving a plaster of it on the sore. God wrought in such a manner—for so wrote Father Junipero himself from San Diego—that he slept all that night until daybreak, and awoke so much relieved from his pains that he got up and said matins and prime, and afterwards Mass, as if he had never suffered such an accident; and to the astonishment of the governor and the troop at seeing the father in such health and spirits for the journey, which was not delayed a moment on his account. Such a man was Father Junipero Serra; and so he journeyed when he went to conquer California. On the first of July, 1769, they reached San Diego, all well, in forty-six days after leaving the frontier. When they came in sight of the port the troops began firing for joy; those already there replied in the same manner. The vessels at anchor joined in the salute, and so they kept up the firing, until, all having arrived, they fell to embracing one another, and to mutual congratulations at finding all the expeditions united and already at their longed-for destination. Here, then, we have the officers and priests, soldiers and sailors, and laborers, mules, oxen and cows, seeds, tools, implements of husbandry, and vases, ornaments, and utensils for the church, gotten together to begin the work of settlement, conversion, and civilization on the soil of California. The first day of July, ninety-one years ago, is the first day of California. The year 1769 is our era. The obscure events that I have noticed must yet by us be classed among its greatest occurrences, although it saw the birth of Napoleon and Wellington.

The number of souls then at San Diego should have been about two hundred and fifty, but the San Carlos had had a very hard time at sea, not reaching San Diego (which place she found with difficulty) until twenty days after the arrival of the San Antonio, which sailed five weeks later. She had, of the crew, but one sailor and the cook left alive; all the rest had died of scurvy. The first thing to be done was to found a mission and to look for Monterey, which from Vizcayno's time had been lost to the world. For founding a mission this was the proceeding:

Formal possession of the designated spot was taken in the name of Spain. A tent or arbor, or whatever construction was most practicable, was erected to serve as a temporary church, and adorned as well as circumstances would permit; a father in his robes blessed the place and the chapel, sprinkling them with water, which also he had first blessed for the occasion, and immediately the holy cross, having first been adored by all, was mounted on a staff and planted in front of the chapel. A saint was named as a patron of the mission, and a father appointed as its minister. Mass was said and a fervent discourse concerning the coming of the Holy Ghost delivered. That service, celebrated with such candles or other lights as they might have, being over, the *Veni Creator Spiritus*—an invocation to the Holy Ghost—was sung, whilst the continual firing of the soldiers during the ceremony supplied the place of an organ, and the smoke of the gunpowder that of incense, if it was wanting.

The mission being founded, the next thing was to attract the Indians. This was done in the simplest manner, by presents of food and cloth to the older ones, and bits of sugar to the young ones. When they had learned enough of their language to communicate with them, they taught them the mysteries of the faith, and when they were able to say a few prayers and make in some sort a confession of faith, they were baptised and received into the fold of the Church. At the same time they were drawn from a wandering life, collected in villages around the mission Church, and instructed in the habits and arts of civilized life. To keep them in the practice of their lessons, spiritual and secular, the father in charge of the mission had over them the control of a master, and for them the affection of a parent, and was supported in his authority by the soldiers at the presidios, or an escort stationed at the mission itself.

This was the mode of accomplishing what Galvez in his instructions declared to be the first object of the enterprise. And in this manner Father Junipero begun the work at San Diego on the 16th day of July. An untoward incident of a very unusual nature in California attended this first essay. The Indians, not being permitted to steal all the cloth they coveted, surprised the mission when only four soldiers, the carpenter, and blacksmith were present, and Father Junipero would have been murdered then at the outset, but for the muskets, leathern jackets, and bucklers, and mainly the valor of the blacksmith. This man had just come from the communion, to which circumstance the fathers attributed his heroism, and although he wore no defensive armor of skins, he rushed out shouting *vivas for the faith of Jesus Christ and death to the dogs, its enemies*, at the same time firing away at the savages.

On the 14th day of July the Governor Portala and a servant; Father Juan Crespi and Francisco Gomez; Captain Fernando Rivera y Moncada, the second in command, with a sergeant and twenty-six soldiers of the leathern jackets; Lieutenant Pedro Fages and seven of his soldiers—the rest had died on the San Carlos or were left sick at San Diego; Don Miguel Constanzo, the engineer; seven muleteers, and fifteen Christian Indians, sixty five persons in all, with a pack train carrying a large supply of provisions, set out to rediscover Monterey. The mortality on board the San Carlos prevented any attempt at that time by sea; that vessel having to be laid up at San Diego, whilst all the efficient men were transferred to the San Antonio, which was sent back with the news and for reinforcements, and lost nine men before reaching San Blas, although she made the voyage in twenty days. Such was navigation on this coast at that time. Portala returned to San Diego on the 24th of June, six months and ten days after his departure. He had been at the port of Monterey, stopped there and set up a cross without recognizing the place. Father Crespi, who kept the diary, said he supposed the bay had been filled up, as they found a great many large sand-hills. This disappointment caused Portala to keep on further towards the north, and at forty leagues distant in that direction they discovered the port of San Francisco, which they recognized at once by the description they had o it. The fathers considered this circumstance as providential. They remembered that when Galvez was instructing Father Junipero by what names to call the three missions he was to found, the father had asked him: "But, sir, is there to be no mission for our father, St. Francis?" and that the visitor general had replied: "If St. Francis wants a mission, let him show us his port, and we will put one there." And in view of the discovery, they thought that it was now clear that St. Francis did want a mission, and had concealed Monterey from them purposely that they might go and find his port; and Galvez to some extent may have been of the same opinion, as they say, for he ordered a mission to be founded there, and a presidio also, as soon as he received the news. However this may be, a question of more historical interest, or curiosity, at least, is whether, notwithstanding that Portala knew the port from description as soon as he saw it, any other white man had ever seen it before. His latest guide was the voyage of Vizcayno, who had entered the port of San Francisco on the 12th of January 1603, and anchored under a point of land called Punta de Los Reyes, namely, in the bight outside the heads and north of Point Bonita.

In the port of San Francisco, as known to Vizcayno, the Manilla galleon San Augustine had been wrecked a few years before. Did a galleon ever enter our bay? Vizcayno was searching for a port to shelter the Manilla trade; if he had seen our harbor would he have ever thought of recommending Monterey? He was doubtless following the pilot who gave the information of the loss of the San Augustine; if that pilot had seen this port would not the specific object of Vizcayno have been to find it again, and not generally to explore the coast to look for a good harbor? Had anything been known of it, would it not have been mentioned by Galvez in his first instructions to Villa, in which he is so earnest on the subject of Monterey? Would he have waited for this news to have given the urgent orders that he did, that this important place should be taken possession of immediately, for fear that it might fall into the hands of foreigners? It seems to me certain that Portala was the discoverer. And I regard it as one of the most remarkable facts in history, that others had passed it, anchored near it and actually given its name to adjacent roadsteads, and so described its position that it was immediately known; and yet that the cloud had never been lifted which concealed the entrance of the bay of San Francisco, and that it was at last discovered by land.

Although Portala reported that he could not find the port of Monterey, it was suspected at the time that he had been there. Father Junipero writes that such was his opinion and that of Don Vicente Villa, of the San Carlos. In the same letter he mentions another matter, and one which disturbed him greatly. The Governor Portala, finding his provisions very short, determined if a vessel did not arrive with relief, to abandon the mission on the 20th of March.

But California was saved at the last moment. The San Antonio came in on the 19th and brought such a quantity of provisions that Portala set out again by land, and Father Junipero himself embarked on the San Antonio, which had proved herself a good sailer and well commanded, and anchored in the bay of Monterey, namely, on the 31st day of May, 1770, and found that the expedition by land had arrived eight days before; and we thus see that the journey from San Diego at that time was made quicker by land than by water. Father Junipero writes that he found the lovely port of Monterey the same and unchanged in substance and in circumstance as the expedition of Sebastian Vizcayno left it in 1603; and that all the officers of sea and land, and all their people assembled in the same glen and under the same oak where the Fathers of Vizcayno's expedition had worshipped, and there arranged their altar, hung up and rung their bells, sung the *Veni Creator*, blessed the holy water, set up and blessed the cross and the royal standards, concluding with a *Te Deum*. And there the name of Christ was again spoken for the first time after an interval of more than one hundred and sixty-seven years of silence. After the religious ceremonies were over, the officers went through the act of taking possession of the country "in the name of our lord the King."

When this news was received at the city of Mexico it created a profound impression. At the request of the Viceroy the bells of the cathedral were rung, and those of all the other churches answered; people ran about the streets to tell one another the story, and all the distinguished persons at the capital waited upon the Viceroy, who, in company with Galvez, received their congratulations at the palace; and that not only the inhabitants of the city of Mexico, but also those of all New Spain might participate in the general joy, the Viceroy caused a narrative of the great achievement to be printed; and which, indeed, was circulated throughout old as well as New Spain. It commences by referring to the costly and repeated expeditions which were made by the Crown of Spain during the two preceding centuries to explore the western coast of California and to occupy the important port of Monterey, which now, it says, has been most happily accomplished; and it is jubilant throughout. Nothing of this sort occurred when they heard a short time before of the discovery of the Bay of San Francisco; and in this authoritative relation it is not even mentioned.

Governor Portala, with the engineer Constanzo, very soon returned to Mexico in the good ship San Antonio, and carried themselves the tidings of their success. We may imagine what a description they gave when we remember that they left San Diego about the middle of April, and that at that season the country through which they passed to Monterey was mottled all over with the brightest and most varied colors. They were the first to behold a California spring in all its boundless profusion of flowers. When they were gone there remained only Father Junipero Serra and five priests, and the Lieutenant Pedro Fages and thirty soldiers in all California; for the captain, Rivera y Moncada, with nineteen soldiers, the muleteers and vaqueroe, was at this time absent too, in Lower California, whither he had gone to bring up a band of two hundred cattle and provisions. It is impossible to imagine anything more lonely and secluded than their situation here, at the time the bells were ringing so joyfully in Mexico on their account. Very soon, however, they began to get on good terms with the Indians, for Father Junipero was not a man to lose any time in beginning his work. And when they came to understand one another, the Indians there, under the pines, told them awful tales about the cross which Portala had set up the year before when he stopped at Monterey without knowing the place; how when they first saw the whites they noticed that each one carried a shining cross upon his breast; and how they were so terrified when they found the whites had gone and had left that large one standing on the shore that at first they dared not approach it; that at night it shone with dazzling splendor, and would rise and grow until it seemed to reach the skies; and how, seeing nothing of this sort about it in the day time, and that it was only of its proper size, they had at last taken courage and gone up to it, and to make friends with it, had stuck arrows and feathers around it in the earth, and had hung strings of sardines on its arms, as the Spaniards had found on their return. For the truth of this story the prudent father would not vouch, but they were still willing to regard it as an omen, and to attribute to it their easy success in converting the natives of those parts, as Father Junipero wrote to the Viceroy for his edification and encouragement. Father Junipero soon removed his mission from Monterey to a more suitable place close by, on the river Carmelo. This was his own mission, where he always resided when not engaged in founding or visiting other missions, or in some other duty appertaining to his office of president of the missions of Upper California. This high office he held for the first fifteen years of the history of California, and until his death, which occurred at his mission of Carmel on the 28th of August, 1784. His activity and zeal in the conversion and civilization of savages are really wonderful, and scarcely intelligible to us. The sight of a band of Indians filled him with as much delight as at this day a man feels at the prospect of making a fortune. He regarded them as so many souls that he was to save; and the baptism of an Indian baby filled him with transport. With what sort of a spirit he worked for these creatures you see pleasantly exhibited in the foundation of the mission of San Antonio de Padua, some twenty or thirty leagues below Monterey. With an escort, a couple of priests, and a pack train carrying all the necessary articles for a new church, he goes off into the mountains, examines all the hollows, and selects a beautiful little plain, through which flowed a small river. Here he orders the mules to be unpacked, and the bells to be hung upon a tree, and as soon as that is done he seizes the rope and begins to ring, crying out at the same time at the top of his voice, "Hear! hear! oh ye gentiles! Come to the holy church! Come to the faith of Jesus Christ!" Father Péyras, who was with him, remonstrates, "What do you stop for? Is not this the place for the church, and are there no gentiles in the neighborhood?" "Let me alone," says Father Junipero; "Let me unburthen my heart, which could wish this bell should be heard by all the world, or at least by all the gentiles in these mountains"—and so he rang away there in the wilderness.

The missions of San Francisco and Santa Clara were not founded for several years after the occupation of Monterey. The wants of the new missions of his jurisdiction induced the Reverend Father President Junipero to take a journey to Mexico to see the Viceroy in person, and although he succeeded to his satisfaction in other things, it was only after much entreaty that he obtained a promise that these two missions should be established after communication was opened by land This was done by Captain Juan Bautista Anza, in 1773, whilst Father Junipero was absent on his visit to Mexico. [Note.—A granddaughter of Captain Juan Bautista Anza is now living in this city. She is the wife of Don Manuel Ainsa, and the mother of a large family of great-grandchildren of the first pioneer who came to Upper California, direct from Mexico by land.] He made his report to the Viceroy in 1774, and came back again with a considerable number of soldiers and families in 1776. In the mean time, in anticipation of his arrival, the San Carlos was sent up to examine the port of San Francisco, and ascertain whether it could be really entered by a channel or mouth which had been seen from the land. This great problem was satisfactorily solved by the San Carlos, a ship of perhaps some two hundred tons burden at the very utmost, in the month of June, 1775. When she entered they reported that they found a land-locked sea, with two arms, one making into the interior about fifteen leagues to the southeast, another three, four, or may be five leagues to the north, where there was a large bay, about ten leagues across and of a round figure, into which emptied the great river of our father, St. Francis, which was fed by five other rivers, all of them copious streams, flowing through a plain so wide that it was bounded only by the horizon, and meeting to form the said great river; and all this immensity of water discharging itself through the said channel or mouth into the Pacific ocean, which is there called the Gulf of the Farallones. This very striking description was accurate enough for the purposes of that day; and as soon as Anza and his people had arrived, and Anza in person had gone up and selected the sites, a party was sent by land and another by sea to establish the presidio and mission of San Francisco. The date of the foundation of the presidio is the 17th of September, and of the mission the 9th of October, 1776. The historian mentions in connection with these proceedings some things which may claim a moment's attention. In the Valley of San José, the party coming up by land saw some animals which they took for cattle, though they could not imagine where they came from; and, supposing they were wild and would scatter the tame ones they were driving, the soldiers made after them and succeeded in killing three, which were so large that a mule could with difficulty carry one, being of the size of an ox, and with horns like those of a deer, but so long that their tips were eight feet apart. This was their first view of the elk. The soldiers made the observation that they could not run against the wind by reason of these monstrous antlers. And after the presidio, and before the mission was established, an exploration of the interior was organized, as usual, by sea and land. Point San Pablo was given as the rendezvous; but the captain of the presidio, who undertook in person to lead the land party, failed to appear there, having, with the design to shorten the distance, entered a cañada somewhere near the head of the bay, which took him over to the San Joaquin river; so he discovered that stream.

Then there are some traits of the first inhabitants of this place, the primitive San Franciscans. They lived upon muscles and acorns, blackberries, strawberries, and fish, and delighted above all things in the blubber of whales, when one was stranded on the coast. They wore no clothes at all, at least the men, and the women very little; but they were not ashamed. They found it cold all the year round, as did the fathers who first took charge of the mission, and to protect themselves, were in the habit of plastering their bodies with mud. They said it kept them warm. Their marriages were very informal, the ceremony consisting in the consent alone of the parties; and their law of divorce was equally simple, for they separated as soon as they quarrelled, and joined themselves to another, the children usually following the mother. They had no other expression to signify that the marriage was dissolved than to say, "I have thrown her away," or "I have thrown him away." And in some of their customs they seemed to have been Mormons. In their marriages affinity was not regarded as an objection, but rather an inducement. They preferred to marry their sisters-in-law, and even their mothers-in-law; and the rule was, if a man married a woman, he also married all her sisters, having many wives who lived together, without jealousy, in the same house, and treated each other's children with the same love as their own. Father Junipero's death closes the first period of our history. It is a period marked by exploits. They are those of humble and devoted, yet heroic missionaries. The story is diversified with only such simple incidents as that, in the summer of 1772, the commander, Pedro Fages, had to go out and kill bears for provisions to subsist on, which formidable game he found in abundance somewhere near San Luis Obispo, in a cañada that still justly bears the name of Cañada de los Osos: and that in 1780 the frost killed the growing grain at Easter. And only one instance of bloodshed attended the happy course of the spiritual conquest. The vicious Indians of San Diego, on a second attempt, murdered one of the fathers and two or three other persons, and burned the mission, which some little time afterwards was re-established. We are told that they were prompted to this deed by the enemy of souls, who was very much incensed at finding his party falling into a minority by reason of the constant conversions of the heathen in that neighborhood. All the seeds that Galvez was so provident in sending up took root and prospered beyond the most sanguine expectations which he could have entertained when he predicted that the soil would prove as fertile as that of old Spain; and the cattle increased and multiplied with an increase without a parallel, so that in short time his purpose, that there should be no lack of something to eat in this country, was fully accomplished.

Our historian is the friar, Father Francisco Palou, one of the followers of Father Junipero, whose life, like a devout disciple, he wrote here at the mission of San Francisco. He was the first priest who had charge of this mission, and his book was written here in 1785. It was printed in the city of Mexico in 1787. It is the first, undoubtedly, but not the worst book written in California. Copies of the original edition may be found in some private libraries of this city, bound in sheepskin, clasped with loops and buttons of the same, and with a long list of *errata* at the end. This volume is of itself an object of interest.

To the work there is a preface which bespeaks the indulgence of the reader, because it was written among "barbarous gentiles, in the port of San Francisco, in his new mission, the most northern of New California, without books or men of learning to consult." There are also the reports of several censors, and both a civil and ecclesiastical license to print it, and likewise a protest, of which the writer is entitled to the benefit at this day. He declares, in obedience to the Church, the Inquisition, and the Pope, that he intends and desires that no more faith should be given to his performance than to a mere human history, and that the epithets he gives Father Junipero, and the title of martyrs which he bestowed on some of the other missionaries, are to be understood as mere human honors, and such as are permitted by a prudent discretion and a devout faith. The narrative is clear and circumstantial, well supported by public and private writings, and obviously true. The miraculous is always introduced as hearsay, and, whilst it does not impeach the veracity of the writer, serves still further to illustrate the times by showing us the simple credulity of the class to which he belonged—the founders and first settlers of California. With the book there is a map. It exhibits the coast of Upper California from San Diego to San Francisco. The only objects visible on it are nine missions and a dotted line, to show the road that the fathers travelled from one to the other, viz: San Diego, San Juan Capistrano, San Gabriel, San Buenaventura, San Luis, (Obispo,) San Antonio, San Carlos de Monterey, Santa Clara, San Francisco, and three presidios, Monterey, Santa Barbara, and San Diego, all lying near the coast, and back all a blank. Looking upon this old map, we realize that California was designed for the Indians. They were to be its people after they were converted and instructed as others had been in Mexico. The missions were to be the towns. The presidios were to protect the missions within, and defend the country from enemies without. Only enough settlers were to be introduced to relieve the government from some part of the burden of supplying the presidios with recruits and provisions from Mexico. For this purpose, pueblos San José de Guadalupe and Los Angeles, one in the north and the other in the south, were established, both in the time of Father Junipero Serra. A small tract of land was given to these villages for their use collectively, and smaller parcels to each inhabitant as his private property. Neither of these pueblos appear on this old map, of such little consequence were they regarded. Father Palou, in relating the rejoicings at Mexico in consequence of the discovery of Monterey, says : " The said extent of three hundred leagues in length"—an accurate measurement of the new dominions of the king in Upper California—"is of fertile lands, peopled with an immensity of gentiles, from whose docile and peaceable dispositions it was hoped they would be immediately converted to our holy faith, and gathered in Catholic pueblos, (villages,) that thus living in subjection to the royal crown they might secure the coasts of this Southern or Pacific ocean." The first grant of land made in California was a tract of one hundred and forty varas square, at the mission of San Carlos, November 27, 1775, to one Manuel Butron, a soldier, in consideration that he had married Margarita, a daughter of that mission. Father Junipero recommends this family, to wit, the soldier and the native Indian woman, to the government, and all the other ministers of the king, " as being the first in all these establishments which have chosen to become permanent settlers of the same." The Indian appears in everything.

In tranquillity this California of the Indians remained for more than fifty years. The fathers built new missions, and continually replenished their stock of converts, which at one time amounted to at least twenty thousand. They planted vineyards, orchards, and the olive. They taught the Indians, to some extent, agriculture and the mechanic arts. They made flour, and wine, and cloth, and soap, and leather, adobes and tiles, and with their villages of disciples about them, lived at ease as well as in peace. There was but one obstacle in their way. A great law of nature rose up to oppose them. The Indian of California was not equal to those of Mexico. He was but a brute. The time never came when he could be enfranchised and trusted to himself, and converted into a Spanish subject as so many races had been further south. The fathers must continue to hold their converts in subjection, or they would return to the heathen state, or even worse would befall them. If the world could have afforded to devote a paradise to such a purpose, and for the Indian, certainly it would have been well if the missions could have lasted forever. I will endeavor to present some of the features and some of the events of this Indian period, as briefly as possible. And here, for whatever of interest I may be able to awaken in the subject, I shall be indebted to Mr. R. C. Hopkins, the accomplished and learned gentleman who has charge of the Spanish archives in the surveyor general's office.

An American audience will of course desire to know something of the form of the political government. Constitution or charter there was none. The government was purely military, outside of the missions. All functions, civil and military, judicial and economical, were united in the person of the commandante of a presidio, in due subjection to his superior, and so on up to the king, an autocrat, whose person was represented and whose will was executed in every part of his dominions. In the archives is to be found a reglamento, which, as the name imports, is a set of regulations for the peninsula of the Californias, Lower and Upper. Its caption expresses that it is for the government of the presidios, the promotion of the erection of new missions, and of the population and extension of the establishments of Monterey. It was drafted at Monterey by the governor, in 1779, sent to Madrid, and approved by the king in 1781. When examined, it is found to adopt the royal reglamento for the government of all the presidios, with such small variations as the circumstances of California required. There are minute provisions for paying, clothing, and feeding the officers and troops, and for supporting the families of the troops, and other persons dependent on the presidios. The number of pack mules to be kept at the presidios, and how the horses are to be pastured, and that four are always to be kept in the presidio ready saddled by day, and eight by night, is prescribed. Another pueblo was to be founded, as was done, namely, Los Angeles. The pueblo of San José had already been founded, two years before. The intent of these pueblos is declared to be to fulfil the pious designs of the King for converting the gentiles, and to secure his dominions. At that date, says the reglamento, the country was filled, from San Diego to Monterey, with an immense number of gentiles, and only one thousand seven hundred and forty-nine Christians, of both sexes, in the eight missions, strung along through all that distance. The manner in which pueblos are to be founded is given; each settler to have his building lot and sowing field of two hundred varas square, that being supposed to be enough to sow two bushels of grain; and the whole together to have commons for wood, water, and pasturage; also a certain number of horses, mules, oxen, cows, sheep, chickens, ploughs, hoes, axes, &c., are to be furnished to each; and the amount of pay—for a settler had his salary for a little while as well as his outfit—his exemptions, and his obligations, are all minutely detailed. Of the first we observe, that for the first five years he is to be free from the payment of tithes; of the latter, that all the excess of his productions beyond his support he must sell at a fixed price to the presidios, and that he must keep a horse and saddle, carbine and lance, and hold himself in readiness for the service of the king. Also, we note that the building lot is a homestead, and cannot be alienated or mortgaged, and descends to the son or (in default of a son, I suppose) to the daughter, provided she is married to a settler who is without a lot of his own; and that after the first five years are past, each settler and his descendants must, in recognition of the absolute property of the King, pay a rent of one-half fanega of corn for his sowing lot. The only trace of a political right that we find in the reglamento is the allowance to the pueblos of alcaldes, and other municipal officers, to be appointed by the governor for the first two years, and afterwards to be elected by the inhabitants. These officers were to see to the good government and police of the pueblos and the administration of justice, to direct the public works, apportion to each man his share of the water for irrigation, and generally to enforce the provisions of the reglamento. This, perhaps, was as much as they ought to have had, for we see in the proceedings on the foundation of San José, that neither the alcalde nor any one of the eight other settlers could sign his name. As a check upon the abuse of their privileges the elections were subject to the approval of the governor, who had also the power to continue to appoint the officers for three years longer, if he found it necessary.

At first California formed a part of the kingdom of New Spain, and was governed directly by the Viceroy of Mexico. In 1776 it was attached to the commandancia general of the internal provinces, which included also Soñora, New Mexico, Chihuahua, Coahuila, and Texas. Afterwards it was a part of the commandancia general of the internal provinces of the west, when Coahuila and Texas, New Leon and the Colony of New Santander had been erected into another jurisdiction, under the title of the internal provinces of the east. The commandante general seems to have had no fixed residence, but to have gone from place to place, wherever his presence might be wanted, and so his orders are sometimes dated from Arispe and sometimes from Chihuahua, both of which now obscure places may be said in their time to have been the capital of California. The Apache and Comanche Indian has watered his horse in their plazas since then. This arrangement did not last many years, and California reverted to the Viceroy again. Laws came from the King, in his council of the Indies, at Madrid, as orders are issued by the commander-in-chief of an army; to the second in command, to wit, the Viceroy at Mexico, from him to his next in rank, we will say the commandante general at Arispe or Chihuahua, from him to the governor of California at Monterey, and from him to the captain or lieutenant in command of a presidio. They took effect only as they were published, spreading as the courier advanced, and from place to place in succession, like a wave, from centre to circumference. They came slowly, but in time every order of a general nature would find its way into the archives of every province, presidio, or pueblo in North and South America, and of every island of the ocean which owned the dominion of the King of Spain. The archives of this State contain a great many, and their counterparts are to be looked for in every public office, from Havana to Manilla, and from Chihuahua to Valparaiso. When wars, or the accidents of navigation, or the urgency of the case, interrupted or rendered impossible communication with Madrid, each viceregent of the King in his department exercised the royal authority. Therefore, in the nature of things, the powers of every governor in his province were practically despotic. And not only the laws, but every other expression of the wishes of the King were transmitted in the same way, travelled through the same circuitous channels, and were received, and published, and executed with the same dignity and formality. Here is an example from the archives:

The King heard that the neighborhood of the presidio of San Francisco abounded with deer of a very superior quality, and desiring to have some for his park, issued an order to the viceroy of Mexico, who in his turn ordered the commandante general of the internal provinces of the west, who despatched an order to the governor of the province of California, who ordered the captain of the presidio of San Francisco, who finally ordered a soldier to go out and catch the deer, two years after the order was given by the King at Madrid. Allowing a reasonable time for the hunt, and for sending the animals to Spain, it will be seen that the King had to wait some time for the gratification of his royal wishes.

Another instance, and the more striking, as the subject-matter belongs to the latitude of the equator, and as it serves to illustrate that the arbitrary government of his Catholic Majesty was paternal and thoughtful as well, I give a translation of the original, complete :

Jacobo Ugarte y Loyola, commandante general of the internal provinces, writes to Pedro Fages, governor of California, as follows :

"ARISPE, *April* 22, 1787.

"On the 20th of November last past, his excellency the marquis of Sonora, (Viceroy of Mexico,) was pleased to communicate to me the following royal order :

"'The archbishop, Viceroy of Santa Fé, (in South America,) on the 2d of July last, gave me an account of a remedy happily discovered by his confessor, against the ravages of the jigger (nigua) in the hot countries of America, which consists in annointing the parts affected by the jiggers with cold olive oil, which causes them to die, and the sacs containing them can be easily extracted—which the King desires should be published as a bando (proclamation) in the district under your government, in order that it may reach the notice of all ; and you shall take care that all those who are afflicted with said insect shall use said remedy, which is as effectual as it is simple.'

"And I insert the same to you in order that you may cause it to be published.   May God preserve your life many years.

"JACOBO UGARTE Y LOYOLA."

And so this valuable specific was made known by a public crier and with a roll of drums, all the world over, even here in California, where the troublesome insect is fortunately unknown.

The couriers, who were the overland mail of that day, on leaving, for instance, Monterey, received a certificate from the commandante of the presidio that he started at a certain hour ; on his arrival at the next stopping place he presented his certificate to the officer in command of the place, who noted the hour of his arrival and departure, and so on at all the stopping places between Monterey and La Paz, in Lower California ; so that if the mail carrier loitered on the way his way-bill would show it.   Such way-bills from Monterey to La Paz, with all these memoranda on them, may be found in the archives.   It was the unfortunate mail rider, and not the government, that people were in the habit of blaming in those days.   These way-bills show that he made the distance from San Francisco to San Diego in five days.   Quiet old days !   But little of a public sort was doing then in California.   There was a dispute that amounted to something like a law suit between the mission of Santa Clara and the pueblo of San José.   It commenced from the very day of the establishment of the latter.   Father Junipero objected to the pueblo being so near the mission, the boundary as at first established running about half way between the two places.   The governor was obstinate and Father Junipero desired that his protest might be entered in the proceedings of the foundation, which the governor refused.   The controversy by no means died out; the head of the college of San Fernando at Mexico, to which all the Franciscans of California belonged, brought it before the Viceroy, praying him not to allow the Indians and missionaries to be molested by the pueblo.   The governor of California was therefore ordered to investigate the matter, and seems to have settled it by making the river Guadalupe the boundary from that time forward.   Again, one Mariano Castro obtained from the Viceroy permission to settle himself upon a place called La Brea, in the neighborhood of the mission of San Juan Bautista ; under this license he applied to the governor to give him the possession of the land, but the priests at San Juan objected strenuously, alleging that the place of La Brea was needed by the mission for its cattle.   This was represented by the governor to the viceroy, who, in the end, told Castro to select some other place, and the mission kept La Brea. We see with what jealousy, and how effectively, the fathers vindicated the title of themselves and their Indian pupils to their California.

For a complete view of the internal constitution of California at that day, two facts, which are exceptional to this ecclesiastical domination, require to be noted.

In 1791, Pedro Nava, commandante of the internal provinces of the west, in a decree dated at Chihuahua, gives to the captains commanding presidios, or recognizes as already existing in them, authority to grant building lots to the soldiers and other residents, within the space of four square leagues. I do not know, but presume, that this power was exercised at San Diego, Santa Barbara, and Monterey, and hence the origin of the towns bearing those names, which, at a later period, come into view as such. At San Francisco, however, there is nothing in the archives, or elsewhere, yet discovered, to show that such a grant was ever made by the captain of the presidio. And in 1795 a commissioner was appointed under the orders of the viceroy to select a place and establish another town, who reported that "the worst place or situation in California is that of San Francisco for the formation of a villa, as proposed." And therefore the villa of Branciforte, so called in honor of the viceroy, the Marquis of Branciforte, was, by great preference, established near the mission of Santa Cruz. It never attained any consequence, and some adobe ruins may now attest its former existence.

Suspicion and exclusion were the rule towards foreigners. On the 23d of October, 1776, the viceroy writes to the governor of California: "That the king having received intelligence that two armed vessels had sailed from London, under the command of Captain Cook, bound on a voyage of discovery to the southern ocean, and the northern coast of California, commands that orders be given to the governor of California to be on the watch for Captain Cook, and not permit him to enter the ports of California." At a later day a better spirit prevailed towards Vancouver, who spent some time in 1793 in the port of Monterey. We have a voluminous correspondence of his with the governor—the letters in English, and written with his own hand. He sets forth the harmonious understanding existing between England and his Catholic Majesty of Spain, and their united efforts in the cause of humanity, and asks assistance in arresting some deserters, and obtaining supplies, &c., which he will pay for with bills on London. Instructions had been previously received by the governor to treat Vancouver well. We see in this amiability between old enemies that the great French revolution was making itself felt on this remote coast. And in some of the letters of the fathers, of a little later period, we find Napoleon spoken of as the great "Luzbel," (Lucifer,) for such he appeared to their imagination in their missions.

The first mention of an American ship occurs in the following letter from the governor of California to the captain of the presidio of San Francisco:

"Whenever there may arrive at the port of San Francisco a ship named the Columbia, said to belong to General Washington, of the American States, commanded by John Kendrick, which sailed from Boston in September, 1787, bound on a voyage of discovery to the Russian establishments on the northern coast of this peninsula, you will cause the said vessel to be examined with caution and delicacy, using for this purpose a small boat which you have in your possession, and taking the same measures with every other suspicious foreign vessel, giving me prompt notice of the same.

"May God preserve your life many years.

"PEDRO FAGES.

"SANTA BARBARA, *May* 13, 1789.
"To JOSEF ARGUELLO."

H. Ex. Doc. 29——19

Twenty years before, this same Fages had sailed on the San Carlos to re-discover and people California. The San Carlos and the Columbia, and Fages the connecting link! The United States of America and California joined for the first time in a thought! It is impossible by any commentary to heighten the interest with which we read this document. Its very errors, even to the gover-nor's ignorance of the geography of his own country, are profoundly suggestive.

The Columbia did not enter the ports of California, but made land further to the north, and discovered the Columbia river.

Fourteen years later, it would appear that American ships were more fre-quent on this coast.

On the 26th of August, 1803, José Argüello, comandante of the presidio of San Francisco, writes to governor José Joaquin de Arrillaga:

"That on the first of the present month, at the hour of evening prayers, two American vessels anchored in the port, (San Francisco,) one named the Alex-ander, under the command of Capt. John Brown, and the other named the Aser, under the command of Thomas Raben; that as soon as they anchored the cap-tain came ashore to ask permission to get supplies of wood and water, when ob-serving that he was the same Brown that was there in the preceding month of March, he refused to give him permission to remain in port; that on the day following, at six in the morning, he received a letter from the captain, (or super-cargo,) a copy of which he transmits, which is as follows:

"PORT OF SAN FRANCISCO, *August* 12, 1803.

"*To the Señor commandante of the port:*

"Notwithstanding your order for our immediate departure from this port, I am constrained to say that our necessities are such as to render it impossible for us to do so. I would esteem it a great favor if you would come aboard and see for yourself the needy circumstances in which we are placed, for during the whole of the time we have been on the northwest coast we have had no opportunity of supplying ourselves with wood and water, the Indians being so savage that we have not been able to hold any kind of friendly intercourse with them what-ever.

"We had several fights with them in the straits of Chatham; the first was in the port of Istiquin, where we were attacked by three hundred canoes, each canoe containing from ten to twenty-three Indians, each one with two or three escopetas and their pistols and spears. Three times in one day they attempted to take the ship, but we defended the same without losing any of our men.

"From this port we went to the Ensenada of Icana, in said straits, at which place we found about a thousand Indians encamped, many of whom came aboard our vessel for purposes of trade, carrying their arms in one hand and their skins in the other.

"After we had been four days in this port, all the Indians came aboard, say-ing that they were not afraid of the Americans, since they were but few, while there were many Indians, who had many arms.

"On the fifth day of our stay in this port, about six o'clock in the evening, three or four canoes came alongside the ship, and, on being ordered to leave, they refused, when our captain seized a gun and fired it in the air, on which the Indians laughed very much, saying he did not know how to shoot, and could not kill; whereupon the captain seized another gun, fired at and killed the Indian, on which the rest retired to the land, and all of them went to a neighboring island; and from ten o'clock at night till eight in the morning they made no further demonstrations against us, at which time we made sail, in the mean time striking upon a rock and somewhat injuring our vessel.

"From this port we went to Juan de Fuca, at which place we learned from the chief, Tatacu, that the chief Quatlazepe had taken the ship Boston; that when the said vessel had been some four days in port, the Indian chief and the captain of the ship, having some difficulty in relation to trade, the captain of the ship said to the chief that he had traded with many chiefs to the north, and that he knew he did not act like an honorable chief; whereupon the chief Pioc-que replied to the captain that he was a bad man.   At this the captain seized a gun and ordered him ashore; whereupon he went to his rancheria and issued an order for the assembling of all the neighboring Indians, from the straits of Juan de Fuca to the point of Nutka, which were so assembled within three days; and, after holding a council, they determined to take the Bos-ton, which they affected in the following manner: At seven o'clock in the morning they went aboard and asked permission of the captain to have a dance, as a ceremony of the renewal of the friendship after their recent dispute. To which the captain replied that he was willing that they should do so. Ac-cordingly, at eight o'clock in the morning, a company of chiefs came and danced on the quarter-deck, having in the mean time ordered their people to arm them-selves with knives, so that while they were dancing they could jump aboard and kill the whole crew, which they did; for while they were dancing they made presents of otter skins to the captain, and also to the sailors, who in a short time had collected on the quarter-deck, when suddenly the Indians fell upon them in their defenceless condition and butchered all save two, who escaped and concealed themselves; the Indians carrying off everything that could be removed during the whole of that day and night, and until twelve o'clock the following day; having in the mean time discovered the two hidden sailors, who, after some cruel treatment, were handed over to the chief, who spared their lives, and they are now at that place. On the following day the ship was beached, and her decks and part of the cargo burnt. Quatlazape has made a fortification at the place where the Spaniards were established.

"This is all the account I am able to give of the matter, and I pray you, in the name of God, to come aboard our ship and see the needy circumstances in which we are placed, destitute of wood and water, and our vessel needing repairs. Trusting in your Christian charity, and that of your nation, we hope to be per-mitted to remain in this port the time necessary to obtain supplies and make re-pairs, since otherwise we shall certainly lose our ship.

"God preserve your life many years.

"JAMES ROWAN."

Times have changed, and Yankee captains are not now so meek in the port of San Francisco. We do not know what John Brown had been doing in March, nor can we vouch for the truth of all the particulars of their adventures on the northwest coast, especially not for the number of escopetas and other arms car-ried by each Indian. The loss of the Boston was doubtless communicated to her owners and the public by John Brown and Thomas Rab(v)en on their return to the United States. The guardians of this port do not note now the arrival of foreign ships by the hour of evening prayers. There was a contrast of national habits then between the shore and the Yankee ships; and the same contrast exists undiminished between the California of 1803 and 1860. From time to time other American vessels, traders to the northwest coast, and whalers, are said to have occasionally entered these waters, but as it was a Spanish colony there could be no American commerce; and it was after the independence, there-fore, that the hide trade sprung up.

With the beginning of the century earthquakes make their appearance for the first time of record in the archives, and with startling effect. I prefer, on this subject, to give the words of the contemporaneous documents:

Account of earthquake at San Juan Bautista, as given in letter of the captain of the Presidio of Monterey, to Governor Arrillaga, on the 31st of October, 1800.

"MONTEREY, *October* 31, 1800.

" I have to inform your excellency that the mission of San Juan Bautista since the 11th instant has been visited by severe earthquakes; that Pedro Adriano Martinez, one of the fathers of said mission, has informed me that during one day there were six severe shocks; that there is not a single habitation, although built with double walls, that has not been injured from roof to foundation, and that all are threatened with ruin; and that the fathers are compelled to sleep in the wagons to avoid danger since the houses are not habitable. At the place where the rancheria is situated some small openings have been observed in the earth, and also in the neighborhood of the river Pajaro there is another deep opening, all resulting from the earthquakes. These phenomena have filled the fathers and the inhabitants of that mission with consternation.

" The Lieutenant Don Raymundo Carillo has assured me the same, for on the 18th he stopped for the night at this mission (San Juan) on his journey from San José, and being at supper with one of the fathers, a shock was felt so powerful and attended with such a loud noise as to deafen them, when they fled to the court without finishing their supper, and that about eleven o'clock at night the shock was repeated with almost equal strength.

" The fathers of the mission say that the Indians assure them that there have always been earthquakes at that place, and that there are certain cavities caused by the earthquakes, and that salt water has flowed from the same.

" All of which I communicate to you for your information.

" May our Lord preserve your life many years.

"HERMENEGILDO SAL——."

San Juan Bautista is the mission between the Monterey and San José, about twenty miles from the former and forty from the latter. The next mention comes nearer home.

Account of earthquake at Presidio of San Francisco, given by Louis Argüello, Captain of Presidio, to Governor Arrillaga, on the 17th of July, 1808.

" I have to report to your excellency that since the 21st of June last to the present date, twenty-one shocks of earthquakes have been felt in this presidio, some of which have been so severe that all the walls of my house have been cracked, owing to the bad construction of the same, one of the ante-chambers being destroyed; and if up to this time no greater damage has been done, it has been for the want of materials to destroy, there being no other habitations. The barracks of the Fort of San Joaquin (the name of the fort at the presidio) have been threatened with entire ruin, and I fear if these shocks continue some unfortunate accident will happen to the troops at the presidio.

" God preserve the life of your excellency many years.

"LUIS ARGUELLO.

" SAN FRANCISCO, *July* 17, 1808."

It could not be said now, if such shocks as these were to come again, that the damage was limited by the *"want of material to destroy."* I acknowledge a preference for one-story houses, and built of wood.

About this time the Russians were first seen in California. " Von Resanoff, chamberlain of the Emperor of Russia, returning from his embassy to Japan, after having inspected, by order of the court of St. Petersburg, the ports, establishments, and trading-houses that the Imperial Russian-American Fur Company possessed, as well on the side of Asia, at Kamschatka, and in the

Aleutian Islands, as on the continent and islands of the northwest coast of America, anchored at the port of San Francisco, in the month of May, 1807." So says the French traveller De Mofras, who visited "California in the years 1841 and '42." An English traveller, Sir George Simson, governor-in-chief of the Hudson Bay Company's territories, who was here in the same year with De Mofras, thus makes us acquainted with one of the parties to a story of romantic love, the first consequence of the advent of the Russians.

"After dinner, (at Captain John Wilson's, in Santa Barbara,) we were joined by the remainder of our party, the Cowlitz having by this time come to an anchor; and we again sallied forth to see a few more of the lions. Among the persons whom we met this afternoon was a lady of some historical celebrity. Von Resanoff, having failed, as elsewhere stated, in his attempt to enter the Columbia in 1806, continued his voyage as far as San Francisco, when, besides purchasing immediate supples for Sitka, he endeavored, in negotiation with the commandante of the district and the governor of the province, to lay the foundation of a regular intercourse between Russian America and the California settlements. In order to cement the national union, he proposed uniting himself with Doña Concepcion Arguello, one of the commandante's daughters, his patriotism clearly being its own reward. If half of Langsdorff's description was correct, 'She was lively and animated, had sparkling, love inspiring eyes, beautiful teeth, pleasing and expressive features, a fine form, and a thousand other charms, yet her manners were perfectly simple and artless.'

"The chancellor, who was himself of the Greek church, regarded the difference of religion with the eyes of a lover and a politician; but as his imperial master might take a less liberal view of the matter, he posted away to St. Petersburg, with the intention, if he should there be successful, of subsequently visiting Madrid for the requisite authority to carry his schemes into full effect. But the fates, with a voice more powerful than that of emperors and kings, forbade the bans; and Von Resanoff died on his road to Europe, at Krasnoyarsk, in Siberia, of a fall from his horse.

"Thus at once bereaved of her lover, and disappointed in the hope of being the pledge of friendship between Russia and Spain, Doña Concepcion assumed the habit, but not, I believe, the formal vows of a nun, dedicating her life to the instruction of the young and the consolation of the sick. This little romance could not fail to interest us, and notwithstanding the ungracefulness of her conventual costume, and the ravages of an interval of time, which had tripled her years, we could still discover in her face and figure, in her manners and conversation, the remains of those charms which had won for the youthful beauty, Von Resanoff's enthusiastic love, and Langdorff's equally enthusiastic admiration. Though Doña Concepcion apparently loved to dwell on the story of her blighted affections, yet, strange to say, she knew not, till we mentioned it to her, the immediate cause of the chancellor's sudden death. This circumstance might, in some measure, be explained by the fact that Langsdorff's work was not published before 1814; but even then, in any other country than California, a lady who was still young would surely have seen a book, which besides detailing the grand incident of her life, presented so gratifying a portrait of her charms."

How strange, as he justly remarks, that Doña Concepcion had never seen that book, though it had been printed more than twenty five years! [General Vallejo, who was on the stand, here informed Mr. R. that this lady had died about eight months ago.]

The Russians, in 1812, came down from the north and established themselves at the port of Bodega, with one hundred Russians and one hundred Kodiak Indians. It is said that they asked permission of the Spanish authorities before doing so. The archives are full, however, of documents from 1812 up, showing the jealousy and fear with which they were regarded by Spain, and afterwards, by

Mexico. They occupied a strip along the coast from Bodega northwards, and only a few leagues in depth, but without any precisely fixed limits.

In 1841 this establishment was at its best, consisting of eight hundred Russians, or Russo-Asiatics, with a great number of native Indian tribes around them, working for wages. It was to circumscribe these intruders that the priests crossed over and founded the mission of San Rafael in 1819, and of San Francisco Solano at Sonoma in 1823, and commenced another at Santa Rosa in 1827. The Russians raised some grain and cattle, and trapped enormously. De Mofras, whom I follow, says that the Kodiaks, in their sealskin boats, made bloody warfare upon the seals, beavers, and especially the otters; that they hunted all the coasts, the adjacent islands, and even the marshes and innumerable inlets of the Bay of San Francisco; and that there were weeks when this bay alone produced seven or eight hundred otter skins, which may be true, but seems to me to be a very large number. In 1842 the Russians all left of their own accord, after having held their possessions, in the character of a Russian colony, for thirty years, as completely as they now hold Sitka, and without apparently paying the slightest attention to the priests or the soldiers who crossed over to look after them. At their fort of Ross, situated amid a forest of gigantic pines, a Greek chapel reared its cross and belfries, with a most pleasing effect. The nearest Catholic mission was but a little way off. Rome and Constantinople here met upon this coast, after a course of so many centuries, in opposite directions around the globe.

While Europe was convulsed, and America shaken, the profoundest quiet prevailed in California. After a long time they would hear of a great battle, or of the rise or fall of an empire, to perturb the souls of priests and other men. But the government had other duties to perform, patriarchal and simple. On the 11th of February, 1797, Felipe de Goycochea, captain of the presidio of Santa Barbara, writes to Governor Borica, as follows:

"I transmit to you a statement in relation to the schools of the presidio, together with six copy-books of the children, who are learning to write, for your superior information. May our Lord preserve your life many years.

"Santa Barbara, February 11, 1797.

"FELIPE GOYCOCHEA."

These copy-books are now in the archives for inspection. As they are the property of the State, I will give samples, which being translated, read: "The Ishmaelites having arrived;" "Jacob sent to see his brother;" "Abimelech took her from Abraham." Good, pious texts, and written in an old-fashioned round hand. Such was the employment of governors and captains in that stormy time; and so it continued through all the period of the mighty conflicts of Napoleon. Even the more protracted commotions of Mexico herself wrought no disturbance here. The dominion of Spain came to an end in California, after fifty-two years of such peacefulness, without a struggle. Mexico having established her independence, California gave in her adherence in the following declaration:

DECLARATION OF INDEPENDENCE IN CALIFORNIA.

In the presidio of Monterey, on the 9th day of the month of April, 1822: The señor military and political governor of this province, Colonel Don Pablo Vicente de Sola, the señors captains commandantes of the presidios of Santa Barbara and San Francisco, Don José Antonio de la Guerra y Noriega, and Don Luis Antonio de Arguello, the captains of the militia companies of the batallion of Tepic and Mazatlan, Don José Antonio Navarrete, and Don Pablo de la Portilla, the lieutenant Don José Maria Estudillo for the presidial company of San Diego, the lieutenant Don José Mariano Estrada for the presidial company of Monterey, the lieutenant of artillery, Don Manuel Gomez, and the reverend fathers, Friar Mariano Payeras, and Friar Vicento Francisco de Sarria, the first as prelate of these missions, and the second as substitute of the reverend father president vicareo foraneo, Friar José Jenan; having assembled in obedience to previous citations (convocatorias) in the hall of the government house, and being informed of the establishment of the kingdom of the empire, and the installation of the sovereign provisional gubernative junta in the capital of Mexico, by the official communication and other documents, which the said governor caused to be read in full assembly, said: that, for themselves, and in behalf of their subordinates, they were decided to render obedience to the orders intimated by the new supreme government, recognizing, from this time, the province as a dependent alone of the government of the Empire of Mexico, and independent of the dominion of Spain, as well as of any other foreign power. In consideration of which, the proper oaths will be taken, in the manner prescribed by the provisional regency, to which end the superior military and political chief will give the necessary orders, and the respective commandantes of presidios and the ministers of the missions will cause the fulfilment of the same to appear by means of certificates, which will be transmitted, with a copy of this act, to the most excellent minister, to whom it corresponds, and they signed,

PABLO VICENTE DE SOLA,
JOSÉ DE LA GUERRA Y NORIEGA,
LUIS ANTONIO ARGUELLO,
JOSÉ M. ESTUDILLO,
MANUEL GOMEZ,
PABLO DE LA PORTILLA,
JOSÉ MARIANO ESTRADA,
FR. MARIANO PAYERAS,
FR. VICENTE FRANCISCO DE SARRIA,
JOSÉ M. ESTUDILLO.

One of the signers of this instrument, Pablo Vicente de Sola, was at that time governor under Spain, and held over for a year as governor still under the kingdom of the empire, as expressed in the declaration, and two others are the chiefs of the ecclesiastical authorities, viz. the prelate of the missions, and the substitute of the reverend father president of the missions. The style does not much resemble our immortal instrument; and, as another difference, we observe that all the parties to it are either priests or soldiers.

The Spanish governors were in all ten. Their names and the time they were respectively in office, as follows:

Gaspar de Portala	1767 to 1771
Felipe de Barri	1771 to 1774
Felipe de Neve	1774 to 1782
Pedro Fages	1782 to 1790
Jose Antonio Romeu	1790 to 1792
Jose J. de Arrillaga, (ad interim)	1792 to 1794
Diego de Borica	1794 to 1800
Jose Joaquin de Arrillaga	1800 to 1814
Jose Arguello, (ad interim)	1814 to 1815
Pablo Vicente de Sola	1815 to 1822 and 1823

Under Mexico the list continues:

Luis Arguello	1823 to 1826
Jose Ma. de Echandia	1826 to 1831
Manuel Victoria	1831 to 1832
Pio Pico, (ad interim)	1832
Jose Figueroa	1832 to 1835
Jose Castro, (ad interim)	1835 to 1836
Nicholas Gutierrez	1836
Mariano Chico	1836
Nicholas Gutierrez, (again for a few months)	1836
Juan B. Alvarado	1836 to 1842
Manuel Micheltorena	1842 to 1845
Pio Pico	1845 to 1846

California, as a matter of course, accepted the republic as readily as the empire. But it was difficult to throw off old habits, and the following document
discloses a temper towards strangers not creditable to a liberal government. It
is of greatly more value, however, as the recorded evidence of the arrival of the
first American who ever came to California by land. Let him tell his own story.

Letter from Captain Jedediah S. Smith to Father Duran.

REVEREND FATHER: I understand, through the medium of one of your
Christian Indians, that you are anxious to know who we are, as some of the
Indians have been at the mission and informed you that there were certain white
people in the country. We are Americans, on our journey to the river Columbia; we were in at the mission San Gabriel in January last. I went to San
Diego and saw the general, and got a passport from him to pass on to that place.
I have made several efforts to cross the mountains, but the snows being so deep,
I could not succeed in getting over. I returned to this place (it being the only
point to kill meat) to wait a few weeks until the snow melts, so that I can go
on; the Indians here also being friendly, I consider it the most safe point for
me to remain, until such time as I can cross the mountains with my horses,
having lost a great many in attempting to cross ten or fifteen days since. I am
a long ways from home, and am anxious to get there as soon as the nature of
the case will admit. Our situation is quite unpleasant, being destitute of clothing and most of the necessaries of life, wild meat being our principal subsistence.

I am, reverend father, your strange, but real friend and Christian brother,

                                        J. S. SMITH.
May 19, 1827.

His encampment must have been somewhere near the mission of San José,
as it was there that Father Duran resided. Who is there that does not sym-
pathise with Jedediah Smith? "I am a long ways from home, and am anxious
to get there as soon as the nature of the case will admit. Our situation is quite
unpleasant, being destitute of clothing and most of the necessaries of life, wild
meat being our principal subsistence. I am, reverend father, your strange, but
real friend and Christian brother."

Thus we came to this country the Browns and Smiths first, and in but an
unhappy plight.

As Jedediah Smith's letter shows, he had been here before. At that time he
had been required to give an account of himself, but had been able to find
vouchers, shipmasters, all of them doubtless from Boston, who had come to buy the
hides which under the new system were now within the reach of commerce:

"We, the undersigned, having been requested by Captain Jedediah S. Smith
to state our opinions regarding his entering the province of California, do not
hesitate to say that we have no doubt in our minds but that he was compelled to
for want of provisions and water, having entered so far into the barren country
that lies between the latitudes of forty-two and forty-three west that he found
it impossible to return by the route he came, as his horses had most of them
perished for want of food and water. He was, therefore, under the necessity of
pushing forward to California, it being the nearest place where he could procure
supplies to enable him to return.

"We further state as our opinions that the account given by him is circum-
stantially correct, and that his sole object was the hunting and trapping of beaver
and other furs.

"We have also examined the passports produced by him from the Superintendent of Indian Affairs for the government of the United States of America,
and do not hesitate to say we believe them to be perfectly correct.

We also state, that in our opinion, his motive for wishing to pass by a different route to the head of the Columbia river on his return, is solely because he feels convinced that he and his companions run great risk of perishing if they return by the route they came.

In testimony whereof, we have hereunto set our hands and seals this 20th day of December, 1826.

WM. G. DANA, *Captain of schooner Waverly.* [L. s.]
WM. H. CUNNINGHAM, *Capt. of ship Courier.* [L. s.]
WM. HENDERSON, *Capt. of brig Olive Branch.* [L. s.]
JAMES SCOTT. [L. s.]
THOS. M. ROBBINS, *Mate of schooner Waverly.* [L. s.]
THOS. SHAW, *Supercargo of ship Courier.* [L. s.]

In extenuation, however, it may be said that Anglo-Americans had long been viewed with uneasiness in this quarter. It was prophesied as early as 1805 that they would become troublesome to California. So wrote a governor in an official letter now in the archives.

In a recent number of a magazine, (Harper's for June, 1860,) Sylvester Pattie, his son, and six others, are said to have been the first who accomplished the journey overland from the United States to California. The dates mentioned in that account show that they could not have reached Lower California, where they first arrived, sooner than 1829 or 1830, as it is said they left the Missouri river in 1824, and remained more than five years in New Mexico. The Patties, therefore, cannot dispute this honor with Jedediah Smith.

After the adoption of the federal Constitution of 1824, by which was established the Mexican United States, the governor of California was called the political chief of the Territory, and was aided by a council known as the territorial deputation. The government of the Territory continued subject to the sovereign congress at the city of Mexico, as formerly that of the province had been to the viceroy. Thus much will be a sufficient introduction for the next paper. It is to be regretted that it was not known to the gentleman who designed the coat of arms adopted for this State.

"In session of the 13th of July, 1827, of the territorial deputation, a proposition was made to change the name of the Territory to *Moctesuma*, the arms of the same to be an Indian with his bow and quiver, in the act of crossing a strait, placed in an oval, with an olive and live oak on either side; the same being symbolical of the arrival of the first inhabitant to America, which, according to the generally received opinion, was by way of the straits of Anian."

The conception is poetical and simple, and differs in this particular widely from the confused medley of incongruous figures with which we have chosen to illustrate our idea of California. The name *Moctesuma* is very significant. It shows how the Mexican, since his independence, has preferred to draw his opinions, as he derives his blood, from the conquered rather than the conquerors. A late but signal triumph of race! California was near losing the name given her by heroes who came across the Atlantic, for one suggestive of a descent from an imaginary people who came across Behring's straits.

The Russians and the American trappers, estrays dropping in from the mountains, seemed to have taught the Californians the value of furs. The government of the Territory very naturally made this new business a source of revenue. They sold licenses to trap. To obtain this privilege was rather a formal matter. Here is an example:

Juan B. R. Cooper petitions the governor for a license to trap with ten boats, for seven months, for otters. The governor refers the petition to the alcalde, to know whether Mr. Cooper is *matriculated in the marine,* i. e., a seaman. The alcalde reports that he belongs to the first class of seamen, and the governor orders a license to be issued to Mr. Cooper to hunt otters from the parallel of

San Luis Obispo to Bodega, two-thirds of the crews of his boats to be natives of the country. There are many others who get licenses, whose names are familiar to the oldest of the living pioneers. Edward McIntosh got his on January 9, 1834, William Wolfskill his September 21, 1833; and many of the old Californians embarked in the same business, as Angel Castro, March 25, 1833, and Juan Bandini on the 9th of April, 1833.

Internal disturbances seem to have commenced in California about the year 1830. The liberal Spanish Cortez of 1813, in carrying out the constitution which they had adopted for the Spanish monarchy the year before, decreed the secularization of all the missions in the Spanish dominions. The design was to make general what had always been done before by special authority—to liberate the Indians from the control of the missionary fathers, and divide amongst them, as their separate property, the land, cattle, and whatever else they had owned in common ; to establish secular priests in the place of regular priests or monks of the religious orders among them, for their spiritual guidance, and in every respect to convert the Indian villages of the missions into Spanish pueblos—the process by which, in so great a degree, society was constructed in all Spanish-American countries, and the ultimate fulfilment of the purpose of the King, everywhere so prominently put forth in colonizing California.

The decrees of the Cortez, not incompatible with the republican form of government, continued after the establishment of her independence to be the laws of Mexico, but very few, if any, of them had been put into operation in California. With the rest, that of secularization remained a dead letter. Enchandia, the political chief, (as the governor was then entitled,) in 1830, very hurriedly, and without consulting the supreme government, published, as the custom of the government was, a set of regulations for carrying this old law into effect. At that moment he was superseded by Victoria, who suppressed the regulations, and put a peremptory stop to the secularization of the missions. Victoria's conduct was approved by the supreme government, but there was a party here warmly in favor of the secularization, and disturbances which were considered serious and threatening ensued, although I do not know that they resulted in bloodshed. The chief promoter of the scheme was sent out of the country by Victoria; and thus, I think, civil strife commenced in California. The occasion was the disposition to be made of the missions, which, we have seen, were once, and for so long a time, so nearly all of California. It was the beginning of the downfall of those ancient establishments, so difficult for us to comprehend, and now so entirely passed away that to recall them is like recalling the images of a dream. What the government of Mexico was opposed to was not the secularization of the missions, but the manner in which it was attempted. The agitation which had been thus commenced resulted in the passage, by the Mexican congress, of the law of the 17th of August, 1833, to secularize the missions of the Californias. Under it the work was begun by Figueroa, the best and ablest of the Mexican governors. At the same time he had two other laws, most fundamentally subversive of the old order of things, to carry into execution. They were the law for the political organization of the Territory, being another of those decreed by the Spanish Cortes in 1813, and the law of colonization, passed by the Mexican congress, August 18, 1824, with the executive regulations, prescribing the manner of its application, dated November 21, 1828. It is evident that this is the true era of revolution in Mexican California. Observing the ancient limits of the presidial jurisdictions, municipal governments were established for each district. Authority was exercised by elective bodies called ayuntamientos, of which the head was an alcalde or judge. This body regulated the economy of the whole district, directly of the pueblo in which it resided, and of every other pueblo in the district, through the intervention of local and subordinate ayuntamientos. This was the separation of the civil functions from the military functions, both of which had been continued in the hands of the commanders of the presidios, as in the Spanish times. Here in San Francisco, and for all the region north of San Mateo creek, east indefinitely, and west to the ocean, the separation of powers took place in December, 1834, at which time the ayuntamiento was established for the civil government of this presidial district, and General M. G. Vallejo, then in command of the presidio, was left with only his military command. In the secularization of the missions, Figueroa advanced so far as to put administrators in possession in place of the fathers, at which stage his proceedings were arrested by a decree of the Mexican President. Ruin was inevitable; it was as rapid as spoliation could make it, and it was soon complete. Governor after governor adopted regulations upon regulations, to secure a faithful administration of the property of the missions, i. e., of the Christian Indians, who inhabited them, and by whose labor all had been built and accumulated. It was to no purpose; and of as little avail was the partial restoration of the missions to the charge of the fathers, by Micheltorena in 1843. The Indian was by nature a very little above the brute; the fathers were not able to elevate him in spite of nature; the administrators stripped him without compunction; and, when the United States conquered the country, he was already exterminated, his destruction complete in ten years. When emancipation began, Figueroa says there were twenty thousand Christian Indians in the missions of California.

Colonization was another idea introduced by the Spanish Cortes in 1813. It was embodied in the Mexican law of colonization of 1824. The scheme was to reduce all the public lands of the State to private property. The Spanish rule before 1813 had ever been to make such grants the exception, and to retain all lands, generally speaking, as the domain of the King. Other Mexican governors may have made informal grants of which nothing appears, but Figueroa was the first to inaugurate the system of which we find the records in the archives. He established a course of proceeding in exact accordance with the law and the regulations, and adhered to it strictly, and executed it conscientiously, and with great intelligence. From the lands subject to be granted are excepted such as belong to pueblos and missions. Of pueblos, i. e., villages, there were but two, San José and Los Angeles, or three, including the unprosperous Villa de Branciforte. Whatever lands these owned were at their foundation surveyed, marked out, and set apart to them, and then recorded. The same course was followed with such of the presidios as were converted into pueblos, as at Monterey, and would have been pursued with the missions when converted into pueblos, if that change had not been arrested. In these cases there could have been no uncertainty as to what lands the governor could grant. With the missions untouched, or incompletely secularized as they were left, there was difficulty. The title of the Indian who had consented to become a Christian and a civilized man, binding as it was upon the king, had always been indefinite as to quantity, and as to the situation of his lands, save that it should be at and about the mission; in which essential particulars it rested altogether in the King's discretion, exercised by the proper officers of his government. The Mexican republic stepped into the same relation to these Christian Indians. That no injustice might be done them, every petition was referred to the priests, and afterwards to the administrators of the missions. They were asked whether the grant could be made without prejudice to the Indians. As they replied so were the grants given or withheld. So it was at least in Figueroa's day, and that, no matter how far the land petitioned for was from the nearest mission. Other governors were neither so exact nor so conscientious as Figueroa. And as, in the hands of the administrators to whom they were delivered over, the missions went rapidly down to complete ruin, it is evident that the lands required for the Indians would become continually less—such would be, and was, the answer of their new guardians to the inquiries of the governor—and finally all was granted, and in some cases, it is alleged, even the missions themselves. Their cattle without the aid of a grant from the governor took the same course. It is not too much to say that when the United States in 1846 took possession of the country they found it passing through a conquest still raw and incomplete. It was the conquest of the missions and the Christian Indians by the settlers of the presidios and pueblos, who at first had been introduced into the country mainly for their benefit, to aid the king and the church in carrying out their pious and humane intentions towards them. Yet it was well that it was so. Who that looks upon the native Digger Indian could wish that a superior race should be sacrificed or postponed for his benefit? We contemplate a miserable result of the work begun with so much zeal and heroism in 1769. But because they failed, we none the less respect the motives and the laborers, whether of church or state.

The unworthiness of the Californian Indian did not altogether deprive him of sympathy. Every government expressed some feeling at seeing him hasten so rapidly to his wretched end. And the just and kind-hearted Figueroa battled for him manfully. In the midst of the complex labors of his administration he was almost crushed by the arrival of three hundred persons, for whom he had to make provision, without resources, and who came under the charge of a director of colonization, instructed by the supreme government, at that time radically democratic, to begin operations by taking possession of the property of the missions and admit the new colonists to a division of it with the Indians. During the winter of 1834-'35 Figueroa and the director carried on an animated discussion in writing, on the subject of the last of these propositions. Figueroa maintained that the missions were the private property of the Indians, and protected from invasion by the constitution. The director insisted upon the letter of the order of. the supreme government. Figueroa said it was improvident, and refused to obey it until he could make a representation to the supreme government on the subject. The end was that some of the partisans of the director attempted an insurrection at Los Angeles, in the spring of 1835, which was easily suppressed, but furnished Figueroa the opportunity to send the director and the heads of his faction back to Mexico. Of these, the principal was the same man who had been sent out of California by Victoria for the same cause, a desire to have a part in the secularization of the missions. The colony, however, remained, and, though numbering but three hundred, was a great addition to the population of California in those days. Among them we find the names of several persons who afterwards became conspicuous in the country, amongst them José Abrego, José Ma. Covarrubias, Augustin Olvera, and Francisco Guerrero.

Figueroa died at Monterey, on the 29th of September, 1835, his death being probably hastened by the effect of the anxiety and vexation of this controversy upon a constitution already broken. At that time his manifesto to the Mexican republic, in which he gives a clear and forcible statement of the whole affair, and an able vindication of his conduct, was going through the press at Monterey. His death seems to have been very greatly deplored at that time, and he is still recognized as the ablest and most upright of the Mexican governors. His work of the political organization of California lasted but a little while; it fell with the overthrow of the federal constitution of 1824, by Santa Anna, in 1836. California then became a department; political chief was changed into governor, and territorial deputation into departmental assembly.

These changes, however, were not fully completed in California until 1839. The department of the Californias was then divided into three districts; the first extending from the frontier of Sonoma to San Luis Obispo, its principal point or seat of administration being the old Mission of San Juan, on the Pajaro river; the second district included the rest of Upper California, the seat of its administration being the city of Los Angeles, which had been promoted to that rank from the original condition of a pueblo, in the year 1835; and the third comprised Lower California, which, after a separation, was now reunited with

Upper California. These districts were divided each into two partidos, of which, consequently, there were four in Upper California. Ayuntamientos were abolished, and a justice of the peace substituted in each partido. For the whole district there was a prefect, who resided at the seat of the administration of one of the partidos, and a sub-prefect, who resided at that of the other partido. In 1843 Micheltorena, acting under extraordinary powers, made some changes in this system, but it was substantially restored by Pio Pico, in 1845, but when again Lower California was thrown off.

With Figueroa everything like stability, and indeed order, passed away. The next year after Figueroa's death, the Californians drove away the governor, and Don Juan B. Alvarado being at that time president of the territorial deputation, was declared governor. After this was done the deputation went one step further and on the 7th of November, 1836, passed these resolutions:

(1.) " California is declared independent of Mexico until the re-establishment of the constitution of 1824."

(2.) " California is erected into a free and sovereign State, establishing a congress," &c., &c.

Public documents for a while were headed " Free and Sovereign State of California." This anomalous state of things lasted until 1838. The demands of the free and sovereign state were not complied with, nor on the other hand was the central government disposed or perhaps able to push the controversy to extremes. In 1838 Alvarado was appointed governor *ad interim;* and constitutional governor in 1839, when we have seen that the innovations of Santa Anna took effect. Whilst California was in rebellion the president of Mexico commissioned Carlos Antonio Carillo as governor. Alvarado refused to recognize him, and accepted the aid of a party of Americans who since the time of Jedediah Smith seem to have found their way into the country. Alvarado prevailed over Carillo; and his appointment as governor *ad interim* compromised the difficulties of those times. Here is a document relating to this contest, which will serve to illustrate California warfare. It is the report of General José Castro to Governor Alvarado, dated the 28th of March, 1838:

" I have the honor to announce to your excellency, that after two days' continual firing without having lost but one man, the enemy took to flight, under cover of night, numbering one hundred and ten men ; and I have determined to despatch one company of mounted infantry, under the command of Captain Villa, and another of cavalry lancers, under the command of Captain Cota, in their pursuit, remaining myself, with the rest of the division, and the artillery, to guard this point," &c., &c.

And here is another of the same period. It now appears that the Americans who sided with Alvarado had fallen under suspicion and into disfavor at about the time that their chief made up his differences with the central government and received his commission as governor *ad interim.* They were all arrested, some fifteen or twenty, perhaps, it is said, by surprise, and sent to Mexico. Amongst them was Mr. Isaac Graham, of Santa Cruz. This paper will also serve as a specimen of California eloquence at that period, and I commend it at the present moment as a model to our political orators.

Proclamation made by the undersigned.

" Eternal glory to the illustrious champion and liberator of the department of Alta California, Don José Castro, the guardian of order, and the supporter of our superior government.

" Fellow citizens and friends : To-day, the eighth of May of the present year of 1840, has been and will be eternally glorious to all the inhabitants of this soil in contemplating the glorious expedition of our fellow-countryman, Don José Castro, who goes to present himself before the superior government of the

Mexican nation, carrying with him a number of suspicious Americans, who under the mask of deceit, and filled with ambition, were warping us in the web of misfortune; plunging us into the greatest confusion and danger; desiring to terminate the life of our governor and of all his subalterns; and finally to drive us from our asylums, from our country, from our pleasures, and from our hearths.

"The bark which carries this valorous hero on his grand commission goes filled with laurels and crowned with triumphs, plowing the waves and publishing, in distinct voices to the passing billows, the loud vivas and rejoicings which will resound to the remotest bounds of the universe. Yes, fellow-citizens and friends, again we say that this glorious chief should have a place in the innermost recesses of our hearts, and be held as dear to us as our very breath. Thus we desire, and in the name of all the inhabitants, make known the great rejoicings with which we are filled, giving, at the same time, to our superior government the present proclamation which we make for said worthy chief; and that our governor may remain satisfied that if he (Castro) has embarked for the interior of the republic, there still remain under his (the governor's) orders all his fellow-countrymen, companions in arms," &c., &c.

The foregoing is signed by seven citizens of note and respectability in the country. When this laurel-laden vessel reached San Blas the Mexican authorities took a different view of the matter. They put General Castro in prison and Graham and his companions in the best hotel in the place, (he says a palace,) and entertained them handsomely until they could send them back to California, which they did at the expense of the government.

In 1839 Captain John A. Sutter, a man who had seen many vicissitudes and adventures in Europe and the wilds of America, arrived in California from the Sandwich islands. By permission of Governor Alvarado he established himself in the valley of the Sacramento, then the extreme northern frontier. He engaged to protect the Mexican settlements extending in that direction under the colonization law (the only vital thing left of the Mexican rule for many years) from the incursions of the Indians, and he kept his word.

In 1841 he obtained a grant of land himself and built a fort, which soon became the refuge and rallying point for Americans and Europeans coming into the country. Over all these Sutter, by virtue of an appointment as justice of the peace, exercised whatever government there was beyond the law of the rifle. Practically his powers were as indefinite as the territorial limits of his jurisdiction. Among those who early gathered around Sutter we find the names of John Bidwell, who came in 1841, and Pearson B. Reading and Samuel J. Hensley, who came in 1843, and many others well known at the present day.

The pioneers of that day all bear testimony to the generosity of Captain Sutter at a time when his fort was the capital and he the government for the American colony in the valley of the Sacramento. In 1844 the numbers of this population had come to be so considerable as to be a power in the State. In the revolution which then occurred Sutter took the side of Governor Micheltorena. But before he marched he took the reasonable precaution, so obviously required by justice to his men, to obtain from Micheltorena a grant of the land for which they had respectfully petitioned. Micheltorena then issued the document known as the General Title.

In this document he declares that every petition upon which Sutter, in his capacity of justice of the peace, had reported favorably, should be taken as granted, and that a copy of this document given to each petitioner should serve in lieu of the usual formal grant. This done, he marched to the south, but was unfortunate, for he was taken prisoner, and Micheltorena expelled from the country. This is the last of the civil wars of California.

In the spring of 1846 General Castro in the north, and Pio Pico, the governor, in the south, were waxing hot against each other, and preparing for new conflicts, when the apparition of Captain Frémont, with his small surveying party of old mountaineers, and the hardy and indomitable pioneers of the Sacramento valley, and the bear flag, put an end to their dissensions. Castro had himself prepared the way for this aggression by driving Frémont and his surveying party out of the Mexican settlements a few months before. The colony on the Sacramento necessarily sympathized with Frémont ; and rumors, more or less well founded, began to run through the valley of hostile intentions towards all the American settlers. But resentment and anticipations of evil were not the sole cause of this movement. There cannot now be a doubt that it was prompted as it was approved by the government of the United States, and that Captain Frémont obeyed his orders no less than his own feelings.

Frémont was still on the northern side of the bay of San Francisco when the American flag was hoisted at Monterey, on the ever-memorable seventh day of July, 1846.

Before the war the government of the United States had fully determined, so far as that matter rested with the Executive, upon the conquest and permanent retention of California as soon as the outbreak of war should offer the opportunity. Orders, in anticipation of war, were issued to that effect, and it was under these orders that California was actually taken. The danger of that day was that England would step in before us. Her ships were watching our ships on the coast of Mexico. The British pretext, it is said, was to have been to secure an equivalent for the Mexican debt due to British subjects; and it is understood that there was a party here who favored this design.

Because Commodore Sloat did not rush to the execution of the orders issued in anticipation of war, on the very first report of a collision between the United States and Mexico, the anxious Secretary of the Navy, dreading to lose the prize, hotly censured him in a letter which reached him after the event had broken the sting of its reproaches, and served only to assure him how well he had fulfilled the wishes of his government. The flag of the United States was no sooner flying than the Collingwood entered the bay of Monterey. There had been a race between the Collingwood and the Savannah. What a moment that was for us, and for the world ! What if the Collingwood had been the swifter sailer, and Sloat had found the English flag flying on the shore ! What if we had been born on another planet ! The cast was for England or the United States, and when the die turned for us, the interest was at an end.

As a feat of arms the conquest of California was nothing for a power like ours. Even more feeble and as much distracted as the rest of Mexico, and with but a nominal dependence upon the central government, but a very little force was sufficient to detach California forever from all her Spanish-American connections. Whatever of military credit there was is due to the pioneers who, under the bear flag, had, before they heard of the beginning of the war, with an admirable instinct for their own rights and the interests of their country, rebelled against any further Mexican misrule, or a sale to the British. The loyalty of their sentiments was beautifully illustrated by the alacrity with which they relinquished the complete independence which appeared to be within their grasp, and turned over their conquests and the further service of their rifles to the country which they remembered with so much affection, and a government from which they would suffer themselves to look for nothing but wisdom and strength, and a tender consideration for the rights and interests of the pioneer.

For three years and a half when there was no war, and for nearly two years after there was a declared peace, California was governed, and for a great part of the time heavily taxed, by the executive branch of the government of the United States, acting through military officers. This I note as an anomaly in the experience of the citizens of this republic.

California separated from Mexico, a new people began to come in from the United States and Europe. But California was remote and yet but little understood. Mr. Webster himself spoke of her as almost worthless, except for the bay of San Francisco, and as though the soil was as barren and thorny as the rocks of Lower California. Emigrants came, but not many—among the most remarkable arrivals being the ship Brooklyn, freighted with Mormons. The soldiers themselves were nothing more than armed colonists. And everything was peaceful and dull, until suddenly, when no man expected, there came a change of transcendent magnitude.

Gold was discovered at Coloma. This was an event that stirred the heart of the whole world. The motives which pervade and most control the lives of men were touched. All the impulses that spring from necessity and hope were quickened; and a movement was visible among mankind. To get to California, some crossed over from Buenos Ayres to Valparaiso, scaling the Andes. The Isthmus of Darien became a common thoroughfare. Peaceful invaders entered Mexico at every point, and on every route startled the drowsy muleteer as they passed over to the Pacific where the coast was nearest, or pushed on directly for California. Constant caravans issued from our own borders, traversed every intervening prairie, and explored every pass and gap of opposing mountains. As the long train descended to the valley, perhaps the foremost wagon is driven by an old man, who when he was a boy moved out in this way from Virginia to Kentucky; and passing still from one new State to another, now when he is grown gray halts his team at last upon the shores of the Pacific. Ships sailed from every port on the globe. The man at the wheel, in every sea, steered by the star that led to San Francisco. So came the emigrants of 1849. The occupation of California was now complete, and she became a part of the world.

The sighs, the prayers, the toiling and the watching of our overwearied countrymen on these long painful journeys are still demanding a railroad to the Pacific.

Eleven years are passed, and have they no voice? We looked out upon a wide expanse—unfenced, untilled—and though nature was lovely, our hearts sunk within us. Neither the priest nor the ranchero had prepared this country for our habitation. We asked who shall subdue all this to our uses? We look again; and now, upon a landscape chequered with smiling farms and dotted with cities and towns, busy and humming like the hive. What magic is it that has wrought this change? On every hand, with one acclaim, comes back the answer. Labor, it is labor. Of our eleven years, here is the lesson. Man's opinions and his passions were but insolence and vanity. Boasting and praise made but the greatness of the passing day. And labor, only labor, has survived. However silent, however humble and unseen, or on what bestowed, it is labor which has created California, and which rules us at this hour. With our own eyes this we have seen, and of our knowledge we know the lesson to be as true as it is old.

California in full possession of the white man, and embraced within the mighty area of his civilization! We feel the sympathies of our race attract us. We see in our great movement hitherward in 1849 a likeness to the times when our ancestors, their wives and little ones, and all their stuff in wagons, and with attendant herds, poured forth by nations and in never-ending columns from the German forests, and went to seek new pastures and to found new kingdoms in the ruined provinces of the Roman empire: or when swayed by another inspiration they cast their masses upon the Saracens, and sought to rescue the sepulchre of Christ from the infidels. We recognize that we are but the foremost rank of that multitude which for centuries has held its unwavering course out of Europe upon America, in numbers still increasing; a vast unsummoned host, self-marshaled, leaderless, an innumerable, moving and onward forever, to possess and people another continent. Separated but in space, divided but by the accidents of manners, of language and of laws—from Scandinavia to California—one blood and one people. Knowledge is but the conservation of his thoughts, art but the embodiment of his conceptions, letters the record of his deeds. Man of our race has crowned the earth with its glory! And still in the series of his works you have founded a State. May it be great and powerful whilst the ocean shall thunder against these shores! You have planted a people; may they be prosperous and happy whilst summers shall return to bless these fields with plenty! And may the name of the pioneer be spoken in California forever!

—

Since the foregoing address was delivered the following letter has been received by Mr. Randolph from Mr. Sprague, a gentleman well known in this city, and interesting as showing the discovery of gold in California thirty-five years ago:

GENOA, CARSON VALLEY, *September* 18, 1860.

FRIEND RANDOLPH: I have just been reading your address before the Society of Pioneers. I have known of the J. S. Smith you mention, by reputation, for many years. He was the first white man that ever went overland from the Atlantic States to California. He was a chief trader in the employ of the American Fur Company. At the rendezvous of the company on Green river, near the South Pass, in 1825, Smith was directed to take charge of a party of some forty men (trappers) and penetrate the country west of Salt lake. He discovered what is now called Humboldt river. He called it Mary's river, from his Indian wife Mary. It has always been known as Mary's river by mountain men since, a name which it should retain, for many reasons.

Smith pushed on down Mary's river; being of an adventurous nature, when he found his road closed by high mountains he determined to see what kind of country there was on the other side. It is not known exactly where he crossed the Sierra Nevada, but it is supposed that it must have been not far from where the old emigrant road crossed near the head of the Truckee. He made his way southerly after entering the valley of Sacramento, passed through San José and down as low as San Diego. After recruiting his party and purchasing a large number of horses, he crossed the mountains near what is known as Walker's Pass, skirted the eastern slope of the mountains till near what is now known as Mono lake, when he steered an east-by-north course for Salt lake. On this portion of his route he found placer gold in quantities, and brought much of it with him to the encampment on Green river.

The gold that he brought with him, together with his description of the country he had passed through, and the large amount of furs, pleased the agent of the American Fur Company so well that he directed Smith again to make the same trip, with special instructions to take the gold fields on his return and thoroughly prospect them. It was on this trip that he wrote the letter to Father Duran. The trip was successful until they arrived in the vicinity of the gold mines, east of the mountains, when, in a battle with the Indians, Smith and nearly all of his men were killed. A few of the party escaped and reached the encampment on Green river. This defeat damped the ardor of the company so much that they never looked any more for the gold mines.

There are one or more men now living who can testify to the truth of the above statement, and who can give a fuller statement of the details of his two journeys than I can.

The man Smith was a man of far more than average ability, and had a better education than falls to the lot of mountain men. Few or none of them were his equals in any respect. * * * * * * *

THOMAS SPRAGUE.

q., *San Francisco.*

APPENDIX 2.

Address on the acquisition of California by the United States, delivered before the Corporate Society of California Pioneers, at the Academy of Music, in the city of San Francisco, on September 10, 1866, on occasion of the sixteenth anniversary of the admission of the State of California into the federal Union. By John W. Dwinelle, a member of that society, president of the Ethno-Historical Society of San Francisco, member of the Ethnological Society of New York, and of the Historical Society of New York.

Mr. President and Brother Pioneers: It has been suggested to me, by the committee through whose hands I received your invitation to address you at this time, that I should give a historical character to my address. I was glad to receive this intimation, for it accorded perfectly with my own desire. The great events of history, when not sufficiently remote to be counted by centuries, are commonly reckoned by decades, or periods of ten years. We are met on the occasion of the sixteenth anniversary of the admission of California into the federal Union of the United States. But, presuming upon your assent, I shall dedicate a portion of these exercises to the celebration of two other historical events of signal interest and importance, namely : the conquest of California by the United States, which took place twenty years ago, on the 7th day of July, A. D. 1846, and the foundation of San Francisco, which was consummated ninety years ago, on the 17th day of September, A. D. 1776. Two decades have therefore elapsed since California has become Anglo-American, and nine decades since San Francisco was inscribed upon the map of political geography. It will therefore be peculiarly interesting on this occasion to cast a retrospective glance into history, and to inquire how it has come to pass that we are here, and by what title we claim to possess this fair California of ours.

IGNORANCE OF EARLY GEOGRAPHERS.

It was only by accident, after all, that Columbus discovered the vast region of continents and islands which are now called America. He was not in quest of new continents, nor of the golden-fruited gardens of the Hesperides. Believing, from inductive reasoning, that the earth was round, but with very imperfect notions of its magnitude, he was firmly persuaded that by sailing in a westerly direction from the coast of Spain, he would in due time arrive on the coast of China, which was then classed as a portion of the Indies ; and when he discovered the first American islands, believing that he had already reached the Indies, he gave to the natives the name of Indians, which inaccurate classification they have ever since retained. Looking over the books and maps of the old geographers, it is curious and wonderful to observe how much they did know, and how much they did not know, of the geography of the northwestern coast of America for more than two hundred years after the discoveries made by Columbus. Although Cortez, when he fell into that inevitable disgrace with which the kings of Spain have always rewarded their greatest benefactors, sent out various expeditions from Mexico for the exploration of the northwestern coast, and even accompanied some of them as far as La Paz, in Lower California, and although the viceroys who succeeded him sent out various expeditions within fifty years after the conquest of Mexico, both by sea and by land, which must have penetrated as far north as the 42d degree of latitude, yet the physical geography of that region remained in the most mythical condition, and the very existence of the Bay of San Francisco was contested as fabulous by the Spanish viceroys of New Spain less than a hundred years ago. There is in the possession of the Odd Fellows' library of this city an engraved map of the world, published at Venice in the year 1546, which is remarkable for its general accuracy, and for the beauty of its execution ; but on this map, at the latitude of San

Francisco, the American continent is represented as sweeping around in a large circle, and forming a junction with that of Asia; while the Colorado, the largest river in the world, rising in the mountains of Thibet, and meandering through a course of 15,000 or 20,000 miles, pours its vast volume of waters into the Gulf of California. In the year 1588, a Spanish captain of marine, named Lorenzo Ferrer Maldonado, published an account of a voyage which he pretended to have made from the Atlantic ocean, through the Northern sea, to the Pacific, and thence to China, giving all its geographical details and personal incidents. This apocryphal voyage proved a delusion and a stumbling-block to historians and voyagers for more than two hundred years, and it was not until the year 1791 that two Spanish frigates, sent out for that purpose by authority of the King of Spain, by a thorough exploration of the extreme northwestern coast, established the fact that a passage through the North sea did not exist, and that the pretensions of Maldonado were utterly false. It is only within a comparatively recent period that the fact has been generally received in modern geography that California was connected with the main continent, and was not an island. In Ogilvie's "America, being the latest and most accurate account of the New World," a most elegant and luxurious folio, published in London in the year 1671, California is laid down as an island, extending from Cape St. Lucas, in the tropic of Cancer, to the 45th degree of latitude, and including the famous New Albion of Sir Francis Drake. The same map is reproduced by Captain Shelvocke, of the royal navy, in his account of his "Voyage Around the World by way of the South Sea," in his Majesty's ship-of-war, published in London in 1726; and in a geographical work published in London in the same year, by "Daniel Coxe, esq.," an account is given of "a new and curious discovery and relation betwixt the river Meschachebe (Mississippi) and the South sea, which separates America from China by means of several large rivers and lakes, with a description of the coast of the said sea to the Straits of Uries, as also of a rich and considerable trade to be carried on from thence to Japan, China, and Tartary." I cannot ascertain that California was relieved of its insular character among geographers until the publication of a map by Father Begert, a missionary of the Society of Jesus, in an account of Lower California which he printed at Manheim in the year 1771, on his return to Germany after his order had been expelled, in 1769, by order of the King of Spain, from the missions which they had successfully established among the Indians of Lower California. Even after it was admitted that California was not an island, but a part of the main land, the most indefinite notions prevailed as to the extent to which the Gulf of California penetrated towards the north; and to the very last of the Spanish and Mexican dominion, when any specific description was given to California in official documents, it was spoken of as a peninsula.

OUR TITLE TO CALIFORNIA.

If a Californian of ordinary historical intelligence were asked by what legal title we assume to possess this country, after following the chain through Mexico to Spain he would probably pause for want of further specific information, or, at the most, suggest that Spain derived her title to California through the right of first discovery. If he were told that all the rights of Spain, and our rights through her, to this land were derived entirely from a grant made to Spain by the Pope, he would undoubtedly be greatly surprised; yet such is the historical fact. Previous to the discovery of America by Columbus, in 1492, the Portuguese had discovered the Azore islands, in longitude 31 west, and on the strength of that discovery claimed that the countries discovered by Columbus belonged to the crown of Portugal, and that the Spaniards should be wholly excluded from them. But the Spaniards refused to admit this pretension, and referred

the matter for decision to the then Pope, Alexander VI. It was then a part of
the law of nations, and of the public law of the world, that the Pope was
the ultimate source of all temporal power; that he could make and unmake
kings, and dispose of all the kingdoms of the earth—powers which he frequently exercised, and against which it were vain to contend. He was, therefore, by general consent, the acknowledged source of all lawful title to land.
He assumed to decide the case thus referred to his decision, and on May 3, A.
D. 1493, determined the matter in dispute between the crowns of Portugal
and Spain by drawing an imaginary line of longitude one hundred leagues
west of the Azores, and granting to the Spanish monarchs all countries
inhabited by infidels which they had already discovered, or might afterwards
discover, lying to the west, and to the crown of Portugal all those lying to the
east of that line. This line was afterwards removed two hundred and seventy
leagues further to the west, by a treaty subsequently made, in the year 1494,
between the Kings of Portugal and Spain; but so thoroughly was the title thus
conceded by the Pope respected by the civilized world that when Henry VII
of England was afterwards about to intrude upon some of the dominions thus
granted to Spain, he abandoned his project on being warned by the Pope to
desist. Our title to California is therefore deduced from the grant by the Pope
to Spain, from Spain by revolution to Mexico, from Mexico by conquest and
treaty to the United States, and from the United States, by the operation of
various grants and political acts, to the State and people of California.

At the time when this partition was thus made by the Pope between the
crowns of Spain and Portugal, the earth was supposed to consist of a large
plain, even although Columbus had been prompted to his discoveries from his inference that the earth was a sphere, because in eclipses it cast a circular shadow
upon the disc of the moon. It was not until the voyage of Magellan, concluded
in the year 1521, by which they reached the Spice islands of Portugal, in the
East Indies, by sailing westward from Spain, that it was proved by actual
demonstration that the earth was round, and the world learned that neither our
spiritual teachers, nor even the Scriptures themselves, were given to us to teach
us lessons in geography.

OUR POSITION HERE NOT AN ACCIDENTAL ONE.

Our position, as possessors of this land of realized promise and of future hope,
is by no means an accidental one. The popular notion probably is that the
acquisition of California by the United States was one of the accidental conse-
quences of our war with Mexico, which broke out in 1846. On the contrary,
the acquisition of California by the United States was the result of plans long
matured and persistently followed, and of a train of causes carefully laid by the
government of the United States, during nearly half a century before its consummation. Nay, more: not only the United States, but the governments of
England, France, and Russia had determined to acquire California; and it was
only by superior promptness and skill that the United States finally became
the winners in the race. The very plan lately attempted to be put into execution by the Emperor of the French, of placing and maintaining an Austrian
archduke upon an imperial throne in Mexico, was not conceived by Napoleon
III. but was matured and published to the world by the government of Louis
Philippe as early as the year 1844, four years before the French revolution of
1848, and was a part of a scheme devised by the French government to prevent England or the United States from getting possession of Mexico, in case
France could not gain it for herself. From this programme, published by the
order of Louis Philippe by Marshal Soult, his minister of war, we shall gather
easily the charges made by France against Mexico before the tribunal of the
public opinion of the world, by which Louis Philippe attempted to justify, in

advance, that intervention in the affairs of Mexico which his government was the first to propose, and which that of Napoleon III has since attempted to effectuate. The following are the principal features of these charges:

LOUIS PHILLIPPE'S BILL OF INDICTMENT AGAINST MEXICO.

Mexico was always prosperous under the rule of her Spanish kings. Private enterprises succeeded; agriculture and mines were successful and remunerative; public works were constructed of utility, magnitude, and permanence; religion and public and private morality prevailed; the finances of the country were successful and prosperous; the people were contented and happy. The attainment of independence from the mother country has completely reversed these happy conditions. There is now no security for property or for private enterprise. The agriculture of the country is becoming reduced to the rudest processes, its products are diminishing from year to year, and the lands are returning to waste; the mines are neglected and deserted, and falling into a state of ruin. Public works are no longer constructed, and those which were erected under the dominion of Spain are mostly deserted and falling into a condition of dilapidation and ruin. The priesthood is becoming corrupt, and public and private morals are rapidly falling to the lowest point of degradation. The finances of the country have long since been in a condition of insolvency, and the expenditures have for many years exceeded the receipts by an annual deficiency of several millions of dollars. The army is composed of bandits; it is recruited by taking from the public prisons convicted murderers and other malefactors, who have yet to serve a term of imprisonment not less than ten years, and granting them a free pardon on condition of their serving five years as soldiers. The officers of the army, who, under the government of Spain, belonged to distinguished and educated families, are now drawn from the most despicable classes, or rise by promotion from the ranks of this bandit soldiery; and the disproportion of officers is so great that the army of 20,000 soldiers is commanded by 84,000 officers, who are entirely deficient in military faith and personal honor; they murder in cold blood their political and military prisoners; they protect robbers and share their spoils; they are accomplices in assassination and murder; and theft is practiced by every one from the President of the republic down to the lowest officers of the custom-house. Republican Mexico has always been the enemy of France, oppressed her commerce, and practiced the most atrocious tyranny upon our citizens resident in her territory. She has discriminated against French products, first by her tariffs, and afterwards in the manner in which she has executed her custom-house regulations. She has, on the most frivolous and unlawful pretences, confiscated the property of French merchants, for which acts of robbery and violence she owes them at this time several millions of dollars, for which she refuses to make them the least compensation. She has thus fallen to the lowest condition of insolvency, brigandage, and ruin. She is a public nuisance and robber on the highway of nations; and any nation, especially those having claims against her, has a right, as a matter of international policy, to interfere and establish a solid government in Mexico, which shall fulfil the obligations of national faith towards the world, maintain order, decency, and morality, and secure life, liberty, and property within her own borders. This can be done only by the establishment of a Mexican monarchy; for republican institutions have been tried there, and have resulted in an utter and hopeless failure. The best citizens of Mexico desire the re-establishment of a monarchy; those who are distinguished for their piety, morality, culture, and the possession of property are willing to pledge themselves in advance to the support of the movement. Some of her most distinguished statesmen, in the face of threats of assassination, have already publicly declared, in the capital of Mexico, that the adoption of this plan presented the only possible hope for the restoration of Mexico to a condition of respectability and prosperity. "But there are certain conditions necessary to the success of this scheme. The new monarchs of Mexico must be Catholic, and must have family ties connecting them with the dynasties which formerly ruled in Mexico. The infantas of Spain, the French princes, and the archdukes of Austria possess these requisites, and any one of them would be unanimously welcomed by the Mexican population. The establishment of any monarchy whatsoever in Mexico is of the greatest importance to the policy of France, for a stable government erected there would at once remove the disabilities and oppression to which our commerce and citizens are subjected in that country; and this can easily be accomplished, for a column of 3,000 infantry, and a few vessels-of-war distributed upon the Atlantic and Pacific coasts are all that is wanted to subdue the empire of Montezuma, whose conquest would be easier to-day than it was in the time of Hernando Cortez!"

LOUIS PHILIPPE ENFORCES THE NECESSITY OF PROMPT ACTION.

But, continues the programme, if a Catholic monarchy is to be established in Mexico, it should be done at once. The English, among all foreign nations, have a preponderating political and commercial interest in Mexico. English subjects own a large portion of the funded debt of Mexico, upon which the annual interest is not paid, although pretended to be secured by an illusory charge upon the customs. She is ready, therefore, at any moment, to make this a pretext for seizing any portion of the coast or territory of the republic. She has already acknowledged the independence of the revolted provinces of Texas, with a view of taking them under her protection, or of establishing even more intimate political relations with them. She has by her intrigues hitherto prevented the United States from acquiring any portion of the Mexican territory; and, if she retains her present influence at Mexico, and still more, if she adds to it by gaining any territory there, or in any other manner, the results cannot fail to be most disastrous to the interests of France.

The United States, too, have for more than forty years looked upon the territories of Mexico with that covetousness of acquisition which has ever distinguished that energetic people. The expedition of Burr would have been hailed with favor if it had been successful, and his acquittal by a jury must be taken as evidence of the popular sentiment in favor of the objects of his expedition. After the purchase of Louisiana from France, and by the treaty of Florida, so called, and by other subsequent treaties, the United States gained a large extension of territory in the direction of the Pacific, and brought down their possessions in Oregon and on the Pacific coast to the forty-second parallel of latitude. They even sought, by other propositions communicated to the court of Spain for the avowed purpose of defining the boundaries between the two countries south of that parallel, and proposing limits which were altogether too vague for geographical or political boundaries, but which they would have found sufficiently specific for the purpose of intrusion, to gain a further extension of territory in the direction of New Mexico; but these latter propositions were indignantly rejected by the Spanish monarchy. But since the establishment of Mexican independence, and the weakness, demoralization and ruin which have resulted from it, Mexico has seemed to the United States to have become an easy prey to their grasping ambition. They have permitted their own citizens to pass in armed bands over their borders into Texas, and there to stir up revolt, which has culminated in successful revolution; they have acknowledged the independence of that country with the view to its annexation to the Union as one of the federal States. A treaty of annexation is at this moment in progress between Texas and the United States, and will doubtless be accomplished as the crowning act of the present adminis-

tration of President Tyler. When that treaty is ratified by the contracting
parties, the military establishment of Texas will be occupied by the forces of
the United States, and war will immediately ensue between the United States
and the Mexican republic. That war can issue in but one result : the armies
of the United States will overrun and occupy the territories of the weaker
republic, and they will be at once and forever absorbed in the domain of the
federal Union. If France, therefore, determines to protect her interests by the
establishment of a Catholic monarchy in Mexico, she should act promptly and
decisively.

LOUIS PHILIPPE CONSIDERS THE DOMINION OF THE UNITED STATES IN MEXICO PREFERABLE TO THAT OF ENGLAND.

But if Mexico is still to exist under a republican government, it is much
better for the interests of France that she should be absorbed by the North
American Union than that England should either maintain or increase her
influence there. The people of the United States have a strong instinct for a
government of law, and even the administration of their famous "lynch law,"
in their newly settled territories, arises from their sentiment of order. Under
their rigid administration, the persons and property of French citizens in Mexico would be protected and respected, and we should not be compelled to make
vain reclamations on the government for official robberies and confiscations.
The sentiment of the people of the United States is favorable and even
friendly to France, and under their dominion we should not have occasion to
complain of odious and hostile discriminations against our commerce, and what
we should gain in these respects, England would be certain to lose. She would
no longer be the nation favored either by the terms of the laws, or by their violation in her behalf, but would be reduced, at least, to a position of equal competition in matters of commerce, which is all that France desires. Our property
would be respected, the lives of our citizens would be secured, and, on equal
terms, we could exchange our products for the agricultural and mineral riches of
Mexico.

GRANDEUR OF THE AMERICO-MEXICAN DOMINION.

This programme of the government of Louis Philippe concludes with a pre-
diction of the future greatness of the United States, which might well excite the
envy of the most enthusiastic eulogist of "the American bird of liberty :"

" If this takes place, the Union will command the Pacific ocean, through that
part of the territory of Oregon which will belong to her—through California and
the western coast of Mexico, Guatemala, Central America, and New Granada.
On the east, she will be mistress of the Atlantic coast, from Canada to the Isthmus of Darien, and thus will threaten the group of islands situated at the entrance
of the Gulf of Mexico, and in the Caribbean sea."

FAILURE OF THE FRENCH PROGRAMME IN MEXICO.

It is instructive to pause a moment and contemplate the results of this proposed scheme for the overthrow of republican institutions and the establishment
of a monarchy in Mexico. Louis Philippe, its responsible author, and the crafty
schemer who prostituted the interests of France to the aggrandizement of his
own family, and who had thus published to the world this libellous imputation
of degeneracy and weakness against the republic of Mexico, was himself, within
four years afterwards, driven from the throne, and his dynasty subverted, without his having the courage to permit a single musket-shot to be fired in their
defence. His scheme has since been taken up by his successor, Napoleon III,
a monarch of greater sagacity, resources, and force of will. But the Mexican

population has not received an Austrian archduke as their emperor with unani-
mous acclamations; a column of three thousand men has not conquered the
Empire of Montezuma; and the republic of Mexico still lives!

ATTEMPTS OF VARIOUS GOVERNMENTS TO ACQUIRE CALIFORNIA.

But while a covetousness of all the territories of the Mexican republic was
thus charged upon some of the great political powers of the world, upon circumstances of mere suspicion, the desire to acquire California was openly avowed
by several of them, and made equally manifest by the acts of others.   France,
in particular, endeavored to qualify herself for the conquest of California, by a
previous exploration of the country of the most thorough and accurate character.
In 1841, Marshal Soult, the French minister of war, detached from the French
legation at Mexico one of its attachés, M. Duflot de Mofras, a gentleman perfectly competent for that purpose, with directions to make a thorough exploration of California in respect to military resources, geography, agriculture, natural
history, meteorology, geology, population, and civil and political history.   This
work he accomplished during a sojourn of two years, during which, as he himself states, he visited every mission, every village, and every rancho in California.   The results of his exploration were published to the world by the French
government at the same time with their programme in regard to Mexico, of which
I have above spoken.   This publication was accompanied with charts of all the
harbors on the coast of California, with their soundings; with the most explicit
and accurate directions for entering them from the ocean; and with plans of all
the forts and presidios of California, which were so accurate that a distinguished
military officer of the United States, to whom I lent them, was enabled to re-
trace, at San Diego, the lines of some of the old fortifications there, respecting
which the officers in command at that station could not obtain any other reliable
information.

I shall trespass upon the patience of my audience by reproducing many of the
details of the report of this remarkable exploration. The inhabitants, said De Mofras,
in substance, are very friendly to France, for they are tired of the republic, and
desire a return to the old form of government.   They hate the Americans, because
they are rapacious, protestant, and republican.   They incline towards France,
because she is monarchical, powerful, catholic, and is of the same Latin race to
which they themselves belong.   They have a presentiment of the approaching
downfall of the Mexican republic, and would hail in advance their annexation
to a strong European monarchy.   The Americans, however, and the English,
have set their hearts upon the acquisition of California.   England has already
offered to take California in payment of that portion of the public debt of
Mexico which is held by British subjects, amounting to several millions sterling,
and to liquidate that debt herself, while the United States have already offered
$5,000,000 for that portion of California lying north of a line of latitude drawn
at equal distances from the bay of San Francisco and that of Monterey.
While I was at San Francisco I visited a fleet of American vessels-of-war
(Wilkes's exploring expedition) lying in the harbor there, and was received
hospitably on board by the officers, who made no secret of the fact that they
were executing a thorough survey of the harbor and of the surrounding country.
During my stay in California I also visited English men-of-war lying in the
same harbor, and evidently sent there for the same purpose.   English men-of-war
are almost always constantly cruising on the coast, as if waiting for a pretext
or opportunity to seize the country.   The Americans have constantly a naval
force upon the coast, with instructions to seize the capital upon probable information of a rupture between Mexico and the United States.   And in the
year 1842, Commodore Jones, upon such a rumor, which afterwards proved to
be unfounded, actually seized Monterey, the capital of California, and raised the

American flag there; but, upon learning that the information upon which he had acted was not true, he restored the place to the California authorities; "yet, in my opinion, having once taken it, he would have done better to have kept it, and also to have seized the port of San Francisco." There are many persons in California who are friendly to France, and who can be very useful to us; one of our countrymen, Maturin, at San Francisco; Baric, a Frenchman, at Los Angeles; Suñol, a Spaniard by birth, who served in the French navy, who speaks our language well, who was on the French brig which Napoleon quitted, in 1815, when he surrendered himself to the captain of the Bellerophon. The most important point on the northwestern coast of the Pacific is the port of San Francisco, which is in reality the key of the northwest coast of America and of the northern Pacific ocean. Captain Beechey, of the royal British navy, in 1813, describes it as being "sufficiently extensive to contain all the British navy, well sheltered, and with good anchorage everywhere, surrounded with a country varied with hills and valleys, partly wooded and partly of fine pasturage, and abounding with cattle of every kind." "It is easy to enter this harbor from the ocean," says De Mofras; "one should, after crossing the bar, lay well to the south, having the island of Alcatraz on a line with the fort, and then, on approaching the gate or strait, one should keep in the centre until Point Bonita is well passed, and then sail well over to the north. There is a dangerous reef, called Blossom rock, which lies on a line drawn from the southwestern point of Yerba Buena island and that of Alcatraz, which is to be avoided; but just behind the point of Saucelito lives an Englishman, who is married to a native Californian, one Captain Richardson, who is captain of the port, and an excellent pilot. There is no military force in California. There are no garrisons at the presidios. The gun-carriages at the forts have rotted away, and the guns, which were mostly cast at Manilla, more than a hundred years ago, lie rusting on the ground. It is perfectly clear that California will belong to whatsoever nation will take the trouble to send there a ship-of-war and two hundred soldiers."

EFFORTS OF THE UNITED STATES TO OBTAIN POSSESSION OF CALIFORNIA.

Having thus giving a résumé of the French report of our own intentions and desires respecting the acquisition of California, I shall endeavor to give an authentic account of them, and of those of other governments. It is true, as above stated, that the English offered to receive Upper California in payment of a portion of the public debt of Mexico; and it is also undoubtedly true that the English were prepared to avail themselves of the pretext of an indemnity for that debt to take possession of California upon any favorable conjuncture. It is also true that the acquisition of California had long been an object much desired by the government of the United States. As early as the year 1835 President Jackson proposed to the government of Mexico to purchase that portion lying east and north of a line drawn from the Gulf of Mexico along the eastern bank of the Rio Bravo del Norte up to the 37th degree of north latitude, and thence along that parallel to the Pacific ocean. This would have included within the proposed cession to the United States all the Bay of San Francisco, and the territory to the north and east of it, and have left to the south the bay of Monterey. This proposition was favorably received by the Mexican government, and would doubtless have been accepted had it not been for the intrigues and powerful remonstrances of the British diplomatic representatives. The American government, however, did not relinquish its designs, nor desist in the execution of its plans for promoting the desired result. It continued to encourage and protect the emigration of its citizens to California. It caused to be made scientific and popular explorations by land, such as those of Frémont, and by sea, such as those successfully and thoroughly made by Wilkes's exploring expedition.

Indeed, it is more than suspected that the main object of organizing Wilkes's exploring expedition was a thorough hydrographic survey of the harbor of San Francisco and its tributaries—a work which was so well accomplished that the maps and soundings of the bays and rivers from San Francisco to Sacramento, which were made on that occasion, are reliable to the present time. What Frémont's instructions were on his last expedition to California is a well-kept cabinet secret, which will probably not be divulged, at least in our time; but it is evident from his course of action that he was directed, in case of receiving reliable information of the breaking out of war, to do all in his power to secure possession of California. It is also very certain that the commanders of the American men-of-war cruising on the coast of California had explicit instructions not to suffer the country to fall into the hands of any other power. And the popular impression is that the English were about to take possession of California, and were prevented only by the seizure of Monterey by Commodore Sloat on the 7th of July, 1846.

MOVEMENTS OF THE CALIFORNIANS IN RELATION TO THEIR ANNEXATION TO A FOREIGN POWER.

Meanwhile the natives of California, with that instinctive apprehension of the coming storm which seems to prevail in the political as well as in the natural world, began to consult upon the policy of preventing the anticipated acts of foreign governments by declaring their independence of Mexico, and placing California under the protection of some great political power. In the year 1836 Don Juan Bautista Alvarado revolted against Mexico, and by the aid of sixty American riflemen, headed by Isaac Graham, drove Gutierrez, the constitutional governor of California, out of the department, and was himself proclaimed governor in his stead. Acting in conjunction with General Mariano Gaudalupe Vallejo and Don José Castro, and aiming at annexation with the United States, he declared California to be completely independent of Mexico, and erected into a free and sovereign state—el Estado libre y soberano de la Alta California—and raised a flag like that of the United States, but with a single star. This revolt was finally abandoned on certain concessions being made by the central government, including the appointment of Alvarado as constitutional governor. In 1842 President Santa Anna sent General Manuel Micheltorena to California as governor and commandant general, with 150 persons to act as officials, and an army of 300 convicts, drawn from the prisons of Mexico.* But he

---

* I should not dare to credit this act of Santa Anna if it were not officially substantiated beyond any doubt. It was published at the time, at Mexico, in *El Observador Judicial y de Legislacion*, 1842, vol. i, p. 372, and also afterwards, in the *Coleccion de los Decretos y Ordenes de Interes Comun, que dicto el gobierno provisional en virtud de las bases de Tacubaya, Mexico: Imprenta de J. M. Lara*, 1850, page 352, under date of February 22, A. D. 1842, and is in the following terms:

"MINISTERIO DE JUSTICIA E INSTRUCCION PUBLICA.

"Exmo. Señor el exmo. Señor Presidente Provisional, en uso de la Facultad que concede et art. 7º de las bases acordadas en Tacubaya y juradas por los representantes de los departamentos, ha tenido a bien disponer: que de los reos sentenciados á presidio que existan en las cárceles de esta capital, se destinen trescientos al departamento de Californias, escogiendo al efecto á los que sengan algun oficio ó industria util; en el concepto de que si al llegar á aquel destino hubieren guardado buena conducta, á juicio del gobierno departamental, se les recajará una parte de su condéna, o se les indultará del todo, segun los servicios que prestaren, y aun se auxiliará á sus familias para que vayan á unirse con ellos, dandoles terrenos y los instrumentos que necesiten para colonizar: (with the purpose of relating a part or the whole of their term of punishment, according to the services they render; and also their families shall be assisted to join them, and lands and implements of cultivation furnished them.)
"Lo que tengo el honor de comunicar a V. E. para su debido cumplimiento, y que se sirva hacer saber esta suprema disposition á los presidiarios que al indicato efecto fueren escogidos.
"Exmo. Señor Gobernador del Departamento de Mexico."

too, after a stormy administration, was forced to retire, in the year 1845, after having stipulated with the insurgents by the treaty of Cahuenga—so styled from the rancho of that name where it was conducted—that he and his adherents might march away with their side-arms with all the honors of war. The crisis of severance from the mother republic became every day more inevitable. Dissatisfied as the Californians were with the exactions and oppressions of the central government, and with the importation from Mexico of a convict soldiery, who graduated from the camp to become turbulent citizens or ferocious bandits, the question of secession from Mexico was freely discussed and its policy approved. They differed only as to what great political power should be invoked for protection and annexation. The departmental assembly of California, in the year 1846, passed a law for the election of delegates to a junta, or extraordinary convention, to be styled "The general council of the united pueblos of the Californias: *el concejo general de los pueblos unidos de California,*" which was to meet at Santa Barbara on June 15, 1846, for the purpose of determining the destiny of California. Meanwhile the resident consuls and agents of the three great powers which were striving for the possession of California — Forbes for Great Britain, Guys for France, and Larkin for the United States—commenced their movements and counter movements, each hoping to gain the predominating influence in the coming convention. But the result of an informal meeting of some of the leading men of California, at the house of Don José Castro, in Monterey, dissipated all these hopes, and showed that the convention, even if held, must prove an utter failure. On that occasion a native Californian, whom it would be invidious to mention, as he is now a loyal citizen of California, but who then represented the monarchical party, spoke as follows : *

"Excellent Sirs, to what a deplorable condition is our country reduced! Mexico, professing to be our mother and our protectress, has given us neither arms, nor money, nor the materials of war for our defence. She is not likely to do anything in our behalf, although she is quite willing to afflict us with her extortionate minions, who come hither in the guise of soldiers and civil officers to harass and oppress our people. We possess a glorious country, capable of attaining a physical and moral greatness corresponding with the grandeur and beauty which an Almighty hand has stamped upon the face of our beloved California. But although nature has been prodigal, it cannot be denied that we are not in a position to avail ourselves of her bounty. Our population is not large, and it is sparsely scattered over valley and mountain, covering an immense area of virgin soil, destitute of roads, and traversed with difficulty ; hence it is hardly possible to collect an army of any considerable force. Our people are poor, as well as few, and cannot well govern themselves and maintain a decent show of sovereign power. Although we live in the midst of plenty, we lay up nothing ; but, tilling the earth in an imperfect maner, all our time is required to procure subsistence for ourselves and our families. Thus circumstanced, we find ourselves threatened by hordes of Yankee emigrants, who have already begun to flock into our country, and whose progress we cannot arrest. Already have the wagons of that perfidious people scaled the almost inaccessible summit of the Sierra Nevada, crossed the entire continent, and penetrated the fruitful valley of the Sacramento. What that astonishing people will next undertake, I cannot say ; but in whatever enterprise they embark, they will be sure to prove successful. Already are these adventurous land-voyagers spreading themselves

---

The alleged design of converting California into a convict colony was only a flimsy pretext for furnishing Micheltorena with three hundred desperate soldiers ; still, it is interesting to know that the intention of making our State the Botany Bay of Mexico was once thus officially announced.

* The speeches which follow were reduced to writing at the time, by the late Thomas O. Larkin, then American consul at Monterey. The first had already been delivered, in substance, in the Departmental Assembly.

far and wide over a country which seems suited to their taste. They are cultivating farms, establishing vineyards, erecting mills, sawing up lumber, building workshops, and doing a thousand other things which seem natural to them, but which Californians neglect or despise. What, then, are we to do? Shall we remain supine, while these daring strangers are overrunning our fertile plains, and gradually outnumbering and displacing us? Shall these incursions go on unchecked, until we shall become strangers in our own land? We cannot successfully oppose them by our own unaided power, and the swelling tide of emigration renders the odds against us more powerful every day. We cannot stand alone against them, nor can we creditably maintain our independence even against them, nor can we creditably maintain our independence even against Mexico; but there is something which we can do, which will elevate our country, strengthen her at all points, and yet enable us to preserve our identity and remain masters of our own soil. Perhaps what I am about to suggest may seem to some faint-hearted and dishonorable. But to me it does not appear so. It is the last hope of a feeble people, struggling against a tyrannical government, which claims their submission at home, and threatened by bands of avaricious strangers from without, voluntarily to connect themselves with a power able and willing to defend and preserve them. It is the right and duty of the weak to demand support from the strong, provided the demand be made upon terms just to both parties. I see no dishonor in this last refuge of the oppressed and powerless, and I boldly avow that such is the step I would now have California take. There are two great powers in Europe, which seem destined to divide between them the unappropriated countries of the world. They have large fleets and armies not unpracticed in the art of war. Is it not better to connect ourselves with one of these powerful nations than to struggle on without hope, as we are doing now? Is it not better that one of them should be invited to send a fleet and an army to protect California, rather than we should fall an easy prey to the lawless adventurers who are overrunning our beautiful country? I pronounce for annexation to France or England, and the people of California will never regret having taken my advice. They will no longer be subjected to the trouble and grievous expense of governing themselves, and their beef, and their grain, which they produce in such abundance, would find a ready market among the new comers. But I hear some one say, "No monarchy!" But is not monarchy better than anarchy? Is not existence in some shape better than annihilation? No monarchy! And what is there so terrible in a monarchy? Have we not all lived under a monarchy far more despotic than that of France or England, and were not our people happy under it? Have not the leading men among our agriculturists been bred beneath the royal rule of Spain, and have they been happier since the mock republic of Mexico has supplied its place? Nay, does not every man abhor the miserable abortion christened the republic of Mexico, and look back with regret to the golden days of the Spanish monarchy? Let us restore that glorious era. Then may our people go quietly to their ranchos, and live there as of yore, leading a merry and thoughtless life, untroubled by politics or cares of state, sure of what is their own, and safe from the incursions of the Yankees, who would soon be forced to retreat into er o wn country."

To these arguments General Mariano G. Vallejo, a native of California, whom we are proud to number among the members of this society, and who has not lost our esteem in consequence of the assaults made upon him by those who have succeeded in confiscating so large a portion of that landed property of the native Californians, whose possession was guaranteed to them by the treaty of Guadalupe Hidalgo, replied as follows:

"I cannot, gentlemen, coincide in opinion with the military and civil functionaries who have advocated the cession of our country to France or England. It is most true that to rely any longer upon Mexico to govern and defend us would be idle and absurd. To this extent I fully agree with my distinguished colleagues. It is true that we possess a noble country, every way calculated, from position and resources, to become great and powerful. For that very reason I would not have her a mere dependence upon a foreign monarchy, naturally alien, or at least indifferent to our interests and our welfare. It is not to be denied that feeble nations have in former times thrown themselves upon the protection of their powerful neighbors. The Britons invoked the aid of the warlike Saxons, and fell an easy prey to their protectors, who seized their lands and treated them as slaves. Long before that time, feeble and distracted provinces had appealed for aid to the all-conquering arms of imperial Rome, and they were at the same time protected and subjugated by their grasping ally. Even could we tolerate the idea of dependence, ought we to go to distant Europe for a master? What possible sympathy could exist between us and a nation separated from us by two vast oceans? But waiving this insuperable objection, how could we endure to come under the dominion of a monarch?—for although others speak lightly of a form of government, as a freeman I cannot do so. We are republicans. Badly governed and badly situated as we are, still we are all, in sentiment, republicans. So far as we are governed at all, we, at least, profess to be self-governed. Who, then, that possesses true patriotism will consent to subject himself and children to the caprices of a foreign king and his official minions? But, it is asked, if we do not throw ourselves upon the protection of France or England, what shall we do? I do not come here to support the existing order of things, but I come prepared to propose instant and effective action to extricate our country from her present forlorn condition. My opinion is made up that we must persevere in throwing off the galling yoke of Mexico and proclaim our independence forever. We have endured her official cormorants and her villanous soldiery until we can endure no longer. All will probably agree with me that we ought at once to rid ourselves of what may remain of Mexican domination. But some profess to doubt our ability to maintain our position. To my mind there comes no doubt. Look at Texas and see how long she withstood the power of united Mexico. The resources of Texas were not to be compared with ours, and she was much nearer to her enemy than we are. Our position is so remote, either by land or sea, that we are in no danger from a Mexican invasion. Why, then, should we hesitate still to assert our independence? We have indeed taken the first step by electing our own governor; but another remains to be taken. I will mention it plainly and distinctly. It is annexation to the United States. In contemplating this consummation of our destiny I feel nothing but pleasure, and I ask you to share it. Discard old prejudices, disregard old customs, and prepare for the glorious change which awaits our country. Why should we shrink from incorporating ourselves with the happiest and freest nation in the world, destined soon to be the most wealthy and powerful? Why should we go abroad for protection, when this great nation is our adjoining neighbor? When we join our fortune to hers we shall not become subjects, but fellow-citizens, possessing all the rights of the people of the United States, and choosing our own federal and local rulers. We shall have a stable government and just laws. California will grow strong and flourish, and her people will be prosperous, happy, and free. Look not, therefore, with jealousy upon the hardy pioneers who scale our mountains and cultivate our unoccupied plains, but rather welcome them as brothers who come to share with us a common destiny."

Upon the conclusion of these remarks General Vallejo and his friends retired in a body from the meeting, and he immediately addressed a letter to the governor reaffirming the views which he had expressed, and declared that he would never assist in any project for annexation to any nationality except that of the United States, or hold any office under any government which proposed to surrender California to any European monarchy; and thereupon he and his supporters retired to their homes. This movement on the part of General Vallejo destroyed the prospects of the convention, so that, although its members were elected, it never met for want of a quorum; and within a few months thereafter California was in the possession of the United States, by the taking of Monterey, by Commodore Sloat, on July 7, A. D. 1846.

ENDEAVORS OF RUSSIA TO OCCUPY CALIFORNIA.

Meanwhile the Russians had for some time been quietly insinuating themselves upon the northern coast of California, with a view to its permanent occupation. In the year 1812 they established themselves at the port of Bodega, having previously obtained permission to do so from the authorities of Spain, for the alleged purpose of maintaining fisheries and hunting for furs. But already, as early as the year 1815, they had established large ranchos in the interior, had purchased cattle of the Spanish inhabitants, and had devoted themselves to the rearing of herds and the production of wheat. During the revolutionary troubles in Mexico, the Russians held themselves to have become the actual owners of the territory which they occupied. About forty miles from Bodega, beyond the river San Sebastian, they constructed a fort, which they called Slawiauski, but which the Mexicans designated as the Fort of Ross. Over this floated the Russian flag, and a military governor was in command, appointed by the Czar of Russia. So carefully was this military colony fostered by its own government, that it possessed one-sixth of the white population of California in the year 1842. But, on the final acquisition of California by the United States, the military colony was withdrawn, and most if not all the Russian population retired at or about the same time.

THESE VARIOUS GOVERNMENTS HAD NO KNOWLEDGE OF THE MINERAL WEALTH OF CALIFORNIA.

When we consider what the causes were which have so rapidly developed California to her present position, it seems surprising to us that the existence of precious metals within her limits was not only not suspected, but was even most authoritatively denied. The acquisition of California was considered desirable by all these nations, because it was known that her conditions of climate and soil were such, that her agricultural sources and productions must be almost incalculable; that she must become the seat of an immense population of a highly civilized and prosperous people, and there form the nucleus of an empire of political and commercial power which must exert a controlling influence over all the coasts of the Pacific ocean. The United States, in particular, found themselves almost in contiguity with the future seat of so much prosperity, wealth, and power, and naturally desired that it should become their own. But although rumors of the existence of gold in California had occasionally been heard, still they had never been verified, or traced to any reliable source; and they were regarded as we now regard the fabulous stories of the golden sands of Gold lake, or those of " Silver Planches," which are said to exist in the inaccessible deserts of Arizona. It seems strange to us, that, when the geological character of this country was so well known and so minutely described, the existence of the precious metals in any large quantity should have been so explicitly denied. De Mofras uses the following language :

"There are no minerals which can be exported from California. The mines of silver and of lead which are situated near Monterey are known only by the result of some very simple assays. Some deposits of marble, of copper and iron, some traces of mineral coal which are found near Santa Cruz, some mines of ochre, sulphur, asphaltum, kaolin, and of salt, have not been examined with sufficient care. The only mine at present operated in this country is a vein of virgin gold near the mission of San Fernando, which yields about an ounce a day of pure gold, and is worked by a Frenchman named Baric.

"The geological constitution of the soil of California is very simple. The base of the Rocky mountains is formed of granites of various colors, sometimes whitish with spots of black, sometimes gray or red ; above are stratifications of gneiss, hornblende, quartz and talcose slate, *similar to those which in Mexico enclose veins of gold*, micaceous schist, and talcose schist."

And yet, with all this explicit description, which gave rise to the recorded suggestion that this geological formation was the same as that which in Mexico contained veins of gold, it never occurred to any one of the statesmen or explorers who interested themselves in the acquisition of California that mines of the precious metals existed within her limits.[*]

OUR GRATITUDE TO THE GIVER OF THIS GIFT.

We have thus shown that our position in California is not an accidental one, but was the result of a long train of causes in which human agencies were actively at work. We should do injustice to ourselves, on this occasion, if we did not give utterance to higher sentiments than those of admiration for the patriotism of our fathers and the skill of our statesmen. We do not entertain those notions of modern atheism, thinly disguised under the epithet of pantheism, which limit the operative creation of God to the diffusion of a thin, gaseous substance throughout infinite space, upon which he set the impress of his law and then went to sleep, leaving the existing universe to be evolved from a succession of vortices. We do not believe that the whole animal and vegetable creations have been evolved from bubbles of albumen, nor even that pantheistical philosophers are only fully developed baboons, however probable this latter might seem. This theory was first popularly presented to the world in a most shallow and unscientific work called *The Vestiges of Creation*, whose author never dared to expose himself to general ridicule by revealing his name, because, just after the publication of his book, Lord Rosse turned his tremendous telescope upon the gaseous pantheistic nebulæ, and instantly resolved them into fixed, starry points. We believe as geology teaches us, that God has often, and at remotely successive periods, interposed in the formation of the physical world, fitting it for the creation and habitation of man. We believe that He still acts in history, preparing great events, rewarding nations and men for goodness, and punishing them for crime. We believe that His adoration is not superstitious, nor prayer an unphilosophical act. "If the Lord had not been on our side— yea, if the Lord had not been on our side," we should not now possess this beautiful and glorious California, nor hope to transmit it as an inheritance to our descendants. To Him, therefore, we pour out our collected tribute of gratitude, and invoke His protection for ourselves and our children.

OUR DUTY TO THE FUTURE.

Standing, as we do, between the mighty past and the mysterious future, recognizing our gratitude to our fathers and our duty to our children, let us this day make a public confession and a solemn covenant. Let us con-

---

[*] In closing the historical narrative, it may be assumed as a fact that the inevitable rupture between Mexico and the United States was hastened by the governments of both countries with the expectation that the existence of war would defeat the plans of the monarchical party in Mexico. It is well known that the friends of Santa Anna, who was then in exile, applied to the American government to pass him through its blockade of Vera Cruz on his proposed return to Mexico, upon the frank representation that although he was the ablest general the Mexicans could have, and would undoubtedly command their armies during the war, yet his presence and influence in the country would prevent the establishment of a foreign monarchy there ; and that the President of the United States, appreciating these considerations, permitted Santa Anna to land at Vera Cruz perfectly free to pursue his own course of action. There are gentlemen of the highest respectability residing in California who came here upon the personal assurance of President Polk, in 1846, that the war should not be concluded until Upper California was secured by treaty to the United States.

fess that those of us who have come into this country since the discovery
of gold in California was announced to the world, came here rather with
the spirit of adventure than with the intention of remaining here as permanent residents; that we came here to gather our share of the mineral
treasures of the land, and then to return to the homes of our youth, there to
spend the remainder of our lives; that, at first, we took no thought to found
here the institutions of a higher civilization, nor even to cultivate social relations; and that, in this solitary isolation to which we condemned ourselves for the
sake of gain, it was true, in a certain sense, of us, as individuals, that "our
hands were against every one, and every one's hand against us." Let us con-
fess that this Ishmaelitish tradition has still a certain influence upon us, and
that we do not devote ourselves as fully as we ought to the preparation for the
great future of California; and let us resolve that this day shall form a new era
in our organized efforts. The faculties of man are threefold, intellectual, moral,
and æsthetic; he has reasoning powers which can be cultivated; a moral and
religious sense which can be elevated; and a perception of the beautiful in
nature and art which can be developed into a source of happiness and refinement.
As of men, so of nations, for nations are but aggregates of men. The man who is
wanting in cultivation of any of these faculties is but an imperfect man; a
nation which is thus deficient can never act a perfect part in the history of the
world. The Greeks and Romans were powerful peoples, highly developed in
intellect and æsthetics, but in religion and morals they possessed only the gross
and sensual superstitions of paganism. The Puritans of New England were
highly cultivated intellectually and morally, but not æsthetically; they were a
strong, stern, and unsocial race. The politicians of the French revolution were
men of powerful intellects, and of high culture in literature and art, but they
were wanting in religious sentiment, and disbelievers in the ever-present working
of an intelligent and personal Deity; so that even Robespierre, contemplating
the threatened dissolution of his political system, cried out in his agony: "If there
is no God, then we must create one!" Deficiency in æsthetic culture is commonly the want of new countries. The want of culture has been ascribed to us in
California; by this is meant the want of intimate and refined social culture, of
the perception of the beautiful in nature and in art—of that beautiful in nature,
and that ideal of human perfection, which the painter strives to perpetuate on
his canvas, the statuary to embody in marble, the poet to crystallize in his
verse, and the musician to bring up from the profoundest depths of the human
soul. The charge brought against us is in a large measure true, as it is always
true of new populations; but we have advanced so rapidly to a high degree of
prosperity that it ought to be true no longer, and we ought ourselves to remove
this great reproach. Let us resolve, then, that we will do all in our power to
develop æsthetic culture in California; that we will not only devote our aid to
the foundation of churches, colleges, schools, and the kindred institutions of
morals, science, and humanity, but also to the cultivation of arts, of the perception of the beautiful, to the advancement of painting and statuary. So shall
we do our duty to the future; so shall come after us generations of Californians
against whom no such reproach can be brought—a perfect race, equally developed in their threefold faculties, by intellectual, moral, and æsthetic culture.

OUR CELEBRATION, TEN YEARS HENCE, OF THE HUNDREDTH BIRTHDAY OF OUR CITY.

San Francisco was founded by a colony of soldiers and settlers who came
up for that purpose from Monterey, overland and by sea, in 1776, and immediately set about constructing a chapel at the presidio, after which the following
proceeding took place, as recorded by Father Palou, one of the missionary
priests who belonged to the expedition:

"We took formal possession of the presidio on the seventeenth day of September, the anniversary of the impression of the wounds of our Father San Francisco the patron of the presidio and mission. I said the first mass, and after blessing the site, (*despues del bendito*,) the elevation and adoration of the holy cross, and the conclusion of the service with the *Te Deum*, the officers took formal possession in the name of our sovereign, with many discharges of cannon, both on sea and land, and the musketry of the soldiers."

The seventeenth of September, A. D. 1776, must therefore be considered the date of the foundation of San Francisco.

Ten years from now San Francisco will have completed the hundredth year of her existence. In ten years most of us, under the ordinary providence of God, will be still living. Let us then, on the hundredth birthday of our beloved city, go up and celebrate it on the plain of the presidio, where she was born. Let us at that time renew the solemn exercises by which the soil was consecrated to civilization : the blessing of holy mother church will not hurt the most zealous Protestant among us. Let us rear mast-high the old flag of Spain, with full military honors, to be replaced with equal honor by that of Mexico, which in its turn shall give place, with "great discharge of musketry and of cannon," to our own national emblem of unity and strength !

CONCLUSION.

It is the singularly good fortune of the members of our society that they have an assured position in the history of California, and one which can never be taken away from them. Whatever the future may have in store for us as individuals, the Corporate Society of California Pioneers has had an existence whose records must always remain in the literature and history of California. Our banner is here, on which our names are inscribed, and that banner will always float at the head of the "innumerable caravan" of the countless generations who are to succeed us—of that column which, like the Macedonian phalanx, widening as it deepens, shall draw its vast recruits as well from the tropical regions of the equator as from the confines of the frozen ocean. Behold the thin mist curling up from the ripple where the sunbeam kisses the western sea! It mounts to Heaven, and on its slight curtain Aurora paints the glories of the rising sun ; condenses itself into the fleecy whiteness which decorates the sky of June ; piles up the mighty thunder-cloud, with blackened base and Alpine peaks of dazzling brightness ; and, at the signal of the far-flashing red artillery" of Heaven, and with reverberating crash, dissolves itself in gentle rain ; descends with refreshing coolness on the thirsty land, rushes in torrents of sheety foam adown the mountain side ; swells the vast river to its grassy brink, and then returns its tributary volume to the mother ocean. So countless as the innumerable drops of rain shall be the people that come after us. So shall they rise up from the mists of the future, filling Heaven and earth and sea with the beauty, greatness, and goodness of their acts, and then return, like us, to the great source from which they came. And among them, what multitudes of unborn painters, sculptors, poets, merchant-princes, generals and statesmen! Unknown they are to us, but sure to be—most of them still sleeping in the vast caverns where repose the unborn generations of mankind. But from the depths of the mists which conceal them, we already hear the reverberations of their heavy tread. The parting haze already reveals the outline of the giant forms of their leaders, but, alas, their faces are veiled ! These are the men for whose coming we are to prepare this California of ours ; these are the men who are to erect on the Pacific coast the imperial throne of the great American empire !

www.ingramcontent.com/pod-product-compliance
Lightning Source LLC
Chambersburg PA
CBHW021214270326

41929CB00010B/1129